Education
for
Effective Thinking

I may be obsessed, or suffering from anthropocentric illusions; but I cannot escape the feeling that the human mind and human curiosity are significant in this world—even perhaps in the cosmos of geological time and intergalactic space. With this impression (or illusion) that the mind is the best of us, and the best of biological evolution, I cannot escape (and neither can you!) the feeling of responsibility to glorify the human mind, and to take it seriously, even dream about its ultimate flowering into something far beyond the primitive muscle-guider and sensation-recorder with which we started.

HARLOW SHAPLEY*

I am convinced that everything that is worthwhile in the world has been accomplished by the free, inquiring, critical spirit, and that the preservation of this spirit is more important than any social system whatsoever. But the men of ritual and the men of barbarism are capable of shutting up the men of science and of silencing them forever.

SINCLAIR LEWIS†

Every educated person ought to know when a thing is proved and when it is not proved, should know how to investigate and analyze the proposition which confronts him, and how to search for solutions, how to talk about it effectively before others, and how to contribute to a discussion on problems of joint interest.

WILLIAM NORWOOD BRIGANCE‡

* Harlow Shapley, from an address delivered at Harvard University.
† Sinclair Lewis, *It Can't Happen Here* (New York, Sun Dial Press, 1935), p. 433.
‡ Professor W. Norwood Brigance, from an address before the American Speech Association, 1946.

Education
for
Effective Thinking

AN INTRODUCTORY TEXT

William H. Burton
LATE, HARVARD GRADUATE SCHOOL OF EDUCATION

Roland B. Kimball
CHIEF, DIVISION OF INSTRUCTION,
NEW HAMPSHIRE STATE DEPARTMENT OF EDUCATION

Richard L. Wing
YORKTOWN HIGH SCHOOL
YORKTOWN HEIGHTS, NEW YORK

 New York

APPLETON-CENTURY-CROFTS, INC.

E 15715

Preface

Thinking as an objective of education. "Teaching students to think" is one of the most commonly expressed aims of education, generally and in almost any subject field. Authorities almost without end could be cited as upholding this as one aim of education. The Harvard Report, *General Education in a Free Society,* to cite but one, says: "Education is not merely the imparting of knowledge but the cultivation of certain aptitudes and attitudes in the mind of the young. . . . These abilities, in our opinion, are: *to think effectively, to communicate thought, to make relevant judgments, to discriminate among values.*" The abilities listed represent a large part of the subject matter of our book.

What is thinking? The word is used carelessly to mean almost any mental operation. Everyone is sure he knows what thinking is. This type of thinking about thinking is useless. We cannot proceed without a definition. All competent texts begin with a definition, and though there is difference in wording, there is a core of agreement on essentials. More will be said of this in Chapter 2.

Terms widely used are: *critical thinking, reflective thinking, problem solving, scientific thinking, straight thinking, clear thinking,* and others.

An acceptable definition is: *Thinking results when there is persistent effort to examine the evidence which supports any belief, solution, or conclusion which is suggested for acceptance, together with the implications and further conclusions of the evidence.*

Thinking occurs when a problem is recognized, when any situation is unclear, and when there is uncertainty as to what the problem means or what should be done. Hypothetical answers are set up which guide the gathering and analyzing of facts and other types of data. Evaluations and judgments take place with due recognition for logical relationships. Conclusions are developed and tested in action. The act of judgment, or drawing of inferences, is central. Unstated assumptions, values, and sentiments must be recognized and appraised. Precision, clarity, and discrimination of language are necessary.

Thinking requires, in addition to the technical skills indicated, the moral conviction that one must think honestly, certain general attitudes, and the avoidance of certain other attitudes. The attitudes are elaborated in Chapter 3.

Can thinking be analyzed? The Harvard Report goes on to say: "the traits are not in practice separable and are not to be developed in isolation. Nor can they even be analyzed in separation. Each is an indispensable, coexistent function of a sanely growing mind."

The report nevertheless proceeds to "analyze each in separation," as do all books on logic or on the psychology of thought. Our book will do the same.

We know quite well that the various abilities used in critical thinking cannot be developed in isolation but must be developed in conjunction with each other through use of appropriate materials and situations. How this is done is usually not set forth in those textbooks which claim thinking abilities as an aim. Inspired teachers do occasionally develop these abilities successfully in students, but this is fragmentary and haphazard.

Can thinking be taught? This is a tricky question. No one can teach anyone "how to think." We can, however, aid individuals to improve the natural abilities they possess and the natural processes which they use. We can aid individuals to recognize and be sensitive to certain conventions and processes of valid thought, to certain pitfalls, fallacies, and sources of error. Certain general methods can be developed by teachers. We have made an earnest effort in this volume to set forth the outlines of these general methods of teaching.

Can such teaching be successful? Exhaustive reviews made by Kimball and Wing of the pertinent research indicate that we can teach students to think more effectively. Findings are summarized in Chapters 12 and 14. A detailed analysis of tests for critical thinking was made by Kimball and indicates that evidence of successful teaching can be secured. Findings are summarized in Chapter 21. Early efforts to teach "how to think" were marked with very little success, but the reasons for failure are now better understood.

Is it worthwhile to attempt the improvement of thinking? Essays and whole volumes by the most distinguished men and women of our times testify not only to the worth and necessity of the effort but to the dire consequences of not improving thinking. Several discussions of this general topic appear in later chapters, but here brief summary statements must suffice. Incomparable improvements in the worth and security of life have resulted from competent thinking. This is true for the individual, the community group, and the nation. There is hope that sound thinking may be applied to international affairs. Incorrect and/or dishonest thinking has precipitated disaster many times in our economic, social, political, and military history. Considerable disaster could still result if we do not "take thought." Every area of human endeavor from rearing children to the management of international relations is affected.

Can ability to think, developed in one area, with appropriate materials and problems, be generalized and transferred to other areas? Ay, there is the rub! Two basic questions have been raised since ancient times and are continuing to the present day:

1. Can men learn to think only within one field of specialization, a limited area, subject, or discipline?

2. Can men, on the contrary, be sensitized to certain general characteristics of valid thinking which might be used in any situation demanding critical or reflective thinking?

Everyone can observe every day the inability of certain distinguished thinkers to operate logically in a field other than their own. Certain historical evidence, however, testifies to the expertness of certain individuals in not one but several fields. Modern investigations of transfer of training give grounds for belief that transfer is possible. Crucial to transfer are the training and skill of the teacher and the intelligence level of the learner.

The scope of this volume. Thinking occurs in all areas of human activity. The general process is basically the same, though certain variations occur with different materials and objectives. Illustrations and incidents, furthermore, can be selected in such wide variety as to be confusing. One volume cannot cover adequately all areas. Each of the modern volumes on logic or thinking sets forth in the preface certain limitations.

1. *The first limitation* grows out of the distinction between logic as the science of valid inference and the psychological descriptions of how the mind works. The leading current books present accounts of logic, with varying amounts of reference to psychological factors. A book is needed which describes the process of thinking but with due deference to logic. Our book is an effort to do this. We include a statement on the relations between formal logic and thinking-in-process.

2. *The second limitation* results from choice of areas for emphasis and from which illustrations are to be drawn chiefly.

The possible areas which might be treated include:

Science, physical and biological, plus some aspects of the social sciences.	*Literature*
	Ethics and morals
	Practical affairs of life
Mathematics	*Law*
Fine arts	*Military strategy*
History	(Others could be listed)

The possible approaches or kinds of thinking would include:

Problem solving, as in the sciences (explanation, discovery, verification, evidential)

Logical, as in mathematics

Making and supporting value judgments

Stating and supporting goals, policies, decisions
Critical analysis, a type of approach which overlaps with and is a part of
   some of the others but exists when a conclusion, assertion, opinion, or
   belief is to be accepted, modified, or rejected
Creative development, as of a new, unique, and not-before-known product

The successful solution of these different types of problems in the various areas of school subjects or life activities requires a different set of procedures in each case. Mathematics, for instance, emphasizes the drawing of
valid inferences from accepted axioms or postulates, the nature of logical
proof. Problem solving commonly turns upon the development and elaboration of hypotheses. Social, ethical, and moral problems use group discussion with exchange of views, the use of tentative conclusions, effort to
obtain consensus through a meeting of minds. The types of thinking presented in this volume will be elaborated in Chapter 15 on general methods.

Each of the major texts currently in use selects a few of these areas and
concentrates on them. One book, for instance, deals with thinking as it
goes on in the physical and biological sciences. A chapter is included on
mathematics but with the suggestion it be omitted by instructors if not useful
in the given situation; chapters on statistics and measurement are also included. Some illustrations from social sciences and history are included but
within the type of thinking chiefly predominating. Nothing at all is said of
historical, ethical or moral, legal, or everyday problems.

A second book includes considerable discussion of logical process in
everyday affairs. There is considerable treatment of semantics in contrast
to the above-mentioned book. No treatment of value judgments, legal problems, and others is included. Still a third book contains an extensive discussion of value judgments and a fairly extended discussion of problems in
the field of history. In brief, all available books quite sensibly set forth
limitations of coverage.

Our book gives special attention to the areas of mathematics, science,
literature, and social studies, and to the kinds of subproblems involved in
each. Extensive reference is made throughout the book to what may be
called "everyday thinking" dealing with the practical affairs of life. Certain
other areas and types of thinking are touched on briefly or omitted. There
is a summary of the relationship between formal logic and thinking as it
occurs in real situations.

Finally, it must be emphasized, this book is a simple, unpretentious introduction. An exhaustive treatment is not the aim. Time and again we
could have extended discussions to far more advanced levels. These levels
are readily available in more technical books which may be used with profit
after introductory insights have been gained. The volume is designed especially for teachers in service and in training. We are quite aware that teachers
must know a great deal more about logic, semantics, and other crucial
matters than we can present in our introductory book.

No unkind criticism is intended, but it is clear that one major reason why schools have done so little about critical thinking is the lack of information and training among teachers. Even among the typical standard texts in various aspects of education itself, several are rejected by a percentage of teachers as being "too advanced," "too sophisticated," "too profound for the students." The teacher-training institutions might give attention to preparing teachers who can handle advanced, sophisticated, or profound texts. Students in many institutions have displayed ability to handle these same texts—under competent instruction. Our aim here is to give teachers an introduction to what it means "to think" and to some of the processes through which the thinking of students may be improved. We hope that further reading and study will be stimulated. The material can be used also, no doubt, in areas of general education far removed from teacher training.

Acknowledgments. We acknowledge with gratitude our indebtedness to the earlier writers, both those who presented simple, beginning accounts and those who presented critical, systematic, and advanced volumes.

The pioneer books in the field were:

John Dewey, *How We Think* (Boston, Heath, 1910; rev. ed., 1933).
Irving Elgar Miller, *The Psychology of Thinking* (New York, Macmillan, 1912).
Julius Boraas, *Teaching to Think* (New York, Macmillan, 1924).

Dewey's book was by far the most widely used even though the writing and organization were far from clear. Bibliographies were not included, and the 1910 edition had no index. Miller's book was widely used during its lifetime, in teachers colleges and normal schools, as was the one by Boraas. These books were well written and simple. Their influence was lost, however, because there were no follow-up volumes. The two were well in advance of interest and understanding.

A period then ensued during which a number of books were written in an effort to explain logic in less formal language, to describe thinking, and to make some application to the affairs of life. These will be listed in the Bibliography. One of the early ones, D. S. Robinson's *The Principles of Reasoning* (New York, D. Appleton, 1910; rev. ed., 1933) with an accompanying volume of readings and illustrations, had good use, but again it was in advance of its times.

Currently there is very great interest in (*a*) teaching students to think, and (*b*) the applications of thinking, particularly of problem solving, in business, industry, and the professions.

Several popular books have appeared in response to the second area of interest, and these are also of use by teachers on all levels. The following are illustrations and probably the best known. Lists here are by no means exhaustive.

Stuart Chase, *Guides to Straight Thinking* (New York, Harper, 1956).

Rudolf Flesch, *The Art of Clear Thinking* (New York, Harper, 1951).
William J. Reilly, *The Twelve Rules for Straight Thinking* (New York, Harper, 1947).
Robert H. Thouless, *How to Think Straight* (New York, Simon & Schuster, 1947).

All these are popular treatments, those by Chase and Thouless being the best organized and written. Those by Flesch and Reilly do not present complete summaries of the thinking process, though Reilly follows the procedure as far as he goes. Flesch has a large collection of anecdotes and other illustrations under catchy chapter headings with no very clear organization. Another book in this group is really on semantics and rhetoric and is very useful in those areas: Monroe C. Beardsley, *Thinking Straight* (Englewood Cliffs, N. J., Prentice-Hall, 1940). A good list of sixteen useful books is to be found on pages 338-339 of David Russell's, *Children's Thinking* (Boston, Ginn, 1956).

Today there is still no book for teachers, though interest is such that several may be expected in the near future. We hope that our book will be useful in this category. Several good books have appeared which present logic and everyday thinking. These have wide use with upperclassmen in college and with graduate students. They can be very useful to teachers. The list is now of some size, the following being illustrations of volumes we have found very useful.

Max Black, *Critical Thinking: An Introduction to Logic and Scientific Thinking* (Englewood Cliffs, N. J., Prentice-Hall, 1946).
Edwin A. Burtt, *Right Thinking: A Study of Its Principles and Methods,* 3rd ed. (New York, Harper, 1946).
Morris R. Cohen and Ernest Nagel, *An Introduction to Logic and Scientific Method,* rev. ed. (New York, Harcourt, Brace, 1936).
Columbia Associates in Philosophy, *An Introduction to Reflective Thinking* (Boston, Houghton Mifflin, 1923).
Harold A. Larrabee, *Reliable Knowledge* (Boston, Houghton Mifflin, 1945).
National Council for the Social Studies, Howard R. Anderson, ed., *Teaching Critical Thinking in the Social Studies* (Washington, D. C., National Education Association, 1942).

The volumes by Black, Burtt, Cohen and Nagel, and Larrabee contain excellent bibliographies. The exercises provided in these volumes are among the most useful materials available anywhere.

Special acknowledgment and thanks are due the library staff in the Harvard School of Education, and to the library staff at Oregon State College, and to various faculty members at Oregon State College. These men and women were of inestimable assistance in finding references and other details, often at the cost of considerable time and energy.

Finally, we thank most sincerely the many students who contributed materially to this project when they participated in advanced seminars at the University of Cincinnati, University of Chicago, Harvard University, and Oregon State College.

The authorship. This volume is a joint product of the authors insofar as it is possible to make it so. Each author was given primary responsibility for certain chapters. First drafts were read critically by the other authors once, and in some cases two and three times. Each chapter, regardless of primary authorship, contains materials supplied by the other writers. We are in agreement on all major questions. Disagreements are few and on subsidiary matters, which in each case have been handled so as to protect the writer or writers in disagreement.

Note to instructors. An intellectual sin of the greatest magnitude would be to teach this book (or any treatment of thinking) as if it were subject-matter-to-be-mastered. An instructor guilty of lecturing this material should be strongly urged to seek a position in occupations making far simpler demands on the intellect than does teaching. Knowing about thinking is one thing, being able to think is quite another. Knowledge is necessary as in any human activity, but doing the thing is the essential.

The ingenuity of the instructor is the crux. Teaching for thinking is as fully an individual matter as is thinking itself. The essence lies in devising methods through which the students do, perform, and experience the processes to be achieved. The exercises accompanying each chapter will be of assistance, as will those in other textbooks referred to in the Preface. New ones will be necessary, designed to fit the particular group and circumstances. The discussion questions for opening the course, found in Appendix A, have been used and revised by the senior author over several years. Some instructors will find them effective; others will wish to develop their own. If used, discussion of these questions should not be hurried. Several class sessions may be devoted to them with profit. Many leads for future analyses will emerge.

Wide reading is provided dealing with the thinking process. In addition (see note at end of Chapter 1), there must be constant wide reading about the current scene and its problems, about anything which concerns people. It is useless to discuss thinking with uninformed individuals.

W. H. B.
R. B. K.
R. L. W.

Contents

Contents

Part I

Reflective Thinking: Definition, Description, and Attitudes Necessary

We do not think enough about thinking, and much of our confusion is the result of current illusions in regard to it.

JAMES HARVEY ROBINSON*

Thinking, like theology and the Terpsichorean arts, possesses a set of principles, conventions, and procedures. It is well to know these. Mere knowledge of principles and processes will not, however, make a prophet out of a village priest, or a creative choreographer out of a chorus girl. Understanding and individual adaptation to situations are the key. So it is with thinking. It is of no avail to recite the characteristics of critical thinking or to repeat in an examination the several phases in problem solving. One must have used and adapted principles and procedures in varied situations.

The major error which must be avoided is to regard thinking as a set of steps or routine, a formula to be operated as set down. A "rule-centered" approach is the death of creative thinking.

The three chapters following contain a description with illustrations which will make clear the chief characteristics of reflective, critical thinking, without reducing it to a formula. The individual is "on his own" in thinking more than in any other activity, but at the same time it is possible to give him some aid. Even though the individual's thinking in given situations is peculiarly his own, it is also clearly and inescapably related to known general processes.

* James Harvey Robinson, *Mind in the Making* (New York, Harper, 1921), p. 37.

CHAPTER 1

Thinking in Action: Illustrations and Description

The failure of modern civilization is partly due to defective logic.

M. K. BRADBY *

A thinking man is the worst enemy the Prince of Darkness can have.

THOMAS CARLYLE

Weird tales of mysterious ruins in the canyons of the Mesa Verde in southwestern Colorado came often to the ears of the first white settlers in that region. Indians told of great houses built of masonry in caves far up the cliffs. The Indians, however, obviously feared the houses and believed them to be inhabited by the spirits of the dead. The houses therefore had not been entered or examined closely by the Indians. White settlers laughed at the "tall tales" of the supposedly superstitious Indians. Everyone knew there could be no such dwellings of masonry and of the size indicated. Early mountain men and miners, however, began telling stories similar to those told by the Indians.

A small party working for the U. S. Geological Survey became interested and employed as guide a talkative old miner who said he knew where the houses were. After failing to find any houses the party became doubtful and demanded that the guide tell them just where they were. "Oh, right up there," he responded, with his pointing hand swinging to take in all the terrain in sight. Still believing the guide "didn't know what he was talking about," the men idly scanned the cliff in the gathering twilight. Suddenly there they were—some small stone houses! The men scrambled up and examined the structures and the next day photographed them. One they named "Two-Story House." Others doubtless had seen one or

* M. K. Bradby, *Logic of the Unconscious* (Oxford, Oxford Medical Publications, n.d.).

3

Who built Cliff Palace?
When?
How long did the
construction continue?
When deserted?
Why deserted?

Six hundred years of silence
intervenes between the
building and desertion
of Cliff Palace.
No records.
No clues.

Answers to the questions were secured, despite six
hundred years of silence, by trained minds.

other of the ruins, but September, 1874, marked the first recorded discovery. [1] The news, however, did not spread. In December, 1888, two ranchmen rode out to look for stray cattle. Laughing still at the Indian tales, the two agreed to keep an eye out for these mysterious stone "cities." As they rode idly along, they rounded a turn and stopped in stunned silence. A stone city filled a large cave from end to end! A quick examination was followed by a month of camping and exploring the find. *Six hundred years had passed since men had lived in what is now named Cliff Palace!*

But how did we come to know it had been six hundred years since the people lived there?!

A difficult problem is analyzed through reflective thought. The ancient citizens of Cliff Palace left no records; they could not write. Imagine the other questions the excited ranchmen asked (and those still asked by the thousands of tourists who visit Mesa Verde National Park)!

Who built these stone houses?
When were they begun?
How long did the building continue to complete these houses?
How long did the builders live here?
When were the houses completely deserted?
Why were they deserted?

A score more questions doubtless arose as to the life, the special activities, the religion of these vanished people. For the moment we will confine questions to those of dates and time. On the one hand, there stood the ruins, silent before those who saw them. On the other hand, there were the questions concerning origin, development, and desertion. In between there was the great blank.

The gap was bridged. The questions were answered. The problems were solved, and with considerable precision! How? The answers were derived by trained minds—minds trained to do critical reflective thinking in the solution of problems. This leads us to the theme of this book. What goes on when one truly thinks? Can we train people to do critical, reflective thinking in solving problems? To anticipate the story: we cannot teach anyone to think, but there is ample evidence to show that we can aid persons to think far more accurately than they ordinarily do. The importance of this for individual and group thinking is almost incalculable. It might often be the difference between survival and destruction. Even for the simple affairs of everyday life, accurate thinking is probably a critical factor in the success or failure of individuals, families, and larger groups.

The answers, or at least some of them:

Beams in some of the houses were put in about the years 1019, 1048, and thereafter.

[1] Don Watson, *Cliff Palace, The Story of an Ancient City* (Ann Arbor, Mich., Edwards Brothers, Inc., 1949). The general facts in these pages were taken from this pamphlet. Specific points will be footnoted later.

Cliff Palace was very probably begun in approximately 1050 and was in construction from then to about 1273.

Cliff Palace was probably completely deserted by 1300, though desertion had been going on for some years.

The years 1276–1300 were years of continuous drought, with 1280 being almost rainless. The Indians had experienced normal rainfall from 1261 to 1272 and expected yearly that the drought would end. When it didn't, they had no alternative other than to move away as their livelihood depended upon farming.

Indians had actually been living in the Cliff Palace area since the beginning of the Christian era, but the building of stone houses for residence and for defense came later as indicated above. The houses were there before William the Conqueror landed on English shores! They were *completed* and *deserted* before Columbus was born, let alone discovered America! They had been deserted for three centuries before the first white men landed on the eastern shores of what is now the United States. The Spanish explorers who were in southwest America a century or so before the landings at Jamestown and Plymouth Rock came within 120 miles of Mesa Verde in 1540. Another Spanish party camped along the same stream in 1776 as did the U. S. Geological Survey party in 1874, but did not see the ruins. The Spanish left written records of some things, but how did we discover the dates from 1300 back to 1019 and earlier? Again the answer is: through the use of trained minds doing critical, reflective thinking in solving problems.

The process of solving the problems presented by the deserted dwellings. A trained physicist and astronomer, Dr. A. E. Douglass, working on climatic problems in the Southwest noted the importance of rainfall in that region. [2] Seeking a method of studying weather conditions prior to the keeping of modern records, he reasoned that any variation in rainfall should be reflected in the annual growth of certain trees. If this were true, he reasoned further, the variation in the annual rings in the trees would give information about climate not available in any other way. This idea was not new with Dr. Douglass: it had occurred earlier to various men including Leonardo da Vinci. The far-flung possibilities of the idea were not developed until the first quarter of the twentieth century. Dr. Douglass

---

[2] A. E. Douglass, "The Secret of the Southwest Solved by the Talkative Tree Rings," *National Geographic Magazine,* Vol. 46, No. 6 (1929). A popular account of the establishment of the first prehistoric chronology. Dr. Douglass published several other accounts in Carnegie Institution bulletins, Smithsonian bulletins, and in the University of Arizona *Tree Ring Research Bulletin.* Other accounts are available in publications of the Universities of Arizona and New Mexico.

N. S. Stallings, Jr., "Dating Prehistoric Ruins by Tree Rings," *General Series Bulletin No. 8* (Santa Fe, New Mexico, Laboratory of Anthropology, 1939); rev. ed. (Tree Ring Society with co-operation of Laboratory of Tree Ring Research, University of New Mexico, 1949). This pamphlet contains a good bibliography of 25 titles.

noted a long definite pattern in more than sixty trees cut within one area. Matching the ring patterns with modern weather records established a relationship between tree ring growth and rainfall. Reasoning was beginning to pay off! Matching patterns from living trees with pieces of old wood from whatever source, provided there was some overlap, extended the annual ring "calendar" backward in time.

To make a very long and very interesting story short, dendrochronology was established, and dated chronologies were established back to the first year of the Christian era. One study using the very long-lived sequoia trees goes back to 1305 B. C. Beams from ancient dwellings were used, including those from the ruins of the Southwest pueblos. So far the objective was still to study and analyze complex climatological problems. The final step, for our story here, came when scientists realized that they could date the building and cessation of building in the ancient deserted buildings through the very beams they were using to study weather. *Trained minds had recognized a problem, had noted evidences, had "thought of" possibilities, had checked their hypotheses or "guesses," and had come up with valid answers.* A seemingly impenetrable mystery had been solved; the age of buildings deserted before Columbus was born had been established!

The reader may be assured that all thinking is not of this remote and complicated type. Everyday problems important to the average citizen will be analyzed a few pages further on. This illustration has been presented because of its novelty, interest, and clear portrayal of certain aspects of thinking. The wealth of detail in this problem has been purposely omitted so that a simple, clearly understandable outline of the major phases of thinking might be presented.

The phases of thinking which have been illustrated. The discussion here will be specific and confined to the illustration used. A general and more inclusive description of the thinking process will be given later.

1. *A problem, with a number of subproblems, was recognized by certain men.* The problem was posed in these questions:

Can we date these mysterious ruins?
When were they built?
When completed?
When deserted?
How long did the construction continue?
Why deserted?

Other subproblems were involved but are not mentioned in this account.

The trained men involved recognized that they would have to "think out" an answer and check it against facts. The thinking started in the mind but was initiated (in this case) by an occurrence in the real world. After the thinking had progressed a bit it was checked against the real world.

2. *A testable hypothesis was set up.* Men examined the facts, such as

there were within the ruins. They were not sure where to look, or what to look for. Doubtless they asked other men for their views, consulted books, and records.

Most important in this case, they examined facts already in their minds; that is, they searched their past experience for anything which might bear on the problem. Two facts from the past were: (*a*) There is a relation between annual rainfall and tree rings, and (*b*) A dendrochronology covering some centuries had been established.

One man, at least, saw a possible connection between the tree ring chronology and the possibility of dating the ruins. A hypothesis came into his mind: *Woods used for beams in these buildings will show a tree ring pattern, and this may overlap with the chronology already established.*

3. *The hypothesis was elaborated:*

a. By reasoning. If overlap could be found between beams in the buildings and the already established tree ring chronology, they would know the dates on which the timbers were cut and presumably placed in the buildings. This would give them a beginning and ending date.

b. By seeking further facts in a place now indicated by the hypothesis and the reasoning. Wood was cut from the beams and compared with tree ring series already proved to be related to the calendar.

4. *The hypothesis was demonstrated to be true* when overlap was found and dates established. The original problem was answered.

5. *The principle produced and verified here was incorporated into our existing system of ideas* and used in dating buildings elsewhere. (The calendar based on diminishing amounts of radioactivity in materials referred to just below can be more widely applied.)

(In areas where such information is available, ancient dwellings, artifacts, and monuments, for example, can be dated by comparing them with similar materials already verified from comparable records, by geologic levels, and the like.)

The answer secured illustrated the process of "thinking about" the facts available, extending the hypothesis by reasoning, and seeking other facts. This, of course, is not the whole story. We shall see that thinking is not the smooth and orderly process it might seem to be from this abbreviated account. The hypothesis and its extension by reasoning were almost simultaneous here. Sometimes it is difficult and time consuming to secure useful extensions. Several hypotheses may have to be examined. Many details will be developed in succeeding chapters. Nothing has been said, either, of the obstacles and pitfalls in thinking, of the controls of observation and inference, of the many serious sources of error, let alone formal fallacies.

Thinking on this particular problem, moreover, ranges over a wider field than indicated here. Problem solvers dealing with ancient civilizations usually study also the implements and utensils of war and peace left behind by vanished peoples, the bones of animals, and other items. In certain archaeological research, as hinted above, answers can be obtained when comparable exhibits are already available.

A mystery seemingly as impenetrable as that of Cliff Palace, namely the origin and placement of the huge stone statues on Easter Island, was recently solved. The facts and circumstances were quite different from those in the Cliff Palace instance, but the processes of critical, reflective thinking operated in each. The account is well worth reading. [3]

Dating by determining the radioactivity of substances. The story of this penetration of ancient secrets is as exciting as any detective story thriller. The summary should be read without fail. [4]

All natural substances and artifacts contain a substance known as carbon-14 which disintegrates radioactively, its atoms exploding one by one. The rates of disintegration are known. A radiocarbon calendar was developed as was the tree ring chronology. The two calendars have been compared on given items with good results. The number of explosions can be recorded by an electronic counter; the amount of radioactivity remaining in the substance is thus revealed, and the age of the substance becomes known.

The ingenuity of the human mind has penetrated another mystery. Charcoal from a fire which burned 30,000 years ago in a cave in Iraq was dated. The ancient men who sat around that fire thirty millenia ago could never have dreamed that the embers would some day figure in complex scientific research. Sandals woven 9000 years ago in Oregon were similarly dated. Modern as well as ancient materials are forced to reveal their secrets. The lid of an Egyptian sarcophagus in one of the best museums was believed to be 2200 years old. Radiocarbon tests showed that it was less than 100 years old! The lid had been cleverly faked to go with the rest of the ancient coffin.

Why do men pursue these remote, complicated problems? Answers in many cases are not of immediate practical value or use, though in other cases answers may be of great import. Man has an urge (though many seem to have lost it!) to know, an urge to base thinking and action on knowledge which he knows to be reliable.

Let us now turn to a problem at the opposite end of the scale, one of great simplicity to adults, though not so simple to the children who dealt with it.

A very simple problem is analyzed. A real-life problem of interest to first-grade children and their parents is presented as a contrast to the very difficult scientific problem outlined above. The account really presents two problems, one for the parents and one for the children.

A first-grade teacher speaking before the parent-teacher association

[3] Thor Heyerdahl, *Aku-Aku: The Secret of Easter Island* (Chicago, Rand McNally, 1958). See also popular articles based on this account of the Easter Island statues, *Saturday Evening Post* (September 6, 13, 20, 27, 1958).

[4] Lyman J. Briggs and Kenneth F. Weaver, "How Old Is It?" *National Geographic Magazine* (August, 1958), pp. 234-255. Earlier accounts of the first steps in this method have appeared from time to time in the *National Geographic Magazine* and in some other general magazines; all of these are excellent reading.

upheld the modern belief that small children can solve real problems appropriate to their level of maturity, even those of behavior and discipline.
Given opportunity and sympathetic guidance they can learn how to do this.
The parents immediately opened a vigorous discussion. Omitting detail,
particularly that which dealt with *subquestions and clarifying the real
issue,* the parents emphasized certain questions:

Can first-grade children really solve problems?
Wouldn't it be better if the teacher (or parent) gave the answers and made the
    children follow her statements?
Can children actually achieve good behavior on their own? (Parents often
    phrased the question like this: Can children get "discipline" in the room
    through their own efforts?)
Assuming that they might maintain discipline, would this get better results
    than teacher-imposed discipline?

Parents *advanced hypotheses* (possible answers) at the same time
they defined the problem and questions. These divided roughly into four:

Children cannot possibly maintain order on their own at that age.
Children could maintain order if given some help in learning how to do this.
The discipline maintained by children, assuming they could achieve it, could
    not be as good as that maintained by the teacher.

A tiny group of parents advanced a fourth hypothesis:

The effort to have children participate in managing their own behavior, even
    if the behavior were not as good as that maintained by the teacher, would
    be desirable because of the training in thinking and in development of
    socially desirable beliefs and habits.

This group got little attention (except from the teacher) because
that type of thinking had not developed far at the time of the incident
here reported. Today this fourth hypothesis is widely accepted.

The parents began *supporting or denying the hypotheses* even as they
advanced them. They *reasoned and referred to experience.* One group said:

Children are too young; they cannot "stay put" long enough to work on a
    problem; they do not know enough; it isn't "natural" for children to do
    this; children must be taught to obey and to respect authority.

A second group stated:

Children often do astonishing thinking on certain problems that arise around
    the home; children must begin somewhere to "learn to think," to take
    responsibility, to learn to "behave on their own." We must train them
    for independence.

Note that most of these are *general statements* accepted and believed
by the parents advancing them. *Specific evidence* was rarely stated, though

several parents cited specific incidents from their homes, and often about the neighbor's children! These were referred to as "facts." No matter how widely circulated and accepted these statements may be, they are neither facts nor reliable evidence. The incidents are single, reported by untrained observers; many factors within the total situation are not known. Sincere individuals often report as "my experience" things that could not possibly have happened. These are honest individuals who have not been trained to distinguish between their experience and *their opinion about that experience*. This aspect of thinking is merely mentioned here for the record. None of the speakers examined in any way the assumptions back of his own statements.

Statements for or against the hypotheses were, thus far, "thought of" by the parents. They came basically from past experience, from reading, and from lectures—and all of these sources had been variously interpreted by the parents. The observations and conclusions were honest but untrained. Many of the beliefs actually came from gossip, old wives' tales, uncritically accepted lore. Again this is mentioned to keep the record straight.

How can parents take the next step, *checking against real facts* or evidences of which they can be sure? First, they might read accounts of valid experiments which have been carried on in real schoolrooms, or observe experiments in progress. Few such accounts were available at the time of this incident. Second, they could, when possible, set up a situation under controlled observation and see what happens. Which hypotheses will be supported or denied wholly or partially by facts already known or produced by further experimentation? The teacher in this case stated that her first grade had been working on these very problems for some time. Interested parents were welcome to observe what went on, and many did so later.

In one period the children came in from recess and grouped themselves around the teacher for their daily "planning" period. The chairman for the month took over, and the teacher went to the back of the room. When asked what needed to be talked about, the group broke into vigorous discussion. The chairman quietly reduced this to orderly taking of turns and waiting until speakers had finished. Real trouble was abroad on the playground! Some boys got on the slides, swings, and bars and refused to let anyone else play on these. There was no "taking of turns." Sand was thrown about in the sandbox, and some projects were trampled or knocked over. Children in charge of collecting the large rubber balls complained that certain children would not give them up; others persisted in throwing them out of reach; others took the balls out of the containers and tossed them away to be picked up again. The children made clear that only a few were causing the "trouble" and "most of us want to take turns and all get some fun."

Reasons were given for improving the situation:

"It isn't fair."
"Some do not get to play at all."
"Taking turns is better."
"Sand could be thrown into our eyes; it isn't nice."
"Some get pushed or knocked down."
"Some get mad and do other bad things."
"So many try to play with one ball that no one has any fun."
The chairman worded the obvious and simple problem, "What can we do about this?"

The children began advancing, supporting, and denying certain solutions:

"We should have rules so everyone gets to play."
"We should do something about those who push people and knock them over."
"Anybody who does bad things after we have rules should be told he cannot play that day." (Other punishments were also suggested.)

To make a long story short, several discussions took place. Simple rules were set up by the group. Varying orders of taking turns were worked out, some alphabetically, some on basis of size of children. The number to play on a slide, bar, or swing at one time was established. Throwers of sand could not play in the sandbox. The determination of how many should play with one large rubber ball (several were available) at a time aroused long discussion. The children themselves proposed an experimental try-out: "Four people at a time and see how that works out." The make-up of this group was such that they abided by their own rules, none resenting the social pressure that was sometimes necessary. Not all groups could do this type of thinking, and none can do it without sympathetic guidance while they learn. Different backgrounds and attitudes could produce groups that would not attack their problems and would be troublesome even under school-imposed rules.

The critical analysis of statements made orally or in print. A third illustration shows that not all reflective or critical thought deals with events; sometimes it is concerned with statements about events. The analysis below will show how the critical aspects may be dominant in a given thought process, with other aspects of problem solving minimized. The abbreviated guide to critical analysis used here is illustrative only. An extended guide will be given in Chapter 15 on general method and another in Chapter 18 on the social studies after further necessary points are developed in Part II. Public speeches and "letters to the editor," examples of careful critical thinking and of extremely noncritical thinking are easily available. The following letter furnishes good material for practicing critical analysis:

Immigration Law Is Defended

To the Editor of The Standard-Times:

Senator Humphrey of Minnesota said our immigration law should be revised. I say it is a good law and should be left alone.

This law protects the American people. It prevents the lawbreakers and undesirables from entering the United States.

The native countries of these immigrants do not want these people back if they become dependents of the state. If their native countries do not want them, why should we let them enter in the first place?

Senator Humphrey says the law has strained our European relations. Why should we care what they think of us? Our law men have thought too much of Europe lately at the expense of America. The Americans in Europe hear very often, "Yanks, go home."

We should come home and leave only a skeleton crew to take care of our money and the way it is distributed. What howls there would be when a good day's work confronted the Europeans—no more liberty bells rubbing each other in their pockets.

The immigration law should be left just as it is, and everyone admitted to our shore should be fingerprinted, diplomat or not.

MRS. BEATRICE PELLETIER
Acushnet

A good thinker, when he hears or reads certain types of materials, will immediately ask questions:

What is the intent of the writer?
What are the main arguments advanced?
Are these arguments supported by facts and reason, given or implied?
Do assumptions, hidden or otherwise, lurk behind statements?
What means of evaluation are used for facts, inferences, assumptions?
Do any obvious fallacies appear; any known methods of checking one's thinking?
Is the language that of an honest thinker, or that of a special pleader, or of a propagandist?
Are terms defined, used consistently; or does meaning shift consciously or unconsciously?
Has the writer supported his conclusion so we can give it belief, or has he failed?

An analysis of the foregoing letter may be summarized briefly as follows:

1. *Purpose, intent, or point of view of the writer.* The letter writer advises against any revision of the present immigration laws. The point of view is isolationist.
2. *Chief arguments used.*
    a. Lawbreakers and undesirables are presently kept out.
    b. If refugees from other countries are undesirable in their native lands, they are undesirable to us.

  c. We should not care what Europeans think of us, whether they like us or not. We can get along alone.

3. *Facts to support arguments.* None, except for reference to appearance in Europe of "Yanks, go home!" Many available facts are ignored or are unknown to the writer. Expression is entirely of personal and unsupported opinion.

4. *Assumptions.* Unsupported innuendo that Europeans do not work now that they get U. S. loans; assumption that they are currently getting such loans. (Several others could be mentioned.)

5. *Evaluation of arguments,* apart from facts and reasoning. The writer:

  a. Fails to take into account immigrants who are neither lawbreakers nor "undesirables," whatever the latter term may mean in absence of definition.

  b. Fails to consider that many potential immigrants are political refugees from Communist countries and might be assets to our country.

  c. Takes up controversial issues far too large for adequate discussion in a newspaper letter.

  d. Failed to consider other hypotheses than the one supported.

6. *Specific logical fallacies. Non sequitur* (several), nonquantitative statements, omission of relevant information or sources thereof.

7. *Emotive language is used to confuse the issue;* distorting hyperbole employed; key terms undefined, for example, "undesirable." Tone is sarcastic, not sober and controlled.

8. *Conclusion.* Wholly unsupported by facts or by the arguments used.

  Careful, critical analysis, therefore, directs us to withhold belief from the purpose and conclusion of the writer. The conclusion may be correct, but there is no way to tell from this letter.

  Thinking appears everywhere in life. An individual may choose his life work, plan a complete change of occupation and residence, or uphold a form of government on either of two general bases. The same holds for such simple problems as deciding what to wear for today's weather, what to take on a week's camping trip, how to rearrange the furniture, which of several routes to take, and many others. The individual may, on the one hand, come to his conclusions on the basis of careful, meticulously scrutinized facts which he has impersonally verified through impersonal standards or which he accepts from reliable authorities. He may carefully define what he is talking about and use specific devices to keep the thinking process on the point. He may deliberately recognize desires or prejudices and attempt to discount them. The individual may, on the other hand, come to his conclusions on the basis of fragmentary, unanalyzed experience, or on the basis of hearsay, or on the advice of persons who know no more than he does. His judgments may be made hastily on the basis of insufficient data; they may be influenced by whims, caprices, prejudices, and the like, whether recognized or not. In short, he may do careful, close reasoning in terms of fact and principle, or he may do "sloppy," superficial, and wishful thinking. The processes of good and poor thinking are far more complex than these introductory sentences imply. Many illustrations and numerous details will be developed in following chapters.

Guidance of thinking very difficult. Few aims of teaching are mentioned as frequently as "teaching pupils to think." [5] Teachers of all special subjects assert freely that one of the outcomes of study in the field is "ability to think." Teachers of music have been heard to dispute with teachers of mathematics and science the relative merits of these subjects with reference to training pupils to think.

One basic reason why better results are not achieved is that the majority of teachers have no knowledge of the thinking process and its development. No carping or supercilious criticism of teachers is intended. The fault lies squarely with the teacher-training institutions, complicated by public indifference to the problem. General ignorance of the intricacies of thinking is the rule with the average citizen, the man-in-the-street. This volume is addressed to the problem of developing understanding of thinking, to teaching so that transfer of processes may take place. This is a first attempt on the level we have chosen, and no claims are made for finality.

A second reason for general ignorance of the topic is that research has been meager and slow to develop. Research on the classroom aspects of guiding thinking is very recent. The canons of formal logic were formulated by competent thinkers centuries ago; research on the actual processes of thought was almost nonexistent until the turn of the century.

Training in thinking necessary and possible. A large section of the public once believed that the mass of the population was incapable of reflective thought and hence could not be trained to think. The data from anthropology and psychology thoroughly refute this idea. Level of native intelligence in the given individual is directly related, of course, to the level of thinking that can be achieved. Any person can be trained, within the limits of his natural intelligence, to think better than he will think without training.

Another belief is that thinking is "natural" and will occur anyway as do breathing or digestion; anyone can think, and everyone does think; hence, training is unnecessary. The average citizen is often amazed and annoyed when it is indicated that he does not think well or at all. Thinking is, in fact, "natural" to the extent that all normal individuals are equipped to do it. Organized, systematic thinking, however, is clearly an acquired ability. Definite, continued experience in problem solving together with analysis of one's processes are necessary.

The school with teachers untrained in the analysis of thought and with a traditional curriculum has often discouraged good thinking in learners. The school has on occasions built up attitudes and habits inimical to good

[5] A detailed analysis of the guidance of thinking, together with the best suggestions we can make, will be found in Chs. 4 through 12.

thinking. Despite the difficulties and handicaps which exist, better methods for guiding problem solving in the classroom are constantly appearing. Research in psychology and education is slowly increasing in amount and value.

The purpose of teaching problem-solving skills is not merely to find the answer to specific problems. The outcomes are far broader and more valuable.

QUESTIONS, EXERCISES, AND REPORTS

1. One or two students may report briefly any cases of thinking in which they have participated, or observed, or read. Cases may be simple or complex and need not be confined to the types illustrated in the chapter.

2. One or two students may report cases of teaching-learning activities which are to stimulate thinking by the learners, in contrast to certain more common practices. (This may not be possible at this stage of the course.)

3. Bring in a brief "letter to the editor," or a paragraph from an editorial, or commentator's column, and make brief critical analysis.

4. List and explain any suggestions you see so far for aiding pupils to improve their thinking. Do not stop with general statements of principle. Give specific applications.

5. List any teaching practices which, on the basis of insight so far, you would suggest eliminating? What new practices now appearing seem justifiable? Have you any new ideas of your own so far?

READINGS WHICH AMPLIFY THIS CHAPTER

DEWEY, John, *How We Think*, rev. ed. (Boston, Heath, 1933), Chs. 1, 6, 7, and pp. 166-168. The latter pages contain the "burglar illustration" made famous in Dewey's first edition.

or

BURTT, E. A., *Right Thinking*, 3rd ed. (New York, Harper, 1946), Ch. 1.

or

BLACK, Max, *Critical Thinking* (Englewood Cliffs, N. J., Prentice-Hall, 1946), Ch. 13.

Readers from this point onward should be on the lookout for accounts of reflective thinking. These will be found in reports of scientific research, invention, or creative thinking of any kind; in philosophic analyses; in autobiographies and biographies. Current publications—both books and periodicals—should be scanned. Two excellent sources are the *Saturday Review* and the *New York Times Book Review Section*. Several other newspapers and magazines contain good brief book review columns. See also index of reviews in the *Readers Guide* and in the *Education Index*.

CHAPTER 2

A General Description of the Thinking Process

> The decisive value of thinking depends upon what the mind is directed to and what logic it accepts for its operations.
>
> JOSEPH JASTROW *

> Few of us take the pains to study the origin of our cherished convictions; indeed, we have a natural repugnance to so doing.
> We do not think enough about thinking, and much of our confusion is the result of current illusions in regard to it.
>
> JAMES HARVEY ROBINSON †

A given presentation cannot proceed without definition of terms and meaning as they are used within that presentation. Definitions for the same term differ a little from writer to writer, but readers should not be dismayed. Different aspects of the major topic are given different emphasis, thus producing some variation in wording. The essence remains the same. So it is with a definition of thinking. Several writers mention that the terms *reflective thought, critical thought,* and *problem solving* are used by different authors to mean about the same thing. Dewey uses *reflective thought* as his major term and practically equates it with *problem solving.* Another important book defines *critical thought* ably in terms of the abilities required, and then several chapters later on gives a list of "the problem-solving aspects of critical thinking." This use of the word *critical* should disturb no one since it is obvious that problem solving does depend upon many critical abilities. Critical analysis may in some cases be the major consideration and other aspects of problem solving minimized, as in the

---

* Joseph Jastrow, *The Betrayal of Intelligence* (New York, Greenberg, 1938), p. 130.

† James Harvey Robinson, *The Mind in the Making* (New York, Harper, 1921), pp. 41, 37.

analysis of the letter to the editor outlined in Chapter 1. Generally in this volume we reserve the term *critical analysis* for the special procedure of analyzing some other person's attempt to solve a problem.

Creative thinking is both a *type* of thinking, "the production of something new, unique, original, not-before-existent," and an *aspect* of critical or problem-solving thinking. Creative thinking will be dealt with as a separate type in Chapter 15. The appearance of creative process will also be noted, as, for instance, in the creation of hypotheses, in the development of insights, "bold guesses", and original conclusions. Critical thinking when stressed in the wrong places may effectively inhibit creative thinking.

Definition of thinking for our purposes. We are chiefly concerned with the type of thinking which goes on in the physical and social sciences, in all the everyday problems confronting men, and in critical analysis of statements of any kind. Two sentences from Dewey define thinking for the purposes of this volume: [1] "Active, persistent, and careful consideration of any belief or supposed form of knowledge in the light of the grounds that support it and the further conclusions to which it tends *constitutes reflective thought*." On another page Dewey states: ". . . *reflective thinking,* in distinction from other operations to which we apply the name of thought, involves (1) a state of doubt, hesitation, perplexity, mental difficulty, in which thinking originates, and (2) an act of searching, hunting, inquiring, to find material that will resolve the doubt, settle and dispose of the perplexity."

We mean by the term *thinking* the critical, reflective search for valid conclusions which solve our problems, resolve our doubts, and enable us to choose between conflicting statements of doctrine or policy.

Can we say in everyday terms what one does when he has to "stop and think"? First, he runs into something which raises a doubt or perplexity in his mind. He does not know the answer and will have to figure it out. Second, he makes sure what the difficulty is and notes the conditions surrounding the situation. Third, he examines the given facts, sets up hypotheses, and searches for more facts both through observation and through memory of similar situations. Fourth, he looks critically at the facts and their interpretations. This necessitates setting up or using known criteria. Fifth, he draws conclusions which seem to be supported by his inquiry, and last, he checks against reality. Throughout, he tries to maintain suspended judgment. The division into first, second, third, and other phases is arbitrary for descriptive purposes only. Thinking is unitary, and all phases go on together. [2]

[1] John Dewey, *How We Think,* rev. ed. (Boston, Heath, 1933), pp. 9, 12.
[2] Other major sources useful here include:
John Dewey, *op cit.,* Ch. 1.
Max Black, *Critical Thinking* (Englewood Cliffs, N. J., Prentice-Hall, 1946), Chs. 11, 14.
Edwin A. Burtt, *Right Thinking,* 3rd ed. (New York, Harper, 1946), Ch. 1.

The problems which initiate thinking may range from simple, every-day matters such as determining how to dress the children for today's weather, to complex, scientific problems such as how to shoot a rocket to the moon.

The term thinking *is often used loosely and carelessly.* The loose and careless use of the term by the average citizen, in contrast to the trained thinker, doubtless has a great deal to do with the citizen's difficulties in thinking accurately. Dewey mentions directly "distinction from other operations to which we apply the name of thought." The various functions loosely labeled as thinking are useful within thinking as here defined but are not equivalent to it.

Remembering is often called thinking. Anything whatever that passes through the mind is, by some, called thinking. Ask someone who is sitting in a "brown study," "What are you thinking about?" "Oh, about the good old days when we were all kids together down on the farm." Ask someone to recall a name or an address for you, and they often reply, "I just can't think of it at the moment." Older people who find they do not remember as well as they once did, often say, "I just can't think as well as I once did." This is all remembering—not thinking as defined here and in other texts.

These reveries consist of random recollections, scene succeeding scene with no necessary connection. These are, as we say, "idle thoughts," a stream of consciousness phenomenon. What goes through the mind may range from the chaotic to a sequence which is vague and accidental, though doubtless pleasant. There is no defined purpose, no real problem, to regulate and make systematic the sequences of remembrances.

Imagining is often called thinking. Two different levels are seen here. First, one classification of things passing through the mind would more properly be called daydreaming. Asked what he is thinking about, an individual may reply, "I was thinking what I would do if I had a million dollars," or "Oh, just dreaming about life in the South Seas." These flights of fancy usually have no regulated sequence; in fact, some impossible things are often "thought of," that is, imagined. Daydreaming of this type can lead into thinking as defined, but it rarely does so. Another person may reply, "I was thinking what I would do if I were the boss." This might be daydreaming with little relation to systematic thinking, or it could be more or less serious. To the extent that this deals with actual conditions, with actual possible changes and improvements, the process would approximate reflective thinking.

Morris R. Cohen and Ernest Nagel, *An Introduction to Logic and Scientific Method* (New York, Harcourt, Brace, 1934), Ch. 20.

Harold A. Larrabee, *Reliable Knowledge* (Boston, Houghton Mifflin, 1945). Use the Index.

David H. Russell, *Children's Thinking* (Boston, Ginn, 1956), Chs. 1, 9, 11, 13, 19.

The second usage is closely related to the first. *Thinking* is often used to refer to things which are "thought of" instead of present to the senses. This may be seen in the fanciful tales told by many poets and prose writers. This kind of thinking occurs also in stories written for children in which there is a sequence but it is not a record of observed facts in the world. Such stories appeal to the freewheeling imagination for which children are noted. Children themselves often make up such stories which are often wild fantasy due to immaturity and lack of distinction between the real and the not real. Sometimes yarns invented by children themselves are, within the limits of maturity and experience, good illustrations of creative thinking. Creative thought and invention are illustrations of dealing with things not present, things which are first "thought out" and then attempted in the real world. These enterprises fit the definition of thinking.

Belief is often called thinking. Remarks are constantly heard, "I think it is going to rain today," "I think you ought to stay home today," "I think business will take an upturn (or a downturn)," "I think that if Mr. X is not elected, we are in for serious trouble." A powerful individual once said to the aldermen of a small town, "If you do not grant us this concession, I think you will see grass growing in the streets of your town." Just for the record, the corporation involved is out of business; and the town in question has almost tripled its population! Public figures often go further and say "I know" instead of "I think." Reflective thinking is almost never involved, only hope, fear, or belief-without-grounds. Any of the remarks could have been based on real thinking, and with careful individuals thinking does so precede. Challenged, the man who has been thinking can outline his evidences and chain of reasoning; the other man cannot, he "just knows."

When Columbus stated that he believed or thought the world to be round, he had listened to others who expressed themselves on this and had himself done reflective thinking based on certain observed facts. He then tried out his belief by making a voyage. Here we have belief which was turned into verified conclusion. Scientific thinking, particularly inventive thinking, is full of illustrations wherein men "thought of" something, believed it so strongly that they tried it out, verifying or disproving their belief. More will be said of this in the readings to accompany Chapter 5 on hypothesis.

A related process should be mentioned here which will be developed later. Men working in and trained for a given field often say, "I think that this will work," meaning "I have a hunch it may work." Coherent backing for the hunch perhaps cannot be outlined on the spur of the moment. Hunches, intuitions, and insights do occur without clear apprehension of the basis. The hunches of trained thinkers occur because they have been dealing with the problem and the data of the field and are steeped in the background. When examined and brought to light, the process back of the hunch can be included in reflective thought as defined. Scientific thinking is often greatly aided (or may be seriously impeded) by this type of thinking. The hunches and intuitions of the average citizen, note well, are not of this order. A small but interesting literature exists on the psychology of hunch or intuition. Interested students may report on it.

Thinking, as defined, is not memory, or imagination, or opining, or believing, or intuition, or insight. But thinking uses all of these. Thinking, as defined, is not daydreaming, or reverie, or a flight of fancy, or building castles in Spain, or "shooting the moon"—though any of these may produce a problem which necessitates reflective thinking of the type presented in this volume.

The term problem *or* problem solving *is also used carelessly.* To repeat, a problem is a situation involving doubt, for which the answer is unknown but can ordinarily be figured out. Some problems (see Chapter 18) cannot presently be figured out. The problem must be understandable to the learner, hence, susceptible to intelligent attack, and must motivate him to want to solve it. The problem-solving process is the critical reflective thinking by which the individual finds his way out of the perplexing situation. A problem which is not understood by the person, which cannot be attacked, and for which he has no desire for solution, is not a problem for the given individual. This is very important for teaching.

Puzzles are of two general types as far as the present issue is concerned. Puzzles involve the unknown and call for solution. If, however, the puzzle is so novel in terms of the individual's experience and motivations that it cannot be attacked intelligently, then it is not a problem for that individual. The learner either has no idea of what to do or has such a vague understanding that he knows where to go to work but not what to do. Blind trial and error are tried. The attitude is one of bewilderment, of *puzzlement* as is often said, and not one of problem solving. This is extremely important because many curriculums and teachers present "problems" which are beyond the comprehension of the learner, with the mistaken idea that this "makes him think." On the contrary, it makes him guess and resort to blind trial and error. The attitude of problem attack does not exist for the given learner, only bafflement. Success in this type of situation is accidental; the method is not likely to be transferred.

On the other hand, puzzles can be classified as problems, as defined above, when they are related to the past experience of the learner, hence are understood well enough to be attacked systematically and also attract his efforts.

The word *question* also refers to two types of inquiry. One type is properly a problem, the other not. First, a question may fulfill all the conditions of a problem described above. These need not be repeated here. Second, a question may refer to a situation for which the person has solutions available and recallable, or for which the sources of answers are known. Requests for information, for directions, for clarification, are questions and nothing more.

A *task* is a job-to-be-done and not a problem-to-be-solved. A task involves known principles and factual elements; the general scheme of the answer is known. The task is to manipulate the known elements for the accomplishment of a known and desired result. This may, and often does, contain instances of problem solving. It is interesting to note that training courses for our armed forces during World War II distinguished between

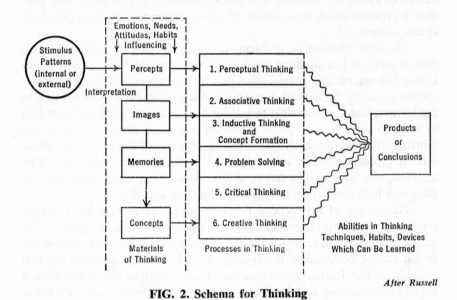

After Russell

FIG. 2. Schema for Thinking

"problems" and "operational tasks." The first includes unknowns and demands an original answer; the second calls for the manipulation of known factors. Even a "calculated risk," the exact nature of which is unknown, is a known factor in such operations.

The typical manuals for laboratory work in many sciences do not have anything to do with problem solving; they furnish recipes to be followed. It is difficult to imagine a method more adequately designed to avoid training in thinking. Some manuals properly list their contents as exercises. The great majority of "problems" in tests for arithmetic, physics, and chemistry are not problems at all, but are simple questions, in some cases tasks.

The factor of *directedness* is stressed by Russell as an aid to distinguishing between kinds and levels of thinking. [3] Thinking may range from

[3] Russell, *op. cit.*, p. 10. Used by permission of author and publisher. "This book" and chapter numbers refer to Russell's book.

the relatively undirected; to that which is directed by the person's past experience, wishes, temperament, and immediate situation; to that which is closely and sharply directed by a stated goal, by some outcome necessary to the individual's progress or safety. These distinctions can be identified in the immediately preceding discussion. The diagram in Figure 2 was developed by Russell to organize the different types of thinking.

The subjective and objective aspects of thinking. Thinking is referred to both colloquially and technically as subjective, perceptual, conceptual, and as objective. The average citizen also refers to "theoretical" and to "practical" thinking in trying to distinguish the subjective from the objective. The interesting misconception in the theoretical-practical contrast will be dealt with in detail in a later chapter.

Sharp distinction between subjective and objective is, in real situations, false. The thinking process is subjective, but it deals with, and must take account of, the objective facts and processes. Thinking is affected by things in the world and in turn affects them. Thinking in some cases must turn to the objective world for its validation; in other cases it brings change in the objective world.

When a problem arises "in the world," suggestions bearing on it arise "in the mind," that is, come from past experience or a recombination of past experiences. This suggestion is then "applied in the world"; reaction is noted "in the mind." Often, search must be made in the world for more suggestions. The total problem-solving process cannot be separated into subjective and objective except arbitrarily for purposes of study. A problem-solving process is a functional interaction between the two.

The so-called objective factors are more likely to affect thinking and to control it more adequately because of their independent existence. Only genuinely stupid persons think in defiance of factors which exist in the real world. The subjective factors are within the control of the individual and consequently are susceptible to gross, even grotesque error. An individual may "think" out the most absurd, nonsensical, and unrealistic interpretations of actuality and come to utterly untenable conclusions, and no one can stop him. In fact, the average citizen does just this. Unless the harsh, irreducible, coercive facts of reality make his absurd "thinking" fatal, painful, or costly, he may continue to hold utterly baseless and useless beliefs. Common beliefs in politics, religion, business, rearing of children, and home medicine illustrate this admirably. Such "thinking" stands in sharp contrast to the thought of first-class business analysts, diagnosticians in medicine, inventors, trained engineers, statesmen, and others.

Training is obviously needed in the control of the inner factors, and particularly in the details of the process. This should be a required part of general education. Trained thinking involves not merely an understanding of certain canons of logic, of the fallacies of thought, but also understanding of the nature of thought-in-process which is very different from formal logic. The thinker must also have a firm desire to think correctly, must insist that he himself follow the principles of thinking regardless of consequences. He must be willing to suffer through periods of suspended judgment, to persist in inquiry. The individual must not only discover how to think; he must ardently desire to think well.

Dewey's analysis of thinking was for long the basis for classroom teaching of problem solving. This description, perhaps because of its brevity, did not make clear the full implication of the process itself. Emphasis fell upon general outlines and major phases; smoothness rather than discursive irregularity was taken as typical. The analysis is a valuable guide to general phases but needs to be supplemented with Dewey's more recent discussion of thought-in-process. The following paragraphs are an abbreviated and rearranged summary of Dewey's original description of thinking: [4]

Origin in some perplexity. We may recapitulate by saying that the origin of thinking is some perplexity, confusion, doubt. Thinking is not a case of spontaneous combustion; it does not just occur. There is something specific which occasions and evokes it. General appeals to a child (or to a grownup) to think, irrespective of the existence in his own experience of some difficulty that troubles him and disturbs his equilibrium, are as futile as advice to lift himself by his boot straps.

A tentative plan is based on analogous experience and prior knowledge. Given a difficulty, the next step is suggestion of some way out—the formulation of some tentative plan or project, the entertaining of some theory which will account for the peculiarities in question, the consideration of some solution for the problem. The data at hand cannot supply the solution; they can only suggest it. What, then, are the sources of the suggestion? Clearly, past experience and prior knowledge. If the person has had some acquaintance with similar situations, if he has dealt with material of the same sort before, suggestions more or less apt and helpful are likely to arise. But unless there has been experience in some degree analogous, which may now be represented in imagination, confusion remains mere confusion. There is nothing upon which to draw in order to clarify it. Even when a child (or a grown-up) has a problem, to urge him to think when he has no prior experiences involving some of the same conditions is wholly futile.

Plan not accepted until carefully examined and criticized. If the suggestion that occurs is at once accepted, we have uncritical thinking, the minimum of reflection. To turn the thing over in mind, to reflect, means to hunt for additional evidence, for new data, that will develop the suggestion and will either, as we say, bear it out, or else make obvious its absurdity and irrelevance.

[4] John Dewey, *How We Think* (Boston, Heath, 1910), pp. 12-13. The revised (1933) ed. contains three new chs. which present in detail the difference between formal logic and thought-in-process.

See also with advanced students, John Dewey, *Logic, The Theory of Inquiry* (New York, Holt, 1938).

See also volumes previously noted in this ch. by Black, Burtt, Cohen and Nagel, Larrabee.

Given a genuine difficulty and a reasonable amount of analogous experience to draw upon, the difference, par excellence, between good and bad thinking is found at this point. The easiest way is to accept any suggestion which seems plausible and thereby bring to an end the condition of mental uneasiness. Reflective thinking is always more or less troublesome because it involves overcoming the inertia that inclines one to accept suggestions at their face value; it involves willingness to endure a condition of mental unrest. Reflective thinking, in short, means judgment suspended during further inquiry, and suspense is likely to be somewhat painful. The most important factor in the training of good mental habits consists in acquiring the attitude of suspended conclusion and in mastering the various methods of searching for new materials to corroborate or to refute the first suggestions that occur. To maintain the state of doubt and to carry on systematic and protracted inquiry—these are the essentials of thinking.

Thought-in-process and formal logic are not the same. The guidance of learning to think in the classroom has for long been under the dominance of formal logic, especially on upper levels. In the lower schools, more or less formal steps are used which are thought to approximate logic. Better procedures which approximate the actual process of thought are now emerging.

Formal traditional logic is the science of valid inference as distinguished from systematic psychological study of how the mind works. Descartes, as long ago as 1637, distinguished between that logic which was useful in explaining to others what is already known and the logic which appears in learning something new. The distinction did not affect teaching until comparatively modern times. Increasing attention is now given to thought-in-process which has its own logic; to the logic of inquiry in contrast to the logic of proof or of post-procedural summary. A section in Chapter 7 will develop the detailed relationships between logic and the thinking process.

The actual process of thought is neither smooth nor sequential. Thought-in-process includes innumerable errors and corrections, digressions, discussions ending in blind alleys, the laborious trial of guesses, the tedious process of evaluating and validating. Terms must be defined and redefined; schemes for classifying one's ideas must be made and often scrapped. There are analyses, selection, and discrimination of ideas. Many, many errors and successes appear before the problem is solved. These and many more are essences of thought-in-process but are not to be seen in the summaries of formal logic. Formal logic is of basic importance but at a stage much further along than beginning thinking. The learner will reach the mature stage only through many experiences in solving real problems.

The individual learns the best methods of proceeding, of avoiding errors, by discovering them within his own problem-solving processes. As soon as sufficient experience has been secured, progress may be expedited through verbal discussion and illustration of more mature logical forms. The young learner does not profit from having the mature forms of logic forced upon him in advance of experience.

Accounts of thought-in-process, once rare, are increasingly available. Early thinkers rarely kept and left accounts of the devious, roundabout processes by which they solved problems. Few gave accounts of the many errors and corrections, the blind-alley excursions, the retracing of steps, the organization and scrapping of schemes of analysis or of comparison, the patient examination of many suggestions valuable and futile alike, the tedious checking and rechecking. Today there is an increasing number of accounts available, well edited and well written. [5] The volumes, noted below, by Conant and by Schwartz and Bishop are particularly valuable. Not enough has been done to uncover the accounts which do exist. Advanced students may well turn to remote sources available in good libraries. Articles reconstructing the records of thinking in specific cases would be welcomed by professional journals and would constitute a valuable contribution.

One of the most famous accounts is the detailed and self-revelatory account of his laborious problem-solving processes left by Kepler, a noted early astronomer. The following descriptive summary is from Whewell: [6]

[5] Paul De Kruif, *Microbe Hunters,* text ed. (New York, Harcourt, Brace, 1932). Contains many excellent illustrations from the work of individual scientists.

James M. Linley, *An Analysis of the Creative Process.* Unpublished doctoral dissertation, University of Southern California, 1938. Many fragmentary accounts available in scattered sources.

Graham Wallas, *The Art of Thought* (New York, Harcourt, Brace, 1926).

[6] W. Whewell, *The History of the Inductive Sciences* (London, John W. Parker, 1857; New York, D. Appleton, 1874, 1901). Many interesting accounts.

D. L. Watson, *Scientists are Human* (London, Watts, 1938).

See also many popular biographies of scientists, inventors, artists. These volumes often contain intimate, explicit accounts of thought-in-process.

W. Whewell, *op cit.,* Vol. I, pp. 291-292.

James B. Conant, ed., *Harvard Case Studies in Experimental Science,* Vols. I and II (Cambridge, Mass., Harvard University Press, 1957).

George Sarton, *A History of Science* (Cambridge, Mass., Harvard University Press, 1959).

John Jewkes, David Sawyers, and Richard Stillerman, *The Sources of Invention* (New York, Macmillan, 1959).

George Schwartz and Philip W. Bishop, eds., *Moments of Discovery*: *The Origins of Science,* Vols. I and II (New York, Basic Books, 1958).

Max Wertheimer, *Productive Thinking* (New York, Harper, 1945).

J. Bronowski, *The Common Sense of Science* (Cambridge, Mass., Harvard University Press, 1953).

Gardner Murphy, *Human Potentialities* (New York, Basic Books, 1958).

The following may be indirectly of interest and use:

N. J. Berrill, *Man's Emerging Mind* (New York, Dodd, Mead, 1955).

John G. Kemeny, *A Philosopher Looks at Science* (Princeton, N. J., Van Nostrand, 1959).

H. R. Hays, *From Ape to Angel, An Informal History of Social Anthropology* (New York, Knopf, 1958).

Bold guessing. Advances in knowledge are not commonly made without the previous exercise of some *boldness and license in guessing.* The discovery of new truths requires, undoubtedly, minds careful and scrupulous in examining what is suggested; but it requires, no less, such as are quick and fertile in suggesting. What is invention but the talent of rapidly calling before us many possibilities and selecting the appropriate one? It is true that when we have rejected all the inadmissible suppositions, they are quickly forgotten by most persons, and few think it necessary to dwell on these discarded hypotheses and on the process by which they were condemned, as Kepler has done.

Reasoning on many errors. But all who discover truths must have *reasoned upon many errors* to obtain each truth; every accepted doctrine must have been selected out of many candidates. In making many conjectures that on trial proved erroneous, Kepler was no more fanciful or unphilosophical than other discoverers have been. *Discovery is not a cautious or rigorous process in the sense of abstaining from such suppositions.* But there are great differences, in different cases, in the facility with which guesses are proved to be errors and in the degree of attention with which the error and the proof are afterwards dwelt on. Kepler was certainly remarkable for the labor which he gave to such self-refutations and for the candor and copiousness with which he narrated them; his works are in this way extremely curious and amusing and are a very instructive exhibition of the mental process of discovery. But in this respect, I venture to believe, they exhibit to us the usual process (somewhat caricatured) of the inventive minds—they rather examplify the *rule* of genius than (as has generally hitherto been taught) the *exception.* We may add that if many of Kepler's guesses now appear fanciful and absurd, because time and observation have refuted them, others which were at the time equally gratuitous have been confirmed by succeeding discoveries in a manner which makes them appear marvelously sagacious, as, for instance, his assertion of the rotation of the sun on its axis before the invention of the telescope. Nothing can be more just as well as poetically happy than Kepler's picture of the philosopher's pursuit of scientific truth, conveyed by means of an allusion to Virgil's shepherd and shepherdess:

> "Coy yet inviting, Galatea loves
> To sport in sight, then plunge into the groves;
> The challenge given, she darts along the green,
> Will not be caught, yet would not run unseen."

Devising tests for false suppositions. We may notice as another peculiarity of Kepler's reasonings the length and laboriousness of the processes by which he discovered the errors of his first guesses. One of the most important talents requisite for a discoverer is the *ingenuity and skill which devise means for rapidly testing false suppositions,* as they offer themselves. This talent Kepler did not possess; he was not even a good arithmetical calculator, often making mistakes, some of which he detected and lamented, while others escaped him to the last.

John H. Hertz, *International Politics in the Atomic Age* (New York, Columbia University Press, 1959).

H. Stuart Hughes, *Consciousness and Society* (New York, Knopf, 1959).

Willingness to abandon false hypotheses. But his defects in this respect were compensated by his courage and perseverance in undertaking and executing such tasks; and, what was still more admirable, he never allowed the labor he had spent upon any conjecture to produce any reluctance in *abandoning the hypothesis as soon as he had evidence of its inaccuracy.* The only way in which he rewarded himself for his trouble was by describing to the world in his lively manner his schemes, exertions, and feelings.

Four important characteristics of thought-in-process may be derived from Whewell's commentary on Kepler's thinking.

1. Bold guessing, taking chances, as well as making inferences carefully based upon the data
2. Much erroneous guessing, "scrapped thought," much waste time and energy
3. Devising careful, detailed checks upon one's suggestions, processes, and conclusions
4. Willingness to give up ideas which will not hold water, no matter how long these ideas have been held, no matter how well liked

Many more subprocesses will eventually be listed and examined.

A summary of the reflective or critical thinking in problem solving stated in everyday descriptive terms. Immediately following there will be a summary of the same thing in formal terms.

1. *A situation for which the answer is unknown* but can be found; a situation which *challenges but does not baffle* the individual seeking the answer.
2. *A period of inquiry,* long or short as the case may be, in which the *confused, indeterminate situation is transformed into a unified and determinate one.*
   a. Terms and limits are defined and redefined.
   b. Suggestions arise from many sources and are deliberately sought for in others.
   c. Discussions, arguments, differences of opinion, exchange of fact and belief take place.
   d. Digressions, blind alleys, useless suggestions, and leads intermingle with valid and conclusive items.
   e. Careful inferences from data, hunches, insights, and bold guesses intermingle with one another.
   f. Plans are made and remade, abandoned, adopted.
   g. Much time is consumed, and much scrapped thought is characteristic; the errors indicated in previous points are not always recognized immediately, nor are correct leads; right or wrong points must often be pursued for some time before validity or lack of it can be determined; many schemes for analysis, for comparison, for organization, are made, improved, abandoned, adopted; ideas once abandoned may be recalled later and prove useful after all.
   (This list is not exhaustive.)
3. *A conclusion is formulated,* checked and corrected, and stated in terms referring directly to the original problem as finally defined. This conclusion is good as far as the facts and reasoning at the time go. It is the "truth" until

further facts or closer reasoning appear which may destroy, modify, or corroborate it.

The three points are not steps in any sense. The process is unified and continuous. Conclusions will spring to mind immediately upon formulation of the problem, even sometimes before the problem is clear. The individual casts about him for information with which to uphold or disprove his first idea. He may examine the problem more closely, he may turn to his past experience, he may examine any promising source of information. The poor thinker is usually satisfied with a haphazard solution or with the first information that comes to hand. This short-circuits thinking and prevents proper analysis. The good thinker suspends judgment, even in the face of seeming certainty, until further inquiry is carried on. Checks are applied; partial conclusions emerge as discussions proceed. A digression may be lengthy; it may be abandoned; and later it may be revived to prove useful. The teacher is to guide without dominating within this confused, discursive, living, dynamic process to the end that it may be organized toward a sensible conclusion.

A summary of reflective or critical thinking stated in formalized and classified form for the purpose of further analysis.

1. *Recognition and definition of the problem.*
2. *Hypothesis.* Formulation of possible solutions or promising courses of action in the search for solution.
3. *Inquiry or search.* Procedures which may be used:
    a. Experimentation—general procedures useful in science
    b. Collection of data, relevant facts, evidence, and authoritative opinion
    c. Reasoning
        (1) Induction
        (2) Deduction   (These three processes will be elaborated in
        (3) Analogy   a later chapter on logic and thinking.)
4. *Decision.* Acceptance of hypothesis established by preceding step.
5. *Test and use* of accepted conclusion.

Certain conditions govern the thinking process.

1. *Attitudes.* The potential problem solver must approach his problem with those attitudes which promote open-minded inquiry and avoid those which inhibit inquiry. (These are elaborated in Chapter 3.)
2. *Linguistic procedures.* Whenever the inquirer uses language it must be precise and nonambiguous. (See Chapter 10 on semantics.)
3. *Errors.* Faults creep into the thinking procedure at each step. The successful problem solver will use procedures for the detection and avoidance of errors. (See Chapter 11, "Errors and Fallacies.")

The vivid, dynamic processes of reflective thought or problem solving cannot be reduced to formulas. The foregoing broad general scheme, however, may be of value for orienting the individual. The specific procedures within the total process will be developed in succeeding chapters.

The dilemma which confronts us at this point is to construct a general outline and an analysis of details which, on the one hand, does not formalize or routinize the process but, on the other hand, is definite enough to be of assistance to anyone engaged either in pondering his own thought processes, or in teaching others to do so. All we can do as teachers is to use problems real to the learner and then sensitize and aid him with the processes of thought which he will use.

The kinds of problems which commonly initiate critical thinking. These are stated in everyday terms for identification and discussion. The general processes of thinking occur in all cases. Differences are partly due to the type of situation, partly due to emphasis on different phases of thinking. Overlap is easily observed. A more formal listing of types will be given in Chapter 15 on general methods of teaching critical thinking:

1. *To find the answer for a real or a theoretical or speculative problem.*
   Common to the physical sciences, to certain levels of technology, and to many everyday activities beyond the trivial or routine. Usually proceeds through suggestion, development, and testing of hypotheses. Problem may be one of: explanation, discovery, verification, evidential summary.
2. *To determine what to do in a given situation, the immediate overt action to take in practical affairs.*
   Common in all everyday affairs, deals with any kind of subject matter, and results in a practical judgment. Usually proceeds through considering one hypothesis, or two alternative hypotheses, rarely a great number. Knowledge is summarized and weighed in light of consequences, and decision made.
3. *To determine goals, attitudes, or policies to control future actions; to reconstruct goals, attitudes, or policies.*
   Common to social sciences, to public affairs generally, to ethical and moral decisions. Usually proceeds through exchange of views in group discussion, tentative conclusions being set up for trial decisions leading eventually to a meeting of minds or consensus. Hypothesizing may or may not be prominent. Testing is usually postponed as trial of policy is longer and less subject to control than scientific hypotheses.
4. *To choose between policies or goals already formulated; to determine the validity of conclusions, beliefs, or opinions expressed by others; to give reasons for supporting one's own expressed belief.*
   Common to situation in Type 3 above, also to analysis of editorials, columns, speeches, advertisements, public or private expressions of any kind. Usually proceeds through examination and evaluation of facts, inferences, sources; through search for assumptions, for bias, or for lack of these things; through search for purpose of speaker or writer; through evaluation of the background and affiliations of the speaker or writer.
5. *To create something new, unique, not heretofore known.*
6. *To draw logical inferences from accepted postulates and axioms; logical proof.*
7. *To make value judgments in ethical and aesthetic fields.*

The Mesa Verde case illustrated Type 1, finding an answer to a problem. The subtype here was explanation. Type 2 may be observed every day as individuals are confronted with situations needing immediate decision. Usually these are neither extensive nor vital, but they may be both. The children and their playground policy illustrated Type 3, together with some of Type 4. The analysis of the "letter to the editor" illustrated Type 4. We do not, in this volume, treat Types 5, 6, 7 in detail.[7]

QUESTIONS, EXERCISES, AND REPORTS

1. Describe any careless or loose uses of the word *thinking* in everyday conversation, in written material.

2. Illustrate erroneous beliefs held by many persons (or by yourself!). Include the absurd, the plausible, and the evidence denying the belief. Explain as well as you can at this stage why such beliefs are held, sometimes by fairly capable persons.

3. Illustrate similarly, if you can at this stage, cases of clearly dishonest thinking.

4. Report in some detail any descriptions you find of the thinking process in given instances. These may be found in biographies, in literary or scientific writings.

5. Explain with illustrations how the serious error of confusing subjective and objective data probably arose. What are the implications both for everyday life and for teaching?

6. Give cases of "bold guessing" that paid off. Include simple everyday cases as well as advanced scientific and creative effort.

Similarly give cases of "bold guessing" which turned out to be seriously in error.

Explain both types of illustration as well as you can.

7. What keeps our "systematic inquiry" systematic? Keeps it from slipping into one or other of the processes listed under loose uses of the word "thinking"?

8. Dewey points out (p. 16) that a person "may not be sufficiently critical about the ideas that occur to him." On p. 7 he points out that many of our ideas came "we know not how"; insinuated into the mind, they become part of our mental furniture almost without our being aware.

Develop the very important implications of this statement.

9. The word THINK is often seen in business offices on a card placed in a prominent position. Teachers are very often heard to exhort pupils to "think." This constitutes a truly serious blunder in each of the cases. What is the blunder, and why is it a blunder?

---

[7] At this point all students should read in Wertheimer, *op. cit.*, the "Introduction," pp. 1-13, and the "Conclusion," pp. 189-215. This will initiate thinking about the differences and likenesses between traditional logic and thinking as it goes on in ordinary affairs. If all is not clear at this point the material should be read again just prior to reading Chapter 7, "Inference: The Heart of Thinking."

Some wag has produced a card which says THIMK. He is a better thinker than those who use the card THINK. Why?

10. If Columbus had come back from his historic voyage and stated that the world was in fact flat, would this be identical with the belief held by those who originally ridiculed his idea that it was round?

11. Dewey makes an important statement in *How We Think,* (on p. 5 of the 1910 edition, on p. 8 of the 1933 edition):

"But to think of the world as flat is to ascribe a quality to a real thing as its real property. This conclusion denotes a connection among things and hence is not, like imaginative thought, plastic to our mood. Belief in the world's flatness commits him who holds it to thinking in certain specific ways of other objects, such as heavenly bodies, antipodes, the possibility of navigation. It prescribes to him actions in accordance with his conception of these objects."

This statement has profound implications for thinking and teaching others. What are they?

State in your own words certain truly stupendous blunders in this respect made commonly and blithely by the average citizen. What can you do about this in your own thinking? (Eventually you will be asked what we might do in aiding others in improving thinking.)

An interesting illustration of Dewey's point that our beliefs commit us to other beliefs was seen some years ago in the case of a Fundamentalist religious leader who taught that the earth was flat. Eventually he took one of the "round the world" cruises! Upon return he was asked by newsmen whether he had not discovered that the world was round—and was he going to maintain his preaching that it was flat. His answer was perfectly consistent with his system of beliefs: "The world is flat—we sailed around it as if around the inside edge of a saucer."

Have you ever heard any other similar cases?

12. Examine the quotation describing Kepler's thinking. Select all statements therein that are *general,* that is, applicable to thinking anywhere by anyone; select those that refer only to Kepler's *individual peculiarities.*

13. List a number of problems the average citizen cannot handle. Why does he insist on trying to come to conclusions on such problems? What are the values and dangers of this? (Distinguish between problems for which there is not at present a fairly complete conclusion, and those for which there are good conclusions whether tentative or final.)

14. What has this to do with democratic values and processes? (Do not answer this glibly or hastily; there are some important implications.)

15. Why does the avearge citizen not see that difficult, controlled experimentation is necessary? Why does he, sometimes, decry "experimentation" and remain unaware that extremely costly social experimentation is going on all the time? Is this all his fault?

16. What is the significance of all this for education?

(This series of questions, particularly Nos. 14-15, can lead to a fruitful discussion of fundamental problems in a democracy. The discussion also prepares the way for analysis later of the need for training thought and of obstacles and resources.)

17. What is the relation of opinion polls to all this?

18. Why are predictions in the social, economic, and political fields so often unreliable? How do you account for those which turn out to be reasonably correct?

What can we do in these fields? What problems confront us?

READINGS WHICH SHOULD BE REQUIRED WITH THIS CHAPTER

BURTT, E. A., *Right Thinking,* 3rd. ed. (New York, Harper, 1946), "Preface" and Ch. 1.

Cite statements from Burtt which clarified, amplified, or limited the ideas derived from this chapter.

ROBINSON, James Harvey, *Mind in the Making* (New York, Harper, 1921).

This reference contains much interesting material which provokes considerable argument among students. Time may be allowed for this with profit, but the discussion must be kept on the present objective: clarifying our meaning for thinking. Discussion must not be allowed to get off onto some of the content.

Cite statements from Robinson corroborating, disagreeing with, or extending points made in this chapter.

Where does "rationalizing" fit into our outline—if it does?

What is the difference between a "rationalized" conclusion and a reasoned conclusion? What is the guidance here for your own thinking; for viewing other people's thinking; guiding learners in this respect?

Give everyday illustrations, general or specific, in which individuals are accused of "rationalizing," or of narrow-mindedness, or of bigotry, or of prejudice, when as a matter of fact they have excellent evidence and reason for the beliefs held.

Is it possible to dislike or be "against" a person, a group, a creed, an institution without being "prejudiced" or guilty of rationalization?

What have the two foregoing questions to do with our major point so far?

OTHER AVAILABLE READINGS, NOT REQUIRED

BLACK, Max, *Critical Thinking* (Englewood Cliffs, N. J., Prentice-Hall, 1946), Ch. 13.

LARRABEE, Harold A., *Reliable Knowledge* (Boston, Houghton Mifflin, 1945), "Introduction," pp. 1-7; 68-73.

CHAPTER **3**

The Development of Attitudes Favorable to Thinking

> We have been dealing so far with the act of reflection as an entirety. There are subordinate unities within the process upon whose character the efficiency of the whole undertaking depends.
>
> JOHN DEWEY *

> Men's prejudices and inclinations impose often upon themselves. . . . Inclination suggests and slides into discourse favorable terms, which introduce favorable ideas; till at last by this means that is concluded clear and evident, thus dressed up, which, taken in its native state, by making use of none but precise determined ideas, would find no admittance at all.
>
> JOHN LOCKE †

The moral to be drawn from the Locke quotation above is clear; we must develop "inclinations" which prevent interference with inference, insofar as this is possible.

Development of a moral attitude favorable to thinking is an important educational aim. Many years ago the student body treasurer in a large university embezzled large sums from the various funds entrusted to him. The faculty committee could not discover the method used, could not even spot the culprit. An accountant-detective was planted among the students and finally caught the student treasurer. At the hearing before the disciplinary committee a professor asked, "We were utterly unable to find how you were manipulating the books—would you mind telling us how you learned the methods you used?" The student, despite the seriousness of the occasion, laughed and said, "I learned all of it in your own course in Municipal Government!" The exposures of graft and dishonesty in city

* John Dewey, *How We Think*, rev. ed. (Boston, Heath, 1933), p. 119.
† John Locke, *Conduct of the Understanding.*

government had made a greater impression than the principles of good government. The student's thinking during the stealing was impeccable, but, to use a common expression, "his attitude was wrong." His "inclinations" had undone him! The first and absolute prerequisite for honest thinking is the desire to think straight. Facts and processes are necessary, of course, but these are not likely to be used properly in the absence of this primary moral conviction. As Samuel Johnson put it: "Knowledge without integrity is dangerous and dreadful."

Thinking within any society is a moral as well as a logical affair. The accepted views of the common good, the general goals of that society are one guide point; the rules of evidence and the canons of logic are the other. "To know the right is to do the right" is nonsense. One must in addition "love the right and hate evil." "Know the truth, and it will set you free" is a childish verbalism. To know the right way of thinking, to know facts (the truth) does not guarantee honest thinking. If one knows the truth and does not like it, the truth will neither set free nor enslave; it will simply be ignored. An individual ridden by attitudes of religious and racial intolerance—with attitudes of antagonism toward certain social or economic classes, for or against international understanding and co-operation, toward social change, toward the inevitable shifts in power between social and economic classes, toward the whole range of pressing social problems—cannot think his way through the problems of the day. The same is true for society generally. A society which expects to get along without civil violence, in fact which wishes to survive, must give serious attention to the attitudes toward fact, thinking, and responsibility for thinking which develop either by undirected social conditioning, or by directed education. Certain attitudes toward facts and correct thinking widely held by some politicians, by some prominent industrial leaders, and by some well-known labor leaders are tragically dangerous nonsense. A prominent Detroit industrialist said angrily to a known and reputable scholar, "You are either a Communist or a thinker!" Competent anthropologists, sociologists, and political scientists regard this situation with real alarm since the prominent leaders possessing dishonest attitudes are in positions of power. ("Don't bother me with the facts, just brief me on the political alignments.")

Thinking may be factually and logically correct and at the same time be morally reprehensible. Dishonesty, self-interest, greed, and bias of various types all influence thinking. Social conventions and pressures ordinarily on the side of honest thinking are in limited areas and on a given issue at a given time are often powerful prime movers to dishonest thinking. Dishonest thinking often pays off handsomely.

A competent thinker must possess the inclination to make honest use of the thinking skills he may possess. Dispositions and attitudes, as has been indicated, are far more powerful determiners of action than are facts and logic. We need to develop unity between the personal moral attitudes toward accepting responsibility, toward honest procedures, with the impersonal principles of good thinking. It is possible to develop certain attitudes which are favorable to honest use of methods of inquiry and testing, to acceptance of facts no matter how distasteful, and it is possible to discourage those attitudes which are inimical to honest thinking.

A number of attitudes dealing directly with the thinking process also need to be developed. The school has proceeded for centuries upon the assumption that human conduct is rationally determined. This but reflects a widely held popular opinion. Common-sense observation, now backed by valid research, shows that this view has no relation to reality. The school in addition to developing skills and habits of thinking must also develop attitudes favorable to engaging in the arduous process. "Some persons would sooner die than think" is a statement attributed to various authors. A wag has added, "And many do!" Many of the books on critical thinking and upon the psychology of thinking seriously urge the development of the necessary attitudes—but few give any suggestions as to *how* to do this. Good suggestions are found in the periodical literature which reports experimental studies on the development or changing of attitudes. The summary in the following pages is not exhaustive but presents what is known to date. Before proceeding further let us define terms.

What is an attitude? An attitude is a relatively constant tendency to act. An attitude is an enduring predisposition to react in a characteristic way, favorably or unfavorably, toward a given person or type of person, object, situation, or idea. An attitude is a feeling for or against something. Attitudes may be intellectual or emotional, but they are usually emotional in base and tone.

Scrutiny of definitions and analysis of research reveal certain typical characteristics:

1. Attitudes are associated with emotions far more than with the intellect. Attitudes are based on feeling more than on knowing.

2. Attitudes are characterized by approach or withdrawal, acceptance or rejection, reaching for or avoidance.

3. Attitudes are directed at persons, objects, situations, processes, more than at images or "ideas."

4. Attitudes may be general or specific; they are capable of being generalized.

5. Attitudes are more constant than not. Thinking and behavior may be predicted under certain circumstances.

6. Attitudes are acquired or learned and may be modified and unlearned.

Attitudes affect thinking for good or ill. The effect of attitudes on thinking has been recognized by writers since ancient times. A pointed statement has been made in modern times by Dashiell: [1]

[1] John F. Dashiell, *Fundamentals of General Psychology* (Boston, Houghton Mifflin, 1937), p. 131.

If we will but stop to ponder the extraordinary degree to which the social life of man is permeated and shot through with his responses to emblems, shibboleths, hackneyed phrases, and epithets, without benefit of first-hand acquaintance and cool-headed analysis of men and issues actually involved, we shall understand the avid interest of the social psychologists and the sociologist in the psychology of attitudes.

Our thinking is influenced far more than the average citizen knows by attitudes, many of which are unconscious (in the everyday meaning of that word). The critical attitude necessary to prevent influence by attitudes inimical to straight thinking is a difficult acquisition.

A famous newspaper publisher under criticism during a national crisis instructed his executives to print small United States flags at the tops of all columns in all papers in the chain. He brazenly stated, "This will be good for business." He counted on an attitude of citizens of the United States; they would react favorably toward the flag. This attitude would be transferred to the newspaper. Critical thinking, further inquiry into the merits of the criticism would be blocked. This blind reaction to otherwise reputable symbols explains the vigorous efforts of certain vested interests among capitalists, labor groups, religious groups, and many others to develop attitudes which block thinking and develop "right or wrong" loyalty to slogans or rituals or symbols. Such an attitude, once built up, can be manipulated with great ease to block or to direct thinking. Manipulation toward socially desirable ends and toward honest thinking is also possible, but those working for these ends desire the attitude to be enlightened and informed rather than blind and unreasoning.

The influence of attitudes on thinking can be observed every day. Research studies confirm the everyday observations. The attitudes of Californians toward Florida and vice versa have achieved the status of stereotypes. Apart from humorous discussions based thereon, there are also some serious blunders in thinking which result. Thinking is influenced in serious measure every day by attitudes toward Negroes, Jews, Catholics, Jehovah's Witnesses, government participation in business, "free enterprise," Russia, liquor, the police, one's own mother or motherhood in general, one's boss, those who agree or disagree with us in politics, religion, child rearing, and many other things. Attitudes on these items vary from person to person, from region to region, even within a family. They are, nevertheless, recognizable and definable. Their effect on thinking can be predicted within reasonable limits. The popularity of opinion polls, the extensive use of propaganda, the ceaseless repetition of certain slogans is indicative of the point under discussion. Stanley Hall long ago said, "Intellect is a mere speck afloat on a sea of feeling."

Warning: Competent thinking may be painful intellectually and socially. Before one undertakes to think seriously he should consider whether it is worth it! He must endure painful suspension of judgment, critical evaluation of everything, including cherished beliefs and ideals; he must slowly and methodically check and test; he must endure the upsetting experience of constantly revising facts, principles, and conclusions. *Thinking demands arduous self-discipline.* Substitutes for thinking are easily available on every hand: in canned editorials, syndicated columns, doctrinal sermons, advice columns, advertisements, neighborhood gossip, and in an unlimited number of clichés, bromides, and slogans. The "organization man" has his thinking done for him by the head office. The nonthinking man runs the risk, of course, of getting the wrong filter on his cigarette.

Thinking will also bring social discomforts. Friends, associates, and others will manifest great impatience with the careful thinker, will ridicule and "wisecrack," will attempt to force him into agreement with conventional wisdom. He will be misinterpreted and misquoted, classified as an "odd ball." He will be regarded as "dangerous" if not "subversive" by the "best people." He would be advised not to be prominent in service clubs or churches and should never apply for membership in the exclusive local clubs. A distinguished teacher and department head was asked, after taking work in the psychology of thinking, if the course had helped her. "Oh yes greatly—but it ruined my social life"! Another student recommending such a course to her grown son was interrupted by her husband who whispered facetiously "Don't take it"!

The critical attitudes necessary for good thinking. Thinking is a matter of strong moral conviction as well as of processes. Certain critical attitudes are necessary.

1. *Intellectual curiosity.* Disposition to be alert and sensitive to problems, their causes, related evidences, possible explanations; to wonder why, or how, or what.

2. *Intellectual honesty, acceptance of responsibility for process and result.* Disposition to accept apparent truth in spite of all inducements to the contrary; to follow evidence and judgment wherever they may lead; to stand up for one's reasoned conclusions together with willingness to change conclusions and beliefs if further inquiry so warrants; to engage in self-criticism; to improve one's own methods.

3. *Objectivity.* Disposition to select objective data; not to rely on hunches, intuition, and subjective observation; to be free from bias or partisanship.

4. *Intelligent skepticism or suspension of judgment; criticalness.* Disposition to delay acceptance of conclusion until all available relevant data have been considered; to accept nothing at face value.

5. *Open-mindedness.* Disposition to consider without bias or prejudgment a wide variety of facts, descriptions, explanations, and interpretations.

6. *Conviction of universal cause-and-effect relationships;* steadfastness in avoiding superstitions, nonscientific, mystic explanations.

Cause and effect in ordinary affairs and within closed systems is a relatively simple matter and easily observable, but in complex matters this is far from the case. Considerable discussion can be found in current publications. A very brief summary will be found later in Chapter 7.

7. *Disposition to be systematic,* to adhere strictly to the problem and to a consequence of ideas; to use outlines, graphs, summaries; to insist on systematic search and check; to be intolerant of confusion and inconsistency. (This is particularly difficult for the average citizen who "bounces off" in any direction as caprice dictates.)

8. *Flexibility.* Disposition to give up a previous conclusion, no matter how attractive, if sufficient contrary evidence is disclosed; to change method.

9. *Persistence.* Disposition to persist in the search for evidence and adequate explanation, never giving up. (Dewey uses the term wholeheartedness to mean enthusiastic identification with the problem, throwing one's self into the undertaking.)

10. *Decisiveness.* Disposition to come to a conclusion; to avoid snap judgments; to avoid balancing and weighing data and conclusions out of all reason; to balance rapidity with gradualism.

Three attitudes are specially valuable in group thinking;

1. *Respect for another's view* if based on evidence and reason; willingness to be convinced by evidence; humility.

2. *Candor and expectancy of candor.* Disposition to speak frankly to avoid withholding facts or arguments, to expect candor from others. (Certain conventional attitudes of tact—as too commonly interpreted—and incorrect views of courtesy are serious blocks to thinking.)

3. *Careful listening.* Disposition to listen with utmost attention. This is far more important in group thinking than is commonly realized. It is (*a*) impossible to present your own facts and views unless you have listened to discover the status and view of the other person. You (*b*) cannot answer arguments to which you did not listen. Reasons you think up while the other person is speaking often boomerang because you did not listen to the opposing arguments.

Attitudes unfavorable to critical, reflective thinking. Sometimes the presence of these is not recognized. Students should become aware of the inimical attitudes and their operations.

1. *Lack of intellectual curiosity; torpidity.* Disposition to be incurious, unaware, indifferent to events, problems, causes, evidences, explanations; to be indifferent to why, how, what. (This is unnatural and is usually due to conditioning in home or school, to malnutrition, or to illness. Should be diagnosed.)

2. *Disposition to flippancy and/or pseudosophistication;* to avoid problems, questions, doubts, even serious inquiries, with a "wisecrack" and impertinent comment. "After all, what does it matter?" "Why get excited?" "Who wants to think?"

This attitude is often a defense against ignorance, fear, or unwillingness to exert one's self.

3. *Intellectual dishonesty.* Disposition and intent to distort, to slant, no matter how ingeniously, facts and inference in line with one's desires, prej-

udices and biases, against disturbance of a comfortable *status quo*. This is often betrayed by selection of cases in support of one's view with obvious rejection of cases in opposition or any negative evidence.

4. *Bias or prejudice for or against (anything)*. The thinker is often naïvely unaware of his prejudice or of the operation of prejudice.

5. *Primitive credulity*. Disposition to believe what one sees and hears without the slightest critical reaction. Discussed in various terms by anthropologists and psychologists, this seems to be a trait developed by primitive peoples and children because at first nothing enters the situation to call into question what one sees, hears, reads. "It says so in the book," with no thought that a liar may have written the book. "I saw it with my own eyes," with no recognition of the necessity for trained observation. Often what one "saw" with his "own eyes" not only did not happen, it could not have happened. "My experience shows (or proves)" often without recognition of (*a*) necessity for trained observation, and (*b*) critical analysis of experience. Often what is cited as "my experience" is the *speaker's opinion of his experience* and not his experience at all. What is already in the mind determines what one sees. The Greeks had a sentence for it: "A man looks out on his world through his ideas."

6. *Undue reverence for the "latest thing," the new or the novel*. Disposition to seize upon any new suggestion or process, to identify with it. This is related to primitive credulity but is often immediately related to personal insecurity. Persons wish to show that they are "up-to-date," "in the swim."

7. *Harmful incredulity; closed-mindedness; undue reverence for what is, for custom and tradition*. Disposition to exalt, to rely upon, to hide behind what is, to hide behind the authority of the past. This, too, is often a defense or desire to follow the path of least resistance and to avoid the difficult job of thinking.

Dogmatism and rigidity; inflexibility. Disposition to state and to adhere to conclusions in disregard of, or even defiance of, obvious facts and logic; adherence to a method and refusal to adapt it to situations. He who "knows all the answers" prevents himself from thinking. (This is not to be confused with steadfast adherence to answers which are adequately supported by fact and logic.)

8. *Disregard for cause-and-effect explanations*. Disposition to accept or to concoct absurd statements of cause and effect; to accept impossible relationships in order to support one's desired conclusions; to accept obvious *non sequiturs;* to believe in superstitions, portents and omens, charms and incantations, "signs" of "good or bad luck," "unexplainable mysteries," "Don't that beat all?" Tendency to magnify coincidence, striking but nonessential characteristics; to explain through use of clichés, slogans, catch phrases, "Oh, that's human nature," "Original sin causes that," "That's the way kids are," "Oh well, it's just one of those things."

9. *Disposition to be tolerant of confusion and inconsistency*, to be indifferent to the necessity for outlines and summaries.

10. *Lack of persistence*. Tendency to quit, not only in the face of difficulty but generally and usually; failure to enter into any situation with wholehearted identification.

11. *Indecisiveness*. Disposition to shilly-shally, to avoid a showdown, to

avoid coming out flatly for or against; tendency to argue and debate beyond any sensible limit.

The attitudes of the thinker affect basically not only what he sees and hears, what he accepts and rejects, but also the very form and method of his thinking. These inimical attitudes may, on occasion, become so strong as to constitute an emotional block to thinking.

The general determiners of attitudes. Since attitudes are so important in critical thinking, we should try to determine what factors influence their development. We can then select methods useful for teaching desirable attitudes and for avoiding undesirable ones. It is not easy to classify the factors which determine attitudes, since attitude research is difficult and still in its early stages. The interaction of innate and environmental factors is very complex. The nature of the individual and of conditioning cannot always be separated as to their influence. Physical, social, and economic environment all affect the individual, whatever his nature. Individual differences in the individuals further complicate the matter. For purposes of temporary convenience, however, we may speak of (1) inborn factors, (2) nondirected external influences, and (3) deliberate institutional influences on attitudes.

Innate propensities. Individuals are doubtless born with factors which affect the kinds of attitudes developed later. Not too much is known. Organic needs can be cited as one factor which affects one's reactions, but even here conditioning enters early. The fact that one is a certain age or sex determines in part the outlook on life and the development of general attitudes. A high or low degree of intelligence, rapidity or slowness of perception, may be factors in shaping attitudes. Differences among individuals in attitudes toward the same thing suggest differences in nature as well as in conditioning. Suggestibility, whether it is innate, conditioned, or partly both, may cause individuals to adopt certain attitudes and avoid others.

Several investigations have attempted to determine the relative importance of one's nature and of outside influences. [2] An early summary of studies indicates that radical attitudes are possessed by individuals of high scholarship and low prejudice; conservative attitudes are related to low scholarship and high prejudice. Intelligence levels between radicals and conservatives do not differ greatly in some investigations; in others radicals are more intelligent. Radicals possess attitudes which are more meliorative, more religious, more moralistic, more sensitive to the opinions of others, more aware of their own inner motives, and more "tender-minded" than

[2] Arthur Lichtenstein, *Can Attitudes Be Taught?* Johns Hopkins Studies in Education, No. 21 (1934).

H. H. Remmers, "Studies in Attitudes: A Contribution to Socio-Psychological Research, Studies in Higher Education, XXVI," *Bulletin of Purdue University,* Vol. 35 (December, 1934).

H. H. Remmers, "Attitudes as Educational Objectives," *University of Washington College of Education Record,* Vol. 7 (1941), pp. 68-75.

conservatives. Conservatives are more mechanistic, self-sufficient, and "tough-minded." One study showed radicals to be superior in reaction time, decision, and free association. Some investigators believe that there is an innate difference between radicals and conservatives (similarly for other contrasting attitude groups) but admit that environment plays a fundamental part and that the two have not been well separated. The volume by Russell contains in Chapter 6 an excellent summary of research on this as far as children are concerned, plus a good selected bibliography. [3]

Normal nondirected external influences on attitudes. We know in general that many attitudes are unconsciously accepted from parents, the community, particularly the socioeconomic segment to which the individual belongs. Social, religious, and political attitudes are early conditioned thus. This is natural in view of the long period of dependence upon parents while children are growing up. The peer society has marked influence, particularly during adolescent and preadolescent years. Social groups of all kinds, from the family to the "great society," affect attitudes. Loved and respected individuals exert notable influence, as do also persons who are not liked or respected.

Protection from opposing beliefs and attitudes, refusal to permit analysis and criticism play a large part in the development of provincial and otherwise undesirable attitudes. Full and free discussion of all views, of conflicting beliefs and attitudes, is more likely to produce desirable attitudes.

Attitudes themselves affect the development of other attitudes. Such attitudes as, for instance, self-interest and greed for money or power play basic roles with adults in shaping dishonest and otherwise undesirable attitudes.

Attitudes themselves, as they develop and become part of the individual, in turn affect the development of other attitudes.

Deliberate educational efforts by the school or by any attitude-forming agency. Planned influences on attitudes, such as those by the school; the church; social, political, fraternal, and government agencies; by publications of any kind; concern us the most. Teachers must not only be informed but must actively participate in these efforts.

Guidance from school and teacher. Research shows that the school is less effective than the home in building attitudes, especially in earlier years of life. [4] Other factors mentioned above have greater or lesser influ-

---

[3] David H. Russell, *Children's Thinking* (Boston, Ginn, 1956). Ch. 6 contains an excellent summary on children's attitudes and the acquisition thereof.

[4] See Russell, *op cit.;* Razran, Sherif and Cantril, Hilgard and Marquis (cited in Bibliography, this ch.); H. H. Remmers and Naomi Weltma, "Attitude Relationships of Youth, Their Parents, and Their Teachers," *Journal of Social Psychology,* Vol. 26 (1947), pp. 61-68; L. Monash, "Why Children Dislike School," *Understanding the Child,* Vol. 16 (1947), pp. 67-70; S. Tennebaum, "Attitudes of Elementary School

ence at different periods. The school has greater influence in later years through its deliberate attempts to develop attitudes. Attitudes unfavorable to the school itself also develop with later years of schooling. Herein lies excellent guidance for administrators, curriculum makers, and teachers.

The influence of the school is about what should be expected because the school, until rather recently, was not consciously concerned with teaching for attitudes. Teachers, furthermore, have not been trained for it or even well informed concerning the nature of attitudes. Attitudes are, in many instances, fixed early and are persistent, indicating the importance of attention to the problem in the home and earliest school years.

Positive influence should result when the following procedures are followed, or avoided as the case may be:

1. The teacher recognizes the development of desirable attitudes as a conscious goal and does not expect them to develop automatically; takes an active and not a laissez-faire part in the development of attitudes.

2. The teacher should exemplify the desired critical attitudes and avoid the noncritical ones.

3. Methods and materials should be adapted to the maturity and experience of the learners and not solely to the importance of the materials and methods. Individual differences should be carefully noted rather than ignored.

4. Direct experience is probably the most valuable but must be supplemented in many instances with vicarious experience. Studies are not conclusive as to the value of various vicarious materials, such as motion pictures, radio and television programs, pamphlets, speeches, advertising, and propaganda devices.[5] Some produce excellent results in one situation and not in another.

5. Rituals and pageantry, much favored by some for patriotic education, are not effective for developing thinking members of a democratic society. An Adolf Hitler could use these techniques to mold a totalitarian society of awesome strength; for our purposes they often produce results that do not stand up under pressure. Attitudes quite antagonistic to the desired attitude often develop due to senseless repetition. Patriotic attitudes are better developed through insight and understanding derived from real experience.[6]

6. Verbal methods are often ineffective. The "safety sermons" and continuous exhortation to "drive safely" and to "avoid accidents" are almost useless in producing the desired attitude.

Children to School. Teachers, and Classmates," *Journal of Applied Psychology*, Vol. 28 (1944), pp. 134-141.

See also summaries by Allport; Murphy, Murphy, and Newcomb; Murchison (cited in Bibliography, this ch.).

See also chapters in some general and educational psychologies.

[5] A considerable literature exists on some of these items, particularly propaganda. Summaries may be made by a student or small committee on any one of vicarious materials and reported for class enlightenment.

[6] There is a very interesting literature on "brain washing" or the changing of beliefs and attitudes through intensive psychological pressures. Twenty or more periodical articles and chapters in books are available. A report may be made.

7. Use of pamphlets and certain modern texts in place of one text in the social studies seems to develop better attitudes than when these materials are not used. This is probably because the pamphlets are timely, dealing with real and current problems.

8. The teacher can profitably encourage questions, criticisms, additions to the class materials, and then ask for evidence of sources.

9. Provocative problems or exhibits may be presented to develop an inquiring attitude.

10. Conflicting references and puzzling contradictions may be offered to induce an attitude of skepticism, but too much of this may encourage a defeatist attitude. (See Chapter 18.)

11. The use of newspapers and magazines, especially on political and economic questions, will encourage an intelligent skepticism to prevent too-ready acceptance. This in turn helps to develop the attitude of asking for evidence, of checking sources, of making critical discriminations.

12. Willingness on the part of the teacher to consider any suggestion, to accord it respect until analyzed, encourages an attitude of wholehearted participation and confidence that one may speak up.

13. Courteously holding everyone for both evidence and consequences should produce an attitude of caution but at the same time one of responsibility.

14. Careful avoidance of dogmatism, arbitrary rejection of pupils' contributions, flippancy, and the like encourages the attitudes of security with beneficial results on many other attitudes.

15. Attitudes should be evaluated through behavior and not solely through verbal responses.

16. The conservative and/or liberal attitudes of the teacher should be evaluated and their effect, for good or ill, on the attitudes of learners noted.

A combination of methods based on the circumstances, level of pupil maturity, specific attitudes under development, resources or the lack of them, and many others is probably best.

Practically all the suggestions made to the teacher for aiding pupils with the various phases of thinking outlined in Part II of this volume also have implications for developing desirable attitudes and avoiding the undesirable. The following items may be mentioned especially: The use of controversial problems, especially those arising in the pupil's own experience, followed by critical reading of appropriate sources. Criteria should be developed for identifying and using correct sources and facts and also for detecting misinterpretations and errors that may arise if backgrounds are inadequate. Criteria are needed for determining the effect of diction, figures of speech, shades of meaning, emotional tone, and the like. (See Chapter 10, "Words: The Symbols of Thought.") The effects of context—verbal, psychological, and physical—may be analyzed. (Again see Chapter 10.) Many others could be noted.

Sometimes the task of the teacher is to change attitudes already possessed. Undesirable attitudes must be unlearned. The same general principles and practices hold.

The influence of school and teacher can, unhappily, be negative. Teachers who demand adherence to the text, to "what the book says," and who demand acceptance of statements and points of view obviously discourage open-mindedness and attitudes of inquiry and discrimination. In one extreme case a textbook had actually slipped through all proof-readings and editorial scanning with a remarkable typographical error. Certain rocks were referred to as "metaphoric rocks." A student suggested that this must be an error and that the text should read "metamorphic rocks." The instructor rapped sharply on the desk and snapped, "We will have no differences with the textbook in here." The students' attitude can only become one of acceptance, lack of interest.

Material which is of no observable use to the student, not related to his purposes, interests, or experiential background, prevents any wholehearted identification with it or any resultant keenness of perception. The student's attitude becomes one of resignation, working for a passing grade.

Material far removed from experiential background arouses no attitude of curiosity. Attitudes of honesty and acceptance of responsibility are not developed because the student sets his own standards of value; don't ask for meaning, don't care, just get by. School attitudes differ here from desired life attitudes.

The exaltation of external standards—marks, prizes, "getting the right answer," "covering the text"—also begets attitudes which facilitate getting along in school but which are not real-life attitudes.

Literature on development of scientific attitudes meager. Periodicals dealing with the various scientific fields contain good articles on the characteristics and desirability of scientific attitudes but almost nothing on the development of those attitudes. The educational journals and text-books contain occasional excellent accounts of teaching for attitude development. The treatment of social attitudes, on the contrary, is well handled in the social science periodicals and in textbooks.

QUESTIONS, EXERCISES, AND REPORTS

1. How, in general, do you suppose the widespread attitudes inimical to effective thinking arose? How did the "scientific attitudes" probably arise?

2. Show in general (specific illustrations if you can) how attitudes of alertness, curiosity, and flexibility are aids to good thinking.

3. Do the same for attitudes of dogmatism, rigidity, pseudosophistication, and caprice as inimical to good thinking.

4. A student cheats in examinations and is not concerned about it but at the same time rigidly refrains from cheating in games and on the playground.

What are the probable reasons for the different behaviors in the two situations?

What is the problem of the school? What is the guidance for teaching?

5. Persons may be observed every day who accept beliefs but refuse the logical consequences of these beliefs. Illustrate this. Indicate what, if anything, can be done.

6. Students are often required to study subjects or topics which are not connected with their experience and hence are not easily understood. No attitude of curiosity is aroused. Students develop an attitude that school subjects are one thing, the affairs outside are another. The material is memorized; the student does not ask what it means in terms of affecting belief and action. The student develops an *attitude of irresponsibility*. Illustrate this from everyday school practice. State what might be done about this.

7. An excellent common illustration of this difficulty is found in certain self-styled "students of the Bible." They quote freely, prove statements with references, often statements flatly contradicted by easily available facts. They claim to be "students of the Bible." They are nothing of the sort. They are quite irresponsible to scholarship. What in reality are they doing when they think they are studying the Bible?

How could you identify a genuine student of the Bible?

8. How in general does one go about developing an attitude of responsibility?

9. A small but good literature is developing on the development of attitudes. Three or four students may report in summary form specific studies on the development of attitudes, particularly those concerned with thinking.

10. The literature on teaching for attitudes is even smaller. Students may report for class benefit any current studies.

11. What principles can we apply here, as a starter, derived from our knowledge of the general principles of learning and teaching?

READINGS

Exercises Nos. 9 and 10 will care for the current periodical or monographic literature.

Students who wish to refresh or to amplify their present understanding of attitudes, nature and development, may read appropriate chapters in any standard text in psychology or in handbooks of psychology.

BIBLIOGRAPHY

ALLPORT, Gordon W., "Attitudes" in C. Murchison, ed., *Handbook of Social Psychology* (Worcester, Mass., Clark University Press, 1935), Ch. 17, pp. 798-844.

BARKER, R. G,, DEMBO, T., and LEWIN, K., *Frustration and Regression: A Study of Young Children,* University of Iowa Studies in Child Welfare, Vol. 18, No. 1 (1941).

BARNARD, J. D., *Teaching Scientific Attitudes and Methods of Science,* Bulletin of the National Association of Secondary School Principals, Vol. 37 (Jan., 1953), pp. 178-183.

BOLCH, C. H., "Examination of Scientific Method and Attitude," *Science Education* (Mar., 1957), pp. 92-97.

BRAMELD, Theodore B., "College Students React to Social Issues," *Social Frontier* (Dec., 1934), pp. 21-36.

CANTRIL, Hadley, "The Intensity of an Attitude," *Journal of Abnormal and Social Psychology,* Vol. XLI, pp. 129-135.

CARMICHAEL, L., ed., *Manual of Child Psychology* (New York, Wiley, 1954).

CHILD, I. L., and DOOB, L. W., "Factors Determining National Stereotypes," *Journal of Social Psychology,* Vol. 17 (1943), pp. 203-219.

CROWELL, Victor L., "Attitudes and Skills Essential to the Scientific Method," *School of Science and Mathematics,* Vol. 37 (May, 1937), pp. 525-533.

FELLOWS, E. W., "Some Social Factors Influencing the Development of Critical Thinking," *Progressive Education* (Nov., 1955), pp. 167-172.

HILGARD, E. R., and MARQUIS, D. G., *Conditioning and Learning* (New York, Appleton-Century-Crofts, 1940).

JONES, Vernon, "Attitudes of College Students and the Change in Attitude During the Four Years of College," *Journal of Educational Psychology* (Jan., 1938), pp. 114-138.

KEESLER, Oreon, "A Survey of Research Studies Dealing with Elements of Scientific Method as Objectives of Instruction in Science," *Science Education* (Oct., 1945), pp. 212-216.

MAUSNER, B., and MAUSNER, J., "Study of the Antiscientific Attitudes," *Scientific American* (April, 1955), pp. 2ff.

MURPHY, G., MURPHY, L. B., and NEWCOMB, T. M., *Experimental Social Psychology* (New York, Harper, 1937).

POLLACK, Jack, "What Are We Doing About Prejudices in Our Children?" *Parents Magazine* (Feb., 1953).

RADKE, Marian, TRAGER, Helen G., and others, "Social Perception and Attitudes of Children," *Genetic Psychology Monographs,* Vol. 40 (1949), pp. 327-447.

RAZRAN, C. H. S., "Transposition of Relational Responses and Generalization of Conditioned Responses," *Psychological Review,* Vol. 45 (1938), pp. 532-538.

RUSSELL, David H., *Children's Thinking* (Boston, Ginn, 1956). Ch. 6 should be read.

SCHOLASTIC MAGAZINE, "Mad Scientists; Youth Attitudes" (Oct., 1956), p. 69.

SHERIF, Muzafer, *The Psychology of Social Norms* (New York, Harper, 1936).

———, *The Psychology of Ego-Involvement; Social Attitudes and Involvements* (New York, Wiley, 1947).

———, and CANTRIL, Hadley, "The Psychology of Attitudes," *Psychological Review* (Nov., 1945), pp. 295-315; (Jan., 1946), pp. 1-24.

THOMPSON, P. K., "Scientific Attitude and Language Arts," *School Science and Mathematics* (Jan., 1956), pp. 50-53.

WRIGHTSTONE, J. Wayne, "Civic Beliefs and Correlated Intellectual and Social Facts," *School Review* (Jan., 1936), pp. 53-58.

Part II

The Thinking Process

Oh! These are hard questions for my shallow wit,
Nor I cannot answer Your Grace as yet.
But if you will give me but three weeks' space
I'll do my endeavor to answer Your Grace.

KING JOHN AND THE ARCHBISHOP OF CANTERBURY*

"Give me but three weeks' space"! Thinking must have been simpler in those days! The following chapters present our best efforts to give a simple but not oversimplified account of thinking as it goes on. Three weeks will not be sufficient. As Goethe once said of learning to read: "One does not learn to read during a complete lifetime." We hope that our chapters will not only give an understandable account but will stimulate an ever-continuing interest in and study of thinking.

* "The Ballad of King John and the Archbishop of Canterbury," Stanza 9, authorship unknown.

CHAPTER 4

Recognized Goals Initiate and Shape Thinking

The formulation of a problem is often more essential than its solution.

EINSTEIN

The earliest known writers on thinking emphasize two points which are repeated by all writers to this day: Thinking starts with a problem. The solution for the problem becomes the goal which guides thinking. An admirable statement was made by Hobbes three hundred years ago. [1] (Spelling and diction have been modernized.)

This train of thought, or mental discourse, is of two sorts. The first is *unguided, without design,* and inconstant; wherein there is no passionate thought, to govern and direct those that follow, to itself, as the end and scope of some desire or other passion: in which case the thoughts are said to wander, and seem impertinent one to another. . . .

The second is more constant; as being regulated by some desire, and design. For the impression made by such things as we desire or fear is strong, and permanent, or, if it cease for a time, of quick return. . . . And because the end . . . comes often to mind, in case our thoughts begin to wander, they are quickly reduced again into the way . . . giving rise to a precept *Respice finem,* that is to say, in all your actions look often upon (the goal) as the thing which directs all your thoughts in the way to attain it.

The discourse of the mind, when it is governed by design, is nothing but seeking, or the faculty of invention, which the Latins called *sagacitas,* and *solertia*—a hunting out of the causes of some effect . . . or the effects of some cause.

[1] Thomas Hobbes, *Leviathan* (Originally published 1651, many modern editions). Quote from early pages of Ch. 3, specific pages differing with editions.

Individuals differ greatly in seeing problems. The differences are not only in seeing problems but in defining them and keeping them in mind—as we say, "staying on the point." One has but to listen to the discussion of a motion in a committee, club, faculty, or city council or to read the proceedings of public bodies to realize how muddled ordinary thinking is on this particular point: seeing the problem and staying on it.

Certain persons do not or will not see problems. Some are insecure individuals who deliberately avoid the problem situations. Disturbances, breakdowns, or other real problems are either refused recognition or rationalized out of existence. "Everything is going well," and "Things are all right as they are," say these persons. Personality development must precede any attempt to aid these individuals to see problems.

A second subgroup is prevented from seeing problems because their lives are lived in pigeonholes and dominated by routines. The operation of rules-of-thumb and procedure along familiar paths will eventually develop a blindness to and disregard for problems which very much need attention. This difficulty is often seen in superintendents of schools and building principals, not to mention public officials and a certain type of minor administrative officer in business or industry. An experienced school principal, when asked in a graduate seminar what her problems were, replied indignantly, "I have none. I'll have you know that I have been a successful principal for twenty years and have no problems." This poor principal does not even know the language of modern education; she does not even know the conditions within her own school. Persons of this type can be aided to see problems only through sympathetic analysis and evaluation of their routines.

A third group includes those who feel in a vague and inexact way that something is wrong. "Something ought to be done about this." The exact nature of "this" and "something" is not recognized and defined. Aiding these people consists of much problem solving under guidance in which definitions are built up, systematic methods are introduced, and other help is given.

The better thinkers see and define problems with precision. Problems are sought, located, and outlined in definite language. The situation is diagnosed, the problem revealed, and systematic procedures developed.

Aiding students to find, identify, and clarify problems, and to stay on them while working. A general prerequisite is a rich, varied, and provocative environment. The learner must have opportunity to observe widely, to deal with many things, to build up a wide background of information and experience. A school devoted to routines, to dull repetition of the traditional form of assign-study-recite, will likely produce thinkers only as individuals revolt against the dreary round.

Class groups will be found with practically no experience with the free process of defining their own problems. Preliminary discussion and experience should be provided so that an intelligent approach may be made and not blind trial and error.

Various problems demand various methods. The genius of the teacher in developing techniques to fit given situations is indispensable. Certain general suggestions for guidance may be made.

1. Encourage, stimulate, and keep alive at all costs the questioning attitude which every child brings to school. Intellectual curiosity is at the door of all worthwhile human thinking, whether in the kindergarten or in the laboratory of theoretical physics.

2. Give much opportunity and practice in stating problems growing directly out of individual and group needs. Use defined terms, precise language, and—where applicable—charts, graphs, and mathematical terms.

3. Discuss directly with students the requirements of a good problem statement. Discussions should deal with an actual problem before the group and not with the abstract characteristics of a good problem. Questions may be asked directing attention to specific phases of the statement.

4. The teacher should state problems well himself when it is necessary for him to do so. The teacher may criticize and analyze his own statements with the class.

5. The teacher may intervene if the problem promises to get beyond experience and information of the learners, or beyond their level of maturity.

   a. Simplifying by suggesting omissions
   b. Dropping problems entirely if the pupils themselves see them as unworkable
   c. Suggesting that a problem be laid aside temporarily, to be taken up later

All this is better done through questioning than through direct decision by the teacher.

6. The teacher may ask questions to direct attention to specific points whenever class thinking reaches an impasse or rules of logic and of evidence are being violated.

7. A problem statement as it emerges may be placed on the board and outlined. Irrelevant aspects are more easily excluded, necessary and available resources noted, a beginning made on sorting hypotheses which will have been appearing throughout the process of defining.

8. Participation by all in the process of definition should be encouraged.

Whenever it is apparent that faulty definition has led the group astray into fruitless exploration of useless hypotheses, try to lead a discussion which will cause them to recognize the difficulty for themselves so that redefinition will result. Recall that certain valuable scientific discoveries came only after several redefinitions of the problem. Pupils will thus learn, it is hoped, the characteristics of a good problem statement and may be stimulated increasingly to state their own.

We do not wish to confuse this simple beginning account but must note that on advanced levels with complex problems the search for hypotheses enters into the defining of the problem. Defining a problem describes the expectations which are being frustrated and the kind of answer which should emerge. Eventually the problem must be stated in terms of the operations which determine the correctness of specific hypotheses, whether observational, logical, experimental, or other. This is doubtless what Einstein meant in saying that "a problem well defined is half answered."

Certain procedures will aid in *clarifying* a problem, once it has been given preliminary statement.

1. Identify and evaluate the key assumptions associated with the problem.
2. Establish definitions for the key words used, a universe of discourse. (See Chapter 10 on words.)
3. Subdivide a compound problem into major parts. This procedure often redirects and redistributes the attack on it.
4. Redefine the problem.

Teachers may aid students *to stay on the problem* by:

1. Holding individuals for the implications of statements made. "Show specifically how that relates to our problem." "That is true and interesting, but does it apply to this part of our problem defining?" "If what you say is true, then how about . . . ?" (Force application to an analogous or similar situation.)
2. Manifesting self-criticism and analysis of his own statements.
3. Occasionally telling students directly but courteously that they are off the point and that the group will have to return to the problem.
4. Tabling a contribution sometimes, with the promise of later discussion when it is applicable.

Defining a problem is not merely an exercise in grammar and diction, though it is good practice in those areas. Certain insights and skills will develop, it is hoped, which will be applicable to other problem situations:

1. Ability to see problems in real situations even though obscured by details; ability to see problems when reading about a situation (that is, not to be carried along in passive agreement while missing the significant problem, not to miss the point through indifference.)
2. Habit of insisting that we know exactly what the problem is at any stage (it may change partially as it develops), before going on with analysis and solution.

Transfer to other situations will be aided by:

1. Looking openly for similarity between characteristics of the problem under consideration and problems analyzed in the past.
2. Noting procedures which helped to unravel, or clarify, complex situations in the past, leading to discovery of the basic problem involved.

The encouragement of questioning, the stimulation of intellectual curiosity. Every child brings to school a wondering, questioning attitude unless his parents have spanked it out of him earlier. Children ask "Why?" "What?" "How?" "What holds the world up?" "Why doesn't an airplane fall down?" "How does medicine cure me?" "Who made God?" "How long ago was once upon a time?" "Why. . . ?" "Why. . . ? What. . . ? What. . . ? How. . . ?" "How. . . ?" With adults and particularly with great achievers in research we call this "intellectual curiosity." Curiosity in children and in great thinkers is the same thing, and probably the most important factor in thinking of any kind.

A story writer has expressed this clearly and at the same time indicated some of the things which kill the wonder and curiosity of the child. [2]

Grown people know that they do not always know the why of things, and even if they think they know, they do not know where and how they got the proof. Hence, the irritation they show when children keep on demanding to know if a thing is so and how the grown folks got the proof of it. It is so troublesome because it is so disturbing to the pigeonhole way of life. It is upsetting because until the elders are pushed for an answer they have never looked to see if it was so, or how they came by what passes for proof to their acceptances of cetrain things as true. So if telling their questioning young one to run off and play does not suffice for an answer, a good slapping of the child's bottom is held to be proof positive for anything from the spelling of Constantinople, to why the sea is salt. It was told to the old folks and that had been enough for them, or, to put it in the Negro idiom, "nobody didn't tell 'em, but they heard." So there must be something wrong with a child that questions the gods of the pigeonhole.

The thing to do is to grab the broom of anger and drive off the beast of fear.

I was full of curiosity like many other children, and like them I was as unconscious of the sanctity of statuary as a flock of pigeons around a palace. I got few answers from other people, but I kept right on asking, because I couldn't do anything else with my feelings.

The greatest intellects ask questions just as do children; in fact, on some questions an astonishing similarity appears. Asking questions may almost be said to have ushered in the modern world. Certainly asking questions did bring a great reform and improvement in thinking from approximately the sixteenth century onward. The fourteenth and fifteenth centuries saw criticism and revolt aimed at the medieval ideas and institutions which had been hampering men. The sixteenth century was the high point. The seventeenth century saw a vast revolution in climate of opinion. And it all came from men who asked questions and sought the answers. [3] As long as Aristotle and the Bible had all the answers, thinking was unneces-

[2] Zora Neale Hurston, *Dust Tracks on a Road* (London, Hutchinson, 1942; Philadelphia, Lippincott, 1944), pp. 21-22.

[3] We mention here of all the many who could be listed: Roger Bacon, 1214–1294, Francis Bacon, 1561–1626; Thomas Hobbes, 1588–1679; John Locke, 1632–1704. Advanced students will find a large literature.

sary, if not impossible. It could even be dangerous. But questions about the world and life were persistent and disturbing; problems arising out of life as it actually was demanded answers. Reasoning from unchallenged assumptions began to give way to fearless questioning of long accepted premises. The transformation of our world goes on. Today the best thinkers in various lines are asking questions about aspects of our universe which were unknown to the original questioners.

Stimulating and keeping alive the questioning attitude—intellectual curiosity. How is this done? Various problems demand various methods. Again the genius of the teacher is a critical factor. Certain general suggestion may be made, however.

The questions and inquiries must be accepted sympathetically and further queries encouraged. *Engage in discussion aimed at pinning the problem down.* This is a normal activity in general education anyway, leading to (*a*) understanding exactly what the problem is, and (*b*) stating it in precise language. *Attention may be redirected to the situation in which the problem appears.* Students may be asked to *examine their own resources* as one means of identifying the problem and the possibility of solution.

Analysis of a problem into its parts or subproblems may come next. All of this leads naturally into considering methods of attack, searching for relevant material, and on into the rest of the thinking process.

The cases in Chapter 1 and those in the latter part of the volume supply content and, it is hoped, understanding of the suggestions here.

Certain negative aspects may be noted. First, as indicated, the problems must be real, preferably growing out of the life and concerns of the learner. *Artificial and ready-made problems are not likely to get real problem-solving thinking.* The "problems" in most science manuals and in mathematics books are practically never problems but are exercises. Texts and manuals can contain real problems which obviously are placed before students. These problems must, however, (*a*) be drawn from real life and from typical activities and (*b*) be accepted by the learner. Passive acquiescence is not valuable. Problems cannot be "assigned" in the ordinary sense of the word.

The attitudes of parents and some teachers, as hinted in an early quotation in this chapter, often discourage the active inquiring attitude which the young child brings to school with him. *Refusal to take the questions seriously, "slapping them down," and even indifference effectually kill the inquiring spirit—and eventually intellectual life.*

The *physical condition of individuals* affects the quantity and quality of thinking. Children cannot be expected to solve intricate problems immediately after a strenuous gymnasium period, or following the class of an *over*zealous teacher.

The formal, traditional school with its *formal assignments, routine study, and fact quizzing is one of the worst offenders.* Schools often manage to destroy all intellectual curiosity before students reach high school. The maligned modern or "progressive" school, properly operated, does an excellent job of stimulating and developing reflective thinking.

The writers have seen a few individual or small-group projects in high school: one problem-solving study in nutrition, another in animal learning, another in the analysis of rumors and how they spread. Currently several illustrations in the field of rocket construction and launching can be seen. A group of college students in physics became so enamoured of the subject that they entered the laboratory on their own time and were setting up and carrying on good inquiries until discovered by the professor. Flying into a rage he forbade them the laboratory, ordering them to put their time on the subject matter of the course! These students had already passed beyond the "subject matter" of the course and were beginning to think within and about that subject matter. This, incidentally, is one of the best ways to learn "subject matter." All these students except one dropped the subject; the one dropped the professor! Going to another college he eventually rendered excellent service in military research.

A group of junior college students became interested in the analysis of "letters to the editor" appearing in the local newspaper. Interest at first centered upon the analysis of the logic and factual content which letter writers presented in supporting their answers to current problems. Spurred by the gross absurdities in most letters, the students developed both a fiendish ability and a high degree of critical analysis in answering the letters with letters of their own. With utmost courtesy it was shown that the original letter writers did not know what problem exactly they were discussing and that they had no facts or command of thought processes. Here again we have an illustration of problem recognition and analysis by students.

Students like these are often looked upon as "odd balls" by classmates and by some teachers. The truth is that they are normal and the classmates are the odd balls. The teachers who fall into this error have long since lost touch not only with the processes of learning and teaching but with the intellectual life of their civilization.

Clarifying and defining the problem may take time, far more than many "assignments," but it is necessary in order to understand exactly what is to be done. Adults and young students often work, even for hours, only to find their efforts wasted through failure to make sure first just what the problem was.

Individual differences in stating problems. In all guidance offered, students must keep in mind that individuals see problems differently because of differing experiential backgrounds, degrees of identification with the situation, general health and vigor, current emotional state, social standards, and what is called "set."

Individuals and groups with specialized interests also differ greatly in seeing problems within a given situation. An automobile crash occurs. The problems seen and formulated will differ considerably between a physician called to the scene and the highway patrolman in charge. The National Safety Council will see still different problems, as will the lawyer for the insurance company, the lawyer for an injured person, and the man on the tow truck. Should there be an odor of liquor at the scene, a representative of the W. C. T. U. would state still another problem. The type of problem determines in part the developing of methods of attack upon the problem.

QUESTIONS, EXERCISES, AND REPORTS

1. What is the *first* thing to do when a problem is sensed? What common errors are made just here?

2. What are the probable reasons why individuals define and clarify problems so poorly?

3. Can you add to or otherwise improve the suggestions given in this chapter for aiding pupils to define and clarify?

4. What is the relation of complacency or contentment to the seeing of problems? Implications for our own thinking and for teaching?

5. Suspended judgment is usually thought of as connected with problem solving, and particularly with accepting conclusions. Show why it is vitally important in defining problems.

6. The statement is made in Ortega y Gassett's *Revolt of the Masses* that the dominance of the masses always means violence; they settle problems with violence rather than in other ways. Why do you suppose this is true? What has this to do with our problem here?

7. Several writers have said, in effect, that a problem well put is half answered but that there are no reliable methods for improving one's ability to formulate problems clearly. Textbooks which contain good illustrations of problem solving give excellent help except on this one item.

    a. Why, do you think, is there so little help on this aspect?

    b. We are thus thrown back on our own observation and ingenuity as teachers. Give specific illustrations from your experience or from observation of classes in which individuals failed or refused to see the problem. What did the teacher do?

    c. Give illustrations from classes dominated by routine. What did, or should, the teacher do?

    d. Report any good illustrations of techniques used by teachers on any phase of this problem.

    e. Report on any recent practical or research summaries appearing in professional magazines.

8. Now we come to the far more difficult phase, identifying and isolating the crucial aspects of the problem. Textbooks have practically no discussions, and the periodicals only a few. Try to locate one or more discussions, but you will probably have to rely chiefly on your own ingenuity. The questions:

How do we aid students (or ourselves) to identify and isolate the crucial aspects of the problem? Try to make at least four points, more if possible.

READINGS WHICH AMPLIFY THIS CHAPTER

Note. Certain of the chapters listed are on the development of hypotheses. Defining problems and the rise of hypotheses go on simultaneously in real situations. Help with the one is often found while dealing with the other. The hypothesis will be discussed immediately following this chapter on the problem.

BLACK, Max, *Critical Thinking* (Englewood Cliffs, N. J., Prentice-Hall, 1946), Ch. 17. Contains excellent discussions of problem cases considerably more complex than Dewey's "burglar" episode and the illustrations in our first chapter.

COHEN, Morris R., and NAGEL, Ernest, *An Introduction to Logic and Scientific Method* (New York, Harcourt, Brace, 1934), Chs. 10, 11.

LARRABEE, H. A., *Reliable Knowledge* (Boston, Houghton Mifflin, 1945), pp. 8-26, and Chs. 4, 5.

BURTT, E. A., *Right Thinking,* 3rd ed. (New York, Harper, 1946), Ch. 2. This reference is quite similar to Dewey and to discussion in this chapter. Note his use of term *universe of discourse.* Do not choose unless others unavailable.

ROBINSON, James Harvey, *The Humanizing of Knowledge* (New York, George H. Doran, 1923). Chapter 1 should be required reading. Whole volume of great value. Several chapters will be referred to later.

Class reports may be made on any of these references, or class discussion can be based on questions raised by students.

GENERAL READING

Knowledge of the processes of thinking is one part of the story. The other necessity is knowledge. Thinking is always about something and always rests on a body of fact and/or inferences about facts. A staggering amount of thinking ranging all the way from everyday trivia to questions of international importance, to basic issues in ethics, goes astray because of lack of information. Individuals constantly develop and state conclusions which range from the nonsensical to the partially but not wholly correct. This is not because they are stupid, dishonest, or malicious. It is because they are uninformed. (There are also dishonest thinkers, but this is not our concern at the moment.)

Wide general reading must accompany any effort to understand and use the processes of thinking. Studying thinking is quite useless unless the obligation to be informed is recognized.

Some students will be primarily interested in political problems, tensions, forms of government, and their workings. Others will read about comparative economic systems and the current arguments about them—the merits and weaknesses of capitalism, socialism, communism. Still others will be interested in social and economic democracy now emerging as did political democracy some centuries back. Questions of ethics and conduct, both for the individual and the group, will engage other readers. Aesthetic standards, argument, and criticism will attract another group, literary standards and criticism still another. Child rearing, city planning, penal reform, comparative religion, scientific discovery, the relation of geography to politics, and any of scores of other areas may attract one or a group of students.

A student cannot read widely over a range of fields. Each will naturally concentrate on his interests. The contributions made to class discussions will contribute to the enlightenment of all. Wide general reading must be an *organized* part of any study of thinking. Lists of old and new books are easily available in book review sections of magazines and newspapers, in library lists, and elsewhere.

NEWSPAPER READING

The regular reading of one—preferably two or three—newspapers, of one or more weekly news commentaries, and of one or more journals of critical interpretation will be essential from this point on. As the following chapters develop, watch the publications for examples of good and bad thinking (or parts thereto). These will be found in quantity in news stories, editorials, commentaries, letters to the editor, and in letters and answers carried in the various advice columns.

1. Note illustrations of careful, shrewd thinking; of careless thinking; of irresponsible thinking; of clearly biased and twisted thinking. Pay particular attention to cases in which known facts are ignored or defied.

2. Note, particularly in letters to the editor, writers who ascribe motives and devious thinking to their opponents, who make statements as facts about their opponents which turn out to be fantastically wrong. Note also the careful, honest thinking of many letter writers.

3. Note, in personal advice columns, the type of information and level of intellect obviously possessed by some of the letter writers. The range will be from incredibly uninformed and childish, to logical, well informed. How do you account for this?

4. Note in contrast letters and answers in specialized columns on medical care, legal advice, child rearing, and other similar ones.

5. Try to explain:
   a. Why letter writers ignore or defy easily available facts.
   b. What motivates a writer who ascribes disreputable motives, devious thinking, to others? Differentiate between those who do it with great rudeness and those who do it courteously.
   c. What probably lies behind misinterpretation of statements which seem to be simple and clear?
      (Discussion to this point must obviously be simple and preliminary. Extended discussion will occur after more study.)

6. Look particularly for news stories, usually simple ones, which indicate clearly that many individuals simply do not read newspapers regularly. This

question is an important one, and students are likely to be startled at what they discover.

7. Do newspapers and magazines have any responsibility for printing letters and commentaries which are clearly out of line with well-known, valid, everyday facts?

Publishers defend this as (*a*) maintaining the free press, and (*b*) as giving opportunity to individuals to be heard. The practice, however, does disseminate incorrect information, baseless beliefs ranging from superstitions and old wives' tales to those which sound "scientific" but which are not. In many cases senseless public controversies are prolonged. Often the misinformation and pseudo-science circulated are dangerous to safety. The practice also undermines the efforts of all other agencies of enlightenment—honest press, the church, the school, and others.

This question will precipitate extended discussion, but this should be confined at this point to quick summaries of student opinion. Later chapters prepare for more detailed analysis.

8. Some newspapers and magazines will reprint statements after facts have been supplied clearly demonstrating the errors in the original statement. What reasons or explanations may be advanced for this?

CHAPTER **5**

The Hypothesis:
The Origin of Conclusions

Science is built up of facts, as a house is built of stones; but an accumulation of facts is no more a science than a heap of stones is a house.

HENRI POINCARÉ

We may stare at facts every minute of our waking day without being a whit the wiser unless we exert our intellects to build upon them or under them.

WILLIAM MINTO

A problem well stated—now what is the answer? The naïve thinker almost always at this point suggests, "We must get the facts." Yes, but what facts, and where do we look? Just to gather facts, as some research workers do, is nothing but busy work. Some writers do, in fact, state that we must "gather data" next after stating the problem. Pearson's statement on this point is sometimes misinterpreted. [1] "The first obligation of a scientist is the careful and accurate classification of facts, observation of their correlation and sequence." This does not mean that gathering data comes first. Elsewhere Pearson says, "The true aim of the teacher must be to impart an appreciation of method and not a knowledge of facts."

A reasonable sampling of books on research and on thinking shows that all but three (one a pamphlet) place the hypothesis next after the problem and as a guide to gathering data. Two books do not make clear just how they do proceed; one lists hypothesis properly and then proceeds to the gathering of data with no further reference to the hypothesis. (A few books on research are written, unfortunately, by men who have done no

[1] Karl Pearson, *The Grammar of Science* (London, Adam and Charles Black, 1900), p. 7. (Other editions are available.)

extensive research.) Dewey and Conant, to name but two prominent authorities, plus other scientists disagree with the statement that gathering the facts comes first. [2]

A hypothesis, or several of them, is necessary as a guide in seeking facts, even in determining what are facts in some instances. Ordinarily it is impossible to get facts, even to find and consult sources of fact without a hypothesis to guide the search. The functional relationship between hypothesis and facts has been illustrated in earlier chapters. They cannot be separated in real situations but may be analyzed separately for emphasis. Observation and collection of facts does, sometimes, take place in the absence of a hypothesis. Early astronomers, for instance, recorded many facts which later enabled Kepler to state laws explaining the orbits of heavenly bodies. Everyone in everyday affairs comes across facts when no particular hypothesis—or even problem—is in mind. Reading and conversation, or lectures, are sources. We note the facts in passing, and these facts often prove useful later. Facts noted thus, however, are related to concepts already in the mind or to the general problems of everyday living. The level of fact and of problem involved will range from simple daily questions to more complex challenges of important affairs. Facts read or heard and unrelated to one's knowledge will be neither noted nor remembered. The effort to memorize facts in advance of problems is futile. Facts and their uses will be presented in the next chapter.

SECTION 1. THE HYPOTHESIS

> Glendower. I can call spirits from the vasty deep.
> Hotspur.   Why, so can I, or so can any man:
>   But will they come when you call them?
> Glendower. Why, I can teach you, cousin,
>   to command the devil.
>   SHAKESPEARE *

Where do our hypotheses come from? Our intuitions, guesses, hunches? From the "vasty deep" of our life experience. Out of the nowhere into the here. But do they always come quickly and easily when we call? No! The authors cannot teach anyone to call even the lesser spirits, let alone "to command the devil"! We cannot give a formula which will ensure that hypotheses come when we call. No one can. We will, however, offer a few suggestions which may be of use.

The hypothesis is a *suggested* answer, an educated guess based on the

[2] J. B. Conant, "The Scientific Education of the Layman," *Yale Review* (Sept., 1946), pp. 15-36.

Carter V. Good, *Introduction to Educational Research* (New York, Appleton-Century-Crofts, 1959). This may be taken as representative of analyses of steps in research.

* William Shakespeare, *King Henry IV*, Part I, Act iii, Scene 1.

facts in the original situation out of which the problem arose. A problem usually suggests to a good thinker not one but several hypotheses. The mind naturally and usually begins at once to suggest answers, to gather evidence, to begin organizing arguments, to make inferences. Here we have the discursive phase of thinking indicated in outline in Chapter 2: good guesses and errors, corrections, redefinition of terms, digressions, shuttling back and forth between facts and hypotheses. Some details were also illustrated in Chapters 1 and 2.

The untrained person, the inexperienced thinker, or the stupid person often seizes upon the first answer (hypothesis). He "jumps to conclusions." He "begins with certainty" and, hence, blocks further thinking. The trained thinker, or the naturally shrewd person, has learned that it is necessary (a) to call up as many tentative answers (hypotheses) as possible, and (b) to look for associations, implications, related ideas of any sort which will lend or deny support to one of the original hypotheses. The trained thinker "begins with doubt" or at least suspended judgment. As Dewey points out, this is not always easy:[3] "Reflective thought is always more or less troublesome because it involves overcoming the inertia that inclines one to accept suggestions at their face value; it involves willingness to endure a condition of mental unrest and disturbance."

All hypotheses when supported by enough facts and reasons to be plausible must then be elaborated even further and subjected to test or proof. The tentative answers must emerge and be stated so that thinking may proceed. Hypotheses may range from very plausible answers to wild guesses, "shots in the dark." Both should be given a hearing. Many plausible guesses turn out to be only remotely related to the problem. Sometimes great advances in intellectual life, both for individuals and for society, have resulted from pursuing what seemed to be "wild guesses."

A number of hypotheses, as stated, are necessary to initiate and guide observation in the search for facts. Many naïve teachers and parents say we must train children in "the powers of observation." There are no such powers which can be trained independently. Everyone can observe, but he must have a direction in which to observe. Darwin long ago said: "How odd it is that anyone should not see that all observation must be for or against some view, if it is to be of any service."

Alternative hypotheses will develop under different value systems and will develop also with historical problems. Problems of critical analysis operate with acceptance-rejection hypotheses, though the hypothesis is often minimized with these problems. Group-type problems will nearly always develop a variety of hypotheses and solutions. The null hypothesis is widely used in research.

The first suggestion, guess, hypothesis, "pops into the mind" spontaneously and automatically. Two or three may come this way, but the

[3] John Dewey, *How We Think* (Boston, Heath, 1910), p. 13.

development of several, and of the more elaborate ones, is a difficult matter. There is no real control; suggestions come, or they do not come. As Dewey says, there is nothing intellectual about it, though what we do with the suggestions is definitely and significantly intellectual.

General factors affecting the emergence of hypotheses. Suggestions just appear, or they do not appear. Some are brilliant, some mediocre, some stupid. The process cannot be controlled directly, but knowledge of the general bases from which hypotheses arise may enable teachers to develop some useful indirect control. The following list is a summary from various sources of the factors affecting the emergence of hypotheses:

1. Native capacity to discern and to discriminate; the "knack" of the individual; originality. This affects the (*a*) ease and promptness, (*b*) extent and variety, (*c*) depth or profundity, of the hypotheses suggested.

2. Intellectual curiosity, or liking for inquiry into causes, relationships, reasons, outcomes.

3. Systematic habit of mind. This rests at first upon the realities of the practical world, later on training. This affects the orderliness and continuity of suggestions.

4. Temperament; the willingness to endure patiently the uncertainty and doubt which characterize this phase of thinking; to suspend judgment.

5. Experiential background, range and type, particularly early experiences resulting in a fund of information.

6. Recent activities.

7. Interests at the moment.

8. Chance or accident. (Not to be confused with "flashes of insight" or sudden discoveries. These always occur to persons well trained and experienced in the given field.)

The teacher may make certain general suggestions. Native capacity, which is crucial, is not susceptible to anything we can do. The whole scheme of modern education, however, is aimed at developing extensive background and at developing some of the skills indicated above. The acceptance and use made of any suggestions or hypotheses are of crucial importance in developing a thoughtful general attitude plus the necessary skills. Possible suggestions of a general nature include:

1. A re-examination of the original situation. "The individual may return upon, revise, restate, enlarge, and analyze the facts out of which the suggestion springs." [4] Sometimes measurement of what was thought to be safely precise is an aid. Clearer definition of the problem, if possible, also aids.

2. Deliberate "casting about" in one's background of experience and reading, looking for similar situations, for related experience and information; consulting other persons; consulting a wide range of references.

3. Deliberate consideration of one's own natural predilections, biases, or even prejudices. This often leads to seeing suggestions which otherwise were blocked. The "personal equation" is important.

[4] Dewey, *op. cit.*, p. 85.

4. Deliberate abandonment of the problem temporarily; turning to some other problem temporarily, or to some recreational activity. To "sleep on it" is good advice, to "think it over." Relaxation brings release of tension which seems to stimulate mental processes. The explanation of this is still in dispute, but all agree that it works. Advice "not to take failure too seriously" is good, provided the problem is not abandoned under that advice.

The teacher may sometimes make the general suggestions more specific. Specific suggestions which can be made include:

1. Call attention to one factor at a time. Break the problem up. This may serve to focus attention on some important or significant characteristic, to eliminate misleading or irrelevant qualities which may be unduly spectacular or otherwise unusual.

2. Warn against being blocked by a verbal or an imaginary whole; select parts for scrutiny. (This only when such a blockade appears.)

Attending to one factor at a time is what is meant by *analysis* in the psychological sense. Analysis is not "picking to pieces" as is often assumed. A mental presentation cannot be "picked to pieces." We can, however, focus upon one feature after another, each exclusively for the time being. This usually stimulates suggestions, guesses, leads. Unskilled thinkers often sit and stare at a problem in apparent bafflement. They seem almost to expect the solution or a hint toward a solution to appear magically. Training enables a student to break the problem up, to look first here, then there, and so on. The more aspects that are consciously considered, the more connections are possible; hence, more recall and suggestion are likely.

3. Suggest related and comparable experiences and problems, analogies, persons, or other sources which might stimulate thinking on the problem.

4. Deliberately encourage pupils to "take a chance"; encourage "hunches," controlled guesses, partial insights. Get as many reasonable hypotheses as possible.

Here we have Kepler's bold guessing. Pupils may sometimes be encouraged to make, and to follow for a time, seemingly wild shots. Successful or unsuccessful, these guesses or hypotheses are likely to lead to fresh angles and new data. At any rate, pupils should be made secure from fear of "being ridiculous." If an idea is ridiculous enough, this will soon be apparent. Many very valuable results have stemmed from suggestions which were laughed at when first produced.

5. Write down hypotheses as given, and then consider each systematically. This often changes the conception of the problem.

6. Maintain a general attitude of tolerance and sympathetic assistance.

The impatient or untrained teacher is often annoyed by the necessities of real problem solving. He is plagued by the seeming irrelevant guesses and suggestions, unaware that these are natural and inescapable. They may be very valuable. The teacher must accompany the class on their excursions after false leads, must follow their immature checking of opinions and facts. The impatient teacher who gives the answer and settles questions robs the learners of the most important phase of problem-solving learning. Emphasis on the *"right answer"* has also interfered with attention to the *process of arriving at the right* answer. The teacher, of course, is to exercise guidance within the process, but he must cheerfully accept the discursive, time-consuming processes of developing thought.

Good teachers recognize that the logic of adult-organized subject matter may not be logical at all to the learners. Organized subject matter is an outcome to be achieved by the pupil through his efforts at solving problems or thinking critically. So also with methods of thinking. A list of necessary skills and expository presentation of the processes may have no effect on younger learners. Later, when they have achieved some understanding through their own efforts and contacts, organized presentations are of assistance.

7. Sometimes the teacher may have to suggest seeking for more cases similar to the original one which set off the thinking. This calls for (*a*) more observation, and (*b*) experimental production of new cases. (This is not to be confused with observation and experimentation aimed at proof or with developing more adequate concepts. This will be treated in Chapters 8 and 9. Here we are concerned only with getting more useful hypotheses.)

Characteristics of a useful hypothesis. These are difficult to state. We really cannot tell the value or usefulness of a hypothesis until we have tested it. Hypotheses which may seem ridiculous at first sometimes turn out to be very productive. A series of poor hypotheses may, as someone has said, at least get rid of the errors.

The list cannot be final; nor does each point apply to all hypotheses. First, the explanation contained in a hypothesis will vary in nature depending upon whether the problem is one of discovery, prediction, explanation, creation, critical evaluation, or other type. Second, the frame of reference within which the thinker is operating at the moment will determine the type and character of the hypotheses stated. For instance, a man is murdered. Several legitimate hypotheses are certain to appear. Which one is selected depends, as said, upon the type of problem and upon who is solving it. The detective will have one hypothesis as to cause of death; the medical examiner may have quite another; the prosecuting attorney may agree with either of the foregoing or may have another hypothesis of his own. A lawyer, a psychiatrist, a newspaper reporter, and particularly the neighbors are all likely to have differing hypotheses.

The following list of characteristics of useful hypotheses is as simple and as adequate as we can make it in view of the various factors involved.

1. *Compatible with existing knowledge;* in accord with known concepts and laws. (Recall previous discussions of the usefulness of wild guesses which seem to go beyond or contrary to known laws and facts. Many discoveries come through differing with accepted knowledge.)

2. *Stated or constructed in such a way that a test is possible.* Deductions from the hypothesis must be testable in some way. Consequences in the world can be inferred and then observed or tested; future events can be predicted and then observed. Tests are not for truth or falsity of the hypothesis, but for adequacy or inadequacy in the given problem.

3. *Answers the question it was designed to answer.*

4. *Stated in defined terms;* free from ambiguity. This saves time wasted in argument based on differing interpretations.

5. *Simple.* When there is a choice between hypotheses which seem to furnish answers to a question dealing with theoretical systems, the simplest is often preferable, that is, the hypothesis which has the fewest elements and furnishes the most direct solution. When simple ones have been exhausted, it will be time for more complex and subtle statements.

The principle that the simplest solution should be selected first is often called the Law of Parsimony: Select that solution which has the fewest residual phenomena. It is often called, also, Occam's Razor, after William of Occam who first stated the principle.

Hypothesis and inference. Inference is the central *movement* in all thinking. It is the *movement* from facts to the tentative explanation (hypothesis), the *movement* from one reason to another either in developing or proving a hypothesis, the *movement* from a reason to predicted facts, and the movement toward acceptance or rejection of a conclusion (the proved or tested hypothesis). [5] The emergence of the hypothesis is an inference. Minor inferential movements take place constantly as the inference is elaborated and finally tested. Inference since it moves from something known to something unknown is peculiarly susceptible to error. There can be no guarantee in advance that the "unknown", the possible but as yet absent conclusions or facts, will be correct or useful. Proof of hypothetical conclusions is always necessary.

SECTION 2. THE HYPOTHESIS IS DEVELOPED AND THEN PROVED OR DISPROVED BY (a) REASONING AND (b) CHECKING AGAINST FURTHER FACTS

Before you try a complicated hypothesis, you should make quite
sure that no simplification of it will explain the facts equally well.
                                                            CHARLES S. PEIRCE

A reasonable hypothesis, once set up, must first be elaborated and proved or disproved either by (*a*) reasoning, or by (*b*) testing against reality. Testing against reality is of two types—observation of further facts in the situation and the experimental production of new facts. Both elaboration of the hypothesis and proving it use the same methods. All this may be a considerable task in important problems, long, drawn out, and difficult. We engage in what Dewey called: [6] "Active, persistent, and careful consideration of any belief or supposed form of knowledge in the light of the grounds which support it and the further conclusions to which it tends. . . ."

Problems in previous chapters illustrate reasoning, checking against

[5] Chapter 7 presents a detailed analysis of inference, its values, dangers, and uses.
[6] John Dewey, *How We Think,* rev. ed. (Boston, Heath, 1933), p. 9.

reality, observing further facts. The cave dwellings on Mesa Verde were physical facts which presented a problem. These facts were examined. Then reasoning entered, known principles were called to mind, movement was from one principle to another. "Wood used in the buildings will show a tree ring pattern." "Tree ring chronology has been authenticated over a long period of time." Back, then, to observing further facts. Wood was taken from the beams in the buildings and compared with the tree ring chronology. Overlap was found, and various dates connected with the buildings were established. A belief then rested "upon grounds which would support it."

The children working on the playground situation had ample facts indicating that a problem of behavior had to be solved. They elaborated the various hypotheses by discussion. They knew that "rules with punishment" plus "agreement on the rules by group members" *might* improve the situation. No easy checking was possible here as with the tree rings. New data had to be produced experimentally, that is, by trying their rules out over a period of time.

The parents' hypotheses are also of interest here. Some held that "entrusting children with control of playground behavior will make conditions worse." "Adult control is necessary to guarantee good order." Other parents held that "Pupil-made rules plus consent might ensure good order." Back of these were assumptions, stated or not: pupils are or are not mature enough to solve problems like this or to maintain order. Again the experimental tryout was necessary. Note in passing that if tryout had been prevented by dominant opinion, thinking and opportunity to learn its processes would have been prevented.

The third illustration dealt with hidden or partially hidden hypotheses and assumptions, not to mention emotional tone which in turn affected all phases of the thinking. "Rigid and exclusive immigration laws will keep out undesirables, to the benefit of this country." The letter presented no facts of any kind; definite errors in reasoning could easily be identified. Other hypotheses were not considered: "Many immigrants are not undesirables but of real benefit to our country." "We may be providing political asylum for persons in danger of their lives in other countries." Others could be listed. Facts could be developed from past history bearing on this problem, though neither facts nor reasoning is likely to be conclusive.

An illustration observed by one of the writers shows proof by reasoning and further indicates that in cases such as this experimental extension is not necessary. Readers may recall the wide publicity given some years ago to the opening of a cornerstone in a Texas town. A live horned toad emerged from the box which had been sealed for forty years! The writer was there and observed with interest and considerable inner glee the wild arguments which raged. Hundreds of citizens *knew* the toad had been in the cornerstone all those years. "With their own eyes" they had seen the toad emerge! In fact, to suggest that a trick was involved for publicity purposes was almost to precipitate violence. Biologists everywhere, in contrast to the "eye witnesses," laughed at the story; they *knew* the toad was not in the cornerstone. The biologists were not even there; they used their informed minds rather than "their own eyes." They reasoned from known principles to an answer which was unassailable. Living organisms cannot survive without oxygen, water, and food; the toad was not in the cornerstone.

The elaboration and evaluation of suggestions and hypotheses may be aided by:

1. Discussing, arguing, exchanging opinions, beliefs, facts.
2. Asking that all statements and beliefs be checked against known facts, accepted principle, or accepted authorities.
3. Suspending judgment until all views have had a hearing.
4. Devising empirical tests.
5. Carrying the checking toward establishing a cause-effect relationship.

The proving or disproving of hypotheses is never final. A hypothesis is at first wholly tentative. The implications are developed by reasoning. Sometimes the implications are tried out in action to get more facts. Both reasoning and testing against reality appear also as methods of proof. The methods of proving a hypothesis, thus arriving at an answer to the original problem or providing grounds for believing the answer, are easily recognized though sometimes difficult to apply.

Students should not be allowed to accept principles, theories, conclusions, without knowing what the act of reasoning or testing includes. Preferably students should engage in reasoning or conduct tests themselves.

Proof, even the best we can get, is always tentative and relative, subject to revision as other facts appear or as new principles are developed. Empirical tests, even extensive experimental work, are not crucial to the point of finality. Acceptance or rejection of conclusions as final, conclusive, or dogmatic is highly undesirable since it forecloses future inquiry. Conclusions are rarely cases of *either-or* but rather of *degrees of this or that*. We accept conclusions with such reservations as "so far as we now know" or "so far as the facts as of now have shown." A good device is to set up balance sheets showing and summarizing evidence for and against the hypothesis under consideration. Chapter 8 will develop the problem and methods of proof in further detail.

QUESTIONS, EXERCISES, AND REPORTS

The first three exercises have nothing to do with education and are admittedly extreme cases. They illustrate the real difficulty of securing, under certain conditions, workable hypotheses. Students, it is hoped, may gain some insight into this crucial factor in all competent thinking. Exercise No. 4 gives students an opportunity to exercise their ingenuity in more typical cases.

1. A fire which destroyed a large circus tent at Hartford, Conn., some years ago resulted in a number of deaths. Every victim was identified and claimed by relatives or friends—except one. The body of a little girl was never identified or claimed. The story had wide publicity in newspapers everywhere. The police, over a period of months, exhausted every resource at their command. False leads appeared, as they always do, but the mystery remained as complete as ever. Not only was no identification made, but no one ever appeared to tell of a missing child anywhere.

Now: this little girl had parents or other relatives. She lived in a neighborhood, known to other adults and to playmates. She attended school somewhere. She must have been known in neighborhood stores and other places. *No one has ever appeared to ask about some little girl who lived, played, and went to school somewhere—but who is now missing.* The little girl disappeared from her life—and no one has missed her. An impenetrable wall stands between the little dead girl and her past life.

Devise as many hypotheses as you can to account for this situation. The facts given are all there are and are sufficient to support a number of hypotheses. (The police followed the same ones you will probably develop and found nothing.)

2. In February, 1957, the body of a little boy about four or five years old was found near Philadelphia. He had been beaten to death. The only clues were the cardboard box and a piece of blanket in which the body was wrapped. Fingernails and toenails had been neatly trimmed; an odd shapped haircut had been given either just before or after death. The hands and one foot were wrinkled as if they had been in the water recently.

The police, as in the Hartford case, exhausted their extensive resources. Four hundred thousand circulars, carrying a picture of the boy's face were posted in police stations, post offices, and courthouses over the nation. The *FBI Law Enforcement Bulletin* alerted investigators everywhere. The American Medical Association circulated a complete medical description, hoping that some doctor somewhere might recognize the boy. Leads developed, but all failed. The police have three filing cabinets full of material—but the boy has never been identified; nor has the slightest clue to his past or to the murderer turned up.

This little boy, like the little girl, lived somewhere. He was known to several adults and presumably to other children. No one has reported a missing boy which fits the case. The impenetrable silence surrounding the case has never been broken.

Devise as many hypotheses as you can to account for the situation. (The police came up with one which could explain the situation but which could not be tested or checked. An excellent account appears in the *Saturday Evening Post* for July 26, 1958, if one wishes further details.)

3. The famous sea mystery "Case of the Mary Celeste" may be recalled at this point. The ship was found in the Atlantic, deserted by the entire crew. Not a sign appeared which would indicate hasty desertion or panic from any danger. Food was on plates in the galley. The sewing basket of the captain's

wife was sitting undisturbed by her chair. Everything everywhere appeared to be in order. The crew had evidently taken to a small boat and was never heard of again. Why did they leave the ship?

What hypotheses can you advance?

A voluminous literature exists concerning the "Mary Celeste," but much of it is in periodicals not ordinarily found in many libraries. Several books are also available. The following are usually accessible and will give sufficient background:

DE LA CROIX, Robert, *Mysteries of the Sea,* translated from the French by James Cleugh, 1st American edition (New York, John Day, 1957)

FAY, Charles E., *Mary Celeste: The Odyssey of an Abandoned Ship* (Salem, Mass., Peabody Museum, 1942).

LOCKHART, J. G., *A Great Sea Mystery* (*The True Story of the Mary Celeste*) (New York, W. F. Payson, 1931). An edition was published in England in 1927.

4. What guidance, if any, can be derived from these rather extreme cases, applicable to education for thinking?

Experienced teachers may illustrate any procedures they have used or observed wherein students were aided to set up hypotheses under difficult conditions in the classroom materials, or in research studies.

Examine a few research studies, and note development of hypotheses.

5. Where do hypotheses come from? What guidance do they offer for education? What do hypotheses do?

6. What is the difference between a hypothesis and an assumption? A hypothesis and a dogma?

7. What is the value of cultivating a variety of possible hypotheses, of examining them freely and fully?

8. Why is it important to have explanatory as well as descriptive hypotheses?

9. What are some of the many everyday errors made by the average citizen in producing and using hypotheses? What guidance for you in guiding students?

10. Describe and/or illustrate how individuals differ in number of suggested hypotheses? In critically examining them?

11. Suggestions and hypotheses are speculative, adventurous, and not warranted in advance. How do we know which are the better, or the best suggestion? How can we keep the process of suggesting on the right track?

12. We have noted that hypotheses which seem plausible at first sight are often found unfit or even absurd when their full consequences are traced out. Others which at first seem remote, even wild, are frequently transformed through being elaborated so that what follows from them is apt and fruitful.

     a. Illustrate the two foregoing statements with commonplace or everyday cases.

     b. Illustrate with more complicated cases of public affairs, or scientific research, of which you have read or heard.

     c. Dewey says a hypothesis may turn out to be useless—the person fails to solve the problem—but that this may be educative. Explain.

13. Read Cohen and Nagel (see Readings below), pp. 197-206. Note the excellent reasoning done by Herodotus in dealing with the problem (explanation) of the Nile overflow. Comment upon the source, nature, and development of hypotheses. Mention of reasoning and proof cannot be excluded, but keep the emphasis here on the hypotheses. Reasoning and proof will be analyzed in conjunction with appropriate chapters.

Examine the illustration from Galileo similarly, Cohen and Nagel, pp. 204-206, 278.

Describe and illustrate errors in forming hypotheses made by the average citizen in similar though simpler cases; by distinguished thinkers when outside their fields of specialization.

Describe skillful development of hypotheses by the average person in a given specific case.

14. Note the exercises in Black (see Readings below), pp. 10-11. Point out the hypotheses which come to your mind as you try one or another of the cases.

Black, Ch. 2, pp. 12-18, bears some relation to our inquiry here. What relations do you see? Do not be confused by the more difficult discussion on pp. 18-25.

State the premises, assumptions, and hypotheses for any selected exercise, Black, pp. 26-30.

15. Summarize from (a) your own experience, (b) observations, or (c) reading any further suggestions for stimulating the rise of hypotheses, over and above those in the chapter.

READINGS

BLACK, Max, *Critical Thinking* (Englewood Cliffs, N. J., Prentice-Hall, 1946), Ch. 2.

COHEN, Morris R., and NAGEL, Ernest, *An Introduction to Logic and Scientific Method* (New York, Harcourt, Brace, 1934), Ch. 11.

LARRABEE, H. A., *Reliable Knowledge* (Boston, Houghton Mifflin, 1945), Chs. 4, 5.

DEWEY, John, *How We Think*, rev. ed. (Boston Heath, 1933), Chs. 6, 7, 11.

Note: Instructors and students who wish greater detail concerning the hypothesis may read with profit Chapters 5, 6, 7, 8, 9, in Larrabee's volume listed above.

CHAPTER 6

Facts: Nature, Source, and Use in Thinking

Facts

In the clumsy clutch of fools
Facts are vain and dangerous tools
Fashioning little save uncouth
Snares to trip the feet of Truth.
But in the deft hands of the wise
What deadly traps they build for lies.

ROBERT G. PECK *

. . . it is the facts which coerce thinking and not thinking that
coerces facts. . . .

STERLING P. LAMPRECHT †

The development of solutions to problems or of conclusions of any sort
depends upon facts and upon subjective data of various types. The facts
are sought for and identified according to some hypothesis which gives
the facts meaning. Facts may then be interpreted to give them value, to
determine cause-and-effect relationships between facts and conclusion, to
make possible prediction. Interpretations may be combined into a theory
which is a guide to further facts and conclusions. Knowledge of whatever
sort, whatever we know about the universe, is based on the interpretation
of facts.

Since facts occur in many complex interrelationships, special attention is given to analysis, as well as to definition and interpretation. The
average citizen, on the other hand, has little or no training and is often

* Robert G. Peek, "Craftsmanship," *Saturday Evening Post* (June 7, 1937), p.
140. Used with the kind permission of author and publisher.

† Sterling P. Lamprecht, *Empiricism and Natural Knowledge*, University of
California Publications in Philosophy. Vol. 16. No. 4 (1940), p. 78.

not even aware of the nature of fact, interpretation, and theory. He is often not aware of his own processes in handling these things. We may represent the situation superficially through the following diagrams:

The careful thinker organizes thus:

observed facts⟶interpretation⟶theory

or

facts determined objectively⟶reasonable interpretations⟶sound theory

The average man builds his system of knowledge on poor substitutes for the above factors:

faulty observation or selection or nonfacts⟶poor interpretation of experiences resulting in unreliable opinions⟶no theory or poor theory

Preliminary definitions. The first step in developing the complex relationships to be outlined in this chapter is to set up definitions.

1. *Fact.* A fact is an event, state of existence, or relationship for which reliable evidence can be found and which entails a minimum of interpretation. Also, a statement about such events, and the like.

2. *Data.* Data are items of basic information, such as dates, weights, records of events, and facts.

3. *Interpretation.* Interpretation is the process of giving meaning to facts or data by making such inferences as generalization, prediction, establishing cause-and-effect relationships.

4. *Opinion.* An interpretation of events which may be true or false, reliable or unreliable, but at any rate is not established.

5. *Belief.* An opinion about which particularly strong conviction is felt, the stress being on the feeling of conviction rather than the established reliability.

6. *Theory.* A theory is a statement of laws and principles which underlie and explain any set of facts, lesser laws, and principles.

7. *Experience.* The sum of events which have happened to an individual.

The Mesa Verde case may be used to illustrate these basic definitions and other important terms introduced elsewhere in this part of the book.

1. *Fact. a.* Observed fact: There is wood in the ruins.
      b. Remembered fact: The wood ring theory has been used in other dating problems.

2. *Hypothesis.* Tree ring patterns may establish the age of this wood.

3. *Assumption.* The wood found in the Mesa Verde ruins was placed there when building began at the settlement.

4. *Interpreted fact.* The wood ring pattern of a sample of the ruins matches that of the criterion pattern.

5. *Theory.* There is a specific relationship between the pattern of rings in a cross section of wood and the history of rainfall in the area where the wood grew. This correspondence will identify the period when the tree was growing and hence the date of the settlement where it was found.

6. *Conclusion.* The Mesa Verde settlement dates from 1019 to 1273. (Provided the assumption above is correct.)

7. *Opinions and beliefs. a.* "They will never figure out when that place was founded." (Incorrect opinion or belief.) *b.* "The settlement dates from 1019. . . ." (Correct opinion.)

8. *Experience.* The sum of all the activities of the archeologists at Mesa Verde, plus their interpretations and reactions. Or, the sum of the activities of the old prospector.

It should be noted that other opinions and beliefs could be any of the above statements, right or wrong.

The foregoing suggests the organization for this chapter:

Section 1. Facts, data, and their sources
Section 2. Interpretation of facts and experience
Section 3. Theory and the facts
Section 4. Teacher guidance in the analysis of experience (Suggestions to teachers for aiding pupils to obtain facts, interpret them correctly, recognize sound theory, and interpret their experience)

SECTION 1. FACTS, DATA, AND THEIR SOURCES

One method of delivery alone remains to us; which is simply this: we must lead men to particulars themselves, and their series and order; while men on their side must force themselves for a while to lay their notions by and begin to familiarize themselves with facts.

FRANCIS BACON

Before starting out to "get the facts," let it be noted that facts are present at all stages of any inquiry. A situation which gives rise to thinking contains facts which must be examined before any inquiry takes place. These initial facts initiate and regulate the formulation of hypotheses which in turn enable us to search for more facts.

Necessity for further definition. The word *fact* is used in everyday discussion, and even sometimes in books on logic and thinking, with no effort to define it. The word is used far more loosely in everyday discourse than in critical thinking. Common usage is often sufficient for minor everyday affairs—*but we must know what we are doing with such usage.* Writers on critical thinking and those engaged in research in the natural sciences reserve the word, as we have seen above, for events or conditions possessing a high degree of objectivity, susceptible to precise measurement or to unambiguous definition, subject to relatively easy verification, and maintaining independent existence in the outside world.

We may now extend the definition of fact to show that there are four different and legitimate senses in which "fact" may be used.

Fact 1. Certain discriminated element in sense perception. The sensory act of observing that lead gives way when struck by a hard object. Cohen and

Nagel point out that inquiry never begins with such facts. We seek them out for the purpose of finding reliable signs which will enable us to test the inferences we make.

Fact 2. A proposition which interprets. "This lead is soft."

Fact 3. A proposition which asserts a generalization. "All lead is soft."

Fact 4. Things existing in time and space, together with relations between them, in virtue of which a proposition is true. "That soft lead out there in front of us, about which we made statements No. 2 and No. 3, is an object."

The control of fact by legal rules of evidence. Here we have a special case in the use of fact. The judge in a courtroom is interested chiefly in determining two things: (1) the facts, that is, what happened; and (2) the legal inference from these facts, for example, who committed the crime? In order to eliminate as much error as possible, a complicated set of rules governs the admission of evidence, that is, data from which the court may determine facts and legal inference.

The *hearsay* rule prevents a witness from quoting other persons, presumably because the absent person quoted cannot be cross-examined by the opposing lawyer. The *"no opinion"* rule and the refusal to accept *"conclusions of the witness"* mean "stick to the facts." This is a safeguard against the notorious disposition of interested parties to present their own biased opinions about matters which the court and jury can perfectly well decide if they have the facts. The interpretation of facts is, of course, allowed in the case of expert testimony by ballistics experts, serologists, meteorologists, and fingerprint experts.

There is a basic distinction between *testimonial* and *circumstantial* evidence. Courts traditionally have placed great faith in eyewitness accounts. Personal identification by a witness and the statement "I saw him do it" usually impress juries strongly and convince them that the facts are as the witness stated. Eyewitnesses are frequently wrong, to be sure, as we point out elsewhere in this chapter. When there are no witnesses, or where there is insufficient testimonial evidence, or confirmation of testimony, the courts depend on circumstantial evidence. A man known to be in debt for a long period suddenly pays off his debts. The store in which he works has been robbed at about this time. Individuals make purchases which are ordinarily out of their line of buying. Their source of funds may be an inheritance, the winning of a large television prize, or a sudden rise in stocks owned, but it may be robbery or embezzlement.

Generally speaking then, legal tradition has established certain rules of thumb by which evidence is restricted to the presentation of information which is most likely to lead to the establishment of the actual facts and to the legitimate inferences from these facts.

The impermanence of facts. The honest citizen going about his affairs assumes—almost unconsciously—that in this confused world there is at least one thing he can count on to stay put, one thing upon which he can rely safely. The facts! A fact is a fact, isn't it? (Not always). Two and two always make four, don't they? (Not always, as any mathematician can explain.) The fact is that facts are not always easy to understand and to manage, do not stay put indefinitely. Facts must first be defined and identified, and their sources validated. Then they must be interpreted and accounted for when used in any kind of thinking. Factness is determined partly by certain "coercive and compelling" characteristics, but in some instances it is determined by definition. Facts are also determined within given systems by the postulates and assumptions of that system.

Contrary to popular opinion, facts are not fixed and unchangeable. A fact may be established for the time and under the given circumstances, but this does not fix it eternally, New instruments, improved methods of observing, more accurate controls, and new assumptions bring changes. The field of modern physics illustrates this. Facts which were accepted for several centuries are being supplemented with new orders of fact more accurately derived. Challenging of old axioms and postulates has the same effect. The flippant statement "Facts, like fish, will begin to smell if kept too long" has been attributed to several writers in the field.

Facts are what William James called the "irreducible, stubborn phenomena," which "cannot be conjured into and out of our world at will." Stubborn and coercive during their life, they are not permanent. [1]

Facts, when clearly valid, have been held in ever increasing respect by everyone from the average citizen to the leading scientists, from the days of Francis Bacon onward. Solutions for our problems and the bases for beliefs held about men and matters must rest upon reliable facts drawn from reliable sources. A modern point of view on factness is ably presented by Larrabee: [2]

To demand the facts is to signify our attention to find out what we are obliged to take account of—that is, to move away from the sphere of the merely possible: guesses, conjectures, and fancies, toward actuality—"the world as it actually is."

Now if we are to make this appeal for confirmation of our knowledge with any success whatever, it is apparent that there must be present in human

[1] Desirable supplementary reading at this point:
Max Black, *Critical Thinking* (Englewood Cliffs, N. J., Prentice Hall, 1946), Ch. 18, and then Ch. 13.

Morris R. Cohen and Ernest Nagel, *An Introduction to Logic and Scientific Method* (New York, Harcourt, Brace, 1934), pp. 199, 201, 217-218, 391-392. The four "senses" in which fact may be used given just above are adapted from Cohen and Nagel, pp. 217-218.

Harold A. Larrabee, *Reliable Knowledge* (Boston, Houghton Mifflin, 1945), pp. 127-130, 138-150 (or all of Chs. 4 and 5 if time permits).

S. I. Hayakawa, *Language in Thought and Action*, rev. ed. (New York, Harcourt, Brace, 1949), pp. 42-44, all of Ch. if desired.

W. P. D. Wightman, *The Growth of Scientific Ideas* (New Haven, Yale University Press, 1953), pp. 29-31 and others if desired. Use the index.

[2] Larrabee, *op. cit.*, extracts from pp. 128-130.

experience, no matter how chaotic and variable it may be in other respects, *some* elements or factors that are relatively stable and orderly. . . .

Whatever in experience is compelling, coercive, inescapable—whatever cannot be conjured into and out of our world at will—deserves the name of fact. . . .

Criteria for verifiability of facts. In a general way we can say that facts are characterized by:

1. *Agreement among independent observers as to the fact;* as to appearance, nature, characteristics.
2. *Reproducibility of the fact* independently of persons. Facts maintain independent existence in the world; they stay put. Facts may be reproduced under controlled experimental conditions.
3. *Agreement among observers* as to the defining criteria.
4. *Frequency of confirmatory observations.*
   a. The number of times an observer reports a fact within a given number of observations.
   b. The percentage of all observers reporting the fact.
5. *Objectivity* of observation and reporting.

It goes without saying that observers must be qualified observers, experts by reason of special training, impartial, credible. As will be shown later, it is at this point that the average individual makes his great blunders in identifying and managing facts. He is neither expert nor impartial.

Sources of and methods of obtaining facts. Facts are obtained by the following methods. All are appeals to experience and range from simple, uncritical observation to sharply controlled observation by trained experts. Commentary will follow the listing.

1. *Observation via the sense organs* of what we see, hear, taste, and the like. (*Cf.* later discussion of first meanings in Chapter 9.)
2. *Observation via instruments of precision,* thermometers, rulers, barometers, altimeters, and many others.
3. *Experimental procedure* for the production of facts to be observed. An artificial situation is set up under controls, with systematic variation of factors and precise measurements of results.
4. *Use of printed sources* such as encyclopedias, statistical reports, historical records, summaries of research, log books, and others.
5. *Use of other persons as sources.* Persons as sources may range all the way from naïve, uncritical individuals, from plain liars, to those who are competent and credible witnesses. To be an authoritative source one must:
   a. Have established credibility.
   b. Have special competence in the field.
   c. Be recognized by other competent authorities.

Uncontrolled observation. The commonest and most widely accepted method for deriving facts is the first one, deriving facts directly from experience through the senses. The average citizen accepts this without question as reliable. A rock, a tree, a color are facts; "ghosties and ghoulies," sea serpents, and campaign promises are not facts. But it is not as simple as that. *The facts of experience are not easy to report sometimes even by well-trained observers.* Curious reports often come from honest and reasonably well-trained observers. We are not here dealing with reports from biased or deliberately dishonest observers. Four nationally known news correspondents were witnesses to the execution of one of the most infamous criminals in our history. They were sitting at close range and had as a sole purpose to report what happened. Their reports agreed, of course, in most aspects but differed in some astonishing ways: "He was gently led to the chair." "He was fairly hustled to the chair." "He was rushed to the chair." "He was held up—stumbling." "His knees were trembling." "His limbs do not tremble; he steps directly and unfalteringly to the chair." Similarly, topflight reporters sitting at ringside for the Dempsey-Carpentier fight did not agree on what happened during the closing seconds of the fight. One even reported an event which is actually prohibited under stiff penalty by the rules.

As this was written, newspapers told of a violent objection by two thousand football fans to a referee's decision giving possession of the ball to the receiving team after a punt. The opposing team and most of the fans asserted that a receiver had been touched by the ball, or had momentarily touched it, thus making it a free ball. Recovery by the team which had punted was, therefore, legal. Motion pictures shown after the game showed that the ball passed two feet from the receiving player! The observation of the referee was right, and the observation of the opposing team and two thousand fans was wrong. The camera observed correctly—as we say, the camera does not lie! (The fans very probably went around telling everyone who would listen that "we saw it with our own eyes!!")

The correction for all this came with the invention of instruments of precision for counting, measuring, and controlling experiments. The average citizen dealing with ordinary everyday affairs need not use the elaborate methods of the scientist in detail, but he should know clearly how facts are derived and verified. Suggestions for introducing children to this vital aspect of good thinking will appear at many points in this volume.

Desirable outside reading at this point will extend the foregoing simple introduction to observation as a method of deriving facts.

Harold A. Larrabee, *Reliable Knowledge* (Boston, Houghton Mifflin, 1945), Ch. 4, pp. 481-485. Note excellent collection of exercises, pp. 156-164.
Morris R. Cohen and Ernest Nagel, *An Introduction to Logic and Scientific Method* (New York, Harcourt, Brace, 1934), pp. 215-217.
Max Black, *Critical Thinking* (Englewood Cliffs, N. J., Prentice-Hall, 1946), pp. 325-340. Note exercises pp. 340-344.

Observation via instruments of precision. Man has invented and developed a large number of instruments (*a*) to correct the inaccurate reports of the senses, and (b) to get knowledge of things in the world which lie outside the powers of our senses. It is far more accurate to say that the temperature is 32 degrees Fahrenheit than to say that it is "around freezing." To say it is 85 degrees is more accurate than to say "It is hot." The foregoing are simple, noncritical illustrations. Precision in temperatures could be a matter of life and death when dealing with chemical mixtures or with illness. Accuracy with measure of weight when applied to drugs could be equally crucial. Other illustrations could be given.

Certain limitations must be noted. Ordinary instruments are not accurate in dealing with minute measurements. All results of instrumental observation must still be interpreted in the light of conditions. This is often overlooked. Mathematical precision is greatly valued; but if the original material is not truly susceptible to mathematical formulation, thinkers are misled by a false objectivity, or "frozen subjectivity."

Experimental procedure. Space will not be used here since this is discussed in Chapter 8 on proof and Chapter 20 on science. Any standard text on methods of research will furnish full accounts of experimental procedure and laboratory methods.

Printed sources. This is probably the chief source of facts for nearly all persons. Printed materials, books, magazines, pamphlets, newspapers, cyclopedias, and many others are widely available and easily accessible. We should note the necessity for criteria for evaluating the reliability and responsibility of printed sources, particularly current ones such as newspapers, weekly journals of opinion, and magazines. (See Chapter 18 on social studies.) These vary from high reliability, as high as can be achieved within a human institution, to practically no reliability at all. Some newspapers and magazines not only distort the facts but will print statements in direct defiance of facts which have been supplied. Encyclopedias are reliable in the sense that they are responsible and try for accuracy; they do, however, occasionally come up with summaries which are open to question, or at least to honest controversy.

The chief point here is that everyone should avoid argument based on ignorance, or on partial facts, but should conscientiously search for valid facts.

Other persons as sources. Individuals vary as do printed sources, from honest and responsible to dishonest and irresponsible. The chief point here is that one should choose his persons. Credibility and competence in given fields can be established within the usual human limitations. Lawyers know more about the law than newspapermen who, in turn, know more about presenting legal matters to the average level of intellect. Doctors do know better than astrologers and clairvoyants. Pediatricians, despite popular jokes, do know more than most parents. Classroom teachers know more about teaching the 3 r's than do professors of chemistry or of history.

MISUSES OF FACT

The appeal to self-evidence. This method of obtaining facts was not listed in the outline above. Facts are asserted to be "self-evident", or a person may cite self-evidence as support for a fact. Hunch, intuition, feeling, revelation, and others are given as bases for facts. The person "just knows" that such and such a thing is a fact. The person citing self-evidence or who "just knows" never seems to be upset because his neighbors may hold the same facts to be utterly false, and on the same grounds —"self-evidence" and "it simply could not be true"!! Self-evidence is not a reliable basis for fact. Self-validation will be elaborated in the following section on interpretation. Inner processes such as hunch or intuition do, under reputable conditions, produce ideas or hypotheses which turn out to be valuable and often lead to important facts.

Refusal to look at the facts precludes progress in thinking. Galileo, in the early seventeenth century, came under criticism and abuse for presenting some new facts revealed by his crude, homemade telescope. The scholars of the day would not look through the telescope but unhesitatingly and flatly denied the existence of Galileo's facts. In a letter to Kepler in 1610, Galileo said:

How I wish we could have a hearty laugh together! Here at Padua is the principal professor of philosophy, whom I have repeatedly and urgently requested to look at the moon and the planets through my glass [telescope], which, with the obstinacy of a glutted adder he refuses to do. Why are you not here? What shouts of laughter we should have at this glorious folly! And to hear the professor of philosophy at Pisa laboring before the Grand Duke with logical arguments, as if with magical incantations, to charm the new planets out of the sky.

The schools of the United States around the middle of the twentieth century were under severe criticism for failure to accomplish certain ends which the critics believed were not being achieved. Dr. Harold G. Shane in an article entitled "We Can Be Proud of the Facts," published in *Nation's Schools* for September, 1957, gave a documented summary of facts bearing upon the criticisms. The school critics, like Galileo's professors, flatly rejected the facts as when the editor of the bulletin of the *Council for Basic Education,* also for September, 1957, wrote, referring to Shane's article: "A professor of education proves, to his own satisfaction at least, that everything is magnificently right about our public schools and the critics are either misled or deliberately misleading. Dr. Shane's statistical evidence seems to us to be highly selective and hardly adequate to his argument."

On another occasion an officer of the same Council examined the *Cyclopedia of Educational Research* and came to the conclusion that the thousands of research studies summarized there were not very good. The cost of the studies must have been well up in the millions of dollars. Independent scholars in all parts of the country participated. A half-century of effort went into the investigations. All to no avail—the facts derived were rejected!

The professors in 1610 refused to look at the facts but unhesitatingly rejected them. The school critics in 1957 looked at the facts and unhesitatingly rejected them. Time marches on, but this does not guarantee that the march has covered any distance.

Two cogent remarks may be of interest here, one made by a world renowned physicist, one by a widely known comedian.

Percy Bridgman: "There is no adequate defense, except stupidity, against the impact of a new idea."

Bert Lahr: "You can't fool me; I'm too ignorant."

Lahr was playing for a laugh, but the implications of his remark are of no mean importance. We might add in passing that while stupidity is the only final defense against new ideas, it is also true that strong prejudice runs it a close second. The Daughters of the American Revolution in convention in 1955 considered a resolution which stated that the United Nations should "cease immediately and completely" from interfering in American affairs. One delegate urged caution, "Let us observe before we condemn, and send observers to the U. N. to see if the rumors of concealed world federalist pressure are true." In other words, let us get the facts. Another delegate stated with considerable vigor that sending observers to get the facts would be a reflection on the dignity of the D. A. R. "Forget about observing. Let's go after them with clubs and what-have-you like our forefathers!"

Fortunately, as we see all around us, there is increasing respect for facts, as well as a growing desire to use them as a basis for thinking. The great scientific advances of modern times are based squarely on this.

Facts may be interpreted with deliberate dishonesty. Emphasis so far has been upon the honest interpretation of facts. Mention has been made of sources of error which may trap any honest person, of mental states which prevent observation of the facts. More will be said of these later in this chapter and in a chapter on sources of error. Dishonesty in using facts is another matter. It is particularly widespread in certain phases of individual and group life. More will be said of this also in the chapter on sources of error. For the moment, the following quotations, serious and flippant, will suffice.

Find the evidence, and then arrange it to suit yourself.

ARTEMUS WARD

Get your facts first, and then you can distort 'em as much as you please.

SAMUEL CLEMENS, *The Idler*

Practical politics consists of ignoring facts.

> *The Education of Henry Adams*

Don't bother with the facts—just brief me on the political alignments.

> A SENATOR (while being briefed
> for an emergency debate in the
> United States Senate)

Don't confuse me with the facts—my mind is made up.

SUBJECTIVE DATA

Data which act like facts in their effect on thinking. Before leaving the discussion of fact, one important and sometimes troublesome area must be summarized. Thinking is affected by the whole range of inner motives, good and bad; compulsions, good and bad; feeling tones; attitudes; beliefs; and prejudices. The presence of these data from the subjective life of individuals must be recognized and taken into account in any piece of thinking. To ignore them is foolish and invites to error. Conclusions and predictions, particularly in the social fields, based on careful consideration of facts as properly defined, do not always agree with what actually happens in the world. The *reasons* why men behave as they do have been overlooked. The illustrative list here is far from exhaustive, but it presents some of the major categories in which subjective data may be found.

Moral and spiritual values, ideals.

Motives, needs, desires or wishes, interests. These may be organic, intellectual, or emotional.

Fears and tensions. Anger, courage, greed, altruism, feelings of elation or depression, feelings of optimism or depression. (Specifics could fill pages.) These may, in addition, be feigned instead of real which further complicates the matter.

Intuitions, hunches, mystical revelations.

Beliefs, dogmas, reasonable or otherwise; *moral convictions; prejudices, bias.*

Attitudes (many could be listed).

Will to believe or to disbelieve. Rationalization, self-deceptions, avoidance of displeasing, acceptance of pleasing.

Fixed ideas, fanaticisms. (May be for or against reputable factors.)

Delusions, fantasies.

Insane aberrations of various types. .

The rigid realist may think he has eliminated the "subjective" with statistics and formulas "only to find that he has overestimated the extent to which human irrationality can be systematized."

When the pamphlet *Feelings are Facts* [3] was published, several physical scientists said emphatically, "But they aren't!" An early statement makes the same point very firmly: [4]

[3] Margaret Heaton, "Feelings are Facts," (New York, National Conference of Christians and Jews, 1952). Originally published by the San Francisco Public Schools.

[4] Reed Bain, "An Attitude on Attitude Research," *American Journal of Sociology* (May, 1928), pp. 942-957.

It is immaterial to the scientist what so-called "subjective" motives or wishes or desires induce people to wear shoes to banquets. It may be pride in small feet, to please wives, to keep the feet dry, or what not. The scientist is concerned only with the fact that they do it. . . . The subjective motives are no more part of his concern than the hypothetical consciousness, drives, and wishes of the atom are concerns of the physicist.

If the scientist here were a married man, or in contact with advertising men, he would discover that "to please wives" is a phenomenon with all the obstinate, coercive power of a fact! The reasons why men wear shoes to banquets are not facts as defined, but they influence thinking—in some instances more powerfully than facts.

Even in the so-called "hardheaded business world" where objective facts are at a premium, the highly subjective data often override the facts. During the boom which culminated in 1929, business firms made use of enormous bodies of precise, objective data, but subjective judgment could not be eliminated. Two silk manufacturers, using identical bodies of precise facts, differed so widely in their subjective reactions to those facts that one borrowed heavily from his bank, increased stocks, and expanded greatly. He went bankrupt. The other liquidated his entire business and stepped out with a fortune. The difference between these men was not on the level of precise statistical fact but in the power of interpretation of the facts, in their opinions about those facts, in their desires, prejudices, and feelings of optimism or pessimism. Similarly, one shoe manufacturer contracted far in advance for hides at the high prices attending the boom. Another cut his inventories to the bone, entered the market after it crashed, and was able to undersell every rival manufacturer because of his cheaply bought raw materials. Again, both used the same objective facts; the difference lay in the interpretation of the data.

Two books illustrate in flippant but deadly manner how even the "big shots" in business and politics can be led astray when prejudice, wishful thinking, or self-interest prevails. These will repay reading and analysis.

Edward Angly, *Oh Yeah!* (New York, Viking, 1931).
Surplus Prophets, a compilation (New York, Viking, 1936).

The first book took the statements of many public men during the years of the depression, followed several of them through a dozen statements, and then compared the predictions with the actual events which came. The second book dealt with pre-election predictions with reference to the New Deal, making comparison with actual events later.

A third book, more serious than those above, contains considerable material bearing on the discrepancy between events and thinking about them.

Clare Boothe, *Europe in the Spring* (New York, Knopf, 1940).

Subjective data are difficult to verify. The inner life of the individual is not subject to observation by others and, furthermore, is complicated by contradictory forces, by easy concealment, or by deliberate falsifying. No one can really know with finality and surety what lies behind the actions of an individual, cannot know the subjective data. As Larrabee says, however: "Yet, we do not, for that reason, abandon our bungling attempts to guess the contents of other minds on the basis of our own experiences."

All we can do is to draw inferences based on our own similar experiences, or upon the appearance or the behavior of the observed person. Reliable knowledge is very difficult to obtain. Even the reports of the person involved are not always reliable. But since this type of data plays a vital part in nearly all situations, the major part in some, we can only try for agreement among observers, similarity between observed situations. Modern research in group dynamics, often sneered at by some physical scientists, is aimed at discovering (among other things) both the open and the hidden factors which influence an individual's thinking and acting.

We *infer* that a person who bumps into a sharp corner suffers the same physical pain that we do, feels the same annoyance or anger. We say that individuals look *"as if"* they were depressed, happy, angry, gay." We may be fooled because the outward manifestations may be faked. We say that someone acts from selfish interest, or for the public good, or for applause. This is, as the lawyers say, "to the best of our knowledge."

Inferences are always subject to error. We cannot examine the facts buried in the minds of the individuals concerned. It is difficult enough when we can agree and acclaim what we think are the thinker's motives. It is a serious matter to impugn the motives of any man no matter how his views may differ from accepted beliefs. Honest men can and must observe the consistent activities, the persistent statements of other men. Honest men may and must draw inferences based on their observation of the acts and statements of other men and upon sincere analysis of the observed phenomena. Are conclusions of the other men based on fair and impartial discussion of affairs? Are they based upon an unacknowledged prejudice, upon a chance for gain?

Larrabee has by far the most detailed and explicit description of subjective data. He uses the term "subjective fact," and speaks of "two orders of fact." We have avoided these two terms for fear of confusing the meaning of fact as defined by physical scientists and as it used in everyday communication. There can be no question, however, as to the crucial importance for thinking of Larrabee's presentation. [5] We give an extended quotation rather than try to abbreviate his statement. Readers are urged to study his chapters.

We should not expect all fact to be of the same type, or equally accessible, or equally easy to establish as "factual" by a single standardized method.

[5] Larrabee, *op. cit.* pp. 130, 128, 132-133.

Rocks are facts, but so are the obsessions of insane people.

What makes this matter of private knowledge of such crucial importance is the fact that within its scope lie some portions, at least, of all of our most profound experiences of value, and the seat of all of our ultimate bases of appraisal. The things by which and for which men live and die have final residues which are private because they lie beyond the possibility of expression in words or deeds. Lovers make momentous decisions on the basis of wordless intuitive estimates of each other that neither of them can coherently express. Many a religious mystic and romantic poet claims to "know what he knows" by intuition or direct assurance from within. If he is called upon to validate his personal feeling of certainty, he is likely to reply that the experience upon which it is based is wholly "ineffable"—that is, incommunicable and therefore unimpeachable by anyone else. The fanatical nationalisms of Europe talk in terms of similar ultimately irrational bases of conviction, the dogmatic *mystiques* of racial power politics, or secular religions.

Larrabee on another page, however, indicates that perhaps we need to be cautious and critical about some of these things:

But the will to believe what is pleasing, whether or not it is contrary to fact, must always battle with the counter-will to find out what is so; and there is abundant evidence that, in the long run, even apparently "vital lies" display poor staying powers. The facts, as we say, have a way of catching up with their most determined ignorers. Men, in other words, are forced to inquire objectively into some matters, if they wish to survive and satisfy their dearest desires.

We may add also, as implied by Larrabee, that there are wholly acceptable explanations for many of the "intuitions," "revelations," and other "mystiques" which appear from time to time. If some are at present inexplicable, let us wait until the evidence is all in.

Their [scientist and mystic] respective preferences for different orders of fact lie at the very fountainheads of their inquiries, in the primary demands which they make on knowing.

The statement "the primary demands they make on knowing" is one of the most important in all Larrabee's discussion. Even if students know little of epistemology, further analysis of this statement will be useful.

There are some particular fields of human inquiry, such as the physical sciences, in which private [data] are relatively unimportant since the goal of investigation can be reached in terms of publicly verifiable data. But there are others, such as the social studies, in which supposedly objective and scientific conclusions are repeatedly upset by a missing "x" which has apparently been overlooked, and which is sometimes characterized as "sheer human perverseness." What has been forgotten is that, while the facts of the exact sciences are preponderantly public facts, those of the social studies are mixtures of public and private facts. In the laboratory sciences, the tests of reliable knowledge are public tests of common perception, by means of which private criteria can be largely eliminated. But in the social studies it is not so easy to distinguish between what is objective fact and what is subjective attitude. Private criteria mingle with public; introspection and external observation aid and abet (and sometimes contradict) each other. Worse still, whatever the social-studies observer may succeed in distinguishing as his own subjective attitude may also be an objective fact of prime importance. The observer is not only a part of what he observes, but the very way in which he observes is also a part of his results. To refuse to acknowledge this state of affairs results in the absurd blindness of "sterile intellectualism".

It is far better to recognize the disturbing presence of the private facts of inner motivation in the picture of human conduct from the very beginning than it is to discover them, in the end, in a mysterious discrepancy between the predictions of "social science" and the ways in which men behave.

We believe that Larrabee is making a point of basic importance for thinking. We do not, however, wish to depart from the stipulated meaning for fact as used in the physical sciences and in everyday affairs.

SECTION 2. INTERPRETATION OF FACTS AND EXPERIENCE

"There are two handicaps to the practice of medicine," Tick had repeated through forty years of teaching. "The first is the eternal charlatanism of the patient who is full of fake diseases and phantom agonies. The second is the basic incompetence of the human mind, medical or otherwise, to observe without prejudice, acquire information without becoming too smug to use it intelligently, and most of all to apply its wisdom without vanity."

BEN HECHT *

The entire history of scientific endeavor appears to show that in our world, comprehensive, simple, and dependable principles for the explanation of observable phenomena cannot be obtained by merely summarizing and inductively generalizing observational (experiential) findings. A hypothetico-deductive-observational procedure is called for and is indeed followed in the more advanced branches of empirical science. Guided by his knowledge of observational data, the scientist has to invent a set of concepts—theoretical constructs, which lack immediate experiential significance, a system of hypotheses couched in terms of them, and an interpretation for the resulting theoretical network; and all this in a manner which will establish explanatory and predictive connections between the data of direct observation.

CARL G. HEMPEL †

EXPERIENCE AND THE INTERPRETATION OF FACTS

Experience is the source of all knowledge, and ultimately all knowledge is tested against experience. Paradoxically, however, the interpreta-

* Ben Hecht, "Miracle of the Fifteen Murderers," *Collected Stories of Ben Hecht* (New York, Crown, 1945).
† Carl G. Hempel, *Fundamentals of Concept Formation in Empirical Science* (Chicago, University of Chicago Press, 1952).

tion of experience may initiate serious errors which prove to be effective booby traps for thinking. As soon as one starts to "invent a set of concepts —theoretical constructs, which lack immediate experiential significance, a system of hypotheses . . . and an interpretation of the resulting theoretical network" he opens a Pandora's box of sources of error.

A fact, says W. H. George, is "a piece of impersonal knowledge." H. M. Tomlinson adds, "Facts can be demonstrated and indexed for reference." But curious things happen to facts when interpreted by different types of individuals. We sincerely hope that Flesch was referring to untrained or casual interpreters when he said, "What are facts? Your mind meets them for a fleeting moment and immediately proceeds to make them over in your image." Elsewhere he says you cannot separate facts from opinions and impressions.[6] Critical thinking necessitates the very greatest effort to distinguish between facts and our interpretations of them. It is always difficult, but we do not give up because of that.

Kinds of interpretation. The human mind almost automatically starts reacting to observed and learned data. It evaluates, classifies, and draws other kinds of inferences. Dullards and many complacent bright persons do not do this and, hence, fall into errors in thinking. The different kinds of inference used in interpretation will be described in the next chapter; briefly they are:

1. *Description.* It is a gray piece of lead.
   Measurement. It is 12 inches long.
   Classification. It is a metal.
2. *Assertion of cause-and-effect relationship.* Hit a piece of lead with a hammer, and it will change shape because it is malleable.
3. *Prediction.* Two ounces of lead will make the fishhook sink to the bottom.
4. *Evaluation.* It is a nice (or an ugly, or an adulterated) piece of lead.

As suggested in the previous section on facts, some interpretation enters into even the simplest observation or determination of fact. "This is a piece of lead" sounds simple, but to say this we must have accepted a definition of lead and have picked out the qualities of the object which identify it to us as "lead." When observations are carefully, systematically, and objectively interpreted, our knowledge increases in a reliable way.

Individuals, however, often interpret casually what they see and hear and refer to this process as "experience." The untrained person does not commonly distinguish between the facts, that is, those things which involve a minimum of interpretation and his interpretation of the facts. "My experience has been" frequently means "The few haphazard observations I made, which I do not remember too well, which I interpreted with considerable bias." In observing facts we often see what we wish to see or expect

[6] Rudolf Flesch, *The Art of Clear Thinking* (New York, Harper, 1951), pp. 25-26.

to see—unless well trained in observation. Our beliefs both biased and unbiased, our inclinations, interests, and conditions at the moment, and many other factors may interfere. The critical thinker must be vigilant to make the distinctions. A good deal of our thinking is actually—and of necessity—concerned with determining the accuracy of our responses to facts. Responses may vary from satisfactory accuracy and adequacy to those which are inaccurate to the level of the ridiculous. Responses when accepted as reliable beliefs affect in turn the thought process of the moment. Many of them may, and often do, exert upon the thinker the same compulsion which we ordinarily get from a reliable physical fact.

Galileo, Pasteur, and Edison all cited their *experience,* but the essence here is vastly different from the *experience* cited by the average citizen in his everyday attempts to prove or refute some statement. This raises several questions. What is really meant by "experience is the basis of knowledge and sources of facts"? Whose experience? How much experience? Are the facts of experience self-evident, or do we have to interpret them? How can experience, the basis of knowledge, and interpretation of experience lead us into gross errors both in knowledge and in thinking?

Experience which has for any particular person been incorporated into his cognitive structure or conceptual scheme after highly critical analysis is one thing. Experience casually met and accepted without the slightest effort to critically evaluate it in the light of systematically organized knowledge is quite another.

A simple, everyday summary of the values and dangers of "personal experience" as distinguished from experience-under-controlled-observation. All experience is *personal* experience. Individuals everywhere will continue to cite it; hence, we had better know what we are doing when we do. The discussion here relates to the common-sense, everyday citation of "my experience" as frequently heard. Everyday experience does have value when used with some regard for the rules of evidence and the canons of logic.

Values. Individuals shrewd enough, or trained, will use personal experience thus:

1. Citation of personal experience which is typical of experiences in that field in an objective manner and in accord with recognized standards of interpretation.
    2. Citation of a personal experience (case or incident) which:
        a. *Reports new information* gained under reputable conditions (measurement, controlled experiment, and the like). An illustration would be new information on the teaching of exceptional children.
        b. *Corroborates and further illustrates* a principle, generalization, or other construct, or which strengthens a practice *already established by valid means.* This extends one's understanding and is useful in explaining to someone else a principle or other construct.

3. Citation of personal experience for the *purpose of asking* for *further clarification* of principles or practices *already established,* or for the *purpose of clearing up individual differences in interpretation.* Often takes this form: "Is this an illustration (or case) of what we are talking about?"

Dangers. Beware of the individual, however, who says, "My experience proves —————," or "My experience refutes —————." A high school teacher after listening to a panel of experts explain some experimental studies involving 30,000 high school students stood up and said quite pleasantly, "I can refute all that because a student I once had —————" !!! This was a case of naïve ignorance rather than brash arrogance which often appears. Simple lack of training in the process of thinking and in canons of evidence was the cause.

A superintendent of schools after listening to a report based on a total of eight hours of individual interviews with 50 per cent of the superintendents in his area said, "The report simply isn't true—my own experience is quite different." Faults here were two, lack of training in analysis of experience, and actual ignorance of what his own experience actually was.

A college graduate hearing that only a small per cent of entering high school students later graduate from college said: "That isn't true; my class went through with no drop outs." His class consisted of nine students in an exclusive private secondary school.

Two quotations point this up:

Experience keeps a dear school, but fools will learn in no other.
BENJAMIN FRANKLIN
Experience is the fool's best teacher; the wise do not need it.
OLD WELSH PROVERB

The so-called "practical" man deals usually with specifics and with sense data. The possibility of general thinking and of conceptual systems is usually undreamed of by the practical man. Despite the glamour which surrounds the "practical" man in our civilization, he is in fact very often a crude blunderer, causing much trouble in everyday affairs. To go beyond the simple, incomplete, and often inconclusive data of the senses and create meanings, generalizations, and concepts requires the process of abstracting common and often hidden characteristics of the data. This opens up possibilities of which the practical man does not even know. It also opens up great opportunity for error as will be shown in a later chapter.

The real, serious, and too-frequent *danger in the citation of personal experience* is: the citation of specific illustrations from personal experience as proof, as being the equivalent of a generalization not otherwise established. The major causes of this and other errors in thinking will be summarized in a separate chapter.

Simple causes of error in interpreting experience. The major cause of error in interpreting experience is ignorance of or failure to apply the criteria cited earlier, usually due to lack of training in observing and reporting. In addition, there are several more immediate and more limited causes of error.

1. One prevalent cause of error is that the huge majority of persons who think honestly that they are reporting the facts of their experience are actually reporting their *opinion or interpretation of* the experience.

2. A related factor is that the opinion (already confused with the event) is often itself incorrect as an interpretation.

3. Some persons actually report as their experience events which are physically or psychologically impossible. But the person "saw it with his own eyes."

4. The basic cause of error, as indicated several times above, is that the average citizen has no knowledge of methods and controls of observation, of reporting observations, of evaluating either observations or interpretations. (Hence, a course in methods of thinking!)

5. Specific practical errors widely observed:

    a. Generalizing from one or from an insufficient number of experiences.

    b. Citation of "experiences" which favor a belief, opinion, or prejudice already held; neglect to cite or refusal to consider contradictory "experiences."

    c. Failure to interpret all accompanying circumstances. (Often an experience is honestly reported but on analysis of the total situation turns out to be quite different in nature, characteristics, and implications from the original report. Competent observers and analysts often upset the naïve reports of the average person.)

    d. Failure to make articulate, to recognize properly the implicit assumptions, prejudices, preconceived ideas of the observer.

    e. Interpreting an "experience" as due to a single antecedent when, in fact, there are several or a constellation of preceding causes. This is the common error of solving a *complex* situation with a *simple* explanation.

    f. Failure to count, to use instruments of precision, to control, to make critical evaluation; depending instead on uncontrolled guesses, estimates, rumor, hearsay, gossip.

Certain individuals, especially those engaged in important activities, have experiences of considerable import. We have mentioned Galileo, Pasteur, Edison, and Einstein. We mention also the man who first broke the sound barrier, the first man to explore the sea with a bathysphere, the first to make a balloon ascension to great heights. We may expect some day to have an individual reporting on the first trip into space, the first landing on the moon, and others.

Unfortunately the experience of one individual, even though he is constantly citing it, is often: (*a*) limited and fragmentary to the level of triviality when considered in the light of the compiled experience of the race; (*b*) incorrectly reported, though in all honesty; and (*c*) incorrectly reported, with deliberate dishonesty.

Self-validation, based on the foregoing, is a fateful error. The very primacy and vividness of personal experience is peculiarly convincing. This leads certain types of thinkers into serious error. Personal experience is accepted automatically as self-validating. The average citizen cites his experience with finality. There is no further appeal. Naïve individuals are actually unable to see the grave error in accepting personal experience as final. Some become quite angry when the accuracy or adequacy of their experience is challenged. Sensitive and naturally logical individuals sense the difficulty at once, though they may be confused at times. Most of us have to learn to mistrust unanalyzed experience—by experiencing the difficulties which ensue from the error!

Nearly everyone trusts experience, opinion, rarely knowing that facts exist going far beyond the fragmentary and meager experience of one person. The really naïve or untrained individual goes even further. He rejects obvious, demonstrable, reproducible facts, so great is his confidence in his own observation and experience.

Adults often parry questions or arguments from children by saying, "When you have had as much experience as I have had —————." This is a real error as often as not. Years of experience are no guarantee that there has been fruitful, educative experience, no guarantee that superior wisdom has resulted. Very often "years of experience" are actually a serious barrier to wisdom. Many who claim "twenty years of experience" have had but one year's experience, repeated twenty times. Their experience may have been the repetition of narrow, limited activities, unenlightened by reading, arguing, comparing; unleavened by doubting, thinking, analysis, let alone by experimental checking. The crucial point is the *kind* of experience with which the years have been filled. The *reactions* of the experiencer are vital. The *analysis* of experience is far more significant than any amount of simple *repetitive* experience.

Interpretations take the form of "opinion" and "belief." *Belief* and *opinion* are terms used, unhappily, very loosely in popular discussion. Many persons base their actions on "beliefs" in the "belief" that such a basis for action is solid. The word *opinion* is quite unthinkingly bandied about. Opinion properly defined and understood is a necessary and useful instrument of thought and of inquiry. Opinion, however, can also be a seductive bawd, ready to lead one down the primrose path of error and fallacy. Let us repeat the original definitions preliminary to making some necessary distinctions.

Opinion. An interpretation of events which may be true or false, reliable or unreliable, but is at the moment unproved or unprovable.

Belief. An opinion which has the connotation of permanent reliability and of conviction on the part of the holder, as a belief in the values of democracy, in the Republican party, in polytheism.

Beliefs and opinions considered as interpretations should be subject to the same standards of reliability. Unfortunately both are often accepted at face value in many cases.

The above definition of "opinion" needs considerable extension. Use should take into account several levels of meaning.

> *Opinion. A formal judgment by an expert or panel of experts.*
>> *a. Judicial opinion.* A ruling, decision, or summary handed down by a judge, a referee, a committee of lawyers.
>> *b. Medical opinion.* A diagnosis, a method of treatment, a recommended public policy given by a physician, a surgeon, or group of medical men.
>> *c. Technological opinion.* A summary and (usually) a recommendation by an engineer, an architect, or other professional expert, or by a board.
>> *d. Political, economic, or social opinion.* Summary or recommendation made by public officials, legislative committees, specialized experts, sometimes by courts. (May deal with taxation, housing, sanitation, control of delinquency, penal policy, and the like.)
>
> *Opinion. A personal interpretation.*
>> *a. Sound concept.* Use of "opinion" with the understanding that it refers to an interpretation which may be true or false, reliable or unreliable, but at the moment is unproved or is indeed unprovable. User carries reservation that he has no deep feelings of conviction about the "opinion."
>> *b. Unsound concept.* Use of an "opinion" without the reservation that it may be an unsound interpretation, a random, unanalyzed notion, not based on fact, an "idea" either irrational or partly irrational, a delusion, an *idée fixe,* or a revelation.

The range of the commonplace concept of opinion may be from one which has considerable basis in fact and logic to one which is completely baseless. The formal and technical meanings for opinion and the commonplace concept as used by careful persons give us little trouble. The unsound use of the commonplace concept which occurs constantly in everyday discourse is a serious blunder in thinking. Let us examine further the serious sabotage of good thinking which results from the indiscriminate use of opinion in the unsound sense.

"One opinion is as good as another." Here we have another detrimental type of reaction to facts. One opinion is as good as another only when the two are equally worthless. Two people holding *identical* opinions, sound or worthless, would have one opinion as good as another, but this is never what is meant. "Everyone is entitled to his opinion, isn't he?" No, he is not in certain fields, such as the physical sciences and mathe-

matics, and in many practical affairs of life. In these fields, "one opinion is as good as another" is pure fatuity.

Opinion in aesthetics is more of a feeling, or an opinion strongly flavored with feeling. In the social sciences there are legitimate differences of belief. Opinions here are or should be strongly influenced by values and facts as we have them. Interpretations will differ but with some basis in fact and principle. Even in aesthetics and ethics the opinion should have some reference to credible sources and support.

An excellent statement is made by Nemetz. [7]

I sometimes think it was the devil himself, who, in order to torment teachers with the suffering of the damned, invented the sentence: "Everyone is entitled to his opinion." Can you imagine how frustrating it is to make a mathematical proof, or to demonstrate why a given argument is invalid, and then out of the mouths of babes comes this soul-shattering rejoinder: "Oh, yes, I see, but that's only your opinion, and everyone is entitled to his own opinion." As if opinions on anything by anyone were like ballots—each to be counted equally. I certainly do not deny that everyone can think as he pleases or even that everyone has the right to think as he pleases. But the assertion that everyone is entitled to his opinion usually is intended to say that everyone's opinion is equally valuable. This view ignores the fact that the mark of an opinion is that it can be right or wrong. However, the right to be wrong is a political right and not an intellectual prize or heritage. To assert that wrong opinions are equally as valuable as right opinions is at least self-contradictory, and a sure way of perpetuating ignorance.

We may add to Nemetz' remarks the additional fact that the man who answers "a mathematical proof" or logical conclusion with the cliché "Oh, that's just your opinion" is betraying *his belief that facts and reasoned conclusions are of the same order as colloquial opinions.* All he has in his mind are random opinions, formed he knows not how, and he assumes that all you have in your mind is the same type of thing. Baseless opinion is all the coinage he has, and the bandying of opinions he believes to be argument or debate. This is further borne out when anyone stubbornly defends "any man has a right to an opinion." He is clearly defending his right to ignorance. He does not know that the difference between two or more enlightened opinions is far, far less than the difference between knowledge and ignorance. To paraphrase another old saw: Be it ever so humbug, there is no belief like my own.

The man who insists on his right to express an opinion should be acutely aware of the bases of opinion. These are: (*a*) facts and logic, *or* (*b*) rumor, hearsay, and gossip, *or* (*c*) ignorance, *or* (*d*) stupidity. Barzun, in *House of Intellect,* says that a man who has the physical right to think as he pleases has the moral duty to think as he ought, that is, in accord with fact and logic. [8]

An apt epigram may be cited here: [9]

OPINIONS

Alas, that the strongest
Are often the wrongest!

Nemetz makes clear distinction between science and mathematics, on the one hand and political policy and decision making on the other. The confusion he is decrying is far more widespread than is thought. A national figure in psychology addressed a college class on a difficult and little-understood phase of mental life. The discussion which followed was opened by a sophomore who said, "It stands to reason that a good deal of this isn't true." Another student, reporting to the class on an article written by one of the most eminent thinkers living, ventured the opinion, "The article is the bunk. The author must be a poor nut with a warped view of life."

Individuals everywhere constantly express opinions and act upon them, on problems they do not understand, on which they have no facts, and to which they have never given ten minutes' study. In streetcars, in offices, at clubs, at social gatherings, everywhere that persons meet, the humblest clerks will be heard expressing opinions in defiance of mathematically precise facts, in defiance of experts. Prime ministers and secretaries of state, not to mention business tycoons, often join the average citizen in this type of discussion. The letters-to-the-editor column in any newspaper will supply daily illustrations. By some this is naïvely called "thinking for one's self," "I do my own thinking." It is the direct opposite of thinking, a flat refusal to think correctly, or at all. Experts are not infallible; blind worship of authority is not implied. The most valid facts are always subject to review if new facts are discovered. A disciplined thinker, however, asks, "What made the man an expert?" "What evidence did he use?" "Are his inferences justified?" Independence in thought consists in careful and exhaustive examination of the facts, in critical analysis of facts and interpretations thereof, in demanding reasonable verification. Impertinent difference of "opinion," stubborn obstinacy in maintaining a belief do not constitute independent thought.

An angry citizen entered a newspaper editor's office and angrily denounced a certain editorial. He ended by hammering the desk and shouting, "And that's my opinion." The editor made a significant comment. "Your statement is not an opinion. You haven't got an opinion on this topic. You have not studied it, or read about it, or taken any time to inform yourself. You aren't even entitled to an opinion on this issue."

[8] Jacques Barzun, *House of Intellect* (New York, Harper, 1959), p. 252.
[9] Georgie Starbuck Galbraith, *Saturday Evening Post* (May 24, 1958), p. 73. Used with the kind permission of author and publisher.

Personal opinion offers itself usually to be accepted. Informed opinion is presented for consideration, critical analysis, possible modification before being accepted or rejected. The average person is far more interested in *establishing his point,* than in determining *which point should be established.*

The social fields, particularly the activities of political affairs, the making of policies and decisions, the organizing of plans of action, present a sharp contrast to the precise fields of science and mathematics. (See Chapter 18.) Diversity of opinion and exchange of views are inevitable and proper. This annoys certain types of persons, but differences here are a sign of vitality. Even in these fields, however, one may not make random assertions, may not express baseless opinions. He must "stay on the point," must cite such facts and sources as there are, must pay attention to the rules of evidence and the canons of thinking. Anyone has the right, really the obligation, to question facts, to examine the methods and controls under which facts were derived, to suggest suspending judgment for further investigation or experiment. No one "has a right to an opinion" in defiance of competent, sufficient, and valid evidence. Attempting to establish something through pooling of "opinion" is infantile even when there exists a slight basis in reality. This not only befuddles discussion but sets up false ideas about validity and proof. The enthusiastic exchange of ignorant opinion is not democratic discussion. Carrying over false ideas of democratic process into the realm of truly democratic decision making is the root of the trouble as Nemetz hints. Carrying this over into precise fields can be due only to naïve ignorance or to stupidity.

Summary statements on the relation of personal experience to knowledge.

1. Personal experience in the simple, noncomplicated, repetitive everyday affairs, experienced over and over again by all individuals, is a reasonably safe basis for knowledge.
2. Personal experience with reference to difficult, complex affairs which are not ordinarily a part of everyday experience varies in value with the persons involved.
   a. Individuals may be seen every day basing their statements on limited, fragmentary evidence, interpreted under bias, with disregard for the canons of logic, and unchecked through use of instruments of precision. Error is almost inevitable.
   b. Individuals in contrast may be seen cautiously scrutinizing their experience, subjecting it to critical analysis; checking it against the recorded experience of other persons; even often subjecting their interpretations to controlled experimentation and precise measurement.

The first type of person is unaware of the nature of facts, of the canons of logic, and of the processes of critical analysis. The second type of person is aware of the necessity for analyzing interpretations, for using a good experiential background of facts, and is respectful of the canons of logic. The first person cannot produce valid facts and knowledge. The second will produce such results in the degree that his knowledge and skill in critical analysis justify.

Human thinking has progressed, over the ages, from the level where immediate experience was the only basis for knowledge to the level of sophistication today on which it is realized that unanalyzed experience produces only confusion. Wise men have long known this, but the average citizen has not yet been brought to that level. Heraclitus said: "Men sought the truth in their own little worlds, and not in the general and common world." Thereby they were deservedly deluded. Francis Bacon put it thus: "God forbid that I should give out a pattern of the imagination for a pattern of the universe."

Experience as a basis of knowledge or proof must meet certain criteria. Treatment is abbreviated here since the major considerations were noted earlier. A summary here will overlap a little with the original presentations.

1. The sense organs through which experience is received must be sound and capable of transmitting the stimulus.

2. The mind which interprets what is transmitted should be as imbued with the scientific and critical attitudes as is possible, free from bias and misinformation.

3. Instruments of precision should be used for counting, measuring, experimenting. Agreed-upon definitions of behavior must be set up.

Where counting and measuring are not possible, there should be reasonably expert observers, and a high percentage of agreement among them.

Observed phenomena should be capable of reproduction, or of repetition under similar conditions, of independent existence, and of public verifiability. (This is impossible with phenomena in the social fields.)

4. Experience must be subjected to critical analysis and to some sort of logical explanation to determine whether it is compatible with existing knowledge and theory.

The expression "compatible with existing knowledge and theory" needs comment. The everyday problems, discussions, and conclusions of the average citizen will almost always be within the limits of the known. Stupendous advances are made, however, by individuals who (1) develop statements which are not compatible with existing knowledge and which challenge and differ with the known, or (2) develop new creative analyses of existing knowledge. Such men as Galileo, Pasteur, Bacon, Steinmetz, Einstein, and others were intimately familiar with existing knowledge before they challenged it. John Q. Citizen does not have the background, and his variations from systematic knowledge are almost always vagaries or whimsies of his mind. Should a Galileo or Edison appear in the average college class, the instructor would be pleasantly surprised and profoundly astonished. The interloper would, in many classes, be eliminated in the interests of a "sound" education.

5. Conscious effort should be made during both the experiencing and the interpreting to guard against the many chances for error leading to unreliabil-

ity or invalidity. This requires adequate criteria and definite training. (Causes of error will be outlined in a separate chapter.)

6. Conscious effort should be made to confine the search to significant data—significant in the light of the problem—and to avoid being led off in pursuit of the striking or the bizarre.

7. Experience must be analyzed in terms of the *time when it was undergone,* in the *light of the hypothesis at the time,* and particularly to see if the experience-at-the-time had as a focus the particular issue now being discussed.

Here again the average citizen goes astray, often quoting evidence from situations which were directed to other points than the one now under discussion, under different hypotheses, and under different social, political, or economic conditions.

A student, for instance, supported the proposition "All athletes are poor students" by citing his experiences as an athlete twenty years ago. He could not have possibly observed, remembered, or interpreted all aspects of his experience twenty years ago since he was not aware of the hypothesis at the time. Colloquially we say, "he wasn't thinking about it then." The hypothesis under which the discussion now arises may be quite a different one.

Many of the lay critics of education who demand a return "to the old days of sound education" are similarly ignorant of all facets of the "good old days." They are also misled by intimate, often poignant memories. Grown-up adolescents often cry for the "halcyon days agone" which never existed in the first place, and which weren't nearly so "halcyon" as rosy memories depict.

An interested student produced a semihumorous summary on the interpretation of facts and meanings, in the form of a roadside traffic sign. He knew, and we all know, that his suggestions do not hold for all occasions. It is difficult to find "a universe of discourse with a fully established conceptual scheme." "Definition" is a tricky jade. The admonitions have nothing to do with competent persons exploring new or limited facts, developing definitions, and trying to find the limits of a universe of discourse. The careful individual dealing cautiously with new and undefined affairs will often need to express "opinions," to use "I agree" and "I disagree." The whole emphasis of his scheme is to cut down on the senseless chatter of much conversation—to cut down on the continuous, absurd, inconsistent expression of opinion, disregard for fact which characterizes far too much of everyday discourse. "I agree" and "I disagree" as used in everyday conversation, when dealing with facts which everyone should know or can easily find in standard references, are at best silly; at worst they are destructive of good thinking and invitations to dangerous blunders.

CAUTION

Rocky Roads and Pitfalls Ahead
Proceed at Your Own Risk
Think Cautiously
Have Your Mind Under Control at All Times

Road conditions to be observed:
   In areas where validated facts are available—
   In areas where definitions are established and known—
   In areas where a conceptual system is established and recognized—

Try to avoid such expressions as:	Try to use instead:
I agree ———	The facts are (or show) ———
I disagree ———	The historical record is (or shows) ———
My opinion is ———	The evidence is ———
My experience shows ——— or proves ———	The conclusion justified by the facts is ———
I maintain that ———	
Well, "all I know is" ———	A reasoned conclusion is ———
	I believe on the following evidence
I take that word to mean ———	(or chain of reasoning) ———
My definition for that word is ———	The accepted meaning for that word in this field is ———

Note: In areas where there are insufficient facts, personal beliefs may be expressed but always with due regard to such facts as we have.

Interpretations of facts may differ widely between persons, resulting in "I agree" or "my opinion is"—BUT—everyone is under obligation to relate his beliefs to the facts and to justifiable inference.

In areas involving values or involving aesthetic judgment, the language of personal preference and belief is used, but again it cannot be used capriciously.

"Human history is long. There is a long record of past experimentation in conduct, and there are cumulative verifications which give many principles a well-earned prestige. Lightly to disregard them is the height of foolishness." Dewey: *Human Nature and Conduct.*

SECTION 3. THEORY AND THE FACTS

"It's all right in theory, but it won't do in practice" is another popular way of reveling in logical absurdity. The philosopher Schopenhauer said all that needs to be said about this sophism. "The assertion is based upon an impossibility: what is right in theory *must* work in practice; and if it does not, there is a mistake in the theory; something has been overlooked and not allowed for; and, consequently, what is wrong in practice is wrong in theory too."
                                                        MAX BLACK *

The *word* theory is one of the most misused words; the *concept* theory, one of the most misunderstood ideas in our thinking. The average citizen is, unhappily, almost unaware of the place and use of theory in any

* Black, *op. cit.,* p. 215. Quotation is from Schopenhauer, *The Art of Controversy,* No. 33.

and all fields. Worse, he is quite unaware of his fantastic blunders in the use of the word and concept.

Definition of theory. The word *theory* comes from a Greek expression meaning to view, to look at, to speculate about, in order to get understanding. Definitions in modern books vary both as to scope and wording. A few books discuss theory, sometimes at length, without ever defining it.

One writer uses the word *theory* "to cover general statements of *all* levels of generality," thus equating theory with generalizations, laws, principles. Another says a "theory is not a law but a set of assumptions from which a set of empirical laws (principles) may be derived." Still another says that a theory is a "set of assumptions from which can be derived by purely logico-mathematical procedures a larger set of empirical laws." Several writers state that there is no hard and fast distinction between theoretical assumptions and empirical laws. The following definitions are given to aid the average student:

Theories are attempts at intelligent interpretation of facts. General theories, if true, are universally true (until new data are discovered). Special theories cover specified sets of facts.

A theory is an effort to construct a more and more inclusive and reliable explanation and instrument of prediction.

A theory is a statement of laws and principles which underlie and explain any set of facts, or sets of lesser laws and principles, and which predicts what is likely to happen under given conditions.

A theory is a set of assumptions from which larger sets of empirical laws may be derived.

The average student who understands the foregoing demonstrates sufficient grasp for ordinary purposes. The advanced student who wishes to go further will find a small but good literature. [10]

[10] Chester I. Barnard, *The Functions of the Executive* (Cambridge, Mass., Harvard University Press, 1938).

Daniel E. Griffiths, *Administrative Theory* (New York, Appleton-Century-Crofts, 1959). Excellent summary statement. See footnotes.

Arthur P. Coladarci and Jacob W. Getzels, *The Use of Theory in Educational Administration* (Palo Alto, Calif., Stanford University Press, 1955).

Andrew W. Halpin, ed., *Administrative Theory in Education* (Chicago, Midwest Administration Center, 1958).

Paul R. Mort and Donald H. Ross, *Principles of School Adminstration* (New York, McGraw-Hill, 1957).

Herbert Feigl, "Principles and Problems of Theory Construction in Psychology," in *Current Trends in Psychological Theory* (Pittsburgh, University of Pittsburgh Press, 1951).

Karl M. Dallenbach, "The Place of Theory in Science," *Psychological Review,* Vol. 60, No. 1 (January, 1953).

John Walton, *Administration and Policy Making in Education* (Baltimore, Johns Hopkins University Press, 1959).

The foregoing references are chiefly to newer books in school administration because the best of the new material is appearing in this field. These books, furthermore, illustrate well the point we are concerned with, namely, the nature and use of theory.

Developments in stating theory in school administration are significant. Books written by administrators and the yearbooks, generally, of the National Association of Administrators are too much made up of "exhortations, how-to-do-it prescriptions, catalogues of opinion, or normative 'status' investigations which do not permit us to generalize beyond the immediate data." [11] A few current statements are moving toward true theory.

Theory emerges when facts and laws become more and more numerous, necessitating unification. Theories are subject to change as new facts and principles are discovered. A theory supplies a guide to further study, to policy making, and to action.

A rather lengthy statement from Hempel is included here since it puts together many terms already used in this volume. [12] The statement is admittedly complicated.

A scientific theory might be likened to a complex spatial network: Its terms are represented by the knots, while the threads connecting the latter correspond, in part, to the definitions and, in part, to the fundamental and derivative hypotheses included in the theory. The whole system floats, as it were, above the plane of observation and is anchored to it by rules of interpretation. These might be viewed as strings which are not part of the network but link certain points of the latter with specific places in the plane of observation. By virtue of those interpretive connections, the network can function as a scientific theory: From certain observational data, we may ascend, via an interpretive string, to some point in the theoretical network, thence proceed, via definitions and hypotheses, to other points, from which another interpretive string permits a descent to the plane of observation.

In this manner an interpreted theory makes it possible to infer the occurrence of certain phenomena which can be described in observational terms and which may belong to the past or the future, on the basis of such other phenomena, whose occurrence as been previously ascertained. But the theoretical apparatus which provides these predictive and postdictive bridges from observational data to potential observational findings cannot, in general, be formulated in terms of observables alone.

The last sentence is a *coup de grâce* to those who insist that we must "not go beyond the facts." He who will not go beyond the facts rarely ever gets as far as the facts. Thinking without a theory can only be chaotic and incoherent thinking. Thinking (or theory making) without facts is likely to result in fantasy. Activities mental or overt (beyond the trivial and the routine) cannot take place without a theory of some sort.

Books in the field of logic or thinking, noted earlier, also contain valuable discussions of theory in relation to thinking. See:

Cohen and Nagel, *op. cit.*, Ch. 20.

Larrabee, *op. cit.*, pp. 71, 165, 140, 454-456.

Black, *op. cit.*, Ch. 19.

Other major texts in this field if available.

[11] See Halpin, *op. cit.* Examine several yearbooks of the American Association of School Administrators.

[12] Hempel, *op. cit.*, p. 36.

Facts, often glorified by the practical man at the expense of theory, cannot be isolated or collected except under a hypothesis which is a tentative theory. The activity is circular, of course; principles or theories (starting as hypotheses) arise as we contemplate the facts of experience, and then the principle or theory is called upon in the search for an interpretation of further facts. We sometimes hear, "Give me a fact, just one single, solitary fact——." This sounds very simple but is in fact impossible. There is no such thing as a "single, solitary fact." Facts are always related to something, or they have no meaning.

Reasons for antagonism to theory in the United States. The major part of our national life has been devoted to the development of our vast continent. We were engaged with the westward migration, conquering the vast distances, plains and mountains, and other physical obstacles. We built the railroads, plowed the new land, dug and mined, drilled for oil, built a huge industrial system. All this dealt with things. Incredible blunders were made by men and governments who lacked theory, but wealth was such that we recovered and went on. We "muddled through" as the British once said of themselves. Muddle or not, our life did glorify the factual, the practical, the handleable, at the expense of ideas about those things.

Specific bases for antagonism to theory. The points here are general but may be read with special reference to the field of education.

1. *Glorification of, and commitment to factualism; commitment to materialism.* "Get the facts" as a doctrine has achieved the status, almost of a dogma, that must not be challenged. Griffiths makes the caustic comment, "That the facts have no interrelatedness seems not to concern those so afflicted." [13] Coladarci and Getzels indicate the handicap to education: [14] "This has tended, historically, to direct education more and more toward the status of a purely empirical discipline without theoretical vehicles to carry the empirical observations and relationships."

2. *Unwarranted respect for authorities, experts, "scientific" facts.* When a view is challenged a certain group will reply in shocked tones, "Why, that is one of Dr. Blank's principles." They never ask under what theory the principles were derived or are applicable. "Dewey says so." (Or Thorndike, or Mort, or Smith, Stanley, and Shores). This group accepts, without inquiry into the theories involved, the results of polls of expert opinion, jury techniques, and the like. The facts that authorities contradict each other and that jury results often differ from the events do not unduly disturb the man who does not think well for himself. He does not inquire into the basic theories involved. He just hunts around until he finds an authority which suits his views.

3. *Unwarranted contempt for authorities, particularly for creative thinkers.* Another group operates in direct contrast to the group above. This is part of the anti-intellectualism which sweeps over any area at

---

[13] Griffiths, *op. cit.,* p. 9.
[14] Coladarci and Getzels, *op. cit.*

given times. The men who produce systematic theoretical explanations are dismissed as "eggheads" and, to compound the error, as "damn theorists".

4. *Fear of theorizing.* This is a very real and important attitude held by man. Theory is held to be impractical, unreliable, unstable. As a school superintendent said, "Can you believe this, or is it just theory?" Others fear theory because it is difficult to produce and to understand if one is not too well educated. A theory is, in truth, the single most practical thing there is. The point is ably expressed by Mort and Ross: [15]

> Theory, in the minds of the authors, is the best and most accurate mental picture of how an organism works, taking into consideration and reconciling all pertinent known facts and phenomena. There is nothing impractical about a good theory. If the theory is a close approximation of truth, the acts which it suggests will be generally wise ones. If it is a bad theory (not close to truth) acted upon, the chances are that there will be many acts of futility. . . . Action divorced from theory is the random scurrying of a rat in a new maze. Good theory is the power to find the way to the goal with a minimum of lost motion and electric shocks.

Theories change in the light of new facts and discoveries. [16] This is not instability but intelligent reconstruction.

5. *Inadequate professional language.* Theory cannot be advanced in a field unless those in it possess clear unequivocal concepts and a terminology to go with the concepts. Every technology in the world has a professional language without which its operations could not be carried on. The word *argot* is used to mean a vocabulary special to any group, trade, or profession. When a circus man, for instance, refers to customers as "suckers," or to paying money to silence a complaint as "squaring the beef," he uses slang. But when he calls the circus grounds the "lot," and the manager's quarters the "white wagon" he is using the argot or special language of his trade. Argot, says Mencken, is quite as respectable when used by circus men as when used by lawyers or diplomats. [17]

Education must develop a professional language. It is the youngest of the academic fields. Errors are being made in the development of this professional language—the same errors made by the older fields when they were on a comparable level of maturity. Professional language development has, furthermore, been inhibited by the sneers of lay citizens about "jargon." This betrays the ignorance of the critics about the nature and necessity of technical language, but it does intimidate some educators. The matter of "jargon" needs further explanation.

Educators, unfortunately, do tend to multiply terms unnecessarily.

[15] Mort and Ross, *op. cit.,* p. 4.
[16] John Dewey, *Sources of a Science of Education* (New York, Liveright, 1929). Use the index.
[17] Henry L. Mencken, *The American Language,* original ed. (New York, Knopf, 1937), Ch. 11. Later revisions are available.

Organized effort to counteract this is well under way, as witness the dictionaries of educational and psychological terms. Educators do also, unhappily, tend to misuse standard terms and their meanings. The term *research* is used constantly when *study* is actually meant. "Research" is used to refer to situations in which *research* could not apply. Books on research are written by authors who have done no research and whose books are not on the subject. "Experiment" is used to refer to unsystematic, uncontrolled, untested, trivial, classroom tryouts. "Workshop" is loosely applied to a dozen or more situations for which there have been standard terms for many decades. Any flubdub of unorganized, discursive interchange of fragmentary opinions is called "group process." "Creative" is applied to things which no single individual could ever have created. The word *theory* itself, as indicated later, is the most misused of any term. These mistaken usages indicate the absence of proper terminology which is necessary to all clear thinking and to theory construction in particular. [18] The unnecessary multiplication of terms, the development of absurd new words for concepts already well named, the crude misuse of terms deserve the taunt of "jargon" and the contempt of all professional educators.

Educators should stand fast for a professional language and against those who apply the criticisms "jargon" and "pedaguese" indiscriminately. In many instances the critics are annoyed because they cannot understand the technical language. Critics who would never dream of sneering at the technical language of physicians, surgeons, and engineers never hesitate to throw taunts at certain other fields, notably, education, church, and government. Incompetent critics should be told that a technical field is not interested in using one-syllable words for the benefit of one-syllable minds.

6. *Frequent tendency to become identified with one's own views.* Here we have the "my experience" blunder again. The person sure that he knows the answers which he has found out the "practical way" is not likely to be open minded or to understand basic theory.

7. *Lack of understanding of what theory is.* The basic difficulty perhaps lies just here. Reasons for our lack of understanding have been hinted at above. Our educational efforts for some generations have not been directed at the understanding of theory as such, except in isolated specialties with advanced students. Industrial and business leaders have made errors in the use of natural resources, in production and distribution, which are hidden behind the great prestige of the men who have money and power. Publications, ordinarily, do not recount the blunders of the

[18] Barzun, *op. cit.* Ch. 11 on language and pedantry is a delightful discussion of the misuse of language. Illustrations show that this error is not confined to education but appears widely in many if not all fields.

Irvin C. Poley, *Speaking of Teaching* (Philadelphia, Germantown Friends School Publication, 1957). If available in local library, students can read with profit and enjoyment Ch. 18, "Sonnet from a Pedaguese: A Note on Educational Jargon."

business elite. A growing and intelligent interest is being shown today by leaders of industry, not only in basic theory but in the history and use of theory. An increasing number of business executives would no longer agree to or support the statement made by a one-time Cabinet member: "Pure research is that done by those who do not know what they are doing." Support is now more likely to be given to basic research dealing with theory. A trend can be seen which is away from trivial inventions, gadgets, and devices. Stereotypes are less and less acceptable.

Prior to World War I, Congress regularly appropriated more money for the control of hog cholera than for research on the health of children. Recently a Congress appropriated more money for price supports for one, not too-important, farm product than it did for research on ballistics. The so-called "practical" won out over the so-called "theoretical." A British scholar of considerable standing once said facetiously, but with an undertone of seriousness, that he believed "the Americans are the chosen people of the Lord and under His special protection—otherwise the nation could never have survived the inconceivable errors made in handling its natural resources." The British, as stated earlier, have also a considerable record for "muddling through"!

Schoolmen are among the worst offenders. Experience and training have given the majority no contact with systematic thinking and its terminology. The nature of the work all too often favors the routinist, the docile and unquestioning individual; hence there is little serious intellectual effort on the part of schoolmen when they are confronted with a new idea or practice. Educational workers far too often tend to reject or "brush off" all new ideas with the words (really epithets as used) "Theory," "Theoretical," "That's all theory," "A good theory, but it won't work in practice," "Is that a sound statement, or is it only theory?" Those using these statements are quite unaware that some of them are self-contradictory and that the user is open to the charge of incredibly incompetent thinking, if not of stupidity. Despite centuries of ridicule the statement about "good theory won't work in practice" persists. A *good* theory cannot possibly fail to work in practice. Otherwise it is *not* a good theory. Sometimes the person trying to operate the theory is incompetent and blames failure on the theory. Again circumstances and absence of resources may prevent the theory from working, but that is overlooked by the operator.

Too often we hear an instructor say, "My course in (administration, or curriculum, or guidance) is a practical course, none of this theory stuff." Two yearbooks issued within recent years by an important association of schoolmen are utterly devoid of any vestige of educational theory. The content is a collection of how-to-do-it prescriptions, summaries of opinion from the membership, a few normative status investigations, together with many exhortations to do the "right" thing. The material not only has no theoretical basis but, what is worse, does not lend itself to any sensible or useful generalizing. The writers of these materials are so busy operating the schools they have never had time to find out why they operate them.

The average schoolworker (and too many outside the school) has his own private meanings for "theoretical," as he uses the word. He means one of the following or similar statements:

1. The idea or practice is one *I never heard of!*
2. The idea or practice is one *I cannot understand* and cannot explain.
3. The practice is one *I am unable to carry out.*
4. The idea or practice is *different* from those I use and if taken seriously would disturb the routines I now use.
5. The idea or practice is one which *I do not intend to exert myself to understand* and use.

Here we have good illustrations of subjective data discussed earlier. These are not the openly admitted reasons for rejection, but they are there. In many instances they are transparently obvious. In others it could not be proved.

Schoolmen and others who decry theory have a theory whether they know it or not. It will be an inadequate, muddled, and often internally contradictory theory—but, nevertheless, a theory! It is impossible to operate anywhere, particularly in relation to facts, without a theory. He who claims to operate "practically," that is, without theory, is like a certain man who

> went somewhere but knew not whither he was going;
> when he got there, knew not where he was; and
> when he got back, knew not where he had been.

The end of the antitheory period may be in sight. Brogan boldly states that the signs are plain. [19] It is increasingly clear that schools cannot be operated on the basis of stereotypes. Devices, techniques, and trivial innovations are not sufficient. Articles and books on theory of administration, for instance, in contrast to those on administrative operations, are increasing.

[19] D. W. Brogan, "The End of Illusion," *Yale Review* (December, 1957), pp. 161-174.

Coladarci and Getzels, *op. cit.*

Roald Campbell and Russell Gregg, eds., *Administrative Behavior in Education* (New York, Harper, 1957).

Daniel E. Griffiths, *Human Relations in School Administration* (New York, Appleton-Century-Crofts, 1956).

————————, *Administrative Theory, op. cit.* Excellent summary statement.

Halpin, *op. cit.*

Paul Mort, *Principles of School Administration* (New York, McGraw-Hill, 1946).

Sources of theory. We are not here particularly concerned with the sources of theory; hence, only brief summary statements are given. First, theory is not personal; it is not something one dreams up. Second, it is not a mere classification. Third, it is not a philosophy. Theory deals with assumptions and rules, with what will happen if certain things are done. Theory is a guide to action; it is a guide to new knowledge and explains this new knowledge.

Traditional sources of theory have been: (*a*) opinions and pronouncements from practitioners, (*b*) surveys of practice, (*c*) deductive reasoning, and (*d*) procedure in other disciplines. Some of these are still useful, but we should desert opinions, questionnaires, check lists, and brief, unorganized interviews. Accurate and detailed descriptions of administrators at work are more important. This extended observational and detailed interviewing technique has been well developed in anthropology and in other social sciences. Two good illustrations from education are seen in:

Neal Gross, Ward S. Mason, and A. W. McEachern. *Explorations in Role Analysis: Studies of the School Superintendency Role* (New York, Wiley, 1958).
Neal Gross, *Who Runs the Schools?* (New York, Wiley, 1958).

A final statement may be of interest here, taken from a discussion of human relations in industry. [20] Good critical analyses are constantly being made in this field.

If we cannot deal with specific events in ordinary terms, we need to break down these events into abstract terms, which will make it possible to compare and contrast incidents from case to case. This is the method of science (namely to set up a theory and tackle the varied facts). . . .

Similarly, we need to work with abstractions in the world of human relations. This is another way of saying we need to work with a theory.

A theory is important to us for two basic reasons.

First, it points out some of the important items [facts] to be observed, described, and analyzed. . . . When observations are made in different terms, the findings do not add up, and science does not grow.

Second, a theory can tell us *how to relate the items* of observation to each other so that we can predict and control behavior on this basis. We often hear people say they will let the facts speak for themselves. *This is an illusion.* The world is infinitely complex, and the facts about it, even in a narrow area of activity, are without number. Furthermore, a fact has meaning for people only insofar as it is *fitted to other facts.* The facts of observation must be organized. We can organize them according to our unconscious preferences. Or we can organize them in terms of a theory. Then at least we know what we are doing and why we are doing it.

Any theory of human relations will select certain aspects for emphasis and leave certain others out altogether. That is always the way with theoretical

[20] William F. Whyte, *Pattern for Industrial Peace* (New York, Harper, 1951), Ch. 11, "A Scheme for Analysis," pp. 157-159.

schemes. They are to be judged not by their inclusiveness but by their workability, to what extent they enable us to account for the behavior we are seeking to explain.

Criteria for a good theory. A theory is an explanation of what we have, as stated earlier, and must indicate the road to new discoveries. Sterility results from dealing only with what we know.

Good theory:

1. Must be based on the scientic data we have, that is, on the objective, reliable, comprehensive, systematic information, and on the operational definitions of concepts in the field under examination.

2. Must explain the essence of the phenomena under examination.

3. Must serve as a guide to action.

4. Must serve as a guide to the collection of facts. (Recall the hypothesis which is a form of theory.)

5. Must serve as a guide to new knowledge and discoveries.

SECTION 4. TEACHER GUIDANCE IN THE ANALYSIS OF EXPERIENCE

I shall try to correct errors when shown to be errors, and I shall adopt new views as fast as they shall appear to be true views.

ABRAHAM LINCOLN

Teachers may aid learners on any level to analyze their experiences critically. Few services are as important as making individuals aware and then critical. First-class teachers, whether using assignments or units, have always provided for some degree of critical analysis of experience as it occurs. The teacher should know, first, the general objectives for which he is working; second, the general procedures leading to critical analysis; and third, the specific techniques that may be used. Too often the general objectives are neglected, thus making for mechanical use of specific devices.

General objectives for the teacher. The following understandings, attitudes, and abilities need to be developed by the pupil as he engages in critical analysis:

Understandings

1. All statements and conclusions must have a basis in (*a*) facts, and (*b*) logically organized sequence of argument.
2. All persons need to learn to be objective and systematic in deriving statements.
3. Rumor, hearsay, gossip, and personal opinion are not evidence and cannot be substituted for facts and logic. Personal experience when properly evaluated produces evidence.
4. Some questions and problems are susceptible to reasonably precise and valid answers—for the time being. Other questions and problems will always have tentative and general answers.

5. Individual differences of interpretation, particularly on nonprecise materials, are inevitable. Certain differences of opinion result from dishonesty in one or more individuals; others are based on wholly honest grounds.

6. All interpretations, honest and dishonest, have demonstrable backgrounds and causes.

Attitudes

These are listed in Part I, Chapter 3.

Abilities

The critical abilities are developed in Part II and are listed in abbreviated form in several places, as in Chapters 4 and 5.

General principles and procedures for the teacher. A few general conditions and principles may be listed. There are others.

1. Provide that within the experiences of the classroom there are *contrasting and contradictory* items. Call attention directly to contrasting reports or interpretations, trying to bring out the effect of different frames of reference, objectives, aspirations, and experiential backgrounds.

Encourage students to refer to their own experiences which are relevant to the problem before the class. The more examples offered, the more opportunity for critical, comparative analysis.

Prevent disregard or "brush-off" of contrasts and contradictions. Do not accept as explanation, "Coincidence," "It's one of those things," "It's a natural," all of which are advanced by individuals who do not really understand the situation or the process of thinking.

This means that free discussion should be encouraged. Search for causes and development of consequences through reasoning (if this—then that), experiment, use of varied sources and references, personal and small group conferences.

2. Keep the aim, topic, or problem before the class as the constant point of reference. Show the bearing on our problem of what you said. What has that to do with the topic?

3. Ask for facts, sources, reasons, backing of any type for all assertions, contributions, conclusions. This keeps students aware of the constant necessity for analysis of experience and what is said about experience.

Classify and evelute with students different sources of data or of authoritative statements.

Do not too quickly condemn statements which seem to your adult mind to be completely illogical. They may be quite logical to the child and are, doubtless, sincere. Careful, sympathetic analysis will help to establish a more mature logic.

Wherever possible have learners compare their conclusions based on "personal experience" with those drawn by experts and based on precise measurement, or controlled experiment, or closely reasoned chain of argument.

Lead through analysis of personal experience to concepts and usage of terms *average, norm, theory, law*.

Aid learner to distinguish between the actual experience and his judgment of it or his "opinion" as to what actually happened. Lead him to see that *description* of an event, or *illustration,* are not *explanations* of that event.

Engage in an open discussion of the nature of *fact* and of *opinion* when argument or confusion results from or turns upon the meaning of each.

Whenever a discussion becomes a battle of opinions per se, or when students jump to conclusions without recourse to facts, you must call attention to the very facts that they have circumvented but which call out for recognition and explanation.

4. Watch for signs of ego-involvement and try to channel it into constructive purposes.

5. Be sure that all views—of majority and of any minorities—are heard and critically analyzed.

6. Allow time for contemplation, greater insight, new data to appear. Delay the formulation of final conclusions. Form buzz groups or committees sometimes to clarify, summarize. Often a discussion may well be put over until a later period.

7. Pinpoint the feeling aspect as well as the cognitive. Lead learners to awareness of their own "feelings" and the effect of feelings on thinking. "Why does he feel (in contrast to think) as he does about this question?"

Work for calm recognition of bias, prejudice, misconceptions, arbitrary beliefs. Once in the open, these are more easily analyzed. Lead to recognition and summary of facts contrary to one's views, particularly one's "opinions."

Nearly anything a student believes because he was born in a certain family, city, state, union, or nation, or which may be identified with certain economic, political, social, business, religious, or educational institution is in one sense a prejudice (but not necessarily so) and should be analyzed.

8. Keep records, thus profiting from all earlier successes and failures in using sources, drawing inferences, proving points. Use a failure constructively and not as a stigma or reproach.

9. Use certain formal devices which aid in clarifying, summarizing, keeping on the track: outlining; tables, diagrams, or graphs; running discourse; a system of recorders and observers.

10. Make use of creative expression wherever it occurs.

11. Establish early a universe of discourse. Define terms. Clarify ambiguous terms. Ask for statement of meaning and restatements as often as necessary to achieve a common understanding.

Illustrative specific techniques. The following suggestions are applicable from primary to high school and college levels. [21]

1. A typical experience is that of visiting a market, the city hall, the fire station (any of many others). Upon return the children tell or write what they saw, draw pictures, and the like. Reports will inevitably differ.

Why, do you suppose, did you differ in reporting the things we all saw together? What factors may account for this? (Several factors are likely to emerge, thus aiding children to see why observing and reporting the very same experiences will differ.) The teacher's own report may be included.

[21] Illustrations here are taken from student papers, here chiefly from summaries by Mary Ward, Marcia Fogg, Jean Hastie, and Alan Buechner.

The same techniques can be used when a small committee has interviewed someone or has used references for class report.

2. Reference books giving differing, sometimes contradictory, accounts of the same events may be consulted. In what ways did the authors differ in reporting the selfsame events or other facts? Why do you suppose they did so? After trying to interpret the differences, students may be sent to the biographies or other sources dealing with the authors themselves to see if differences can be explained. (All this holds both for reporting and interpreting facts or events.)

Which of the differing accounts did *you* prefer? Why? (This reveals to the student the presence in his own thinking of the factors influencing the author.)

3. During a reading lesson, or in reading literary classics, the class might come across accounts of experiences of a child or children of their own age levels; of the same or different social, economic, or geographic status. How do the related experiences differ from yours? How are they similar? Develop as many contributing factors as possible from the report given.

4. Relate or give a written account to the class of a situation which is of interest and which could happen to the students themselves. What would you do and why? Class can then analyze the differing responses to the identical situation.

5. Role playing affords excellent illustrations of differing reactions with opportunity to analyze and explain.

Have several pupils play the part of Mother helping with homework, of Father trying to find out exactly how the neighbor's window got broken, of another child trying to extract a given promise or favor from another, and other roles. Why did *you* act as you did? Can you explain why your classmate presented different actions?

Now reverse roles. Did you feel natural? Did anything happen which helped you to understand the thoughts and actions of the other person?

6. Use of amateur planning, mistakes, failures. The children plan an experience beyond their capacities. Let them go ahead; then analyze what happened. Why do you think we made that mistake, failed in this point? Just where did you begin to see we had gone wrong? How will that help us with another experience?

Have any student relate an unsuccessful experience; then ask the others what they think caused the trouble. How would they have reacted before they heard the account? After hearing it?

7. Use of pictures, films, mock-ups, and the like. Relate what you thought was going on. Why did that attract your attention? Get several reports, and analyze why they differ. Do any of you think that things might have happened differently from the events shown in the film? Why?

What can you tell of the life, occupations, climate—perhaps of the social customs and religion of the people shown in the film—from things that were shown? Account for your answers.

8. Semantics: definition of terms, use of words, interpreting statements. Do you see how interpretations of experience differ from person to person due to language?

What did *you* mean by that word? What evidently did your classmate mean? What makes you think that the word means what you say it does? (This item will be developed further in Chapter 10 on words.)

9. Accounts of an incident, accident, quarrel, or co-operative effort on the playground or near the school and involving the school. The same can be done for incidents at home. What did you see? How did it happen? Where were you when it happened? How do you account for these differences in reports of what you all saw? Incidents may be staged for observation without warning to the class.

10. A girl reports in her homemaking class that she cooked something at home which was a complete failure, but she doesn't know why.

Let us do it over again at school under controlled conditions. The girl looks up the necessary food facts and theory, plans the procedure, uses the specified ingredients, checks with the instructor. The cooking is then done and checked at every point with procedure and results at home. Differences in the experience appear which account for the differences. This type of exercise can be used in various courses.

11. Listen to a lecture, radio, or television presentation of a topic in your field or to your interest. Write down at the time comments on any statement which gets your attention for good reason. Later, do you still believe that the statements and your reactions for or against were correct? What caused you to agree or challenge in the first place? What caused changes in your views on later thought (provided you did change on some points)?

We may re-emphasize that individuals learn by experience many things that are not so. They are quite unaware of this. One of the most important tasks of the school is to make them aware and critical. Analysis and experience with fact finding, checking, and proving are necessary at all levels.

The use of such specific techniques, and many others, carried on in the light of the general aims set forth earlier will aid pupils to analyze critically what happens to them and to others—their experiences. It should develop the habit of caution in accepting experience at face value.

The critical importance of developing skill in the analysis of experience. Discussion in this chapter has been somewhat longer than with other topics. The basis of knowledge, of inference, and conclusion is involved. Personal experience, for reasons given, will continue to impress individuals and will be cited as proof. But it also must be integrated with publicly demonstrated knowledge. Aiding students to analyze their personal knowledge in the light of objective knowledge is a sensitive and fateful procedure. We cannot ask individuals, especially in education, to give up their personal beliefs based on personal experience in the light of objective knowledge *unless these individuals genuinely understand the discrepancies between the two, and why these discrepancies occur.* To omit or neglect the comparison-for-resolving-discrepancies is to run serious risk of replacing complete acceptance of personal experience by complete acceptance of principles which are not truly understood and, hence, easily deserted. This is more serious in education and the social sciences generally than in the physical sciences. Objective data in the education and social science fields are legitimately subject to a range of interpretations. They do serve to disprove many traditional assumptions, but they do not in all cases provide unambiguous guidance for teaching or teacher education. They are far superior to the uncontrolled conclusions of the untrained observer, but without careful comparison the untrained observer will not know this. Personal experience inevitably flows into the gap left by the absence of basic principles both in teaching and in the everyday affairs of life. To suppress or to ridicule personal experience without sympathetic efforts to aid in its analysis may only drive it underground where its influence will be even less obvious and subject to control. *Comparison between inferences drawn from reliable, objective data and from personal experience must always be made and discussed.* [22] When this is done with due respect for the rules of evidence, the real and the apparent contradictions will be clearly seen. Some will disappear; some will need to be further analyzed. The comparison, however, must be made by the learner himself, or in class discussion. It can't be omitted in favor of imposition or conclusions.

PRELIMINARY EXERCISES

Two preliminary inquiries will be of interest and value to all students if the necessary materials can be made available. These inquiries afford a direct and easily understood entry to the difficult problem of fact and interpretation.

1. The April, 1949, issue of *Harper's Magazine* contains an astonishing article by Milton Mayer, "How to Read the Chicago Tribune," pp. 24-35. This affords an introduction not only to the place of facts and to critical reading, but also to a whole range of problems dealing with the press.

Mayer analyzes in the light of known and demonstrable facts an article which appeared in the *Chicago Tribune,* November 14, 1948. He documents 112 errors in detail. The article occupies 57 inches of space in *Harper's,* using the usual type. The documented criticisms occupy 113 inches of small, single-spaced type. The whole analysis is a monumental affair.

---

[22] Note. The authors here deliberately omit discussion of a more fundamental approach to this whole matter which should engage the attention of advanced scholars in the field. The present volume is a book for beginners. What is further needed is the development of basic theory or systems to serve as bases for the "objectivization" of a teacher's personal experience somewhat analogous to that used by competent physicians and others. A theory for classifying observed behavior should enable one to decide upon specific actions on the basis of the systematized behavior of the past. Perhaps this cannot be done in the social sciences or, at least, not easily done. The use of statistical methods in education does not help; nor do experimental methods, if carried on as they often are, without regard to a theoretical system which bridges the gap between the observations and operations of the practitioner (teacher) and measurable, testable quantities. Graduate schools should be interested in this.

Harper's is usually available in college libraries or in city libraries. All students should read this article and present their views pro and con in class.

If the magazine is not available so that all may have access to it, the instructor should describe or read a substantial section to the class.

2. The September, 1959, issue of *Cosmopolitan Magazine* contains an article, "Multi-Million Dollar High School Dilemma," by Dr. Eugene Stull, principal of the school.

The article contains 5 statements which are amply supported by known facts, 20 that are contradicted by known facts, 5 that are doubtful but which may be sound, 5 doubtful which are probably not sound, and 7 inferences based on insufficient or nontypical data.

We are chiefly interested in the 20 statements which are contradicted or questioned by valid and available data.

Files of *Cosmopolitan* are usually found in city libraries. Students should read the article, select any one or two unsound statements and proceed to summarize relevant data. Use the *Encyclopedia of Educational Research,* the *Education Index,* the various indexes of psychological research, the *Readers Guide,* and any other useful source.

(The designation of correct, noncorrect, and doubtful statements is based on our best knowledge and judgment. There may be errors in our interpretations. The statements labeled nonfactual, however, will stand up since large amounts of data are available.)

3. Read the article "All the News that Fits the Pattern," in the May, 1949, issue of *Harper's Magazine.* Make a similar analysis of current news insofar as facts can be obtained. Students may at least gather from two to six accounts of the same event and attempt to make a summary which is more nearly truthful than any one account.

4. The foregoing exercises concentrate on inaccurate and/or dishonest handling of facts. Newspapers and magazines also present accounts of events, and of movements behind events, which are accurate in the highest degree. Find a magazine article or a connected series of articles in a newspaper which are models of factual reporting, so far as we can determine, and show how you checked the facts.

5. In each of the foregoing four exercises make an effort to explain why the reports are patently inaccurate; why the accurate accounts are as they are.

QUESTIONS, EXERCISES, AND REPORTS

The following exercises are but samples; the list may be extended greatly by any college instructor. Elementary and secondary teachers may develop similar exercises in any subject area for use with pupils.

Special note on all exercises wherein we analyze the thought of another person. These exercises particularly, and some to come later, deal with the critical analysis of someone's facts and use of facts, terms, and logical processes. This poses a special hazard:

1. When we reconstruct the logic of another person, we can never say that we have actually duplicated his processes. All we can say is that this is our honest summary based on such evidence as is contained or implied in the state-

ment by the other person. On the other hand, the original speaker or writer is responsible for acceptance or explanation of any reasonable inference drawn from his remarks.

2. When summarizing a well-supported and logically organized proposition, list the factual references, the valid evidences, the proper logical processes used. Do not dismiss a piece of good thinking by referring to the person involved as "bright," "clever," "intelligent," "shrewd." These blur the situation. A sharp, critical analysis will show how "clever" the person is far better than these colloquial words with varied meanings.

3. When summarizing an incompetent piece of thinking, list the factual materials of which the individual is evidently unaware. List actual logical errors. List the biases which seem obvious, the rationalizations which may indicate psychopathic, or neurotic ego-involvement. Do not dismiss with the colloquial words, "ignorant," "stupid," "biased," or in some cases "neurotic."

4. Give everyone the benefit of reasonable doubt when noting possible bias or prejudice.

5. Above all, avoid the irresponsible procedure observed in so much conversation and argument. Individuals constantly try to say what others meant or thought. "What you really meant was——." "You say this, but what you meant was the opposite." "You evidently believe that——." This is almost immoral in its lack of responsibility for one's own utterances.

SECTION 1. FACTS, DATA, AND THEIR SOURCES

The following exercises deal with facts and thought processes. Sources of the statements are given and may be consulted for total context. Select any one, and:

a. Restate (when necessary) in simplest terms the crux of the statement.
b. Define terms as we honestly believe the author uses them.
c. List assumptions which seem clearly to be in the writer's or speaker's mind, whether implicit or explicit.
d. List factual materials which support or deny the statement.
e. Watch carefully for important differences of meaning for certain key terms, or shifts in meaning during the discourse. Speaker or writer may be using one meaning, listener or reader another.

1. "In the light of intellectual history and of modern psychology, it does not seem unreasonable to report that the best, if not the only, way by which the teacher can promote fruitful thinking is to promote knowledge and to inspire respect for the laboriously and painfully ascertained facts that constitute human culture." Ben D. Wood and F. S. Beers, "Knowledge versus Thinking," *Teachers College Record,* Vol. 37 (1936), p. 496.

2. "But it is doubtful, to say the least, that teaching or syllabi of any kind could ever make thinkers out of the vast majority of students now in high school and college."
(Same reference as preceding question, p. 495)

3. "The chief effect of reinforcement of old solutions is to facilitate new (different) solutions."

4. "Success breeds success; students should be protected from failure."

This statement and its opposite occur widely in both psychological and educational literature.

5. "Only analysis of antidemocratic propaganda in terms of total social context can provide us with effective means of dealing with the disease at its roots."

6. "Only that man knows who knows that he knows and can so exhibit his technique that others may know that he knows or may know by the same token that he does not know." T. V. Smith, quoted by Larrabee in *Reliable Knowledge, op. cit.,* page 27.

This volume by Larrabee is a veritable mine of materials of this type. Note exercises at ends of appropriate chapters and also long list of study questions dealing with the exercises, pp. 639-669. Note that Larrabee identifies by name all persons and places involved. This should be done in all cases where you make exercises for your own classes.

7. The following exercises deal with facts and process as did the foregoing ones, but with special reference to our own field, education. Knowledge of standard educational literature is necessary, either known from past study or looked up now.

Several class discussions may be devoted to reports based on any selection from these or similar references:

BURTON, W. H., "Get the Facts: Both Ours and the Other Fellow's," *Progressive Education* (Jan., 1952).

————, *Scientific Criticism Aids Education,* Bulletin of the National Association of Secondary School Principals (Dec., 1958), pp. 172-179.

CUNNINGHAM, Earl C., "A Quack Quacks Back!" *Journal of Teacher Education* (March, 1958), pp. 61-73. A commentary upon Albert Lynd's *Quackery in the Public Schools* (Boston, Little, Brown, 1950) which should be examined statement by statement along with Cunningham's analysis.

————, "The Wastelands of Professor Bestor," *Journal of Teacher Education* (June, 1959), pp. 158-172. Commentary on Bestor's *Educational Wastelands* (Urbana, Ill., University of Illinois Press, 1953). See also the rest of the symposium of which Cunningham's article was a part, pp. 173-210.

HAND, Harold, "Black Horses Eat More than White Horses, " American Association of University Professors *Bulletin* (June, 1957), pp. 266-279. Use the *Education Index* to find other articles by this able writer.

McDOWELL, Bruce, "A Bill of Rights for Classroom Teachers," *Phi Delta Kappan,* Vol. XXXX (May, 1959), pp. 330-332. Repeated in brief in *Education Digest* (Sept., 1959), pp. 34-36. Replies are also found in *Phi Delta Kappan* (Oct., 1959), pp. 32-35. This article is written with feeling and sincerity but is almost entirely innocent of factual backing. (We will examine this article for logical errors when we come to Chap. 11.)

SCOTT, C. W., and HILL, Clyde M., *Public Education Under Fire* (Englewood Cliffs, N. J., Prentice-Hall, 1954). This volume is a mine of rich material on educational controversy. Both sides are quoted copiously and in full. Friendly and unfriendly critics of the schools are included equally. The volume includes sources for Bestor, Lynd, and Smith. In addition the *Bulletin* of the Council for Basic Education should be consulted.

KEATS, John, and BECK, Robert H., "How Well Are Our Teachers Being

Taught?" *Better Homes and Gardens* (May, 1958), pp. 51-54. Two articles plus rebuttal giving two sides of the question.

Select any article or part of a book from the foregoing list or from other more recent publications.

  a. For any one of the various summary conclusions found which is not properly supported by factual references, list samples of the materials which have been overlooked or omitted.

  b. List references to valid factual material which contradicts, or modifies in any way, or otherwise partially changes any one of the conclusions.

  c. For any conclusions which you believe to be wholly or partially illogical, present an analysis (as it seems to you) of the processes which must have been used to produce the conclusions stated.

  d. Has the selected writer used the word *fact* correctly? Has he kept facts and conclusions from facts separated?

Note. Instructors and students should be on the lookout for current contributions to the controversy over schools.

8. Students interested in any field other than education (art, music, engineering, public policy, or what not) may present discussions similar to those indicated for education.

9. "The use of legal force in changing beliefs and attitudes is frequently a psychologically sound procedure." David Krech and Richard Crutchfield, *Theory and Problems of Social Psychology* (New York, McGraw-Hill, 1948), p. 512.

Analyze this under same questions as the preceding quotations. Do not answer this one too quickly or glibly. Students may fall into a serious error in interpreting this one.

10. A graduate class studying group dynamics and social process was asked to list in writing any questions developing from the initial contacts and demonstrations. One administrator turned in the following list:

  a. In the face of the accusations that the American people are immature generally (Overstreet, Streicher, Bell, Wylie), isn't there a necessity to insure that leadership be more strictly limited than is implied in the group process? Who, for example, is to judge the relative worth of contributions?

  b. Since the idea of democracy is historically based on Graeco-Hebrew-Christian ideals, can we expect to develop democratic morality without adopting the religious premises underlying it?

  c. Isn't the interpretation of democracy (as applying to economic and social orders) somewhat revolutionary insofar as capitalism is still the dominant economic theory in America? (In other words, is the school a forerunner of change, or is it the function to reflect the present culture?)

  d. Since the democratic process will not work without a developed democratic conscience, must not the educator insist that the home and family be held *primarily* responsible? If this is so, should the school continue to broaden its activities which parents thrust upon it—extracurricular activities, nursery and prenursery schools, camping experiences, and sex education, for example?

(1) Reconstruct as honestly as possible the conceptual system under which this man is operating.

(2) List the obvious assumptions.

(3) Then proceed as in earlier exercises to list factual materials pro and con, logical processes which are defensible or otherwise.

11. An address by Superintendent John W. McDevitt of the Waltham, Mass., Public Schools stimulated much lively discussion among Boston elementary teachers before whose association the address was made. In the absence of a manuscript from Superintendent McDevitt, statements here are as reported by the teachers: "The use of authority over other persons is legitimate in order to get things done. Authority is a proper instrument."

a. List bodies of factual material, and indicate logical processes which support Superintendent McDevitt's statement. (One or two references only.)

b. List bodies of factual material or logical processes which would contradict, modify, or alter the proposition. (One or two.)

c. Attempt to reconstruct the thought processes of the superintendent in arriving at the proposition.

d. The preceding item raises another problem: Could the proposition be valid under one conceptual system and not under another? What then becomes the problem? (This is an important question for all thinking.)

A second statement as reported by the teachers was: "The use of fear to control and manage children is legitimate and effective."

a, b, c as in first part of Exercise 11.

d. A student may volunteer to report (more extensively than in a) the scientific literature on the effect of fear upon human personality. Materials are available in considerable volume in physiology, psychology, psychiatry, psychotherapy, and group dynamics. A quick summary of representative studies is sufficient as an exhaustive study is not necessary here.

12. Another statement, probably from a different source, was reported: "Any child who gets into the sixth grade is capable of doing sixth-grade reading. If he does not do it, it is the teacher's fault."

a, b, c, d as in first part of Exercise 11.

13. A certain group of high school teachers object to receiving practice teachers, saying that the work of the children suffers.

a, b, c as in first part of Exercise 11.

14. We come now to a case which is not actually an exercise here but rather an illustration of procedure which is highly desirable.

Newspapers recently carried long accounts of controversy over manuscript versus cursive handwriting as taught in the Brookline, Mass., schools. Newspaper accounts contained numerous expressions of opinion, arguments bandied back and forth, statements by patrons, and the like. No reference to the excellent body of valid factual evidence appeared in the newspaper accounts. Inquiry directed to Superintendent Ernest Caverly gave us the following:

> "We have gone farther than most communities in carrying manuscript writing throughout our entire elementary school system, and indeed now into the High School. It is inevitable, therefore, that we should have some protest from those who think we are not teaching our children to write as other people do. On the other hand, our Handwriting Committee, under the leadership of Miss Mary K. Carter, has studied this subject intensively for ten or more years, and has come to the conclusion that as far as speed and legibility of handwriting are concerned there is no justification for changing from manuscript to cursive at any time. May I ask you at this point to read pages 332 and 333 of my annual report for the calendar year 1949, a copy of which is enclosed."

> "You have spoken of evidence concerning the use of manuscript writing. This was mentioned in Miss Carter's report of March, 1953, and also has been brought to the attention of those who are sufficiently interested to make inquiry. For example, specific reference has been made to an article by Ruth Strang in the *Journal of Education* for September, 1951, and to favor the other point of view to an article by Dr. H. Callewaert, M.D., in the *Journal of Educational Research,* 1947–1948, pages 1 to 12. Still further, I have written the American Medical Association to check on a statement which alleged that the medical profession 'felt that perfect posture is impossible where manuscript writing is used exclusively.' The reply which I received from Dr. Donald A. Dukelow of the A.M.A. is definite in stating that he has been 'unable to find any reference that would indicate that the medical profession has any opinion on the relation of manuscript writing to posture.' "

The pages in the superintendent's report and the report by Miss Carter contained a wealth of specific factual evidence. The superintendent's letter closes with a statement with which we are familiar and sypmathetic: "Even when we explain the facts and give all the evidence, we must still expect some will be unconvinced."

   a. Students may wish to offer comments on the foregoing presentation.

   b. Watch for and report similar instances in educational controversies, in other public discussions.

15. Illustrate the errors made by the average citizen, or any untrained observer, in deriving and dealing with what he calls facts. Illustrate particularly his confusion between facts, opinion, and belief.

16. Illustrate carelessness in use of the word *belief.*

17. Illustrate refusal to look at facts—and this is not confined to the average citizen. Illustrate dishonesty in deriving and interpreting facts.

18. Examine editorials, speeches, and educational publications for illustrations of good and bad use of facts and interpretations thereof.

19. Examine summaries of findings under the Pure Food and Drug Act with relation to use of fact and nonfact in advertising, in labels, and the like. This can be a very enlightening experience.

SECTION 2. INTERPRETATION OF FACTS AND EXPERIENCE

1. What is meant by a "hypothetico-deductive-observational" procedure?

2. What is the difference between learning the facts and learning from the facts?

3. Watch for correct use of experience as a basis for fact or conclusion; watch for gross errors here. Watch for self-validation.

4. Illustrate briefly the four points on page 89.

5. What are the probable reasons why individuals insist "one opinion is as good as another," and "everyone is entitled to an opinion"?

6. Illustrate from everyday discourse, newspapers, reading, or anywhere, the expression of nonsensical opinions.

7. When is it desirable and effective to use a generalization? When a specific illustration? Illustrate the serious (often humorous) errors here.

8. Recall from Chapter 2 reference to problems not handleable by the average citizen. Have you any further comment now?

SECTION 3. THEORY AND THE FACTS

1. How do you account for the almost diametrically opposed views on practice and theory, as between the average citizen and the trained scholar?

2. A widely used text in education was characterized by the Superintendent of the Reading, Mass., schools as "too theoretical to be usable." Asked to list the theoretical statements, the Superintendent proposed in all sincerity and seriousness that "a committee be appointed to determine which statements were theoretical and which not." He meant also that the committee define "theoretical," a term which is in standard usage in learned discourse.

    a. Within what universe of discourse was the Superintendent operating?

    b. If a similar universe were to govern technical fields, what would likely happen? (What, in fact, does happen all too often because of this?)

    c. What historical facts and semantic principles could be cited to support or contradict his proposal to determine the meaning of "theoretical" and to select theoretical statements by committee vote?

    d. A seeming paradox appears here: The meanings and definitions for all words are originally determined by consensus and can only be so determined—but—a proposal to determine a meaning by consensus at a given time may be pure absurdity.

    e. Under what circumstances is this true (thus explaining the seeming paradox)?

    f. What would happen if we determined at the time and on the spot by consensus meanings for: vitamin, corporation, neutron, diagnostic test, reading readiness, lawn mower, and whiskey? (The last two queries are important for your own thinking.)

A student pointed out that the text in question contains chiefly descriptions of actual practices in many school systems, statistical summaries of practices, principles and supporting text derived from analysis of widely observed and reported practices. The Superintendent then said: "I am proceeding on the 'premise' that the book does not contain descriptions of practice. You are proceeding on the 'premise' that it does."

    g. Show that the word *premise* is used correctly here or that it is not.

    h. Use of the word *premise* as above reveals a number of important facts about the processes used. What might some of them be?

    i. Under what circumstances could a "practice" be judged to be "theoretical"?

    j. Attempt to reconstruct the thought processes of the Superintendent which led to (1) the proposal to determine *within a known universe of discourse* the meaning of a basic term (*theoretical*), and (2) the use of the word *premise* as above.

    3. Recall the article by McDowell listed above in No. 7 of the Exercises for Section 1. The author cited as one of his "Teachers Rights" freedom from having to follow "high sounding theories." Asked to illustrate the theories, Mr. McDowell very courteously listed eight. Not a single one was a theory! One or two could be labeled as mere whimsies of a professor's mind. Read the original point on theory. Explain as nearly as you can how the author probably fell unto the error of discussing "theory" with illustrations which did not remotely approximate theory.

    4. The foregoing incident focuses on a widespread difficulty in educational circles. The words *theoretical* and *practical* are widely used with obvious error in their definition. The Superintendent's proposal would be simply incredible in any other technical field, but he cannot be criticized for this because he is obviously following usage by many persons within the profession, untrained in semantics.

    Many schoolworkers from teacher to administrator do, of course, know what they are talking about when they use these words. Careful inquiry over a period of ten years shows, however, that many do not. On the basis of your own contacts with this:

    a. Can you add to the list in the text any further meanings for the terms *theoretical* and *practical?* Any further reasons for holding these views?

    b. All this has serious implications for the professional status of education, and particularly for preservice training of teachers. Develop in considerable detail what some of these implications might be.

SECTION 4. TEACHER GUIDANCE IN THE ANALYSIS OF EXPERIENCE

    1. Illustrate any two or three of the 11 points on pages 111-113.

    2. Report for comment any systematic procedures used or observed by you similar to those points made by Miss Ward and Mrs. Fogg.

    3. Illustrate any original efforts of your own.

    (The points in this section are not ordinarily achieved by casual or incidental efforts. Careful, systematic planning is necessary.)

CHAPTER 7

Inference:
The Heart of Thinking

> In every case of reflective activity, a person finds himself confronted
> with a given present situation from which he has to arrive at, or
> conclude to, something else that is not present. This process of
> arriving at an idea of what is absent on the basis of what is at hand
> is *inference*.
>
> JOHN DEWEY *

We have described in previous chapters how problems are recognized and
analyzed, how hypotheses are sought and elaborated, how facts are gathered and identified. Succeeding chapters in Part II will present: (1) the
nature of proof, (2) the role of concepts, (3) the role of language, and
(4) the nature of error in thinking.

THE NATURE OF INFERENCE

Inference in logical terms is the act of concluding that propositions
before us imply new propositions. Inference occurs in many varied situations and of varied degrees of complexity. The moment after a wife spots
strange lipstick on her husband's collar, inference (among other things)
occurs. An automobile owner sees a pool of water under his car and
infers that the radiator leaks, or that the water is a residue from that which
dripped off the car after a heavy rain. Inference occurred when Archimedes leapt from the tub shouting "Eureka." Cases of thinking in earlier
chapters contained several illustrations of inference of different levels of
difficulty.

Inference is a precarious process. As stated briefly in Chapter 5, inference is the central *movement* in all thinking. It is the *movement* from

* John Dewey, *How We Think,* rev. ed. (Boston, Heath, 1933), p. 95.

123

facts to the tentative explanation (hypothesis), from one reason to another, from a reason to predicted new facts, toward acceptance or rejection of a conclusion. Thus, inference is the heart of thinking. It is often referred to as a "leap" or "jump." The thinker observes facts which are real, can be measured, or otherwise handled, and then he "leaps" to an explanation. Dewey has described the necessities here more clearly than other writers:[1]

Systematic inference, in short, means the recognition of definite relations of interdependence between considerations previously unorganized and disconnected, this recognition being brought about by the discovery and insertion of new facts and properties.

The function of reflective thought is, therefore, to transform a situation in which there is experienced obscurity, doubt, conflict, disturbance of some sort, into a situation that is clear, coherent, settled, harmonious.

What is important is that every inference be a tested inference; or (since often this is not possible) that we discriminate between beliefs that rest upon tested evidence and those that do not, and be accordingly on our guard as to the kind and degree of assent or belief that is justified.

The leap or inference, in the words of a popular song, "flies through the air." There is no guarantee of any kind in advance that the leap will land safely. The process of inference, leaping from known things to unknowns, from present, observed facts, to possible but—at the moment—absent facts, is peculiarly susceptible to error. The individual's temperament, his experiential background, his standards, values, prejudices, likes and dislikes, selfish interest at the given moment, and many other considerations may insinuate themselves, thus causing error within the inferential process. One difference between a trained and an untrained thinker at this point lies in the rigor with which inferences are subjected to testing and proof. Regulation, such as we can give, transforms inference into an acceptable belief. Causes of error and a number of standard fallacies are presented in a separate chapter later.

All control of inference is indirect. A brief summary is made here for the record.

1. Certain desirable *attitudes* must be developed. (See Chapter 3.)
2. The *nature and use of facts,* and of other phenomena which act like facts, must be understood. (See Chapter 6.)
3. *A system of ideas, a conceptual system,* must be built up within any given field. The concepts serve to interpret facts, sometimes are changed by new facts, enable reasoning to take place because of the relationships between concepts. (See Chapter 9.)

[1] John Dewey, *How We Think* (Boston, Heath, 1910; rev. ed. 1933). The first quotation is from the 1910 ed., p. 81. The other two are from the 1933 ed., pp. 100-101 and 97.

4. *Methods of testing and proving* must be selected or devised and used. (See Chapter 8.)

The formal nature of inference. As a psychological act, inference may happen rapidly, instinctively, and there is little we can do to train anyone how to have correct inferences in all situations. But when the ideas preceding an inference are analyzed and expressed in verbal form, we have the materials of the subject of logic; from these materials we can gather useful principles which may guide us in interpreting future inferential chains of thought. The assumption behind this analytic procedure is that whenever ideas, or their expression in verbal form, follow a certain *pattern,* they have the same inferential validity, no matter what variation there may be in subject matter detail.

Logical inference is divided commonly into *deduction* and *induction.* Deduction is the process of arriving at propositions which follow necessarily from prior general or general and particular propositions called premises. Induction is the process of arriving at general propositions of some degree of probable truth from particular matters of fact. In most reasoning cases there is a mixture of deductive and inductive processes.

DEDUCTION

Deduction historically has been the subject matter of formal logic, a science established by Aristotle and refined by later logicians such as Duns Scotus, Frege, Peirce, Russell, Tarski, and Whitehead. Modern refinements in symbolic logic have increased the importance of deductive logic as a foundation for mathematics and theoretical science.

In simple terms, the approach of logicians is to assume that the language of statements (not commands, questions, or exhortations) can be organized into propositions which assert some description, offer a choice between alternatives, or pose a condition. Elaborate systems of rules are then evolved by which we can determine whether certain combinations of propositions of these types do imply valid conclusions.

Categorical statements. One pattern of deductive argument is the array of categorical statements traditionally presented in syllogistic form. Example:

> All philosophers are wise.
> Some Greeks are philosophers.
> (Therefore) Some Greeks are wise.

In this three-part argument, called a syllogism, the first two propositions, or premises, imply the third. A combination of statements that have this form implies a *valid* conclusion. Whether or not the premises are true in themselves does not affect this validity.

Syllogisms of this type can also be solved by means of diagrams, such as the circles of Venn.

Alternation. An alternation is an argument containing propositions of the form "Either . . . or. . . ." This opposition of possibilities seems simple at first, but it is important to observe that the word *or* is ambiguous in English. In formal logic it is taken to mean "either *A* or *B* or both." But in common speech it may also mean "either *A* or *B* but not both (the exclusive use).

An example of an alternative argument of the second kind is found in a speech made by Secretary of State Dulles at a NATO meeting several years ago when he was discussing the need for German forces to help defend Western Europe: [2]

The missing element in making Europe defensible at this time is the lack of any German forces. Those who oppose the European Army with its twelve German divisions have proposed no alternatives. The theoretical alternative is that Germany might be made a member of NATO and recreate its own national forces, but of course, the French have a veto, and I am told that they would be even more opposed to that than . . . to the European Army. The United States could not keep large forces in an indefensible Europe.

The alternatives proposed here are:

> Either (1) Germany should contribute twelve divisions to the European Army,
>
> Or   (2) Germany should be made a member of NATO and recreate its own national forces,
>
> Or   (3) Europe should be left without German forces and (so Dulles asserts) be indefensible.

According to the argument, alternatives (2) and (3) are unacceptable; therefore, alternative (1) is mandatory. Once the alternatives are made explicit, the inference is obvious. The greatest source of error or disagreement from a political rather than from a logical standpoint is in the value of the alternatives proposed and the reasons for accepting or rejecting any particular one.

Another source of trouble lies in the possibility that all possible alternatives have not been presented. For example, in the above argument the possibility of neutralizing Germany was not explicitly mentioned, though its unacceptability is implied by the third alternative of Mr. Dulles. This problem, again, is beyond the purely logical scope of the alternation.

Conditions. The typical conditional argument has this form: "If . . . then. . . ." To refer to the Mesa Verde story:

> If the ring patterns of wood specimens match the established criterion pattern, then the wood dates from the eleventh century.

[2] Quoted from *Time Magazine* (May 4, 1953).

The patterns match.
Therefore, the wood is from the eleventh century.

Here again the inferential process is rather obvious in a simple case like this, but the material facts in the case, such as the reliability of the criterion pattern, require careful scrutiny. The ring pattern theory itself was established by largely inductive processes. Errors of sampling might occur.

Another source of error is the possible confusion between "necessary" and "sufficient" conditions. A necessary condition is one required for the consequence it implies; a sufficient condition is one which is adequate to imply a consequence but which may not be the only adequate condition.

A summary of logic brings to light the following useful considerations. The brief sketch given here of formal logic is clearly too brief to accomplish much in the training of logicians. Further detail is omitted since it is readily available in standard books on logic and symbolic logic, including Quine, Cohen and Nagel, and many others. We do not believe, furthermore, that a study of formal logic in great detail is necessary for the preliminary understandings we are presenting. There are, however, several ideas from formal logic which are useful in critical thinking.

1. *Techniques in the analysis of sentences.* Logic teaches us to analyze important statements in order to find out their basic structure —that is, whether they are in the form of descriptive classifications, "if . . . then. . . ." propositions, "either . . . or. . . ." alternations, or whether they are not assertive at all and merely make rhetorical comment or demand.

2. *Concentration on material truth of premises.* The distinction between validity and material truth reminds us to check propositions asserting a fact to make sure they are true before we draw inferences from them.

3. *Awareness of the importance of assumptions.* Important ideas in an argument are often taken for granted, or are neither explicitly stated nor proved. In ordinary conversation, for instance, we often omit one of the vital premises or even the conclusion because it seems to be quite obvious. Sometimes the assumed proposition will bear looking into. We are also reminded not to fall into the trap of merely restating one of the assumptions as a conclusion—circular argument.

4. *The relevancy of arguments.* Although it seems obvious that premises used in an argument should be related to the main issue, we often find that irrelevant matters are dragged into discussion, such as the personality of the disputants, appeals to popular prejudice, and red herrings of various waters.

5. *Recognition of logical fallacies.* The history of the study of logic has produced many and varied lists of logical fallacies, whose

formulation serves as a warning to avoid procedures which would render an argument worthless. A list of some fallacies is given in Chapter 11.

Although some high school students probably can comprehend an introduction to formal logic, we do not believe this is the most effective way to improve everyday critical-thinking skills. On the other hand, the efforts of the teacher will be more productive if she has some notion as to what formal logic is and, equally significantly, what it is not.

Limitations of formal logic. In spite of the valuable ideas which we may gain from reflection upon the points above, there are certain limitations to the utility of formal logic for our purposes.

1. *Formal logic is difficult to learn.* The vocabulary is cumbersome and medieval. In relation to the value of applying logical analysis to common problems, it would not seem feasible to introduce courses in formal logic in schools below the college level.

2. *Many conclusions reached by logical analysis are obvious enough to be determined by simple inspection.* If analysis is desired, Venn diagrams or other similar techniques could be applied.

3. *Logicians are not as much concerned with the material truth of the premises and conclusion*—that is, with whether the propositions are true according to conditions in the physical world—*as they are with internal validity*—that is, the formal relationships between propositions. In ordinary problem solving, the material truth is of utmost importance. Thus, logically:

> All cats have two heads.
> I am a cat.
> (Therefore) I have two heads.

The conclusion is valid, but not materially true.

4. *Formal logic has a post-mortem aspect* in that it deals with the product of thought rather than with the process of thought. It is more useful in analyzing arguments already advanced than in creating new ideas.

5. *Formal logic has a restricted range of applicability* considering the variety of problems that we are concerned with in this book.

It has become fashionable in some circles to decry logic, or at best to dismiss it with mild contempt. "Logic enables you to go wrong systematically," said the noted inventor Charles Kettering. This is not fair unless we have in mind the limitations the critics have in mind. Logic can clearly be an obstacle to thinking if there is insistence upon too rigid a use of ancient, fixed frames of reference. Thinking on typical problems depends upon and demands creativity, upon dealing with a clutter of unsorted, undefined realities. These often cannot be fitted into neat categories. The real point is that some have overconfidence in logic. It is not a hocus-pocus to be applied indiscriminately, but it is useful when properly regarded.

The place of formal logic in problem solving. The ways of solving a problem are many and varied, depending upon the nature of the problem under study, the field of operation, the purpose of the solver, his attitudes, and ability to interpret and explain the problem. Formal deduction is one of many processes useful for the analysis of thought.

Although we cannot in general recommend lengthy study of formal logic for the young student, the teacher would well profit from courses in the subject or from the study of such excellent books as Cohen and Nagel, Black, Quine, and many others. At this point it may be well to re-read Max Wertheimer, *Productive Thinking* (New York, Harper, 1945), "Introduction" and "Conclusion," pages 1-13 and 189-213.

Note on assumptions. As indicated above, assumptions, especially those which are implicit, may make or break any piece of thinking. They need serious scrutiny. Everyday thinking falls into many errors through failure to recognize and examine assumptions.

An assumption is anything treated as true without examination. An assumption is anything "taken for granted." When assumptions are stated and made explicit we can then assess their influence on the argument. The implicit assumptions are those which need serious analysis. Often the person is quite unaware of his own assumptions.

Deductive and inductive inference rest on premises, some of which may be unexamined assumptions. Deduction rests wholly on premises which are assumed to be true. Sometimes they are not true, or conditions may change so that once-safe assumptions are no longer sound. In all careful thinking it is necessary to analyze critically all assumptions and to assess their bearing on thinking.

Illustrations of assumptions. These are to be found in all areas, from advanced abstract thinking to the everyday exchanges between friends.

1. *Axioms or postulates in geometry are all assumptions* which are taken for granted.

This is necessary for any logical or deductive thinking, but the challenging of axioms (assumptions) as conditions change may lead to very valuable advances in thinking.

2. *Explicit assumptions occur constantly* in editorials, lectures, documents of any kind.

For instance, in a famous document, the Declaration of Independence: "We hold these truths to be self-evident, that all men are created equal, that they are endowed by their Creator with certain unalienable rights, that among these are life, liberty, and the pursuit of happiness."

The signers of the Declaration firmly believed in the explicit assumptions set forth above. These assumptions, as interpreted by our forefathers, were not the assumptions accepted by King George III and his ministers.

The argument based on the assumptions is wholly convincing to loyal Americans but not to the Ministers of the Crown.

3. *Implicit assumptions occur in most statements, documents, and the like.*

Again from the Declaration of Independence: "He has affected to render the Military independent of and superior to the Civil Power."

The implicit assumption here is that "the Military should not be independent of and/or superior to the Civil Power." Today, in the Western World at least, this assumption is explicit and very important. The United States has always had civilians as cabinet members for war, or the army, or the navy. Peoples with different conceptions of the state, of government, and of the relation of citizen (or subject) to state make different assumptions.

4. *Everyday conversation and thinking abound in unrecognized, implicit assumptions.*

This is one important reason why so much ordinary thinking goes so far astray.

"This medicine cured my cold right up. You should try it." This simple sentence abounds in unstated assumptions: "My cold was of the same nature as yours. My constitution is of the same general nature as yours. My state of health, digestion, and metabolism at the moment are the same as yours. I have no allergic or other antagonistic reactions to the drugs in this medicine, and neither do you." (Others can be stated.)

A student could not find any books by Dr. Ortega y Gassett in the college library. Inquiry revealed that he had proceeded on the assumption that Gassett was the last name as it is in English. He was unaware of the Spanish custom of adding the maternal ancestral name in order to distinguish between persons of the same paternal name.

"You ought to spank your baby hard for that." "We did, and it cured him." Assumptions are that small babies learn through spanking, that no other factor entered into the "cure," that all babies will react alike. Worse, there are assumptions that no bad emotional effects will ensue, that there are no alternative methods to spanking. (Many others can be listed.)

Political recommendations, social proposals, sales promotion programs often rest upon the assumption that public enlightenment, belief, and reaction have not changed in fifty years. Often they rest on assumptions based on incorrect sampling.

We must constantly be aware of a serious (and exasperating) blunder which occurs often when examining a proposed new departure in government, business management, military strategy, education, child rearing, methods of constructing buildings or roads, new machinery, or in any of the myriad fields of human endeavor. If the frontier thinker cannot prove in advance that his idea will work, the assumption is usually made by naïve thinkers that the opposite must be true—the idea will not work. Page Galileo, Pasteur, Edison, Steinmetz, and Einstein, to mention but a few! A much more correct method of thinking would be to examine the proposal in detail, to plan limited tryouts, and to examine conditions making for success or failure.

Some of the current widespread criticisms of the schools, of teaching, and of educational results are correct. The great majority of them are quite out of keeping with the facts, largely because of the implicit assumptions (rarely explicit) of the critics. Assumptions are made that a class school is superior to a democratic one, that only a selected class should go on to higher education, that education is concerned with the mind only, that formal discipline has never been disproved, that education was once quite effective but has been ruined by new and superficial ideas.

INDUCTION

Induction, as defined earlier, is the process of reasoning from particular to general. Broadly conceived, it includes science as a whole and so, like deduction, is too vast a subject to be treated in these pages with any degree of thoroughness. There are, however, certain broad purposes of induction, recognition of which provides a general orientation to many kinds of problems.

Purposes of induction. Three common purposes of inductive reasoning are: (1) to assert or discover causes, (2) to make predictions, and (3) to provide a description.

1. *Cause.* John Stuart Mill in his *System of Logic* described five methods by which causes may be identified: [3]

> The method of agreement
> The method of difference
> The method of concomitant variation
> The method of residues
> Joint method of agreement and difference

The method of agreement can be illustrated through considering the problem, "What caused the food poisoning?" If we find that sick persons on a picnic ate all different kinds of different things, except that every sick person had had a serving of chicken salad, we may conclude that the eating of the chicken salad, the one circumstance common to all the cases of poisoning, may have been the cause of sickness. These methods do not eliminate the need for painstaking research and imaginative conjecturing and rejection of certain causal factors, but as Cohen and Nagel say: [4]

---

[3] Discussion of these methods can be found in Morris R. Cohen and Ernest Nagel, *An Introduction to Logic and Scientific Method* (New York, Harcourt, Brace, 1934), and similar references.

[4] Cohen and Nagle, *op. cit.,* p. 267.

"They are of undoubted value in the process of attaining truth. For in eliminating false hypotheses, they narrow the field within which true ones may be found."

The method of *concomitant variation* is defined to mean that when *two kinds of events vary in the same way,* there is causal relation. The Mesa Verde story illustrates this. Botanists have noted that the way ring patterns of trees vary is similar to the way rainfall cycles vary. They conclude that the rainfall affects the growth of trees and consequently the ring pattern.

The *method of differences states* that if events leading up to the occurrence of a phenomenon and the events leading up to cases in which the phenomenon does not occur *are the same except for one thing,* that thing may be causally connected with the phenomenon under question. Illustration is found in the famous search for the cause of yellow fever. The human guinea pigs were smeared with infected blood, were in contact with infected persons, wore clothing cast off by victims of yellow fever. Other factors held for all the human volunteers. *But only one of the individuals was bitten by a mosquito, and he caught yellow fever.*

The very notion of a "cause" is a troublesome concept. Attempts to define a cause usually end up with some such definition as this: "A cause exists when a constant relation exists between two circumstances or when one event invariably precedes another under similar circumstances." But the common idea of causation is influenced by two common human tendencies, the tendency to simplify and the propensity for conceiving physical events in terms of human action and motivation. In most people's minds, the word *cause* calls into consciousness the idea of a human agent actively working to bring about some action. Thus, "The cause of death was that the accused struck a knife into the victim's heart." In human affairs, this kind of event is often associated with concepts of "blame," "intention," "responsibility." (For example, the Army policy of fixing "responsibility" for every occurrence of damage or error.) When carried over into nonhuman areas of cause and effect, these anthropomorphic concepts tend to blur the problem. In weather prediction, for example, factors of temperature, humidity, wind direction and velocity, and their conjunction "cause" rain or some other weather condition. This kind of relation has to be conceptualized in a different way from those of the knife murder.

Causes are often complex and different in their immediacy. "What were the causes of World War I?" Many volumes have been written on this subject, and the authors usually are obliged to point out that some factors are "underlying" and others "immediate." The shooting of the Archduke at Sarajevo was an "immediate" cause. Underlying causes included nationalistic attitudes, ambitions of national leaders, historical European antagonisms, mercenary motives of munitions makers, and traditional concepts of international relations. It is thus an oversimplification to say "Germany started the war," or "An assassin was the cause of the war."

It is obvious that causes precede effects. It also appears obvious that one event which precedes another is not necessarily its cause. Yet the error of making this assumption is one of the commonest kinds of false inference. The Latin name *post hoc, ergo propter hoc* has been given to the kind of fallacy by which we assume that some event which has preceded another is its cause, when in fact it is not. Examples of this kind of thinking are legion: "I drank a glass of whiskey every day, and in ten days my cold disappeared." "The cause of juvenile delinquency is women's suffrage" ("progressive education," "Prohibition," "repeal of Prohibition," "depression," "prosperity," "jazz," "swing," "rock and roll," "World War I," "World War II," "fear of World War III," and so on).

To cite an actual case of *post hoc* inference, here is a comment about alleged effects of the fine summer school program organized at Rochester, Minnesota for school children. [5]

> There is indication that the program may be having a healthy effect on the entire student body. Recently Rochester senior high students took the Iowa Tests of Educational Development. . . . Results showed the school-wide average to be in the top eight per cent of all senior high schools tested in the United States.

Although the claim of cause and effect is stated somewhat guardedly, the reader is supposed to accept an unjustified conclusion. As far as the description in the article goes, we do not know whether the Rochester students would have scored in the ninety-second percentile before the summer sessions began, or perhaps even higher. Many other factors affect scholastic performance besides summer sessions. One obvious factor is the selected nature of Rochester school children, many of whom are the sons and daughters of doctors and other professional people at the medical center and who may be atypical of school children who take the Iowa tests.

Naturally there is no clear-cut boundary between causal inference and descriptive or predictive.

2. *Prediction.* Predictive inference has been the field of operation for charlatans of all sorts from soothsayers to astrologists and also the domain of amazing feats of accurate prognostication, such as the prediction of of the existence of hitherto unknown planets from their gravitational effects on other planets.

Underlying most prediction are the assumptions that constant factors are in operation, that nature is uniform, and that it is possible to assert with relative assurance that similar combinations of factors in the future will bring about similar results. In the case of reliable subject material such as the chemical elements, it has been possible to predict the discovery of new elements to fill in the periodic table, for example, and to do so with reasonable hope of success. In other domains, such as human personality, the assumption of consistency of factors is less reliable. Our State Department must spend much energy predicting the reactions of Soviet leaders to moves in the political sphere planned by the United States, with limited hope of success. In warfare, the "calculated risk" has been recognized as a necessary element of planning.

Another source of error in prediction is imperfect analogy between past situations with known consequences and present or future events whose outcome we would like to predict. How often we hear the claim that war is at hand because the world situation is "just like" the situation in 1939. These are difficult problems of course, and we do what we can.

3. *Description.* A common type of inductive inference is that in which a description of some phenomenon or condition is obtained. The Gallup poll is one example of a descriptive procedure. The pollsters attempt to arrive at significant descriptions of this sort: "Sixty per cent of the people polled said yes when asked if they approved in general of the president's actions." In chemistry a description is this: "Sodium burns when exposed to oxygen." In each case the truthfulness of the inference depends upon correct interpretation of data obtained through careful sampling processes.

SAMPLING

In inductive inference we are often unable to examine all the data in existence. If, for instance, we wish to determine the color of whales, it is physically impractical to observe every whale in existence. It is insufficient on the other hand to observe one whale, since he may be atypical. So we are reduced to observing some whales and assuming that the remainder are similar. This procedure introduces an amount of uncertainty, so that inferences of this sort have only a certain amount of *probability*. For instance, we may sample one hundred whales, all black, but miss the albinos. This probability of success in describing depends upon the quality of the sampling process used to obtain our computational data.

The basic requirement for a good sample is that it be representative of all the individual items in the universe or population under study. In order to obtain representative samples, the method of *random* sampling is often used. By this method the individual samples are selected by chance, so that no systematic bias can creep into the sampling. Thus, if we are interested in learning the average intelligence of the members of a certain race, it will not do to examine only those members who have gone to college. One random technique would be to arrange an entire group alphabetically by name, or according to height, and select every tenth one for examination.

Failure to obtain random samples has led to many faulty surveys. One of the most famous was the *Literary Digest* poll of 1936. Millions of queries were sent out to people to find out which candidate they favored for president. The mailing list was drawn from telephone directories and lists of auto owners. It happened that the sample of telephone and auto owners systematically favored the Republican candidate, whereas the proportion of Democrats in the population of voters as a whole were not represented proportionally in the sample. The poll predicted a Republican victory, but the Democrat Roosevelt won by a large margin.

Faulty sampling procedures are often found in educational studies. The kind of questionnaire soliciting a voluntary return often introduces a bias factor. In surveys where actual return of the questionnaire can be influenced by the traits of co-operativeness and dependability or by request for responses favorable or unfavorable to an individual, a systematic bias may affect the survey, since those who elect to return the questionnaire may be more on one side of the fence than those who neglect to do so. [6]

The popular human pastime of making hasty generalizations stems from faulty selection of samples or instances from which to make general inferences. Very often *insufficient cases are considered,* as when people denounce a product because of one bad experience with it. Sometimes the *instances observed are not representative* because they are exceptional, striking, or selected according to some bias. In other cases, *contradictory instances are ignored* either because of poor sampling procedure or deliberate prejudgment. Illustrations of poor inference because of these procedures could be given without end. One has only to think of the many rash statements he has heard about members of other racial and national groups to provide himself with many examples.

Statistical methods. When we wish to arrive at numerical descriptions of the samples we study, or when we wish to make inferences which can be quantified in some fashion, various statistical methods are helpful. Because the field of statistics is a complex one, only an intuitive development of some of its most common elements can be presented here. Further readings are suggested in the footnotes.

Generally speaking, statistical inquiries are of *two* types. The *first* type of investigation requires only a description of the samples observed. Measurements of central tendency, such as the arithmetic average or mean, or the "middle figure" or median, or the most frequent figure (mode) reveal an important characteristic of the group. Figures of this sort tell us nothing about an individual member of the group, but they do give a generalized indication of the average accomplishments or charac-

[6] J. P. Guilford, *Fundamental Statistics in Education and Psychology* (New York, McGraw-Hill, 1950), p. 178.

teristics of the group. Descriptions of "spread" or dispersion within the group also are meaningful. For this purpose we may merely report the range of scores, or we may refine this by reporting quartiles or percentiles. More complex but more general descriptions of dispersion are indicated by standard deviations, probable errors, and related measures. Correlations of various sorts describe the extent to which two or more sets of data appear to be related.

By and large, descriptive statistics are descriptive and nothing more. Although they inform us about the characteristics of the group under study, they permit no substantial conclusions based on comparisons of groups or comparisons of individuals within groups. Such conclusions are inferences and must be supported by some general theory of statistical probabilities. (See list of common errors below.)

It is the *second* type of statistical inquiry which is more commonly associated with scientific studies. Ordinarily, we hope by observing a sample to be able to reach conclusions regarding the total population which the sample represents. When we use the data of our sample to obtain information about the total population, we are engaging in inferential statistics and must observe its procedures and limitations. [7] It is equally important to recognize that there are available techniques which permit us to compare averages between two or more groups in order to judge whether one group is truly superior to another, that there are methods to study correlations in order to make plausible inferences concerning the significance of the correlations, that there are available processes to make reasoned comparisons of percentages.

In a world where statistics are so often invoked as crucial evidence, the careful thinker will inquire as to the significance of the data and the logical basis for any inferences drawn from that data. Although this may be an oversimplification, perhaps the amateur statistician may safely limit himself to an understanding of good sampling techniques and a comprehension of the distinction between "chance differences" and differences which are significant when tested by established laws of chance or probability. Without some understanding of statistics, the modern man leaves himself painfully vulnerable to some of the commonest and most blatant forms of deception. [8]

[7] For a thorough, but sometimes technical treatment of statistical inference, see the very excellent volume by H. M. Walker and J. Lev, *Statistical Inference* (New York, Holt, 1953).

[8] For further reading, consult the following:
Cohen and Nagel, *op. cit.*, pp. 151-172, 302-322.
D. Huff, *How to Lie With Statistics* (New York, Norton, 1954).
H. A. Larrabee, *Reliable Knowledge* (Boston, Houghton Mifflin, 1945), pp. 356-472.
Q. McNemar, *Psychological Statistics* (New York, Wiley, 1949).
Walker and Lev, *op. cit.*

Some of the more commonplace errors in the use of statistics are these:

1. *Drawing inferences about individuals from measures of a group,* or vice versa. The average reading score of a certain class does not give us the right to infer much about the reading score of any individual in the group.

2. *Ignoring or misinterpreting factors which influence data used in a statistical study.* A common example is the allegation that since Latin students score high on intelligence tests or do well in college, Latin study was the cause of the success. Actually a more reasonable explanation is that the same factors which induced students to take Latin and allowed them to do well in it contributed to their success in other endeavors. Similar misinterpretations are made about cigarette smoking and ownership of cars among students.

3. *Ignoring the errors usually present in statistical studies.* Intelligence test scores are more often than not misinterpreted, one form of misinterpretation being the attachment of greater confidence in the accuracy of individual scores than they merit.

4. *Making sampling errors,* as described above.

ANALOGY

Analogy, the process of reasoning by comparisons, can be shown to be a kind of inductive procedure, [9] but it is so widely used in common practice that it deserves separate, if brief, treatment. How often we hear reasoning like this: "Conditions in Europe are nearly like those of 1914. We can expect war." Or, "Teachers in Scarsdale, New York, can earn up to $13,000 a year. Our district should adopt a similar scale." The reliability of such analogies as these depends upon the following conditions:

1. The elements of comparison should be real and significant rather than forced or imaginary.
2. There should be numerous points of comparison rather than a few, if possible.
3. There should be no crucial points of difference.

These conditions are rather obvious, but it is amazing how often they are ignored. A noted United States senator was once quoted as saying, "Middle-of-the-road politics is as poorly advised as driving down the middle of the road." This attack on moderate politics, the famous method of the compromise, has a small measure of truth to it, as most poor analogies do. But it ignores the crucial point of difference, namely, that the traffic on a highway is controlled by a convention which rules that vehicles must travel on the right-hand side and by the physical fact that the speed and momentum of motor vehicles render a defiance of this con-

[9] Cohen and Nagel, *op. cit.,* pp. 286-288.

vention automatically disastrous. No such automatic, physical collision occurs, say, when a budget figure somewhere between the high estimate and the low estimate is adopted.

Analogy is also the essence of figurative language, for example, metaphor. This subject is treated in Chapter 10.

In the preceding pages we have briefly touched upon the subject of inference and its components deduction and induction. Vast and difficult as this topic is, a person can hardly begin to command the processes of critical thinking without an understanding of the concepts and procedures merely hinted at in this book. The reader is urged to expand his knowledge in this field by further study of the references quoted.

EVALUATIVE INFERENCES

Difficult problems arise when we try to prescribe procedures for dealing with value judgments, that is, with questions of what is the right thing to do (morals or ethics) and what is beautiful or artistically worthwhile (aesthetics). The scientist in his field reasons about his evidence to find descriptions of *what is* or *could be*. But the person concerned with a value judgment tries to determine *what should be,* a purpose of a different order. Conclusions about physical events can be quite confidently checked, but conclusions about conduct and ideas of beauty are derived from theories resting upon assumptions which cannot be definitively challenged or supported. Some religious creeds, for example, rest upon articles of faith rather than fact.

The problems of ethics and aesthetics have been debated since the days of Plato (*Philebus, Republic, and others*) and Aristotle (*Ethica Nicomachea*). In the course of history satisfactory answers to the basic value questions have not been discovered. We do not pretend to have any new answers, and the ethical and aesthetic question is not our prime interest in this book. But there is a worthwhile distinction which bears upon our critical problem.

Basically, a value judgment involves two processes or levels of thought. The first is the assumption of some governing value system, and the second is the application of this system to individual actions. Thus, a person may adopt fundamentalism, that is, belief in the literal precepts of the Bible, as his guide to conduct. Then for his individual actions he must decide whether each act is in conformity with his fundamental value system. Concerning the choice of a basic value system we have little to say. We cannot prescribe methods for determining whether Buddhism is superior to Mohammedanism or whether modern or classical art and music set superior standards for appreciation. But in the phase of value judgments where individual actions are to be praised or condemned according to basic value systems, many principles of inference enumerated in this chapter apply.

One of the fundamental inferential considerations dealing with values is the principle that basic assumptions should be made explicit or kept in mind. More human time has been wasted in futile argument about details of religious difference than in any other human pursuit we can think of, chiefly because the participants failed to observe that they were arguing from different assumptions.

Another logical consideration is that of consistency, although it is not always decisive in value disputes. There is considerable reason for requiring that what I find moral or beautiful today I also value tomorrow. This does not mean to say that I may not like popular music today and go to a concert of classical music tomorrow, however.

Inductive principles relating to cause-and-effect determination, prediction, sampling, description, and the use of analogy may also play a part as we appraise value evidence and, in a sense, fit it to a system of values.

To illustrate these points, let us consider the value problems of the Amish, a religious sect in eastern and central United States. According to reports, the Amish use no electricity in their homes, do not own automobiles, and dress in very plain, though distinctive, styles. These practices are derived from the literal interpretation of certain passages in the Bible. To dispute this basic creed would be to challenge the entire value system of the Amish which is a problem of the first order (and which we prefer to dodge). To question individual practices, such as the alleged fact that they ride in automobiles, though they do not own them, and use gasoline engines, though not electric ones, is to dispute on a level where common inferential processes may be used. Is an automobile ride contrary to the scriptures or *analogous* to other trivial departures from basic principle? Is a gasoline engine fundamentally different from an electric one? Is its use likely to *cause* dissension over values? These second-order judgments can be made more successfully by the use of common types of inference.

A clear summary of this distinction between determination of basic "Goods" and practical actions is made by Dickinson. [10]

It is the part of Reason, on my hypothesis, to tabulate and compare results. She does not determine directly what is good, but works, as in all the sciences, upon given data . . . noticing what kinds of activity satisfy, and to what degree, the expanding nature of this soul that seeks Good, and deducing therefrom, so far as may be, temporary rules of conduct . . . Temporary rules, I say, because, by the nature of the case, they can have in them nothing absolute and final, inasmuch as they are mere deductions from a process which is always developing and transforming itself.

[10] Goldsworthy Lowes Dickinson, *The Meaning of Good* (1901), pp. 86-87; quoted in Stephen E. Toulmin, *The Place of Reason in Ethics* (Bradford, Percy Lund Humphries and Co., Ltd., for Cambridge University Press, 1953).

A very clear and simply expressed exposition of the role of inference in value matters is to be found in Toulmin's book, just cited. The reader is invited to examine this reference and others suggested by it.

QUESTIONS, EXERCISES, AND REPORTS

1. Inference has been referred to as a "leap in the dark." Why is this a significant area for study? How do you know that your inferences are "any good," that is, valid and reliable? Illustrate.

2. Contrast briefly, with illustrations, systematic inference with unsystematic. What is the bearing of this on our general problem?

3. What is meant by "regulation transforms inference into proof"?

4. State explicitly and illustrate the relation of (a) observation, and (b) experimentation to reasoning.

5. What are some factors which affect one's reasoning process?

   a. Illustrate how judgment may be thrown off because of the misleading nature of prominent characteristics.

   b. Illustrate how subtle-and-difficult-to-observe items may really contain important clues.

   c. How does one eliminate irrelevant items? How aid students to do it?

6. Why does the average citizen not demand proof for your inferences or for those he reads, or produce proof for his own? He will likely say that "one opinion is as good as another" or "everyone is entitled to his opinion." Have you anything to add to this since studying it in Chapter 6?

7. Recall at this point Exercises 13 and 14 from Chapter 5 on hypothesis. Do you wish to add anything to your discussions then?

8. Illustrate from everyday life the use of categorical statements, alternation, and conditions, as used on a simple problem.

9. Illustrate with simple everyday cases any one of the five useful considerations derivable from logic.

10. Illustrate similarly the limitations of formal logic.

11. Illustrate from your own experience, or from observation or reading, the uses and dangers of assumptions.

12. Recall the case of the Mary Celeste, used in Chapter 5. Have you anything to add to your understanding now in the light of this chapter?

13. A classic example from a Sherlock Holmes story may be used here. The account appears in the Unit "A Pattern for Effective Thinking" in Appendix D and hence is not repeated here.

   a. Answer the exercise presented there.

   b. Write a very brief case study in which a pupil known to you is described as was the watch. We will then hand these cases around the class so that each student may interpret the facts and draw inferences which sound reasonable and plausible.

14. The classic type of detective story was an exercise in inference. So also is much real-life detection. Report a case known to you, or read about, with commentary on the inferential process. Such cases may be presented to

the class to allow them to draw the inferences. (The modern-type detective story, "slug 'em and shoot 'em," does not supply any illustrations of thinking ordinarily.)

15. In April of 1930 a Pullman porter was found to be missing. Later his body was found about a quarter of a mile from the railway. He had been tied to a sapling; his skull had been fractured; and there was a deep wound under his left arm. A trail of blood and footprints led from the tracks to the body and back again. No further tracks were found.

The train was going 70 miles an hour at that point and had not stopped for seventeen miles. The car door was not open; but a window was open, and the screen was gone.

Police and coroners jury were unable to advance a single theory (inference) to account for the facts. Other facts were related, but the foregoing gives the essentials. Can you make any reasonable inferences?

16. Illustrate from real life errors resulting from the typical pitfalls of the inductive inference. These errors are observable constantly.

   a. A generalization based on simple enumeration.
   b. A generalization which is descriptive but not explanatory.
   c. Generalizing from a single instance.
   d. Generalizing from insufficient or nontypical cases.
   e. Ignoring contradictory cases.

17. Give illustrations, if you can recall them, of historical experiments which were performed to overcome difficulties due to rarity, subtlety, or fixity of cases so that a valid generalization could be drawn.

Do the same for educational research or from everyday experience if any have been observed by you.

18. Illustrate proper use of any one of the inductive purposes.

19. Illustrate from everyday intercourse any one of the errors made in inferring from statistical data.

20. An archaeologist recently reported that he had uncovered valid evidence supporting the Biblical story of the flood. Without knowing all the details, can you suggest other inferences that might be drawn from his data about sediment, inundation, marks on high ground, and the like?

READINGS WHICH SUPPLEMENT THIS CHAPTER

DEWEY, John, How We Think, rev. ed. (Boston, Heath, 1933).

BLACK, Max, Critical Thinking (Englewood Cliffs, N. J., Prentice-Hall, 1946), Chs. 1, 2, 14, 15, 16.

COHEN, Morris, R., and NAGEL, Ernest, An Introduction to Logic and Scientific Method (New York, Harcourt, Brace, 1934), Chs. 8, 11.

LARRABEE, H. A., Reliable Knowledge (Boston, Houghton Mifflin, 1945), Chs 3, 4, 5.

Readings of a far more technical nature than our presentation here are available in any modern book on logic, or critical thinking, or on scientific methods.

CHAPTER 8

Testing Conclusions: The Final Step

> With what ease do they indulge in daydreams, when they invent
> innumerable worlds and measure the sun, moon and stars, and the
> earth, as though by thumb and thread, and render a reason for
> thunder, winds, eclipses and other inexplicable things, without the
> least hesitation, as though they had been the secret architects of all
> the works of nature or as though they had come down to us from
> the councils of the gods.
>
> ERASMUS *

There are those among us who, as Erasmus hints, have explanations for
everything. Proof or support for the explanation does not disturb these
individuals. The average citizen practically never provides any proof for
his statements or demands any from you for your statements. The citation of an example is regarded as proof. Specific cases and illustrations are
not distinguished from proof. The average citizen is not wholly to blame.
Professors, preachers, salesmen, parents, and confidence men regularly
cite a specific case as if it proved a general principle. This is not because
people are dishonest. It is because they are ordinarily unaware, *first,* of the
necessity for proof and, *second,* of the nature of proof. Many individuals
also discuss problems for which they could never under any circumstances
secure proof themselves. "After all the desire to attain the truth is a later
and relatively undeveloped human motive compared with the more vital
and voluminous motives of social approval." [1]

Once we have concluded any piece of human thinking, it is necessary
to test or prove the conclusion. Checking has been going on, of course, at
all stages—definition of problem, developing hypotheses, gathering data,

* Erasmus (paraphrased and abbreviated).
[1] Morris R. Cohen, quoted in W. G. Ogburn and A. Goldenweiser, *The Social
Sciences* (Boston, Houghton Mifflin, 1927), p. 453.

142

and drawing inferences. The hypothesis which has been carried through to a conclusion gives, when proved, some evidence that the preceding processes have also been correct.

Supplying proof for our wide-ranging statements is, however, imperative. Conclusions on any level are never reliable until "tried out." Dewey states the matter admirably: [2]

> What is important is that every inference be a tested inference; or, (since this is often not possible), that we discriminate between beliefs that rest upon tested evidence and those which do not, and be accordingly on our guard as to the kind and degree of assent or belief that is justified.

To prove a thing means to test it. We often hear it said that "we must put it to the test." The old saw "The exeception proves the rule" *really* means that an exceptional case will truly *test* the rule. Unless a rule accommodates exceptional cases as well as routine ones, usually it is no rule at all. The word *prove* derives from the Old French *prover* which in turn derives from the Latin *probare, to test*. Often in contemporary usage we interpret the saying as indicating that a rule is proved because only a few rare exceptions can be found and thus a large number of nonexceptions exist to corroborate or "prove" the rule.

What constitutes proof? The modern literature on proof is astonishingly meager. Writers on mathematics and the teaching of mathematics have a fair amount of material, but it is naturally on one kind of proof, that accepted for mathematical problems. Books on logic, a few of them, do not carry the word *proof* in the index. Others have accounts of varying length and worth, meager to very good. The nature of legal proof has an extensive and authoritative literature, but this type of proof is not too useful to the average citizen.

Suitable definitions are difficult to frame. We need also to bring in the concepts of test and of evidence in order to define proof.

Proof. The process of establishing a fact or truth; also an operation for testing the accuracy of a previous operation; the guarantee of validity which such a process implies.

Test. A decisive trial, or any method of examining a conclusion to support a proof.

Evidence. Any data, testimony used as a means of proving or supporting the validity of some allegation or conclusion.

Proof is a rather broad term which differs in the way it is used from one kind of problem to another. In geometry, it consists in the logical sequence of statements building up to some conclusion. In the law court, proof is a network of relevant evidence, reference to principles of law, and inferences from the evidence in the particular case to the principle

[2] John Dewey, *How We Think,* rev. ed. (Boston, Heath, 1933), p. 97.

of law. In historical research, proof may consist in the discovery and interpretation of some document or artifact.

Testing in common parlance is the application to a conclusion or
contention already established of some independent trial or special proof.
Thus, the *test* pilot climbs in the airplane which has already been constructed according to rigid principles of aerodynamics and actually flies it
to see in an empirical way what it will do. A test of a principle of physics
may consist in some kind of demonstration by which the conclusions of
the physicist may be put to trial. Of course, the two terms *testing* and
proof are sometimes used loosely and interchangeably.

Evidence derived through any of several means of testing is the basis
for proof. Determination of proof is easier in some areas than others.
Mathematics, the natural sciences, and mechanics are not too difficult, but
the social sciences present serious problems. Variables are more numerous
and often unpredictable when dealing with human relations. The seeker for
proof in the social fields may make the mistake of too strict analysis and
precise measurement for material unsuited to such treatment. He may go
to the other extreme and make broad generalizations which cannot be
easily proved or disproved.

The search for proof. The average citizen, as indicated earlier, has no
inkling of the necessity for having standards of judgment, criteria, postulates, against which to judge his conclusions. The Egyptians, however, hit
upon this idea over 2,000 years ago. We have not done too well in dis-
seminating this idea through education.

The total story of the development of proof and the realization of its
necessity fills many pages and can only be hinted at here. A few of the
outstanding historical events are listed here as illustrations of the long,
rough road which responsible men have followed in the search for proof.

The search may have begun with the Egyptians looking for ways of
determining land boundaries after the annual Nile floods. Geometry
evolved, but even more important was growth of the concept that rules
could be set up to which everyone would agree. The Greek leaders developed geometry to a high degree. As some writer has said, the Greeks "left
off telling tales and began to give reasons" in conceptual terms. About 600
B.C., Thales began asking for proof of the agreed-upon mathematical laws.
He demonstrated proof for six theorems which had been used without
question for years. Pythagoras went further, pointing out that he could
state that a theorem was true or false and that his hearers could do nothing
unless they had some proof. Additions to methods of proof were made from
time to time by Plato, by Aristotle, by Euclid, and by others. Postulates
were laid down, and proof consisted in showing that conclusions followed
logically from the axioms.

The appeal to objective fact and the beginnings of scientific or objective methods are customarily assigned to the seventeenth century, though

the necessary ideas had been developing from the thirteenth century. Galileo (1564–1642) is said to have experimented with falling bodies, measuring their rate of acceleration in 1589. Kepler (1571–1630) offered proof in 1609 that Copernicus had been right—the earth and other planets did move around the sun. Newton (1642–1727) offered proof of the hypothesis of universal gravitation in 1679. The various Newtonian laws stood until modern times when Einstein's hypotheses suggested that revisions were in order. Pages could be filled with developments up to the present day. These few illustrations must suffice to indicate the story. Francis Bacon (1561–1626), the great name in the development of inductive methods based on observation, published his *Novum Organum* in 1620. The inductive method, proof by looking to see, took its place beside the deductive method of determining validity by logical inference from agreed-upon axioms.

The men of the sixteenth and seventeenth centuries made it safer to challenge any so-called absolute truth. They hinted at developments which came later. Proof by demonstrated fact derived from controlled experiments emerged.

Men have used many other methods of seeking proof, but these will not be described in detail since they contributed only indirectly or not at all to modern methods of proof. Men early consulted oracles, soothsayers, and witch doctors whose statements were accepted as proof. Modern man has not entirely deserted this method. Trial by ordeal was common in medieval times. Witches were thrown in the water; and if they floated, they were proved innocent. If they sank, they were proved guilty. Secular and religious authority were accepted as sources of truth. Religious authority for centuries undertook to pronounce on many affairs now regarded as belonging to science. Civil power became the authority for many procedures and beliefs. Appeals have been made to custom and tradition, to personal experience, to trial and error. The methods of organized, systematic, objective inquiry are superior to all of these. [3]

[3] This abbreviated citation of certain highlights must be supplemented through related reading.

Modern popular accounts:

Harold A. Larrabee, *Reliable Knowledge* (Boston, Houghton Mifflin, 1945), Chs. 3, 4, 10-17. Select passages through the index.

James Harvey Robinson, *The Mind in the Making* (New York, Harper, 1921), Chs. 8, 9, 11, 12, 13.

Modern more-systematic accounts:

Wm. A. McCall, *How to Experiment in Education* (New York, Macmilllan, 1923).

Samuel Chester Parker, *A Textbook in the History of Modern Elementary Education* (Boston, Ginn, 1912), Ch. 6.

Daniel S. Robinson, *The Principles of Reasoning*, rev. ed. (New York, D. Appleton, 1930).

Original classic references:

R. L. Ashley, *Early European Civilization* (New York, Macmillan, 1917).

Acceptable modern methods of determining proof. Out of the long, long story so briefly illustrated here, a number of procedures have emerged.

1. *Experimental corroboration as proof.* An experiment is the deliberate setting up of a situation and conditions based on the requirements of the tentative conclusion to see whether the results theoretically indicated by the hypothesis do occur. Experiments, for instance, were set up to test the hypothesis that the democratic operation of a classroom would result in better learning, better interpersonal relations, and in the acquisition of the skills of group thinking. Other hypotheses were that authoritarian management of classrooms or laissez-faire management would result in less learning, poorer interpersonal relations, and no progress in group skills. Class operation went on for a period under the different hypotheses, and results proved all three hypotheses to be correct.

Justifiable acceptance of conclusions comes if the experiments show that the inferred consequences do appear. The experiment must account only for the hypothesis under test and not for other hypotheses. The accepted conclusion is held to be valid until and unless new facts appear which question that validity.

An experiment may show that the conclusion is not verified and, hence, not acceptable. The competent thinker takes this not as a failure but as an indication that the preceding steps in thinking may need reexamination: definition of the problem, developing of hypotheses, gathering data, drawing inferences. The processes used to prove the hypothesis should also come under review.

At the moment, some very provocative experiments are being proposed to test the theory of relativity. This theory has been based on reasoning and on observed facts. One proposal is to build a clock accurate to the second over long periods of years, put it in orbit in outer space, and then compare time signals with an identical clock on the earth. This would give experimental data bearing on the hypothesis that time goes faster or slower at given altitudes—or faster at some, and slower at others. Other ingenious experiments are being suggested for modern theories in

James Creighton, *An Introductory Logic,* 4th rev. (New York, Macmillan, 1920).

Thomas Fowler, *The Elements of Inductive Logic,* 3rd rev. (Oxford, Clarendon Press, 1876).

W. Stanley Jevons, *The Principles of Science, A Treatise on Logic and Scientific Method,* 2nd rev. (London, Macmillan, 1924).

J. Welton, *The Logical Bases of Education* (London, Macmillan, 1919).

F. A. Westaway, *Scientific Method: Its Philosophical Basis and Modes of Application,* 3rd rev. (London, Blackie & Son, 1924).

Matthew T. McClure, *An Introduction to the Logic of Reflection* (New York, Holt, 1925).

R. D. Carmichael, *The Logic of Discovery* (London, Open Court Publishing Co., 1930).

Special reference to relation of deductive and inductive methods.

In above lists: Creighton, Fowler, Jevons, Robinson, D. S., Welton.

physics, as they have also been suggested in the past for what was theory then.

Mill's various methods presented in Chapter 7 on inference can be used to secure a degree of proof as well as to develop hypotheses.

2. *Verification by observation.* Experimental tryout is not always possible. We deduce from the hypothesis, therefore, further events which may be expected to occur if the hypothesis is true, or if it is not. We then observe events as they occur to see if they corroborate or contradict the hypothesis.

Classic illustrations are found in astronomy. Certain observed phenomena, plus a theory of movement of heavenly bodies, indicate that a new planet should be observable at a certain place. Sometimes observation had to wait upon the development of more powerful telescopes, but planets were found by observation where the reasoning said they should appear.

Simpler cases are found in the current scrutiny of schools. Parents and committees often come to school to observe (and thus, verify) whether spelling or arithmetic is being taught as it was in their own school days. Observers visit Russia—and would like to visit Red China—to determine if reported developments there are observable or not.

Even simpler cases occur in such everyday problems as whether to change residence, to take a vacation now or later, to discipline children in various ways, to change positions. Facts from various sources and of varying values are considered, and a decision is made. Events are then observed to see if the decision now acted upon is corroborated or contradicted. The validity of the proof depends upon the ability of the thinker to in-interpret the evidence supplied by the events.

3. *Reasoning.* Often there is no chance to apply a reasoned conclusion, to observe its operation under controlled conditions. Observation of events may be impossible or difficult because of the rarity and subtlety of the corroborating (or contradicting) events or because of the time intervals which may elapse between occurrences. Belief is given to the conclusion on the basis of other facts or beliefs already validated or at least accepted. Many conclusions in scientific fields are of this type, based on reasoning from one belief to another, with no experimental verification at the moment. Histories of science give several such cases.

The important relationship between reasoning and experimental verification was illustrated by the case of the proposed experiment with a clock to check up on the theory of relativity. The relationship to proof by observation was shown in the illustration from astronomy.

Reasoning is checked for internal consistency:

1. Is the reasoned conclusion in accord with systematized knowledge in the given field as at present constituted? Conclusions and beliefs are to be checked against known facts and accepted principles and against recognized

authorities in the absence of demonstrable facts; sources are to be revealed.

2. Is the conclusion in line with the conceptual system in the given field as at present constituted? Conclusions which differ from accepted concepts are usually wrong, but they should be investigated. New discoveries often come from radical theories which challenge the old and accepted conclusions. Cause-and-effect relationship, or other necessary connection, is to be sought.

3. Are assumptions, attitudes, prejudices, opinions, and beliefs explicit or implicit? These should be discussed openly. Opinions should be labeled as such; so also with facts and all subjective data. Thinking out loud often brings assumption and other hidden items into the open.

4. Are the many levels of explanation in any situation made clear?

5. Is open discussion given to disagreement among authorities? Are bases of agreement or disagreement made clear? (Very often dramatizing the implications of two divergent views is very helpful.) Often two views turn out to differ only in trivial consequences and not in important implications.

The teacher may aid learners here by:

1. Holding always for relation of suggested reasons to the problem.

2. Slowing down the processes of generalization, even of hypothesizing, in order to prevent premature judgments while engaged in examining data.

3. Aiding learners to give up untenable views without loss of security, aiding them to see that mistakes, even failure, may lead to new and better hypotheses and conclusions.

Other procedures can be added.

The checking of reasoning obviously necessitates using all the points developed in preceding chapters in Part II. The list here is an illustrative sampling. Readers may wish to develop lists under other organizations.

4. *Legal proof.* [4] The hypothesis in any legal case is the allegation made by the prosecution. Proof must be built up through a complicated pattern of rules of law, of rules of evidence; inference from evidence; conclusion, and establishment of an analogy between the rules of law and the evidence in the case. Proof of guilt or innocence is established. "See Chapter 6 on legal facts.)

The kind of proof depends upon the nature of the problem. The teacher should be aware of the fundamental kinds of problems under attack since the mode of proof varies. In physical science courses we can have experimental proof. In social sciences the problem may be normative, historical, critical, or other. The following outline, not intended to be exhaustive, gives examples of different kinds of proof possible for various kinds of problems.

[4] A considerable literature exists dealing with legal proof which is in striking contrast to discussions of proof in other fields. The two references here are samples:

Albert S. Osborn, *The Problem of Proof* (Newark, N. J., Essex Press, 1926). Detailed discussion of scores of types of evidence. Good bibliography.

Erle Stanley Gardner, *The Court of Last Resort* (New York, William Sloane Associates, 1952). Excellent discussion of famous cases which have been reopened. Crux is usually the evidence and type of proof used in court.

KIND OF PROBLEM	POSSIBILITY OF PROOF

Scientific

Does the battery additive DX-2 prolong the life of a battery?

Experiment: Comparing life of batteries with and without DX-2.

What support is there for the theory of relativity?

Tests, designed to check theory empirically.

Is the Salk vaccine effective?

Statistical survey of incidence of polio in children with and without shots.

Were the Mesa Verde buildings built about 1019?

Independent test using Carbon 14 method.

Normative

Will integration be successful in Little Rock?

Try out, with results judged according to agreed (?) norms.

Mathematical

How can we prove that the interior angles of a triangle total 180°?

Logical deductions from accepted premises which themselves appear compatible with the real world.

Empirical measurement of various triangles.

Historical

How much tribute did the Athenians collect in 447 B.C.?

Estimated figure corroborated by discovery of tablet bearing exact figures.

Legal

Who killed Cock Robin?

Confession, corroborated by circumstantial evidence.

Practical (for example, low-grade scientific)

Is this radio tube bad?

Test it, or replace it.

Aesthetic, ethical

Is this painting or act of high value?

Value judgments in terms of stated norms. One possible, though debatable, test of values is survival. Does it last?

Critical

The re-examination of evidence and proof in any of the above constitute a critical problem.

Conditions necessary for testing or proof. First, the persons doing this must be competent to carry on the necessary processes. The persons testing for proof may or may not be those who carried on the original inquiry. *Second,* the plan of procedure must correspond to the conditions and assumptions of the original procedure. *Third,* the results must be consistent within the given framework. *Fourth,* the proof must account adequately for the hypothesis under test and not for other hypotheses or conclusions.

Implications for the teacher and education. We cannot prove or disprove every statement of whatever type we make, hear, or read. Time does not permit. Education does have certain clear responsibilities growing out of the need for proof and out of the impossibility of always getting it. *First,* teaching should always bring to students an awareness of the need for testing whenever testing can be done, the need for getting proof wherever possible. *Second,* we should develop skills in the operation of various techniques for testing. Skills in analysis and discrimination must also be developed so that tested conclusions can be distinguished from assumptions, mere assertions of opinion, from guesses. *Third,* there should be developed a sincere attitude of preference for conclusions that have valid bases of proof and, *per contra,* an attitude of rejection toward those which do not have such bases. *Fourth,* we should develop the belief, recognition, and attitude that tests and proof are always tentative and subject to revision.

QUESTIONS, EXERCISES, AND REPORTS

1. How would you prove or test the following conclusions previously reached (but not necessarily true)?
   a. A pound of feathers falls faster than a pound of stone.
   b. A spider has six legs. (Compare Aristotle.)
   c. Pupils learn better when room temperatures are 72° than when they are 80°.
   d. Antihistamines effectively reduce cold symptoms.
   e. *Pi* is about 3 and 1/7.
   f. Geraniums grow better in damp soil.
   g. The closed shop is unconstitutional.
   h. The old Viking boat found underground in Stockholm dates from the period 800–900 A.D.

2. What do you do in problematic situations when you can find no answer in which you can believe, that is, no answer with sufficient proof? (Give more than one alternative.)

3. Recall once again the discussion of Herodotus and the Nile; of Galileo and his early experiments. Do you wish to add anything to previous discussions?

Examine similarly the cases in Black, (see "Readings" below), Chs. 1, 2, 14.

4. At the 33rd annual conference, 1959, of the Secondary Education Board, an organization of the private preparatory schools, Dr. J. F. Gummere, secretary of the board and headmaster of the William Penn Charter School in Philadelphia, made an interesting statement as reported in the *New York Times*: "The independent school is not plagued by certification requirements for teachers, which too often sacrifice knowledge for theory. The teacher who is educated according to our standards is the answer to the whole question of education. . . . [We have] freedom from bureaucratic control." (Other remarks were made at the conference concerning the superior teaching in independent schools.)

The statement, although given as a conclusion, is actually a hypothesis.

a. How would you go about getting proof supporting or denying the hypothesis? (Break it up into its several parts first.)

b. The private schools present along with excellent teaching cases of teaching so bad as to be incredible. Might the same hypothesis account for the bad teaching as well as the good? If you think so, what becomes of the statement about good teaching? If you think not, explain.

c. Every political subdivision in the world, save one, has some form of teacher certification, as they do for physicians and surgeons, lawyers, architects, and others. This does not prove that certification is correct or deny that there are abuses here and there in administering certification. But it does raise some interesting questions.

(1) Is the age-long development of certification all wrong, and are the private schools right?

(2) Advance arguments showing how absence of certification would make for better teachers in general? Poorer?

(3) Cite specific evidence that the private schools might indeed be better off than they are if certification held.

5. If you recall any classic experiments or cases where proof was badly needed and eventually secured, report for class discussion.

READINGS

BLACK, Max, *Critical Thinking* (Englewood Cliffs, N. J., Prentice-Hall, 1946), Chs. 1, 2, 13, 14.

COHEN, Morris R., and NAGEL, Ernest, *An Introduction to Logic and Scientific Method* (New York, Harcourt, Brace, 1934), Ch. 11.

DEWEY, John, *How We Think*, rev. ed. (Boston, Heath, 1933), Chs. 6, 7, 11.

CHAPTER 9

The Role of Concepts in Thinking

Empirical science, we noted earlier, does not aim simply at a description of particular events: it looks for general principles which permit their explanation and prediction. And if a scientific discipline entirely lack such principles, then it cannot establish any connections between different phenomena: it is unable to foresee future occurences, and whatever knowledge it offers permits of no technological application, for all such application requires principles which predict what particular effects would occur if we brought about certain specified changes in a given system. It is, therefore, of paramount importance for science to develop a system of concepts which is suited for the formulation of general explanatory and predictive principles.

The vocabulary of everyday discourse, which science has to use, at least initially, does permit the statement of generalizations, such as that any unsupported body will fall to the ground; that wood floats on water, but that any metal sinks in it; that all crows are black; that men are more intellectual than women; etc. But such generalizations in everyday terms tend to have various shortcomings: (1) their constituent terms will often lack precision and uniformity of usage (as in the case of "unsupported body" and "intellectual," etc.); and, as a consequence, the resulting statement will have no clear and precise meaning; (2) some of the generalizations are of very limited scope (as, for example, the statement dealing only with crows) and thus have small predictive and explanatory power (compare in this respect the generalization about floating in water with the general statement of Archimedes' principle); (3) general principles couched in everyday terms usually have "exceptions," as is clearly illustrated in our examples.

In order to attain theories of great precision, wide scope, and high empirical confirmation, science has therefore evolved, in its different branches, comprehensive systems of special concepts, referred to by technical terms. Many of these concepts are highly abstract and bear little resemblance to the concrete concepts we use to describe the phenomena of our everyday experience. Actually, however, certain connections must obtain between the two classes of concepts; for science is ultimately intended to systematize the data of our experience, and this is possible only if scientific principles, even when couched in the most esoteric terms, have a bearing upon, and thus are conceptually connected with, statements reporting in "experiential terms" available in everyday language what had been established by immediate observation.

CARL G. HEMPEL*

Concepts were invented by man for describing the world around him. Very early man discovered that some objects, events, processes, and regions have similar characteristics. He then grouped the various phenomena in terms of the discovered similarities on the basis of size, weight, location in time or space, causation, function, and others. Concepts range from ideas about very simple things to high-level abstractions, rather far removed from the object level. Thinking, progress, and development in all fields of human endeavor rest upon the accuracy of our concepts.

Man also invented symbols for conveying the meaning of concepts. Early symbols were quite closely related to the original objects, such as cave drawings, early picture writing, hieroglyphics. Modern language systems range from relatively simple to quite complex. The extensive use of symbols is a major characteristic of modern cultures.

The concepts and the symbols serve communication but also are vital to reasoning and to the discovery of new relationships. Service in reasoning was illustrated by the cases in Chapter 1; also by Archimedes in stating a new relationship regarding objects, force, and water displaced; and again by Einstein and his theory of energy. Economy is also seen when hundreds of objects, colors, and living organisms can be reduced to a small number of categories.

The long quotation from Hempel, above, is included because it bears on several important points. The necessity for concepts has already been illustrated in previous chapters and is summarized again below. An important additional point is the emphasis on (1) the shortcomings of everyday concepts based on immediate experience, and (2) the necessary relation between our first, evolving, more-concrete concepts and the final, validated concepts. The average citizen is prone to trust his immediate "common-sense" concepts and to condemn others as "theory." Individuals are found also who insist on "common-sense" concepts based on limited, fragmentary experience even when these are flatly contradicted by valid concepts based on extensive investigation. These points were briefly touched upon earlier in Chapter 6. One other point is of importance here.

* Carl G. Hempel, "Fundamentals of Concept Formation in Empirical Science," *International Encyclopedia of Unified Science*, Vol. II, No. 7 (Chicago, University of Chicago Press, 1952), pp. 20-21. A basic treatment, but too difficult for beginning students. Excellent for advanced students with some scientific background.

We cannot think well in any field of knowledge without knowledge of the systematic concepts on which that field rests. Advanced levels in any discipline are based on complex, specialized, often hard-to-understand concepts. Illustrations from any field, used in this volume, are deliberately limited to less-difficult concepts, as is necessary with beginners. Hempel presents the use of concepts in everyday thinking and the scientific systematization of concepts as well when he shows that concepts enable us to connect, explain, and identify events and to predict what may happen next.

All fields, as Hempel indicates, have systems of basic concepts which have been verified in greater or lesser degree. The most important thing, in fact, to be learned in any field—biology, chemistry, geography, meteorology, medicine, anthropology—is the system of concepts on which the field rests. Anthropology is included in the list to indicate here that the social fields are, despite differences in the nature of data and controls, slowly evolving basic concepts.

James long ago stated the opinion that the best-educated man was he who had the largest store of general meanings. Russell recently stated this cogently:[1] "The clarity and completeness of a child's concepts are the best measure of his probable success in school learning because meaning is fundamental to such learning. The adult's concepts determine pretty well what he knows, what he believes, and thus in large part what he does."

Definition of a concept. Some writers make very heavy going in defining a concept. This is probably necessary in technical fields and for advanced thinking. Simple definitions can be made which tell us what we need to know:

A concept is a defined idea or meaning fixed by, and as extensive as, the term used to designate it.

A concept is the amount of meaning a person has for any thing, person, or process.

A concept is a suggested meaning which has been detached from the many specific situations giving rise to it and provided with a name.

A concept is a logical construct capable of interpersonal use.

A concept is a word or other symbol which stands for the common property of a number of objects or situations.

Concepts are established meanings on which we can rely with assurance. They have a verbal form as well as a mental and physical; for instance, *democracy* is a word used to refer to the idea of democracy, which in turn is about some real situation. There is danger of verbalism when a person confuses the verbal with the mental kind of concept, or with the event itself. Certain incorrect teaching methods, also described later, are

[1] David H. Russell, *Children's Thinking* (Boston, Ginn, 1956), p. 120. This book contains the best summary to date of concept formation and use by children. Chapters 5 and 8 should be read in connection with the present treatment. These will be referred to again later.

likely to develop considerable confusion between real understanding, grasp of meaning, and mere word saying. Concepts based solely on reading or listening are not as reliable as those based on varied real experience.

Basic concepts in physics include mass, energy, work, light, heat, and sound. In mathematics currently there is much emphasis upon meaning rather than on manipulation only. Concepts include, fraction, integer, whole number, size, ratio, quantity, and the like. The social fields use such concepts as monopoly, socialist, public opinion, capitalism, conservative, standard of living, nationalism and internationalism, conservation, community, basic needs, and interdependence. Geography uses latitude, longitude, zone, region, and others.

The value and use of concepts. Their immediate use has been demonstrated in the several illustrations of thinking given previously. There is more to it, however.

1. *Concepts give us a relatively stable, relatively permanent system of knowledge.* A vast array of facts, a great collection of generalizations, particularly if on different levels, would be confusing. It could not even be remembered. Knowledge which is interrelated, however, can be sorted out and grouped. Everything which may describe, explain, or otherwise enlighten us about force, heat, latitude, acid, capitalism, or any other topic may be gathered up by the mind and grouped. This gives us the concept, a psychological construct. Major and minor aspects are discriminated and arranged accordingly. The knowledge thus grouped can be recalled and used because it is systematized.

Basic treatments in any field will reveal a systematic statement of concepts with related knowledge subsumed under proper headings. An illustration of serious error in this process was revealed through examination of a number of high school texts in physics. The concept *air* was used as a guide. Nearly every fact in the whole range of physics was found placed under air in one text or another. Air was presented as a subpoint under nearly every other major topic in one text or another. The writers of these texts had no clear understanding of the basics or of interrelation of knowledge in the very field they were presenting.

Concepts are, of course, as already indicated, subject to change as new facts are discovered. Another type of change in meaning must be noted which is not due to new knowledge. Change in meaning is often introduced in the heat of argument or other discussion. Sometimes this is an honest mistake, the speaker not being clearly aware that he has shifted. Sometimes, unfortunately, the shift is deliberate and dishonest for the purpose of misleading someone.

2. *Class concepts and abstractions enable us to generalize.* This is a great saving of time and effort. Great numbers of specific cases are covered which otherwise might have to be referred to individually. This enables us:

    a. To carry understanding quickly from one thing to another.
    b. To identify individuals, thus placing them within the system.
    c. To supplement our knowledge of any specific thing through drawing on the total connotation of the concept.

    3. *Concepts provide a framework and guideposts for thinking.* Each of the examples in preceding chapters illustrated the part played by concepts in thinking. The Mesa Verde story showed a meteorologist using known concepts from his field and from dendrochronology. The answer to the riddle of the buildings depended upon use of these concepts. The case of the toad in the cornerstone, humorous as it was in part, illustrates the use of concepts which settled the matter with finality. The children's solution to the playground problem was tentative. Concepts enabled them to set up a policy which would then be tried out in experience.

    When Darwin's evolutionary hypothesis was announced, a contemporary scholar said that the hypothesis, if demonstrated (and he thought it could be demonstrated), would destroy the value of all the natural history museums in Europe. Skeletons and animals had been grouped on concepts of relationship which were destroyed by the new evolutionary hypothesis. The commentary on Darwin's hypothesis speaks of "destroying the value of the museums" *as then arranged.* Suspended judgment is always a characteristic of good thinking; but occasionally scholars, even some prominent ones, are so reluctant to see their present ideas "overthrown" or "destroyed" that they resist new data and new hypotheses. It has been said that the Dead Sea Scrolls of recent discovery were not welcomed at first by a certain few scholars who were reluctant to see their comfortable structures of thought "overthrown" or at least partially reconstructed. The attitude of these scholars was inimical to proper thinking about basic concepts. New facts constantly refine concepts.

    A fifth-grade teacher, to give an everyday illustration of concept use, showing a sand table made by her children was somewhat taken aback when a parent remarked, "It would have been better, I think, if the upland animals had been grouped in typical terrain, the plains animals, the river animals, for example, similarly. As it is, you have them all living together." The teacher said in some embarrassment, "Why do you know—that's what the children kept saying"! The children had a better grasp of certain concepts than had the teacher. Usable concepts at the term level here would include river animals, mountain animals, upland country, and perhaps even habitat could be introduced. Concepts on the proposition level, "animals which live together should be grouped together," "sand table models should be like real life," would be appropriate.

    Concepts are far more important in everyday thinking than is sometimes realized. A good deal of everyday behavior is necessarily reduced to habits and routines. But sometimes habits and routines may be insufficient for meeting a new situation, that is, adapting behavior to a dynamic, changing society which produces these new situations quite regularly in everyday life. Concepts are the instruments which enable us to adapt behavior to situations. The many meanings and possible "cues" to adjustment contained in a concept give the individual many choices. Concepts common to many everyday problems are honesty, courtesy, civility, the Golden Rule, selfish interest, greed, competition, co-operation, common good, and others.

Concepts have use and importance far beyond everyday affairs. Valid concepts are necessary for understanding the social, economic, and political life around us. Included here would be such important concepts as balance of power, favorable trade balance, free trade, protective tariff, mercantilism, capitalism, socialism, communism, coexistence, treaty, barter, international banking, and many others.

The validity and proper use of concepts might play a basic part in the safety of our country and society. Concepts can be wrong, muddled, even stupid; but they are still concepts and affect our thinking. History shows several cases in which basic concepts, particularly in religion or in social relationships, have retarded whole societies and insured their backwardness. Examples are caste in India, ancestor worship in China, the master race idea in several societies. Segregation, or blacks-must-be-separate, is an issue in two great countries at the moment. The concept of a class society is in contrast with the concept of upward mobility. Many contrasting concepts making for better civilizations could be cited.

Races and nationalities sometimes called backward are often the victims of stronger nations which hold concepts of colonialism and exploitation, often camouflaged by concepts of manifest destiny, white man's burden, and God-given dominion over palm and pine. Many believe that the backward peoples, so-called, are inherently less intelligent than the people of more advanced civilizations. This is a serious error; intelligence is distributed among all peoples. Children in our own society are sometimes judged to be dull or backward on the basis of an intelligence test which was not adapted to the children's experiential background and social class beliefs.

Concepts which do not grow out of reality are dangerous instruments. People act on the basis of "ideas in their heads," but the actions take place in a real, objective world outside their heads. Clashes are often disastrous, sometimes fatal, to those who adhere to ideas in their heads which are flatly contradicted by facts in the world. A concept that is retained in the face of reality becomes a stereotype but loses none of its power over thinking. Havelock Ellis phrased this well: [2]

We cannot remain consistent with the world save by growing inconsistent with our own past selves. The man who consistently—as he supposes "logically"

[2] Havelock Ellis, *The Dance of Life.* Any edition, preface.

—clings to an unchanging opinion is suspended from a hook which has ceased to exist. I thought it was she, and she thought it was me, and when we came near it weren't neither one of us—that metaphysical statement holds, with a touch of exaggeration, a truth we must always bear in mind concerning the relation of subject and object.

We all react to the crucial problems of the day—political, social, or economic—in terms of the concepts in our minds at the given time. We may vote for men in key positions for reasons that are trivial or are of profound import. The extent of our concepts and our insight into the situation determines our reactions.

Misnaming concepts and confusing one concept with another are serious errors. Two brief illustrations from the field of professional education are given, but the difficulty appears in all fields, particularly in popular discussion. A college catalogue recently listed a course titled: "Administration in Urban Cities." Here indeed is confusion compounded. Concepts, as indicated later, are first formed, the idea is developed, and then a name is attached to the mental picture. The name *city* is attached to a well-known idea or concept: many people living together in an incorporated municipality under various forms of government and with certain other conditions and conventions which could be listed. Someone here made a curious error in adding the concept *urban* which means belonging or pertaining to a city. It is difficult, if not impossible, to figure out what, if anything, went on in the mind of the person who arrived at the term *urban cities*. The illustration is unusual and of trivial import but illustrates a common error in everyday discourse, namely, misnaming concepts and the careless attaching of names to ideas.

A truly serious detrimental error is seen in the widespread misuse of the concept and name *workshop* when discussing teacher education. The term has suffered from the unhappy tendency in education to seize on a new term and apply it to whatever one is doing. Leaders in the field are unanimous in presenting a justifiable concept of a workshop and in condemning sharply the "bandwagon" thinking which applies the *name* workshop indiscriminately to other well-defined concepts such as panels, group discussions, conferences, and committee meetings. Old-fashioned institute-lecture sessions with no participation of any kind by the audience have been labeled workshops. The workshop came into teacher education in 1936 and had been used in other fields for decades if not for centuries. The concept set forth in all fields, and specifically in education, has been consistently supported by all writers. [3]

A workshop is just what the name implies, a shop in which work is accomplished. Problems from real situations are brought in by the participants. Objective materials are produced in answering these problems. To

[3] An excellent literature is available, chiefly in pamphlets and in the periodicals.

label otherwise-legitimate concepts and procedures as workshops is shoddy thinking. To name an institute-lecture program a workshop has been called a *reductio ad absurdum*. To label a one-day conference a workshop is a reduction beyond absurdity and approaches intellectual bankruptcy. A misuse which defies comment is that of a legislative committee which announced "a citizens' workshop on the tax program on Thursday from 9:15 to 11:30 A.M." A state Parent-Teacher Association convention announced that while shortening the total program they had protected the Monday morning workshop by lengthening it twenty minutes. The Committee on Diagnostic Reading Tests, Inc., holds annually various excellent and useful meetings but names them indiscriminately. Half-day or single-day sessions devoted to reading research papers are named "workshops." Commenting on the indiscriminate naming, Dr. Frances Triggs, secretary for the Committee, says that it is silly to judge a meeting by its name. A half-day spent discussing research papers is enough to make marked gains in understanding. Correct, but that is not what a workshop does. Naming a hatrack a hayrake will not enable it to do the work of a hayrake. Numerous college catalogues list "one-day workshops."

The concepts *workshop, conference, symposium, panel,* and *group discussion* each have their own meaning, characteristics, processes, and goals. The goals to be achieved in a workshop cannot be touched upon, let alone achieved, in a one-day symposium.

This extended discussion of workshop naming is given *first* because it is, sadly, too typical of many similar blunders in educational discussion, and *second* because of the evils such errors bring. *First* it gives aid to the enemies of professional educators who assert that educators are not too well educated and are careless thinkers. *Second,* it perpetuates and compounds confusion in a field which very much needs to clarify its concepts and labels. *Third,* and worst of all, misapplication in naming and using the workshop concept prevents the real workshop from emerging. When the name is applied to the very outmoded processes which the workshop was designed to replace, then indeed, Time marches backward.

The meaning of meaning. Meaning as the content of concepts has been mentioned several times, so perhaps we had better define or describe it. What is meaning, and how does it develop? Where does meaning come from in the first place? How does meaning get associated with words? In analyzing these and similar questions we enter an area in which much spade work remains to be done. Advanced scholars are still engaged in controversy over the meaning of meaning. The importance of ultimate definition cannot be denied; nor can differences between experts on this be disregarded. A simple definition, but not oversimplified, can be set up for everyday use. The authors of the famous book, *The Meaning of Meaning,* state that the word *meaning* is used by everyone everywhere, but that its own meaning is not well defined. [4] Another writer expresses pessimism about defining meaning and believes that any discussion of symbols and meanings is "headed straight for a fog bank." [5] Nevertheless, a sensible working definition must be set up.

Meaning is the total significance for any thing, person, process, or situation built up by an individual as he has experiences with it. Meaning is the grouping of ideas, knowledges, beliefs, feelings, and impressions of any and all kinds attached to the item.

Meanings differ according to circumstances, usually involving a selection from the total meaning available. Considerable confusion in thinking results from failure to take this into account. Chapter 10 on words will develop this matter further.

How do meanings arise and become stable enough to be recorded in the dictionary? [6] The average person assumes that meanings are created full blown by dictionary makers. Needing a meaning, you turn to this source; but the dictionary, an indispensable tool, cannot supply meanings *in toto* or for a given situation. Some further detail will be given in the chapter on words.

Meanings arise and are refined through one or more of the following methods:

1. Meanings are determined by direct and continuous experience. These are the literal or sense meanings and are fairly specific.

2. Meanings are determined by reflection upon experience, by abstracting and interrelating various phases of experience.

3. Meanings can be derived from "nonexperience." Certain abstract words, as explained in Chapter 10 on words, are removed from the concrete level. They are theoretic constructs made up from formulas, or from consideration of ideal but nonexistent conditions. Meanings of this type are found in mathematics, for instance, and with social or political "fictions" or abstractions. Non-Euclidean geometry, for instance, in its beginnings had no connection with reality but did have meaning. Today it does have use in explaining certain phases of the real world.

The general process is through discrimination, then generalization, with symbolization appearing as maturity increases. Meaning and concepts develop slowly out of many experiences as indicated above. First, some gross feature is discriminated and used as a core; then, generalization ap-

---

[4] C. K. Ogden and I. A. Richards, *The Meaning of Meaning* (New York, Harcourt, Brace, 1938 and 1953), Ch. 9. Difficult reading.

[5] Frank Lorimer, *The Growth of Reason* (New York, Harcourt, Brace, 1929), p. 72.

[6] There are two points involved here: (1) the development of meaning, and (2) the attachment of meanings to words. We are concerned here with the first point. The second will be presented in the following chapter on words.

pears to broaden the meaning as more experiences occur; and finally, words
are used to clarify, to extend, and to communicate meanings.

*First in the development of meaning is the discrimination of things,
persons, processes, and other items from the immediate experience.* A baby
learns through repeated experience that certain sights and sounds *mean*
that he will soon get a bottle or warm food. Other activities *mean* that he
is going out in his perambulator. *Meaning* in the accepted sense is probably not present at this stage. All that an observer can do is infer that
"bottle" equals "nice-taste-warm-good-mama-smiling-no-pain-in-tummy-
sleepy." Repeated experiences, particularly if varied, eventually carry the
baby well beyond these beginnings. As he explores his world, examining
and manipulating everything he can seize, he learns meanings or concepts
for *soft, hard, will-roll, sharp, will-cut,* and many others. The baby who
laboriously develops a concept for *bottle* eventually grows up to achieve
meanings, concepts, and symbols for *food, hungry, eat, taste, balanced diet,
eat-your-vegetables, vitamins, calories, reduce-your-hips.*

The acquisition of language speeds up the process since explanation
and illustrations can be described. Asking questions as soon as language is
under control further improves the process of achieving meaning. At first,
both the core of the meaning and the language are very specific and limited.
Students will enjoy at this stage the book by Ruth Krauss, *A Hole Is To
Dig,* which gives a collection of the limited and specific concepts possessed by young children: "Feet are to put shoes on," "A nose is to blow,"
and many others.

Generalizing from experiences is eventually followed by discrimination between and within experiences. A concept includes necessary items
and excludes those not significant for the meaning. [7]

*The second level in developing meanings is more precise, sensory dis-
crimination within a pattern, plus increasing use of words.* There is more
deliberate analysis of the immediate stimulus field, together with recall and

---

[7] For a detailed description of the various stages in development of meaning see:

William H. Burton, *Reading in Child Development* (Indianapolis, Ind., Bobbs-
Merrill, 1956). Ch. 2 is entirely devoted to this topic. Parts of Chs. 8 and 9 deal
with meaning-as-related-to-words. Two-page bibliography on research in development
of meaning, concepts, and their relation to thinking.

Paul McKee, *The Teaching of Reading in the Elementary School* (Boston,
Houghton Mifflin, 1948), Ch. 3.

Wm. S. Gray, ed., *Promoting Growth Toward Maturity in Interpreting What Is
Read,* Supplementary Educational Monographs, No. 74 (Chicago, University of
Chicago Press, 1951).

Wm. S. Gray, ed., *Reading in Relation to Experience and Language,* Supplementary Educational Monographs, No. 58 (Chicago, University of Chicago Press,
1944).

Ogden and Richards, *op. cit.* (1953 ed.). Difficult reading.

Ruth Krauss, *A Hole Is to Dig: A First Book of Definitions* (New York,
Harper, 1952).

Books by Stuart Chase, S. I. Hayakawa, and H. R. Huse, listed elsewhere, are
also of value.

analysis of related past experience, plus aid from the experiences of others. This will not be illustrated in detail as it is well known to observant persons and can be seen in everyday experience. (See also Exercise No. 6.)

The third level clarifies and extends meanings and creates new abstract ones, chiefly through use of language. Emphasis in early stages is on first-hand experience. Many valuable meanings are achieved through interaction with language symbols, oral, printed, or written words. Eventually, as indicated earlier, meanings can be derived from "nonexperience." Listening and reading are added to first-hand experience as avenues to meaning and concept formation. Functional language study is an important part of concept development, whereas the neglect of language in home and school contributes to retardation of such learning. While words can contribute mightily to the development of meaning, it is also true that words can be a real detriment to such learning. Words not within the learner's experience or vocabulary, words with odd meanings, can all confuse learners at any age and prevent concept development. The school has the important task of aiding learners to achieve and use concepts in thinking while at the same time avoiding the development of verbalisms.

There is more to it than these brief paragraphs indicate, but this should enable students to proceed at this point. Extended reading is indicated in the Bibliography. Exercises at the chapter end will provide for extension of the treatment here.

The school and concept development. Obviously the development of concepts is a major task of general education as well as a part of training in thinking. The following summary of principles may be of aid to teachers:

1. Concepts are usually achieved incidentally to the pursuit of an interest, problem, or purpose of some sort in real life.

2. Concepts may be sought through vicarious experience by individuals of wide experience and of maturity.

3. Concepts, other things being equal, are more accurate if based upon many varied experiences.

4. Concepts are clarified and extended through analysis, reflection, generalization, and discrimination. These processes are stimulated when a person finds that his concepts do not work in new situations, when he encounters different concepts, when someone challenges his concepts.

5. Concepts are not achieved quickly or at a given time. They are never fixed or final; the process of discrimination and generalization goes on continuously.

6. Concepts are achieved through an active dynamic process, not through a formal or so-called "logical" process.

How do the principles affect teaching methods and the program of instruction? What can the teacher do every day to assist learners in concept development?

1. Learners should be provided with as rich and varied environments as circumstances permit. The school must often compensate for a meager neighborhood environment.

2. Learning situations and activities should be provided to make it possible for learners to come into contact with numerous and vivid, clear-cut examples of things, persons, processes, and relationships for which concepts are being achieved.

3. The examples of things, persons, processes, and relationships should be met so far as possible through direct experience. The direct experience should be supplemented by vicarious experience obtained by means of motion pictures, radio and television programs, dramatizations, lectures, pageants, and many types of printed materials.

4. Learners should be stimulated to reflect upon and to analyze experiences, illustrations, meanings, and the process of developing concepts. Reflection and analysis are almost certain to result if the learning situations are lifelike and meaningful to the learners.

5. Learners should be encouraged to state their understanding (meaning growing into concept) in simple everyday terms, as far as possible. This is a simple direct test for the possession of meaning; a verbalist (see "Verbalisms" below) cannot state meanings in everyday words (see No. 7 below).

6. Learners should be encouraged to illustrate concepts with specific situations drawn from their own experience. (Again, a verbalist cannot respond in this manner.)

7. Learners should be encouraged to express concepts, particularly those that are somewhat hard to put into words, in a variety of ways in addition to verbal statements—as, for example, drawing pictures, making models, using formulas, carrying on dramatizations. (Often a pupil says, "I know that, but I cannot explain it." When this occurs the teacher should give him the opportunity to demonstrate his understanding by any means that he may choose. If he cannot express "what he knows" in some manner or other, the teacher should assume he does not know.)

8. Learners should be encouraged to evaluate several accounts of the same event, process, motive, or act which differ somewhat, or may even be contradictory, and to derive an explanation which can be defended.

9. Learners should be encouraged to explain and evaluate critically their own concepts and the processes through which these were developed, to give arguments in support of these concepts and against conflicting concepts.

10. Learners should be taught to avoid meaningless repetition of words that they have read or heard. (See "Verbalisms" below.)

11. Learners should be studied through observation, interviews, personality tests, and the like to determine their experiential backgrounds, tendencies, attitudes, and interests. The information thus gained should be used in making adjustments to individual differences and needs.

Levels of concepts. The purpose of the teacher is to help the child develop increasingly widening concepts and help him utilize these in his further thinking. An example of this is from *ship* to *transportation* to *interdependence*.[8]

Even a concept such as *ship* is not simple. The teacher must always make decisions as to the phases which are essential for understanding. When one thinks of a ship one thinks that:

It floats on water.
It carries people and goods.
It is run by machine.
It takes men to operate a ship.
There are different kinds of ships for different purposes.

These statements represent the simplest level of a concept. A somewhat more complicated level would include all the foregoing plus recognizing and solving problems, thinking, reasoning, generalizing, and seeing relationships. For example:

While ships carry people and goods they are slower than airplanes. If a man wished to cross the ocean rapidly would he use a plane or a ship? How would you send an automobile, a diamond ring, medicine, badly needed in another country?

A still more complicated conceptual level includes all the foregoing plus attitudes of weighing values, making practical personal decisions, predicting future events, and estimating possible outcomes.

Actually, the questions used on the second level involved the relationship between such concepts as ship, airplane, size, and speed. To be sure that a concept is thoroughly understood there must be considerable development and use of the concept on the second level. Simple beginnings on the second level can be made even in the first grade.

Bradfield and Moredock present a good statement showing the types of activities teachers may use to aid learners' progress toward ever higher levels of concepts.[9]

Level   I. Imitating, duplicating, repeating.
Level   II. Level I plus recognizing, identifying, remembering, recalling, classifying.
Level III. Levels I and II plus comparing, relating, discriminating, reformulating, illustrating.
Level IV. Levels I, II, III plus explaining, justifying, predicting, estimating, interpreting, making critical judgments, drawing inferences.
Level   V. Levels I, II, III, IV plus creating, discovering, formulating new hypotheses, new questions and problems.

Serious errors in aim and method of teaching occur to the detriment of concept formation. These appear everywhere. They are even encouraged

[8] J. Murray Lee and Dorris M. Lee, *The Child and His Curriculum*, 3rd ed. (New York, Appleton-Century-Crofts, 1960). Ch. 4 contains several discussions of concept formation.

[9] James M. Bradfield and H. Stewart Moredock, *Measurement and Evaluation in Education* (New York, Macmillan, 1957).

somewhat by the overwhelmingly verbal nature of the traditional school. The modern school with emphasis on activity and experience does better, but even there one serious error often occurs.

1. *Concepts are given out ready-made.* A certain type of teacher evidently believes that *telling* is equivalent to *teaching* and that *hearing* words amounts to *understanding*. This teacher usually tests learners by calling for repetition of the words, but with no reference to the meaning or use of the concept. "I just told you yesterday, but you don't seem to understand." (Neither does the teacher, but that's another story!) This general view is to be seen in curriculums which begin with statements of the principles or concepts in the field. Supposedly these will then be illustrated and experienced until understood. *First,* it is overlooked that these basic concepts were developed in the first place by bright, mature adults. We now expect little children to grasp them on sight. *Second,* concepts develop over long periods of time and through many experiences. Mature learners can often grasp them quickly because they have already a wide background of experience. The young learner cannot; hence he memorizes the words and gets verbalisms instead of meanings.

An enlightening comment is made by Boroff in his article, "Imperial Harvard":[10]

Students and faculty talk about the "Exeter Syndrome"—a term which applies to secondary school graduates, especially from Exeter, who are overprepared for Harvard.

"At fifteen," a faculty member explained, "they are handling the verbal ingenuities of the Metaphysical Poets. They're living off intellectual capital they haven't fully earned."

"Even students who have no right to do so take ideas seriously," a professor remarked.

One cannot resist the comment that many distinguished persons who advocate copying the private school system by public schools may not be too familiar with either private or public schools.

Concepts in real situations are achieved or discovered, not accepted and given acquiescence with no further ado. The attitude of the learner is not that of absorbing, but of groping, hunting, searching, trying one thing after another. The attitudes favorable and unfavorable to good thinking listed in Chapter 3 may be recalled here.

2. *Activities and experiences are not carried through to the level of concept derivation.* Some modern schools have much activity—many things are going on; experiences are being undergone—but all this is not, as we say, "intellectualized." The student is not stimulated to attempt generalizing. General meanings, interpretation, and concepts do not emerge.

3. *The learner is allowed to remain submerged in specifics.* This may be regarded as part of the preceding point but is stated separately for em-

[10] David Boroff, "Imperial Harvard," *Harper's Magazine* (Oct. 1958), p. 30.

phasis. This occurs with those teachers who see only, live only, for "facts." The children are drilled on memorizing vast accumulations of facts of many kinds—but they do not understand any of them. A famous war correspondent was noted for his fact gathering together with the fact that he never seemed to sense the significance of some of the tremendous events he recorded. One reviewer disposed of one of the correspondent's widely known books with a one-line critique: "Mr. Blank was there—but he didn't think." We all know persons who are full of "fascinating facts" but who do not *know* anything.

The foregoing paragraph must not be interpreted as relegating facts to nonimportance or nonsignificance. A fact by itself has no meaning; nor does a collection of them by themselves. Facts are, however, the basis of all ideas and mental manipulations. There is no such thing as a "mere" fact. Our point is that the method of arriving at facts and using them when once obtained is the important thing. One cannot collect great masses of fact and then make some concepts. He may not even be aware of what we call concepts. Properly handled, facts and concepts develop together in real situations.

The proper use of specifics and of generalizations. In everyday discourse, specifics and generalizations (concepts) are often badly mishandled.

The chief typical uses of specifics are:

1. As one of a series out of which some type of concept is built, generalization, law, principle.

2. As items in developing deductive implications of a selected generalization.

Other uses of specifics in discussion include:

1. To illustrate a known and reliable generalization to one who is ignorant of it or slow to comprehend it. This is in reality building up a generalization for him. The specific illustrates and builds up the general concept and should not be used to prove the concept.

2. To secure concreteness and vividness in argument which comes from the citation of cases. The specific does lend vividness and emphasis but cannot prove the point.

3. To point out weakness in a too broad or improperly based generalization.

4. To make an analogical statement. There are not enough specifics, or the data are too complex to be readily understood.

5. To avoid acceptance of an unpleasant generalization through citing of an exception. This is conscious or unconscious dishonesty. We should make a conscious effort to overcome the tendency to ignore unpleasant truths.

The typical uses of generalizations are:

1. The embodiment of the essential characteristics of a class.

2. The organization of conflicting data or the explanation of a puzzling specific.

3. The carrying on of deductive inquiry.

Other uses of generalizations include:

1. To carry on discussion with individuals competent to think in these terms.

2. To avoid entanglement in the variations of specifics in local meanings; to avoid, as we said, "submergence in specifics."

3. To avoid the necessity of explaining troublesome, rare, or subtle specifics. (This may be in some instances conscious dishonesty.)

4. To avoid recognition and facing up to unpleasant or disturbing specifics. (This is very often conscious dishonesty.)

Several of these ideas have already appeared in Chapter 7.

Verbalism. [11] **Words can be substituted for meaning as well as carry it.** Learning words seems to possess an evil magic. As has been hinted, the outcome of a learning experience may be not a meaning or concept but a verbalism. Clichés, bromides, old saws, claptrap, and empty words come to have a standing of their own without reference to meanings. The unrealistic, symbolic world created by and within the school accepts verbalisms as valid and meaningful. Verbalisms substituted for concepts make for untold confusion in thinking.

A backward high school class gave some simple, homely concepts they had derived from study of certain poetry. "One who does his best will be respected." "He who does good work will be liked." The teacher harshly rejected this and demanded that the children see "truth, wisdom, and beauty" in the poems. The children do not know what this means, but they will quickly learn to say it. A junior high school class which asked a simple question about a piece of music was given this advanced concept: "Harmonic tempo of music is usually in inverse ratio to the melodic tempo." The children cannot possibly understand this concept; but, even though it is difficult to remember, they will have it ready for the examination papers.

High school and college teachers sometimes accept from students "original" themes or reports which have been copied or slightly paraphrased from encyclopedias or other references. The students might as well have been copying Chinese as far as their development of concepts has been concerned. Unhappily, the fields of patriotism and loyalty are too often areas of gross confusion in this respect. Memorizing the Constitution

[11] For further development of these ideas see: H. R. Huse, *The Illiteracy of the Literate* (New York, D. Appleton-Century, 1933).

See also William H. Burton, *The Guidance of Learning Activities,* 2nd ed. (New York, Appleton-Century-Crofts, 1952), pp. 119-127, 28-41, 137-143. Note particularly the dozen or so references in footnotes, pp. 30-36.

or repeating pledges for which the background is missing are accepted in place of the more arduous procedures necessary for the development of real concepts here. In recent years we have seen much development in the teaching of meanings (concepts) in arithmetic instead of stopping with manipulations within computation.

The school is not the only sinner here. Verbalisms are heard regularly in the form of pompous nonsense from prominent pulpits; specious pleading and legal sophistry from respectable (*sic*) lawyers; the lovely words of public officials denying their responsibility for graft, corruption, and disaster which are clearly owing to their own incompetence and dishonesty; the twitterings of socially prominent, but intellectually incompetent, persons. Verbalisms are not only substituted for concepts, they prevent concepts from emerging. Ludicrous blunders in thinking occur.

The dilemma in the school is that, despite the obvious dangers of *verbalism,* the use of *verbal methods* and of learning through words is legitimate and necessary. Education could not be achieved without use of verbal vehicles of vicarious experience. Common-sense definitions have been assumed to this point. The nontechnical definitions below will organize thought further.

A verbalism is a statement which is empty of meaning. It is an empty sequence of words. Words are substituted for meanings and facts. The statements sound well; they are socially acceptable; they ease one past a situation; but they have no reference to facts or actions based on the words. *Vox et praeterea nihil*—a voice and nothing more. The average citizen recognizes the situation—even though he is a constant user of verbalisms—when he refers to *claptrap, empty words, lip service.*

Verbal methods of teaching are methods which use words, oral or written, through which to convey meanings. Verbal methods are necessary. Verbalisms can be avoided if verbal methods are based on (*a*) experience known to be possessed by the learner, (*b*) a level of maturity sufficient to handle abstractions, and (*c*) teaching methods designed to avoid the pitfalls of vicarious experiencing.

The end result of any type of experience can be either verbalism or a genuine meaning. Genuine meanings result from reputable verbal methods as noted above and elaborated in standard texts on teaching. Verbalisms result usually because of (*a*) violation of these methods; or (*b*) imposition of verbalism in advance of, with disregard for, or in defiance of experience; or (*c*) the teacher's naïve, uncritical acceptance of verbalisms which in turn confirms the habit of verbalizing.

Concepts must be validated. The general means for proving beliefs was outlined at the close of Chapter 5 on the hypothesis and in Chapter 8. Concepts are to be accepted as valid, first, if their extension by reasoning develops no contradictions in implications with known concepts already verified. Startling new discoveries will, of course, be exceptions here. Proof by reasoning is not final; only check with reality can be that. In some situations, however, we cannot check immediately, sometimes not for a long time; hence, we accept a reasoned chain of argument. Second, we may observe the operation of the concept when applied to the outside world. Sometimes this consists of the critical observation of uncontrolled events as they occur, sometimes of the experimental production of events under controlled observation.

QUESTIONS, EXERCISES, AND REPORTS

1. List a few basic concepts in some field with which you are familiar. In education. In psychology.

2. Various points on pages 155-156 are somewhat difficult. Give specific illustrations from everyday affairs.

3. Give a specific illustration of the importance of concepts in everyday thinking.

4. Give a specific illustration wherein proper use of valid concepts (or the opposite) played a vital part in a political, economic, or social crisis.

5. Illustrate the confusion resulting from misnaming concepts or of confusing one concept with another.

6. Illustrate concept development by little children (preferably a case you have observed). By elementary school children in any subject field or area of activity.

7. Describe methods used by a teacher deliberately aimed at the development of certain new concepts. Any original efforts of your own?

8. The text, pages 164-168, describes errors made in high school and college courses in methods used to convey concepts to students. Some of the errors are almost incredible. Illustrate the three mentioned in the text with specific illustrations from your experience or reading.

9. Show what useful concepts do or do not result from learning:
   a. The capitals of the states.
   b. The list of products grown in subtropical regions.
   c. The computation of cube root.
   d. Why the United States returned the Boxer indemnity money.
   e. How the Gettysburg address is regarded and why.
   f. To recite from memory the Constitution of the United States.
   g. Hamlet's soliloquy, passages from The "Lady of the Lake."
   h. The argument in Burke's speech.
   i. The square of the hypotenuse of a right angle triangle is equal to the sum of the squares of the other two sides.

10. Illustrate the different levels of concepts which may be adequate for learners of different levels of maturity and experience.

11. Verbalisms are decried as educational outcomes. At the same time it is clear that verbal methods and verbal learning must be widely used. Verbal learning is quite satisfactory under certain circumstances.
   a. List and analyze one or two crucial major *educational* problems raised by this situation.

     b. List and analyze three or four important *teaching* problems con-
fronting the classroom teacher here.

     c. What has all this to do with our chief theme—improving thinking?

    12. A candidate for teaching completes the required courses for a major
in science and is certificated to teach science. He is, however, wholly ignorant
of what it means to be scientific.

     a. What does it mean to be scientific?

     b. Does it make any difference in his teaching whether he knows
what it means to be scientific?

     c. Should his training in science affect in any way his views in art,
religion, ethics, economics, and politics? Why or why not?

     d. How could he major in science and yet be "unscientific"?

    13. A group of high school science teachers studying at a university
under the current program for the improvement of science teaching angrily
rejected certain suggested methods of teaching with the statement that the
methods were "inapplicable to high school teaching."

    The methods in question have been in use widely in high schools for
approximately a third of a century. They were originally developed in a university high school.

    We are not here concerned with the tragic ignorance of these teach-
ers. We are concerned with the basic ignorance of fundamental concepts in
science and teaching and learning.

     a. How did their reaction demonstrate ignorance of basic concepts
in teaching and learning? (Do not confuse ignorance of the facts
with ignorance of concepts.)

     b. How did their reaction demonstrate their ignorance of certain
basic concepts in their own field—science?

    14. Why do you suppose James said that the man possessing the great-
est number of general meanings or concepts is the best-educated man?

    15. Some years ago a writer, decrying the decline of serious reading;
the easy response to headlines, slogans, and clichés; and careless reasoning said
that democratic life might be endangered by "The Great Stupidity." What do
you think he meant? What has this to do with our chapter?

    16. The public is clearly becoming less able to think about many serious
problems, less able to make good judgments in public affairs. This is not a
carping criticism but a recognition of an obvious situation. Blame is often put
upon the public schools for this situation.

    What are the real causes for this condition? What can be done about
it in school or elsewhere?

READINGS WHICH AMPLIFY THE CHAPTER
AND BEAR ON THE QUESTIONS

DEWEY, John, *How We Think,* rev. ed. (Boston, Heath, 1933), Ch. 10, pp.
149-164, "Understanding: Conception and Definition," may be skimmed
for quick introduction; Ch. 12, pp. 179-189, "Systematic Method: Control of Reasoning and Concepts."

RUSSELL, David H., *Children's Thinking* (Boston, Ginn, 1956), Chs. 5 and 8 very enlightening.

BURTON, William H., *The Guidance of Learning Activities,* 2nd ed. (New York, Appleton-Century-Crofts, 1952), "Verbalisms." Use the index.

———, *Reading in Child Development* (Indianapolis, Ind., Bobbs-Merrill, 1956), Ch. 2.

KRAUSS, Ruth, *A Hole Is to Dig* (New York, Harper, 1952).

GENERAL READINGS, BEGINNING

BROWNELL, William A., and HENDRICKSON, Gordon, "How Children Learn Information, Concepts, and Generalizations," in *Learning and Instruction,* Forty-ninth Yearbook of the National Society for the Study of Education, Part I (Chicago, University of Chicago Press, 1950), pp. 92-128.

CURTI, Margaret W., "Child Development: Concepts," *Encyclopedia of Educational Research,* rev. ed. (New York, Macmillan, 1950), pp. 175-177.

Any recent text on educational psychology will usually have a chapter dealing with concepts. For instance:

THOMPSON, George G., GARDINER, Eric F., and DiVESTA, Francis J., *Educational Psychology* (New York, Appleton-Century-Crofts, 1959), Ch. 15.

GENERAL READINGS, ADVANCED

HEMPEL, Carl G., "Fundamentals of Concept Formation in Empirical Science," *International Encyclopedia of Unified Science,* Vol. II, No. 7 (Chicago, University of Chicago Press, 1952).

COHEN, Morris R., and NAGEL, Ernest, *An Introduction to Logic and Scientific Method* (New York, Harcourt, Brace, 1934), Ch. 2.

HEIDBREDER, Edna, "The Attainment of Concepts: III, The Process," *Journal of Psychology,* Vol. 24 (1947), pp. 93-138.

HUMPHREY, George, "Abstraction and Generalization," in *Thinking: An Introduction to its Experimental Psychology* (New York, Wiley, 1951), Ch. 9, pp. 265-307.

SAMPLE INVESTIGATIONS

BURTON, William H., and others, *Children's Civic Information, 1924-1935,* University of Southern California Educational Monographs, No. 7 (1936).

DEUTSCHE, Jean M., *The Development of Children's Concepts of Causal Relations* (Minneapolis, University of Minnesota Press, 1937).

HEIDBREDER, Edna, "The Attainment of Concepts: VI, Exploratory Experiments on Conceptualization at Perceptual Levels," *Journal of Psychology,* Vol. 26 (1948), pp. 193-216.

MELTZER, Hyman, *Children's Social Concepts, A Study of Their Nature and Development* (New York, Teachers College Bureau of Publications, Columbia University, 1925). An early and valuable study.

PIAGET, Jean. Several volumes by this author bear on concept formation.

SMOKE, Kenneth L., "The Experimental Approach to Concept Learning," *Psychological Review,* Vol. 42 (1935), pp. 274-279.

VINACKE, W. Edgar, "The Investigation of Concept Formation," *Psychological Bulletin,* Vol. 48 (1951), pp. 1-31.

HALL, Stanley, "The Content of Children's Minds on Entering School," *Princeton Review* (May, 1883), pp. 249-262. This is the great classic in the field. It dealt with information, but inferences are easily made concerning concepts. Many early textbooks in education cite the study, and it is still of value.

Hall's study was duplicated in Kansas City in 1883. An account is found in SMITH, Theodate L., *Aspects of Child Life and Education* (Boston, Ginn, 1907).

Several similar studies were made in foreign countries, and these are briefly noted in the Burton reference above, Ch. 3.

CHAPTER 10

Words: The Symbols of Thought

There are masked words abroad, I say, which nobody understands.
JOHN RUSKIN

There are trivial ways of studying language which have no connection with life, and these we need to clear out of our schools. But a deeper and more thorough study of our use of words is at every point a study of our ways of living. It touches all the modes of interpretive activity—in techniques, and in social intercourse—upon which civilization depends.
I. A. RICHARDS *

—except ye utter by the tongue words easy to be understood, how shall it be known what is spoken? for ye shall speak into the air.
I CORINTHIANS 14:9

The general area of semantics. Semantics is the study of the meanings of words. It enters into critical thinking whenever ideas are exchanged through spoken or written language—that is, in nearly every kind of problem. In recent years we have become increasingly aware of the fact that two persons can start with the same information and describe it in ways that are different because of the words they choose. The language can differ in its emotional suggestiveness, its abstractness, or its use of figures of speech, and in other ways.

John Brown, who attacked the Federal arsenal at Harper's Ferry is described by some as a "hero," by others as a "traitor," "symbol of humanitarianism," "a common murderer." It is a historical problem to decide what actually happened on the night that John Brown's party raided

* I. A. Richards, *Interpretation in Teaching* (New York, Harcourt, Brace, 1938), p. ix.

the arsenal. But it is a semantic problem to decide which words to use in describing the raid.

In our daily life we see advertisements which make use of clever tricks with words to entrap the unwary reader. Politicians attempt to sway our opinions by the use of exaggerated labels for their opponents and by persuasive words describing their own plans for the future. A study of word meaning can be a protection to the average citizen.

Is the description of a given event accurate? Is a news story true, or even in some cases within the bounds of possibility? Are advertisements factual—always, sometimes, never? Is an editorial or commentary unbiased, based on all known facts, or do hidden assumptions and feelings creep in? All this leads to a study of context and definition. We will also take up the varied meanings for one word and shifts in meaning.

Semantics is one approach to the study of language function. The processes and skills of communication are obviously a part of this. Meaning, accuracy, and communication are basic to good thinking which is the subject of our volume.

Semantics and concepts. Clearly, the study of words cannot be separated entirely from the things they stand for or from the concepts in our minds which the words suggest. To show the connection between semantics and concept formation, we represent them as parts of a triangle:

Whenever we see or hear a word, such as *whale,* there are three things involved: the *word,* or symbol, *whale;* the actual mammal itself, which we call the *referent;* and the idea or *concept* of whale which we have in our minds. In the last chapter we were concerned chiefly with the way concepts are learned, for instance, in science classes of elementary schools. In this chapter we are concerned with the relationships between the *word* and the *concept,* the *word* and the *referent,* and the interrelationships of all three.

Semantics and grammar. Semantics is not to be confused with grammar, or the study of the formal structure of language. Semantics, as the root shows, is concerned with signification of language, whereas grammar is commonly used in school merely to supply a vocabulary for the correction of errors in usage. [1] The school often places more stress upon form than on content. Edna Ferber, long ago, addressing the National Council of Teachers of English, asked why they devoted so much effort to form and so little to getting content worth dealing with. The situation could be changed by the addition of work in semantics to the curriculum.

Proper training in language is not readily available. We are, however, seriously handicapped in studying meanings and use of words because schools generally have failed to provide systematic training in the nature

---

[1] The word *semantics* is derived from the Greek verb *semainein,* to "signify," from *sema,* a sign. The subject was first used in 1897 by Michel Breal in his *Essai de semantique.* The word appeared in English in 1900 in a translation of this essay.

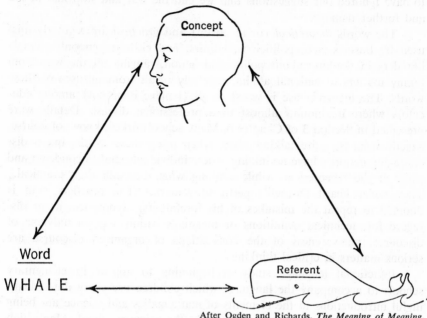

After Ogden and Richards, *The Meaning of Meaning.*

FIG. 3

and use of language. Time is spent on grammar, rhetoric, and certain "trivial ways of studying language." People in general know very little about language, about the nature, characteristics, and uses of words. Everyone knows that words are used to convey thought. Many evidently do not know that words may be used to confuse thought or to conceal the absence of thought. The average citizen is constantly bamboozled by the magical or suggestive power of words and yet may not be aware of the power. He is fooled by incantations, soapbox oratory, speeches by politicians, commercials on radio and television. He keeps right on believing things that he reads or hears—or he develops an equally paralyzing cynicism about language and facts.

Some common mistakes in the meanings of words are merely funny, but other mistakes can be deadly serious. A tragic case was seen toward the end of World War II when errors were made in translating certain words in Japanese peace feelers and in their replies to our approaches. The war was probably prolonged and many lives lost. The Japanese word *mokusatu,* which in formal discourse means "to ignore," has in less formal situations the meaning "refrain from comment." The latter leaves the door open for further discussion. The original dispatch received at American headquarters was translated correctly in terms of the general tone of the note—to withhold comment at the moment. The newsmen, knowing less Japanese, put it on the wires as "to ignore." The Japanese were thus said to have ignored our suggestions that we end the war and stop loss of life and further damage.

The words *theoretical* (or idealistic) and *practical* are regularly misused by businessmen, politicians, editors, and citizens generally. Tragic blunders in thinking about policy and action, ranging all the way from family matters to national affairs, regularly result from misuses of these words. The incorrect use is worst of all (believe it or not) among educators where it amounts almost to a professional disease. Details were presented in Section 3 of Chapter 6. Many schoolworkers know, of course, exactly what they are talking about when using these words, but a discouraging majority have no inkling. These individuals tend to condemn and sneer at the "theoretical" while exalting what they call the "practical." They never heard Disraeli's pertinent remark, "The practical man is doomed to repeat the mistakes of his forefathers." Ignorance of, or disregard for, technical definitions or meanings within a given universe of discourse, unawareness of the conventions of organized discourse are serious matters in critical thinking.

Functional language study is beginning to appear in elementary schools to accompany the language which children use every day. Meaningful introductions to the elements of mathematics and science are being provided more frequently, particularly in the primary school. Many high schools and colleges are experimenting with courses in the history of language, language usage, semantics, and propaganda analysis. These may eventually take the place of some of the arrant nonsense being taught about grammar and rhetoric.

The study of language as such, with special reference here to words and their uses, is a huge problem. It is far more serious than the foregoing simple paragraphs indicate. A single chapter cannot do more than present an outline of points bearing upon our main theme, critical thinking. We have here presented a bare-bones summary which we hope will be of use. Advanced students can and should go much further. References are found at the end of the chapter.

Critical analysis of factors affecting meaning not commonly stressed in school. We are again handicapped by the schools' neglect of the necessary training. Four problems are involved.

1. *Schools generally do not give training in critical thinking.* Educative experiences in critical analysis can be given in any subject area or learning activity. One objective of teaching in Latin, algebra, and science is commonly alleged to be an effort to teach thinking through formal discipline in the subject. Overwhelming evidence testifies to the failure of this approach. The present volume is one of several which presents some of the ways in which critical thinking can be experienced by learners. Within the area of critical thinking, specific training in semantics should be given in several subject fields.

2. *Home, school, and life generally inhibit or suppress the critical attitude.* This is a general point applied here specifically to accepted meanings and beliefs. [2] Conventional meanings and doctrines which are acceptable and comfortable are demanded. Criticism or analysis of shibboleths and verbalisms—the search for real meanings—is ruthlessly crushed. To think, and especially to think critically about accepted beliefs in suburbia, is to be an "odd ball."

3. *Reading-for-critical-evaluation is still widely regarded as something over and beyond "learning-to-read."* The advanced treatments of teaching to read present critical evaluation of word meaning and of what is read as an integral part of learning to read. Many textbooks and manuals do not do this. Countless classroom teachers know little or nothing about it.

4. *Reverence for the printed word—reluctance to react critically to anything in print—is a part of our primitive credulity.* Some writers regard this as one of the chief problems here. The problem is widespread and of serious proportions. This, like the second point above, is again a general point affecting all thinking, but here it is related specifically to semantics. Development of a critical attitude through experiences with a wide range of meanings, with shifts in meanings, and particularly with dishonest manipulations of meaning is necessary. "It says so in the newspaper" is heard on all sides as a guarantee of truth. (With some, appearance in the newspaper is taken to mean the statement is not true, or at least it is biased. This is still a case of lack of critical analysis.) "It says so right on the bottle" sold many bottles of fake medicine in the old medicine shows. It still does when applied to political and economic "bottles."

Learning experiences in critical analysis of language can be provided. Functional language courses and meaningful approaches to subject fields are, as indicated earlier, beginning to appear. Every teacher in any field can incorporate learning experiences directed toward critical analysis and interpretation of language and meaning. Simple checking against reality begins on preprimary levels. On higher levels, criteria can be developed for determining the effect of diction, figures of speech, shades of meaning, emotional tone, and the like.

MEANING

Word meaning. The general nature of meaning and its development were presented briefly in the preceding chapter on concepts. We are in the present chapter concerned with a special aspect of meaning, namely, meaning-for-word.

[2] For a vivid and provocative treatment of this problem as it relates to economic life in current American society, see John K. Galbraith, *The Affluent Society* (Boston, Houghton Mifflin, 1958).

Words are symbols. The words in any sentence are signs. A sign is an event or object which causes us to react in a certain way in accordance with our past experience with similar events and their consequences. In Pavlov's famous experiment with his dog, the sound of the bell was a sign to the dog. The bell sound was associated with food in the dog's past experience and caused his mouth to water when he heard it. Most words we use are far more complex and subtle than simple signs like bells. The analogy, however, enables us to make certain points and distinctions which will be useful later.

A little baby is constantly in the presence of adults who are always using certain vocal noises, or words, in relation to things, persons, processes. The baby hearing these vocal noises, or words, comes to associate them with the meanings he has built up through repeated experiences. He attaches the word to the meaning and thus completes Comenius' famous brief summary: "Things, Meanings, Words."

A word is a purely arbitrary symbol. The choice of any particular word to represent a referent and to produce an idea is purely an arbitrary matter. There is no natural or necessary connection between a word and its referent. Using the triangle of reference presented earlier, we may note that different nations have different names for the same thing—*dog, chien, hund,* for example. This point may seem obvious at first, but there have been stages in human history when a word has been taken to be identical with its referent, as in the case of the Egyptian word-god *Khern,* or when words have been assumed to have special power of their own as in the cases of *sesame, hocus-pocus, abracadabra.*

Many words have origins so far in the past that we can only speculate on how they became connected with their present referents. The word for *father,* cognate in most European languages must have come from some remote Indo-European word like *pitar.* With other words, remarkable shifts in meaning occur through the process of constant oral use. *Nice,* for instance, comes originally from a Latin word, *nescius* meaning ignorant. *Villain* comes from *dweller in a villa* or hamlet.

Meanings are not determined by the dictionary, as is commonly thought. Actually editors of dictionaries try to find out how words are being used in literate circles and then record this usage. Precaution must be taken in looking up words in a dictionary to note the special senses of words in particular situations and to avoid substituting approximate synonyms.

At the concept level, the ideas associated with a word, or with the referent for a word, are built up by direct experience, by reflection upon experience, or by stipulation, that is, deliberate agreement to attach a certain meaning to a word. This process was discussed at length in the preceding chapter.

CONTEXT

A word, as we have seen, possesses no meaning of its own but derives its meaning from context. The great difficulty is to keep this in mind. The matter is not as simple as it sounds. Dictionaries describe the standard meanings of words. People build up through experience fairly uniform concepts of word meaning. The particular meaning of a word at any special time is, however, determined by its context. Many think of context as verbal only, the immediately surrounding words and sentences. We deal with three types of context: the verbal as just described, the psychological, and the physical. The psychological and the physical contexts may often be more important than the more familiar verbal context. The various aspects of context may be fused in real situations; they are listed separately here for discussion.

The basic problem in the interpretation of language is to find out exactly what the other fellow was thinking when he said what he said.

1. *The word, or verbal, or symbol context;* the language surrounding the word

The passages just before or after a word serve as clues to the special sense in which a word is to be taken. In order to select the meaning which is indicated by the context, the reader must possess a knowledge of the standard meanings of the word, or be able to infer the meaning from the context. This meaning may, of course, be figurative.

2. *The psychological context*

No word means exactly the same thing to two different persons because each individual has a different background of experience with each word. The mental image constructed for a word varies from person to person according to the following factors.

> The reader's or listener's:
> *a.* Experiential background, meager or rich
> *b.* Education, his organized knowledge, his capability and special preparation
> *c.* Point of view as affected by his various assets, liabilities, and pressures; his socioeconomic status, political and religious affiliations; his temperament, opinions, and prejudices
> *d.* Emotional status, his general mood and temperament, any special emotional set that he may have had at time of writing
> *e.* Purpose or intent, what he seeks to accomplish
> *f.* Interpretation of tone of voice (or writing), mannerisms, accent, tricks of eloquence or rhetoric

3. *The physical context*

This has to do with the conditions under which the referent exists. The objects and relations in the world, about which we talk and use symbols, also vary from time to time and under various circumstances. There is a changeableness about things which we must take into account constantly when we communicate to each other about them. As some Greek scholar pointed out, we never can step into the same river twice because the particles in the river are ever changing and moving on. There are background, planning, and limiting conditions which must be considered. For example, we can use the word *modern* to describe a school system or motel accommodations. But the word will be meaningless unless we know the time, the region, and the standards set for the use of this term.

The symbolic, conceptual, and physical contexts of a word are linked together in an infinitely complex combination of interacting elements. Sometimes the contexts are easy to understand, sometimes impossible, but we must attempt to take them into account as far as we can in order to achieve successful interpretation or communication.

A point often overlooked is that the reader or listener while interpreting words is affected by the same factors that influence the author or speaker. The reader has a psychological content of his own—experiential background, schooling, point of view, emotional status, purposes in reading or listening. His physical status and surroundings all affect his interpretation.

Meaning for word differs with context. The changes in word meaning according to context may be illustrated through 12 different uses of the common word *book*.

1. Tolstoi wrote a book. (An ordinary book)
2. A jug of wine, a book of verse, and thou . . . (Small book)
3. Pass in the books, students! (Textbooks or workbooks)
4. It is written in the Book. (Bible) The Book of Job. (A division, section, or part)
5. The first six books of the Aeneid will be read. (Division of an epic)
6. The book profit was high. (Account book)
7. Sullivan wrote the music, and Gilbert wrote the book. (Libretto)
8. He was booked for bookmaking. (Registered at the police station; taking bets)
9. The court threw the book at the convict. (Total possible charges)
10. A book of tickets is missing. (A booklet)

The total significance of words in a phrase, sentence, or paragraph may depend, as already hinted, upon the context of the surrounding passages. To put it negatively, it may be difficult to know what a phrase or sentence means unless we know the surrounding context. To quote passages out of context, and thus confuse meaning, is a common device in persuasive prose with the purpose of embarrassing an opponent. Example: Several years ago in a "letter to the editor" concerning a House bill to admit additional immigrants to the United States, Representative Judd of Minnesota was quoted as saying the bill "will do just as much good to our

enemies as if it were written in the Kremlin. . . ." What Judd actually said
was:

Let me say at the outset that I, of course, approve the stated purpose of
this bill. . . . But I regret the limitations of the bill. . . . (and for the Congress
of the United States to pick this moment to pass this legislation in its present
form is to do just as much good to the enemies of everything you and I believe
in as if it had been written in the Kremlin itself.)

This type of rank misquotation is a violation of the context principles
stated above.

The analysis of context always necessary. The indifferent person, the
one who "believes what he reads," or who casts aside as "difficult" anything not understandable at first glance cannot avoid serious blunders in
thinking, errors in drawing conclusions, with resultant disasters in action.
This is commonly to be observed all around us.

The foregoing outline of context clearly indicates the orderly procedure for analyzing total context. The following abilities need to be cultivated for the analysis of verbal context:

1. The ability to choose the key surrounding words to use as context
clues in determining the meaning of a word
2. The ability to recognize and interpret phrases, clauses, and paragraphs
as important segments of the total context
3. The ability to determine the quality of the language, its correctness,
clarity, appropriateness, literary appeal
4. The ability to glean from language something about the author, such
as his probable experiential background, education, viewpoint, emotional status,
purpose or intent
5. The ability to detect attempts to distort, exaggerate, or suppress meanings through the use of tricky language and, in the case of speaking, through
eloquence and mannerisms
6. The ability to translate language, to express meaning in one's own
words in place of those of the author

Outlines for the analysis of psychological and physical context will
be found in Chapter 18 under the headings "External criticism" and "Internal criticism." Students may amplify any of these outlines to suit
situations.

The adequacy of the meaning achieved by the reader or listener depends upon the skill and completeness with which he has examined the
total context.

The art of intelligent reading implies the ability to make distinctions between what is thought and what is fancy, what is suggestion, emotion, or
scheming. And above all, it demands translation into terms of motive.

What is involved . . . is reading with *translation,* that is, translation into motive, authority, probability, and into meaning as expressed by one's own words. [3]

Shifts of meaning. The ways in which words do differ may be summarized:

1. The same words may have different meanings or different shades of meaning in different contexts. Words differ:
   a. From family to family, locality to locality, community to community, and within each of these.
   b. From time to time.
2. Different words may express the same or virtually the same meanings.
3. Words differ greatly in definiteness of meanings, some having broad, class, or group meanings; others having very specific meanings.
4. Some words, such as *democracy, freedom, honesty,* do not refer to things that we can see, hear, touch, taste, or otherwise handle. They have no final referents.
5. Words used in special fields and in technical discussions must have agreed-upon meanings and must be used consistently. Necessary as this is, it can become a handicap to thinking if the dynamic nature of life and of language is ignored, thus delaying necessary changes in standardized terms. Technical and stipulated meanings usually differ from everyday or colloquial meanings.
6. Word meanings may shift within a given discourse.
   a. Naïve, unnoticed shifts
   b. Deliberate and intentional shifts

Unlike mathematical symbols, the symbols of language are slippery things. They do not stay put; they carry multiple meanings, which shift from time to time and differ from place to place; their ostensible references are overlaid with meanings of a nonrational character. [4]

THE NEED FOR DEFINITION

Preceding pages have made clear that we must determine meaning as closely as possible and must use word meanings consistently in all discourse. Too many long arguments end up with one party saying, "Oh! If that's what you mean, I agree." Engaging in discussion without having defined terms is an exercise in futility.

Dewey has some cogent words on this: [5]

A constant source of misunderstanding and mistake is indefiniteness of meaning. Because of vagueness of meaning we misunderstand people, things, ourselves; because of ambiguity we distort and pervert. Conscious distortion

[3] H. R. Huse, *The Illiteracy of the Literate* (New York, D. Appleton-Century, 1933), pp. 98 and 8.
[4] Commission on the Secondary School Curriculum of the Progressive Education Association, *Language in General Education* (New York, Appleton-Century-Crofts, 1940), p. 17.
[5] John Dewey, *How We Think,* rev. ed., (Boston, Heath, 1933), pp. 159-160.

of meaning may be enjoyed as nonsense; erroneous meanings, if clear-cut, may be followed up and got rid of. But vague meanings are too gelatinous to offer matter for analysis and too pulpy to afford support to other beliefs. They evade testing and responsibility. Vagueness disguises the unconscious mixing together of different meanings, and facilitates the substitution of one meaning for another, and covers up failure to have any precise meaning at all. *It is the aboriginal logical sin—the source from which flow most bad intellectual consequences.* Totally to eliminate indefiniteness is impossible; to reduce it in extent and in force requires sincerity and vigor. [Italics ours.]

. . . the meaning that exclusively and characteristically attaches to . . . terms . . . is set forth in definition. . . .

The following passage from the *Congressional Record* illustrates failure of a discussion in Congress because one representative failed either to seek or to accept a definition of the main topic. In fact, he seemed ignorant of the fact that definition is necessary.

Mr. Dingell: Mr. Chairman, will the gentleman yield?

Mr. Knutson: I yield to the gentleman from Michigan.

Mr. Dingell: The gentleman was corrected on that statement in the hearings to the effect that there is only one tin mill in the U. S. located down in Texas, and it came in only recently during the war.

Mr. Knutson: Oh, we have been making American tinware for years and years and years.

Mr. Dingell: That is not a tin mill.

Mr. Knutson: I am standing by my statement.

Mr. Dingell: Not tin mills. The gentleman cannot stand on it.

Mr. Knutson: I am talking about the manufacture of tinware.

Mr. Dingell: That is a different story, tinware and tin mills.

Mr. Knutson: If the gentleman wants to argue the difference between Tweedledee and Tweedledum, I will be glad to yield some time to him later.

Mr. Dingell: There is no such difference here now. A tin mill is different from tinware.

Mr. Knutson: I am too busy to argue the difference.

Mr. Dingell: I am very sorry the gentleman cannot differentiate . . .

Mr. Knutson: Sit down, and I will handle this. . . .

Mr. Dingell: I will sit down when I am good and ready. . . .

And so the processes of democratic government make their way toward momentous decisions. To paraphrase an old saw: Clarity uncovers a multitude of sins.

The need for definition has not prevented the best logicians and psychologists from differing on the nature of definition and on the acceptability of certain methods of defining. The details of careful defining can become quite complicated. Walpole, in fact, gives 25 different "roads to definition." The leading writers themselves say, however, that the intricate details are not necessary in every day usage. For our purposes here we use a simple statement: *Definition is some process by which we make clear to another person what the meaning of a word is.*

Definitions, like anything else in the world today, are relative. They change in base and in content as new ideas come along. Physical concepts, for instance, were usually defined in terms of properties or characteristics before Einstein. There is now a tendency to define in terms of operations. Newton's discoveries wrought a similar change in concepts which had been based for centuries on Aristotelian thought.

Definitions are needed for various purposes:

1. *To remove ambiguity or vagueness.* Ambiguity occurs when there are two possible referents for a single word. Vagueness is the term for the condition in which the word does not clearly define the referent.

2. *To introduce and explain any new term,* for example, *turbojet, slip stream,* and the like. The previous generation similarly had to define *rubberneck, jaywalker.* Today, attention is given to such terms as *beat generation.*

3. *To extend a new meaning for an old term,* for example, the *id* of Freud, or *set* in psychology.

4. *To limit terms temporarily by stipulation,* for instance, "Let *x* equal the speed in miles per hour." This form of definition is necessary in scientific discourse.

5. *For system building in science.*

A need for definition exists whenever key terms are unclear, in fact, when any term used in discourse is not clear.

Methods of definition or identification. Writers, as indicated above, do not agree on all details and methods. A common scheme for definition or identification is as follows:

1. *By genus and differentia.* This is the classical method. First, the general class to which a referent belongs is named; then, the ways in which the referent differs from other kinds of things in the general class. For example: *whale,* a mammal (*genus*) which lives in the sea and is shaped like a fish (*differentia*).

2. *Comparison.* "Like a porpoise, only bigger."

3. *Synonym.* "Cetacean."

4. *Pointing.* "That's a whale over there."

5. *Example.* "Moby Dick was a whale."

6. *Translation.* "*Walfisch*," "*baleine*."

7. *By operations,* that is, meaning for a scientific term lies in the operations, the things done to establish its validity. Meaning can be tested by data furnished by direct observation.

The operational definition has been given considerable impetus in the writings of physicist P. W. Bridgman who said, "The true meaning of a term is to be found by observing what a man does with it, not by what he says about it." This type of definition can be applied to some areas outside the sciences. Carl G. Hempel, presents a good illustration of operational definition (in *Fundamentals of Concept Formation in Empirical Science,* Chicago, University of Chicago Press, 1952, page 41):

Thus, the operational criteria of application for the term "diphtheria" might be formulated in terms of various symptoms of diphtheria; these would include not only such symptoms as are obtainable by the "operation" of directly observing the patient but also the results of bacteriological and other tests which call for such "operations" as the use of microscopes and the application of staining techniques.

Many writers accept the first method above as the only respectable one. [6] But the choice of method depends on purpose at the time. The first method, generally good, is not always effective, for instance, in defining relations.

Errors in the use of definition. Many of these are very common and constantly confuse thinking.

1. *Failure to define.* Commonest of all faults is the simple failure to define when definition is needed. Education textbooks contain many words which need constant redefinition—*progressive, need, functional.*

2. *Search for the "true" meaning of a word.* We often hear individuals asking, "What is the *real* meaning of that word?", as if each word had some one eternal, unchanging reference. As shown in preceding pages, many words have several meanings and change from time to time.

3. *Failure to accept stipulation.* Even after a writer has declared that he is using a word in a special sense, there are individuals who will ignore this stipulation and try to use the word in some extended sense.

4. *Careless use of synonyms from the dictionary.* Although most dictionaries list synonyms for words defined, these synonyms are often only approximate in meaning and can be used in some idiomatic manner. For example, *exacerbate* is defined as "to make bitter." But you cannot say, "Angostura exacerbates Manhattans."

5. *Use of difficult words in definition.* It is of no great help if the definition is harder to understand than the word defined. Consider the famous definition by Samuel Johnson of *network:* "Anything reticulated or decussated, at equal distances, with interstices between the intersections."

6. *Circularity.* Usually words should not be defined in their own terms, as *Chauvinist:* "one obsessed by chauvinism." But there is no sound objection to defining a Monagasque as an inhabitant of Monaco.

Quantification. A subject related to definition which needs attention is the use of words which imply quantity but are vague in their reference. Such vagueness is conveyed by words like *some, many,* or by the total

[6] Hugh R. Walpole, *Semantics* (New York, Norton, 1941), Ch. 6.
See also Max Black, *Critical Thinking* (Englewood Cliffs, N. J., Prentice-Hall, 1946), Chs. 9, 10, 11. Somewhat difficult to read but exercises at ends of chapters, especially Ch. 11, are very stimulating.
Huse, *op. cit.,* Ch. 8.

omission of quantifying words. In *Newsweek,* July 14, 1958, Raymond
Moley in a discussion about school costs said:

> The major increase in expenditures has been caused by three factors: (*a*)
> inefficient use of teachers' time and of school plant; (*b*) excessive cost of con-
> struction by the addition of vastly excessive accessories for community use, not
> for teaching children; and (*c*) the dilution of the curriculum by such courses
> as marriage and family relationships, grooming, junior homemaking for boys,
> beauty care, date behavior, stagecraft, square dancing, and fly-casting.

Granting that this is a highly compressed summary of more detailed material read by the author, we still may be misled by the nonspecific quantitative words like *excessive, vastly,* and *dilution.* Notice also that we cannot
judge from this passage how many courses such as "marriage and family relationships . . ." have been added, and it may be that the number
of fly-casting courses in American schools is not significantly large. Before
forming a judgment about the cause of increasing school costs, we would
need to have the quantities more carefully defined.

REFERENTIAL LANGUAGE

Referential language is the type of language we use every day to
convey facts or to talk about things neutrally. Political and economic discourse, description of current events, discussions of controversial questions, editorials, and advertisements, together with verbal materials from
many other areas, all need to be scrutinized to make sure the language is
truly referential. Referential statements are subject to verification through
checking with sources, with statistics, or with other corroborating materials. When a hidden emotive purpose lies behind a presumably neutral
analysis, considerable confusion can result.

EMOTIVE LANGUAGE

Mathematics is often regarded as the most objective of symbol systems. When we assert that nine times six is fifty-four, this statement arouses
little feeling. Its reference is neutral in respect to emotional content.

But even with numbers the human mind associates emotion. "Thirteen at a table," "seventh son of a seventh son," "three on a match"—associated as they are with superstitions, these numbers arouse an emotional
response which can be considered separately from the referential or cognitive meaning, even though the emotion is always dependent to some degree
upon the "pure" reference of a word.

The term *emotive* is used, of course, to suggest that words to which
it is applied arouse the basic emotions—such as hate, fear, love—in some
amount, ranging from obvious to subtle. Such a response is sometimes

highly desirable, as, for instance, in the case when we hear "Fire!" or "Look out below!"

Sometimes the emotional response is *premature* or misguided; it may interfere with the rational consideration of a problem which should precede action. The newspaper headline "Man Is Slain" is less stirring and prejudicial than "Man Is Murdered." Sometimes, also, the emotive word suggests an approval or disapproval, a moral or aesthetic judgment without openly admitting it. We can, for instance, describe a persistent effort as "stubborn" or "pig-headed." The chief difficulty, however, is that the emotive term may give a referential distortion. At some time or another, both major political parties in this country have been called the "party of treason," in most cases because they had done something which was considered to be inimical to the interests of the country, as, for example, when they advocated joining the United Nations. Although "treason" is a colorful word and highly emotive, it does not fit the referent action in the case stated if we accept the common definition of treason as a deliberate attempt to overthrow the government.

Another illustration of the attempt to attach unfavorable emotional tone to an otherwise sensible idea is found in an address given before several educational conventions by Dr. Joel Hildebrand, emeritus professor of chemistry at the University of California, one-time Dean of Liberal Arts, and one-time President of the American Chemical Society. Speaking to "Education in the Light of the Satellites," Hildebrand quotes with approval the statement of a high school teacher who names units of instruction, "eunuchs of instruction, they never produce anything." Units of instruction cannot be emasculated by renaming them. This procedure, to make a mild double pun, would be nonoperational.

A proposed scheme for the analysis and criticism of emotionally toned discourse. The following outline is proposed by Black.[7] The discussion and exercises in his book are very useful.

1. Begin by reading the passage slowly, carefully, and calmly several times, noting any points in the utterance which seem to deserve further examination. (You will pardon this insistence upon so elementary and obvious a point. Experience shows that once the excitement of the chase has been aroused, there is a tendency to "discover" sinister or profound implications in a passage, before even reading it with any degree of attention!)

2. State the general intention and context of the utterance. (E.g., "This is a report of a new scientific discovery made to an audience thoroughly familiar with the general background, and made by a man who is trying to suppress all that is personal in the circumstances he is describing." Or "This is an advertisement whose main object is to arouse curiosity concerning a mysteriously labeled new product; it is designed to appeal especially to women to make them more receptive to later 'follow-ups.' " It is useful also to try to determine the evidence

[7] Black, *op. cit.*, pp. 160-161. The page references and other notations within the quotation refer to materials in Black's original presentation.

used in arriving at this verdict concerning the general nature of the symbolic situation.)

3. Extract the words and phrases in the passage which are particularly effective in conveying the desired suggestion. (Crude instances of this, such as those discussed in the last section, are easily detected. More subtle suggestions, e.g., those due to the general style of a passage, may easily escape notice. It is an excellent practice here, as throughout this training, to compare one's results with those of those working independently on the same passage. Hunting down the reason for disagreement will often bring to light unsuspected resources of the language used.)

4. Make the suggestions of each word explicit, and combine the partial suggestions in a single statement. (This has been illustrated by the analysis preceding version C above. You will soon find, on trial, that the suggestions of a word or phrase can be made explicit only in a largely rough and approximate way. Paraphrasing the implicit content largely neutralizes its emotive influence. Instead of extracting the implicit content in this way, a useful variation is to rewrite the original passage reversing the emotive effect of the critical terms, as illustrated in statement D above.)

5. Formulate, in neutral language, the impersonal content of the original passage. (The products of steps 4 and 5 should together approximate in informative content to the original passage.)

6. Determine the evidence in favor of the original passage, as now elaborated. (But beware of assuming that the speaker is arguing, and not "just telling." Compare what was said on this point on p. 60 above. At this stage anything said in part 1 concerning the criticism of thought may be relevant. But what are we to say about the criticism of feeling? When is a man justified in expressing hate, indignation, approval, etc.? These questions, important as they are, take us out of the subject matter of this book into the fields of ethics and aesthetics. They illustrate the limitations of logic.)

To summarize: if we accept the emotive connotation of a word uncritically, we may overlook the fact that the language leads us (a) to *prejudge*, (b) to *accept a disguised approval* or disapproval, or (c) to *believe a distorted reference,* or (d) to do all three.

It is a useful practice to analyze prose passages, detecting expressions used emotively and determining what the references are when the emotive connotations are removed. As an example, consider the analysis of the following passage from the *Life* editorial criticizing modern American education.

But the trail blazers in education have to fight a war on two fronts. If they can persuade a community to increase a school's learning content, they must still reckon with the powerful educationists on accreditation boards and within [the] school administrations who continue to confuse the aims of education by their half-blind devotion to the practical techniques of the teacher and utopian "life adjustment" of the pupil.

This passage contains some highly emotive words and statements:

"trail blazers"—Complementary term referring to educational pioneers of
   whom the editor approves. Saturated with the approval felt of early settlers
   in America.
"reckon with"—Suggests a contest or struggle with some formidable and perhaps evil force.
"educationists"—A word recently coined to make use of the derogatory effect
   of the suffix -ist, which suggests a faddist, an adherent to a false cause,
   someone superficially playing a role. Here used to refer to adherents of
   "progressive" education.
"continue to"—Suggests "continue in spite of good reason to the contrary."
"confuse by half-blind devotion"—Means indirectly, "They disagree with us.
   They are wrong." The "blind" figure of speech has the connotation "unable to make correct judgments."
"practical techniques"—Not emotive, but "devotion to practical techniques" is
   intended as a criticism of what is regarded as excessive requirements in
   pedagogy for teaching credentials.
"utopian"—Standard derogation for "hopelessly ideal."
" 'life adjustment' "—Here the quotation marks mean "so they foolishly say
   or believe." Life adjustment is held by the *Life* editor to be outside of the
   scope of school aims.

When this is somewhat shortened and the emotive implications made explicit, it means something like this:

> Persons attempting to increase the subject-matter training of teachers and
> increase the proportion of time spent in school on such subjects as English
> and mathematics will be opposed by professional educators who believe that
> teachers should be well trained in method and that one of the aims of educa-
> tion is that pupils be equipped to make adjustments to the various social
> problems of life. We think that the professional educators are wrong in this
> belief. Wrong, stubborn, stupid, idealistic. Hooray for those termed "trail
> blazers."

Such a version is less interesting to read and more time-consuming to construct, but it helps us avoid unwittingly accepting the innuendoes of the
original.

   We may recall also at this point the discussion of attitudes in Chapter
3. Of particular importance are alertness or vigilance, objectivity, criticalness, and intellectual honesty.

FIGURATIVE LANGUAGE

   A figure of speech is an expression in which an object or action is
described in terms which literally mean something else. The commonest
type of figure is the metaphor which we may illustrate in this fashion. [8]

[8] Other figures:
   Simile. An expressed metaphor: "like a lion in the fight"; "as hot as a fire-
cracker."

Suppose we use the term *whale* to refer to something which is not a "fish-like mammal," as in this phrase, "a whale of a story." In this case the word *whale,* which does not normally or literally denote stories, is used because the size of the whale suggests some quality of magnitude in a picturesque way to the referent "story." We are expected to overlook details other than magnitude which do not apply to the "story," for instance, shape, habitat, blubber. Radio commentators constantly refer to a game being reported as a "whale of a game." Animal metaphors are rather common because of our habit of attributing certain definitive characteristics to animals: "dog of an unbeliever," "a lion at bay," "to chicken out," "weasel words." The unwary or naïve thinker may take a metaphor literally, thus making a "whale" of an error in his thinking—usually a whole school of whales! [9]

Figurative language is also seen when a singer or a work of art is characterized as "out of this world," or as deserving a "rave" notice. Cigarette and automobile advertising are filled with hyperbole which often parts company with any real fact in the matter. Euphemism and hyperbole are escapes to a never-never land wherein crude reality does not intrude on sweet scented fantasy. (To use a hyperbole.)

Uses. Figurative language is an essential kind of speech in much the same sense that emotive language is. Its uses can be classified under these heads:

1. *Illustration.* Normally we do not find much figurative language in science, but even there it has its uses, particularly for illustration: "The earth is flattened at the poles, like an orange."
2. *Picturesqueness, "color," "imagery."* Perhaps one of the commonest uses of figures is to add an imaginative quality or emphasis to literal expressions. For instance, in sports: "mouse-trap" play, "stealing home." Figures are often found in poetry because of this quality.
3. *Economy.* Often a figure expresses a complex idea in a few words. Try, for example, to express the idea of "stealing home" in a word or two.
4. *Essential statement.* Figures are not purely decorative. Many of our basic terms are metaphors or dead metaphors. In psychology, for instance, the problem of describing mental activities has obliged authors to borrow metaphorically from common experience:

Metonymy. One word used for another it suggests: "throne" for "king."

Synecdoche. The part for the whole: "all hands on deck." The whole for the part: "the smiling year (spring)." The material for the thing made: "ivories."

Personification. Attribution of human qualities to things not human: "The sun smiled down."

Hyperbole. Exaggeration: "higher than the moon."

Euphemism. A softened expression: "passed away" for "died."

[9] This illustration does not account for "dead" metaphors, that is, words which were originally figurative but which have been so commonly used that we do not think of them any longer as figures: for example, a "head" of lettuce, the "foot" of the bed, a "crane" (derrick).

    a. Gestalt—"a sudden flash when things are seen in fresh relation to each other."

    b. Thinking is "restrained speaking and action." [10]

    c. The brain is "like a telephone exchange." [11]

Dangers. Although figurative language is a necessary and normal kind of speech, it sometimes leads to misunderstanding.

1. *Misinterpretation.* Sometimes the incautious reader or listener takes a figure literally, that is, he accepts the analogy between the referent being described and the imaginative object with which it is being compared in more respects than the writer intended. A famous example occurred a few years ago when Charles Wilson compared union and nonunion workers with good hunting dogs and lazy dogs to the degree that each group exhibited initiative. The irrelevant and denigratory connotations of the word *dog* were accepted as part of the intended meaning of the figurative comparison in spite of Wilson's denials.

2. *Emotive effect.* Figures are frequently emotive in the sense of the previous section on emotive language and with the concomitant dangers.

3. *Mixture.* Sometimes writers will combine several figures in an incongruous mixture.

    The coolness between Toy and Kelly reached a boiling point in 1938 when Kelly. . . . (From the Flint, Michigan, *Journal*)

    They do not mean that the urge to get skilled is dead. They simply mean that we are not tapping the source. If we are smart enough to adjust—to go forward or backward or to the side—we will hit the nail on the head and ride along on the crest of the child's own urge. (From *Understanding Your Child*, by James L. Hymes, Jr.)

    Such mixtures of figures are repugnant chiefly for stylistic reasons, but the confusion of figurative references sometimes makes it hard to understand what the writer means, as in the second example.

ABSTRACTION

Communication without the use of abstract terms would be possible only in a primitive society where each object and every single action had a separate name. If you wished to speak of *people* in such a society, you would have to name them separately—*John, Robert, Julia.* You couldn't use the word *food;* you would have to name each item individually.

Suppose now that as a member of this society you tired of your limited vocabulary and wished to observe, for instance, that all the Johns, Roberts, and Julias had two legs. You might then *abstract* this quality from those individuals and invent the word *biped.* From the same individuals you could abstract, or select, other qualities and assign terms such

[10] E. G. Boring, H. S. Langfeld, and H. P. Weld, *Foundations of Psychology* (New York, Wiley, 1948) p. 474.

[11] J. F. Dashiell, *Fundamentals of Objective Psychology* (Boston, Houghton Mifflin, 1928), p. 569.

as *whiteness* or *brownness, vertebrate, viviparous.* If you observed that some of your fellow beings were unusually slow about changing their ways, you might go as far as to invent a highly abstract term *conservative.*

In actual primitive societies it is rather common for the people to abstract a property such as *fertility,* personify it, deify it, and worship it as if it were some real thing. This illustrates one of the dangers of abstraction about which we will speak later. This tendency to abstract and to generalize, that is, to invent a new word as a name for a class or group, is a natural one. It can be cultivated consciously. These abstract words, troublesome as they are, are extremely useful in communication and in thinking. The chief source of difficulty is that the words have no tangible referents.

Levels of abstraction. Language has proved to be too complex to admit of any clear-cut classification of kinds and levels of abstraction. But there are four rough groupings which can be identified as an aid in the use and control of abstract terms.

1. *Concrete terms.* "Words designating immediately experienced qualities are concrete par excellence." [12] Such are words like *sweet, hard, red* when they are used to characterize and thus identify objects. Words that point out things, places or time, such as *this, now,* and *here* are also concrete.
2. *Class concepts.* It is convenient to have terms by which we can refer to all members of a class of things having certain characteristics in common. For example, we may call *criminal* a class concept for all persons who have committed serious offenses against the law. *Japanese* is a classificatory term for all persons with racial origin in Japan. Other class concepts are *gentleman, undergraduate, hillbilly.* (Even the Greeks had a word for hillbilly, namely *Boetian* after a rural district.) *Fruit, furniture, thing* are other illustrations.
3. *High-level abstractions.* For want of a better term, we will thus designate those words whose meaning is particularly far removed from the concrete level or which are especially complex. In this category we include words like *beauty, truth, liberalism, socialism, honor, democracy.*
4. *Theoretical constructs,* the hypothetical concepts used by scientists to carry thinking forward. Many words in science are made up or borrowed from their common use to represent concepts constructed from formulas or hypotheses or ideal conditions. Classic examples are *phlogiston* and *ether.* Modern illustrations are *mass, force, proton, absolute temperature.*

Mass, for instance, is a metrical concept in physics and is defined as the quotient of the weight of the body divided by the acceleration of gravity. This is highly abstract and requires a high degree of conceptualization. The referent is no simple object. Such constructs are abstract but precise. They are introduced into scientific discourse jointly by (*a*) setting up a theoretical system formulated in terms of them, and (*b*) by giving this system an experimental interpretation which in turn confers empirical meaning

[12] John Dewey, *Logic: The Theory of Inquiry* (New York, Holt, 1938), p. 351.

on the theoretical constructs.[13] All this is extremely difficult to understand fully, and therein lies guidance for the average citizen.

Dangers. Of the uses of abstraction we need not speak because they must be obvious from the preceding description. There are certain errors in thinking, however, which may be introduced through the misinterpretation of abstract words.

1. *Misuse of class concepts* (*through overextension*). Although it is useful to have a term which refers to all persons of Japanese ancestry, there is a tendency of the human mind to form a mental image of a Japanese type and to assume that each new person who may be called Japanese resembles this stereotype. Such a practice ignores the fact that every Japanese is an individual and may be quite different from the stereotype.

There is also a human tendency to attribute the connotation of regularity to a person designated by a class concept which pertains to behavior. For example, we think of a criminal violating the law constantly, even though our definition of criminal may cover people who have committed only one crime or who have reformed. A fourteen-year-old Los Angeles girl who ran away from home was found in a bar in San Francisco. A Los Angeles newspaper referred to her the next day: "Young barfly found in San Francisco."

To some, all intellectuals are "eggheads" with certain known characteristics; to others, all nonscholars are "blockheads" with certain known characteristics. The only difficulty is that this is not true. A newspaper publisher, very contemptuous of educated people, constantly referred in editorials and lectures to "starry-eyed professors." He lost his audience one night when he was asked from the floor which was the worst—a "starry-eyed professor" or a "cockeyed publisher." Businessmen, some of them, blame everything on "corrupt labor leaders" and imply all such leaders are corrupt. Labor leaders, some of them, blame everything on "parasitic and predatory capitalists" and imply that all capitalists are parasitic.

2. *Oversimplification of complex terms.* A natural tendency of the mind is to simplify things as much as possible and yet to be fascinated by the symbols of profound and complex ideas.

Many high-level abstractions are so complex that they are misapplied to referents which do not satisfy the conditions of a complete definition of the word, sometimes not any of the conditions. Figure 4 (But Isn't He a "Communist?") illustrates the complexity of the term *communist,* applied freely to persons to whom the definition applies only partially or not at all. Patriotic societies and veterans' associations (some of them) are very prone to apply the term *communist* to anyone who differs with them, even though the person so labeled satisfies no part of the real definition. To apply it carelessly or, especially, to apply it deliberately for propaganda purposes makes for incredible errors in thinking. Often a worthy and desirable end is blocked by such misuses.

[13] Carl G. Hempel, *Fundamentals of Concept Formation in Empirical Science* (Chicago, University of Chicago Press, 1952).

Fig. 4. But Isn't He a "Communist"?[14]

That is—
One who believes

that private enterprise = espouses as a "cause"—especially with commitment to the political party? ... 1
    = entertains as a live possibility? ... 1a

(His program)
is to be

= in all industries, agriculture, and public services? ... 2
= in basic industries, and utilities, such as mines, hydroelectric power, railroads, telephones, and telegraph systems? ... 2a

= ought to be ... 3
= will inevitably be ... 3a

= through overthrow by force   = in a revolutionary mass movement? ... 4
     = indirectly, by support of Russian advances? ... 4a

replaced = through successful political party action? ... 4b
= through the working of economic processes? ... 4c

by collective ownership = vested in the government? ... 5
= vested in co-operative associations? ... 5a

and operation = by the owning public agency? ... 6
= by lease to private agents under public control? ... 6a

of the means of production and distribution = of all economic goods and services? ... 7
= not including luxuries? ... 7a

(His philosophy)

and who is motivated by an ideology assuming
(1) a "class struggle" between capitalist and landlord owners and dependent workers = proletarian wage earners? ... 8
= all unpropertied or small-propertied workers? ... 8a

(2) a solution of the struggle by the equalizing of possessions = to the point of equality between everybody? ... 9
= to the point of reduced and functional inequalities? ... 9a

(3) a negative role for religion = for the Church as as aligned with property interests? ... 10
= for religious faith in itself an irrelevant? ... 10a

14 Used through the kind permission of Professor A. D. Sheffield, retired professor of English, Wellesley College.

Comment on Variable Elements in the Definition

This tabular display of meanings for a word of controversy is meant as a semantic approach to sanity. The passions now stirred by tensions with Russia are denying to reason its access to basic questions about a collective economic order, for real thinking stops when "communist" becomes a mere smear-word. The mischief is to more than the persons unjustly "smeared." Our own economic system gets cut off from fruitful criticism when dissenters come to be simply repelled as political lepers.

What the sheet aims to give is a sufficiently full definition, with each of its elements (numbered 1, 2, 3, etc.) showing an alternative understanding (numbered 1a, 2a, 3a, etc.) which is either currently held or responsibly suggested. The two may not exclude each other, but the alternative in "-a" tends to be less "extreme."

1a. The greater spread of acceptance for "belief" in this sense gives communism a present "sword of Damocles" function, making for social consciousness in capitalist power-holders.

2a. Much argument on issues of private vs. public enterprise takes in all business statically as either pure-private or pure-public. Actually we have gradations from individually owned small business all the way up to "public utilities" and to great corporations with price controls that become a virtual power of taxation.

4. In speaking of revolution by force, "leftists" are often unclear whether it is being *intended* or just *prophesied*. If pressed, they put it that propertied holders of power will, when political majorities vote economic change, start violent resistance. But people who *talk about force before the incriminating event* seem to court the "woe unto him by whom the offense cometh."

4a. Russia today, of course, is "communist" only as committed in purpose by an oligarchy administering *state socialism* for a people now nationalistic in temper.

7a. Early revolutionary writers did not think of the wage earner as aspiring economically to much above security and to the simpler comforts of living. With the present mass-indulgence in radios, hairdos, etc., their view of distribution problems—as in Bucharin's *A B C of Communism* (1921)—must seem laughably naïf to the party intelligentsia of today.

8., 8a. The shift here marks a realistic recognition of the "lower-middle" class, and a program with adaptations to members not self-conscious as "workers."

10. The prejudice has, of course, historic grounds (for example, Luther and the Peasant Revolt, the Spanish bishops and the Spanish Civil War), but it makes no allowance for the relativities of a church institution in its changing civilizations.

10a. The relevance of faith to social change depends on the level of aspiration to which a movement may rise, and to powers of leadership felt as drawn from a creative source of human good.

A word that designates an adherent or associate of a party based on a school of thought has a meaning composed of ideas of theory and action all subject to qualifying in the course of national and world experience. They are "conditioned variables." For purposes of economic and political argument at a given time the variables *as then generally understood* compose a *true enough* in its general reference to serve in profitable communication. But at a time of inflamed feelings a stereotype is evoked out of its wild-oats extremes, and the name puts anyone named in a class beneath arguing with.

Among consequences that may be really "subversive" is a surreptitious change in the U. S. Constitution by which committees of Congress become courts privileged to entertain accusations of a kind that automatically punish without needing to be proved.

This definition with its alternative components illustrates the complexity of the word *communist*. The smear connotations, which would further complicate the matter, are left out. The diagram also shows how a person subscribing to the views designated by *a* or *b* could be mistaken for the other or more radical type of socialist.

3. *Acceptance of emotive overtones.* Many abstract words are emotive in connotation, as just illustrated with *communist, capitalist, blockhead*. Appropriate precautions should be taken with such words.

4. *Hypostatization, or assigning real existence to abstract ideas.* [15] The abstract concept, which was artificially created as an aid to communication, is treated as if it referred to something which actually does exist. The German "state" for Hitler was something more than a mere symbol for the people living together under one government in central Europe. It had assumed in his mind a real, compelling existence for which he justified the most outrageous actions. Similar process and result can be seen in some of the actions of the Crusaders. The communists doubtless see the "state" as did Hitler.

In philosophy and theology, hypostatization frequently becomes a serious barrier to progress. *Virtue, truth, conscience, liberty,* and *idea* are words which have often been used without sufficient attention to their qualities as abstract terms.

We are fooled and we fool others if we think we are dealing with real things in the world when all we are doing is using words or—worse—substituting words for things. As a famous anthropologist has said, "Primitive man cannot distinguish between order of ideas in his head and order of things (or facts) in the world." Primitive man is not alone in this.

The situation sometimes degenerates to the level where honest and useful abstractions, or fictions, [16] representing honorable ideals or aspirations become slogans, stock phrases, even wisecracks. These degenerate

---

[15] See C. K. Ogden and I. A. Richards, *The Meaning of Meaning* (New York, Harcourt, Brace, 1946). Extensive discussion of hypostatization and other misuses of abstract terms.

[16] C. K. Ogden, *Bentham's Theory of Fictions* (New York, Harcourt, Brace, 1932).

Walpole, *op. cit.,* Ch. 8.

forms of legitimate terms take the place of thought and eventually interfere with it.

Procedures for interpreting abstract language. Abstract words need to be carefully handled. Over a century ago, Jeremy Bentham in his book *Theory of Fictions* prescribed a method for interpreting abstract terms with a minimum of confusion. We can (*a*) paraphrase the complex term by using the simplest and most concrete words possible. For *freedom*, describe some of the conditions under which free people live; for *beauty*, describe some things commonly called beautiful. Then (*b*) do consciously what we often do automatically, namely, provide a simple mental picture of some process or object which will symbolize the abstraction. Draw a picture of the referent. When using the words *mass* or *immovable*, one may see the Rock of Gibraltar. This won't do for immovable today with the explosive power of hydrogen bombs able to move almost anything. For *power*, many nowadays see an explosion of such bombs. *Crime* for some always brings up a picture of handcuffs. These two controls are not absolute but help to avoid some of the pitfalls of abstraction. Without these controls, as Richards and Walpole suggest, "our ideas would be much woolier than they should be."

Summary of Semantic Fallacies and Errors

1. *Failure to define.* Vague or ambiguous use of words.
2. *False reference.* Deliberate; or (unconscious) in writing application of words to inappropriate reference, for example, a lie.
3. *Context errors.*
   a. Words quoted out of context.
   b. Words interpreted without regard to context.
   c. Words assumed to derive their meanings from dictionaries by fiat rather than from immediate context. (The dictionary fallacy.)
4. *Etymological fallacy.* Assumption that the best current meaning of a term can be found by analyzing its roots; that original meaning is the true one.
5. *Emotive errors.*
   a. Objective meaning distorted, blurred by emotive use.
   b. Emotive connotation accepted uncritically.
6. *Figurative fallacies.*
   a. Figures of speech taken literally.
   b. Figures mixed.
7. *Oversimplification of complex terms.*
8. *Classification errors.*
   a. Attribution of imagined class qualities to a member of that class.
   b. Connotation of regularity given or accepted in the use of class concepts.
9. *Reification.* Abstract terms treated as if concrete. Attributing objective or "real" existence to things represented by abstract words.
10. *Utraquistic fallacy.* Confusion of process and product, for example, "perception," "conception," "government."[17]

[17] For further discussion, see Ogden and Richards, *op. cit.* p. 134.

11. *Mistranslation.*
    a. Inaccurate substitution.
    b. Overanalysis of translation for subtleties of connotation.
12. *Amphiboly.* Syntactic ambiguity; dangling relative clauses.
13. *Spurious morphological ambiguity or false derivation.* Similarity of mean-
    ing between two words is assumed because of similarity of forms. "Are
    you a poster or an imposter?" "He is uncouth, but she is couth."

QUESTIONS, EXERCISES, AND REPORTS

   1. For what varying purposes do we use language?
   2. Look up the word histories of: sycophant, rival, chivalry, gossip,
person, ambition. (Or select any others.)
   3. Define: due process
              necessary and proper
              "equal" in "All men are created equal."
   4. A Tulane psychologist, Dr. Loh Seng Tsai, trained a rat to select
from three doors the one marked with two images which led him to his dinner.
One door was marked with one image while the others were marked with two
and three images respectively. The three doors were interchanged, but the one
with two images always had food behind it. Dr. Tsai claimed that in learning
to pick the door with two rather than one or three images the rat showed that
he had the quality of "reasoning".
   Does this performance by the rat fit the definition of reasoning?
   5. Contrast the emotive qualities of the following pairs:
              house—home
              lie—prevarication
              bureaucrat—civil servant
              youth—juvenile
              (Or select other current paired words in common usage.)
   6. Analyze and illustrate the use of the following words as emotive terms:

communist	progressive
socialist	liberal
fascist	conservative
un-American	reactionary
egghead	businessman

   7. The following news item appeared in the *Los Angeles Times,* February 9, 1959.

   "Hugh Hardyman testified in a $100,000 civil rights damage
   suit in Glendale Superior Court that on November 14, 1957, during
   a meeting of the La Crescenta–La Canada Democratic Club, several
   men wearing American Legion hats filed into his house. One of them
   stepped forward and addressed the group.

   [This man] said that the assembled group was un-American and
   that their activities would not be tolerated in Glendale, the witness
   said.

   [Another witness] testified that [a Legionnaire] told the audience of some fifty persons that they had 'ten minutes to leave,' or else they 'would be put out forcibly.' "

    a. Define un-American.

    b. What differences in meaning or interpretation in this case led to the difference of opinion about the meeting?

    c. Is it un-American to hold any kind of meeting? To hold it in a private home?

    d. Is it un-American to enter a man's home for the purpose of breaking up a meeting on private property? To threaten violence to any who disagree with you? To threaten private citizens without presenting evidence of misconduct?

    e. Why do you suppose the Legionnaires did not proceed through legal channels, presenting evidence in duly constituted courts, securing a warrant, and employing officers of the law?

    f. Is the violation of law and of Constitutional rights, un-American or patriotic?

    g. The group may have been subversive and un-American in views. From the news item given, cite the evidence which led the Legionnaires to believe that subversion was present.

    8. In the 1958 election campaign, Vice-President Nixon defined a "radical" as a man who "believes in excessive or unlimited government spending." Analyze the possible linguistic basis for this definition, telling whether it is legitimate or not, whether it could be stipulative, and what other semantic problems enter into the definition.

    (Note other cases of this kind in current news stories and in magazine articles. Take care to include all shades of opinion and all common sources: politicians, business leaders, labor leaders, scholars, columnists, editors, and others.)

    9. Tell in what ways the following fit the definition of theoretical construct:

heat	proton
energy	phlogiston
pressure	

    10. What are the dangers in the uses of the following generic terms:

liar	Negro
lady driver	teacher
Yankee	

    11. Read the following (from *Time Magazine,* December 27, 1948):

    Davis Knight had lived in Mississippi all of his 23 years except for his three years in the Navy. He married blonde, blue-eyed Junie Lee Spradley and farmed a poor piece of land. One night the county police arrested him. Knight was a Negro, they said; Junie Lee was white. In Mississippi that kind of marrying was against the law.

    Knight said they were wrong. But a relative, irked by an old family feud, had dug up Davis Knight's genealogy. His great-grandfather had been Cap'n Newt Knight, who deserted the Confederate Army and set up "The Free State of Jones" in Jones County.

Cap'n Newt had had children by Rachel, a Negro slave girl. Rachel was Davis Knight's great-grandmother.

Through succeeding generations the Knights had married white men or women. Davis Knight's own parents had not known of the Negro strain in their ancestry. The story the relative dug up would affect a number of other families in the neighborhood, all sprung from the loins of Cap'n Newt and Rachel. Last week a court in Ellisville convicted Cap'n Newt's great-grandson of miscegenation, sentenced him to five years in jail.

Analyze the problem of classification here.

How would you define *Negro?* How is *Negro* legally defined?

12. Expand the following abstract terms:
   a. liberal
   b. politics
   c. freedom
   d. imperialism

13. Point out the ways in which this metaphor is mixed (from a letter in the *Wilmington* (Del.) *Journal-Every Evening*):

In recent past, PTA's have sprung up like dewdrops after Spring showers, and have taken the ball and practically run wild. Of course, sooner or later, they will have their wings clipped. Maybe they are bumping into road blocks already.

Try for fun to draw a picture of the referent here: dewdrops springing up, seizing the ball, running wild, getting their wings clipped, bumping into road blocks.

ADDITIONAL QUESTIONS

Some instructors may wish to use the following questions before using those above; others may wish to omit them entirely.

1. Describe for class analysis any curriculum materials or classroom procedures which are aimed at modern, functional teaching of language in contrast to formal treatment.

2. Illustrate from everyday life how various factors suppress critical analysis of meanings.

3. Duplicate the changes of meaning with context as in the case of *book* in the text. Particularly illustrate the effect of psychological and physical context.

4. What factors cause basic meanings to change historically?

5. Word meanings may change within discourse.
   a. Distinguish, with illustrations, between deliberate and unnoticed shifts.
   b. Why do speakers and writers shift meanings?

6. Bring in illustrations of figurative language, both misleading and properly used. Of emotive language. Look particularly for mixed metaphors. Apply Black's six points to cases of emotive writing. Analyze certain abstractions in common usage today which seem to be causing confusion.

7. What is the meaning of the statement: "The ostensible reference of some words is overlaid with meanings of a nonrational character"? How does this come about? Guidance for teaching language? For use of language in critical thinking?

8. The semantic fallacies listed in the chapter have been, many of them, illustrated in answering the foregoing questions. Bring in illustrations for analysis for those which have not yet been covered.

9. Read with critical attitude the following statement which shows the widely different meanings for words which turned up after everyone had presumably agreed to definitions and meanings.

   a. Explain as well as you can how these differences appeared for words which presumably had been agreed upon.

   b. What weaknesses and mistakes in the negotiating process now become apparent?

   c. Prepare a fairly extensive summary of guidance you can derive from this, (1) for your own thinking, (2) for teaching.

(The material is used here with permission of Professor A. D. Sheffield, retired professor of English, Wellesley College.)

The Statement

National X expects to pay wages in its plants and offices as good as or better than prevail for similar work under similar conditions in the communities in which it operates.

What the president therefore proposed and the union accepted as a solution of the case was that a new contract be drafted, including a schedule of the hourly rates then paid, and that a Board of Arbitration be constituted to judge whether the rates did in fact conform to the *policy* of the company set forth in the language above quoted. The contract was signed, the strike called off, and the negotiators sat down to a dinner together with everybody feeling that their difficulties had been solved.

When, however, the appointed arbitrators began hearings on the issue as put in these terms, it became evident that policy-words make trouble when they are treated as contract-words. As the testimony and argument proceeded, every key word in the pronouncement had different meanings urged as *the right* meaning according as the speaker was a witness, lawyer, or official of one side or of the other. The result was a web of multiple meanings that can be displayed as follows:

Multiple Meaning Implicated in a
Statement of Wage Policy

"National X intends to pay *wages*

(1) hourly wage rates
(2) wage *totals* for compared spans of employment

in its plants and offices as good as or better than *prevail*

(1) are received by most employees
(2) are paid by most firms
(3) are paid by most firms, not counting firms that are deemed not properly comparable
(4) appear by averaging the showings of the firms compared

for similar work

(1) operationally and descriptively similar
(2) of like *ratings* on job "factors" as compared item by item
(3) of nearly the same *total* ratings for the compared aggregates of job-factors rated

under similar conditions

(1) *work* conditions in the plant
(2) *company* conditions (financial status, or social level of labor policies and practices)

in the communities

(1) localities taken *distributively* —comparisons for the NX plant in each being made with *local* plants
(2) localities taken *collectively*— comparisons for one plant may be drawn from *all* NX communities

in which it operates."

(1) operates its manufacturing or processing plants
(2) does business, whether of manufacturing or of selling its products

(A. D. Sheffield, December, 1940, by permission)

A summary of the conflicting interpretations of word meanings was then prepared:

"National X intends to pay   =(1) hourly wage *rates**
wages   =(2) wage-total for compared spans of employment†

in its plants and offices as   =(1) in amounts of weekly "take"†
good as or better   =(2) in weekly amounts *relative to the number of weekly hours* required to earn them*

than *prevail*   =(1) are received by most employees
                                 =(2) are paid by most firms*
                                 =(3) are paid by a sampling of firms, passing over such as are deemed not properly comparable
                                 =(4) appear by *averaging* the showings for the firms compared†

for similar work   =(1) operationally and descriptively similar jobs   as compared job with job*   as compared *class* with *class* of job†
                                 =(2) of like *ratings* on job "factors" as compared item by item
                                 =(3) of like *total* rating for the compared *aggregates* of job-factors rated†

under similar conditions   =(1) *work* conditions in the plant†
                                 =(2) *company* conditions (financial status, or social level of labor policies and practices)*

in the *communities*   =(1) localities taken *distributively*—comparisons for the NX plant in each being made with local plants†
                                 =(2) localities taken *collectively*—comparisons for one plant being drawn from *all* the NX communities

in which it *operates*."   =(1) operates its manufacturing or processing plants†
                                 =(2) does business, whether of manufacturing or of selling its products*

* Union-preferred meaning
† Company-preferred meaning

A STUDY OUTLINE FOR MORE DETAILED ANALYSIS

Students whose previous contacts with semantics may have been brief may wish to follow this suggested outline:

WALPOLE, Hugh, *Semantics* (New York, Norton, 1941), Ch. 4, "Symbols." DEWEY, John, *How We Think,* rev. ed. (Boston, Heath, 1933), pp. 230-235.
1. What is the difference between a sign and a symbol?
2. What are some examples of words treated as things?
3. Dewey's (pp. 233-234) metaphorical use of the words *fence, label, vehicle,* is quoted by other authors (for example, Richards, *Meaning of Meaning,* p. 133). Can you select an illustration from Dewey to show how this threefold distinction applies?

WALPOLE, *op. cit.,* Ch. 5, "Contexts." DEWEY, *op. cit.,* pp. 280-282.
1. Which of Walpole's three kinds of context is Dewey writing about on p. 280?
2. On p. 153, Dewey. What is the connotation of the word *deposit?* What might this term mean in other contexts?
3. What other theories of meaning are widely accepted? (Compare "Language," pp. 92-94.)
4. What are some of the implications of the context theory for education?

WALPOLE, *op. cit.,* Ch. 2, "Emotive Language." HUSE, H. R., *The Illiteracy of the Literate* (New York, D. Appleton-Century, 1933), Ch. 4, "Figurative and Emotive Use of Words." (See also HAYAKAWA, S. I., *Language in Thought and Action,* rev. ed. (New York, Holt, 1949), Ch. 5.
1. Reduced to one sentence, what is the chief point made in Huse, Ch. 4?
2. Huse discusses three figurative uses of words and a fourth, emotive use.
   a. State as briefly as possible and in everyday words the chief point he makes under each of the four uses. Give everyday illustrations with special reference to thinking.
   b. What are the legitimate uses of each?
   c. What are the real and serious dangers for thinking in the uncritical use of each?
   d. Can figurative expressions be considered "emotive"?
   e. Which of the "emotive" words on p. 41 are also metaphors?
   f. What in general is the remedy for the evils?
   g. State two or three principles designed to aid us in avoiding the dangers.
   h. Cite examples of figurative and emotive expressions from Huse or Walpole.
   i. Dewey, p. 147, line 29, uses the word *manipulating.* Do you consider this an "emotive" use?
   j. (For mature students only). What are the subclasses of emotive usage?
   k. What documents from U. S. history might be used as exercises for the study of the above topics?

OGDEN, C. K., and RICHARDS, I. A., *The Meaning of Meaning* (New York, Harcourt, Brace, 1938 and 1953). WALPOLE, *op. cit.*, Ch. 6, "Theory of Definitions." DEWEY, *op. cit.*, Ch. 10.

1. What one simple principle aimed at better thinking and discussion could be laid down concerning definition?
2. What else is required besides the willingness to define before mutual understanding can be attained?
3. Notice how Dewey follows his own advice in Ch. 1 by defining a key term. Notice on p. 15 of Dewey, line 9, how reference to his definitions is needed.
4. What terms are used in this course in the oral discussions which need better definition?

WALPOLE, *op. cit.*, Ch. 8, "Fictions." HUSE, *op. cit.*, Ch. 7, "Abstractionism." DEWEY, *op. cit.*, Ch. 15 and pp. 200-202.

1. Can you suggest a better word than *fictions* for Walpole to use?
2. What dangers arise in the interpretation of abstractions?
3. What techniques might be used in interpreting abstract writing in order to avoid misunderstanding?
4. On p. 201 of Dewey, can you find any nouns that are not abstractions?
5. Dewey, p. 90. What is meant by *freedom?*
6. Can you think of any abstract terms commonly used in educational literature which are vague or misleading?

WALPOLE, *op. cit.*, Ch. 7, "Metaphor."

1. Find the metaphors in the passages in Dewey starting on p. 200 "If we add . . ." and ending on p. 201 ". . . and more extensive inference."
2. In what way do the metaphors above:
   a. Increase the effectiveness of the expressions?
   b. Convey Dewey's meaning indirectly?
3. On p. 230 of Dewey, express the ideas behind the following metaphors in nonfigurative language:
   a. "Tool" of thinking.
   b. Intellectual "barrenness."
   c. A "sham" of thought.
   d. Chief "instrument."
   e. Severest "indictments."

OPTIONAL READING

For enlightenment and amusement, students might read the following:

Huse, *op. cit.*, Ch. 5, "Word Magic"; Ch. 6, "The Suggestive (Hypnotic) Effect of Words."

Did you, while reading Ch. 6, catch yourself falling into the very error discussed? Give everyday illustrations, preferably from your own experience.

P. 57. Do you have to be hypnotized to find the effort of reflective thought difficult? What is the significance of your answer here?

P. 60. Interpret and illustrate the points in the last two sentences on this page.

P. 61. Do the same for the sentence toward the bottom: "It is often observed that people repeat their own falsehoods so frequently that they come to believe them." (This is often said facetiously, but the real point is deadly serious.)

P. 67. How do you think we might train individuals to "refuse to cooperate in the cruder forms of suggestion . . ."? General statements are all that are possible at this point.

P. 69. Develop in some detail the significance of the long paragraph in the middle of the page.

Write a brief summary, in either outline form or as a list of numbered points, of the principles and facts derived from this discussion of words. One page should do it. Some points of reference are (a) guidance of thought as it develops, (b) resources for good thinking, (c) sources of error.

Clichés, bromides, and slogans. This topic, highly entertaining and deadly serious, had to be omitted because of space. A student or committee can well pursue it and make a class report. The following references are but starters:

Jonathan Swift published in 1738 the *Complete Collection of Genteel Conversation Now Used in the Best Companies of England.* Probably one of the earliest collections.

Bergen Evans and Cornelia Evans, *Dictionary of Contemporary American Usage* (New York, Random House, 1957). A similar modern summary.

Gustave Flaubert, *The Dictionary of Accepted Ideas,* translated by Jacques Barzun (New York, New Directions, 1954).

Gustave Flaubert, *Bouvard and Pecuchet,* translated by T. W. Earp and G. W. Stonier (New York, New Didections, 1954). This is a novel but also an excellent account.

Bergen Evans, "Fell Swoop on a Fine Cliché Kettle," *New York Times Magazine* (July 27, 1958), pp. 13 ff.

Joseph Wood Krutch, "Great Cliché Debate (Continued)," a reply to Bergen Evans, *New York Times Magazine* (August 31, 1958), pp. 13 ff.

Hackneyed words, trite expressions, stereotypes. These are less pretentious than clichés but nevertheless serious detriments to good thinking. Make a collection of expressions used again and again by writers, speakers, and in conversation. These meaningless verbalisms appear everywhere. Some writers include lists of these under "bromides" above.

BIBLIOGRAPHY

BLACK, Max, *Critical Thinking: An Introduction to Logic and Scientific Thinking* (Englewood Cliffs, N. J., Prentice-Hall, 1949), Chs. 9-11.

———, *Language and Philosophy* (Ithaca, N. Y., Cornell University Press, 1933).

BLOOMFIELD, L., *Language* (New York, Holt, 1933).

CARNAP, Rudolph, *The Logical Syntax of Language* (New York, Harcourt, Brace, 1937).

CARROLL, J. B., *The Study of Language* (Cambridge, Mass., Harvard University Press, 1953).

———, "Communication Theory, Linguistics, and Psycholinguistics," *Review of Educational Research* (April, 1958), Ch. 1. Excellent current bibliography of 59 titles.

CHASE, Stuart, *The Tyranny of Words* (New York, Harcourt, Brace, 1938).

———, *The Power of Words* (New York, Harcourt, Brace, 1954). An enlightening popular treatment.

DEWEY, John, *Logic: The Theory of Inquiry* (New York, Holt, 1938).

FLESCH, Rudolf, *The Art of Plain Talk* (New York, Harper, 1946).

GLEASON, Henry A., *An Introduction to Descriptive Linguistics* (New York, Holt, 1955). Good introductory treatment.

HAYAKAWA, S. I., *Language in Thought and Action*, rev. ed. (New York, Holt, 1949). Extensive bibliography.

HEMPEL, Carl G., *Fundamentals of Concept Formation in Empirical Science* (Chicago, University of Chicago Press, 1952).

HUSE, H. R., *The Illiteracy of the Literate* (New York, D. Appleton-Century, 1933). Out of print but worth reading if available in college library.

KORZYBSKI, Alfred, *Science and Sanity* (Lancaster, Pa., Science Press Printing Co., 1933). The original book in the field of general semantics. Some controversy with more recent writers.

LANGER, Susanne K., *Philosophy in a New Key* (Cambridge, Mass., Harvard University Press, 1942; also in Pelican Books, 1948).

LARRABEE, Harold A., *Reliable Knowledge* (Boston, Houghton Mifflin, 1945), Chs. 7, 8. Good footnote bibliography. Excellent exercises.

MORRIS, Charles, *Signs, Language, and Behavior* (Englewood Cliffs, N. J., Prentice-Hall, 1946).

OGDEN, C. K., *Jeremy Bentham's Theory of Fictions* (New York, Harcourt, Brace, 1932). See also Bentham's original volume.

OGDEN, C. K., and RICHARDS, I. A., *The Meaning of Meaning* (New York, Harcourt, Brace, 1946).

Progressive Education Association, *Language in General Education* (New York, Appleton-Century-Crofts, 1940).

RICHARDS, I. A., *How to Read a Page* (New York, Morton, 1942).

———, *Interpretation in Teaching* (New York, Harcourt, Brace, 1929).

———, *Practical Criticism* (New York, Harcourt, Brace, 1929).

WALPOLE, Hugh, *Semantics* (New York, Norton, 1941). A much simplified account.

(A number of advanced books are available in college libraries.)

CHAPTER 11

Errors and Fallacies in Thinking

Oh ye Gods! What thick encircling darkness blinds the minds of men.

OVID

Whom the gods intend to destroy, they first smite with blindness.

SOPHOCLES

"Logic! Good gracious! What rubbish!" exclaimed E. M. Forster's Old Lady, "How can I tell what I think till I see what I say?"

A statement credited variously to Voltaire or to one of his biographers holds that "Men will continue to commit atrocities as long as they believe absurdities." Today we may add that men can and do precipitate disasters in economic, social, political, military, and other areas, as long as they think without regard to reliable knowledge and valid processes. The results of bad thinking affect not only atrocities, disasters, and affairs of state, but also the everyday affairs of the average citizen.

The relation between thinking and a great military disaster is cogently stated in this paragraph: [1]

Failure at Stalingrad was the product of grand delusions. Hitler *thought* the Russians were beaten at the beginning of the 1942 summer campaign. Hermann Goering *thought* the German troops, after encirclement, could be supplied by air. Paulus *thought* the Nazi leaders could not leave an army to perish. Underlying these fantasies was the root insanity: the *conviction* that

[1] Gordon Harrison, "Delusions Brought Disaster," *New York Times Book Review* (Nov. 16, 1958), p. 40. A review of Heinz Schroeter's *Stalingrad,* translated by Constantine Fitzgibbon from the German, *Stalingrad: Bis Zur Letzen Patrone* (New York, Dutton, 1958).

208

German military might could and should subdue the world. In the last days of Stalingrad a doctor remarked that "we [the German people] attached too much importance to ourselves, and now we have to pay for our arrogance with our lives." This is an *insight* which makes impertinent the effort to fix on Hitler or any other individual the blame for what happened.

Three hundred thousand lives were lost; the battle was lost, and doubtless also the war.

In the early days of World War I, the British high command was unable to think in terms of the obvious facts. A century or more of war against poorly armed natives in various far countries had grooved military thinking. The Germans sat safely in concrete pillboxes while the British sprayed them with shrapnel. Mounting losses and a vigorous campaign in the press were necessary to change the tactics. The strategy of some of our West Point trained officers during the early Indian Wars in the far West does not make too good reading. Thinking suited to one type of warfare had first to be broken down and new ideas developed.

The early days in the development of marketing co-operatives presented some interesting illustrations of kinds of thinking. A brilliant lawyer who had made a national name in this field addressed a huge gathering of wheat farmers who were in trouble in marketing their grain. After his address and in the discussion groups, thinking turned on these ideas: "What does a lawyer know about raising wheat?" "We don't need a city slicker to tell us how to farm!" "The guy couldn't run a tractor!"; and many others. For two days the lawyer and committee tried to get the discussion on marketing. The final address was a masterpiece of brevity delivered in that courteous and deadly calm tone which is much more convincing than bluster:

Gentlemen, you are right—I am a city lawyer. You are right—I do not know anything about farming. You are right—I cannot run a tractor. I do not even know the difference between kinds of wheat. I do know the national and international grain markets intimately and in detail. You are evidently too stupid to distinguish between raising and marketing wheat. I leave you to your excellent methods of raising wheat which you have demonstrated you cannot sell to advantage. Gentlemen, I bid you good day.

So saying, he picked up his briefcase and walked out. The group refused to pay his fee. After another year of bad marketing the lawyer was invited back and collected a fee for each appearance. Bad thinking costs money.

The father of two boys managed them with an iron hand, "I believe in discipline." The boys were absolutely subservient, did as they were told, spoke only when spoken to, were ordered about regardless of what they were doing. Teachers and a child psychologist tried to point out the dangers but were answered, "I know I am firm—but I know the boys will

respect me for it when they grow up." Teachers tried to point out the immediate effects on schoolwork and on conduct. The child psychologist said
quietly that the boys would run away from home before they were sixteen.
The parent said he thought not. One boy ran away twice before he was
fifteen. The other developed the typical aggressive resentments, bullied
smaller children unmercifully, became insolent to all adults outside the
home. Neither got along in school, despite good general ability. Bad thinking here worked tragic damage to personality and conduct, not to mention
future success.

Cases could be multiplied without number. Emphasis here is necessarily on bad thinking. Reference has been made elsewhere to many cases
of excellent thinking.

Early efforts to list errors and sources of error. Primitive peoples seem
not to have thought about thinking, taking it largely for granted. Many
individuals are still in that stage. The great discovery made by the Greeks
was that one could think about thinking. They were the first to pry into
the workings of the mind. Great intellectual achievements took place in the
Greek city states from approximately the fifth century B. C. The interesting
story of these developments is told elsewhere. For the moment we will
examine the matter of errors. One group, the sophists, became so well
known for slippery argument that Plato criticized them severely, and his
remarks are probably the first to deal with fallacies in logic.

Scholars since early times have made classifications of errors and of
sources of error. When modern scientific thinking was just beginning,
Francis Bacon made a classification of "Idols" which, as idols often do,
lead the mind astray. [2] An abbreviated definition is given here:

Idols of the Tribe. Foundation in human nature itself, and in the tribe
or race of men.

Idols of the Cave or Den. Foundation in the particular mental or bodily
constitution of each individual; also in his education, his conversation with
others, reading; in authority of those he admires; in differences in impression
made on his mind when preoccupied or predisposed, or when indifferent and
settled. Heraclitus said: "Men look for sciences in their own lesser worlds and
not in the greater or common world."

Idols of the Market Place. These spring largely from one cause: intercourse and association through language.

Idols of the Theater. Basis is in the learned or taught philosophical systems; in inadequate or inaccurate demonstrations.

A detailed listing of the specific Idols as given by Bacon will be found
in Appendix B. Bacon's designation and illustrations are subject to some
revision in the light of modern knowledge, but his basic idea is good today.
We need, particularly, to be cautious about Idols of the Tribe as being

[2] Francis Bacon, "Aphorisms Concerning the Interpretation of Nature and the
Kingdom of Man," in *The Great Instauration,* Part II (1620), any ed.

rooted in "human nature." We know far more about this than in Bacon's day. Individuals are heard on every hand excusing certain blunders in thought or action or refusing to correct certain errors in thinking with the slogan, "Well, that's human nature." "He can't help that, it's human nature."

The naïve layman does not know there are several score conceptions of human nature, not just the one he uses. Most cultures begin with some conception or other of human nature and then try to make living personalities conform to the predetermined culture pattern. The uncritical and unrealistic acceptance of the concept of "original sin" as a part of the human nature complex has encouraged complacent acceptance of many social evils, such as slavery and hideous atrocities committed in the name of religion.

Even worse is acceptance of the ancient superstition, "Human nature does not change," or "You cannot change human nature." Dreadful blunders in thinking are excused with those clichés. If human nature could not, in fact, be changed, then churches and schools should close their doors, since the improvement of human nature is one of their chief responsibilities.

The routine nonsense about "human nature" is absurd in the light of modern knowledge. One writer, Gardner Murphy, says we do not yet know enough about human nature to relate it to the great issues of the day. Interesting references here are:

Ellsworth Faris, *The Nature of Human Nature* (New York, McGraw-Hill, 1937).
Paul Grabbe, in co-operation with Gardner Murphy, *We Call It Human Nature* (New York, Harper, 1939).
Gardner Murphy, *Human Potentialities* (New York, Basic Books, 1958).
Volumes by Ashley-Montagu and by other anthropologists are very useful here.

John Locke analyzed the causes of bad thinking in two different organizations, of which the following is a summary. The original organizations are found in Locke's *The Conduct of the Understanding,* any edition, Section 3, and in *Essay Concerning Human Understanding,* Book IV, Ch. XX.

1. *Dependence on authority. Individual does not think.* Dependence on authority is both an error and a cause of other errors.
   Beliefs are accepted from others without critical reaction.
   Principles are accepted by children from beloved parents, teachers, priests. These principles come to be almost sacred, and to question them is offensive in high degree.
2. *Dogmatic cast of mind. Individual refuses to think.* May overlap with foregoing point.
   The testimony of others is denied and refused, sometimes the testimony of one's own senses.

3. *Strong emotions, feelings. Thinking is blocked or twisted.*
4. *Circumscribed experience.*

The purpose of the outlines which follow, in Sections 1 and 2, is to list sources of error, the kinds of error, and to fit the latter to the problem-solving framework. Texts on logic and on thinking, popularly presented, contain such lists. The very names of the formal fallacies differ somewhat over the years, and from text to text. A given error may be traceable to a combination of causes which are themselves in different groupings. Any outline, no matter how systematic, will contain overlap and cross reference. All authors agree that this is inevitable. Outlines differ, therefore, in basic scheme and in placement of items. Schopenhauer attempted a collection and, after finding forty devious methods for confusing thought, gave up in disgust!

Our treatment is designed to aid teachers and the average citizen who does not know the language of formal logic, particularly of symbolic logic, and to aid the classroom teacher who may wish to stimulate learners to improve their thinking. Language, classification, and illustrations are therefore drawn from everyday communication and problems. The formal fallacies have been explained, so far as possible, in everyday terms following the formal title.

SECTION 1. POSSIBLE SOURCES OF ERROR

A number of schemes can be presented, as has been stated. This is but one of several which could be devised. Anyone can construct another which he may like better. The specific errors will be described and, to a limited degree, will be illustrated in Section 2. Certain major categories have already been treated in earlier chapters and will be abbreviated and cross-referenced here.

I. *Sources of error resident in the thinker.*
   A. *Intellectual equipment or training.*
      1. An inferior quality of mind limits the ability to carry on the various processes outlined in earlier chapters necessary for critical thought or problem solving.
      2. Meager, limited experience with, incomplete knowledge of the techniques of thinking. (Ability present but untrained or badly trained or handicappd by lack of experience.)
      3. Deficiency in skills of co-operation and interaction (group process); deficiency in understanding of and skill in use of language as a means of communication.
   B. *Impulsive emotional nature.*
      1. Emotional states so severe as to interfere with thinking at all. One acts, as we say, in an unreasoning manner.
      2. Emotions and sentiments and strong personal interests can also lead

to specious or sophistical conclusions, to rationalization, or to conscious dishonesty.

Emotion can also lead one to seize a conclusion hastily to end the emotional discomfort or to delay unduly through great fear of coming to a wrong conclusion.

3. Deficiency may exist in essential state of interest or wholehearted participation.

4. The need for security, the desire for survival, and the need to feel useful can both aid and interfere with thinking.

C. *Attitudes.* A chapter has been devoted to attitudes favorable and unfavorable to good thinking. A few salient unfavorable attitudes will be repeated here for the sake of emphasis.

1. Attitudes of primitive credulity, complacency, dogmatism, or flippancy often prevent thinking at all.

2. Attitudes of impatience toward careful observation of data, toward controlled methods of inquiry, toward necessary suspension of judgment will lead to hasty or ill-considered conclusions.

The same results may flow from attitudes of intellectual dishonesty, from absence of a critical attitude.

3. Lack of alertness, curiosity, flexibility; tendency to eternal balancing of arguments and conclusions, thus delaying or preventing conclusion and action.

Acceptance of line of least resistance; indifference to problems and the necessity of "doing something about them." Will to think is absent or dormant.

D. *Physical and mental health.*

Permanent defects in sense organs, congenital or acquired.

Neuroses, fixations, instabilities.

Fatigue, illness, pain.

II. *Sources of error resident in the conditions; in the interaction between and among persons and between persons and environmental factors.*

A. *The nature of the problem itself.*

1. The problem may be too difficult for the person or group attempting the solution; a long, complex process of inference and checking may be beyond the abilities available for the given individual or group.

2. Data may not be available for the solution of the problem; nonexistent; unobtainable at the moment.

3. Data may be so highly technical that interpretation is difficult or impossible for average individuals.

4. Instruments of precision for gathering data may be nonexistent or at the moment unavailable.

5. Checking or testing results may be technically difficult or sometimes impossible at the moment.

B. *Distractions due to:*

1. Noise or other physical interruptions.

2. Pressure or harassment due to deadlines or other time limits.

3. Lack of economic security.

C. *The limitations of language are a potential source of error.*

1. The evolutionary and inexact nature of language as an instrument of thought and of communication may often hamper thinking.
2. Verbal symbols always possess some degree of vagueness, often ambiguity.
3. Quantitative symbols under certain conditions may also be vague and/or ambiguous.

(See Chapter 10 on words for further elaboration of these points.)

D. *Certain social conditions are incompatible with good thinking.*

1. Various media of guidance and communication, parents, teachers, newspapers, radio commentators, promulgate erroneous beliefs which may become conventions of discourse and behavior and are inimical to effective thinking.
2. Certain groups of persons may exert detrimental influence on thinking:

   School
   Peers
   Relatives
   Pressure groups, religious, political, economic, social class, or other. (These groups may often actually suppress thinking, quite apart from the nondeliberate blocking or warping of thought.)
3. The custom or fashion (growing out of several points already made) that accepts rhetorical and oratorical statements, verbalisms, high-sounding ideals, without insistence on data, referents, reasoned chains of evidence. (Much polite conversation, political and economic discussion, preaching and religious discussion, interchange of opinion and experience about child rearing—and many others— display very ineffective thinking and often absence of thinking.)
4. Ineffective thinking acquires social approval. (Or, negatively, society makes no demand in ordinary affairs for rigorous, consistent, and systematic thinking.)

The checking of errors in one's own thinking or the detection of them in any kind of materials is not a simple task of checking against the list of sources above. A given error may have several causes, or the real cause may be hidden behind a specious cause. All the tricks of confusing and diverting thought may be used to distract.

Insufficient intelligence is a relative term. Students well able to solve problems on a certain level at a given level of maturity may be quite unable to solve problems on another level. There is a moral here for those parents and teachers who select impossible problems for children on the theory that the harder the problem, the better thinking will result. No thinking, or badly confused thinking, will result.

Emotional blocks may frustrate the thinker and keep him from thinking coolly or efficiently. Certain emotions, we may note in passing, are aids to thinking. The normal emotions of pride and self-respect can become serious blockades to thinking if an individual feels he will "lose face" by admitting he was wrong. The argument for an accepted belief then becomes a matter of pride and not of facts and logic. This can be reversed, as Rousseau pointed out long ago. To feed a feeling of superiority, an individual may differ with others no matter what stand is taken—"With believers he is an atheist; with atheists he is a believer." (*Émile,* Book IV). Even some competent scientists are slow to give up an idea if the new one, no matter how well demonstrated, tends to upset a comfortable system already accepted.

Prejudices are usually highly emotionalized beliefs. Descartes once said: "A man can more easily burn down his own house than get rid of his prejudices." A modern counterpart by Einstein has it: "It is disheartening to live in an age when it is possible to split the atom, but impossible to break down a prejudice." Vivid, emotional experiences, unfortunately, have greater weight than rational ones. We may match the scholars above with a quotation from a homely humorist of the American frontier, Artemus Ward, "Find the evidence, and then arrange it to suit yourself."

SECTION 2. A LISTING OF ERRORS AND FALLACIES

A man who has committed a mistake and doesn't correct it is committing another mistake.

CONFUCIUS

Kinds of errors. Mistakes in thinking may be made in all stages or processes of solving a problem. Traditional discussions of bad thinking have emphasized the logical fallacies. Error may result from poor attitudes, lack of productive hypotheses, failure to employ any satisfactory method of solution, or through succumbing to tricks used by others to becloud the issue or to divert one from the essential issues.

Some of the following items are properly *fallacies,* that is, kinds of illogical reasoning; others are more broadly *errors in thinking,* that is, procedures which do not help to solve the problem at hand.

I. *Attitudinal errors*
  A. Lack of intellectual curiosity; torpidity.
  B. Disposition to flippancy and/or pseudosophistication.
  C. Intellectual dishonesty.
  D. Bias or prejudice for or against (anything).
  E. Primitive credulity.
  F. Undue reverence for the "latest thing," the new or the novel.
  G. Harmful incredulity; closed-mindedness; undue reverence for what is, for custom and tradition.
  H. Disregard for cause-and-effect relationships.
  I. Disposition to be tolerant of confusion and inconsistency.
  J. Dogmatism and rigidity; inflexibility.
  K. Lack of persistence.
  L. Indecisiveness.

II. *Gross methodological errors* (Errors in details of method are listed a
few pages further on.)
  A. Failure to define problem at all.
  B. Failure to advance hypotheses.
  C. Failure to look for evidence, to employ suitable methods of experi-
     mentation or of proof. Failure to examine data even when given.
     Failure to seek expert advice.
  D. Failure to give rational consideration to relations between data and
     propositions.
     1. Failure to reason from facts to generalizations at all.
     2. Failure to reason from generalizations to facts.
  E. Failure to reach a conclusion, or to test conclusions reached.
  F. Failure to use conclusions in appropriate applications.
III. *Errors in interpretation*
  A. Definition.
     1. Words whose meanings are vague, complex, or ambiguous, used
        without definition.
  B. Context.
     1. Words are quoted out of context.
     2. Words are interpreted without regard to context.
     3. The "dictionary fallacy." Words are believed to get meanings by
        fiat from dictionaries. (And not from contexts in part.)
  C. Emotive connotation.
     1. Objective meaning distorted, blurred by emotive.
     2. Emotive connotation accepted uncritically.
     3. Emotive verbalisms or glittering generalities. Words that are nearly
        empty of objective reference but loaded with connotations of
        approval or disapproval offered and accepted as though they were
        objective. For example, "democratic," "traditional."
  D. Complexity.
     1. Complicated terms used or accepted for one component meaning
        only. (Oversimplification)
  E. Classification.
     1. Connotation of regularity given or accepted in use of classifiers
        (existential, evidential, characterizing, adjectival terms). For ex-
        ample, "drunkard," "thieving."
     2. Attribution to a member of a class qualities of the class in gen-
        eral. For example, "All Aryans are blond."
     3. Converse of 2.
  F. Abstraction.
     1. Abstract terms vague, failure to exemplify or make concrete.
     2. Reification. Abstract terms treated as if concrete.
        a. Personification.
     3. Utraquistic fallacy. Confusion of process and product. For ex-
        ample, "perception," "conception," "government."
  G. Quantification.
     1. Terms used which are vague in quantity. For example, "some,"
        "many," "most."

H. Figurative fallacies.
    1. Figures of speech taken literally.
        a. Euphemism.
        b. Hyperbole.
        c. Metaphor, metonymy.
    2. All references of figurative terms taken to apply to the referent under discussion.

I. Ambiguity.
    1. Words with several distinct meanings used without indication as to which meaning is implied.
    2. Equivocation. Deliberate ambiguity. Especially in case of words shifting meaning within discourse.

J. Quibble.
    1. Unnecessarily fine distinctions made.

K. Gross verbalism.
    1. Use of words individually or collectively whose meanings are not significant, in such a way as to imply that they are significant.
       A grievous offense against the law of the Lord is often rendered. A green fence around the lawn of the Lord.

L. False reference.
    1. Deliberate application of terms to inappropriate references, as calling an honest man a thief.

M. Jargon.
    1. Use of technical terms not understood by audience or in circumstances where nontechnical terms are adequate.

N. Translation.
    1. Mistranslation of a foreign language.
    2. Analysis of translated term as though it were original form of expression. For example, analysis of King James Bible terms (written in Hebrew and Greek originally).

O. Etymological fallacy.
    1. Assumption that the best current meaning of a term can be found by analyzing its roots. Ignores changing meanings.

P. Accent.
    1. Misunderstanding arises when certain words in a sentence are stressed.

Q. Amphiboly (Syntactic ambiguity).
    1. Words in sentence put in such an order that confusion arises. Dislocated relative clauses, for example.

IV. *Errors in identification or definition of the problem*
A. Failure to analyze problem properly.
    1. Failure to discover what principles are involved.
    2. Failure to determine what persons are involved.
    3. Failure to locate specific points of conflict.
B. Failure to recognize pattern of problem, that is, whether it is normative, descriptive, discovery, critical, creative, legal, or the like.

V. *Errors in hypothesis*

    A. Infertility: failure to produce any, or sufficient, or imaginative hypotheses; failure to advance alternative hypotheses.

    B. Irrelevancy: ridiculous hypotheses.

    C. Impracticability: hypotheses that cannot be tested.

    D. Proliferation: too many hypotheses.

VI. *Logical errors* (Subdivided into inductive, deductive, and other)

    A. Inductive.

        1. Insufficient instances. Judgments about people of other nationalities after observing one or two.

        2. Instances not representative. Judgment about French people after seeing only shopkeepers and Folies-Bergère.

        3. Contradictory instances ignored; throwing out cases which seem to contradict the rule.

        4. Instances of accidental or temporary concomitance only.

        5. *Post hoc ergo propter hoc.* Events which follow others are assumed to be caused by them.

        6. False cause. General attribution of causation to wrong subject.

        7. Statistical fallacies. [3]

            a. Drawing inferences about individuals from measures of a group.

            b. Interpreting statistical averages as representing strictly invariable relations within a group.

            c. Imputing causal significance to correlations.

            d. Inferring significant connection between two types of events on the basis of the observation that they are frequently associated.

            e. Assuming that correlations between samples invariably reflect correlations of populations.

            f. Nonrepresentative sampling.

            g. Use of absolute numbers instead of percentages to show trends.

            h. Making comparisons on the basis of units or classifications which do not retain the same value or meaning for the different groups compared.

            i. Neglecting to consider differences in method of collecting statistical data.

            j. Employment of different units of measurement to make comparisons.

            k. Neglect of methods of testing consistency of data.

            l. Forgetting that statistics are abstract, and that they, therefore, omit many qualities which are not selected for attention.

            m. Comparing data out of their contexts, when the latter, if included, would vitiate the comparisons.

            n. Assuming falsely that all other variables except those measured and compared remain constant.

---

[3] Items a through k are adapted from Morris R. Cohen and Ernest Nagel, *An Introduction to Logic and Scientific Method* (New York, Harcourt, Brace, 1934), pp. 316-322.

Items l through s are taken as they are from H. A. Larrabee, *Reliable Knowledge* (Boston, Houghton Mifflin, 1945), pp. 401-402.

    o. Extrapolating on the assumption that no new factor has entered or no old one has changed in importance.

    p. Compare *c* above.

    q. Claiming greater precision in the conclusions than is warranted. by the nature of the materials and units used.

    r. Compare *a* above.

    s. Supposing that figures about masses of individuals convey information concerning the interrelations of the individuals in groups.

B. Deductive. The Classical Fallacies which are broadly deductive.

    Deduction may be defined: the process of drawing from assumptions or from established generalizations which are implicit in them but which are not obvious; reasoning from general to particular.

    Deductive errors are then drawing inferences which are not justified by the assumptions or generalizations.

    Examples of such errors: Making a judgment concerning a given individual on the basis of an accepted generalization. A particular course of action is recommended on the basis of a general criterion of action.

    Some of the following are not strictly "logical" fallacies, but errors caused by introducing false assumptions.

    1. Presumptive (false assumptions made).

      a. Exceptions ignored ("Accident").

        (1) Description: the assumption is made that what is true in general is true under all conditions; real exceptions are disregarded.

        (2) Examples:

          (*a*) All people who do not pay import duties are smugglers. (Envoys have immunity.)

          (*b*) All students off grounds are truant. (Some have permits.)

      b. Exceptions overvalued ("Converse accident").

        (1) Description: the assumption is made that what is true under some circumstances is true in general; exceptions are regarded as typical instances.

        (2) Examples:

          (*a*) Some movies are harmful to children; therefore, all movies should be banned.

          (*b*) Some high school graduates are failures; therefore, the high schools fail generally in their duties.

      c. Begging the question (*Petitio principii*).

        (1) Description: assuming the conclusion to be proved:

          (*a*) Stating the conclusion in changed form in the premise.

          (*b*) Assuming a debatable proposition.

          (*c*) Reasoning in a circle (*Circulus in probando*), that is, using two propositions to prove each other.

        (2) Examples:

          (*a*) It is wrong to flirt because it is not right to make love insincerely.

(*b*) Capital punishment is wrong because it is wrong to take human life.

(*c*) The Koran is indisputable because it is the sacred word of Mohammed.

(*d*) Maiming the umpire is un-American.

   d. Complex question (*Plurium interrogationum*).

     (1) Description: questions are asked in which certain facts are implied to be true or false, the question being framed so that a direct answer involves admission of the assumption.

     (2) Examples:

(*a*) Have you stopped beating your wife?

(*b*) Why are school teachers absent-minded?

(*c*) Did you win by cheating or paying the referee?

2. Irrelevant (off the point at issue—*Ignoratio elenchi*).

The speaker or writer really proves a proposition other than the one he claims he is proving. He succeeds in substituting and getting debate on a conclusion which is not the original point at issue. This may be done deliberately to mislead, or without awareness in the course of a long and complicated discussion.

   a. You're another (*Tu quoque*).

     (1) Description: an action is excused by charging that another person or group under the same conditions would do the same thing. (Both might be wrong.)

     (2) Examples:

(*a*) The Republicans would use patronage if they were in power.

(*b*) You would have kept the money if you were in my shoes.

   b. Argument against the man (*Ad hominem*).

     (1) Description: arguments are directed for or against the personal qualities of someone instead of to the issue; attributing bad motives or prejudices.

     (2) Examples:

(*a*) Mendelssohn's music was banned in Germany because he was a Jew.

(*b*) Hitler was ridiculed because he was once a paper hanger.

(*c*) The testimony of beautiful women is credited by a jury without basis in fact.

   c. Argument to popular prejudice (*Ad populum*).

     (1) Description: appeal is made to prejudices.

     (2) Examples:

(*a*) Vote against the damnyankees!

(*b*) Keep the Pope out of the White House!

(*c*) Do you want a Senator Yamamoto?

   d. Argument employing threats (*Ad baculum*).

     (1) Description: intimidation is used to force agreement.

     (2) Examples:

(*a*) Sign this or else.

(*b*) Might makes right.

e. Appeal to reverence or authority or prestige (*Ad verecundiam*).

  (1) Description: apparent weight is given to argument by quoting some ancient and revered authority, by appealing to some long established precedent. Or a contemporary authority may be invoked. Repeated affirmation eventually begets authority, as does also a confident manner. False credentials may be brought in. The fallacy exists when the authority cited is inappropriate.

  (2) Examples:

    (*a*) What Washington said in the eighteenth century is necessarily valid today.

    (*b*) What was good enough for my grandfather is good enough for you.

    (*c*) According to Pegler. . . .

    (*d*) The Chinese argument—appealing to one's ancestors.

f. Appeal to pity (*Argumentum ad misericordiam*).

  (1) Description: appeal to sympathies, feelings, pity, instead of to more cogent arguments.

  (2) Examples:

    (*a*) Socrates in Plato's *Apology* ridicules this appeal and illustrates it in reverse: ". . . someone . . . prayed and entreated the judges with many tears, and how he produced his children in court, which was a moving spectacle, together with a host of relations and friends; whereas I, who am probably in danger of my life, will do none of these things."

    (*b*) "Don't make your child unhappy because you haven't a television set." Much advertising uses this appeal.

g. Appeal to the purse (*Argumentum ad crumenam*).

  (1) Description: a mercenary appeal is made instead of a constructive argument.

  (2) Example:

    (*a*) A new school building will raise taxes.

h. *Argumentum ad captandum vulgus.*

  (1) Description: any argument, cliché, slogan, to "catch the crowd."

  (2) Examples:

    (*a*) Many advertising slogans.

    (*b*) Most propaganda devices; glittering generality, testimonials, plain folks, bandwagon.

3. Other.

  a. Objections.

    (1) Description: it is reasoned that if there are any objections at all against a proposal that it should be rejected. It ignores strong favorable arguments.

    (2) Examples:

(a) Do not deposit your money; the banks may fail.

(b) The Marshall Plan helps some people who do not deserve it.

(c) Vivisection hurts dogs.

b. Appeal to ignorance (*Ad ignorantiam*).

(1) Description: attempt to support an argument by claiming that the opposite cannot be proved; negative proof.

(2) Examples:

(a) It has never been disproved that our souls return in the bodies of dogs.

(b) It cannot be disproved that the study of mathematics improves the mind.

c. *Non sequitur*. (It does not follow.)

(1) Description:

(a) Generally, an illogical conclusion.

(b) Specifically, a conclusion drawn from true premises, but which does not logically follow; or complete lack of connection between premises and conclusion.

(2) Examples:

(a) I tried hard in the exam; I should get an "A."

(b) He has a Ph.D.; therefore, he must be a good teacher.

d. Misuse of analogy.

(1) Failure to state explicitly the characteristics of the resemblance and consequent failure to make the analogy clear.

(2) An insufficient resemblance even when stated.

(3) Failure to state explicitly the characteristics in which the two factors differ. Unlikeness or "disanalogy" is often important.

(4) Resemblance is imaginary or forced or on trivial points.

(5) Used as a striking or attention-getting statement and not honestly as part of the argument. (Similar to red herring device below.)

VII. *Rhetorical devices for confusing thought in group problems*

The following rhetorical devices are used by individuals in argument with other people. These devices are classified as errors because they prevent or delay the systematic, logical presentation of evidence and the objective solution of a problem involving conflicting interests. The occasion for such techniques may be the courtroom, the legislature, or the home when a child seeks to divert Mother's attention from incriminating evidence, and many others.

A. Confusing.

1. Extension of an opponent's proposition by contradiction or misrepresentation. Raising objections which are irrelevant.

2. Evasion of a sound refutation by the use of a sophistical formula, slogan, or cliché. For example: "The exception proves the rule." "Good in theory but won't work in practice." "That is an idealistic or Utopian proposal."

3. Nonexhaustive dilemma. Presenting alternatives which do not include all possibilities. "Vote for the Democrats or for ruin."
4. Use of the fact of continuity between two things to throw doubt on a real difference.
5. Special pleading. Use of arguments whose other consequences one will not accept. Condemning or commending a proposition not on its merits but because of practical consequences to the reader or listener.

B. Diverting.
1. The red herring. The weakness of a position is concealed by turning attention to some issue other than the one under discussion. A side issue is dragged in to distract attention. Minor side issues are often played up in political campaigns to distract attention from major issues. Dictators stir up war scares to distract attention from social crises at home. (Dictators are not the only ones to do this!) Dishonest newspapers usually play up a small-time criminal or one without friends or influence to distract attention from the newspaper's own connection with big-time crime or vice.
2. Statement of doubtful proposition in such a way that it fits in with the thoughts, beliefs or prejudices, or habits of the reader or listener.
3. Overcoming resistance to a doubtful proposition by a preliminary statement containing a few easily acceptable ones; sometimes by others far worse than the original proposition. Often are also irrelevant.
4. Speculative argument about an ideal situation rather than the actual one; talking about what *ought* or *should* be the case instead of facing the actual situation. Others are worse off than we are.

C. Delaying or blocking.
1. Gradualism. "This is not the time to do this." "Must not move too fast." "Better be slow and sure."
2. Academic detachment. "There is much to be said on both sides." "Well, you really cannot tell about this."
3. Affectation of failure to understand.
4. Bland statement that "No issue is involved," "We have no complaint," "Others are worse off than we are."
5. Aggressive raising of objections constantly, usually coupled with refusal to do anything else. Reject all proposals instead of working for amendment or compromise.
6. Repeat affirmations over and over regardless of the facts which have been brought out.
7. "There comes a time." "It is high time." "Now is the time." These expressions usually indicate that the speaker intends to consider the facts or propositions no further. An arbitrary and dogmatic conclusion or inference is about to be imposed—if the speaker has the power to impose. It also often means that the speaker will pay no attention to further facts or reasons, will not answer challenges to his position.

"CONVENTIONAL WISDOM," A SERIOUS BLOCK TO THINKING IN ALL FIELDS AND ON ALL LEVELS

The only crime is ignorance.

(Attributed to various authors)

Ignorance is the curse of God.
Knowledge the wing wherewith we fly to Heaven

SHAKESPEARE
King Henry VI, Part II, Act IV, scene 7

Every law which originated in ignorance and malice, and gratifies the passions from which it sprang, we call the wisdom of our ancestors.

SYDNEY SMITH

When foreign affairs were ruled by autocracies or oligarchies the danger of war was in sinister purpose. When foreign affairs are ruled by democracies the danger of war is in mistaken beliefs.

ELIHU ROOT

The future of mankind will be greatly imperilled if it is left to be worked out by ignorant change, or ignorant opposition to change.

JOHN STUART MILL

The preceding organization of errors is along logical lines with equal space allotted to each type. There are a few kinds of errors, though, which deserve more space because of the frequency with which they interfere with good thinking. This classification may be more easily recognized by the average citizen. Among major types of faulty thinking we may note, among others:

1. Uncritical acceptance of conventional ideas, a form of credulity.
2. Uncritical rejection of new ideas, or harmful incredulity. Failure to be open-minded even about radical new ideas which inspection would show to be at least plausible.
3. Uncritical acceptance of impossibilities.

Attitudes are involved in these as well as cognition and experience, but specific attitudes which cause faulty thinking are often themselves the results of bad thinking. One who is anti-Catholic, or anti-Protestant, or anti-intellectual or one who is favorable to these groups will often be influenced for or against ideas and conclusions depending upon their sources. Other forms of rigidity of thought may be listed. The following typical illustrations may be duplicated every day by everyone.

Uncritical acceptance of conventional ideas, beliefs, standards. Studies of beliefs and their sources show that individuals until sensitized or trained are greatly influenced by the beliefs and ideas of those around them.

Watch out for the person who says, "Why, everyone knows that!" "Why, that's always been true!" "You can't change things like that!" We have already referred to the genuinely stupid cliché, "You can't change human nature." The odds are very great that persons using these expressions will make incredible blunders in thinking. The effect of "custom or tradition," of social approval, of ineffective thinking in certain areas is serious and deserves considerable attention.

The executive of a huge industrial concern recently delivered a hard-hitting address on the necessity of competition for economic advance and listed several other benefits. There has been no real competition for over a quarter of a century in the field where he is engaged. This man was not lying or even trying to propagandize. He believed his statements. He had been misled by more than a century of encrusted thinking. Competition is a factor in human endeavor, but it is not a blanket prescription.

Spokesmen for associations of manufacturers and other types of business concerns have stated on occasions that certain forms and amounts of taxation are forcing some firms to curtail expansion and causing business failures. This could well be true, but on one or two occasions that statement has been made during a time of booming expansion of business. A great newspaper once ran an editorial pointing out that the policies of the national administration in Washington were destroying American business and enterprise. The financial page of the same newspaper was filled with enthusiastic reports of unprecedented prosperity and expansion. Again, these men were not lying, though propaganda undoubtedly entered in some measure. Most of them believed what they said. They were victims of "age old" wisdom and failure to look at the emerging facts. Certain writers assert that consumer prices always fall during recessions, but scrutiny of the facts shows that on a half-dozen occasions in modern times prices fell insignificantly and actually rose on one occasion. A page could be filled with illustrations from economics and politics. The reader is referred to the volume by Galbraith listed at the end of the following discussion on harmful incredulity. Chapter 2 should be read by all students.

While poking fun at other fields we should not overlook our own fields of teaching, and education generally. A good deal of intellectual furniture there should long since have been relegated to the attic. Improved teacher training has driven out many outmoded ideas, but many such as the following are still the "conventional wisdom" of some teachers and large numbers of laymen.

"Child prodigies, and bright children generally, are sickly and neurotic and fade early." "All children are quite capable of doing the work if they would only try." "The child can easily adjust to life and the social order *after* he has learned what the school has to give." "College students with high grades do not succeed nearly so well in life as the 'all-around' man who may have averaged 'C' but who has learned much from athletics, college life, and the like." "A child is born with an instinctive knowledge of right and wrong; the conscience is present from birth."

Several score equally absurd ideas could be listed. The typical arrangement of the school into the 8—4 grade is actually a conventional hand-me-down with no justification whatever in fact. We are making some progress in overcoming this particular bit of crystallized thinking.

Harmful incredulity, uncritical rejection of new ideas. Hand in hand with uncritical acceptance goes uncritical rejection, failure to be open-minded. No one wants to be so open-minded that his brains fall out, but in far worse state is he who cannot open his mind at all. Caution and discretion are always desirable, but today's unprecedented scientific discoveries make it equally desirable to take a look at any new idea which comes along.

Two quotations are of interest:

There is no adequate defense against the impact of a new idea except stupidity.

PERCY BRIDGMAN

Gegen Dummheit die Götter selbst kämpfen vergebens.

SCHILLER

In 1828 a debating society of young men asked the school board in Lancaster, Ohio, for the use of the schoolhouse to argue the question as to whether railroads were practical. The school board replied:

You are welcome to the use of the schoolhouse in which to debate all proper questions; but such things as railroads and telegraphs are impossible and rank infidelity. There is nothing in the Word of God about them. If God had designed that his intelligent creatures should travel at the frightful speed of fifteen miles an hour by steam, He would have clearly foretold it through His holy prophets. It is a device of Satan to lead immortal souls down to hell.

These men *knew*. Public discussion and thinking were blocked—at least locally and temporarily! The jet plane was as yet undreamed of. As this was written a "letter to the editor" in the *Portland Oregonian* strongly decried space exploration and travel, saying: "If God had intended us to travel in space he would have built a bridge."

The automobile manufacturers of the United States at a meeting some years ago discovered that they were planning to build more than 250,000 cars the next year. "We are ruining a good business! The American public will never be able to buy so many." John D. Archbold, a top figure in the early oil business, then confined to Pennsylvania, heard that large oil fields were reported possible in other areas. He said, "I will drink all the oil ever discovered outside of Pennsylvania."

Many decades ago the natives under the protection of the British navy were thrown into a panic when new warships arrived with but one funnel. An effective warship had two funnels and always had had. The British must be on the downgrade. The suggestion was seriously made that a dummy funnel be placed on the ships. Primitive intellects react alike whether in the Persian Gulf or in Times Square.

The Wright brothers' flight at Kitty Hawk in 1903 was reported briefly in five newspapers and refused by sixteen! [4] The *Daily News* in Dayton, Ohio, home of the Wrights, ran a paragraph on an inside page, headed "Dayton Boys Emulate Great Santos-Dumont." The editor knew so little he confused two basically different types of flying machines. Simon Newcomb, a prominent American astronomer, stated with finality that it was impossible to fly a heavier-than-air machine. In 1905, Wilbur Wright claimed to have flown 24 miles in 39 minutes, but nobody paid much attention. In 1908, the "crazy" Wrights were thought to be "duping" the War Department when they demonstrated a biplane and asked $25,000 for it! The telegrapher who sent in stories said he didn't believe a word of what he was transmitting. A free-lance writer wired the *Cleveland Leader* that he had seen the machine in flight. He was told, "Cut out the wild cat stuff. . . . We can't handle it." The *New York Herald* on receipt of the same story wired curtly, "Confine yourself to the facts." The *Herald* did, however, send one of their own staff to see what was going on and then fired him for reporting that he had seen a man flying! This reporter tried the story on a leading magazine and was told, "Your manuscript does not qualify either as fact or fiction"! (The *Herald* reporter was later reinstated!)

The writer while teaching in a small rural town read in the paper of the German feat in World War I of shelling Paris from a distance of 75 miles with a new gun, the Big Bertha. No doubts occurred in his mind. On arrival at the village post office, however, he found a scene of hilarious uproar. "Wow, did you see this fool story the newspaper has today?" "You'd think they'd have better sense than to print nonsense like that." With much laughter and thigh slapping, the village elders agreed the story was fantastic. "Why, that'd be shooting as far as from here to Portland."! That settled it. The Germans could not be shelling Paris from that distance. (The United States and Russia, as this was written, shot satellites several hundred thousand miles.)

A group of distinguished news correspondents were traveling to England at the outbreak of World War I. One of them reading in the ship's library suddenly threw his book across the room exclaiming, "Bosh! How can a great writer produce nonsense like that!" The book by H. G. Wells predicted that some day small mobile forts would go clanking over battle fields with men and guns; soldiers would be dropped by parachute behind enemy lines and on strategic points. The newsmen agreed that the ideas were fantastic. The same correspondents a short time later were sending stories about the "tanks" introduced by the English. The parachute troops did not appear in that war but did soon after.

On October 15, 16, 17, 18, 1953, the *Boston Herald* carried four remarkable editorials under the heading "The Weapon of Knowledge." The whole story is long and interesting. We can reproduce but one high light here.

[4] Fred Kelly, *The Wright Brothers* (New York, Harcourt, Brace, 1943).

On April 16, 1953, the Air Force used a new weapon in Korea. This was the result:

For eight days all MIG's were grounded.

In the 60 days after it was used there were 21 per cent fewer Red sorties, and 22 per cent fewer MIG's engaged U.S. planes than in the 60 days previous.

In March and April, before the new weapon was used, we lost four Sabre jets shooting down 53 MIG's. In May and June we only lost one Sabre while shooting down 107 Communist planes.

Our losses were cut 300 per cent while enemy losses jumped more than 100 per cent.

The effects of the new weapon were felt on Communist air fields in China, Russia, and halfway around the world in Poland, Czechoslovakia, and other satellite countries.

What was the new weapon? Was it some atomic shell? Or a new electronic gunsight?

No. It was something which can be more powerful than any of those weapons. It was knowledge.

The weapon which kept the MIG's on the ground for eight days was a program based in part on information which came out of the green book-bags and intellectual foreheads of the members of Harvard University's Russian Research Center in Harvard Square.

The studies at that center have been called a "form of insanity" by Senator Homer Ferguson and a "lot of professor theories" by Senator McClellan. They both seem to forget the practical results of a group of academic people who studied something called nuclear fission.

There are moments when it seems as if the Senate might profit from understanding some "professor theory"! The *Herald* editorials went on to tell in detail of the insight gained into the Communist mind by the studies of the Institute. Over 600 daily newspapers and magazines a month are translated. Teams interviewed scores of those defecting to Western countries in Europe. The knowledge gained was broadcast by leaflets dropped widely on Communist air fields. Communist generals were forced to put political reliability ahead of flying and combat ability. The handicap to them and advantage to us were very great. The whole story has many ramifications, but this brief excerpt serves to illustrate the power of knowledge and the absurdity of rejecting "fool theories."

Sometimes the refusal to entertain new ideas, the determination to maintain the old ones, is further complicated by twisted logic. The real leaders in the business and industrial worlds are aware that we are living in a changing world and that new concepts of government, of production, and of capital and profits are bound to be presented by scholars dealing with those areas. The second-raters in business have the greatest contempt for new ideas and for the men who produce these ideas. A standard answer, derogatory without logic, is to say, "Well, those men never met a payroll." By what twisted logic a standard procedure from one field is used to measure the ability in another field is beyond comprehension. To reply in kind, one might answer, "Others who never met a payroll include Confucius, Socrates, Jesus, St. Augustine, Cardinal Mercier, Martin Luther, Percy Bysshe Shelley, Copernicus, Galileo, and Einstein." We might add, to give the already twisted logic one more twist, that among those who do meet payrolls easily and promptly are the heads of gangster mobs and crime syndicates.

Even the scientists, sacrosanct since Sputnik, in some cases have real difficulty with new ideas. The stimulating and entertaining article by Stevenson, listed below, should be read. Many illustrations are from medicine where, if anywhere, there should be open-mindedness. Stevenson has coined the term *harmful incredulity* which should take its place along with the term *primitive credulity* used by many anthropologists.

Two quotations may give point here:

My Brethren! I beseech you, in the bowels of Christ, to consider that you might be wrong.

OLIVER CROMWELL

It is not bigotry to be certain we are right; but it is bigotry to be unable to imagine how we might possibly have gone wrong.

G. K. CHESTERTON
The Catholic Church and Conversion

The following are but a few of the many good books and articles available which, in one way or another, deal with "conventional wisdom."

J. Donald Adams, "The Egghead vs. the Muttonhead," *New York Times Magazine* (Nov. 23, 1958), p. 14.

N. J. Berrill, *Man's Emerging Mind* (New York, Dodd, Mead, 1955).

John K. Galbraith, *The Affluent Society* (Boston, Houghton Mifflin, 1958). See especially Chapter 2. See also other books by this author.

H. R. Hays, *From Ape to Angel* (New York, Knopf, 1958).

H. R. Isaacs, *Scratches on Our Minds* (New York, John Day, 1958).

H. J. Muller, *The Uses of the Past* (New York, Oxford University Press, 1957).

Ian Stevenson, "Scientists with Half-closed Minds," *Harper's Magazine* (Nov., 1958), pp. 64-71.

The uncritical acceptance of impossibilities. An equally serious error is the direct opposite of the two just presented. This can be as truly dangerous as are all serious errors in thinking, but on some occasions it has produced world-wide hilarity. One illustration is given in some detail, but several pages could be filled with other illustrations far less humorous than this one.

Dr. Gustav Albrecht of Altadena, California, studied and photographed the growth of the *Yucca whipplei* for many years when he conceived the idea of a magnificent scientific spoof. The beautiful bloom widely seen on our Southwestern deserts is carried on a stalk which grows from 10 to 20 feet within two to three weeks and then dies. He wrote an article carried in the *Scientific Monthly* for October, 1952, claiming that the photographs of the growth of the stalk (actually taken one week apart during the period of growth) were taken at *one-second intervals!* He invented a long-dead German botanist, Dr. Ferdinand Grünspann (*Grünspann* is the German word for verdigris), as the discoverer of the variety *schuss Yucca* (schuss means to shoot up). Albrecht also invented a 20-volume *Handbuch der Yucca* (Leipzig: *Schmutzig Verlag,* 1893) written by Grünspann. (*Schmutzig Verlag* means "Dirty Edition") The article contained a dozen or more clear cues that the article was a piece of whimsical buffoonery in scientific vein! The *Scientific Monthly* carried it as such. Now, what happened?!!

The science editor of a leading New York newspaper called long distance asking for photographs to reproduce, having already published an article headed "Stalk Grows 10 Feet in Two Minutes." The science editor of the *Christian Science Monitor* caught on to the joke but thought it was a hoax. In exposing the hoax he unwittingly contributed to the gaiety of the occasion, "You can tell from the shadows cast by the plant and by the person standing by it that at least eight hours elapsed during the growth." A seed company wrote for seeds or cuttings. Several botanists were very angry and denounced Albrecht savagely. A London Sunday paper reprinted the original article as fact. The Royal Horticultural Society, however, went on a determined hunt for Grünspann and his 20-volume *Handbuch.* Having checked the facts, as good thinkers should, they recognized the story for what it was, a piece of entertainment.

The huge majority of botanists and other scientists caught on at once and in turn wrote genuinely witty commentaries filling four pages in the *Scientific Monthly* for November, 1952, and January, 1953. One botanist spoofed Albrecht in turn by claiming that the latter had not seen Grünspann's second edition, illustrated, published by *Schmutzig und Drecker Verlag* ("Dirty and Filthy Edition").

We have space for but the one illustration, but the general point is important. [5] There can be too-easy acceptance of new ideas, especially when the source is respectable.

Attitudes and inner convictions mislead thinking. Often the persons making errors here are not aware of their inner blocks. When they are aware, we have dishonesty and not error. Pages could be filled with illustrations; in fact, two small books have been so filled, covering a relatively short period of time and dealing with economic and political issues only. [6]

[5] The accounts of this incident are well worth reading in the issues of the *Scientific Monthly* indicated above. Another article appeared in *Horticulture,* published by the Massachusetts Horticultural Society, for August, 1953.

[6] Edward Angly, compiler, *Oh Yeah* (New York, Viking, 1931). Dealt almost entirely with newspaper headlines and public records.

September 17, 1928. Roger W. Babson, economist, addressing National Business Congress, Wellesley Hills, Mass.

"If Smith should be elected with a Democratic Congress, we are almost certain to have a resulting business depression in 1929—The election of Hoover and a Republican Congress should result in continued national prosperity."

October 5, 1928, campaign speech at Gary, Ind., by Charles Curtis, vice-presidential candidate.

"Stick to the full dinner pail. You have been enjoying Republican prosperity. If you want to continue to enjoy prosperity of the administration of Calvin Coolidge, vote for Hoover."

July 27, 1928, campaign speech by Herbert Hoover, San Francisco, Cal.

"The outlook of the world today is for the greatest era of commercial expansion in history."

Hoover and the Republicans were elected.

October 24, 1929. Headline, *New York Herald Tribune.*

"Stocks off 5 Billion in Severest Break of Wall Street History."

October 25, 1929. Herbert Hoover in statement to the press.

"The fundamental business of this country, that is, production and distribution of commodities, is on a sound and prosperous basis."

December 2, 1929. Monthly Review, National City Bank, New York.

"There are no great failures, nor are there likely to be."

October 17, 1931. Dun's Review. "Amount of Liabilities in Failures (first nine months only)":

1929	$332,425,638
1930	473,043,174
1931	531,776,004

Statement after statement by top-flight industrialists and by government officials was flatly contradicted by facts and developments. The few competent scholars who raised voices of doubt from before the crash were dismissed as prophets of doom and as "damned theorists." Statements by many industrialists were flatly contradicted, not in general but by the facts from within their own firms.

Note carefully, however, that this type of error is not peculiar to Republicans and to industrialists. Illustrations can be drawn from every field and group.

A study reported by Spindler indicates that inimical attitudes are formed early and are vigorous. [7] A hundred or more students preparing to be teachers were given certain projective techniques to which to respond. One open-ended sentence was, "Intellectuals should. . . ." Forty percent of

---

Surplus Prophets, compiler not named (New York, Viking, 1936). Dealt with statements from prominent leaders as quoted in newspapers.

[7] George D. Spindler, "Education in a Transforming American Culture," *Harvard Educational Review* (Summer, 1955), pp. 145-156.

―――, *The Transmission of American Culture,* the Third Burton Lecture. (Cambridge, Mass., Harvard University Press, 1959).

the students responded, "be more sociable, more practical, more down to earth." Twenty percent said, "keep it under cover, drop dead, shut up." Only thirty percent said, "apply their intellect, study, think." Ten percent were unaccounted for. Sixty percent of prospective teachers in this sample want intellectuals to be more like less-intellectual individuals or think of them as individuals to be avoided and to be prevented from contributing. The blunders in thinking which will result over the years, unless the attitudes are changed, can only be tragic.

QUESTIONS, EXERCISES, AND REPORTS

Introductory Discussion

The following references will be of value here. Some others are available. Students are asked to turn in any other references found which are of value.

BURTT, E. A., *Right Thinking,* rev. ed. (New York, Harper, 1946), Ch. 4, "How Wrong Thinking Occurs"; Ch. 5, "Hindrances and Aids in the Correction of Wrong Thinking."

FLESCH, Rudolf, *The Art of Clear Thinking* (New York, Harper, 1951). Various chapters.

KEYES, K. S., Jr., *How to Develop Your Thinking Ability* (New York, McGraw-Hill, 1950). A popular account of details.

KEYSER, C. J., *Thinking About Thinking* (New York, Dutton, 1926).

REILLY, Wm. J., *The Twelve Rules of Straight Thinking* (New York, Harper, 1947 edition). Ch. 2. Another popular summary.

STEFANSSON, V., *The Standardization of Error* (New York, Norton, 1927).

———, *Adventures in Error* (New York, McBride, 1936).

THOULESS, R. H., *How to Think Straight* (New York, Simon & Schuster, 1947 edition). Mixture of popular and more formal.

Analysis of studies of prejudice, scapegoating, and of propaganda techniques is of value here.

1. What do you believe to be the *chief* reason why thinking is prone to error? (There will be legitimate differences of opinion here, but analysis of the answers will reveal a number of basic points.)

2. State explicitly how, up to a certain point, the physical world and practical affairs—the necessities of life—automatically check wrong thinking and aid in keeping thinking straight.

Show how, on the other hand, the practical world often directs, encourages, and confirms the worst kind of erroneous thinking.

Why is the natural discipline of the practical world inadequate? (Two or three major reasons may be advanced here.)

3. Dewey points out that "logical attainment in one direction is no bar to extravagant conclusions in another," and that "natural intelligence is no barrier to the propagation of error, nor large but untrained experience to the accumulation of false beliefs." DEWEY, John, *How We Think* (Boston, Heath, 1910; rev. ed. 1933), p. 23 of 1933 edition, and p. 21 of 1910 edition.

Illustrate from your general reading how a savage who is expert in one aspect of life will yet gravely relate the most preposterous yarns about other phases of the same area.

Illustrate the same thing from the life of modern man, preferably yourself and your neighbors. Particularly note this in speeches, editorials, articles.

Can an individual ever judge or think well outside his field of interest and specialization? (Do not answer this too quickly. Time should be given to analysis of views on this.) How might he be aided to overcome the difficulties here?

The two references here will be of value:

ROBINSON, James Harvey, *Mind in the Making* (New York, Harper, 1921), pp. 65-147.

————, *The Humanizing of Knowledge*, rev. ed. (New York, George F. Doran Co., 1926), Ch. 5, "Science vs. Lore, and the Current Hostility to a Scientific Attitude of Mind."

4. Granting for the moment that "primitive credulity" is a characteristic of human thinking, can you develop a plausible explanation showing how it might have arisen?

5. Illustrate the common tendency to buttress an incorrect belief with additional errors. Why is this done, do you think?

6. What makes the difference between looking at the mercury to foretell rain and looking at the entrails of a fowl for the same reason? How did we ever get away from these superstitions?

7. Dewey, *How We Think,* p. 24: "Even today correct beliefs about the constitution of nature are held by the great multitude merely because they are current and popular rather than because the multitude understands the reasons upon which they rest."

Illustrate this. Explain the significance and implications of this statement, particularly for education, popular enlightenment, mass media, and the like.

8. Dewey, *How We Think,* p. 24: "Only systematic regulation of the conditions under which observations are made and severe discipline of the habits of entertaining suggestions can secure a decision that one type of belief is vicious and the other sound."

Explain the significance and implications both for everyday discourse and for education.

9. Dewey, *How We Think,* p. 25: "When such regulation is absent, dreams, the position of the stars, the lines of the hand, are regarded as valuable signs, and the fall of the cards as an inevitable omen, while natural events of the most crucial significance go disregarded."

Illustrate from various levels how "natural events have been disregarded" with results from trivial to disastrous.

Illustrate specifically how many "nook-and-cranny superstitions once universal" have been destroyed.

10. Duplicate from your observation or reading the particular type of bad thinking illustrated in the incident of the lawyer and the wheat growers; in disciplining children harshly on the basis of belief that this will breed respect later.

Cite a case of blundering conclusions by competent thinkers when operating outside their own fields. (This may have been covered by an earlier exercise, but if not cite and analyze here.)

Students who wish may read at this point:

BACON, Francis, *The Great Instauration* (any edition). The section headed "Novum Organum" and, within that, the "Aphorisms Concerning the Interpretation of Nature and the Kingdom of Man"—paragraphs 38 (xxxviii) through 69 (lxix).

LOCKE, John, "An Essay Concerning the Human Understanding," *Of Wrong Assent, or Error* (any edition), Ch. 20, Bk. IV.

11. Illustrate from your own experience or reading any two or three of the *Baconian Idols* (listed in Appendix B).

12. Do the same for Locke's causes of error as listed in our text.

13. What, if anything, can be done to cure one of dependence on authority?

14. What plausible explanations can you advance for the closed mind? How might it be changed? How should we handle a person with closed mind in a discussion?

15. Do individuals really believe the arguments they use when self-interest or other emotional factor is obviously twisting thinking? What are the educational implications of your answer? What usually happens when you point out rationalizations to individuals using them?

16. What is meant by "dogmatic principles"? Why is this so very difficult to handle? How do you try to handle it in your own thinking?

17. How do you suppose that authority and dogmatic principles (among the worst sources of error) came to be so widespread?

18. Why, basically, do you think we fall into the errors listed by Bacon and Locke?

SECTION 1

1. Illustrate specifically the operation of any two or three of the major sources of error as outlined in Section 1. Pay particular attention to the school and to educational processes as causes of error.

2. The original attempts by Bacon and Locke to classify sources of error do not differentiate clearly always between *primary* sources and what we may call *secondary* sources which themselves grow out of the primary. There is also argument over the inherent or acquired status of some of the points. This argument we may avoid. We have in Section 1 attempted to outline the primary sources of error. This outline is not final or sacrosanct.

The student who wishes to do so may develop an outline of "Primary Sources of Error" which he believes to be better than that available here. He will thus see the necessary and/or unnecessary overlap, contradictions, differences by level of thinking involved, and the difficulty of avoiding extensive cross reference. Students need not be limited by the categories here set up. Any of several possible schemes of classification is acceptable, provided it is consistent and adequate.

The student attempting this must be reasonably well informed as to current facts about nature-nurture, the general outlines of the dynamics of behavior in living organisms (what causes them to act in order to preserve themselves and to grow).

Analyze any one of the Idols in the light of modern knowledge in psychology, sociology, anthropology, and psychiatry.

3. Show how many errors in thinking are actually taught by schooling and by training as distinguished from education.

4. Give some suggestions for distinguishing between "errors with intent" and those without intent.

5. A group of students concocted the term "life's minor stupidities" to refer to actions which are done, as we say, "without thinking," or because "I wasn't paying attention." Such actions range from the trivial and mildly annoying to those which can be dangerous to safety and life. Successive classes have compiled a list of several hundred.

Innocuous "stupidities"

Writing "rush" on the outside of a letter
Touching paint to see if it is really wet
Pushing the elevator call button just after someone else has done so
Stopping squarely in the doorway—in a narrow hall—on a crosswalk
    to converse, blocking many other people from proceeding
Honking the horn in an auto jam
Expressing opinions on all subjects
Stacking dishes too high

Dangerous "stupidities"

Rocking the boat
Taking medicine in the dark
Taking medicine recommended by friends or neighbors
Pointing a supposedly empty gun at another person
Pulling trigger to see if gun is loaded
Signing legal documents without reading them
Trying to beat a train to a crossing
Publishing (by newspapers) of names and addresses of key witnesses to
    gang murders, robberies, or the like

Watch for these and many others in everyday affairs. Make a list. Attempt to explain some of them, particularly the serious ones. What has this to do with thinking?

One bank has a printed check list of 16 items which is sent to depositors with returned checks, statements, and the like with appropriate "errors" checked. Be on the lookout for similar materials.

Watch for lists which appear quite often in popular magazines, headed "Do you believe this?" The lists consist of conventional beliefs, stereotypes, and "minor stupidities" which are widely believed. Test yourself and your friends, and report.

Certain references are of interest:

DUNHAM, Barrows, *Man Against Myth* (Boston, Little, Brown, 1949).

EVANS, Bergen, *The Natural History of Nonsense* (New York, Knopf, 1949).

———, *On the Spoor of Spooks, and Other Nonsense* (New York, Knopf, 1954).

GARDNER, Martin, *In the Name of Science* (New York, Putnam, 1952).

HUSE, H. R., *The Illiteracy of the Literate* (New York, Appleton-Century-Crofts, 1933).

JASTROW, Joseph, *The Betrayal of Intelligence; A Preface to Debunking* (New York, Greenberg, 1938).

WARD, Henshaw, *Throbbing: A Seat at the Circus of the Intellect* (Indianapolis, Bobbs-Merrill, 1926).

WIGGAM, Albert Edward, *Sorry But You're Wrong About It* (Indianapolis, Bobbs-Merrill, 1930). This is one of the oldest books in this field and one of the most interesting.

SECTION 2

The following references will amplify the summary in the text.

BLACK, Max, *Critical Thinking* (Englewood Cliffs, N. J., Prentice-Hall, 1946), Ch. 12, "Assorted Fallacies." (Instructors may wish to use several of Black's many excellent questions at the close of the chapter.)

BURTT, Edwin A., *Right Thinking*, 3rd ed. (New York, Harper, 1946), Ch. 14, "Further Problems in the Study of Forms."

COHEN, Morris R., and NAGEL, Ernest, *An Introduction to Logic and Scientific Method* (New York, Harcourt, Brace, 1934), Ch. 19, "Fallacies."

LARRABEE, H. A., *Reliable Knowledge* (Boston, Houghton Mifflin, 1945). Two popular references will be useful:

CHASE, Stuart, *Guides to Straight Thinking* (New York, Harper, 1956).

KAMIAT, Arnold H., *The Critique of Poor Reason* (Privately printed by the author), (New York, 1814; Printing Crafts Bldg., 1936). This is not available in all libraries. A lively little book with many good ideas.

The analysis of the extensive lists in this section may be handled in any of several ways. Groups of students may select any list or part thereof for attention. Two committees may work on the more extensive lists.

1. Two points are to be covered. *First,* illustrations are to be found in everyday conversation, in editorials, articles, lectures, books, and the like. *Second,* ways of handling these and of eventually avoiding them if possible should be developed and analyzed by the class.

Pay particular attention to everyday illustrations of rhetorical devices for diverting, delaying, or confusing thought. Pay particular attention to clichés, slogans, and the like.

Avoid simple, trivial illustrations; look for those of some seriousness.

2. "Conventional wisdom." Note in everyday discourse the specific instances of (*a*) uncritical acceptance of conventional ideas, (*b*) uncritical rejection of new ideas, (*c*) uncritical acceptance of impossibilities. After illustrating these in everyday affairs, note and cite the same things in important political, economic, educational, medical, or other fields.

3. Comment briefly on the following:

> All millionaires must have exploited resources or persons.
>
> All labor leaders are hoodlums.
>
> Poverty is conducive to righteousness.
>
> Money cannot buy everything; we are happier without it. Those who have it are unhappy.

Statistics never proved anything. (Or can be used to prove anything.)

Gentlemen prefer blondes.

Coming events always cast their shadows.

Truth is stranger than fiction.

4. Conventional wisdom is embodied in proverbs, of which there are thousands. The fact that proverbs can be found flatly contradicting each other does not seem to bother those who quote proverbs and use them in thinking. There is now a good literature on proverbs, their origin and nature. Collect a large number of commonly heard proverbs, and consult also the printed summaries. Explain the general origins of proverbs, their persistence in human communication and thinking, their obvious wisdom in some cases, their more than obvious illogicality in others. Summarize also relation of proberbs to reality, and to thinking.

5. Analyze in terms of thinking involved:

When Grover Cleveland was mayor of a certain city he tried repeatedly to get the engineering department to undertake certain projects around the city. Time after time this department was "too busy," was "understaffed," had "no money available," could not do it "at this time."

A project appeared in which there appeared great opportunity for prestige, and perhaps for some "rake-offs." Immediately the engineering department, despite the huge size and complexity of the project, clamored for it, demanding it as being within their department of public works. Mayor Cleveland wrote them and listed every one of the previous excuses—a long list—and stated that he could not think of imposing this on the understaffed, overworked, and underfinanced department. The contract was given to outside operators.

A small town threatened with a smallpox epidemic called in the state health officer for advice. At a meeting which lasted most of the night the council contradicted, wrangled with, and refused every request of the trained health officer. Voluminous facts were cited on the results of vaccination but were rejected without hesitation by the council. The meeting ended with no plans, precautions, or measure of any kind being achieved.

For some years after the Soviet government came to power, newspapers in the U.S. carried regularly stories that the government was about to fall, was in precarious shape, was threatened with uprising, and even several reports that it had fallen. Forty years later none of these things had happened.

During recent years Soviet newspapers have regularly reported economic distress in the United States; the capitalist system is breaking down; workers are starving and about to revolt. None of these things have happened so far.

The important thing in all this is not to find errors, and especially not to be merely amused by some of the odd ones, but to take steps to avoid these many fallacies ourselves and to teach so that students are alerted and provided with means to combat them.

Analyze at some length any proposals for improving our abilities to detect, avoid, and counteract fallacies and errors in thinking. This is the important part of this whole discussion, and ample time may be devoted to it.

6. Examine now the books and articles listed in Chapter 6, Section 1, Exercise 7, for logical errors and fallacies. Pay particular attention to the volume by Scott and Hill which gives excellent material on both sides of the school criticism controversy. Pay particular attention also to the article by McDowell and to the answers thereto. This article though written with obvious sincerity is written also in complete unawareness of logical principles and of systematic argumentation. Analyze one or two of the more astonishing errors. Look especially for arguments which actually prove the opposite of what the author intended.

7. The following contrasting quotations from *Time Magazine* are from a study made by Milton S. Gwirtzman, editor of the *Harvard Crimson,* and published therein on November 4, 1955. (Quotations are by permission of the *Harvard Crimson.*)

July 23, 1951. The subject of [the President's] 1952 intentions came up again in his weekly press conference. The President wasn't saying anything, just acting deliberately mysterious. It has become an unprofitable inquiry and a stale joke.

January 24, 1955 . . . he [the President] has skillfully refused to commit himself on 1956.

July 11, 1955. Adroitly he fielded questions about a second term.

March 14, 1955. At [the President's] news conference last week, his 1956 intentions seemed to be on the mind of almost everyone of the 188 reporters present. . . . both the questioners and the answerer were obviously enjoying the banter.

April 2, 1951. Never in U.S. History had the cost of living been so high. Between January 15 and February 15 the consumer's price index jumped 1.3 per cent to 183.8.

July 4, 1955. After a considerable shift in domestic economic policy, the U.S. is more prosperous than ever before. (The consumer price index was not included in this quotation; it was 192.3.)

October 16, 1950. For 18 years, roly-poly George E. Allen bobbed around Washington like a pneumatic rubber hose.

January 28, 1946. Last week [the President] eased his croniest crony, George E. Allen, into the Board of Directors of the Reconstruction Finance Corporation.

August 12, 1946. George is all the more remarkable because, to the naked eye, he is a clown.

December 14, 1954. Last week . . . [the President] chatted quietly with . . . golfing companion George E. Allen, Washington lawyer and friend of presidents.

See also the *New Republic,* issues February 2, 16, and 23, 1959, for similar analyses of *U.S. News and World Report, Newsweek, Time.*

a. Attempt to explain the contrasting quotations as they stand.

b. If necessary examine the original files for additional information.

c. Make a brief similar study of news treatment currently or from files over a period of some weeks or months. (This can be a very important exercise.)

An editorial in the Pendleton, Ore., *East Oregonian,* written by J. W. Forrester, Jr., and quoted here with his permission, contains two sharp indictments of *Time Magazine;*

Those persons or groups whose thinking disagrees with that of the editors of *Time Magazine* become victims of a nasty journalistic practice. *Time* doesn't concede that the beliefs of those it opposes could be honestly arrived at.

It's brutal. And it's amazing that *Time* has been doing it for so long under the guise of being a news magazine and getting away with it. *Time* is a journal of opinion, not a reporter of the news. And there isn't any propaganda trick that its editors haven't mastered.

d. Examine magazines other than *Time*—weekly, monthly, or quarterly— which report news. Examine also radio and television news reports. Summarize and report any evidence that can be derived from the reports showing prejudice, bias, or honest, objective reporting.

Supplement your observations through study of articles on this topic as they appear in magazines and books.

Be on the alert for your own bias or prejudice in examining current, controversial material. Apply also the same critical analysis to the attacks on magazines and papers as you do to the periodicals.

CHAPTER **12**

Summary of Research on Factors Affecting Critical Thinking

"All but the most thoughtless and impulsive will, in short, use their minds before giving credence to others' reports and try to collect evidence before trusting their own surmises. The world is too full of error and falsehood to make any other course mentally or physically safe."

JACQUES BARZUN and HENRY F. GRAFF *

INTRODUCTION

Prior to about 1900 the general belief was that thinking was a purely logical process. If one wished to understand how to solve problems, one had only to understand the canons of logic. If one wished to teach problem solving, this was done best (and perhaps solely) through the consideration of subject matter organized in accord with rigorous logical standards. And if one wished to measure competence in thinking, this could be done very simply by noting how many problems the individual could solve correctly.

For years philosophers and educators had sensed the inadequacy of such an interpretation, but it was not until the turn of the century that the issue was brought into the psychological laboratories for closer scrutiny. The Würzburg group headed by Külpe and Marbe, Binet in Paris, and Woodworth in England independently and virtually simultaneously began directing their research at the processes of thinking rather than the products of thinking. Variations of their approaches have appeared during the intervening years, but the emphasis on *process,* not *product,* has remained.

* Jacques Barzun and Henry F. Graff, *The Modern Researcher* (New York, Harcourt, Brace, 1958), p. 89.

240

Research designed to reveal the process of normal human thinking is not without its pitfalls. In many respects this type of research is severely handicapped. Perhaps Gardner Murphy's trenchant observation best expresses the difficulty which we face:

It is not thought of the Aristotelian type, but thought as a tension-reducing mechanism that appears in domestic conflict and in political controversy. . . . But the experimental psychologist with his impersonal laboratory environment and mimeographed problems virtually requires his subjects to "park their culture outside." [1]

Indeed it will be wise for the reader to bear this thought in mind as we examine the research on human thinking and the experimental attempts to improve thinking.

One further word of explanation may help the reader to get full value from this chapter. Although a very great number of research studies dealing with the process of thinking have been published, by and large they are unrelated, one to the other. Except for brief sequences of experimentation where several studies have been stimulated by concern for a particular aspect of thinking, there is a real tendency for each study to be discrete, specific, individual, distinct. Motivated by different purposes, shaped by different psychological constructs, and limited by the usual restrictions which characterize research with human subjects, these studies do not readily and obviously lend themselves to neat summaries.

Yet some pattern is needed. Although research clearly indicates that thinking is influenced by many factors, these factors may usefully be grouped into four major categories in the following fashion: (1) intellectual factors, (2) personal-emotional factors, (3) experiential factors, and (4) procedural factors.

These distinctions, as the reader quickly will note, are necessarily arbitrary and somewhat blurred. They tend to overlap and, in a sense, are artificial. Their function, however, is to permit a structured discussion of the research, not to set up any rigorous scheme for mutually exclusive and jointly exhaustive classification. For such a function they appear adequate.

INTELLECTUAL FACTORS

INTELLIGENCE

If one were asked to rate in order of importance those factors which determine ability to think critically, surely many persons would rank intelligence first. In fact, some might even insist that intelligence is the only significant factor, though, as we shall see, such persons would be mistaken.

As part of a comprehensive experiment in the improvement of critical

[1] Gardner Murphy, "The Freeing of Intelligence," *Psychological Bulletin*, Vol. 42 (1945), pp. 1-19.

thinking skills of high school seniors, Glaser (20) [2] reported several relationships between these skills and measures of intelligence. He found that the correlation of scores made on the 1939 edition of the Watson-Glaser Tests of Critical Thinking with Otis Gamma scores was .48 (N = 127). Correlation with school grades, occasionally viewed as a rough approximation of intelligence, was a mere .12. The test manual for the 1949 edition of the Watson-Glaser Critical Thinking Appraisal reports a correlation of .41 with the A.C.E. Psychological Examination scores of 758 Brooklyn College "Presophomores." For the same group, a correlation of .37 is reported between critical-thinking scores and performance on the Co-operative General Culture Test.

Even lower, but still positive, relationships between intelligence and "tests of critical thinking and knowledge" are reported by Furst (17). Certain features of his experimental design, particularly the uniformly high intelligence of the subjects and the uncertain validity of his critical thinking tests, leave the results open to question. But they do corroborate Glaser's findings that intelligence and critical-thinking ability exhibit only moderate positive correlation.

Other aspects of problem-solving ability, when correlated with general intelligence, reveal essentially the same pattern. Alpern (1) found that the ability of high school students to devise or choose tests of scientific hypotheses correlated .53 with I.Q. (N = 123). Also working with high school students, Techman (63) reported that the more intelligent students tended to be better at reaching conclusions on science items. Atkins' study (2) with grade school children indicated that there was no relationship between a pupil's intelligence and his tendency to favor authority versus experimentation as the means of testing science hypotheses.

Miller (47) made an extensive analysis of the relationship between ability to identify various logical fallacies and other factors, including intelligence. The results of his study suggest that there is a definite rank order of difficulty and that this order is essentially the same, regardless of the intelligence of the subject.

Tests of inductive reasoning were administered to grade school pupils by Long and Welch (35), who noted a correlation of .28 (N = 93) between test scores and Otis I.Q. Two studies of arithmetic problem solving by Hansen (25) and Johnson (31) show definite relationships between this skill and intelligence.

In Chapter 14 we describe the several experimental programs of classroom instruction deliberately organized to improve some aspect of critical-thinking skill. At this point, it is of interest to note that these experiments generally indicate that students of lower intelligence profit more, relatively speaking, from such instruction than do the high-ability groups.

[2] Numbers in parentheses refer to listing in the special Bibliography of Research Studies at the end of this chapter.

The consistently positive relationships reported between general intelligence and various thinking skills suggest the possibility that there may be some general critical-thinking ability. Billings (5) set out to test the hypothesis that a person will be as good at reasoning in one field as another, provided he has equivalent backgrounds. A group of 146 college students were taught the facts and techniques necessary to solve selected problems in geometry, arithmetic, physics, mechanics, economics, sociology, and geography. Intercorrelations between various test scores were computed. The average of 29 such correlations was .67 (method of averaging not indicated), apparently supporting the hypothesis. However, the very fact that the subjects were college students suggests they already shared unusually high ability and academic background. Other studies seem to indicate that success in critical thinking in one field will not, per se, guarantee good thinking in all areas.

ACADEMIC SKILLS

In what respects are academic skills and subject matter knowledge, or the lack of them, a factor in critical thinking?

Obviously, certain specific facts and special skills are necessary, or at least helpful, if one is to handle competently problems in the various subject matter areas. No research seems needed to establish this. Hence, it is no surprise to note that Hansen (25) reported that skill in arithmetic problem solving was clearly related to "ability to perform the fundamental operations of arithmetic" and to "arithmetic vocabulary." Alpern (1) found that previous study in science was slightly associated with the ability to test scientific hypotheses. Similar conclusions are implied, at least in an incidental fashion, by a host of other studies. It is extremely important that teachers not misconstrue these results. Even though academic skills are *necessary,* they are not *sufficient.* A wide variety of studies by Burack (8), Burack and Moos (9), Bloom and Broder (6), Duncker (16), Horrocks (29), Maier (40, 43), and Maltzman and others (44) have established clearly that knowledge of the principles in a particular field of knowledge in no way assures that these principles will be properly applied in problem-solving situations.

These results bring into sharp focus one of the major problems which confronts the classroom teacher. Just what teaching techniques will best close the gap between *understanding* a principle and effectively *applying* that principle in a new problem situation? A major purpose of this volume has been to suggest some answers to this question.

READING SKILLS

Most of our everyday problem solving goes on at the verbal level. Perhaps this is why research persons have given an unusual amount of attention to the relationship between various reading skills and skill in thinking clearly. The studies by Alpern, Glaser, and Techman previously cited indicate moderate positive correlations (in the order of .35) between general reading skills and competence in critical thinking.

Any temptation to interpret these findings as an indication that problem-solving skill is assured if one can read well is dispelled by the work of Gans (19). She showed that ability to read with comprehension does not necessarily signify ability to discriminate between relevant and irrelevant material. Persons with high ability to comprehend what was read often were quite unable to read *selectively* in order to solve problems.

Due in part to Gans' work, the concept of a generalized reading ability beyond the primary grades has been subjected to close study. Such a concept apparently must be rejected. Husbands and Shores (30) have concluded that different reading abilities are required in different problem situations. With this as a point of departure, Shores, in collaboration with Saupe, developed a "Test of Reading for Problem Solving in Science" (57). The results of their studies with this instrument indicate the reading skill needed for solving science problems differs significantly from what might be termed "general reading ability." Hansen (25) reached a similar conclusion, noting that skill in arithmetic problem solving seemed to bear no relationship to either speed of reading or reading comprehension as measured by the Gates Silent Reading Test. Although Maney (46) reported that there was a substantial relationship between literal and critical reading in science, she found no relationship between specific critical reading skills (special vocabulary, key ideas, sequence, and the like) and general and literal reading. Sochor's (59) study of literal and critical reading in social studies showed these two skills to be unrelated.

SUMMARY AND IMPLICATIONS

1. Intelligence definitely is a factor in thinking ability. Other things being equal (which they never are), the higher the level of intelligence, the higher the level of thinking ability. Ability to do inductive and deductive reasoning and facility with abstract symbols appear to be the two intellectual traits which most closely associate intelligence and clear thinking.

2. Intelligence clearly is not the only factor involved in problem solving. None of the correlations reported are particularly high. As a matter of fact, the correlations reported appear to indicate that less than half of the variability in problem-solving skills may be accounted for by intelligence test scores. It thus appears that classroom teachers have much opportunity to improve thinking skills, regardless of the intelligence level of their students.

3. A good understanding of the content and procedures in a particular academic field is necessary, but not sufficient, for problem-solving skill in that particular field. The teacher must seek ways to make subject matter

a means to an end (improved ability to apply the subject matter in problem solving), not an end in itself.

4. There seems to be no general reading skill which is associated with problem-solving competency. There is a high degree of specificity in types of thinking required in different reading situations. Similarly, particular reading skills are important for particular types of problems. Relatively little has been done to clarify the exact constellation of reading skills required in a given problem setting.

5. The ability to think clearly can be improved among individuals of virtually all intelligence levels. Certainly it appears that this is true for all intelligence levels encountered in the public schools. (See Chapter 14 for a complete review of experimental efforts to accomplish this.)

PERSONAL-EMOTIONAL FACTORS

RIGIDITY OR "SET"

Virtually every theoretical analysis of scientific thinking emphasizes the need for flexibility, for fluency of hypotheses, even for an occasional "controlled guess." The absence of this inclination has come to be called rigidity or *set*. Set may be thought of as the tendency to persevere in a given mode of thinking when it is no longer the best one to use.

Gestalt psychology, particularly under the leadership of Duncker and Wertheimer, has been responsible for much of the research into the nature and influence of "set," or, to use the Gestalt expression, *Einstellung*.

The first exhaustive study of set was accomplished by Luchins (38) in 1942. Using his now-famous "water jar" problems, supplemented on occasion with other set-inducing arrangements involving maze tracing, word identification, and geometric proofs, Luchins showed conclusively that most persons are susceptible to set in some degree. Susceptibility appears largely independent of age, sex, intelligence, or level of schooling, although children of grade school age appear to have the greatest difficulty in recovering from set.

While much of Luchins' early work was concerned with developing a better understanding of basic psychological attributes of rigidity, many studies followed which were concerned with its relationship to problem-solving efficiency. Maier (41) had observed that when attempting to solve a problem, persons tended to pursue a single, "habitual direction." He speculated that this "directive tendency" might be (*a*) nothing more than behavior which results because more fruitful responses do not occur, or (*b*) a mental function which is so firmly established that it actually *blocks* the appearance of more fruitful processes. Maier's experimentation indicated that "habitual direction" is actually an inhibiting force which decreases the likelihood that the thinker will achieve new directions, even though the necessary knowledge and processes may be within his command. Numerous other studies support the conclusion that mental rigidity restricts both the versatility and effectiveness of the problem solver.

Solomon has shown (60, 61) that rigid persons are less able to grasp and apply the various factors which constitute the scientific method and are less able to organize ideas into comprehensive wholes. The tendency is for the rigid person to be narrow, isolated, specific, concrete in his thought processes.

Most studies suggest that rigidity is a generalized characteristic of personality, permeating all thought activities. The work of Rokeach (54), Cowen and Thompson (15), and Solomon point to this conclusion, although the evidence is hardly overwhelming.

It does seem safe, however, to interpret the research as indicating that an individual's thinking ability will be handicapped in relation to his susceptibility to set and his difficulty in overcoming set. If it is correct that set is a general trait, its influence will make itself felt in all types of problem-solving activities. This being the case, what means do we have for increasing flexibility of thought?

Before examining this issue, it is only fair to observe that some might argue that rigidity has its desirable characteristics. There is evidence, for instance, that persons who adopt a set, routine, mechanical approach to thinking activities can handle certain types of problems with greater speed and efficiency. Gaier's (18) detailed study of eleven high school students in a social studies class is a case in point. His subjects were ranked on rigidity as indicated by an individual Rorschach record. When these rankings were compared with rankings on various sections of a comprehensive examination in social studies, the rank order correlation between rigidity and knowledge of specific information was .73. This would seem to indicate that the conventional sort of high school curriculum, with its subject-matter-centered approach, *rewards* and *encourages* the rigid, mechanistic thinker. As might be expected, the rank order correlation between rigidity and ability to apply principles in new situations, or to critically compare ideas, was almost exactly reversed $(-.71)$.

Thus it may be concluded that the rigid individual will be efficient when handling highly structured, specific materials but will be inept at interrelating materials and applying old ideas in new situations. If this is true, no detailed argument is needed to support the contention that in a democratic society flexibility of thinking is to be preferred to rigidity; there would seem to be a net gain if we sacrifice some small degree of efficiency in "routine thinking" in order to achieve a more universal ability to attack the issues that are unusual, peculiar, singular.

The problem is how to promote this flexibility.

The most obvious device for preventing set is to warn the subjects to be alert for it. Moderate success has been reported by Maier (41), Guetzkow (21), and Luchins (38). In a second study, Luchins (39) examined techniques which might be of more enduring value or more general applicability. Three separate ways of reducing set were compared: (1) verbal warnings to avoid set, (2) presentations of problem material to de-emphasize the "law" which applied, (3) presenting problems in concrete rather than symbolic form. No technique was truly effective at any age level.

Rokeach (55) suggested that when the thinker is in a hurry he is forced to perceive the problem narrowly and tends to solve it in a rigid, "efficient" manner. Although he did discover that nonrigid solutions were produced more frequently when subjects were unhurried, even under optimum conditions over fifty percent of the solutions followed the *Einstellung* pattern.

Common sense would lead us to expect that groups would suffer less from set than would individuals. Taylor and Faust (62) report results which support such a judgment. Unfortunately, even though groups were less prone to set, they also seemed to be highly inefficient, requiring many more man-minutes per correct solution than individuals. A later study by Lorge and others (37) suggests that this matter of inefficiency may not always be significant; sometimes groups are more efficient as well as more productive.

Many persons have noted that after prolonged work on a problem, thinking "gets into a rut." Starting a search in any given direction tends to blind the worker to other possibilities. One effective device for breaking up this sort of set appears to be the simple expedient of putting the problem aside for several days. Although no experimentation on this possibility has been reported, many experienced thinkers give testimony out of personal experience regarding its efficacy.

These generally discouraging findings seem to indicate that, if we are to enjoy any success in our efforts to make students' thinking more flexible, our approach must be of a fundamental nature. Luchins contends that public school pupils have been so thoroughly grounded in mechanistic, *Einstellung*-type problem-solving methods that any relatively superficial attempts to alter this behavior are unlikely to be successful. In his opinion, only a change to a flexible, problem-centered curriculum will truly remedy the situation. "Our schools may be concentrating so much on having the child master the habits, that the habits are mastering the child."

Luchins' blunt statement actually is a challenge to all teachers!!

EMOTIONAL STRESS

Earlier in this chapter we observed that the subdivision of topics must be arbitrary. Emotional stress is intimately affiliated with intellectual rigidity. Probably emotional stress reflects itself in thinking solely through rigidity of method. Research, we hope, will eventually investigate the possibility of emotion's resulting in haphazard method, or no method at all. In any case, the importance of emotional stress as a factor in clear thinking warrants its separate consideration.

Emotional complications accompanying *frustration* have been shown to induce rigidity. Christie (11) found that persons tend to cling even more tenaciously to a given scheme of attack under frustrating conditions. The fact that the "solution method" failed to work at all in the frustration situation did not make the subjects more disposed to abandon it. Rather, that fact served to imbed the method even more firmly into their cognitive structure. Luchins (39) found identically the same thing in an experiment with grade school children.

Studies also have been made investigating the effect of *anxiety* on thinking ability. Beir (3) noted that "individuals who are faced with threat and are in a state of anxiety show a loss of abstract abilities or, more specifically, face a loss of flexibility of intellectual function. . . ." Cowen (13, 14) reported that experimental groups under no emotional stress produced fewer *Einstellung* solutions and required less time to solve than did those under conditions of stress.

By ranking his subjects for anxiety as well as rigidity, Gaier (18) found that while anxiety did not impair knowledge of specific information (rho = .34), it was associated with poor performance on examinations which required flexibility and originality. Rank order correlations for scores on analysis, applications, and synthesis were respectively −.48, −.61, and −.42.

From these findings it appears that under conditions of emotional stress, the individual feels that his security is being challenged. When he detects a pattern or technique, as in the *Einstellung* problems, his tendency may be to view it as "something he can count on." As a consequence, he is most reluctant (and perhaps unable) to give up that pattern when it no longer is appropriate. If emotional adjustment is normal, this stress threat is absent and the subject finds it easier to alter his mode of response to varying problem situations.

Attention to mental hygiene, then, may be one fundamental approach to the problem of reducing the tendency to resort to stereotyped behavior patterns in lieu of original thinking.

BIASES

An ancient proverb states "A man views the universe through his ideas." This very fact accounts for one major barrier in clear thinking. Duncker (16) and others have pointed out that a person attacks a problem by establishing a "search model" and seeking the solution within the framework of that model. While a variety of circumstances appear to contribute to the shaping of a specific search model, the prejudices, values, and biases which the individual entertains compete mightily with the others. Under certain conditions they dominate the others.

This domination appears to be most complete when the problems are concerned with emotionally toned subject matter. Lefford (32) found that syllogisms involving neutral subject matter were solved correctly more frequently than syllogisms of equivalent logical validity involving emotive subject matter. When neutral items preceded emotional ones, more correct responses to the emotional items were obtained, whereas presenting the emotional items first tended to inhibit correct responses to the neutral items that followed. Apparently some sort of "set" to be logical was developed in the first situation while a "set" to be "emotional" or "partial" was created in the second.

Lefford's conclusion that "accurate and unbiased reasoning is rare in an affective stimulus situation" has been confirmed by Morgan and Morton (49). Emotionally toned syllogisms again were used as experimental material. After a detailed analysis of their data, these investigators concluded that approximately one-third of the "deciding influence" which determined choice of response could be attributed to "the personal convictions of the respondent."

Biases may also be introduced by more or less extraneous outside circumstances. An especially significant form of outside pressure is that of majority opinion. Asch (22) placed individuals in a situation where they found themselves consistently contradicted by other members of the group in simple perceptual judgments. There was a marked tendency toward conformity, although certain extreme differences in independence were noted. Berenda (4) has demonstrated that the judgments of grade school pupils are very susceptible to pressure from teachers and peer groups.

These findings relate only to thinking in emotionally toned circumstances. O'Connor (50) examined the influence of prejudice and bias on reasoning problems which were devoid of emotional content. College students were compared on ethnocentrism, "intolerance of ambiguity," and "abstract reasoning ability" (performance on syllogisms). Ethnocentrism and abstract reasoning were negatively related, the partial correlation with the effect of school grades held constant being $-.30$. Ethnocentrism and intolerance of ambiguity, on the other hand, exhibited a positive correlation of $.55 (N = 57)$.

This sort of experimental evidence has given rise to a rather widespread belief that most erroneous conclusions are the result of the individual's desire (or compulsion) to believe that which appeals to him. It is entirely possible, however, for incorrect deductions to result from trivial, impersonal circumstances associated with the problem. A few experiments have been completed illustrating that when equally favorable hypotheses are available, there is a strong tendency for thought to proceed along the line of least resistance. If the hypotheses are associated with a numerical or alphabetical sequence, the one occurring first tends to be favored; if associated with magnitude, the largest tends to be favored, for example. Hence the desire of political candidates to have their name printed at the top of the ballot? Apparently, even trivial biases are of real significance in many situations.

Attitude Toward the Problem

In a sense, this entire section is concerned with attitudes, but it seems desirable that we isolate for specific consideration the influence on effective thinking of the subject's general relationship to the problem.

Bloom and Broder (6) reported that good and poor problem solvers differed distinctly on two sorts of attitudes. One is their attitude toward the problem—their general problem-solving approach. Subjective appraisals of problem-solving performances indicated that good solvers are more aggressive, confident, tenacious, and attentive to detail. The other significant area of difference was the attitude toward the solution. Good solvers had faith in reasoning as contrasted with faith in guessing. The poor solvers felt that one either "got it" right away, or not at all; they could see no reason for persistent, hard thought on a problem. While good solvers relied upon independent analysis, poor ones depended upon "feelings" and "impressions." The less able students tended to proceed on a quasi-emotional basis, selecting answers in accord with their individual value systems and then confining their efforts to justifying their choices.

The tenacity with which subjects attacked a problem under varying degrees of confidence that a solution was possible was measured by Robinson (53). Large individual differences appeared, but there was a definite and consistent trend for the amount of time spent until abandonment to vary directly with the designated probability that the problem was solvable. When subjects were given the opportunity to choose from varying numbers of solution patterns of equal promise, all tended to spend progressively less time before giving up the first choice in favor of an alternative one as the number of available alternatives increased.

Although confidence facilitates problem solving, and discouragement inhibits it, we must not assume that all types of "negative attitudes" interfere with effective thinking. For instance, Gaier's (18) subjects were rated on negativism, that is, on their tendency to be critical, to oppose, to disagree. Even though we might anticipate that this kind of attitude would diminish problem-solving effectiveness, this was not the case. Rank order correlations between negativism and examination performance indicated no relationship between the two.

Summary and Implications

1. Under appropriate circumstances most people can be influenced to adopt stereotyped behavior patterns, to adopt a particular "mental set", with respect to a problem. If the problem is not routine or mechanical,

this type of behavior will diminish the person's effectiveness in solving the problem. Usually it does this by limiting the appearance of fruitful hypotheses, or imaginative "search models."

2. Mental rigidity tends to permeate many aspects of an individual's personality configuration. This basic personality trait has much influence on the ability to think clearly.

3. Experimental attempts to lower rigidity have not been notably successful. The most useful technique is to recognize that emotional stress heightens rigidity. The development of a favorable emotional climate in the classroom through regard for the principles of mental hygiene probably will be as helpful as anything. Frustration, anxiety, and discouragement should be avoided. A more sensible organization of the program of instruction may be just as important as good mental hygiene. A rote, mechanistic, subject-centered approach will reward rigidity, and consequently foster it. A flexible, imaginative, problem-centered program will reward diversity and creativity and thereby reduce stereotyped behavior.

4. Values, prejudices, and biases influence thinking. Problem solving is significantly distorted by emotionally toned materials or by majority pressures which run counter to the solution advanced by the individual. When dealing with emotionally weighted situations, teachers should be alert for these nonrational influences and help the students to identify and overcome them.

5. Persistence, aggressiveness, objectivity, confidence, and rationality characterize effective thinking. Unreasoned guesses, self-justification, and lack of attention to detail characterize poor problem solving. Teachers can learn much about the problem-solving characteristics of students through an analysis of their thought protocols on an individual basis. Once the specific difficulties are isolated, a guide for remedial instruction has been achieved.

EXPERIENTIAL FACTORS

FUNCTIONAL FIXEDNESS

What we have chosen to call "functional fixedness" probably is quite similar to mental rigidity. We distinguish between the two because the former seems to focus attention on the individual's relationship to external physical objects and influences, while the latter is more accurately thought of as an internal, affective trait of personality. It is true that any attempt to distinguish beween the two will appear somewhat forced, and separate treatment here is not intended to imply that the two characeristics are separate in actual practice.

Wertheimer chose the term *functional* to describe the role which the problem elements fulfilled when they met the structural requirements of the problem. [3] He felt that it is not enough to seek common elements among various problems. These common elements must be seen as things required by the structure of the problem; they must be "functional" with respect to that structure. Persons who persist in attempts to fit the elements into a structure which is not appropriate to the problem suffer from one type of "functional blindness."

Though this phenomenon admittedly is a type of "set," it is an internal rather than an external influence. Dunckner (16), however, has expanded this concept by suggesting that functional fixedness not only embraces the manner of structuring the problem elements but also includes the manner of utilizing the materials of thought brought to bear on the problem from outside the problem itself. He devised certain ingenious test situations to illustrate and examine this phenomenon. Essentially, these situations entailed (a) giving one group of subjects a problem where certain of the materials needed in the solution were presented in a functional role quite different from the role they would play in the solution pattern, and (b) giving a second group the same problem without this "pre-utilization" of the solution materials. For example, a problem might require that a box be used as a platform. One group would receive the box in the role of "container"; the second group would receive it in a neutral context. The influence of functional fixedness was then estimated from the difference in the number of correct solutions offered and in terms of the amount of time required to solve the problem.

After a series of experiments involving mathematical problems, Duncker concluded that the same sort of fixedness which associates with physical objects also influences conceptual or thought material. His hypothesis to explain this is that "thought material is from the very beginning more thoroughly imbued with perceptual functions." Alleviation of fixedness, then, depends upon avoiding concepts which are too "image-bound." The difficulty is not that one starts with a specific structure and is unable to shift to a new one, but rather that he starts with a specific structure and *merely* shifts to other specific structures. Only by starting with adequate, *generalized* structures will this obstacle be surmounted.

Other experimenters have followed Duncker's trail. In general, two conclusions stand out. *First,* fixedness in one situation does not reliably indicate that the person will suffer from fixedness with other objects in a different situation. That is to say, susceptibility to fixedness varies not only among individuals, but within a given individual as he works with different materials and different problems. *Second,* there is clear evidence that an individual with more diversified experiences is less subject to functional fixedness; he enjoys greater flexibility in using his experiences effectively to solve problems.

Several investigators, but most notably Bloom and Broder (6), have

[3] Max Wertheimer, *Productive Thinking* (New York, Harper, 1945).

pointed out that poor problem solvers often possess all of the relevant information needed to solve a particular problem, yet are unable to do so. They are unable to bring this information to bear on the problem. Under guided questioning they are readily led to the appropriate solution; left to their own devices, they might never achieve it. When this phenomenon is viewed in the light of the research described above, it seems plausible to suggest that the information these students possess has been acquired through specific, unrelated, narrow, isolated experiences. The failure to generalize the experiences has seriously restricted their value in subsequent problem situations where these experiences actually were essential for solution.

Maier used the expression *direction* to denote fixedness, observing that it is that condition or tendency which orients a person to a problem in a particular manner. Direction determines the pattern in which past experiences will be organized and brought to bear on the problem. One of Maier's (40) experiments indicated that mere experience, or even pertinent experiences, may not be adequate for solving a problem. Solution is achieved only when the thinker has the proper direction so that his experiences are integrated in terms of the goal. Another experiment by Maier (41), previously cited, showed that acceptance of one direction tended to block the appearance of other, different, directing tendencies. Apparently this is simply another way of saying that functional fixedness has occurred. Still further study by Maier (43) indicates that even though past experiences with pertinent elements of the problem situation serve to facilitate solutions, these experiences are most profitably utilized if the subject is assisted in selecting the proper direction.

But how is direction achieved? Duncker has suggested that two heuristic tendencies come into play during problem solving: (1) analysis of the situation, that is, analysis of the area of conflict or uncertainty and of the materials, and (2) analysis of the goal. Reid (52) has shown that subjects assisted in analyzing the problem goal performed significantly more efficiently than did those who were not specifically goal-oriented. A further analysis led Reid to conclude that the contribution of goal analysis is its directive tendency. It permits the thinker to substitute for the original goal an intermediate one which is simpler and more readily attained, but which also serves as a mediating stage en route to the total solution. Without goal analysis, subjects usually "start with the materials of the problem." The result then is fixedness, inflexible structuring of the problem in a single, and usually unproductive, context.

To this point, only the influence of *quality* of experience has been considered. Effective thinking also is modified by the *quantity* of any given experience. Although its effect is not as subtle as that of quality, it is of particular importance in fostering fixedness and rigidity. Without citing specific studies, suffice it to note that the bulk of the evidence indicates that a large number of similar experiences which verify a particular hypothesis will increase the difficulty of abandoning that hypothesis in favor of a new and incompatible one, even when such a shift is appropriate. These findings only serve to underscore again the great need for diversity of experience and for emphasizing generalities rather than specifics.

AGE TRENDS IN THINKING ABILITIES

Everyone has observed that as children grow older they are able to solve more difficult problems. Inevitably this suggests the question: At what age are children able to solve reasoning problems?

Maier (42) defined *reasoning* or *productive thinking* as "the ability to combine or integrate isolated experiences." This skill he contrasted with *learning* or *reproductive thinking,* "the ability to associate or combine contiguous experiences." After exposing children to a maze test which required a "reasoned" solution, Maier concluded that it was not until children reached a mental age of five years that truly rational problem solving, as distinguished from associative learning, appeared.

There are at least a half-dozen studies which suggest that the ability to think effectively in situations requiring reasoned conclusions appears at an even earlier age. For our purposes, the question is not particularly significant. It is clear that by the time children enter school they are able to handle situations which demand rational thinking. By inference, this means they are ready to profit from instructional activities which help them to develop this ability.

Studies of inductive reasoning abilities in children have been made by Long and Welch (34, 35, 36). Comparisons of children aged four to six with children aged six to eight indicated that the two groups are very similar in their ability to discover independently the inductive principle underlying a given problem, but the older children profit more from hints and are better able to generalize their solutions. Although some of the children are able to reason inductively without help, a definite increment in this ability appears about age nine to ten (38). The whole period of adolescence appears to be marked by a distinct and pronounced development in reasoning. It is not until late adolescence, however, that efficiency in inductive reasoning approaches that in deductive reasoning.

Miller (47) has reported that, although particular types of logical fallacies are more difficult than others, at least for senior high school students, the order of difficulty is independent of sex, grade level, mental maturity, and even scholastic standing.

THE DIFFICULTY REDUCTION TENDENCY

All human thinking is dependent upon the recognition that a problem exists and needs to be solved. Further, the problem must be within the intellectual and experiential comprehension of the prospective solver, or there really is no problem in any meaningful sense of the word. And yet, people regularly are confronted with problems which exceed their capabilities. What is the usual manner of meeting a problem which, in its original form, is totally beyond the capacity of the solver?

Hildreth (28) has suggested that the typical response is a "difficulty reduction tendency." Persons faced with problems which surpass their understanding and experience are inclined to substitute simpler mental responses for the appropriate ones. A new goal, which is achievable by the solver, replaces the goal set by the problem. Usually the new goal and the original one are related; the substitution is not completely arbitrary and fickle. But the individual has to "deform and assimilate" the problem "according to a mental structure of his own." Hildreth states that this sort of response is actually more common than random guessing or simply giving up, and that it appears at all intellectual and age levels.

Experimental verification of this hypothesis apparently has not been attempted. Perhaps the most valid confirmation can be derived from the research of Chrisof (10) and Bloom and Broder (6). Chrisof reported definite instances of behavior designed to avoid, not resolve, perplexing factors. The thought protocols recorded by Bloom and Broder show that poor solvers readily deform a difficult problem into one which they can solve.

To comment that such a procedure is undesirable is indeed trite. But it underlines the fact that effective thinking is not necessarily improved by a problem-centered curriculum. Unless the problems are meaningful and manageable, they will just reinforce inadequate thinking techniques rather than foster productive ones.

THE VALUE OF MISTAKES

Great pains have been taken to alert educators to the fact that "success breeds success." Earlier we pointed out that consistent, prolonged failure restricts effective thinking. Does this mean that pupils should always be protected from mistakes and failure in their thinking experiences? Not at all!

Even as we recognize that a steady diet of failure would be extraordinarily disruptive, we should bear in mind that mistakes also can contribute to greater efficiency in thought. A study by Morgan (48) led him to observe that under certain situations "success tended to inhibit the efficient use of inductive processes, whereas failure instigated a critical analysis of both failures and successes."

After a thorough analysis of the function of mistakes, Duncker (16) was able to make an important distinction. He stated that (a) mere *recognition* that something does not work leads only to a variation of the old, useless proposal, but (b) *realization* of why it does not work leads to a variation of process which corrects the conflict. Here, it seems, is the crux of the mattter.

SUMMARY AND IMPLICATIONS

1. Functional fixedness appears to be another aspect of psychological rigidity. It operates to retard effective thinking by decreasing the versatility of the thinker in his manipulation of both thoughts and materials. Diversity of experience and assistance in generalizing the significance of specific experiences will help to reduce this obstacle.

2. "Direction" or orientation of the search model is most productive when the solver has developed his orientation through an analysis of the problem goal.

3. Frequent confirmations of a particular hypothesis, or of a particular approach, increase the difficulty of relinquishing that hypothesis or technique when it is appropriate to change. Again, diversity of experience seems to afford the best protection against this difficulty.

4. School children of all ages are capable of solving problems requiring some degree of insight and reasoning. Indications are that abstract and inductive reasoning capabilities mature most rapidly during adolescence.

5. The common response to problems which exceed the intellectual capacity and experiential background of the individual is to convert them into less complex problem situations within the individual's capacity. Learning experiences which are beyond the ability of the student ordinarily will be deformed into something he can assimilate, although it is virtually a certainty that he then will assimilate something quite different from what the teacher intended.

6. Mistakes can be a valuable device for teaching the improvement of thinking. The crucial point is that the teacher must be sure that mistakes do not act as barriers, but as guideposts.

PROCEDURAL FACTORS

There is general agreement that the process of thinking varies among individuals. That is to say, it is quite probable that different people may consider the same problem and arrive at the same answer, but by thought processes that are not at all similar. It also appears that certain processes are more productive than others. Consequently, much experimental effort has gone into the determination of optimum procedures of thinking and the determination of those circumstances which encourage persons to adopt this procedure.

Basically, the same experimental design characterizes virtually all of the research on this aspect of thinking. The procedure has been to present subjects with problem situations and have them either "think out loud" as a solution is attempted or recapitulate their thought processes after the solution effort. Detailed thought protocols thus are recorded and available for close study. The difficulties inherent in this research technique have resulted in most studies being completed with only small and sometimes select samples of subjects. The generalizations which will be presented must be read with this in mind. However, most of this kind of research has been done with care and thoroughness, and the generalizations can be offered with reasonable confidence.

"INSIGHT" AND "TRIAL AND ERROR"

Much, and possibly all, of the controversy which has persisted with regard to the concepts of "insight" and "trial and error" seems caused by extremist definitions of these two concepts. The point of view of the authors is that there is nothing antithetical between the two procedures. In fact, there is evidence to suggest that in most thinking each type of behavior appears. Duncker's (16) description of the process can be construed as supporting this view. He suggested that "The final form of a solution is typically attained by way of mediating phases of the process, of which each one, in retrospect, possesses the character of a solution and, in prospect, that of a problem." He divides the solution process into two major stages: (1) the "stage of explications" wherein the goal and the premises of the problem are explored (this presumably being the period of trial-and-error activity) and (2) the stage wherein a decisive relation "snaps into place" (the moment of insight).

Hartmann (26, 27) found that even when subjects attempted problems which elicited either total success or total failure, instantaneous solutions were quite rare. However, sudden solutions, following extended delays characterized by adoption, rejection, and modification of a variety of working hypotheses, were relatively common. His findings led him to declare "Learning [thinking?] can and does occur either by means of continual trial-and-error activity with ultimate association of correct responses or through insight, that is, through an immediate appreciation of the function of the various elements of the total situation." Hartmann's work, confirmed by five or six independent studies, suggests the following levels of insight:

1. *Immediate* or instantaneous, where the solution is grasped as a whole through some leap in thought.
2. *Gradual,* where the solution seemingly matures as the thinker investigates through trial and error a variety of possibilities. Solutions may be complete or partial, depending on whether adequate "closure" is achieved.
3. *Sudden,* where the period of trial and error seemingly is ineffectual, yet has been a necessary preliminary to the sudden emergence of the total solution.

Studies of productive thinking at the level of genius are rare and usually depend upon reconstruction of the occasion. Yet those which have been made by Hadamard (23) and Patrick (51) indicate that process does not differ fundamentally from that which appears at lesser intellectual levels. It is quite easy to distinguish four phases: (a) Preparation, (b) Incubation, (c) Illumination, and (d) Elaboration. It probably is fair to suggest that these same stages can be detected in genuine productive thinking by average persons, albeit on a more pedestrian plane.

There is consensus that insightful thinking is more "elegant," more efficient, and more fundamental as a higher intellectual process. This emphasis on the desirability of fostering insightful techniques is significant to teachers. The following suggestions may prove useful:

1. Problem situations should be interesting, but not so stimulating as to arouse an emotional response.
2. Because insight tends to be unstable in nature, correct solutions should be followed up with several repetitions.
3. Children should be taught to vary solving procedures at an early age. "Problem-solving rules" and habitual modes of attack should be minimized.
4. Problems which are in some respect unique, out of the ordinary, which require an approach different from the routine one, should be presented as often as feasible.
5. Persistent failure and discouragement should be circumvented.
6. When prolonged blocking of progress is encountered, pupils should be encouraged to put aside the problem and to return to it at a later time when a fresh approach is more probable.
7. Children should be encouraged to attack the "whole problem," to seek broad relationships, to penetrate to the true structure of the problem.

ABSTRACT AND CONCRETE: CONCEPTUAL AND PERCEPTUAL

The modes of solution which Duncker observed in his research led him to theorize that, in general, one of two principles tends to be followed in thinking. The *first,* and more "banal," he labeled "situational analysis." In this approach the thinker concentrates on the materials of the problem. The *second,* and more "elegant," he described as "goal analysis." Here the thinker focuses attention on the needs of the problem, on the structure which must be completed if a solution is to be accomplished.

Several other investigations have produced supporting evidence. Hanfmann (24) and Simmel (58) labeled the processes as the *conceptual approach* and the *perceptual approach.* Conceptual thinkers utilized goal-directed behavior and detached, abstract thought. Perceptual thinkers depended upon a sort of situational analysis involving constant, close contact with the problem materials; thought processes tended to be concrete, specific. There appears to be a tendency for conceptual-type thinkers to be superior, but the results are not conclusive. Perhaps the results are not typical because the subjects investigated were of unusually high intelligence and well educated. It also should be kept in mind that a given individual does not adopt one or the other of the procedures as his exclusive approach. He will switch from one to the other, even though clear preferences often are evident. When the approaches were in conflict, for instance, when the subject forced himself to use one method exclusively regardless of the need of the situation, thinking became much less efficient.

Rokeach (54, 55) has demonstrated that there is a relationship between preferred method of thinking and ethnocentrism, with ethnocentric persons inclined to favor concrete solving methods and nonethnocentrics favoring abstract procedures. He also noted that concrete methods are preferred when subjects are hurried; abstract methods tend to be used when the subject takes time for analysis prior to any overt solving activity.

THE INFLUENCE OF THE PROBLEM SETTING

We have already emphasized that problems never are considered in a vacuum. The atmosphere associated with the problem will itself interact with the thinker and become an influential part of the thinking process. This point has been brought out in our discussion of biases, set, and fixedness. There are other subtle ways in which the problem setting impinges itself upon the solution model. Some of these will now be considered.

Sells (56) has shown that the over-all "tone" of a problem has a definite influence on the solution offered. Syllogisms expressed in a negative manner tended to elicit negatively phrased responses; those stated affirmatively encouraged the selection of affirmative responses. This suggests that persons adopt a "mental set" consistent with the problem atmosphere and because of this find it a simple matter to accept a solution which reflects that atmosphere.

Several workers have investigated the effect of presenting essentially the same problem in varying settings. Brownell and Stretch (7) presented grade pupils with arithmetic problems in settings of varying familiarity. About one-half of the group were consistently good or poor, regardless of problem setting, but the others showed a definite lowering of solving efficiency when familiarity was decreased. The interference caused by unfamiliar problem settings seems to concentrate itself at the conceptual level; unfamiliar settings increased the errors in *choice of operations* but not in the *accuracy of computations*.

Whenever problem settings are made more complicated, even though the same principles may be involved, effective thinking is hampered. This conclusion certainly is no surprise. It is interesting to note, however, that success in applying a given generalization at a particular level of difficulty is not a reliable index of a person's ability to apply the same principle at more difficult levels. Similarly, it is much more difficult to discover a general principle when the problem is made more complex. One investigator

(27) has suggested that difficulty in discovering the solution principle of a problem increases "as the cube of the complexity (of the problem)."

Problem settings which are impersonal would be expected to permit a more objective analysis than would those which involve the thinker on a personal basis. Marks (45) structured the very same problem situation in two settings—one personal, the other impersonal. The number of successful solutions produced under impersonal conditions was significantly greater than for matched subjects working under personalized conditions. Marks felt that the difference in performance was due to a lowering of the ability to analyze objectively the problem elements. This conclusion is enhanced by Mark's demonstration that the number of correct solutions under impersonal conditions no longer is significantly greater if the subjects in each situation are presented with a list of the problem elements in need of analysis.

METHODOLOGICAL CONSIDERATIONS

It might be suspected that certain specific problem-solving methods are applicable within the broad framework defined by "abstract" and "concrete" or "conceptual" and "perceptual" modes of attack. If that were true, some indication of the relative efficiency of the various methods would be available. Nine so-called problem-solving techniques (for example, location of the crucial aspect of the problem) were studied by Burack (8). The purpose of his research was to evaluate the contribution which each of the nine methods made to more effective problem solving. The results certainly are not encouraging for those who would like to equip school pupils with a set of rules for improving thinking and problem solving. Burack's major conclusions were that (a) The nature of the problem largely determines the effectiveness of any specific solving technique, and (b) It is quite possible that nonmethodological intellectual traits and abilities are more important than are the specific methods used.

SUMMARY AND IMPLICATIONS

1. Although "insight" and "trial and error" are distinct in their extreme manifestations, they may be thought of as representing different sections of the continuum of problem-solving behavior. Not only are they compatible with each other; in most problem situations both types of behavior will characterize the thinker's efforts.

2. As a general rule, insightful activities are to be preferred in most situations requiring reflective thought. Certain conditions which facilitate insight have been suggested (see p. 258).

3. Individuals tend to subscribe consistently to a particular mode of thinking when attacking problems. These modes can be classified as (1) abstract, conceptual, general, oriented toward the problem goal, or (2)

concrete, perceptual, specific, oriented toward the problem materials. For most situations, the former appears to be most effective.

4. A problem situation always presents itself in a particular context. That context becomes a definite factor in tempering the solution process; sometimes it facilitates impersonal objectivity, generalization, and direction; sometimes it inhibits or distorts them. Teachers should choose learning activities which are relatively free of "tonal effects" in order to help the student direct his attention toward the basic intellectual techniques needed for rational thinking.

5. Efforts to isolate and evaluate specific problem-solving techniques have not been successful. Indications are that they never will be, as particular problem situations appear to demand particular solving techniques. Hence, any hope for a neat set of "rules for thinking" is presently a forlorn one. The purpose of this entire volume is to help the teacher recognize the vast diversity of situations and techniques which the thinker must be prepared to handle and to suggest some classroom procedures which will make both teachers and students better thinkers.

QUESTIONS, EXERCISES, AND REPORTS

1. Select some factor which influences thinking ability, such as intelligence, emotion, rigidity, memory, and locate one or more recent research studies directed at this factor. Give a summary report and critical evaluation of the studies.

2. This chapter suggests four major groupings for the factors which influence thinking. If you were writing the chapter, how would you organize the summary of research? Explain your answer.

3. Page 258 lists suggestions for teachers interested in helping children develop "insightful responses." Prepare a similar list for helping children acquire other desirable thinking skills. (For example: skill in analysis of goal, in flexibility of approach, in testing hypotheses.)

4. Just how significant are the reservations implied by the quotation from Gardner Murphy which appears on page 241? Cite any recent research studies which seem to have been designed to overcome the objections presented by Murphy.

5. A number of reports should be made and used for class discussion. Experienced teachers should present in some detail their handling of any of the factors presented in this chapter, particularly those which interfere with thinking. How was the situation detected? What procedures were used to aid the learner?

BIBLIOGRAPHY OF RESEARCH STUDIES

Note: Only the research studies cited in this chapter are listed. These studies were selected because they were especially significant. However, at least an additional two hundred studies have been made. New ones continue to appear regularly. Thus, the reader must understand that this bibliography is really nothing more than an *introduction* to the research on thinking.

1. ALPERN, M. L., "The Ability to Test Hypotheses," *Science Education,* Vol. 30 (1946), pp. 220-229.

2. ATKINS, J. M., "A Study of Formulating and Suggesting Tests for Hypotheses in Elementary School Science Experiences," *Science Education,* Vol. 32 (1958), pp. 414-422.

3. BEIR, E. G., "The Effect of Induced Anxiety on the Flexibility of Intellectual Functioning," *Psychological Monographs,* Vol. 65, No. 365 (1951).

4. BERENDA, R. W., *The Influence of the Group on Judgments of Children* (New York, King's Crown Press, 1950).

5. BILLINGS, M. L., "Problem Solving in Different Fields of Endeavor," *American Journal of Psychology,* Vol. 45 (1934), pp. 259-272.

6. BLOOM, B. S., and BRODER, L. J., *Problem-Solving Processes of College Students* (Chicago, University of Chicago Press, 1950).

7. BROWNELL, W. A., and STRETCH, L. B., *The Effect of Unfamiliar Settings on Problem Solving,* Duke University Research Studies in Education, No. 1 (1931).

8. BURACK, B., "The Nature and Efficacy of Methods of Attack on Reasoning Problems," *Psychological Monographs,* Vol. 64, No. 7 (1950).

9. BURACK, B., and MOOS, D., "Effect of Knowing a Principle Basic to Solution of a Problem," *Journal of Educational Research,* Vol. 50 (1956), pp. 203-208.

10. CHRISOF, C., "The Formulation and Elaboration of Thought Problems," *American Journal of Psychology,* Vol. 52 (1939), pp. 161-185.

11. CHRISTIE, R., "The Effect of Frustration upon Rigidity in Problem Solution," *American Psychologist,* Vol. 5 (1950), pp. 296-297.

12. COOK, T. W., "Amount of Material and Difficulty of Problem Solving, II: The Disc Transfer Problem," *Journal of Experimental Psychology,* Vol. 20 (1937), pp. 288-296.

13. COWEN, E. L., "The Influence of Varying Degrees of Psychological Stress on Problem-Solving Rigidity," *Journal of Abnormal and Social Psychology,* Vol. 47 (1952), pp. 512-519.

14. COWEN, E. L., "Stress Reduction and Problem-Solving Rigidity," *Journal of Consulting Psychology,* Vol. 16 (1952), pp. 425-428.

15. COWEN, E. L., and THOMPSON, G. G., "Problem-Solving Rigidity and Personality Structure," *Journal of Abnormal and Social Psychology,* Vol. 46 (1951), pp. 165-176.

16. DUNCKER, K., "On Problem Solving," *Psychological Monographs,* Vol. 58, No. 270 (1945). Translated by L. S. Lees.

17. FURST, E. J., "The Relationship Between Tests of Intelligence and Tests of Critical Thinking and Knowledge," *Journal of Educational Research,* Vol. 43 (1950), pp. 614-625.

18. GAIER, E. L., "The Relationship Between Selected Personality Variables and the Thinking of Students in Discussion Classes," *School Review,* Vol. 60 (1952), pp. 404-411.

19. GANS, R., *A Study of Critical Reading Comprehension in the Intermediate Grades,* Teachers College Contributions to Education, No. 811 (1940).

20. GLASER, E. M., *An Experiment in the Development of Critical Thinking,* Teachers College Contributions to Education, No. 843 (1941).

21. GUETZKOW, H., "An Analysis of the Operation of Set in Problem-Solving

Behavior," *Journal of General Psychology,* Vol. 45 (1951), pp. 219-244.
22. GUETZKOW, H., ed., *Groups, Leadership, and Men* (New York, Carnegie Press, 1951).
23. HADAMARD, J., *The Psychology of Invention in the Mathematical Field* (Princeton, N. J., Princeton University Press, 1945).
24. HANFMANN, E., "A Study of Personal Patterns in an Intellectual Performance," *Character and Personality,* Vol. 9 (1941), pp. 315-325.
25. HANSEN, C. W., "Factors Associated with Successful Achievement in Problem Solving in Sixth-grade Arithmetic," *Journal of Educational Research,* Vol. 38 (1944), pp. 111-118.
26. HARTMANN, G. W., "Concept and Criteria of Insight," *Psychological Review,* Vol. 38 (1931), pp. 242-253.
27. HARTMANN, G. W., "Insight vs. Trial and Error in the Solution of Problems," *American Journal of Psychology,* Vol. 45 (1933), pp. 663-677.
28. HILDRETH, G., "The Difficulty Reduction Tendency in Perception and Problem Solving," *Journal of Educational Psychology,* Vol. 32 (1941), pp. 305-313.
29. HORROCKS, J. E., "The Relationship Between Knowledge of Human Development and Ability to Use Such Knowledge," *Journal of Applied Psychology,* Vol. 30 (1946), pp. 501-508.
30. HUSBANDS, K. L., and SHORES, J. H., "Measurement of Reading for Problem Solving: A Critical Review of the Literature," *Journal of Educational Research,* Vol. 43 (1950), pp. 453-465.
31. JOHNSON, J. T., "On the Nature of Problem Solving in Arithmetic," *Journal of Educational Research,* Vol. 43 (1949), pp. 110-115.
32. LEFFORD, A., "The Influence of Emotional Subject Matter on Logical Reasoning," *Journal of General Psychology,* Vol. 34 (1946), pp. 127-151.
33. LING, B. C., "The Solving of Problem Situations by the Preschool Child," *Journal of Genetic Psychology,* Vol. 68 (1946), pp. 3-28.
34. LONG, L., and WELCH, L., "Reasoning Ability in Young Children," *Journal of Psychology,* Vol. 12 (1941), pp. 21-44.
35. LONG, L., and WELCH, L., "Factors Affecting Efficiency of Inductive Reasoning," *Journal of Experimental Education,* Vol. 10 (1942), pp. 252-264.
36. LONG, L., and WELCH, L., "A Comparison of Reasoning Ability of Two Age Groups," *Journal of Genetic Psychology,* Vol. 62 (1943), pp. 63-76.
37. LORGE, I., and others, "Problem Solving by Teams and by Individuals in a Field Setting," *Journal of Educational Psychology,* Vol. 46 (1955), pp. 160-166.
38. LUCHINS, A. S., "Mechanization in Problem Solving: The Effect of *Einstellung,*" *Psychological Monographs,* Vol. 54, No. 6 (1942).
39. LUCHINS, A. S., and LUCHINS, E. H., "New Experimental Attempts at Preventing Mechanization in Problem Solving," *Journal of General Psychology,* Vol. 42 (1950), pp. 279-297.
40. MAIER, N. R. F., "Reasoning in Humans, I: On Direction," *Journal of Comparative Psychology,* Vol. 10 (1930), pp. 115-143.
41. MAIER, N. R. F., "An Aspect of Human Reasoning," *British Journal of Psychology,* Vol. 24 (1933), pp. 144-155.
42. MAIER, N. R. F., "Reasoning in Children," *Journal of Comparative Psychology,* Vol. 21 (1936), pp. 357-366.
43. MAIER, N. R. F., "Reasoning in Humans, III: The Mechanisms of Equivalent Stimuli and Reasoning," *Journal of Experimental Psychology,* Vol. 35 (1945), pp. 349-360.
44. MALTZMAN, I., and others, "Some Relationships Between Methods of In-

struction, Personality Variables, and Problem-Solving Behavior," *Journal of Educational Psychology,* Vol. 47 (1956), pp. 71-78.

45. MARKS, M. R., "Problem Solving as a Function of the Situation," *Journal of Experimental Psychology,* Vol. 41 (1951), pp. 74-80.

46. MANEY, E. S., "Literal and Critical Reading in Science," *Journal of Experimental Education,* Vol. 27 (1958), pp. 57-64.

47. MILLER, E. H., "A Study of Difficulty Levels of Selected Types of Fallacies in Reasoning and Their Relationships to the Factors of Sex, Grade Level, Mental Maturity, and Scholastic Standing," *Journal of Educational Research,* Vol. 49 (1955), pp. 123-129.

48. MORGAN, J. J. B., "The Value of Wrong Responses in Inductive Reasoning," *Journal of Experimental Psychology,* Vol. 35 (1945), pp. 141-146.

49. MORGAN, J. J. B., and MORTON, J. T., "The Distortion of Syllogistic Reasoning Produced by Personal Convictions," *Journal of Social Psychology,* Vol. 20 (1944), pp. 39-59.

50. O'CONNOR, P., Ethnocentrism, Intolerance of Ambiguity, and Abstract Reasoning Ability," *Journal of Abnormal and Social Psychology,* Vol. 47 (1952), pp. 526-530.

51. PATRICK, C., "Creative Thought in Poets," *Archives of Psychology,* Vol. 28, No. 179 (1935).

52. REID, J. W., "An Experimental Study of 'Analysis of Goal' in Problem Solving," *Journal of General Psychology,* Vol. 44 (1951), pp. 51-69.

53. ROBINSON, E. E., "An Experimental Study of Two Factors Which Produce Stereotyped Behavior in Problem Situations," *Journal of Experimental Psychology,* Vol. 27 (1940), pp. 394-410.

54. ROKEACH, M., "Generalized Mental Rigidity as a Factor in Ethnocentrism," *Journal of Abnormal and Social Psychology,* Vol. 43 (1948), pp. 259-278.

55. ROKEACH, M., "The Effect of Perception Time upon Rigidity and Concreteness of Thinking," *Journal of Experimental Psychology,* Vol. 40 (1950), pp. 206-216.

56. SELLS, S. B., "The Atmosphere Effect: An Experimental Study of Reasoning," *Archives of Psychology,* Vol. 31, No. 200 (1936).

57. SHORES, J. H., and SAUPE, J. L., "Reading for Problem Solving in Science," *Journal of Educational Psychology,* Vol. 44 (1953), pp. 149-158.

58. SIMMEL, M. L., *A Study of Qualitative Individual Differences in Thinking and Problem Solving.* Unpublished Ph. D. thesis, Radcliffe College, 1949.

59. SOCHOR, E. E., "Literal and Critical Reading in Social Studies," *Journal of Experimental Education,* Vol. 27 (1958), pp. 49-56.

60. SOLOMON, M. D., "Studies in Mental Rigidity and the Scientific Method, I: Rigidity and Abilities Implied in Scientific Method," *Science Education,* Vol. 36 (1952), pp. 240-247.

61. SOLOMON, M. D., "Studies in Mental Rigidity and the Scientific Method, II: Mental Rigidity and Comprehensiveness," *Science Education,* Vol. 36 (1952), pp. 263-269.

62. TAYLOR, D. W., and FAUST, F. W., "Twenty Questions: Efficiency in Problem Solving as a Function of Size of Group," *Journal of Experimental Psychology,* Vol. 44 (1952), pp. 360-368.

63. TECHMAN, L., "The Ability of Science Students to Make Conclusions," *Science Education,* Vol. 28 (1944), pp. 268-279.

SUPPLEMENTAL BIBLIOGRAPHY

The references given here will help the reader to gain further background in the research and theory on human thinking. Although not every one of the references is a report on research, each presents thoughtful summaries of research and suggests useful interpretations of the results.

BARTLETT, F. C., *Thinking: An Experimental and Social Study* (New York, Basic Books, 1958).

BRUNER, J. S., GOODNOW, J. J., and AUSTIN, G. A., *A Study of Thinking* (New York, Wiley, 1956).

HUMPHREY, G., *Thinking: An Introduction to Its Experimental Psychology* (New York, Wiley, 1951).

JOHNSON, D. M., *The Psychology of Thought and Judgment* (New York, Harper, 1955).

KATONA, G., *Organizing and Memorizing* (New York, Columbia University Press, 1940).

LEE, D. M., and BINGHAM, A., "Intellectual Processes," *Review of Educational Research,* Vol. 29 (1959), pp. 185-196. This article reviews the material on thinking which appeared in the preceding six years. Contains an unusually complete bibliography.

PIAGET, J., *The Psychology of Intelligence* (New York, Harcourt, Brace, 1950).

PRICE, H. H., *Thinking and Experience* (Cambridge, Mass., Harvard University Press, 1953).

RUSSELL, D. H., *Children's Thinking* (Boston, Ginn, 1956).

RYLE, G., *The Concept of Mind* (London, Hutchinson House, 1949).

VINACKE, W. E., *The Psychology of Thinking* (New York, McGraw-Hill, 1952).

Part III

The Teaching Process and Learning to Think

Let us now sum up the meager yet certain fruits of our long analysis.

EDGAR ALLAN POE

The preceding chapters have set forth in detail the abilities and attitudes necessary for good thinking. The chapters in Part III are designed to show the utilization and development of those abilities through school processes.

The basic abilities. The following summary is based on the development of the various abilities in separate chapters. It is for quick and ready reference with all chapters in Part III.

One may be said to think effectively to the degree that he behaves in any of the following ways;

1. Recognizes and defines problems, identifies issues.
2. Formulates, extends and verifies feasible hypotheses.
3. Collects, selects, or selectively recalls relevant data, differentiates between reliable and unreliable sources, between factual and nonfactual sources.
4. Recognizes reliable experiments.
5. Draws reasonable inferences regarding cause and effect, logical implication, valid generalization, reliable prediction, and accurate description.
6. Recognizes and evaluates implicit assumptions, uses postulational arguments logically, recognizes relevant value systems and uses them reasonably.
7. Recognizes errors and fallacies.

8. Comes to decisions or conclusions, tests them, applies them to pertinent situations.

9. Applies semantic principles to language employed.

The attitudes favorable and unfavorable to thinking. These have been presented in detail in Chapter 3; the following is a brief listing of key ideas:

1. Intellectual curiosity
2. Intellectual honesty
3. Objectivity
4. Intelligent skepticism
5. Open-mindedness
6. Conviction of cause-and-effect relationships
7. Disposition to be systematic
8. Flexibility
9. Persistence
10. Decisiveness

Attitudes valuable in group thinking.

1. Respect for another's views
2. Candor and expectancy of candor
3. Careful listening (tendency to)

Attitudes unfavorable to effective thinking

1. Lack of intellectual curiosity
2. Intellectual dishonesty
3. Bias or prejudice for or against (anything)
4. Primitive credulity
5. Harmful incredulity; the closed mind
6. Disregard for cause-an-effect relationships
7. Unsystematic procedure, tolerance of confusion (tendency to)
8. Dogmatism and rigidity; inflexibility
9. Lack of persistence
10. Indecisiveness

All the suggestions for teaching contained in the following chapters are based on the assumption that every effort will be made by teachers to give opportunity for the exercise and development of the abilities and attitudes known to be essential for thinking.

CHAPTER 13

Skill in Thinking as an Aim of Education

> The aim of education is precisely to develop intelligence of this independent and effective type—*a disciplined mind.*
>
> JOHN DEWEY *

> We state emphatically that, *upon its intellectual side, education consists in the formation of wide-awake, careful, thorough habits of thinking.*
>
> JOHN DEWEY †

> There is not adequate enough theoretical recognition that all the school can or need do for pupils, so far as their *minds* are concerned, is to develop their ability to think.
>
> JOHN DEWEY ‡

> Education is not merely the imparting of knowledge but the cultivation of certain aptitudes and attitudes of the mind . . . abilities [which] should be sought above all others—these are in our opinion: to think effectively, to communicate thought, to make relevant judgments, to discriminate among values.
>
> *General Education in a Free Society* §

The first thing to say about teaching individuals to think is that a formal outline of thinking and teaching to think would handicap, if not nullify,

---

* John Dewey, *How We Think* (Boston, Heath, 1910).

† John Dewey, *How We Think,* rev. ed. (Boston, Heath, 1933).

‡ John Dewey, *Democracy and Education* (New York, Macmillan, 1916).
It is odd that Dewey's critics so often charge him with being "anti-intellectual" in view of these and many more statements stressing the intellectual discipline as an aim of education. Dewey actually has, as will be noted later, the very best criticism available of those educational methods which fail to make for the disciplined intellect.

§ Report of the Harvard Committee, *General Education in a Free Society* (Cambridge, Mass., Harvard University Press, 1946), pp. 64-65.

efforts along this line. A general, flexible scheme is, however, not only possible but necessary. This volume presents what the authors believe to be a workable procedure. We hold that people can be taught to think more effectively through thinking.

SECTION 1. GOALS AND VALUES OF EDUCATION FOR THINKING

Schools have always placed stress on "teaching to think," but actual results have been negligible. *First,* the knowledge about thinking-in-process has not been available. *Second,* teachers generally have not been well informed on the nature of thinking and have received practically no training in teaching this. *Third,* popular notions about "thinking" are mostly nonsense, but the existence of these ideas has handicapped the schools. *Fourth,* a good deal of success in life can be achieved without thinking very much, or well. Events marching on have demonstrated the serious necessity for greater knowledge and skill in thinking.

The values accruing from thinking. Several values that come from thinking can be listed from everyday observation, with more important ones to come from more analytic viewing.

Thinking enables us:

1. *To direct our efforts toward a purpose or end; to govern our actions in an orderly and systematic way, instead of on caprice, or through mere routines, or on inadequate information.*

To say this another way; we are better able to meet our problems intelligently instead of impulsively or, as we say, "without thinking."

2. *To anticipate difficulties or problems and thus to prepare in advance.*

Everyone has observed the confusion, in serious cases, the panic which results when the unexpected happens. Emergencies may be tiny or enormous, occur anywhere from the nursery to international affairs. Many years ago, a serious collapse and cave-in happened on a construction project involving the subway in mid-Manhattan. Before the dust had settled, before those in the vicinity knew what had happened, the police had the area under control. "Control stations" appeared as by magic; danger spots were roped off; firemen, electric and water department men were working to control problems in their respective areas. Newspapers and citizens gave unstinted praise to the authorities—at the same time, wondering openly how a real disaster was under control almost in moments. The Police Commissioner explained it easily. "Such a collapse is a possibility in any large operation involving extensive excavation with heavy buildings nearby. We not only plan for just such accidents, but the fire and police teams are given practice on specific and potential danger spots. A complete plan for this very collapse had been reposing on the Commissioner's desk for some time. One phone call, and this plan went into operation."

The field of health and sanitation, particularly in the control of certain diseases, supplies many excellent examples of thinking in advance of a possible and probable problem. The primitive peoples tried to get rain for their crops by dances and other ceremonies. Modern man constructs extensive irrigation systems (as some intelligent primitive people did also) and ensures water in advance of need. He is even now experimenting with the seeding of clouds and similar measures to precipitate moisture from the clouds at points of special need.

3. *To increase steadily the meaning content for things and for symbols.* The development of meaning and the crucial part played in thinking by concepts has already been developed. Suffice it to note here that the more man thinks, the more numerous and more extensive his stock of meanings becomes. This enables anyone so disposed, to do constantly more effective thinking. Eventually, creative thinking will emerge for all in degree commensurate with native equipment. Dullards who think rarely, or not at all, and the average person of limited experience do badly in solving problems or in making discriminatory judgments partly because of the meager store of meanings possessed. One of the marked and sure differences between educated and noneducated men appears here. A person of native shrewdness and alertness, but without much formal education, often shows the value of thinking by the store of meanings he derives and keeps. As Mill long ago pointed out: [1] "To draw inferences has been said to be the great business of life. . . . It is the only occupation in which the mind never ceases to be engaged." Thinking both increases our store of meanings and increases the efficiency of thinking (drawing inferences) because of these meanings.

4. *To contribute to the stability and security of life for both the individual and society.* The foregoing points are all important and can be given attention in classrooms at all levels, in fact, in the preschool rearing of children.

The huge majority of men are not merely uninformed, they are misinformed about themselves, about the natural world, about the civilization in which they live. It is neither unkind nor supercilious to say that the uninformed and the unintelligent make up the great majority. This is just a fact to be faced and perhaps remedied if we recognize it in time. The few topflight thinkers make possible the advances of civilization but have little to say about managing that civilization. Currently this situation is being questioned. One way out of this dangerous gap between trained minds and the rights of the mass of citizens is through education—general education, plus specific training in the nature of thinking.

[1] John Stuart Mill, *A System of Logic* (New York, Longman's Green, 1925), paragraph 5 of introduction. Many other editions are available.

The gap between the knowledge and the skills of thinking possessed by the uninformed and the informed is incredible. When beliefs
about man, nature, and civilization held by both groups coincide, it is not
because the majority understand the reasons which support the belief.
Coincidence of belief has been due, until modern times, to the fact that
the scientific belief appealed to the emotions or coincided with another
belief already held by the less informed. Scientific conclusions which run
counter to popular notions, particularly in religion and politics, and latterly
in economics, have little chance of acceptance. Even in medicine there
are still found beliefs stubbornly held by the crowd which are flatly contradicted by simple, easily apprehended facts. General education and attention to the process of thinking, as stated above, are necessary.

A simple illustration, abbreviated here, is found in the public reaction
just after the turn of the century, to smallpox vaccination and in current
reaction to proposals for fluoridation of drinking water. Antagonism to
vaccination was widespread and sometimes violent until a long, slow
campaign of public education and dissemination of incontrovertible facts
changed public opinion. Vaccination as a prerequisite to school attendance,
or to foreign travel, is now taken as a matter of course. Similarly, the popular delusions about and antagonism to fluoridation are bound to suc-
cumb to facts as these permeate the mind. Many similar illustrations could
be given.

The uninformed run the world mostly and have precipitated many
minor and major disasters. The present crisis and revolution going on in
the world is complex and due to many causes, but one of the causes is unquestionably the type of conventional thinking which has dominated the
world. This is particularly true of what we may call conventional wisdom
in economics, in the relation of so-called advanced and backward peoples,
in political or diplomatic procedures.

A remark of obscure origin, but attributed to various prominent persons, is "Some people would rather die than think!" The trouble is that
many do—and in their blundering carry other people with them. Cassius of
the "lean and hungry look" was condemned by Caesar: "He thinks too
much; such men are dangerous." Far more dangerous are the men who
think little or not at all.

The inescapable interdependence of the peoples of the world causes
events anywhere to have effects everywhere. The sequence of events today
proceeds at breathless pace. The events, their causes, and their effects cannot be ignored. Too little thinking, marked inability to interpret events
and to develop valid bases for our beliefs and actions could be dangerous.
The individual and society both suffer from too little thinking. Ortega y
Gassett, in his *Revolt of the Masses,* pointed out that the direction of society is being taken over by "a new type of man who is not interested in
the principles of civilization, not in this or that civilizaton, but of any

civilization." A civilization cannot exist without a culture which is the total of enlightenment and refinement resulting from intellectual and aesthetic endeavors. If the advocates of the classic languages and history, to mention but one, only knew it, their subject matters could be of enormous value in enlightening everyone on the nature of civilization, its developments and its downfalls. Devotion to mythical and mystical "values" instead of the solid enlightenment of their pupils about their materials has handicapped the situation. The school generally has not done too well with this momentous aspect of education.

Education has basic and perhaps fateful tasks. *First* it must aid individuals to transform whatever natural capacity they have into trained processes of thought. *Second* it must sensitize individuals to the natural tendencies to error within their own minds, to aid in destroying the conventional wisdom which consists largely of "accumulated and self-perpetuating prejudices" acquired over the ages. *Third* it must alert all individuals to those pressures of the social environment which not only lead to error in thinking and in belief, but also retard the acceptance of beliefs resting clearly on valid and demonstrable fact and inference. *Fourth* it must develop respect for thinking and a willingness to engage in this by-no-means-simple process. This includes development of a moral conviction, namely, that one is obligated to think straight—that is, in terms of facts and regulated inference.

The only safeguard against myth, superstition, and patterned conventional thinking is vigilant and systematic regulation of our methods of thinking, of defining and finding facts, of discrimination of reliable from unreliable sources, of drawing inferences, and of testing our beliefs before acceptance.

SECTION 2. TRAINING IN THINKING IS NECESSARY FOR VARIOUS REASONS

The values and skills of thinking do not accrue automatically; do not develop by themselves. The natural capacities possessed by everyone need training and development. Locke pointed this out cogently: [2]

No man ever sets himself about anything but upon some view or other, which serves him for a reason for what he does; and whatsoever faculties he employs, the understanding with such light as it has, well or ill informed, consistently leads; and by that light, true or false, all his operative powers are directed. . . .

Temples have their sacred images, and we see what influence they have always had over a great part of mankind. But in truth the ideas and images in men's minds are the invisible powers that constantly govern them, and to these

[2] John Locke, "The Conduct of the Understanding," an abstract from the *Essay in Human Understanding*. Available separately and in collections.

they all, universally, pay a ready submission. *It is therefore of the highest concernment that great care should be taken of the understanding, to conduct it aright in the search for knowledge and in the judgments it makes.*

The following indictments of bad thinking are drawn from life in the United States. The illustrations apply equally to any other people—the Americans are not alone in this. The difficulty is common the world over. Every faker knows of certain weaknesses in human thinking and takes advantage of them, as does every agent of special interests. Individuals, groups, and large federations of groups are led astray. Many wonder what to believe, and what not to believe. Training in reading for meaning, for sharp, critical evaluation of what is read or heard is of utmost importance for everyday thinking. This is far more complex than is commonly supposed, as we shall presently see. Without such training, however, thinking is led astray at every turn.

During World War I the late President Eliot of Harvard made this sharp commentary which is as applicable today as then: [3]

Since the United States went to war with Germany there has been an extraordinary exhibition of the incapacity of the American people as a whole to judge evidence, to determine facts, and even to discriminate in the prophecies of prominent administration officials, both State and National, in the exhortations of numerous commissions which are undertaking to guide American business and philanthropy, and in the almost universal acceptance by the people at large, day by day, of statements which have no foundation, and of arguments the premises of which are not facts and events, but only hopes and guesses. It is a matter of everyday experience that Americans can not observe with accuracy, repeat correctly a conversation, describe accurately what they themselves have seen or heard, or write out on the spot a correct account of a transaction they have just witnessed. These incapacities are exhibited just as much by highly educated Americans as they are by the uneducated, especially if the defects of their education have not been remedied in part by their professional experience.

A third of a century later another president of Harvard, Dr. Nathan M. Pusey, makes a statement on the teaching of critical thinking:

The job of the university is to educate free, independent, and vigorous minds, capable of analyzing events, of exercising judgment, of distinguishing facts from propaganda, and truth from half-truth and lies.

The *New York Times* (November 10, 1953) commented editorially on President Pusey's remarks:

This principle ought to be hammered home. It ought to be understood on campuses and everywhere else. We are in no danger, now or ever, of too much

---

[3] Charles W. Eliot, *Certain Defects in American Education and the Remedies for Them,* Teachers Leaflet No. 5 (Washington, D. C., United States Bureau of Education, Department of the Interior, June, 1918), p. 7.

thinking. The danger lies in the peanut-sized brain and foghorn-sized voice and then only if we put them in positions of power. The cure is more education, not less.

Hitler said men and nations should "think with their blood." His views seem not to have been successful. Still others in all nations would turn thinking over to a few competent thinkers at the top, believing that today's problems are too big and too complex for ordinary men to solve. This would soon result in the end of democracy. There is no alternative; men must learn how to think as well as they can, must learn what characterizes a competent authority in given fields. We must all turn to authorities at times, but a part of thinking is to be able to discriminate between authorities and those who are merely in positions of authority.

Another illustration of uncritical thinking is found in public reaction to the unprecedented barrage of criticism directed at our public schools, beginning in the 1940's and continuing in some measure today. Legitimate criticisms may be made of certain weaknesses in the schools. These are known to schoolmen far more clearly than to outsiders. Efforts at improvement go on steadily. An incredible amount of criticism was, however, worse than nonsense. Bizarre and fantastic statements were made. Others were made with no basis in fact, still others in flat defiance of large bodies of valid facts. A few criticisms were voiced which were flatly contradicted by legal provisions governing certain aspects of education. Inferences were drawn and conclusions stated with finality by persons who were completely uninhibited by the nature of facts and the rules of evidence. The tragic aspect was not the criticisms but public reaction to them. Fact and fantasy were accepted equally. Careful reasoning was not critically distinguished from sophistry, or from downright chicanery.

Hidden purposes and assumptions masquerading under pleas for "improvement," for "basic knowledge," were undetected by the average citizen. The real purposes in some cases were to cut the tax bill, to curtail enlightenment in certain areas. Assumptions included outmoded beliefs about learning, and undemocratic views on classes in society. Some of the critics were, themselves, unaware of their own assumptions. The Russian satellite added guilt feelings to the complex of causes back of criticism. There are, as stated, real weaknesses in the schools, but the general public was unable to distinguish between factual criticism, special pleading, and plain lying. A large amount of factual evidence is readily available, but neither it nor its sources were generally known. A further tragic commentary was that many persons of distinction in their own fields had no hesitation in voicing senseless criticisms.

The schools and the schoolmen were not without blame in the situation. For a long time, attention to "teaching to think" was not serious, despite many repetitions of the phrase. Schoolmen, furthermore, were not at first very skillful in presenting the real facts and the valid conclusions about schools and learning.

The values of thinking may be nullified through lack of training. The process of thinking can lead astray—and to wrong beliefs as readily as to correct conclusions. The sources of error and the general fallacies leading to error were summarized in Chapter 11. The presence of untested and unverified ideas in the mind is a prime cause for acceptance of other wrong beliefs. Ideas in our minds, along with other factors, govern our actions. Pestalozzi long ago said, "Mankind is the victim of his ideas." Books have been written under such titles as "Ideas are Weapons," "Ideas have Legs," "Ideas have Consequences." Today we are engaged in an ideological warfare for the control of men's minds. "Brainwashing" has emerged as a technique for controlling men's minds and nullifying their accustomed methods of thinking. Norman Angell wrote in *The Unseen Assassins* that thinking was often "assassinated" through the presence of ideas in the mind which are "unseen," that is, not articulated by the thinker.

An unquestioned high level of intelligence is, as Dewey puts it,[4] *"no barrier to the propagation of error, nor [is] large but untrained experience to the accumulation of fixed false beliefs. . . . Logical attainment in one direction is no bar to extravagant conclusions in another."*

As these chapters were being written the author observed a Nobel prize winner in chemistry discussing education and the schools generally. The mind which won a world-renowned prize in one field showed itself to be, in another field, naïve, uninformed, capable of gross blunders in logic. The mind which followed faithfully the conventions of evidence and inference in one field showed no such adherence to the laws of evidence in another. A mind incapable of making fantastic blunders in chemistry did so repeatedly when discussing education. A one-time president of the American Chemical Society did the same thing, not only making serious blunders in thinking but repeating them in defiance of ample facts to the contrary.

A distinguished professor of education, and a statistician at that, undertook to discuss group dynamics before an interested group. His intellectual ability has been attested by several original contributions in advanced mathematics, but in discussing group processes he disregarded fact and logic repeatedly. Even worse, he betrayed a vigorous emotional bias. A one-time president of the American Psychological Association was guilty of serious errors of fact and inference in discussing the same subject. The president of a famous Ivy League college said quite recently that the study of Latin was still the single best training for rigorous, logical thought. Perhaps he had not studied Latin.

Francis Bacon, eminent in the beginnings of modern scientific thought, who gave us many of the early standards for good thinking in the physical

[4] Dewey, *How We Think, op. cit.* (1910 edition), pp. 20-21.

world, was, in the field of health, the slave of helplessly incompetent ideas. He dosed himself regularly in the spring with rhubarb, nitre, saffron, and many other chemical concoctions. He kept flowers and sweet herbs on his table to ward off fevers. None of the primitive peoples described in Fraser's *Golden Bough* held any beliefs more weird than some of Bacon's. Oddly enough it was Bacon's fidelity to "looking for the facts" that caused his death. The idea came to him that very low temperatures would prevent or greatly retard the putrefaction of meat—an idea known today to every schoolboy. Bacon had a chicken plucked and drawn and then went to a snow bank to stuff the chicken's body cavity full of snow and to bury the whole fowl in snow. He caught pneumonia and died.

Captains of industry, highly successful in manufacturing or commerce, often discuss foreign affairs with assurance and aplomb, hold forth on domestic affairs, or even upon technical problems, but with no facts and no knowledge of the systematic controls of thinking. The ignorance and illogicality of businessmen and industrialists are obscured by the prestige accorded money and power. They are, however, fully as uninformed and absurd in their thinking outside their special fields as are professors, doctors, lawyers, engineers.

All this is far less a criticism of physicists, professors, and industrialists than it is a tribute to—shall we say the versatility of—the human mind! The mind is, in fact, one of the most versatile instruments in the universe! This "versatility" is sometimes good and sometimes evil. Just how versatile the mind is may be indicated first by a few rather tragic generalizations. The mind is fully capable of:

1. Evolving a sublime set of values and convictions, stating them persistently and consistently; and at the same time and without embarrassment justifying actions in flat contradiction of the announced values and convictions.

2. Maintaining, with no embarrassment whatever, two flatly contradictory sets of opinions, convictions, beliefs, sometimes even facts.

3. Substituting words (verbalisms) for action in situations which actually can be solved only by appropriate action.

4. Refusing to accept either intellectual or moral responsibility for conclusions, judgments, speech, or action; operating with no awareness of what constitutes responsibility for beliefs, words, or action.

5. Failing to distinguish between:

Fact and opinion.

Reasoned conclusions and unsupported beliefs, sometimes even lore, superstition, old wives' tales.

Evidence and rumor, hearsay, and gossip.

What was actually observed, and the observer's opinion of what was observed.

The criteria of fact and evidence, the canons and controls of the thinking process, and the complete absence of these; bias and prejudice and their opposites.

The general situation is satirized by Chesterton:

The sentimentalist, roughly speaking, is the man who wants to eat his cake and have it. He has no sense of honor about ideas; he will not see that one must pay for an idea as for anything else. He will have them all at once in one wild intellectual harem, no matter how they quarrel and contradict each other.

The difficulty is by no means confined to sentimentalists—or perhaps far more persons are sentimentalists than we think!

Anyone wishing specific illustrations need only look around him, need only read the *Congressional Record,* "letters to the editor" in any newspaper, listen to the speeches of politicians, study the prophecies of businessmen about the state of the economy, listen to professors of chemistry telling how to rear children. A very brief but hilarious and telling summary of incompetent thinking by prominent men and women is found in Edward Angly's *Oh Yeah,* published by the Viking Press in 1931. Out of print now, it is available only in larger libraries. A more serious treatment is found in *Surplus Prophets* dealing with pre-election predictions about the New Deal and the actual outcomes some years later. A scholarly summary of wild ideas held by the popular mind at one time or another is found in Charles Mackay's *Extraordinary Popular Delusions and the Madness of Crowds,* originally published in 1841, now available in modern editions. A modern exposé of pseudoscientists and their fantastic pronouncements done with hilarious humor is Martin Gardner's *In the Name of Science,* Putnam's, 1952. Two books by Joseph Jastrow contain devastating summaries on fakers in thinking, *The Story of Human Error,* 1936, and *The Betrayal of Intelligence,* 1938. Also of interest are David Starr Jordan's *The Higher Foolishness,* 1927, and D. W. Hering's *Foibles and Fallacies of Science.* Three books in lighter tone but with serious import are Bergen Evans, *The Natural History of Nonsense,* Knopf, 1949; his *The Spoor of Spooks,* Knopf, 1954; and Leo Gurko's *Heroes, Highbrows, and the Popular Mind,* Bobbs-Merrill, 1953. Numerous essays are also available both on the idiosyncrasies and the achievements in thinking, Bertrand Russell's *An Outline of Intellectual Rubbish* being an example.

A Short Introduction to the Study of Human Stupidity, by Walter Pitkin, Simon and Schuster, 1932, makes entertaining and enlightening reading. A more extensive treatment filled with incredible specific illustrations is Paul Tabori's *The Natural Science of Stupidity,* Chilton, 1959. [5]

---

[5] Every book on logic or on thinking which we used over the years, particularly in preparation of this book, contained one or more errors, usually minor, in the very subject being discussed. One or two interesting contradictions on logical matters occurred between books. The authors of this volume are not arrogant enough to believe that they have made no mistakes, though all three have given special scrutiny to this. Anyone finding errors (not misinterpretation or items on which primary sources themselves disagree somewhat) and reporting them will have our gratitude— and will receive an autographed copy of the revised text.

The achievements of trained minds bear witness to the value of training. The remarkable flexibility of the mind does not always manifest itself in ridiculous beliefs and conclusions. The miraculous advances of our civilization result from creative but orderly thinking, among other things. An interesting summary of scientific thinking to the turn of the century is found in W. Whewell, *The History of the Inductive Sciences,* published by the D. Appleton Company in 1901. An excellent summary for advanced students is W. P. D. Wightman's *The Growth of Scientific Ideas,* Yale University Press, 1953. A recent volume, *Harvard Case Studies in Experimental Science,* edited by James B. Conant, supplies many specific accounts of thinking done by scientists. The two volumes of the late George Sarton's *History of Science* (Harvard University Press) are of great interest. It is to be hoped that the six other volumes contemplated by Dr. Sarton will eventually be completed by other scholars.

A remarkable book dealing with the intellectual achievements of Americans in literature, economics, philosophy, history, politics, law, and architecture is found in Henry Steele Commager's *The American Mind,* Yale University Press, 1952. The descriptive bibliography covers twenty-two pages and opens up a huge area dealing with the thinking of our people. Treatments limited to selected topics are found in Barrows Dunham's *Man Against Myth,* Little, Brown, 1949, and N. J. Berrill's *Man's Emerging Mind,* Dodd, Mead, 1955.

The worth of good thinking is amply attested by the achievements of good thinkers in philosophic, artistic, scientific, and applied fields. Matching those who are ruled in part by superstition, who hold irrational beliefs, who cannot distinguish fact from opinion, are those who invented the wonder drugs (so-called), terramycin, and the Salk vaccine; who split the atom and harnessed its power to drive a submarine and who are even now thinking out ways to use this new and awesome source of power for peacetime uses in the service of civilization. Pages could be filled with listings of examples of good thinking; in fact, books have been so filled.

The foregoing digression was necessary to correct any misinterpretation which might be placed on the emphasis at this point on errors and tendencies to error in thinking. Not only do many do excellent thinking, but we note the ease and prevalence of errors for the sake of emphasizing the necessity for training.

The natural discipline of events, of life experience, is not sufficient. The self-made man often boasts that he learned what he knows in the University of Hard Knocks. His thinking has been shaped by hard facts and practical necessity—and not by theories learned in books. He has risen to an executive position from nothing, let us say, or he has made a million dollars. He asserts, therefore, that his thinking must be sound. These very assertions indicate that, whatever the merits of his thinking in given specific affairs, he does not understand too much about thinking. As some anony-

mous critic has said, "Most self-made men should have hired an architect."
All honor to the self-made man who has made something of himself and
contributed to the social good. The coercive facts, the stark necessities of
life, do shape thinking. There are, however, definite and serious limitations
in learning to think through raw experience alone. Definite errors, sometimes serious, appear because of lack of knowledge of all factors in thinking
and of general theory in any given field. The worst handicap, probably, for
the self-made man is unawareness of his own limitations.

Thinking which affects directly pride or pocketbook is likely to be
reasonably accurate, though not *necessarily* so. Thinking which does not
affect the satisfaction or security of the individual, at least not directly or
seriously, is more than likely to be wrong. As stated earlier, it is quite
possible for intelligent individuals to entertain beliefs and conclusions that
are absurd. Plain ignorance of facts, susceptibility to conclusions favored
by emotions, unawareness of the power of implicit assumptions, and other
factors may easily lead one astray.

An old saying has it thus: "Power corrupts, and absolute power corrupts absolutely." Power is a fateful factor in confusing thinking; *power
to control* is confused with *knowledge or logic*. Industrial executives, army
officers, teachers, to mention but a few, are in position to issue orders with
power to enforce the orders. Incredible blunders are made; serious disasters
result in given instances; but the person with power sees only that what he
ordered was done. The whole operation may be based solely on power with
no reference to facts or good thinking.

Many mistakes made by parents and teachers in disciplining children,
by employers in managing employees, grow out of this serious blunder—
confusing power to enforce with good thinking. Parents say they *know* how
to rear children because they can *control* children, can reward or punish,
can "discipline" them. The child is ordered to behave in a certain way. He
does so—as long as his parents are in sight! "You see," say the parents, "the
child's behavior is as desired; we *know* how to handle him." Teachers think
they *understand* human behavior merely because they can *control* it, can
pass or fail, reward or punish pupils. Employers believe they *"know* how
to handle labor" merely because they have *power* to hire and fire—that is,
control—labor. The rise of union power prevented arbitrary firing of employees and showed many executives and managers to be quite unable to
think in meeting the situation. The labor unions as they gain in power are
making many mistakes through confusing this power with knowledge, insight, good thinking. Many Southerners say of the Negroes, "We *know* how
to handle them," failing to see that all they have is *control*. Parents, teachers, and others in authority over persons admit freely that they are ignorant
of physics and chemistry, rarely dispute a doctor's prescription, but do not
see that this is because they cannot *control* the behavior of the molecules

or physical forces, are ignorant of the facts and thinking back of diagnosis and prescription.

Persons with power can override facts and logic—for a time. Eventually facts catch up. The person who has been confusing power with good thinking is then buried, sometimes even with honors. Unfortunately facts do not always catch up within one lifetime, whereupon innocent peoples must often pay the bill for the bad thinking of their leaders.

Finally, it must be noted that many social factors, conventions, and conventional beliefs or standards actually encourage thoroughly bad thinking and absurd conclusions. The practical affairs of life do aid thinking to a point and in certain areas; they can just as easily lead thinking into tragic error.

Training in thinking is necessary if we are to transform everyday thinking into systematic, orderly processes for arriving at reputable beliefs and guides to conduct. This may be the most important aim of education.

SECTION 3. THE PRIMARY RESOURCES FOR EFFECTIVE THINKING ON WHICH TRAINING MAY BE BASED

We cannot, as has been stated, teach anyone to think. We can only aid individuals and groups to use better the capacities they have and the resources which are readily available. The outline below lists those basic conditions which, to the degree that they are met, make possible effective thinking. These factors, as has been made clear in preceding chapters, do not operate in isolation, but blend together and contribute to any on-going thought process.

I. Certain resources are part of the native endowments of the individual thinker.
   A. Intellectual ability.
      1. The higher the degree of native intelligence, the greater the individual's potential for effective thinking. (Note that intelligence may manifest itself in very different ways with various individuals.)
      2. The higher the level of mental vigor, energy, alertness, curiosity, and flexibility, the greater the individual's potential for effective thinking. (Recall Chapter 3 on attitudes.)
   B. Emotional drives and their control.
      1. A hierarchy of emotional drives motivates and shapes the pattern and effectiveness of thought, inducing the individual to accept particular goals and particular means of achieving them.
      2. Emotional control, natural or acquired, frees thinking from certain distorting influences:
         a. One's normal desires and appetites.
         b. Extreme emotional states.
         c. Hasty, impetuous decisions (all problems demand varying degrees of patience and persistence.)

C. Physical and mental health.
1. A sound body, physical energy, and vigor normally facilitate effective thinking.
2. Mental health, as in B 2 above, plus freedom from fanatically held beliefs, *idées fixes,* and the like.
D. The capacity for group co-operation.
Effective thinking may be assisted by man's social and intellectual inclination to work out solutions in co-operation with other men. Group solutions for some kinds of problems will be superior to solutions by individuals, and for other problems, vice versa.
II. Certain resources are a part of the environment within which the individual is or has been situated.
A. Experiential background.
1. Experiences which have been broad and nonspecific equip the individual with the store of generalizations necessary for effective thinking.
2. Adequate training in the processes of thinking improves effectiveness.
B. Material conditions.
1. Instruments of precision and complex computing devices are available and applicable.
2. Adequate and reliable sources of information are readily available.
3. Immediate physical comforts such as time, quiet, and economic well-being are more generally available. (Note that some excellent thinking has been done under conditions very poor in economic stability.)
C. Social conditions.
1. There exists a means of communication of reasonable standardization and precision, that is, a universe of discourse.
2. Certain social influences encourage effective thinking:
   a. The operation of certain tried customs and traditions having a rational basis is now almost automatic.
   b. Fellow men may insist on certain standards of precision (verbal or mathematical), on fidelity to objective reality, on conclusions for which reasoned chains of evidence can be shown.
   c. Social inducements such as fame and prestige, material gain, often are rewards for the successful thinker.
3. Efficient management of many practical affairs does, to a certain extent, enforce correct thinking.
4. A growing body of psychological knowledge has led to:
   a. A better understanding of the processes involved in effective thinking.
   b. Improved techniques for developing the individual's capacity for thinking more effectively (within the limits of native endowment).

Obstacles to effective thinking. The only insuperable obstacle to effective thinking is native stupidity. The factors listed above, however, when present in low degree or meager amount, or absent, are likely to make for ineffective thinking and to be sources of error. A detailed discussion of errors, sources of error, and fallacies was presented in Chapter 11.

SECTION 4. BRIEF RÉSUMÉ OF EARLY EFFORTS TO IMPROVE THINKING THROUGH EDUCATION

The account of the several approaches the school has made to "teaching learners to think" is abbreviated. Little success has been achieved though current proposals may be more fruitful.

Courses in formal logic on the college level. Courses of this type at one time occupied a major place in college curriculums. The number is decreasing, but in early days practically every college stressed these courses. Elementary courses have been tried from time to time for students entering college, and a few with high school students. Little effect on thinking resulted, and this became increasingly realized. More is now known also about thought-in-process and a new type of course is appearing, as we shall see below.

Formal discipline in college and secondary school. An early view held that thinking was a separate faculty of the mind which could be trained through special or formal exercises. Certain subjects, notably Latin, Greek, and mathematics, were believed to be typically intellectual and logical. Finally, it was held that this "faculty" of thinking, once trained, could then be used when and as needed, transferred to any and all problems. This is the theory of "formal discipline," based on the now long-discarded "faculty psychology." Today no psychologist nor any competent educator believes this theory, even though it still dominates the minds of large numbers of high school and college teachers. Many of the severe critics of public schools of the Bestor-Smith-Lynd-Adler type base their suggestions, among other things, on this theory, albeit unconsciously in some instances.

The story of this theory and its eventual destruction is long and interesting and should be known to all who have had beginning courses in psychology or the history of education. Recall that Latin and Greek were placed in the curriculum in the first place (apart from the training of priests) for content and use, not for training thought. This reason was not advanced until the subjects began to come under fire in modern times as being without use to modern students as *general education*.

Educational theorists began challenging formal discipline long ago, notably Herbart about 140-150 years ago. The following quotation from a modern critic, the late Alfred North Whitehead, is given at length because of the powerful and unequivocal language used. [6]

> The mind is an instrument, you first sharpen it, and then use it; the acquisition of the power of solving a quadratic equation is part of the process of sharpening the mind.

> I have no hesitation in denouncing [this idea] as one of the most fatal, erroneous, and dangerous conceptions ever introduced into the theory of educa-

[6] Alfred North Whitehead, *The Aims of Education* (New York, Macmillan, 1929), p. 17. Pocket edition also available.

tion. The mind is never passive; it is a perpetual activity, delicate, receptive, responsive to stimulus. You cannot postpone its life until you have sharpened it. Whatever interest attaches to your subject matter must be evoked here and now; whatever possibilities of mental life your teaching should impart, must be exhibited here and now. That is the golden rule of education, and a very difficult rule to follow.

Experimental evidence delivered the final blow with conclusive findings. Not one iota of evidence has ever been found that, first, certain subjects teach "thinking" better than others. No subject has a monopoly on thinking or on training to think. Second, the evidence shows conclusively that there is little or no carry-over (transfer) through formal exercises. (Conditions for successful transfer are summarized later.)

The intellectual value of any subject lies not in its internal, pre-organized structure, but in its power to set pupils to examining grounds for their beliefs and to checking bases for conclusions. The real point, as shown by modern research, is the method of teaching. Genuine problems must be developed, the process of thinking developed within the specific conditions of the situation; but above all, the teacher must know exactly what it is he is teaching for. There has been in the past too much reliance on mystical values transferred by some miraculous means. Orata has a very blunt statement: [7]

Do we want transfer, and if so, what, in terms of ideals, attitudes, beliefs and habits, do we want transferred; and what provision should we make in method of learning and teaching, administration, and the like, in order to bring about transfer in the form and amount we desire? . . . First, the teacher should know what it is that she wants the children to transfer to other fields. Second, she must learn by experience or experiment how to teach for transfer, and third, go ahead and do it.

Thinking is not a separate, unitary, faculty of the mind. It occurs in various forms under varying conditions. Individuals differ considerably even when following the known conventions of good thinking. They also differ markedly in the conditions under which they both learn and improve thinking. [8]

Formal approximation of "steps" in thinking. Between 1890 and approximately 1920, teachers were brought up on Herbartian methods brought back from the University of Jena by a number of young Americans who went there to study. Herbart's "five formal steps" were an approxima-

[7] Pedro T. Orata, "Transfer of Training and Educational Pseudoscience," *Mathematics Teacher*, No. 5 (1935), pp. 278-281.

[8] Evidence of the failure of transfer through formal discipline and use of special subjects is summarized clearly in the *Cyclopedia of Educational Research* under headings: "Transfer of Training," "Formal Discipline." More detailed summaries are found in the statements by Thorndike, and by Orata, which are available in the periodical literature, and also in brief monographs.

tion of certain aspects of thinking but were hopelessly formalized and became more so in the hands of rank-and-file teachers. The first four steps were "inductive," designed to lead the student through the inductive process of making generalizations. The fifth step, "application," was the deductive use of this generalization on a new case or illustration. The student would thus learn the major formal processes of thinking by being put through this formula in all subjects where it would fit. Other similar approaches have been made. Suffice it to say, first, that the approximation of thinking was very crude at best and, second, no provision was made for what we now know to be an essential of thinking—free-ranging inquiry to develop both hypotheses and data, attention to cases which did not fit the narrow formula, attention to diverse checking in real situations.

Another formula often seen in arithmetic classes directs children to proceed through certain steps: "What is asked?" (or "What am I to find?"); "What is given?"; "What do I know?"; "What process or processes should I use?"; "What is the probable answer?"

Weaknesses are: first, this puts more trust in a formula and ignores personal and situational factors. These factors are important, often crucial, as summaries of research will show. Second, the formula may appeal to adults as "logical," but may not be used by all adults. Research has shown that it is not used by children who do good thinking on their own. It is better not to impose formulas but to start with the procedures children use and gradually lead them to discover and understand better methods.

Teaching of the sciences designed to improve thinking. In modern times the most extensive effort to improve thinking was through the natural sciences. Scientists were, obviously, excellent thinkers. Discoveries by scientific thinkers have affected every phase of our lives. The average citizen can see this easily even though he does not always understand some of it. Training in scientific subjects must surely produce good thinkers. A point not clear until quite recently was, unfortunately, given less attention than it deserved. Scientists outside their chosen fields—many of them—made absurd blunders. Today when scientists are in the forefront of attention, speaking on various aspects of life outside their specialties, it is quite apparent that certain processes and controls of thinking have *not been generalized* by men who are excellent thinkers within a specialty. The sciences have not, in some cases, produced good thinkers, even among the scientists. (Recall the question raised in the "Preface" concerning the possibility of learning to think in such manner that the processes could be carried over to other fields.)

The type of science introduced into the schools, unhappily, was "recipe following" or "cookbook" science. Laboratory manuals dictated every step the student took. The text supplied facts and generalizations. Science teaching of this type, almost universal in high schools, and wide-

spread in college, is an excellent procedure for the inhibition and discouragement of thinking. Science as currently taught has produced no
widespread improvement in scientific thinking. Even more unhappily,
critics of education today have made it fashionable to ridicule teaching
methods—techniques and *devices*—and to demand *subject matter* in large
doses. Both are necessary. Science teachers generally know their subject
matter, but their teaching methods are often such as to defeat all the aims
of the subject matter.

Properly taught by teachers who understood how science materials
are derived and compiled in the first place, these subjects quite conceivably
could aid students to develop desirable habits of thinking. Direct attention
to the process of thought, its safeguards, fallacies, and subprocesses may
be very helpful, especially on upper levels. Attention can be given to the
actual methods of experimentation and discovery. Teachers here and there
have become famous for doing this very thing. The writer has observed
students in various high schools carrying on such projects as: experiments
in nutrition using small animals, analysis of cosmetics and drugs in common use, participation in various civic projects, planning a new gymnasium with the architects, observing police courts and police methods, par-
ticipating through working for election boards. Texts are also being revised
away from their sixteenth-century content. Tragically, there are still schools
which do not attempt to teach sciences well, let alone teach for transfer
of thinking skills. An extreme case was reported in the *Boston Herald,*
November 21, 1957: Waltham (Mass.) high school spent $7334 more on
athletics than on science and mathematics combined. Money and public
understanding are necessary for advances in any educational area.

Extravagant claims have been made for mathematics, especially algebra and geometry, as subjects par excellence through which to "teach
thinking." Unfortunately for all the brave claims and high hopes, the cold,
hard data from research do not support the claims. A few eminent mathematicians have even stated their opinion that training in thinking within
the limited and precise field of mathematics may actually handicap an individual when he meets problems within the nonprecise, discursive, unsys-
tematically organized areas of everyday life. Both Dr. Robert Oppenheimer
and the late Albert Einstein have commented on the greater difficulty of
deriving valid results in the social areas. Both urged attention to reflective
thought in these areas in their own right. A number of instructors in
mathematics have made earnest efforts to rewrite basic texts in this field
so as to bring out the relationships between mathematical reasoning and
thinking in everyday affairs. (See Chapters 19 and 20 for discussion of the
relation of mathematics and science to teaching for transfer of thinking
skills.)

Familiarity with the mental processes of great thinkers. This method
of introducing students to the process of thinking, plus the claim that there

will be transfer has been advanced several times over a period of years. A clear statement appears in the Harvard Report, *General Education in a Free Society*, page 110: "Long-continued close contact with excellent work, the best of its kind, has a formative and ordering power, especially on minds still plastic, growing, and active in imitation."

The Harvard Report was here chiefly concerned with the norms and potentialities of living, with developing a unifying factor within our culture, and with transmission of our literary heritage. The implications for the thinking process, however, are inevitably included. There is no evidence that thinking can be trained in this manner, except with some of the bright students. Imposition of subject matter is not the best approach to the dynamic, changing, and precarious processes in thinking. "Active imitation" is meaningless with reference to learning to think.

Two very different interpretations and practices are observed. First, a number of distinguished scholars in colleges everywhere present carefully detailed and systematic *lecture* accounts of thinking by great men of science, by writers, and creative artists. The *reading* of scientific case studies is having considerable vogue currently. Many professors claim that such lectures and readings "cannot help but improve the thinking of the students." Evidence does not exist, as stated above, that listening to or reading about embalmed thinking improves the thinking of the passive observer.

The second method is not confined to listening to or reading about given instances of high-level thinking. The cases are subjected to aggressive, critical analysis, are evaluated and compared one with another. Free discussion or "wrangling" about the methods used is encouraged. Two results are claimed which seem reasonable: (*a*) increased *understanding* of scientific thinking, and (*b*) sensitivity to the attitudes and methods of scientific thinking. Effects (*c*) on the actual thinking of students are claimed or implied. Evidence is not available on the last point.

The use of case studies in science or other fields as a method of developing critical thinking in students is presented in some detail in a later chapter. The author of that chapter carefully points out that chief benefits are in understanding of the "tactics and strategy" of science and in the identification of the attitudes and processes of the thinker; that even understanding and identification of the process will not always be achieved automatically. He further emphasizes that thinking can be learned, so far as we know now, by performing the processes of thinking and that teaching even there must be for transfer; that frequent opportunities must be provided for exercising thinking as well as talking about thinking. He then outlines a number of illustrations and procedures.

Free self-expression as method of learning to think. Plans for teaching students to think were, until the present century, those of imposition or "discipline." Partly as reaction to the restraints of these methods and to their obvious ineffectiveness, partly due to increasing knowledge about the learner and his processes, there arose the idea that freedom for self-expression was also important in thinking and learning to think. Freedom is, in fact, vital to thinking, particularly in the crucial processes of creating hypotheses and of inference. (So also is "discipline" as we shall see later.) Creativity, individuality, self-expression, freedom—all of them basic in thinking—came to be interpreted as "let them do as they please." To repeat the old cliché, liberty became license.

Progressive education which properly realigned the balance between subject matter and learner, and which is responsible for most of the admirable reforms in education, got the blame for this tragic misinterpretation of freedom. The literature of progressive education nowhere contains a single paragraph giving a basis for what happened in certain classrooms. Even Dewey, usually blamed as the high prophet of uncontrolled freedom, as the enemy of systematic instruction and subject matter, has published some of the strongest indictments of senseless "freedom." Newspapers and magazines carried scores of "jokes" about "letting Willy express himself," and about the riotous uproar in so-called "progressive schools." The public prints in sacrificing fact and principle for a temporary "wisecrack" did great damage to education. The uncontrolled type of classroom freedom was due solely to misinterpretation by superficially trained teachers. It was never as widespread as was supposed. Freedom properly used is a factor in teaching students to think. The balance between discipline and freedom will be summarized a few pages further on.

Attention to thought-in-process. This is a comparatively recent development, though a few instructors on the college level have tried it. Two factors were involved. First, there had been long continued criticism of the rigid formality of Aristotelian logic, plus a natural development of new ideas about thinking. Second, popular interest in thinking increased as a natural response to the increasing complexity of our life, the complexity of problems confronting the average citizen. A few authors attempted to popularize the term *dynamic logic* for thought-in-process, a term which would have had considerable merit. Logicians and semanticists frowned on this, holding properly that logic had a standard definition which had been used for centuries. The new term would cause more confusion than good. Two of the best writers in the field make the distinction clear and at the same time indicate the value of both views: [9]

The traditional view of logic as the science of valid inference has been consistently maintained against all attempts to confuse logic with psychology, where by the latter is meant the systematic study of how the mind works. . . . On the other hand, the pedagogical applications of psychological logics have not been ignored.

[9] Morris R. Cohen and Ernest Nagel, *An Introduction to Logic and Scientific Method* (New York, Harcourt, Brace, 1934), p. iv.

Other writers, without confusing the two, include good material on how thinking takes place. Writers in logic, as well as in psychology and education, are increasingly presenting accounts of thinking as it actually goes on, in advanced scientific inquiry and everyday problem solving and in critical analysis.

Two procedures have emerged. *One,* give courses in the psychology of thought itself to students capable of this. Teaching deliberately for transfer might enable individuals to carry principles and processes over to use in various areas. *Two,* teach all regular courses so that the processes of critical thought are made clear. Again, teaching for transfer is the key.

Transfer of training and teaching for transfer. Several references in this and other chapters indicate that transfer of training is the crux in improving the thinking of students. Controversy has largely died out due to the derivation of experimental evidence during the past half-century.

The older theory of formal discipline—that is, transfer due to formal exercises in given subjects such as Latin, mathematics, or the like—has been definitely disproved. The evidence is conclusive and easily understood. Summaries are available in several places.

Two theories have been proposed in modern times. Thorndike suggested that transfer took place only and if the learner recognized specific "identical elements" either in content or process between two situations. Psychologists of the conditioned-response school have upheld the view that learning is specific and that transfer can only occur when there are identical elements shared by two situations. The belief is held that learning does not generalize. Critics pointed out that recognition of identity between two or more situations was actually generalizing. Other criticisms were voiced which need not interest us now in view of the experimental evidence. Judd, on the other hand, advanced the theory of transfer through generalizations. Meanings and principles were the vehicles of transfer. The Gestalt psychologists advanced the idea of "insights" which extended Judd's theory. Understanding and insight by the learner were all-important. The implications of each theory for the curriculum and for methods of teaching were of the greatest importance.

What does the experimental evidence show? Scores of studies were made. The scholarly summaries by Orata give the best composites. In 1928 his analysis of 99 studies showed two things. First, the amount of transfer shown by the investigations was:

Appreciable transfer............................ 49.5 per cent
Considerable transfer........................... 32.3 per cent
Very little transfer............................. 8.08 per cent
Inconclusive or invalid .... 5.07 per cent
No transfer or negative transfer................. 5.05 per cent

The second point of Orata's analysis was that the studies showing little or no transfer dealt with content difficult to generalize and that there was steady increase of transfer with material easier to generalize. In 1941, Orata showed that transfer occurred through conscious generalization in about 70 per cent of the studies, and through identical elements in 30 per cent.[10]

What are the characteristics of modern theory of transfer? Several can be listed, of which method of teaching is the most important.

1. Transfer is not automatic.
2. Transfer is not inherent in any subject, but it is possible from any field. Transfer is not dependent upon a set of formal exercises, but on methods of teaching which utilize lifelike situations as to materials, methods, problems.
3. Transfer is facilitated by teaching directly for conscious transfer.
4. Transfer varies. There is much transfer (*a*) on common things easy to generalize, and (*b*) by persons of good intelligence. There is little on items difficult to generalize, and by duller individuals.

Our volume has tried to present an analysis of thinking as it operates, plus methods of teaching which will aid the learner to generalize and to transfer. The effectiveness of any procedure for securing transfer seems to depend upon the training and ability of the teacher.

Discipline and freedom in teaching to think. Before turning to an account of general methods of teaching we may summarize the prickly problem of discipline and freedom in thinking and in teaching.

The disciplinary groups operated on the basic belief that the mind is, by nature, illogical. Logical forms must be developed through absorption of ready-made, logically arranged subject matter. Method of teaching becomes the rigid operation of a set of "steps," of mechanical devices, of formulas externally imposed. This view is widely reflected in much public discussion, among certain college professors, and among certain private school people. The slogans are: "Make them work"; "Pour it on"; "Three hours' homework"; "Discipline"; "Make everyone take science and mathematics"; "Hard work and more hard work"; "Get tough."

Hard work at what? And for what purpose? The mind does not become logical no matter how hard a student works if mere difficulty is the point. Several experimental studies show that home study of the traditional type has no effect on desirable learning. (The modern type of outside work may have considerable effect.) The student will not become logical through working in conformity to adult-prepared logically organized subject mat-

---

[10] Pedro T. Orata, *The Theory of Identical Elements* (Columbus, O., Ohio State University Press, 1928).

Pedro T. Orata, "Recent Research Studies of Transfer of Training with Implications," *Harvard Educational Review*, Vol. XI (1941), pp. 359-378.

ter. A very good thinker, René Descartes (1596–1650), pointed this out quite a while ago.

The student will not become logical as he is forced through some "steps," or a scheme, external to his own natural processes. Creative thinkers are not developed in any line by stuffing them with subject matter. Rebellion against rigid disciplinary methods, while annoying to the school, indicates that some intellects are breaking through and trying to think.

The believers in freedom make the identical error the disciplinary group makes: They believe the mind is naturally illogical. Their methods of curing this are, however, the direct opposite of those used by the disciplinary group. Let the mind grow in its own way, without harmful restraints or impositions. The slogans are: "Just turn them loose, and they will learn to think"; "Do not interfere with self-expression"; "Creativity must be allowed free rein"; "You never can tell when a great idea will turn up"; "Felt needs"; "Personal problems"; "Spontaneous interest"; "Individual initiative"; and others. All these are valuable, as are discipline and hard work—when properly understood.

Freedom from what? And for what purpose? No one ever learned to think under conditions of uncontrolled, uninhibited freedom. Even if the pitfalls and errors were miraculously avoided, even if some continuity and system did emerge, the expense in time and money would be insupportable. And more crucial than the other questions, just what is freedom? Therein lies the crux, just as it did in the question "hard work for what?" Freedom, like discipline, can become an end in itself, activity for activity's sake. Rebellion against the boredom of pointless, undirected freedom, while annoying to the school, indicates that some intellects are breaking through and trying to think.

Results of misunderstanding discipline and freedom. Each group has misunderstood the meaning of its own key word. The results of imposition are not "disciplined" habits of thought, but the docile operation of imposed procedures. Dreary apathy results from the dull activity of following the formulas in a laboratory manual. Worst of all, conformity is demanded and secured *in the very areas where free play of the intellect is necessary.* This is a far cry from the free-ranging, original, chance-taking thinking which is the result desired.

The results of pointless freedom are lack of continuity and system, acceptance of fuzzy, inadequate reasons for one's beliefs, and eventually a demand for continual stimulation by new trivia. Uncritical, unsystematic, immature processes will result which cannot serve the purposes of critical thought. Boredom and antagonism to school and to learning, resulting in refusal to exert effort, will eventuate.

Discipline and freedom, properly defined, are inescapable necessities in good thinking. Discipline is not imposition; freedom is not a gift. Discipline is not the rigid following of formulas; freedom is not casual, capricious attention to transitory interests.

Discipline and freedom are both powers which can be achieved only through experience and effort.

Discipline is the power to hold fast to the moral conviction that one must think straight, must follow facts wherever they lead, must accept conclusions which are contrary to one's emotional desires, must draw inferences which can be validated, must avoid stating fool conclusions which are not susceptible to checking, must persist through difficulties, must accept conclusions only after critical scrutiny.

Freedom is the power to make choices and decisions. Plato long ago defined a slave as one who must accept his decisions from another. Freedom is power to tackle any problem, to consider any facts or conclusions though some of them may seem absurd, to draw inferences as one sees the facts. Freedom is emancipation from whim and impulse, from bias and prejudice, which interfere with thinking. Freedom enables one to defy conventional wisdom when this seems clearly justified.

Discipline and freedom must be *self-regulated,* or they are worthless. Discipline and freedom are two sides of the same coin. Discipline is power to accept, to use, and to regulate freedom. Freedom is the power to use discipline in the pursuit of one's chosen purposes and to reject irresponsible capriciousness.

Discipline and freedom achieved through experience. The mind, contrary to widespread belief, has natural tendencies to generalize, to draw inferences, to be critical, to accept and reject conclusions on evidence. This can be seen in very little children. The fact that it cannot be seen in some adults is due to life circumstances rather than to native inability to think. The natural activities of the mind will not be elaborated here since some accounts were given in earlier chapters. Any of the references on the development of meaning or upon children's thinking will supply details.

Problems which are real to the learner will invite all his powers and skills of inquiry. Critical inquiry directed at these real problems reveals the inescapable necessity of discipline in the sense of critical, cautious analysis, and of systematic procedure. Inquiry, at the same time, reveals the necessity for freedom from conformity, either to predetermined processes or to conventional wisdom.

The student learns to think the way he learns everything else, through doing thinking. He deals with problems and hypotheses, with facts, with wide-ranging guessing and inferring, with controls, pitfalls, and errors. He learns through acceptance those attitudes and systematic controls (discipline) which are inescapable if he is to think straight. He learns those attitudes and skills of concocting hypotheses and inferences, even of "wild guessing" (freedom) by noting results. Subject matter, incidentally, is covered in greater amount and with greater understanding under freedom than under imposition. Discipline there is, in quantity, but it is not external and imposed; it is internal and accepted. It is derived through noting the power of "stubborn, coercive, impersonal facts," by the demands of acceptable proof, by the results of "scrutiny of beliefs in the light of grounds which support them." Freedom there is, in quantity, but it is not the irresponsible freedom of caprice or impulse. It is personal responsibility derived through noting what "pays off" in thinking and what does not.

The task of the school is to provide ample opportunity to exercise the process of thinking, to the end that the natural tendencies to reflect and to draw inferences will be transformed into attitudes and habits of systematic inquiry.

QUESTIONS, EXERCISES, AND REPORTS

1. Give specific illustrations from your experience or observation for each of the first three values accruing from thinking.

2. Illustrate specifically the gap between the knowledge and skills possessed by trained thinkers and by the average citizen. Several cases should be cited by different students.

3. The fourth value is of considerable import, both for everyday affairs and for national issues.

   a. Duplicate the cases of vaccination, fluoridation, pasteurizing, from today's reading and observation.

   b. Duplicate cases in which eminent scholars make senseless statements—"sound off," as we say colloquially—outside their own fields.

   c. Duplicate cases in which wealthy industrialists, powerful labor leaders, or others prominent in public life make statements for which they are quite unqualified.

   d. Illustrate, from observation or reading, excellent attitudes and response by eminent thinkers when called on for expressions outside their fields. How did they respond? Report also any procedures used to inform themselves.

4. What, in general, is the relation of ordinary school procedures to the achievement of the first value? What important changes are needed so that the school may aid pupils in achievement of this value?

5. Why, in general, does the average man not profit more than he does from the second value?

6. How does the savage man ward off danger, disease, and the like? Can you cite the persistence of the essence of these methods among uneducated modern men? Among some who might be expected to know better?

7. Can you state the third value in another way?

8. The fourth value is more remote than the others. What can the school do about this one?

9. Do you wish to add any other values than the four listed?

10. What did a recent writer mean when he said "ideas are weapons"?

11. Norman Angell once wrote a book entitled *The Unseen Assassins,* presenting the view that ideas are the unseen assassins. What did he mean, and what is the relation of his view to our present discussions?

12. The list of contradictions, page 277, was discussed in one of the preliminary sessions.

>   *a.* Can you improve on the illustrations you gave then for the first three points? Reference may be made to all levels, from public affairs to everyday conversation.
>
>   *b.* The fourth point can be observed every few minutes in ordinary social conversation. Can you improve on your earlier discussion?
>
>   *c.* The same for the fifth point.
>
>   *d.* Do you wish to add any commentary of any kind concerning this list, over and beyond the views expressed in the early session?

13. Instructors and students who wish may include a class report and discussion on any one or more of the books listed on page 278 dealing with curious and absurd errors.

14. The same may be done with the books dealing with the achievements of good thinking.

15. Illustrate how everyday events and necessities often fail to discipline thinking.

16. Do the same for the confusion between power (or control) and knowledge.

17. Should there be any additions, omissions, or corrections to the list of resources?

18. Section 4 on the early efforts to teach thinking is largely informative. Instructors and students should feel free to add, omit, or correct any point.

19. What are the factors which make training of thought necessary? (This does not refer to the values accruing from training thought.)

20. Dewey says in *How We Think* (Boston, Heath, 1910), p. 25:

>   "Education has accordingly not only to safeguard the individual against the besetting erroneous tendencies of his own mind—its rashness, presumption, and preference of what chimes with self-interest to objective evidence—but also to undermine and destroy the accumulated and self-perpetuating prejudices of long ages."
>
>   What is the importance and the educational significance of this
statement?

ADDITIONAL READING BEARING ON THE TOPIC

ROBINSON, James Harvey, *Mind in the Making* (New York, Harper, 1921), pp. 3-29.
A. *On the purpose of Robinson's volume:*

1. Support your agreement or disagreement with the second sentence on p. 3: "If the majority . . ." Why, then, do we not get on with the business of developing a decent world?

2. Can you describe or define in your own words "the unprecedented attitude" to be created? Is anything being done nowadays about this?

3. State, in not to exceed a sentence each, the suggestions Robinson makes for achieving this "unprecedented attitude," pp. 6-11. What is the greatest obstacle to achievement of this desired attitude? Other obstacles?

B. *On the three disappointed methods of reform:*

1. Illustrate the futility of the *first* method? Why does it not work? Under what circumstances would it work? That brings us to what method? Where have we met this first method before in education courses?

2. Why does the second method not work? Could it?

3. Are Robinson's views on the results of liberal education, published in 1921, still valid, or are they badly outmoded?

4. The chief obstacle to enlightenment through social studies for citizenship is . . . ? Is his view here valid today or outmoded?

5. What is the relation of pp. 24-29 to our present topic?

6. What would happen if people used facts which are obvious to anyone with an open mind and which can be validated with simplicity and ease: To your politics? To your religion? To social conventions? To rearing children? (Add any other areas.)

READINGS FOR SECTION 3

The following deal chiefly with resources for thinking and, while somewhat discursive, do contain considerable valuable information. Surprisingly little is available on the topic.

BURTT, E. A., *Right Thinking*, rev. ed. (New York, Harper, 1946), Ch. 6.

LARRABEE, Harold A., *Reliable Knowledge* (Boston, Houghton Mifflin, 1945), Ch. 1.

RUSSELL, David H., *Children's Thinking* (Boston, Ginn, 1956), Chs. 12, 13.

CHAPTER **14**

A Summary of Research on Methods of Teaching Critical Thinking

Research is formalized curiosity. It is poking and prying with a purpose. It is a seeking that he who wishes may know the cosmic secrets of the world and they that dwell therein.

ZORA NEALE HURSTON *

Unfortunately a great deal of advice on how to teach is based on theorizing unsupported by sound research in teaching method or without reference to the research which exists. One has the impression while reading research literature in education that there is a pitifully small group of researchers who write articles read only by the other members of the group. In the field of critical thinking there is also great need for additional research, but one can find a small amount of reliable reports of experiments which demonstrate the effectiveness of certain methods of teaching critical thinking.

The scope of this chapter. In this chapter we will concentrate on a few important studies which are more than vague exhortations, or over-brief reports of experiments which may or may not have been conclusive; in short we will concentrate on reports of research which fit the following description:

Criteria for inclusion in this chapter:
1. The objectives of the experimental proposal include some of the abilities or attitudes listed in our definition of critical thinking.
2. Anticipated results of the experiment are stated as hypotheses.

* Zora Neale Hurston, *Dust Tracks on a Road* (London, 1942; Philadelphia, Lippincott, 1944), p. 91.

3. An actual tryout of some instructional method for improving critical thinking has been made.
4. The instructional method is described in sufficient detail for the reader to be able, with some imagination, to reconstruct the method.
5. Some valid method of testing is reported by which the effectiveness of the method is ascertained.
6. Samples of test items are included so that we may decide for ourselves by inspection whether genuine critical responses are needed to obtain a right answer.
7. The data accumulated from the testing program are clearly described and competently interpreted.

Assumptions made by researchers. The experimenters in the studies which will be mentioned in this chapter make a few common assumptions which it would be well to bring up here. One assumption is that critical-thinking abilities and attitudes may be analyzed into a number of components for the purpose of instruction and evaluation. This matter has been discussed earlier in the book. A representative list of critical abilities was given in the introductory pages to Part III. Another assumption is that these abilities may be validly and reliably measured by paper-and-pencil tests. This subject will be taken up in Chapter 21.

One assumption sometimes made, which we do not accept, is that ability to get correct answers on test items based on the special vocabulary and procedures of formal logic necessarily means that the subject has critical-thinking ability. This problem was discussed in Chapter 7. We refer here, of course, to certain experiments in which students were drilled on syllogisms for some period of time and then tested on control of syllogism patterns with the implication that this kind of activity is "critical thinking," or even "logical thinking" in a somewhat extended sense.

METHODS OF TEACHING CRITICAL THINKING IN SECONDARY SCHOOLS

Methods in science courses. Of the several experiments in the field of teaching science, two are particularly instructive, one by Higgins and another by Boeck.

In 1940–1941, Higgins (17)[1] conducted an investigation with 240 tenth-grade biology students in New York State to find out if an experimental teaching program would result in improved scores on three tests of inductive ability. Experimental classes, matched in intelligence (Henmon-Nelson Tests of Mental Ability) with control groups, were given brief instruction on "the scientific method with special consideration

---

[1] Numbers in parentheses refer to listing in the Bibliography at the end of this chapter.

of the subordinate concepts which are involved in the formulation of the hypothesis or generalization." They studied experimental procedures and tried to identify experimental factors and write conclusions, using as materials of instruction the résumés of 30 experiments taken from journals in the field of biology. Students and teachers collectively analyzed the experiments and discussed the various conclusions reached by the class members with respect to accuracy, completeness, or the degree to which the conclusions went beyond the data.

Three tests were used to measure the students' ability: (1) to judge whether conclusions went beyond items of data supplied, (2) to judge whether conclusions were true or false, and (3) to sense patterns (Thurstone Test of Induction). On the Thurstone test there was an initial difference in favor of the experimental group, and on the other tests three out of nine subsections showed scores favoring the experimentals. But on the tests where the experimental and control groups were even in ability, the comparison of pretest and post-test scores showed the experimental groups to have improved significantly in ability to judge conclusions and identify "complete" and "beyond data" conclusions.

Boeck (5) made a study in 1948–1949 to compare the effectiveness of the "inductive-deductive" approach in the chemistry laboratory with that of the "deductive-descriptive". One class selected at random from classes in chemistry at the University of Minnesota High School and seven classes from other high schools about the same size were used as controls. The techniques and materials in all control classes were similar. Laboratory exercises as described in a representative published laboratory manual were carried out after the general principles involved had been thoroughly discussed in recitation periods. No provisions were made for student planning of experiments or for the solution of real problems under laboratory conditions. Such was the "deductive-descriptive" approach.

The experimental class used the laboratory to obtain data for the solution of a series of problems which the students "had a real desire to solve." The pupils planned the mode of attack on the problems with the guidance of the teacher and were encouraged to recognize the value of controlled experiments, basic assumptions, clear records, good laboratory techniques, and careful observations and to draw conclusions of their own from data they had collected.

At the beginning of the experiment Boeck administered the Terman-McNemar Test of Mental Ability and his own achievement tests designed to measure knowledge of facts and principles of chemistry. At the end of the experiment the achievement exams were readministered, and three laboratory exams were given: the first, a performance test for evaluating technical skill in handling apparatus; the second, a test in which students criticized commonly-found poor laboratory techniques; and the third, a "resourcefulness" test. On these examinations in the laboratory, the experimental group was superior to the other University High class at the five per cent level of probability and to the outside classes at the one per cent level. The experimental method was adopted for use generally in the University High chemistry courses.

This experiment is particularly interesting in view of the frequent criticism of "set problems" in science laboratory courses.

Methods in mathematics courses. There has been considerable literature on how to teach mathematics in such a way as to improve the critical abilities of pupils, especially in one area of mathematics—geometry. Several important experiments have been conducted in this field.

In a historical sense Harold Fawcett's study, *The Nature of Proof* (9), has been the most influential, inspiring several other experimental studies. Fawcett's book, published in 1938, was designed to "describe classroom procedures by which geometric proof may be used as a means for cultivating critical and reflective thought and to evaluate the effect of such experiences on the thinking of pupils." For a period of 68 weeks an experimental class of 25 high school sophomores and juniors established from 25 to 34 geometric theorems and, in addition, studied the following topics: recognition of the need for definition, introduction to space concepts, undefined terms, definitions and assumptions, definition in nonmathematical situations, implications of definitions and assumptions, inductive proof, detecting the factors which determine conclusions, and the recognition of assumptions in nonmathematical arguments. Three unmatched control groups studied geometry in the conventional way.

Measurement of the experimental group and the controls was accomplished by administering the Ohio Every Pupil Test in Geometry and Fawcett's Nature of Proof Test and by collecting reports by parents, reports of observers, and cases of voluntary contributions of pupils in class. The Nature of Proof Test consisted of a series of described situations which presumably led to conclusions and on which the pupil was asked to comment concerning facts omitted, assumptions made, terms needing definition, and main topic presented.

To determine the relative achievement of the experimental group and the one control class in the same school, comparison was made between the actual achievement of the control class on the nonmathematical material with the predicted achievement for this class based on the scores of the experimental class. Interpretation of these scores, which greatly favored the experimental class, together with analysis of the other measures, such as testimonials and reports of parents, convinced Fawcett that his experimental procedures were successful in improving the reflective thinking of the special class. The cumulative evidence from the tests and the reports indicates that some critical abilities were improved by Fawcett's method, although we do not know exactly which. One fault in the experiment is that the experimental group scored higher as a class on the intelligence test than did the control group, a fact which suggests that some of the achievement of the special class may have been due to superior general intelligence rather than to superior instruction.

In 1950 Lewis (25) reported the use of the Watson-Glaser Test and the Co-operative Interpretation of Data Test to measure the effectiveness of a plane geometry course in which such topics as the need for clear definition, assumptions, direct deductive proof, interpretation of data, and induction were introduced through geometric materials. The logical principles were applied to nonmathematical materials such as school happenings, advertisements, news reports, magazine articles, and selections from the history of science. In the two control classes the usual textbook method was employed. Test results when interpreted showed a significant difference in favor of the experimentals on the written tests. Other evaluative procedures, reports by nongeometry teachers, anonymously-answered questionnaires filled out by the students, and a monthly essay on topics related to reasoning were interpreted by Lewis to indicate improvement in critical thinking on the part of the experimental class.

Similar results have been reported by Ulmer (39) and Gadske (12). Kimball (22) prepared sets of eleven resource units for the teachers of six experimental classes in New Hampshire high schools:

1. An introduction to geometric method
2. Some fundamental geometric concepts
3. Deductive proof
4. Similarity, proportion, and analogy (See Unit VII, Appendix D.)
5. Quadrilaterals and areas
6. Locus
7. Circles
8. Co-ordinate geometry
9. Indirect reasoning
10. Regular polygons and circles
11. A pattern for effective thinking (See Unit VIII, Appendix D.)

No attempt to teach critical-thinking skills directly was implied. The units stressed geometric content and followed the sequence usually found in standard texts. Ways were suggested to present the content as a means of introducing, demonstrating, and ultimately generalizing those aspects of the process of critical thinking which that content illustrated.

Five control classes comparable in ability and from comparable schools were taught by conventional methods.

At the end of the course it was found that the experimental classes made scores significantly higher than the control classes on the post-test Watson-Glaser Critical Thinking Appraisal. On the ACE Test of Critical Thinking the experimental group did better than the controls, but the differences were not significant at the five per cent level. Gains on a Critical Thinking Rating Scale made by Kimball were highly significant for the experimental group, but the control classes were actually rated lower by their teachers at the end of the course than at the beginning. On a standardized geometry achievement test the experimentals did slightly better than the controls but not significantly so.

Kimball's study shows that supplementary units when used by interested teachers will result in significantly greater growth in critical-thinking skills and without loss of content mastery.

The previous studies were all conducted in geometry classes, but some experimentation has also taken place in other kinds of mathematics classes. In a summary of his doctoral study done under the supervision of Harold Fawcett, Oscar Schaaf (35) has reported certain methods used in algebra classes which had positive results in teaching students to generalize. An experimental class of ninth graders at the University School, Ohio State University, matched with a status group from the Columbus public schools, worked from special lesson sheets according to which they developed algebraic principles heuristically and applied these and other generalized principles to nonalgebraic situations. For example, the study of graphs led to examination of the graphed performance of a Buick Special in terms of gasoline consumption at different speeds and the consideration of a dozen or so possible conclusions which one might draw, correctly or incorrectly, from the graph.

According to results on algebra tests and on an essentially nonmathematical generalization test, the experimental class (1) made significantly greater improvement in their ability to draw conclusions which were justifiable extrapolations and interpolations of data, (2) made significantly more improvement than the status group in ability to recognize conclusions that were not justifiable extrapolations and interpolations of accepted data, (3) became noticeably more cautious when generalizing from data both surrounded by and relatively independent of an emotive context, and (4) made significantly greater improvement in interpreting graphical and tabular data. Incidentally, the experimental students did equally as well as, if not better than, the status group on the conventional algebra tests.

Methods in language arts courses. The most important contribution to the experimental literature of critical thinking is the monograph of Edward Glaser (14) published in 1941. The purposes of the experiment were to develop techniques for stimulating growth in critical thinking, to construct measures of such growth, and to find out what relationships exist between critical thinking and other factors.

For ten weeks, four experimental classes in the twelfth grade studied the following eight units:[2]

[2] Five of these units (1, 2, 3, 5, and 8) have been published in a book by Violet Edwards (8). They were used in the program of the Institute for Propaganda Analysis.

1. Recognition of the need for definition
2. Logic and the weight of evidence
3. The nature of probable inference
4. Deductive and inductive inference
5. Logic and the method of science and some characteristics of scientific attitudes
6. Prejudice as a factor making for "crooked thinking"
7. Values and logic
8. Propaganda and "crooked thinking"

Four control classes, matched in age, average school grade in the preceding year, and intelligence (Otis), studied the regular senior English work in the New York City and Newark high school curricula, namely, English, prose literature, and a study of newspapers. These courses of study also included among their objectives the development of ability to think critically.

To measure the results of the special instruction, Glaser used a battery of six tests he and Professor Goodwin Watson constructed. The subtests are entitled, "Tests A1 and A2: A Survey of Opinions," "Test B-AR: General Logical Reasoning," "Test C: Inference," "Test D: Generalization," "Test E: Discrimination of Arguments," and "Test F: Evaluation of Arguments." Other sources of data for evaluation were essays written by the experimental students about the special instruction, letters or papers from the teachers of the experimental classes, expressions of opinion from other teachers, and records of interviews and additional testing with selected pupils from the experimental group.

On the Watson-Glaser tests as a unit the experimental group made a significantly greater average gain (C.R.=6.09) than the control group. Critical ratios of 1.94, or better, favoring the experimental group were found for the subtests A1 and A2, B-AR, D, and F, indicating that the instructional material and methods were successful in improving students' ability to hold consistent beliefs, to think in accord with the rules of logic, to avoid rash overgeneralization, and to understand the following four principles relating to proof: (1) the necessity for accepting inferences which follow from accepted premises, (2) the importance of definition, (3) the conditions of validity of indirect arguments, and (4) the illogicality of *ad hominem* arguments. Evidence from the other evaluative devices confirmed the conclusion that critical behaviors of the members of the experimental classes were improved.

Glaser's experiment is the most thorough and convincing of the proposals for teaching critical thinking. The design and statistical treatment are sound; the methods may be studied in detail; and the tests are carefully constructed. These tests, incidentally, have been revised. (40) For comment on the later form, see Chapter 21.

An interesting study in view of the controversy about the relationship between reading ability and critical-thinking ability is that of Brownell (6), who ran an experiment in Whittier, California, to test the hypothesis that general training in a 28-week reading course would produce significant gains in ability to think critically as measured by the Watson-Glaser test. As a definition of "reading," Brownell used Gray's phrase, "intelligent interpretation of printed symbols." Critical thinking was defined after Glaser as a threefold combination of "thoughtful attitude," "knowledge of methods of logical inquiry and reasoning," and "skill in applying methods of logical inquiry and reasoning."

Two ninth-grade "core" classes were matched on performance on the Watson-Glaser test, the Progressive Achievement Test: Reading, and the California Test of Mental Maturity. Both classes studied the usual core materials, but two hours a week for 28 weeks the experimental class used methods and procedures "patterned after Gray's *Reading in the High School and College,*" (presumably chapters 4 and 6 of the 47th Yearbook of the National Society for the Study of Education). Post-test results showed that the mean gain of the experimental class in total score was significantly greater than the mean gain of the control class (probability at the two per cent level). Brownell concluded that improvement in reading ability results in improved ability to score higher on the Watson-Glaser test of critical thinking. He also raised the question as to whether this test can be used as a measure of critical thinking as something apart from reading ability. Our views on this subject have already been expressed in Chapter 12. We might add here that *reading* can be defined in such a way as nearly to coincide with critical thinking. When this is done, it is a matter of little importance whether we name the crucial abilities *critical thinking* or *critical reading,* especially when the testing is done by a printed instrument.

Methods in social studies courses. Although many chapters have been written on methods of improving critical thinking in social studies classes, very few supply proof of effectiveness. Of course, the experiment of Glaser, previously described, could have been conducted in social studies as easily as English, considering that both courses commonly carry "critical thinking" as an objective.

There are, however, several noteworthy attempts to evaluate the effectiveness of antipropaganda instruction in social studies classes. Interest in propaganda was encouraged by the Institute for Propaganda Analysis which flourished in the 1930's. Publicity was given to "seven tricks of propagandists," seven ostensibly effective and obviously neat classifications stigmatized as propaganda devices: "name-calling," "glittering generalities," "transfer," "testimonial," "plain folks," "card stacking," and "bandwagon." There were also studies like those of Biddle (2) which seemed to show that knowledge of these tricks was a protection against undue influence by propagandists.

Osborn (30) designed an experiment to test the usefulness of the proposal to teach propaganda resistance by a study of the seven tricks. Twenty pairs of social studies classes in Iowa high schools were the subjects, with one class in each pair designated as experimental. At the beginning of the experiment Osborn had a six-day unit on "Public Opinion and Propaganda" taught to the experimental groups. Four weeks later he tested both groups with the Peterson and Thurstone Capital Punishment Attitude Test and his own test of achievement on knowledge of capital punishment. The same day he gave both groups a reading selection entitled "Why Capital Punishment is Necessary," followed immediately by the alternate forms of the two tests. Two weeks later all subjects took form B again of the Peterson and Thurstone attitude test. With this procedure, Osborn hoped to find out whether the six-day unit had any effect on the amount of change in attitude induced by the one-sided article on capital punishment. He found that there was a statistically significant shift in mean attitude score of both experimental and control groups in favor of capital punishment, but that the mean difference between the two groups in shift was not significant, either for the test given immediately after exposure to the biased article or for the delayed test. He concluded that the emphasis on the "form" of propaganda, on the "tricks" in other words, was not effective. He speculated that more success in developing resistance to propaganda might have been achieved by emphasis on the content as well as on the form of propagandistic materials.

Osborn noted that there were certain limitations to his investigations: for example, only propaganda in printed form was used; only one social issue was brought in; and the students may have responded to the attitude test in a manner which they believed would please their teachers.

Jewett (19) reported an investigation in which more elaborate methods were used to develop resistance to propaganda. Two units were studied by 121 pairs of juniors and seniors in four Minnesota high schools. In the first unit, lasting three weeks, the experimental classes studied the tricks of advertising and propaganda in magazine articles and newspaper columns. During this phase the students made summaries and lists of techniques and appeals used by propagandists. In the second unit, taken up a few weeks later, they studied for two weeks the use of emotional and vague words, tabloid thinking, stereotypes, overgeneralization, scientific methods of thinking, weak and strong argument, and probable inference.

A comparison was made between the students in the experimental classes and the controls, who had been matched on the basis of intelligence, ability to read, and ability to detect and analyze propaganda. The tests used were the Jewett Propaganda Test and three of Glaser's tests used also by the Institute of Propaganda Analysis—Generalization Test, D2; Strong and Weak Argument, E2; and the Inference Test, C2. The Jewett test consisted of several groups of three articles, each to be ranked by the subject according to the relative amount of propaganda contained in it. Validation was accomplished by having 20 "authorities and experts in the fields of propaganda, reading, and testing" judge the items for "propaganda" content, "propaganda" being undefined.

The results were that the experimentals showed a "highly significant superiority" over the controls on the Jewett test and on the generalization test when a comparison of pretest and post-test scores was made. The experimental classes "failed to distinguish better between strong and weak arguments" than the control groups. The experimental groups made a small amount of growth on the inference variable.

The miscellaneous quality of the special instruction makes it difficult to determine which phases of the instructional method were the most effective, but it does appear that the five-week unit did help students discriminate on gross measures of propaganda and to be more cautious in making generalizations on the basis of insufficient data. Jewett's teaching method went far beyond the study of seven tricks of propaganda and possibly for that reason obtained more positive results than the instruction of Osborn.

METHODS OF TEACHING CRITICAL THINKING IN ELEMENTARY SCHOOLS

Research into methods of teaching critical thinking at the elementary school level has been reported in very few articles, and what there is seems inadequate to form an organized report. One reason for this is the lack of standardized tests of critical thinking at this level. In the references listed at the end of the chapter, Nos. 13, 15, 16, 17, 20, and 27 are a few of the scattered articles dealing with experiments at the elementary school level.

PROPOSALS FOR TEACHING CRITICAL THINKING WHICH ARE OUTSIDE THE SCOPE OF THIS CHAPTER

There are many suggestions for teaching critical thinking which do not meet the criteria established at the beginning of this chapter.

Some articles describe what may be effective methods of teaching some phase of critical thinking but do not report a testing program. Examples of such articles are those by Ferrell (10, 11) and Thursfield (38) in history, Sams (34) and Kottmeyer (23) in English, Coutant (7) in foreign language, and Stewart (36) in combined science and social studies.

Other articles report a testing program, but the evaluative procedures are not soundly designed. An example of this type is furnished by Kay (21) who attempted to measure the effectiveness of a program for teaching students to analyze their own thinking, find conclusions, tell whether two authors agree or disagree, and discover inaccuracies and omissions. Kay gave a homemade test to 385 pupils, but apparently there were no control classes or any other way to determine whether the reported improvements of the students were due to practice with the test or to other uncontrolled variables. No data on the tests were given at all, except the statement that increases ranging from 5.7 per cent to 22.3 per cent over pretest scores were obtained on post-tests. It is difficult to appraise such an evaluative program.

A third class of studies is the kind which is on such a large scale that in spite of an elaborate testing program it is not possible to identify details of method or tell which details were effective. One example of this type is the Quillen-Hanna study (31) which attempts to compare the "problem" approach with the "topical" and "chronological." Great masses of statistical data are supplied on the testing results, but the methods are described in idealized form, that is, as they should have been taught in the numerous classes in which the 1106 student subjects were studying social studies.

There are also many articles in print which urge various methods for teaching critical thinking but which report no tryout. Doubtless many of these exhortations contain valuable suggestions, and one can only wish that more of them would be tried out under reliable experimental conditions.

Several yearbooks have been published which contain suggestions for instruction in critical thinking. The 13th Yearbook of the National Council for the Social Studies, for example, contains many potentially useful proposals and sage reflections on critical thinking, which have, however, been determined to be outside the scope of this chapter.

The implications for method of psychological studies dealing with factors affecting critical thinking have already been listed in Chapter 12.

CONCLUSIONS

In order to spell out the methods of teaching critical thinking which we have accepted as being established by reliable research, we repeat here the techniques described in the preceding pages.

In biology:
1. Instruction on the scientific method with special consideration of the subordinate concepts which are involved in the formulation of the hypothesis or generalization
2. Study of experimental procedures, identification of experimental factors
3. Study of résumés of experiments, writing conclusions from data read about
4. Discussion of conclusions thus reached by other class members with regard to accuracy, completeness, and the degree to which the conclusions go beyond the data

In chemistry:
1. Student selection and planning of experiments

2. Encouragement of students to:
   a. Recognize the value of controlled experiments
   b. Recognize basic assumptions
   c. Make clear records
   d. Use good laboratory techniques and careful observation
   e. Draw conclusions of their own from data they collect

In geometry:
1. Establishment of theorems inductively
2. Study of definition
3. Study of assumptions
4. Study of inductive proof
5. Study of factors which determine valid conclusions
6. Presentation of above matters in nonmathematical contexts—for example, advertisements, news reports, magazine articles, and selections from the history of science

In algebra:
1. Development of algebraic principles through method of self-discovery
2. Application of certain algebraic principles to nonmathematical materials
3. Discussion of extrapolation and interpolation of data

In language arts, use of following units:
1. Recognition of the need for definition
2. Logic and the weight of evidence
3. The nature of probable inference
4. Deductive and inductive inference
5. Logic and the method of science and characteristics of scientific attitudes
6. Prejudice as a factor making for "crooked thinking"
7. Values and logic
8. Propaganda and "crooked thinking"
9. Reading methods, as prescribed by William Gray

In social studies:
1. Propaganda analysis when reinforced by above units

It must be observed here that in the above lists, although we may have confidence in the complex of methods successfully used in a particular area, we cannot in every case be certain of the efficacy of a particular technique.

Although the above list might be increased by the addition of conclusions from studies which do not quite meet our criteria for inclusion or which may have been overlooked, the impression must be clear to all that there is a shocking lack of genuine research in this field of critical thinking which receives a disproportionately large amount of lip service.

EXERCISES

1. Why do you suppose that conventional laboratory techniques in high school science are not more effective?

2. Why do you think that geometry continues to be taught so widely in the conventional way when clear evidence exists to show improved methods?

3. Outline a course of study in your own field which embodies the established research in this area.

4. Describe in broad terms the features of an experiment which would be useful in adding to our store of established methods for teaching critical thinking.

5. Read the following references (15, 16, 20, 27), and report on findings which you think would be valuable as suggestions for methods of teaching critical thinking in the elementary grades.

6. Can you find any of the Glaser units which would *not* be useful in your subject field?

7. Can you find a study which should have been included in this chapter? First student to report such a study will receive a free copy of the revised book.

8. Select one of the following chapters in this book: 17, 18, 19, 20, and pick out the recommendations which are supported by research and those which are not.

9. Select one of the college studies (1, 4, 24, 26, 32 in the Bibliography for this chapter), and determine whether the conclusions might be useful at the high school level.

BIBLIOGRAPHY

1. ALDRICH, Julian C., "Developing Critical Thinking," *Social Education*, Vol. 12 (Mar., 1948), pp. 115-118.

2. BIDDLE, William W., *Propaganda and Education* (New York, Bureau of Publications, Teachers College, Columbia University, 1932).

3. BINGHAM, N. Eldred, "A Direct Approach to the Teaching of Scientific Method," *Science Education*, Vol. 33 (April, 1949), pp. 241-249.

4. BLEDSOE, Joseph C., "A Comparative Study of Values and Critical-Thinking Skills of a Group of Educational Workers," *Journal of Educational Psychology*, Vol. 46 (1955), pp. 408-417.

5. BOECK, C. H., "Teaching Chemistry for Scientific Method and Attitude Development," *Journal of Experimental Education*, Vol. 19 (1951), pp. 247-253.

6. BROWNELL, John A., "The Influence of Training in Reading in the Social Studies on the Ability to Think Critically," *California Journal of Educational Research*, Vol. 4 (1953), pp. 28-31.

7. COUTANT, Victor, "Foreign Language Grammar and Reflective Thinking," *Modern Language Journal*, Vol. 27 (1943), pp. 386-393.

8. EDWARDS, Violet, *Group Leaders' Guide to Propaganda Analysis* (New York, Institute for Propaganda Analysis, 1938).

9. FAWCETT, Harold P., "The Nature of Proof," Thirteenth Yearbook of the National Council of Teachers of Mathematics (New York, Bureau of Publications, Teachers College, Columbia University, 1938).

10. FERRELL, Francis H., "An Experiment in the Development of Critical Thinking," *American Teacher*, Vol. 30 (1946), pp. 24-25.

11. ———, "Critical Thinking," *Education Digest* (Jan., 1949), pp. 14-16.

12. GADSKE, R. E., *Demonstrative Geometry as a Means for Improving Criti-*

cal Thinking. Unpublished Ph.D. dissertation, Northwestern University, 1940.

13. GANS, Roma, *A Study of Critical Reading Comprehension in the Intermediate Grades* (New York, Bureau of Publications, Teachers College, Columbia University, 1940).

14. GLASER, Edward M., *An Experiment in the Development of Critical Thinking* (New York, Bureau of Publications, Teachers College, Columbia University, 1941).

15. GUNDERSON, Agnes G., "Thought Patterns of Young Children in Learning Multiplication and Division," *Elementary School Journal,* Vol. 55 (April, 1955), pp. 453-461.

16. HANSEN, C. W., "Factors Associated with Successful Achievement in Problem Solving in Sixth-grade Arithmetic," *Journal of Educational Research,* Vol. 38 (1944), pp. 111-118.

17. HIGGINS, Conwell Dean, "The Educability of Adolescents in Inductive Ability," *Science Education,* Vol. 22 (1945), pp. 82-85.

18. HYRAM, George H., "An Experiment in Developing Critical Thinking in Children," *Journal of Experimental Education,* Vol. 26 (Dec., 1957), pp. 125-132.

19. JEWETT, Arno, "Detecting and Analyzing Propaganda," *English Journal,* Vol. 29 (1940), pp. 104-115.

20. JOHNSON, J. T., "On the Nature of Problem Solving in Arithmetic," *Journal of Educational Research,* Vol. 43 (1949), pp. 110-115.

21. KAY, Sylvia, "Critical Reading: Its Importance and Development," *English Journal,* Vol. 35 (1946), pp. 380-385.

22. KIMBALL, Roland, *An Investigation of the Relationship Between Certain Aspects of Critical Thinking and Instruction in Geometry.* Unpublished Ed.D. dissertation, Harvard University, 1958.

23. KOTTMEYER, William, "Classroom Activities in Critical Reading," *School Review,* Vol. 52 (1944), pp. 557-564.

24. LAHTI, Arnold M., "The Inductive-Deductive Method and the Physical Science Laboratory," *Journal of Experimental Education,* Vol. 24 (1955), pp. 149-163.

25. LEWIS, Harry, "An Experiment in Developing Critical Thinking Through the Teaching of Plane Demonstrative Geometry," *Mathematics Teacher,* Vol. 43 (1950), pp. 411-413.

26. LYLE, Edwin, "An Exploration in the Teaching of Critical Thinking in General Psychology," *Journal of Educational Research,* Vol. 52 (Dec., 1958), pp. 129-133.

27. MACLATCHY, Josephine, "Variety in Problem Solving," *Education,* Vol. 61 (1941), pp. 453-457.

28. MASON, J. M., and WARRINGTON, W. G., "An Experiment in Using Current Scientific Articles in Classroom Teaching," *Science Education,* Vol. 38 (Oct., 1954), pp. 299-304.

29. "Teaching Critical Thinking in the Social Studies," Thirteenth Yearbook of the National Council for the Social Studies (Philadelphia, McKinley Publishing Company, 1942).

30. OSBORN, Wayland, "An Experiment in Teaching Resistance to Propaganda," *Journal of Experimental Education,* Vol. 8 (1939), pp. 1-17.

31. QUILLEN, I. James, and HANNA, Lavone A., *Education for Social Competence* (New York, Scott, Foresman, 1948).

32. ROBBINS, Irving, and WILSON, Phyllis C., "Improving Reasoning Ability

on Educational Problems," *Educational Research Bulletin,* Vol. 34 (Nov., 1955), pp. 205-209.

33. SALISBURY, Rachel, "A Study of the Transfer Effects of Training in Logical Organization," *Journal of Educational Research,* Vol. 28 (1934), pp. 241-254.

34. SAMS, Henry W., "Composition and Logic," *Journal of General Education,* Vol. 6 (1952), pp. 268-279.

35. SCHAAF, Oscar, "Student Discovery of Algebraic Principles as a Means of Developing Ability to Generalize," *Mathematics Teacher,* Vol. 48 (May, 1955), pp. 324-327.

36. STEWART, Bruce, "Applying Scientific Method to Social Problems," *Social Education,* Vol. 11 (1947), pp. 123-125.

37. TECHMAN, L., "The Ability of Science Students to Make Conclusions," *Science Education,* Vol. 28 (Dec., 1944), pp. 268-279.

38. THURSFIELD, Richard E., "Developing the Ability to Think Reasonably," *Seventeenth Yearbook of the National Council for the Social Studies* (1946).

39. ULMER, Gilbert, "Teaching Geometry to Cultivate Reflective Thinking," *Journal of Experimental Education,* Vol. 8 (1939), pp. 18-25.

40. WATSON, Goodwin, and GLAZER, Edward M., *The Watson-Glazer Critical-Thinking Appraisal* (New York, World Book, 1952).

41. ZAPF, Rosalind, "Superstitions of Junior High School Pupils, Part II: Effect of Instruction on Superstitious Beliefs," *Journal of Educational Research,* Vol. 31 (1938), pp. 481-496.

Lengthy bibliographies containing many articles and books on the subject of this chapter may be found in

42. LEE, Dorris May, and BINGHAM, Alma, "Intellectual Processes," *Review of Educational Research,* Vol. 29 (April, 1959), pp. 186-195.

43. RUSSELL, David H., *Children's Thinking* (Boston, Ginn, 1956).

CHAPTER **15**

Teaching for Thinking: General Methods

Let me hasten to assure the reader that I shall not propose that a course in logic be added to the high school curriculum. Quite the contrary! If the reforms I suggest succeed, I shall find, I hope, that I have talked myself out of the job of teaching elementary logic in college, for the course will become obsolete, as it should. Is it not ridiculous, when you stop to think of it, that we introduce the high school student to correct reasoning in mathematics, to the experimental method in the physical sciences, to reasoning about controversial political questions in his debate courses, and then send him to college to take a course in logic to find out correct methods of reasoning? *It would be ridiculous, at any rate, if the high school courses really taught the student how to reason correctly.* At present, the college course in introductory logic is necessary as a remedial course, painfully undoing the harm done to students' thinking powers in their high school years. But, I repeat, if and when the goals I shall outline are attained, and the parts of logic pertinent to each of the subjects taught in high school are incorporated into the training in those subjects, the need for the remedial course in logic at the college level will disappear. And that will be a great advantage to both higher education and democracy.

CYNTHIA A. SHUSTER *

The quotation from Miss Schuster hits the nail squarely on the head: develop classroom methods through which students will learn to think as a natural consequence. Personal and social aims of education will be served, to be sure; essential subject matters will be utilized, but the processes of reflective or critical thought will be stressed as aims in their own right. The direct opposite is still too true in many classrooms. The

* Cynthia A. Shuster, "Can We Teach the High School Student to Think?" *Educational Research Bulletin*, Vol. XXXVII, No. 4 (April 9, 1958), pp. 92-93.

rest of this chapter will develop some ideas as to how all this can be done.

The organization of instructional units. The nature and use of units and of assign-study-recite procedures is fully set forth in standard texts on principles of teaching. [1] Students are assumed to have this background, in fact, cannot profit from this volume without it. A brief summary must suffice here.

Efforts to organize subject matter for instructional purposes around desired outcomes and not in terms of the logic of the subject matter have been appearing since ancient times. The use of disjunctive assignments has been under fire for a long time. Systematic efforts at improvement developed, however, in comparatively recent times.

The term *unit* was first used in 1926 by Morrison, [2] who pointed out that there must be some external organization of subject matter and experiences [3] which best correlates with the internal learning products we wish the learner to achieve. Morrison emphasized functional learning outcomes in contrast to the common memorization of subject matter. Critical thinking is clearly one of the most important functional outcomes.

The subject matter unit and the experience unit. The first serious effort to clarify and systematize the definition was made by Caswell and Campbell in 1935. Their scheme dominated until 1950, though amplifications

[1] For quick review consult: Mildred L. Biddick, *The Preparation and Use of Source Units* (New York, Progressive Education Association, no date, probably 1940). Out of print. Very useful.

James B. Burr, Lowry W. Harding, and Leland D. Jacobs, *Student Teaching in the Elementary School,* 2nd ed. (New York, Appleton-Century-Crofts, 1958). Use the index for much excellent material. Note bibliographies.

William H. Burton, *The Guidance of Learning Activities,* 2nd ed. (New York, Appleton-Century-Crofts, 1952). Extensive detail, Chs. 12, 13, 14. Note extensive reference to other good sources.

J. Murray Lee and Dorris M. Lee, *The Child and His Curriculum,* 2nd. ed. (New York, Appleton-Century-Crofts, 1950), Ch. 7 for excellent brief summary.

I. James Quillen, *Using a Resource Unit,* Bulletin in the Problems of American Life Series, published by National Association of Secondary School Principals and the National Council for the Social Studies (National Education Association, 1942). Older reference with good material.

B. Othanel Smith, William O. Stanley, and J. Harlan Shores, *Fundamentals of Curriculum Development* (Yonkers, N. Y., World Book, 1950 ed.). Ch. 23 is the only discussion of details in process units. Excellent bibliographies. Note: this chapter is not included in the 1957 revision.

Ruth G. Strickland, *How to Build a Unit of Work,* Bulletin No. 5, U. S. Office of Education (Washington, D. C., 1946). Elementary school level.

J. G. Umstattd *Secondary School Teaching,* rev. ed. (Boston, Ginn, 1944), Ch. 9.

[2] H. C. Morrison, *The Practice of Teaching in the Secondary School,* rev. ed., (Chicago, University of Chicago Press, 1931), Ch. 2.

[3] NOTE. A formal outline for "teaching to think" would defeat its own purpose. Worse, if followed in an unimaginative fashion it would actually handicap thinking and learning to think. A general schematic procedure, or several of them, is however not only possible but necessary. This chapter implies not a formula but rather a general guide.

and clarifications were made chiefly by Hopkins, Burton, Lee and Lee, Macomber, Hockett and Jacobsen, and Umstattd. [4]

A. Subject matter units
1. Topical
2. Theme, generalization or principle
3. Survey
4. Problem
B. Experience units
1. Unit based on pupil purpose, need, or interest
2. Unit based on a pupil problem

The basis for the classification is obvious but is not actually adequate. It did, however, represent a great step forward, and classroom practice was affected favorably. Subject matter and experience are essential in any learning situation and occur in all organizations from the most formal to the most functional. More basic than either is the learning product achieved by the pupil, and this appears in later analyses.

The process unit. Smith, in 1950, re-emphasized that subject matter and experiences must be included in all learning. [5] This resulted from the revolt against overemphasis on formal subject matter. Smith pointed out that another factor was attention to thought-in-process resulting from our growing understanding of instrumental logic. Patterns of thought and effective habits of thinking were emphasized as basic outcomes of learning, fully as important, if not more so than substantive outcomes derived from subject matter. Smith proposed three types of units based on the processes of thinking:

1. Units of verification and discovery. These are designed to ascertain laws, generalizations, explanations, descriptive principles.
2. Normative units. These are designed to make decisions, formulate policies, reconstruct goals, and the like.
3. Units of criticism. These are designed to examine and critically evaluate statements or assertions, proposals of any kind, conclusions, doctrines, plans.

[4] Hollis L. Caswell and Doak Campbell, *Curriculum Development* (New York, American Book, 1935), Ch. 15.

L. Thomas Hopkins, *Interaction* (Boston, Heath, 1941), Ch. 7.

Burton, *op. cit.,* 1944 ed., Chs. 9, 10; 1952 ed., Chs. 12, 13, 14.

Freeman G. Macomber, *Guiding Child Development in the Elementary School* (New York, American Book, 1941), Chs. 2, 3, 4, 5.

John A. Hockett and E. W. Jacobsen, *Modern Practices in the Elementary Schools,* rev. ed. (Boston, Ginn, 1943), Ch. 3.

Lee and Lee, *op. cit.,* Ch. 7.

Umstattd, *op. cit.,* Chs. 6, 7.

[5] B. Othanel Smith, "The Normative Unit," *Teachers College Record* (Jan. 1945), pp. 219-228.

Smith, Stanley, and Shores, *op. cit.* (1950), Ch. 23. (This chapter does not occur in the 1957 revision.)

The similarity of these to the types and processes of thinking presented in foregoing chapters is obvious. We will return to this a few pages further on.

Smith bases his scheme upon the assumption that the most efficient type of unit is one which parallels the thought processes involved when the problem is analyzed in actual practice. This assumption is a valuable contribution—but a very broad one. A second assumption is that there is enough similarity in different specified problems to make a general approach useful. This also has value, but it must be noted that variations among actual problems confronting students or citizens are enormous. Any number of overlapping situations can be listed. We add, therefore, first, the assumption that whatever and whenever a given thought process comes into play, the teacher should be ready to assist students in handling it. A second assumption is that despite certain general likenesses, it may be profitable to distinguish between subtypes within the broad classifications.

Patterns and skills in thinking thus become outcomes of instruction along with substantive outcomes derived from subject matter and also with personal-social-moral developments from experience. The teacher who prides himself on "covering the text" or on "mastery" of subject matter cannot teach learners to think. He cannot teach, but that is not yet widely recognized.

One definition for all units with differentiation in terms of emphasis. In 1944 and 1952, Burton proposed that we abandon the effort to distinguish between units in terms of subject matter, experience, and process and agree on characteristics which would fit all units. A long story can be summarized as follows:

A unit is any combination of subject matter content and outcomes, and thought processes, combined in learning experiences suited to the maturity and needs of the learners; which clearly serves the needs of those learners; which is a whole with internal consistency determined by immediate and ultimate goals.

The basic assumptions are:

The important thing is to provide a combination of subject matter materials and of process which will have real value for the learner, that is, aid him in continuously integrating his learning.

Integration by the learner is aided sometimes by one thing, sometimes by another.

Emphasis either upon subject matter or upon experiences will be determined by the levels of maturity, the experiential background, the purposes, needs, and interests of the learner. These factors inescapably determine which experiences will be educative, that is, will enhance the integrating growth of the learner.

The education of *little children,* of *beginners* on almost any level, and of classes *in the area of general education* will proceed best via units wherein direct experience predominates over the vicarious. The purposes and immediate needs of the learners will largely determine the amount and complexity of the subject matter to be included and the degree of attention to be given to processes of study or thought.

The education of students who have *adequate reading ability,* who have achieved sufficient maturity *to learn through verbal abstractions,* and who are entering upon *areas of specialization* which involve a look to the future will proceed best via units in which greater use is made of vicarious experience. Ultimate social goals and the more remote personal goals, with due regard for the necessity for challenge now, will largely determine the amount and complexity of subject matter and the degree of attention to be given to processes of study or thought.

General aspects of unit organization. The details of unit procedure are available in any of the general textbooks referred to in preceding chapters. The following abbreviated outline is for quick reference only.

Title

I. *The overview.* A brief statement of the nature and scope of the unit. Any of several forms may be used. This is for the teacher's guidance.

II. *The teacher's objectives.* These should be stated in complete declarative sentences, not in single words or fragmentary phrases.

III. *The approach.* A brief account of the most probable introduction or initiation of the unit. Two or three approaches may be prepared by the teacher since various levels of maturity, interest, and ability must be motivated. The teacher prepares in advance, but the preplanned approach is modified in the classroom as the actual development of the unit is worked out co-operatively with the learners.

IV. *The planning and working period.* These are treated together since they merge. (In fact, all phases of the unit merge and appear at any time.)

Indicates briefly how planning will be done, either in advance or co-operatively, of questions, exercises, readings, experiments, excursions, reports, interviews, group discussions, development of study habits, setting up committees, exercises for organizing, summarizing, memorizing, practicing, encouraging creative effort.

V. *The pupil's aims or objectives.* States the major and minor outcomes which it is hoped the pupil will achieve. These usually emerge out of the approach. Contrary to the belief of many untrained teachers, the pupil's objectives are *not* announced in advance by the teacher. They emerge from the approach and are discovered by the pupils.

VI. *Evaluation techniques.* This should not be a mere listing of tests, scales, descriptive methods, and the like, but should show how each one to be used is related to the desired outcomes.

VII. *Bibliographies.* Those useful to the teacher in planning instruction, and those useful to the learners.

VIII. *Audio-visual aids, materials, and the like, with sources.*

The daily sequences and events within the unit as it proceeds also need to be planned from time to time. Details will be found in most standard texts.

Organization of units with special reference to teaching critical think-

ing. The listing to follow is neither perfect nor final. It is based on the historical development of unit teaching by Morrison, Burton, and Smith, plus the thought and experience of the present writers. We were unable, after extensive discussion, to develop a listing free from criticism. We could not devise mutually exclusive categories. Overlap and other inter-relationships exist within our list as they do in all other lists in print. We have added descriptive and explanatory sentences which we hope reduce the difficulty somewhat. Problem solving, for instance, occurs in all think-ing but is conventionally thought of chiefly in connection with the sciences and with practical problems of everyday life. Critical analysis, given here as a type of thinking, is a form of problem solving, but from a point of view and with data far different from scientific exploration, discovery, or veri-fication. Other illustrations could be given.

The units suggested for our general purpose in this volume are basically the same, with differentiation in terms of emphasis on given phases of the thinking process.

Conventional problem-solving units dealing with (1) explanation, (2) discovery, or (3) verification. Units dealing with (4) weighing of evidence where experimentation ordinarily could not be used. Units deal-ing with explanation, discovery, or verification are the kind most frequently used in the physical and biological sciences where facts are available and basic, or in any field where there is need to ascertain laws, generalizations, explanations, or descriptive principles. The method applies also in those phases of social sciences where facts can be derived and verified.

The classic cases in science are those in which experiments are set up to determine a new substance, a new law, or to test some hypothesis already expressed. The details of the process are those already presented in the early chapters of this book: recognition of the problem, generation of hypotheses, collection of data, coming to conclusions, testing the con-clusions through reasoning or experimentation. The essence lies in the checking and testing of the hypotheses and conclusions. Without this, trial and error might predominate.

The fourth type of problem is not readily organized under the cate-gory of explanation, discovery, verification. The evidential problem deals with thinking activities or situations which involve choice but do not ordinarily permit or receive controlled experimentation to verify the wis-dom of the choice. The kind of event involved is, in a sense, nonrepeatable. Events are often restaged or dramatized during an investigation, but this is not the same as reproducing the original event.

Our listing, it will be noted, expands that by Smith and gives some details.

1. *Explanation; seeking causes.* A given situation calls for explanation as in the case of the Mesa Verde ruins, the statues on Easter Island, or what caused our raspberry bushes to die.

    a. The problem is defined, analyzed into subproblems and questions if necessary.

    b. Hypotheses (preferably several) are developed.

    c. The hypotheses are tested:

        (1) Elaborated through reasoning.

        (2) Through collection of data.

        (3) Through experimental reproduction or production of data.

    d. Conclusion is drawn on basis of reasoning and the data we get through experimentation.

2. *Discovery.* To develop a new generalization or a new process; that is, how to manufacture synthetic vitamins, how to treat delinquent children, how to identify and stimulate gifted children.

    a. Problem is stated and examined, subproblems listed when necessary.

    b. Various suggested processes (hypotheses) are stated.

    c. The suggestions (hypotheses) are tried out experimentally.

    d. Testing here is usually a very long verification process.

3. *Verification.* Usually deals with testing to prove or disprove the worth, use, dangers, advantages of some substance, any alleged physical phenomenon, a broad theory, an educational hypothesis.

    a. Problem is defined operationally. Problem is usually clearly before the individual or group to start with.

    b. Little or no hypothesizing enters this type of problem; the null hypothesis is often used.

    c. An experimental design is evolved.

    d. Evaluation is nearly always statistical, or quantitative.

    e. Conclusions grow out of the statistical summary or quantitative statement—usually the last statement therein.

4. *Evidential.* Weighing evidence as in the legal determination of circumstances surrounding a crime; weighing evidence in many everyday problems, such as choosing which college to attend, purchasing a home, determining whether to change positions, making plans for the next vacation.

Normative units. This type of thinking arises within groups. [6] Value systems are involved. The problem is to formulate, or to reconstruct, goals or policies and to make, or to reconsider, decisions. Facts are as necessary as in any other type of thinking, but the striking characteristic here is the differences, often conflicts, of opinion and belief. Several value systems may be revealed during discussion, and some effort to resolve differences must be made. This all calls for the reconstruction of the personal system of beliefs and values. All kinds of bias and slant may enter. The necessity

---

[6] The type of thinking here discussed so briefly is of far-reaching importance and ramifies into many areas of human endeavor. For a more extended account, see R. Bruce Raup, George E. Axtelle, Kenneth D. Benne, and B. Othanel Smith, *The Improvement of Practical Intelligence,* rev. ed. (New York, Harper, 1949), Ch. 10 and elsewhere. Difficult to read but a valuable reference. First published in 1943 as the 28th Yearbook of the National Society of College Teachers of Education.

for securing such facts as there are from valid sources is important. Solutions in this area come through consensus or a meeting of the minds.

For instance, the question "Should we have socialized medicine?" will touch off thought processes in which the aspects emphasized will differ from those emphasized in the factual units of verification. Loyalties, emotional and otherwise, to various interpretations of "free enterprise," "individualism," "democracy," "public welfare," "charity," and many others will enter and will often override facts. Social norms of varying import and varying degrees of honesty or dishonesty also enter. The problem content is social-moral in contrast to strictly factual. Even the little children trying to develop a playground policy illustrate all this in simple fashion. The discussion by the parents illustrated the process even more clearly.

The general pattern of reflective thought as outlined in detail in this book holds as it does in all thinking. Points of emphasis, types of data admitted, and the controls, together with methods of checking, will differ.

1. A group finds itself in a situation in which there is conflict over aims, policies, or current beliefs. The issue may be political, economic, or social.

2. The points of conflict within the group, or within an individual's life if it is a personal problem, must be located and defined first. Discussion is aimed at bringing into the open and stating the differences of social beliefs. The words used, the means suggested, the type and number of facts cited are all important. One's opinions, for instance, have nothing to do with formulas for shooting a rocket to the moon, or determining the efficacy of vaccination, but they determine with some finality for the time being whether Negroes shall attend hitherto white schools, whether a bright boy from the wrong side of the tracks shall be elected governor.

3. The contrasting normative positions and beliefs should be openly stated, examined, and "talked out" in an effort to reconstruct some of them and reach a consensus or group policy. Smith, Stanley, and Shores suggest such questions as:

    a. How did these norms originate? What group of people advanced them, and for what interests?

    b. How did I come to accept or reject these norms?

    c. Have the social conditions changed to such an extent that their validity is now questionable? In other words, do the factual conditions now support any of the contrasting positions?

    d. Are any of these norms consistent with the norms of democracy?

4. Communications should be kept open, trial votes taken, decision delayed as long as is reasonable in the interests of obtaining consensus.

5. A new policy is formulated if the norms can be reconstructed sufficiently to reduce the conflict, if not eliminate it.

6. The new policy or program is put into operation and the consequences observed and judged by the extent to which they uphold a fundamental philosophy—in our case, the democratic values.

These units are prominent wherever the "activity" curriculum is operating, in broad field courses in social living, in the core curriculum. In real life this is the kind of thinking which dominates most discussion of public affairs and policies. While facts are not dominant at first, the outline above indicates how they must enter eventually insofar as they are available.

Public discussion indicates daily the need for understanding of this type of thinking. Political speeches, "letters to the editor," editorials, and personal columns make astonishing blunders here, even though they often show remarkable ability to maintain balance in this difficult type of thinking. The chief weakness is ignorance of, or defiance of, such facts as exist. The 1958 convention of the Daughters of the American Revolution, for instance, gave serious attention to a resolution stating that fluoridation of public drinking water was part of a Communist plot to subjugate the people of this country. A few minutes in any public library or a note to the American Medical Association would supply the pertinent facts at once. The play of social beliefs and political philosophies is clearly implied in this illustration.

Smith, Stanley, and Shores state the purpose of these units very clearly. [7]

The working out of normative units in actual classroom practice requires not only that individuals come to perceive the social issues—and the facts, social norms, and interests at play in the issues—but also that they become aware of and study their own views, desires, prejudices. It is patent that the resolution of social issues requires a reconstruction of the characters of the persons involved in them. For characters are themselves in conflict, and if consensus is to be attained so that action can ensue, these characters must somehow be brought into harmony. The purpose of the normative unit, then, is to enable individuals to learn, in co-operation with other persons, how to think through issues in the interests of common action and the common good.

Units of criticism. The problem here is to determine whether a statement heard or read, or made by one's self, has sufficient basis to be valid, hence acceptable. Obviously, this again calls for emphasis upon certain parts of the thinking process, in this case on critical scrutiny and critical judgment. Occasion for highly critical judgment occurs many times daily as one reads newspapers, journals of opinion, listens to radio or television, to sermons, sales talks, political statements. The critical attitude and the processes of critical judgment are paramount.

Illustrations of this type of thinking have been given in previous pages through reference to "letters to the editor," to editorials and columns, and to so-called news magazines which are actually journals of opinion. This type of thinking so necessary in everyday life is tragically neglected in school. This is partly due to the practically total absence of training of teachers in this type of thinking. Public pressures also prohibit the school from discussing certain issues. (The same public then bitterly criticizes the

[7] Smith, Stanley, and Shores, *op. cit.,* p. 567; pp. 565-566.

schools when pupils turn up ignorant of crucial everyday issues!) In one Southern California city, the United Nations and UNESCO may not be mentioned by any teatcher on pain of dismissal. Certain selfish interests backed by powerful newspapers see to it that the growing generation is kept in ignorance of important aspects of life today. Thirty miles away, another city has a first-class program on international affairs and relations between nations. An enlightened group got this started in advance of contrary influences and happily received good backing from the local newspaper. The day after Stalin's death, a quick check by newspapers and interested individuals showed that, so far as could be discovered quickly, no teacher in a large Massachusetts city had dared even to mention this momentous event. The event itself, of course, was known to every student who could read the daily newspaper. People who wish to coerce the thinking of others should realize that persons are far more influenced by events than by words about them. The thing to do is to prevent the events. This is much more difficult than censoring discussion.

Units on propaganda and on resistance to it are appearing in increasing numbers and are of some help. They are, unfortunately, largely confined to exposing the tricks of propaganda and to the misuse of language to persuade and to mislead. Sustained programs for the development of a critical attitude and for development of skills of critical judgment are rarely found.

Units of criticism may appear in any subject area as well as in many nonschool activities. Two points precede the critical analysis:

1. A proposition, assertion, conclusion, policy, or program, read or heard, comes before an individual or group. Choice must be made.

2. The statement must be clearly stated, apprehended, and analyzed before it can be evaluated. This calls for definition of terms, summary statements.

The analysis may take various forms and use various questions. We suggest the following as one method:

1. What is the *purpose, intent, or viewpoint* of the writer or speaker? Who are the sponsors of the speaker, of the statement, policy, or program? What are their affiliations and possible motives?

2. What are the *chief arguments* used? State in compact form in a written list.

3. Are these arguments *supported by fact and reason,* given or implied?
    a. What facts are used? State these in a list.
        Has the writer or speaker collected, selected, or selectively recalled relevant evidence?
        Has he differentiated between reliable and unreliable sources; verifiable and unverifiable data? Between the essential and the incidental?
        Has he recognized the necessity for adequate data?
    b. What basic reasons are used? List.

Has the writer or speaker differentiated between observational statements, logical definitional propositions, meaningless propositions? Discriminated between referential, emotive, and figurative language? Recognized stereotypes and clichés?

c. Does the writer consider any other hypotheses than the one he supports?

4. What *assumptions* appear openly or lurking implicitly behind statements? Does innuendo appear? Openly or under guise of fact?

5. What standard means of evaluation are used for the facts, the reasons, the arguments, the conclusions? Does the writer evaluate his own data, and particularly does he recognize and evaluate his assumptions?

6. What fallacies appear? Errors? Methods of checking for one's fallacies or errors?

7. Is the language referential, emotive, or figurative? Is it the language of an honest expositor, a special pleader, or a propagandist? Is the tone sober and controlled? Sarcastic? Ironic? Deliberately misleading? Are terms defined and used consistently, or does meaning shift consciously or unconsciously? Are connotations and denotations correct?

8. Has the writer supported his conclusions so that they invite justifiable acceptance?

The citizen or student then makes a judgment of acceptance or rejection, and operates under that judgment, noting consequences.

The above eight-point summary is for quick reference. Each point has considerable supporting detail. The details for Point 1, for instance, were given in Chapter 10 when dealing with verbal and psychological context. Point 3 c was elaborated in Chapter 7; Point 5 in Chapter 8; Point 6 in Chapter 11 and Point 8 in Chapter 8. We present below a brief outline of details subsumed under Points 3 and 4.

Questions to ask about the facts used. Other points can be added to this summary as desired.

1. Are the statements of fact which are offered as evidence (a) reports of observations? (b) inferences from what has been observed? (c) "hearsay"?

2. Are the statements of fact reliable? (a) Who made them? (b) Is he a competent witness? (c) What was his purpose in reporting the facts? To make news? To eulogize? To discredit? To convey accurate information?

3. Under what conditions were observations made? (a) Casual observation? (b) Carefully controlled experiments? (c) Under emotional stress?

4. To what extent did the reporter depend on memory?

5. Are all the facts presented as evidence relevant to the question? How might irrelevant facts be used to serve a writer's or speaker's purpose? To divert interest or attention from other facts? To stir feeling? To shape attitudes and dispositions toward the issue? To change perspectives?

6. Are all relevant facts, both for and against, presented?

7. If all the information pertinent to the question cannot be presented, is the selection a typical and fair sampling?

8. Do the facts necessarily mean what the author interprets them to mean?

Can they be given other interpretation? How can the same facts be taken to mean a different thing? What is the relative evidential value of the facts? (The latter is the problem of "weighing evidence.")

Questions to ask about principles and assumptions which underlie the reasons.

1. How did I come to accept the principles, or to reject them? (*a*) By unconscious imbibing? (*b*) Coercion of custom? (*c*) Careful thinking? (*d*) Warranted trust in authority? (*e*) Appeals of eloquence?

2. What has been the history of given principles and arguments? (*a*) How did they come to be formulated? (*b*) What kinds of ends were the principles and arguments designed to serve—the common good, interests of limited group, or a partisan bias?

3. Have the principles underlying the arguments been transmitted through decisions that are the products of rigorous thinking, or through unconsciously accepted tradition?

4. What effect have the principles had on institutions?

5. Has the situation to which they applied or from which they were derived (social, economic, or political) changed sufficiently to warrant new principles?

6. What idealistic justifications have been offered in support of the principles? Have these justifications been so interpreted to justify the views or practices of a partisan group?

7. Are the principles consistent with other accepted principles? Are they supported by known facts?

8. What would the consequences be if we acted upon the reasons advanced in situations . . . ? (Outline real situations here). Would we be willing to accept the consequences?

9. What unconscious controls—tastes, interests, temperament, prejudices, and the like—may have led the author to select the principles and arguments used? To give facts their meanings, rather than some other alternative principle? (This one overlaps with the statements given elsewhere on interpretation of context). [8]

The case study method. A case is a detailed account of events leading up to some type of difficult problem. The written or printed summary brings realistic detail to the student through which he can project himself into the situation and see the issues vividly. This brings the learner as close to actual participation as is possible. Students may develop case materials as well as use them for practice in critical thinking.

The use of cases as instructional material is, perhaps, best known in

---

[8] The two summaries on fact and principle were adapted from a pamphlet by the late Fred C. Hood. This is an excellent reference on this type of thinking but is out of print and difficult to find. Large college libraries usually have it:

Fred C. Hood, "Developing the Ability to Assess the Results of Thinking," *University of Illinois Bulletin,* Vol. 45 (Feb., 1949). This pamphlet deals with other aspects of thinking as well.

Many of the standard texts in critical thinking and some in psychology also contain material of value.

law schools. Case studies and case work have had great development also in medicine, psychiatry, clinical psychology, child study, guidance and counseling, delinquency, and therapy. The method is increasingly used in anthropology, sociology, economics, political science, business administration, and educational administration. Further discussion is given in the later chapters on science and on social studies.

A case may be handled in any of several ways, but the following is a typical outline:

1. The specific instance to be studied, be it an institution, a type of community, a local or national policy, a controversy, or any of many others, must first be clearly recognized. The circumstances giving rise to the inquiry (the original facts) must be examined and interpreted. Differences in interpretation of the original situation, differences in social norms, differences of values, differences of opinion must be brought into the open. This may or may not be prominent, depending on the problem.

2. Hypothesizing may or may not be prominent.

3. A series of guide questions will be developed around which the case will be developed and analyzed. These will include things to find out, to do, and to exercise judgment upon.

4. Data of all types will be collected from a wide variety of sources.

5. Classification and analysis of data follow.

6. Tentative conclusions, often only summaries, will emerge and be compared with standards or norms already in existence. Sometimes the norms will be reorganized.

7. Conclusions are in the form of summaries, supplemented by suggestions for actual or desirable action.

Practice is given in the various aspects of thinking, particularly critical analysis.

The general texts in principles of teaching tragically neglect the case method. The best sources are introductory texts on research methods from which easy adaptations to instructional situations can be made. Any standard text will be satisfactory, such as:

Carter V. Good, *Introduction to Educational Research* (New York, Appleton-Century-Crofts, 1959), Chs. 7 and 5. Ch. 7 contains excellent abbreviated accounts of specific case studies.
See also:

Pearson Hunt, "The Case Method of Instruction," *Harvard Educational Review* (Summer, 1951), pp. 2-19. Good bibliography up to that date. Excellent discussion of general theory and method. Extensive trial of case methods in the Harvard Business School preceded the preparation of this statement.

Joseph C. Bailey, "A Classroom Evaluation of the Case Method." Available in a pamphlet, together with Dr. Hunt's article, distributed by the Harvard Business School Association.

Creative thinking, its stimulation and expression. Two aspects must be mentioned. First, creativity appears in all thinking. The development of hypotheses is a case of creativity, mentioned earlier. The recognition of hidden and remote relationships between data and problem illustrates creative insight. The production of insights which cut through confusion to reach the heart of the matter, the sudden flash of so-called inspiration, or intuition are all creative processes. Second, creative thinking is a unique type of thinking of major proportion with products of its own. It is on a par with problem solving, determining values and goals, and critical determination of conclusions. Creativity in this sense means the production of something new, unique, not-before-existent; a musical composition; an invention. Creativity is not confined to the fine arts, as many think, but appears in any field of human endeavor.

Creativity in either sense has been tragically neglected by the schools and in some instances actively repressed. Today there is growing emphasis upon creativity, as it is recognized that we are dealing not with special talent, but with originality, inventiveness, and new insights which appear as normal characteristics of all persons. The trait or ability differs with individuals as do all other characteristics. A tradition of creativity, originality, and inventiveness in the school can be developed to replace the currently dominant tradition of passivity, acceptance, or acquiescence.

Suggestions for stimulating creative thought. The stimulation of thinking of any type is difficult, as we have seen. Stimulation of creative thought is doubly difficult because of its subtle character and because of our limited understanding of its nature and development. There is no formula for stimulating creativity any more than there is for any kind of independent intellectual endeavor. We do know some things as previous chapters pointed out. The following list is not final or dogmatic.

1. The first factor or criterion is free expression by the learner under meaningful purpose, with appropriate regard for level of maturity, experiential background, and interest.

2. Opportunities should be provided and spontaneous expression encouraged.

Conversations, everyday experiences, experimentation with media and materials, and self-initiated projects of all kinds and levels give rise to creative expression.

3. Creative expression should be received with expectancy and encouragement.

Some of it may appear crude to some adults, but it may be excellent for the pupil's level of maturity. The imposition of adult standards and techniques should be avoided.

4. Negative comments, laughter at first attempts, and comparison with standards beyond the learner's level are discouraging.

5. Taste, standards, and skills will develop with maturity and experience.

Avoid drills on techniques in advance of need and use.

Give aid in response to needs and insights of pupils at the time.

Wait patiently for development of maturity and skill—but give opportunity constantly for skills to appear and to develop.

6. Periods of relaxation, contemplation, rumination, even of daydreaming and idleness, should be provided. These are necessary for the emergence of creative expression.

7. Provision should be made for change of work, dropping a project temporarily.

8. The improvement of any and all types of thinking eventually contributes to creative thinking and vice versa.

9. Periods of systematic training may be provided eventually for those who have special talent or wish to specialize. The public school, however, is chiefly concerned with creativity as a part of the general development of all children.

Landis gives three good suggestions in relation to stimulation of creativity in art which apply to all fields. [9]

1. The child must have something to express.

2. The child must be made aware of the possibility of expressing his feelings and ideas in art materials.

3. The child may be helped to understand, enjoy, and appreciate the materials, organization, and the meaning of his work and the work of others.

This indicates the necessity of understanding and identification with whatever the learner is trying to express or create.

List of general characteristics. The reader may wish to add more items to this list.

1. Creative expression is uncertain—it comes, or it does not come.

2. Creative expression is easily stimulated, repressed, or destroyed with finality in little children.

3. Creative expression is favored as a rule by freedom from compulsion, but this is not universal.

4. Creative expression is aided by order and regularity of effort, once production is under way, by a place and facilities for work.

5. Creative periods of work are marked by intense concentration and absorption, sometimes by complete dissociation.

6. Creative expression is not "imagination" in the popular meaning of the term.

7. Creative expression is not mere revolt.

8. Creative expression is not mad, turbulent, "temperamental."

Phases of a creative act. Nearly all writers analyze the phases through which creativity proceeds. We emphasize, as in earlier chapters, that thinking cannot be reduced to a routine, a formula, a set of steps. The

[9] Mildred M. Landis, *Meaningful Art Education* (Peoria, Ill., Charles A. Bennett Co., 1951).

four phases are merely a very rough description of the creative process and are not a precise account of the behaviors involved. [10]

1. *The phase of preparation,* of achieving familiarity, of securing experiences, of becoming absorbed, of initial efforts to achieve.

2. *The phase of incubation.* The problem is dropped, either for rest from it, relaxation, or because of other necessary activities. The problem may or may not recur consciously. New ideas, insights, partial solutions occur spontaneously. Stages of preparation and of incubation may overlap.

3. *The phase* (*sometimes a moment*) *of illumination,* of inspiration, of insight, of fulfillment.

4. *The phase of revision,* of elaboration, of polishing.

These phases, actually, are true of all operations. All learning or thinking rests upon experience and information gained therefrom. New ideas, flashes of insight, and inventions do not occur to uninformed minds. We should distinguish between minds *furnished* with facts and knowledge acquired functionally in meaningful situations and minds *stuffed* with facts acquired through rote memorization or forced upon them in advance of sufficient maturity. Stuffing pupils with subject matter as such, seemingly demanded by many critics of the schools, will not of itself produce original ideas. The other phases are self-explanatory and are not unduly different from the same phases in any type of thinking. [11]

[10] The best critical analysis of the four "phases" or "stages" is found in David H. Russell, *Children's Thinking* (Boston, Ginn, 1956), pp. 311-313. This volume is also the only complete summary of research on various aspects of children's thinking. The whole book is a valuable reference on thinking, with Ch. 11 of special value on creative thinking.

[11] A rapidly growing bibliography attests to the increasing interest in creative thinking. Accounts of the creative process are now available dealing with several fields. The references below are sharply selective since we cannot give here an extensive general bibliography.

Catherine Patrick, *What is Creative Thinking?* (New York, Philosophical Library, 1955). This is a general account of the creative process. The bibliography of 209 titles introduces several dozen studies in specific fields: art, music, literary composition, mathematics, medicine, surgery.

H. C. Lehman. Ten or more specialized studies are available, mostly in scientific and psychological journals. Use the *Readers Guide* and psychological indexes.

Raymond F. Loewy, *Never Let Well Enough Alone* (New York, Simon and Schuster, 1951). This deals with creativity in industrial design, advertising, and business promotion. Excellent reading. Few such books are available, and any found should be reviewed by students.

Breiastes Ghiselin, *The Creative Process* (New York, Mentor Book, New American Library, 1952.) Available in hard cover also.

Use the card catalogue to find volumes by Hughes Mearns, Charles S. Crow, and Samuel S. Slavson.

Look also for biographies, autobiographies, and private journals of writers, artists, musicians, scientists, and inventors. Excellent materials are available.

The literature of aesthetics, philosophy, religion, and mysticism contains some enlightening accounts. Books on the history of science or of particular scientific fields are good sources.

Modern textbooks on psychology and on principles of teaching are increasingly including treatment of creative thinking and of means of stimulating it.

The use of group process in thinking. Several statements have indicated that while some problems may be solved either by individuals or groups, still other problems may be solved only by groups. Problems necessitating group process are those of the normative type, chiefly of determining goals, of policy making, and of organizing programs of group action. Problems of this type are not solved by precise measurement or controlled experimentation; they are solved by a meeting of minds and consensus.

Democracy depends for its existence on group thinking. Modern times have forced us to realize the importance of human relations, of working and getting along together in groups. On the international level, the most obvious danger lies in the inability of groups, raised to the national level, to get along. The mechanisms of co-operation, of interaction, of interchange, and particularly of group thinking and decision do not exist on that level.

The democratic method of solving problems of concern to the group and reaching decisions is one of free discussion wherein all are at liberty to express their views. Common agreement is reached through the interaction of individuals of all types and of all levels of insight within the group. Decisions are then understood and invite loyalty. Care must be taken to preserve individual freedoms while arriving at a consensus, and afterward.

The democratic method frees creative power in astonishing ways as no other method can. A group engaged in solving a problem which is real to them will find need for many kinds of ability, many types of skill and insight. Contributions to the common problem may come from any and all members of the group. Group discussion is not random discourse, as some seem to think. The atmosphere must be free and permissive, but there must be order and continuity. Control is exercised by the problem and related facts. Any member of the group may ask that discussion which strays be brought back to the point. Summaries and tentative conclusions should be made from time to time, looking toward eventual consensus. Control through prescribed directives or through power of a chairman or an organized minority may seem to bring smooth operation, but it will not beget good thinking or growth in thinking skills.

General characteristics of group process in thinking. The solution of a problem by a group of people working together does not always proceed according to the most logical arrangement of ideas. The solution must often be based not on a scientific prediction or summary, but on the desires and values of the people involved. The level of maturity of the group, its cultural and informational status, and the kinds of procedures used may enhance or inhibit the attainment of the best solutions.

The solution of social problems by group thinking is a very recent development in human history. The oldest and commonest method is that in which a person or small group in power dictates goals and policies, decisions of any kind. Examples of group thinking on problems proper for this type of procedure may be found all the way from a rural community considering and voting a renovation of a one-room rural school, or fire protection means and methods, from larger groups deciding upon an extensive system of freeways, or slum clearance, up to the national Congress making laws and determining policies. (See Chapter 18 on social studies.)

1. *A problem arises of concern to the group;* which involves choice in terms of values and insights; which is solvable through "meeting of minds" or consensus, rather than by more precise methods.

2. *The problem is defined* and may be redefined a number of times. This is sometimes a long and arduous process, much more difficult than definition of a problem in the physical sciences.

3. *The problem is analyzed and explored at length* in order to guarantee understanding by the group. The exploration includes:

   a. The facts in the situation as in all thinking.

   b. The varying values, experiential backgrounds, and levels of maturity within the group.

   c. The hidden objectives, if any, of individuals or of subgroups.

4. *The general process of thinking then ensues* as outlined in earlier chapters. Orderly, sequential processes of thinking do not occur even in controlled scientific problems. The processes of group thinking are far less sequential than in science. Details have been described earlier. Teachers, many of them, regard all this to be a waste of time and training in bad habits. The opposite is true. No one can learn to think without thinking, to achieve the many difficult skills of group thinking without engaging in group thinking. Errors are made; time is consumed; but unless there is genuine confusion and disorder this is a necessary phase of learning to think, either as an individual or as part of a group.

5. *The experience of the group should be voluntarily extended beyond its own resources.* A group cannot chat itself to truth. Uninformed persons pooling their ignorance cannot achieve sensible decisions. Material and personal resources will be used and invited.

6. *The machinery and organization necessary* for co-operative process develops out of the situation, is not set up in advance (beyond simple necessities for getting started).

7. *Summaries, tentative conclusions, and straw votes* are made continuously, both to delay a too-early final conclusion and to work toward consensus.

8. *Evaluation,* both of process and conclusions, goes on continuously.

9. *Conclusions are accepted as tentative,* and their consequences tested in actual situations; consequences on persons, groups, and situations.

Great value attaches to allowing differing values, biases, levels of insight to appear through free discussion. Many individuals are quite unaware, first, that there are basic and serious differences in attitude, in standards, in likes and dislikes, and, second, that many of these are acquired, as we say, "unconsciously." It is very enlightening to discover that beliefs held uncritically since childhood are not accepted by many educated people, to discover that one has little or no basis for many of the values which he upholds vigorously. Getting these out in the open often clears the way toward a consensus which would not be achieved as long as members of the group were directed by beliefs and motives which were not expressed.

Guide lines for participants in group thinking. The fifteen points listed below were prepared for the Michigan Study of Secondary School Curriculum several years ago by J. Cecil Parker and are used here with permission.

1. Each person should do his own thinking. Don't try to "save time" by telling the group the right answer. The leader is not a group instructor, but a social engineer, trying to arrange conditions so that each will do creative thinking.

2. Group discussion is not a debating society. We do not argue for the fun of it. The issues are of great importance; wise men disagree in their views; our task is to find more truth than we bring to any group meeting. We are in a co-operative quest. Our thinking is creative rather than combative.

3. Ask yourself which ideas, experiences, and differences are basic, fundamental, and most worth discussing.

4. When discussion wanders, restate the question and get a new start. Sometimes, if the sideline is especially important, put it up to the group. "Shall we follow this interesting issue that has come up, or shall we return to the plan of discussion originally adopted?"

5. Make short statements, not speeches.

6. Do not pass any important matter that is not clear to you. Sometimes, individuals hear unfamiliar terms and assume that everyone else must understand; hence they fear it would be humiliating to ask for explanations or illustrations. This is untrue. Have you not often been glad when someone else asked for clarification on a point on which you had been none too clear? Others may profit too, but you are in the group to learn, and you must not hesitate to ask.

7. If you find yourself talking more than other members of the group, train yourself to pass over minor points and to speak on only a few carefully chosen issues.

8. Use special care to be fair to positions represented by a minority or not represented at all in the group. If you are aware of a position not being adequately represented, present it as its adherents would like to hear it stated; then explain your disagreement.

9. Challenge contributions you cannot fully accept. Do not keep your disagreements quiet in the mistaken notion that it is better manners to pretend to agree when you do not. Make inquiry concerning the assumptions involved in the contribution.

10. The "either-or" attitude is on the whole not fruitful. Search rather for new means which enable both sets of values to be pursued without clash. Our concern in co-operative thinking is not simply to choose between two ways we now know, but if possible to find a way of integrating the values of both,

thereby creating an improved solution. However, avoid smoothing over differences. Differences should be probed with questions to make them clear and sharp.

11. When there is some confusion over a diversity of opinions expressed, a minute of silence can do much to help members rise to a clearer perspective of what has been said. In suggesting this pause, the chairman should restate the precise issue under discussion. After the pause the members may be more able to co-operate in detecting the root of the disagreements. This may be in the partial nature of the experience and evidence used, or in a difference in the sense of values. Try to keep in mind some ends everyone else wants.

12. Be on the lookout for different uses of the same word. Call for illustrations whenever this difference becomes confusing. Do not wrangle over a verbal definition.

13. Trust the group. There is no person in it who is not superior to the rest in at least one respect. The experience of all is richer than the experience of any. The group as a whole can see further and more truly than its best member. Remember that every member of the group is an individual just as you are.

14. For every discussion there is available a limited amount of time. Each individual should help make it possible to utilize the time more effectively. To attempt too much in too short a time fosters a habit of slipshod and superficial thinking.

15. Summarize (1) whenever a major point is finished before going on to the next, (2) whenever the discussion has been fairly long drawn out or confused, (3) shortly before the close of the period. Try to use the words of members of the group, rather than your translation.

Another set of guides, bringing out two or three points not included in the foregoing, is taken from Miel: [12]

1. Give full opportunity for every member of the group to contribute every suggestion that occurs to him.

2. Keep the gathering of suggestions as a phase of the discussion separate from the evaluation of the suggestions. (This usually ensures a more impersonal discussion of suggested solutions.)

3. Allow plenty of time for pooling of facts and harmonizing of conflicting values.

4. Before final votes are taken, use straw votes to uncover minority opinion early in the process. In this step allow each voter to register as many choices as he wishes.

5. Seek for a consensus by allowing full discussion of the minority view before entertaining formal motions.

6. If after adequate discussion the group is still fairly evenly divided as to the proper course of action on a given matter, consider whether or not a decision really must be made at the time. Often it is better to postpone making the decision until further study can be made by all parties.

7. If a decision of some sort must be made, have it understood that the

[12] Alice Miel, *Changing the Curriculum: A Social Process* (New York, D. Appleton-Century, 1946), pp. 139-140.

decision is a trial one whose results will be carefully reviewed in order that the large minority will co-operate as wholeheartedly as possible.

Groups trying group discussion for the first time often follow parliamentary procedure (Robert's Rules of Order). This is natural in view of past experience. The preceding pages should make clear that "rules of order" are a definite handicap to free democratic discussion. There must be order, but the chairman and the group will be responsible for keeping it subordinate to the free discussion. Free give-and-take motivated by purpose and engaged in by sincere individuals, will not need rules of order.

Group process is susceptible to misapplication and misuse. Procedure may not be kept problem centered, may deal with problems of no use or meaning to the group. Fictitious problems, problems too difficult for the group, or problems susceptible to solution through reference to precise data available in known sources will not initiate or sustain group thinking.

Group process, furthermore, does not work with certain types of individuals. These are the individuals who simply do not respond to this method, even with explanation and experience. Tensions, frustrations, antagonisms, and disintegrative conflict appear which destroys reflective thinking. The unintentional pressure of the group situation often causes some individuals to desert opinions and standards which would be of real use if maintained in the thinking. Other individuals, sensing group pressure, no matter how unintentional that pressure may be, resort to stubborn stands and dogmatism. Pressure distorts judgment even when no pressure is intended. Another difficulty is the "hidden agenda," that is, the private opinions and conclusions which are quite different from those expressed in group discussion. Properly used, however, group discussion in any type of thinking frees creative power in astonishing degree.

Group process may be defeated through lack of balance in the group, as, for example, too many administrators within a group of teachers (or any type of worker), or too few administrators. Administrators may "throw their weight around" with groups which dare not fight back. Insufficient information, or insufficient preparation of any kind, on the part of those making up the group will prevent thinking. Absence of a general policy governing the problems discussed is a prime cause of difficulty. Insufficient time for discussion (often a device by those controlling a group) will wreck the process and confidence in it. Machinery is not set up for getting data, particularly opinions of groups outside the one working on the problem. Lack of structure or direction is fatal. Structure and control are exercised by the group but must be exercised. Definite training and experience for gradual development of skill are necessary. Group process is not random conversation, or entertainment, or a pleasant way to pass the time. It is a difficult and complex process for which there must be orientation and training.

Critics of the process should not overlook that (*a*) group thinking is a very recent achievement in human history, and (*b*) the nature of group thinking and the necessity for attaining it are not yet clearly understood.

The effect of group process upon problems which may be and usually are tackled by individuals. One point should be noted in passing, namely, that co-operation among several persons will enhance the ability of the individuals to solve individual problems. This contradicts much common opinion, and not a little among certain academicians.

1. Research shows clearly that pairs or groups of students solve more problems than individuals though they may take longer. [13] Groups also learn more than individuals. One study even shows that correct judgments of a group of persons will be increased significantly over the average for their own individual responses.

2. Conflicts of opinion, challenges to the adequacy of evidence for assertions and beliefs appear in greater number in group discussion than in the case of the individual working alone. This leads to critical discrimination.

3. A far wider range of information and sources appears in group thinking than in individual thinking.

4. Group thinking which often starts with muddle ends up with more organization and systematization than individual thinking.

5. Individuals in the group learn to "give and take," to respect other's opinions while demanding proof, to give in without "getting sore."

Bibliographies on group thinking. Attempting to give a current listing of references is futile. Literally scores of books and hundreds of pamphlets and magazine articles are available. New materials, furthermore, are appearing constantly. The card catalogue and the guides to periodicals will supply more material than can be used.

Chapter summary. As pointed out elsewhere, thinking is not produced through formal exercises in certain so-called intellectual subjects. Neither is it produced through exposure to excellent thinking done by others and embodied in various types of documents. Two or more surveys of research support these negations and do show, so far as we now know, that if a subject is taught with the express purpose of developing intellectual habits improvement will result, particularly for the academically brighter students. The whole view and hope in our volume is that students may be given practice in the process of thinking and made conscious of their own processes in solving problems and in coming to critically discriminated conclusions. It is a sad commentary on modern life and education that many men are quite familiar with operations of the calculus, and of intricate machines, but are childishly naïve about the operation and processes of their own minds.

Implications. The teacher interested in improving habits of thinking will analyze his course of study to see which purposes, subject areas, and

---

[13] Russell, *op. cit.* See p. 267 for compact and readable summary.

processes may be involved; he will then aid the students to solve the pertinent problems according to the most efficient methods and teach them what he can of the general processes to be used.

Naturally the processes vary considerably according to the purposes and subject matter of the particular unit. An experiment to test a proffered theory may stress the procedures of the laboratory and require a minimum of original hypothesis. A scientific problem in which the aim is to discover some new drug, for instance, will demand fertile hypotheses. An explanatory problem in history will require much reading of factual material and hypotheses of an entirely different sort. The teacher must use his initiative in determining the most useful processes for the problem at hand. In later chapters more detail is given on the special processes useful in mathematical, scientific, literary, and social problems.

Furthermore, the nature of the individual processes varies according to the subject matter and purpose. Thus, the collection of data in chemistry is quite different from the collection of data in a social problem such as racial integration.

QUESTIONS, EXERCISES, AND REPORTS

The contents of this chapter constitute a summary of materials which should be known to students using this volume. Time should not be used to "teach" this chapter. Students who are not familiar with current principles and practices of teaching cannot do what is now called for, namely, tell how the discussion of thinking can be applied in teaching. There are practically no references on this, though there is an ample supply on principles of teaching.

The discussion should deal with procedures used or proposed for use by teachers in the group.

1. List current factors and practices in school which are obstacles to and interfere with learning to think. Why do you still use these procedures?

List current factors and practices which facilitate and encourage effective thinking. Why are these not more widely used?

2. Report briefly for class analysis any units or other types of lessons which you have used in teaching any phases of reflective thinking.

3. Outline similarly any new units you are currently developing.

Dewey, in *How We Think,* rev. ed. (Boston, Heath, 1933), makes cogent remarks upon certain phases of teaching on pp. 35-36, 46-47, 49-52, 52-54.

4. Pp. 35-36 contain some statements which, if related to current educational practice, would be truly devastating. Make one or two applications to the current educational scene, and develop the implications for teaching.

5. The closing paragraph of the section on pp. 46-47 contains, in half a page, a collection of the chief errors, misconceptions, and general stupidities widely distributed among secondary teachers. Why do these persist in the face of unanimous disapproval by trained thinkers and valid evidence to the contrary?

6. What are the implications for curriculum and instruction of pp. 49-52? Make several points.

7. Pp. 52-54 again refer to gross blunders in several phases of the educational process. Why do these errors persist? (Some remote and fundamental points should be developed here in addition to the more obvious ones.)

READINGS

The footnotes include the chief materials necessary here. Readers should be on the lookout for any new books or articles treating of general principles of learning and teaching.

CHAPTER 16

Teaching for Thinking: Elementary Education

> To the psychologist the mind of the child still gives an impression of appalling chaos.
>
> CLAPAREDE *

> Our present-day knowledge of the child's mind is comparable to the fifteenth-century map of the world—a mixture of truth and error.
>
> ARNOLD GESELL †

> I have dared to believe that providing a basis for the understanding of children's thinking may eventually help many people to think more clearly.
>
> DAVID H. RUSSELL ‡

A myth still widely current among laymen is that children cannot think or reason. We have ample evidence to the contrary. Children do, in fact, think and reason at a very early age. [1] They are but exercising a natural tendency of all human beings. The acuity and directness of children's thinking is often embarrassing to adults whose thinking has been warped by the acquisition of conventional wisdom. Children do, however, make odd, often hilarious, blunders in their thinking. This is the natural result of lack of maturity and experience. Odd and contradictory—sharply acute at one time, naïve and blundering at another—children's thinking is important. This is especially true before they have learned from adults how to use various substitutes for thinking. The very freedom and *seeming* chaos

---

* Claparede, Introduction to Jean Piaget, *The Language and Thought of the Child*, p. xii.

† Arnold Gesell in 1950.

‡ David H. Russell, *Children's Thinking* (Boston, Ginn, 1956), Preface.

[1] Russell, *op. cit.* A monumental volume containing a careful and critical summary of known research on the topic.

335

of children's thinking is at once a real difficulty and a very great opportunity for the teacher.

General reasons for mixture of good and bad thinking in children. Children's thinking lacks logical consistency at times for the general reason that there is insufficient maturity and life experience.

1. *Absolutistic tendency dominates.* Relativity has not yet been sensed; differences and degrees within a total event are not recognized.

2. *Egocentricity dominates.*

3. *The real is not yet distinguished from the not-real,* the objective from the subjective, what happens in their minds from what happens in the world.

4. *Ability to abstract* and generalize, though present from an early age, *develops very slowly.*

5. *Abstract relationships are not well understood,* particularly cause-and-effect relationships.

> Children are greatly influenced by accidental associations in time and space.
>
> In some instances children deal with an unanalyzed whole situation; in others they cannot seem to go beyond the specifics. (This is related, of course, to 3 and 4 above.)

The thinking of little children (and of many adults!) is highly personal and narrowly individualistic. The aims and desires, the pride of the individual, his peace and comfort are the controlling factors. Limited personal experience is the criterion of validity. This can be observed continually in everyday intercourse. Little children are intensely partisan. Every child asserts that his dad can lick any other dad in the neighborhood and that his mother is the prettiest of all. Children assert and sincerely believe that their toys, dolls, sleds, and dogs are better than any other. Children almost unconsciously assume the religious and political beliefs of the family. Doubt and critical analysis do not, at first, appear.

Dad meanwhile takes it for granted that his home town, his automobile, his house, his children, his country club, his political party, and his church are the best, if not in fact perfect. Criticism or analysis is resented. In every automobile accident it is "the other fellow" who is to blame. The bulk of social discussion among adults consists of the defense of views expressed by the individual but for which he has little or no data or knowledge. The belief has never been scrutinized "in view of the grounds which support it."

Egoism is wholly natural with children, since childhood is and can only be egocentric. Pride and self-esteem are valuable in adults, but undue egocentrism carried into adulthood is a form of infantilism and is a serious handicap to the individual and, if widespread, to the social order. Happily, natural growth, increasing experience, and deliberate schooling aid children to modify the characteristics of early childhood and to develop ever more useful characteristics of thinking.

Children are not analytic about their conclusions; nor do they yet have the idea that what they believe must meet the approval of other persons. A conclusion which is pleasant is acceptable; "I like" and "I want" are sufficient bases for belief and action. Events are blamed on causes with which, often, there could be no real connection. The natural egocentrism prevents little children from seeing the "other fellow's side." Persons or events are good or evil, pretty or ugly; gradations must wait upon further experience. Thinking is influenced by juxtaposition in time and space, no matter how accidental. Nonsignificant associations and placement within a pleasant or unpleasant total situation result in judgments on persons, events, and actions as desirable or undesirable. Accusations of "guilt by association" are, however, not confined to childhood!

The conclusion that children cannot think or reason is, however, not justified. Children at any age can solve problems which are real to them and within the limits of their store of meanings, facts, and skills. The thinking at first will lean toward the specific, the concrete, and the nonverbal, but it is nevertheless thinking. Abstractions are difficult for them. Research shows that children at three may manifest the rudimentary beginnings of reasoning. Odd mistakes and "funny remarks" are often greeted with laughter and cited as evidence that children cannot think. Many of these incidents are, in fact, excellent evidence that children do think—and think directly to the point. They do not think as adults do; they are not inhibited by custom and taboo. As stated above they are not sure of the limits of reality; they do not understand cause and effect very well. The funny conclusions are quite justified, however, within the limits of the child's knowledge and skill. Adults constantly voice beliefs and conclusions that are far "funnier" than anything children can achieve—but no one can detect them except an expert in the given field. Thus, much incorrect thinking among adults goes unchallenged.

Part of the argument over children's thinking turns upon definitions of reasoning and problem solving, upon the type of problems often given to children in earlier days. Reasoning in the sense of formal, systematic analysis, using abstractions, stating and developing hypotheses, checking conclusions, does not appear in children's thinking. It does not appear in the thinking of many adults. Children are thought not to reason when, in fact, the problem is quite beyond their levels of maturity and experience.

As a child grows, he plays increasingly with other children. He plays games; he forms friendships; he carries on feuds. He talks with the postman, the delivery boy; he assists his parents. Thus the child is socialized, the egoistic tendencies are modified through social contacts; absolute judgments begin to give way to judgments involving degrees and levels. The immovable objects and irresistible forces of the outside world collide with the developing personality. The real from the unreal is increasingly discriminated. A store of reliable knowledge begins to build up. Eventually he separates events from surrounding circumstances. Let it be noted for the record that social pressures and events in the real world may and often do encourage the irrational and the unjustified conclusion. School training is needed.

Children's thinking begins to take on logical consistency as maturity and life experience modify original tendencies.

1. *Absolute judgments begin to give way* as there is increasing discrimination of degrees and levels, of differences of opinion.

2. *Increasing sensitivity to others* and to the group slowly breaks down egocentrism and purely subjective bases for decision.

3. *Increasing reference is made to the real world;* the real is discriminated from the unreal.

4. *Ability to abstract and generalize increases.*

5. *Relationships* between facts, processes, and persons, particularly of cause and effect, are increasingly understood.

> Increasing ability is seen to separate the accidental and incidental from the real event.

> Increasing ability is seen to discriminate parts from wholes and to handle each for itself.

Immaturity and maturity of thought are not separate, disjunctive levels. One does not end and the other begin at a definite age. Progress from one to the other is gradual, uneven, and irregular, between aspects of thought, and from one individual to another. Not all children are illogical; not all adults are logical. Some children manifest early certain aspects of maturity in remarkable degree; many adults never do. This part of this volume has been developed as a sincere effort to aid development from immature to mature thinking.

Encourage the questioning attitude. Children come to school bubbling with questions about all manner of things. Any item in the environment will set off a barrage of comment and question. In Chapter 3 we stressed the value of encouraging, stimulating, keeping alive the questioning attitude. Curiosity, intellectual and otherwise, is at the root of all thinking.

"Why do high mountains have snow, they are closer to the sun?" "Where does milk come from?" "Why do bees make honey?" "Why doesn't an airplane fall down?" "How do they know it's going to snow tomorrow?" "What does the post office look like behind the windows?" "What do the men back there do?" "How can dirt walls keep back the sea water in Holland?" "What does the janitor do?"

Questions like these may lead into simple or more extended problem-solving and thinking activities. A later chapter will give illustrations of questions and problems raised by older children.

Curiosity, contrary to public opinion, is not a faculty or power; it is a name given to certain tendencies to action. The first manifestation in babies is probably of physiological origin, an urge which drives to the handling, manipulating, exploring, reaching, and "fooling around" so typical of very small children. Curiosity on this level is not intellectual, but without these activities there would be no basis in knowledge for later intellectual endeavors. The second stage is still aimed at facts or knowledge rather than intellectual processes. Children learn they can ask questions in order to find out more than they can by manipulating things. "Why doesn't it bounce?" "What makes it do that?" "What is it?" This is the first stage carried over in the social situation. Causes and relationships are not really the goal, only more facts, more information. Children are often more interested in asking questions than in paying continued attention to explanatory answers. Third, curiosity becomes intellectual when the answers become important. The learner really wishes to know why things happen as they do; in other words, causal relations are sensed. Problems needing answers appear both in the physical and the social worlds. The learner's curiosity is now a factor in learning more than mere information. Answers, furthermore, may not be immediately apparent. A series of relationships may need to be understood, with judgment suspended meantime.

Curiosity, one of the roots of all learning, is easily destroyed through inept teaching. Children may become indifferent to events, may learn not to ask questions, may become flippant, if squelched often enough. Older persons seek security in rigid dogmatism, harshly repressing any interest in new ideas. With still others, curiosity becomes meddlesome interest in the affairs of others, backfence gossip.

Curiosity may also become an intellectual driving force of incredible power. The questioning attitude notable in young children is the same attitude which drives scientists to penetrate the innermost secrets of the universe, sends medical research men on the quest of cures for "incurable" diseases, causes engineers to discover new ways of managing the physical world.

The teacher must respect and keep alive the poking and prying of little children from which knowledge results. Inquisitiveness, asking others, must be encouraged and stimulated until it becomes ability to find out things for oneself, ability to "think up" new hypotheses to be followed. The school must lead "curiosity" over into vital problem solving and more critical inquiry which constitutes thinking.

A store of facts, meanings, and processes must be acquired through direct experience with things, persons, and situations. Preprimary and primary level. Evidence exists showing that thinking based on knowledge and understanding is superior to that based on memorization or upon formulas. The degree of understanding or meaning developed by the learner is related to the kind of instruction given. The type of instruction which enables learners to organize previous experience into meanings is better than other methods. Jersild has said: [2]

> Careful studies of the thinking of children have shown that the chief cause of faulty reasoning on the part of those who are gifted with good intelligence is lack of information; and that the same child may be logical and incisive in reasoning about a question on which he happens to be informed and yet quite illogical in reasoning about another topic on which he happens to be ignorant.

We have noted in earlier discussions that quite a few distinguished scholars, when operating outside their field of specialization, often do just what the children do! They reason quite illogically on topics on which they are not informed.

The nursery school, kindergarten or other preprimary unit, and the early primary should be devoted largely to giving children as many varied experiences as possible with multiple aspects of their environment, not forgetting the social environment. These contacts should be as numerous and as varied as maturity and emotional stability permit.

The process of achieving factual knowledge and meanings, with the beginning of insight into relationship, is a natural one, but it progressively needs guidance. Parents and teachers give this at first; later the learners themselves participate. The first implications are simple. Babies and very small children should be free to wriggle, to squirm, to reach, to kick, to crawl around. A baby explores his world by seizing everything he can get his hands on. He examines, manipulates, destroys, conserves, hides, bites, eats, throws away, steps on, tries to take apart, tastes, listens to all manner of objects. This is one of the most important phases of his life and learning.

Babies learn not only facts and meanings, but they learn about human reactions. They learn to influence human reactions for their own purposes —and this is rudimentary thinking. Chapter 9 on concepts contained an account of some of the details of the process of deriving meanings, and these need not be repeated here. With increasing maturity and experience, children learn to judge, to discriminate, to choose, and to reject. They learn why they sometimes fail, sometimes succeed. They thus learn to take one type of failure in stride, to persist in attacking another type.

Little children learn also many things about the behavior of others and its relation to their own affairs. The acquisition of language speeds the process of learning and thinking. Definitions can be called for; children

---

[2] Arthur T. Jersild, from a speech before the American Psychological Association in Minneapolis, Minn., quoted in *New York Times* (Sept. 4, 1957).

See also:

William A. Brownell, "Problem Solving," *The Psychology of Learning*, Forty-first Yearbook of the National Society for the Study of Education, Part II, Ch. 12, particularly pp. 436-437, and Bibliography, pp. 441-443.

Ernest Horn, "Language and Meaning," *The Psychology of Learning, op. cit.,* Ch. 11 and Bibliography.

can be asked to tell why they believe as they do, can be asked for proof. [3] Eventually engaging in co-operative projects with other children greatly extends their knowledge of persons and their behavior. [4] In upper grades, participatory planning of units and projects gives ample opportunity for exercising all the phases of thinking set forth in Chapters 4 through 12. This is getting ahead of the study however.

Self-expression and creative learning. Early experiences build backgrounds of fact and meaning, to be sure, but the experiences must not be confined to the manipulative. Teachers can guide natural activities toward organization of ideas, toward very simple generalization, toward use of new facts in other situations, toward giving reasons (causes) for certain events. Children should be encouraged to ask questions, to "guess" at what should be done, to seek information in various places. In this way, discovery, creative thinking, and discrimination will be introduced if only on most simple levels. Dramatic play, not too well understood by the layman, is an effective learning device in general, and particularly with certain phases of thinking.

Extension of experience through visits and excursions, and through group planning and discussion. Schools have for long extended children's experience by taking excursions to various places. Visits usually begin with the school and its immediate environment; then come the home neighborhood, the community, and, with older students, more remote regions. City children may visit a farm, rural children various aspects of a city. Visits are common with primary children to the post office, a fire station, a store, an airport. Short trips are made by train. The important thing is that these excursions are not merely for information. A co-operatively planned excursion gives excellent opportunity for the exercise of all aspects of thinking, from locating and defining a problem (reason for going), through questions to be answered, material to be gathered and organized, answers derived and checked. This can begin with very little children and in upper grades attain fairly complex levels.

The process is group discussion rather than imposition by the teacher. This gives additional experience in thinking with others, learning how different individuals react and think, and learning to participate in give and take. The necessity for and methods of compromise are learned. Decision

[3] Good scientific studies exist showing the relation between experience and the meanings, attitudes, and behavior of children. The American studies are listed at various points in Russell's volume, already noted. These studies are also referred to in William H. Burton, *The Guidance of Learning Activities,* 2nd ed. (New York, Appleton-Century-Crofts, 1952), p. 30. Some older foreign studies are listed in William H. Burton and others, *Children's Civic Information,* 1924-1935, University of Southern California Educational Monographs, No. 7. (1936), Ch. 3.

[4] It would be futile to attempt to list here all the materials, pictures, blocks, tools, models, exhibits, animals, plants, pictures, and the like, which should be available in preprimary and early primary. The teacher's guides issued by city, county, and state school systems contain scores of pages dealing with this.

making is explored. Discussion over what was learned and particularly on the validity of inferences drawn from the observations can be very valuable.

Co-operative planning of more extensive projects and units. The processes initiated in preprimary continue throughout school. The details of co-operative unit planning are given in standard texts on teaching. Suffice it to repeat here that ample opportunity is available for all aspects of thinking.

Course of study opportunities for improving thinking in typical subject areas. Generalists cannot presume to discuss details in a wide variety of subject areas. Many excellent volumes are available on the teaching of reading, arithmetic, language, history, geography (or social studies), science, and health. The materials in city, county, and state courses of study or teachers' guides also cover many pages. Reports may be made on these materials with special reference to aiding learners to improve thinking. Our volume can deal with the process of thinking itself.

Specific suggestions for guidance of the thinking process. Suggestions for stimulating and aiding children's thinking all the way from discovering and defining problems to the checking of conclusions have been set forth in copious detail in Chapters 4 through 12. These suggestions will not be repeated here. Instructors and students may wish, however, to make a mimeographed summary for ready reference.

Thinking, as we have seen, uses specific facts, general ideas or concepts, inferential processes. These are stored in the memory in the form of percept, images, concepts, principles, generalizations, and in the form of habits or skills of judgment. These function everywhere in all thinking but particularly in creative, critical, reflective, problem-solving thinking. Children start dealing with all these from earliest years. When should educational guidance begin? Just as early as possible, certainly long before school entrance.

Summary: general principles for guidance of children's thinking. The general principles of learning which serve as guides for teachers hold here as elsewhere. These are available in texts in psychology and on principles of teaching. The following list was made with the guidance of children's thinking in mind.

1. The development of the abilities and skills in thinking should be thought of as a goal of the total school program and not as the outcome of special subjects or projects. The processes of thinking may be generalized and verbalized with older learners, but on lower levels there must be permitted considerable free, personalized, spontaneous procedure.

2. Occasions for thinking will occur most frequently when teachers encourage pupils to raise questions of their own, to evaluate statements by teacher and classmates, to "talk back" as necessary.

Adult authority and demands for conformity reduce the creativity, the critical judgment children use.

Encouragement to present personal problems without fear will stimulate thinking. Admonitions to "think" or "think hard", and other exhortations do not produce thinking.

3. Evidence exists showing that teaching can assist in the development of inquisitiveness, experimentation, and creative production. The problem-solving process can be aided by teaching organized to that end.

4. Occasions calling for thinking must be real to the children, must deal with their purposes and activities, and must be sufficiently diversified to stimulate flexibility and creativity. Imposed or isolated situations are not effective.

5. Occasions for thinking must be related to the learner's maturity, experiential background, readiness.

6. The materials and processes must be within the understanding of the learner, must be available, must be found and identified with reasonable ease.

7. The formal processes of thinking cannot be imposed; they must be discovered and developed by the learner. Balance between conformity and spontaneity will merge at first through the learner's own experiences and may be aided later by direct instruction.

8. A wide range of individual differences in all aspects of the thinking process must be accepted.

9. Varied attacks on problem solving and thinking generally are more effective than following one more-or-less set pattern. Varied experiences are more effective than repetitious experience.

10. Emphasis should be chiefly on developing understanding of the processes and reasons for correctness and not solely on correct response.

11. Assistance should be given not through supplying the right facts, processes, or answer, but through questions and suggested alternatives, calling attention to factors hitherto unnoticed.

Testing solutions in action is one of the best suggested aids and is a cure for verbalizing without sufficient backing.

12. Children need to observe and read widely, but stuffing them with subject matter does not produce thinking.

13. Thinking is affected by numerous factors: motivation, set, social-class mores, peer-group values, teacher personality, the situation, learner's own emotional nature (insecurity, cocksureness, perfectionism, complacency, satisfaction with mediocre work), and own personality factors.

14. Children need time for "thinking it over" (or, with older learners, contemplation); they must search their background, recall similar situations and decisions. They cannot be hurried to immediate decisions.

15. Inability to solve problems in a given area may be caused by weakness in some given aspect of the process, not the total movement: unfamiliar vocabulary, insufficient reading skill, weakness in computation, poor definition of terms and language usage generally, and others. Learners need aid in identifying subsidiary causes of error.

QUESTIONS, EXERCISES, AND REPORTS

1. Illustrate with specific incidents the clear and sharp reasoning often done by very small children. The odd blunders made. Why the blunders?

2. Illustrate types of subject matter and problems given children in early days upon which they could not possibly reason. Early schoolbooks will supply good illustrations.

3. Give specific incidents which you have observed illustrating the five points on page 336. What factors brought about the development in the given cases?

4. Report briefly a case study of some child observed, or some casual observations you have made illustrating the five points on page 338.

5. Explain how the meaning for "curiosity" possessed by most persons and by many teachers is erroneous.

6. What is the significance of the earliest type of curiosity for child rearing? For nursery school and kindergarten?

7. What is the significance of the second level for child rearing? For the elementary school?

8. What is the significance of the third level for child rearing and for schooling? What is the importance of "intellectual curiosity"?

9. How can you tell when children's questions are (sometimes) a show-off device? How handle?

10. Show in some detail how curiosity is discouraged or inhibited. How the alternatives to curiosity develop.

11. An excellent source of suggestions, and of lessons in which critical thinking is an aim definitely provided for, is the teacher's guide or course of study. Report for class analysis some specific illustration from this source.

12. Report for class analysis any lessons or parts of lessons which you have worked out for the express purpose of aiding children to improve their thinking.

READINGS

BINGHAM, Alma, *Improving Children's Facility in Problem Solving* (New York, Teachers College Bureau of Publications, Columbia University, 1958). Well-written, easily read materials for elementary teachers. Slight mixup on place of hypothesis but easily managed.

BLACKWOOD, Paul E., *How Children Learn to Think,* U. S. Office of Education Bulletin No. 10 (Washington, D. C., Federal Security Agency, 1951).

BOLTZ, Jozeph K., and others, *Problem Solving* (Detroit, Mich., Detroit Public Schools, 1956).

GESELL, Arnold, and ILG, Frances L., *The Child from Five to Ten* (New York, Harper, 1946). See also other books by Gesell and associates.

JERSILD, Arthur T., Speech before American Psychological Association in Minneapolis, 1957. In *Proceedings* and also quoted in *New York Times* (September 4, 1957). See also his *Child Psychology.*

MIEL, Alice, and BROGAN, Peggy, *More than Social Studies* (Englewood Cliffs, N. J., Prentice-Hall, 1957).

PIAGET, Jean. See any of several books on children's thought and development by this author.

RUSSELL, David H., *Children's Thinking* (Boston, Ginn, 1956). This is the best over-all summary both on research studies and on classroom operations. Bibliographies are extensive and exhaustive. Special attention to this whole volume is recommended.

SEASHORE, R. H., and VAN DUSEN, A. C., *How to Solve Your Problems* (Chicago, Ill., Science Research Associates, 1950). Deals mostly with problems of older children and adolescents, but much can be applied to younger children.

STRANG, Ruth, *Helping Children to Solve Problems* (Chicago, Science Research Associates, 1953).

SYMONDS, Percival M., "How Do Good Habits of Thinking Begin?" *Childhood Education,* Vol. 23 (1947), pp. 309-314.

THORNDIKE, Robert L., "How Children Learn Principles and Techniques of Problem Solving," in the Forty-Ninth Yearbook of the National Society for the Study of Education, Part I (Chicago, University of Chicago Press, 1950), pp. 192-216.

TREANOR, J. J., "Teaching Pupils to Think," in *The Packet,* Vol. 6 (Boston, Heath, 1951), pp. 22-27.

UPDEGRAFF, Ruth, and KEISTER, M. E., "A Study of Children's Reactions to Failure and an Experimental Attempt to Modify Them," *Child Development,* Vol. 8 (1937), pp. 241-248.

Standard texts in general psychology, child psychology, and educational psychology often have useful chapters on thinking and training for thinking.

Progressive Education issue for March, 1953, is devoted to this topic and contains excellent articles.

Association for Childhood Education, International, 1200 Fifteenth St., N. W., Washington, D. C., often has pamphlets or other short treatments on this topic.

CHAPTER 17

Teaching for Thinking: Language Arts

A list of the vices of reading should put first, as worst and most disabling, the expectation that everything should be easily understood. Things worth thought and reflection cannot be taken in at a glance.

I. A. RICHARDS *

Learn to read slow: all other graces
Will follow in their proper places.
WILLIAM WALKER †

O gracious God! how far have we
Profan'd thy heavenly gift of poesy!
DRYDEN ‡

Words are wise men's counters—they do but reckon by them; but they are the money of fools.
HOBBES §

The scope of conventional English classes. One of the tragic paradoxes of education is that the subject called *English,* which must by definition include every fascinating story or idea expressed by the imaginative mind of man, is regarded by the majority of students as being unendurably boring. Even after twelve grades of pain and boredom the graduates of this system have less than a satisfactory control of expression and understanding of the printed or spoken word. Not that they are any worse off than students of

* I. A. Richards, *How to Read a Page* (New York, Norton, 1942), p. 12.
† William Walker, *The Art of Reading.*
‡ Dryden, "Elegy on Mrs. Killegrew."
§ Hobbes, *Leviathan.*

346

equal capacity fifty or a hundred years ago, but they are still not as well educated in language skills as they ought to be.

What has their experience in English consisted of? Typical moments in an English class are these:

1. Review of "who" and "whom." Half of the class have had this review eleven times before. Half of these will never get it and don't care; the other half got it five years previously and are inexpressibly bored.
2. Rhapsody by the teacher on some questionable piece by Longfellow.
3. Composition. The girls are all writing about "How to bake a cake." The boys, "How to make bookends." All will sooner or later write on "What the American flag means to me."
4. One unhappy student gives an oral report on a book which the other students have not read. Report consists of a plot summary and a recommendation that the others read it.
5. Movie is being shown: "The Tale of Two Cities." This film is twenty years old. The sound track sounds like Bugs Bunny with a cold, and the entire story has been cut to twenty minutes.

Even more tragic is the story of what is not being taught in English classes —the content of this chapter. We believe it is possible to improve the English course of study so that it is more comprehensive than at present and more interesting.

Traditionally the subject of English has been limited to the study of literature and practice in composition with stress on the rules of grammar (in some schools) and on spelling. Occasionally, oral reports are required for training in speech. Ability to read critically has often been asserted by English teachers to be another concern of language instruction, but as Howard Anderson says in the introduction to the 1942 Yearbook of the National Council for the Social Studies: "they have accepted critical thinking in principle without bothering to define the terms precisely or to do much by way of direct instruction to see that this goal was achieved." In terms of the scope of the material read in most English classes, the limitation to literary works seems narrow; a broader view is that English should be the study of language as a means of communication for all kinds of ideas—expository as well as literary.

The view that English should include critical thinking and analysis of expository prose is of special significance to the authors of this book. We believe that in the teaching of literature attention should be directed to the possibilities of literary criticism as a method of increasing understanding and, thereby, appreciation which, after all, is our main objective.

So far in this chapter we have accepted the traditional place of English in the curriculum as an independent subject, as though it were possible to separate language study from the other subject fields which often provide its content. This view of compartmentalized language study is misguided. And whenever language study can be combined with or inserted into other subject areas, such as history, much more profitable study of language will result. In cases where this cannot be done, the organization of English used in this chapter will apply.

To make another reservation, it is obvious that we cannot speak of English as though there were only one grade level, or of English students as though they were all of one level of ability. We do believe that the ideas presented in this chapter are susceptible to modification or simplification to fit most high school grades and pupils. Co-ordination in curriculum construction will ensure that identical material is not repeated in successive grades. Such modifications to grade level and student ability are by our assumption implied throughout the chapter.

OBJECTIVES OF ENGLISH TEACHING

Condensed into three items, the aims of English teaching may be asserted to be:

1. To improve the pupil's ability to express his ideas, both in speech and writing, with clear, idiomatic, and interesting language.
2. To increase the pupil's ability and desire to understand and appreciate literature.
3. To increase the pupil's ability to read or listen to expository material critically and with comprehension.

SPECIFIC CRITICAL ABILITIES IMPLIED BY STATEMENT OF OBJECTIVES

The abilities requisite for understanding and appreciation of literature include:

1. The ability to make critical verdicts about new literature in keeping with some value system.
2. The ability to discern the sense, tone, feeling, intention, and special rhythmic, figurative, and formal effects of poetry.
3. The ability to make valid descriptions of a piece of prose literature, or of dramatic literature.
4. The ability to avoid critical errors, such as critical presuppositions and stock responses.

Broadly speaking, the criticism of expository prose or the composition of it may require any or all of the critical abilities listed in the introductory pages to Part III and developed in Part II. In review these are the abilities: to recognize and define problems, to formulate feasible hypotheses, to handle data reasonably, to recognize reliable experimental method, to draw reasonable inferences, to recognize and appraise assumptions, errors, and fallacies, to come to sound decisions, and to apply semantic principles to the language employed.

ORGANIZATION OF UNITS

Course work designed to train students in these abilities can be arranged in various ways. One possible organization would be the following:

1. *Introductory Unit:*
   a. Semantics
   b. Problem-solving processes (See Chapters 3 through 8 on attitudes, recognition of problems, hypothesis, facts and data, inference, testing solutions.)
2. *Literature Unit:*
   a. Introduction to literary criticism
   b. Examination of various types of literature
3. *Unit on Expository Prose:* newspapers, magazines, books, speeches, possibly propaganda literature
4. *Composition Unit:*
   a. Writing and discussion for Unit 2
   b. Writing and discussion for Unit 3

The ingenuity of the teacher will suggest many other ways of organizing this material, such as the integration of introductory units with presentation of prose and poetic selections, or the intermixture of expository and literary materials. The method of handling composition implied above is that it should be a part of each of the other units, not something separate from the main content of the course.

UNIT 1: INTRODUCTION

If the pupils in a particular English class have never before been exposed to semantics or the other critical ideas described in this book, it may be advisable to spend a few weeks with introductory activities dealing with general critical topics before beginning the expository and literary units. The chapters in this book, Part I, as well as the unit outlines in Appendix D will suggest to the teacher the ideas which he may desire to present to the class.

Semantics, being the science of word meanings, is entirely within the scope of a language course, according to our conviction. The other chapters in Part II of this book are concerned with material which is important in the comprehension of written matter in general. Often it is impossible to say whether a certain problem is linguistic or nonlinguistic, as, for example, the determination of the factual nature of a statement. Adequate treatment of the unit on expository prose would be impossible without some understanding of assumptions, fact-opinion analysis, inference, and common fallacies.

UNIT 2: LITERARY CRITICISM

Some authorities on the teaching of literature stress historical background, chronology, biography of authors, and arrangement of the literature by periods of style. Others, impressed by the social themes in literature, emphasize its sociological implications. These points of view are important and even paramount with some literary works, as, for example, "Old Ironsides" and the didactic effects of Goldsmith's "Deserted Village"; but we would like to urge that special attention be paid to the critical analysis of literature as the focus of method.

Not that we wish to raise a generation of critical gadflies, and we have heard the warning about how it is easier to be a critic than to be correct. But we take our definition from Saintsbury: "Criticism is the endeavor to find, to know, to love, to recommend, not only the best, but all the good that has been known and written in the world." (*A History of Criticism*) Or, in agreement with Cazamian: [1] ". . . it is rightly felt that if the . . . student . . . of literature is to be capable of an intelligent appreciation, he must go beyond the passive enjoyment of what he reads; he must be instructed, partly at least, in the mysteries of the art . . ." In the treatment of all kinds of literature—poetry or prose, lyric, drama, novel, short story, or essay—the first effort should be to understand the meaning of the author and the second to decide whether his product is good.

Understanding requires an examination of the basic meaning of a work, the author's intention, tone, and basic ideas. For each form of literature there are special elements of analysis which aid in the exchange of ideas about the work. For instance, there is the concept of meter in poetry, plot in drama, and focus of narration in novels. The pupils should be made aware of these basic concepts; the terms should be made not an end in themselves but a means to understanding the work under study.

The dangers of excessive analysis and insufficient attention to techniques which encourage appreciation are so great that special warning must be given against formalism in analysis, that is, against the study of analytic terms for themselves and not as an aid to understanding. What we need is a reasonable combination of meaningful explanation—analysis plus all the known devices for inducing appreciation: sympathetic treatment, build-up, sincerity, selection of works appropriate to the age and capacity of the pupils, and proper de-emphasis on examinations. Certain kinds of literature, such as poetry, may require more explanation than others, such as romantic novels. Good judgment on the part of the teacher is essential.

Evaluation of a literary work, a highly subjective undertaking,

[1] Louis Cazamian, quoted in Cleanth Brooks and Robert Penn Warren, *Understanding Poetry* (New York, Holt, 1950), p. xx.

usually proceeds upon the assumption of underlying criteria of literary excellence. Such criteria are realism, interest, success in accomplishment of intention, appropriateness of media, clarity of thought and language, originality and imagination, and avoidance of triteness, sentimentality, and monotony. Dogmatism upon these criteria should be avoided with the utmost care. Each work will of itself suggest what areas of discussion will be most fruitful; no formula can be devised for the evaluation of all kinds of literature.

Intensive reading of the kind recommended by Richards (see introductory quote) is time-consuming. The number of literary works closely examined in a term cannot be very large. This does not mean that every poem or story must be closely analyzed, but it does mean that the amount of literature "covered" will be less than in the ordinary textbook.

Teaching of poetry. Too often from lack of inspiration about methods of presenting poetry, the teacher resorts to such techniques as the counting and names of figures of speech or kinds of meter; "inspirational" and overenthusiastic interpretation; lecturing on historical background with insufficient attention to the verses themselves; nonspecific comment, such as "This poem has beautiful imagery"; concentration on the social message of poetry; or, in general, the superficial treatment of a large number of poems, of which only the titles remain familiar for long.

A sounder point of view is that a relatively small number of poems should be intensively studied. Enjoyment, present and future, is the aim, but this comes through understanding—and understanding through careful analysis—of the many different aspects of poetry, such as sense, feeling, tone (the attitude of the author toward the reader), intention, imagery, metrics, and form. The assumption here is that familiarity does not breed contempt, although the danger of excessive analysis is a real one.

The philosophy of criticism to which we subscribe in the main is that of I. A. Richards. In a series of books about language and literature he presented many ideas which have been adapted in detail and further discussed by others. [2] There is much of Richards' influence in Zahner's *Language in General Education.* [3]

In *Practical Criticism* Richards describes an imaginative experiment he performed at Cambridge University. He had a number of students comment freely upon thirteen poems, authors undisclosed, so that he could analyze their comments. From this analysis Richards produced a list of ten problems in the criticism of poetry:

[2] I. A. Richards, *Practical Criticism* (New York, Harcourt, Brace, 1929); *Interpretation in Teaching* (New York, Harcourt, Brace, 1938); *How to Read a Page, op. cit.*; with C. K. Ogden, *The Meaning of Meaning* (New York, Harcourt, Brace, 1936).

[3] Louis Zahner and others, *Language in General Education* (New York, D. Appleton-Century, 1940).

1. Making out the plain sense
2. The apprehension of sense and feeling
3. Interpretation of imagery
4. Reaction to poetic form
5. Irrelevant association and stock responses
6. Sentimentality
7. Inhibition
8. Doctrinal or dogmatic assumptions
9. Technical presuppositions
10. General critical preconceptions

For further study of these points the reader is invited to peruse Richards' fascinating book.

The best application of critical principles in an anthology to our knowledge is *Understanding Poetry* by Brooks and Warren. [4] This book of poems, organized according to dominant interest in narration, description, metrics, tone and attitude, imagery, or statement and idea, contains some masterful analyses of well-known poems which the English teacher may study with great profit. As an introduction to this book, turn to the devastating criticism of Kilmer's "Trees" or to the sensitive comments on Keats's "Ode to a Nightingale." Here are some excerpts from the critique on "Trees": [5]

This poem has been very greatly admired by a large number of people. The fact that it has been popular does not necessarily condemn it as a bad poem. But it is a bad poem.

First, let us look at it merely on the technical side, especially in regard to the use Kilmer makes of his imagery. . . . The comparison is that of [a] tree to a human being. If the tree is compared to a human being, the reader has a right to expect a consistent use to be made of the aspects of the human being which appear in the poem. But . . . [in] stanza two . . . the tree is metaphorically treated as a sucking babe, and earth, therefore, as the mother. . . . But [in] the third stanza . . . the tree is no longer a sucking babe, but, without warning, is old enough to indulge in religious devotions. But that is not the worst part of the confusion. Remember that the tree is a human being and that in the first stanza the *mouth* of that human being was the root of the tree. But now if the branches are "leafy arms", the tree is a strangely deformed human being.

The fourth and fifth stanzas maintain the same anatomical arrangement for the tree as does the third, but they make other unexpected changes: the tree that wears a "nest of robins in her hair" must be a grown-up person, a girl with jewels in her hair; the tree with snow on its bosom is a chaste and pure girl, for so the *associations* of snow with purity and chastity tell the reader; and the tree that "lives with rain" is a chaste and pure young woman who, although vain enough to wear jewels, is yet withdrawn from the complications of human relationships and lives alone with "nature", i.e., rain, or might be said

[4] Cleanth Brooks and Robert Penn Warren, *op. cit.*
[5] *Ibid.,* pp. 274-278.

to be nunlike, an implication consonant with the religious tone of the poem.

[Kilmer] tries to convey the tree as a babe nursed by mother earth, as a devout person praying all day, as a girl with jewels in her hair, as a chaste woman alone with nature and with God . . . and therefore presents a picture thoroughly confused . . .

But . . . there are other difficulties on the technical side. The rhythm is not well chosen. It is monotonous. Each stanza has the same rhythm, with a full pause at the end of a couplet and no pauses within the lines. The effect is sharp and pert, with no impression of thoughtfulness or of competent control on the part of the poet. This is especially inappropriate for a poem which pretends to treat a serious subject. . . .

> Poems are made by fools like me.
> But only God can make a tree.

This is perfectly true, but by the same line of reasoning God makes the poems too, through his agency in man . . .

But why has the poem been popular if so bad? It appeals . . . to a stock response which has nothing to do, as such, with poetry. It praises God and appeals to a religious sentiment. Therefore people who do not stop to look at the poem itself or to study the images in the poem and think about what the poem really says, are inclined to accept the poem because of the pious sentiment, the prettified little pictures (which in themselves appeal to stock responses), and the mechanical rhythm.

Contained in this persuasive commentary are remarks about imagery, metrics, theme, feeling, and sense. As a guide to topics which may be profitably discussed in the analysis of poetry, the following questions may be used:

What is the author's *intention?* What effect is he trying to create?
What is the plain *sense* of the poem? Can you paraphrase it?
What is the *tone* of the passage?
What is the *feeling?*
What is the *theme?*
Is the *verse form* appropriate to the theme of the poem? Are the variations of *meter* appropriate?
Is the *imagery* effective, consistent enough? Original?
What *sound effects* are intended? Are they successful?
Is the poem sentimental? Convincing? Realistic?

Many of the above considerations are also useful in the analysis of prose.

Teaching of prose literature and drama. Novels and short stories present fewer problems of understanding to high school students than poetry, and the chief stress should be on the enjoyment which students get from their reading. But the meaningfulness and appreciation of narrative literature can be enhanced by the intelligent discussion of its merits. In order for such discussion to proceed in orderly fashion, some common concepts of narrative structure, such as plot, character development, setting, diction, and focus of narration, should be introduced. An excellent reference for this form of literature is Brooks and Warren, *Understanding Fiction.* [6]

Similar principles apply to the treatment of drama. Unenlightened people see a play and walk away, never commenting on it except to say, "Good play," or "I didn't like it." Although we do not aim for shallow dilettantism, it does seem that we can teach a number of our students to conceive interesting thoughts about plays and discuss them with other neocritics. Under the heading "drama" we should include motion picture plays and television plays.

UNIT 3: EXPOSITORY PROSE

If we take the broad view of education, that it should prepare the pupil for civic responsibility and reasonable conduct in society, education must find some way in which to provide training in reading and understanding the mass of expository material which is produced by those who wish to influence the citizen's life. Every day he is faced with newspaper articles and editorials, advertisements, speeches on television, arguments from insurance salesmen, wives, and shopkeepers. In order to vote intelligently, buy wisely, and make sensible decisions on all manner of subjects, the citizen must interpret this mass of expository ideas which he faces. The total of suggestions for handling this material is the subject matter of this entire book, but there are certain linguistic aspects which belong particularly to the field of English, provided we do not arbitrarily restrict language education to literature.

A typical example of expository matter to be dealt with was the "letter to the editor" analyzed in Chapter 1. In the analysis of that letter were included these specifically linguistic considerations: purpose, essential meaning, identification of factual and nonfactual-type statements, tone, emotive language, figurative language, and (lack of) definitions of key terms. These topics should be touched upon in the basic units of any general English course.

A complete analysis of an editorial, for instance, would include the following topics:

1. General purpose, intention of writer.
2. Main point in argument; organization of argument; individual arguments.
3. Analysis of factual-type statements.
4. Assumptions.
5. The means of evaluation used.
6. Fallacies and weak arguments.

[6] Cleanth Brooks and Robert Penn Warren, *Understanding Fiction,* 2nd ed. (New York, Appleton-Century-Crofts, 1959).
Cleanth Brooks and R. B. Heilman, *Understanding Drama* (New York, Holt, 1942).

7. Language, consistent definition, tone.
8. Conclusion adequately supported; could conclusion be supported by arguments not presented in article; possible arguments not used?

Details and subpoints under the eight statements were included in Chapter 15, pages 320-322, and in Ch. 17, page 353, and are not repeated here.

Some kinds of prose are so complex and full of abstractions that it is necessary to translate them into simpler language before they can be fully understood. This process is extremely rewarding as an exercise by itself on passages of real importance. An example of such analysis is given in *How to Read a Page* by I. A. Richards. Richards and C. K. Ogden have developed a vocabulary of primary words called "basic English," 850 words with which nearly any passage of English can be translated. [7] The use of this vocabulary requires much time and hard work, especially in the beginning. But the practice of rephrasing difficult bits of language is not without merit. For example, a complex sentence can be broken down into simpler English as in the following sentence from Carlyle, *On Boswell's Life of Johnson:*

"The stupendous Fourth Estate, whose wide world-embracing influences what eye can take in?"

Translated (not in basic English), the sentence means something like this:

"Newspaper writers print their ideas in papers which many people read and because of which they change their ways of acting. The extent of these changes is greater than we can understand."

Such paraphrasing compels the reader to search for the basic meaning of a passage and gives insight into language usage in general.

Specific activities. Specific procedures for training students to handle expository matter includes long- and short-term units on the analysis of publications, such as newspapers, magazines, and pamphlets; the frequent examination of letters, speeches, editorials, commercials, articles, and other prose types of language; intensive reading of difficult passages; and the study of controversial material in the line of propaganda.

If a term project is required, it can be designed to fit the critical aims of the course. A sample prescription for a term paper assigned in a combined course in English and U. S. history at Long Beach, California, was worded as follows:

1. *Topic:* Select some currently important political, economic, or social problem connected with United States history or government.
2. *Treatment:*
   a. Analyze the problem and its history.
   b. Describe possible solutions.

[7] C. K. Ogden, *Basic English* (London, K. Paul, Trench, Trubner, 1930).
I. A. Richards, *Basic English and Its Uses* (New York, Norton, 1943).

    c. Give a critique of at least one article or book on the subject. In-
    clude enough of the criticized selection to permit the reader to
    appraise your critique.
    d. Give your solution to the problem.

An interesting and profitable activity is to make a study of the local
newspapers on the basis of their political bias, editorial policies in general, selection of news items, views of columnists, tenor of letters to the
editor, nature of feature articles, and so forth. A similar analysis of news
magazines is valuable. This could be a long-term unit or concentrated in
two weeks.

Much material for analysis of point of view is easily available through
such organizations as:

    The United States Chamber of Commerce (and local chambers also)
    The National Association of Manufacturers
    Various trade organizations; house organs
    The American Federation of Labor (and the C.I.O. separately or in con-
      junction with the others)
    Local labor union papers

What is their general attitude on questions of public interest, government
regulation, social security, foreign aid, government spending, and the like?
Do they use straight news techniques, or are propaganda devices easily
observable?

The resolutions adopted at the annual conventions may be obtained
from such organizations as:

    The American Association of University Women
    The Daughters of the American Revolution
    The American Association of University Professors
    The American Legion
    The Veterans of Foreign Wars
    The National Education Association
    The Taxpayers Association

These documents make interesting subjects for analysis, particularly if
they happen to be on the same subject, as, for instance, when the AAUW
and the DAR make resolutions on similar topics.

If the teacher desires to go into propaganda analysis as a distinct
unit, there is much material readily available. The scope of propaganda
study is broadened if the following definition is adopted:

Propaganda is any planned attempt to influence the opinion of groups
of people toward some preconceived end. Usually the word *propaganda* is
taken in a narrower sense as an improper attempt to sway opinions in an
undesirable direction. The seven tricks of the propagandist, as described
by the Institute for Propaganda Analysis in the 1930's, were:

1. Name calling. (Compare the *ad hominem* argument.)
2. Glittering generality. (Various inductive fallacies appear.)
3. Bandwagon tactics. Adopting winning causes. (*Ad populum* and others.)
4. Card-stacking. Withholding negative evidence. (Inductive fallacies, withholding evidence, and other devices for tampering with the facts.)
5. Transfer. Influence by association of ideas.
6. Testimonials. Mostly biased.
7. Plain folks. (Compare *ad populum*.)

Our opinion about these devices is that they are too broad in application and that the fallacies listed in Chapter 11 are more precise in definition. But the propaganda study is interesting and provides a different approach to the same problems.

UNIT 4: COMPOSITION

Content. It is a commonly expressed objective of English teaching that the students should learn how to express themselves clearly and according to current standards of usage, both in written and spoken language. It is equally common to hear complaints that this objective is not attained. Such complaints are not new. One continuing cause of failure to teach composition adequately is that stress in English courses has more often been on form than on content. In spite of complaints to the contrary, thousands of patient English teachers spend hours correcting spelling and punctuation, but lack a technique for correcting content. It hardly needs to be argued that what is said in a paper is more important than the way in which it is said, provided an important topic is being discussed. Here again is a difficulty. The topics set for composition are often trivial or uninteresting.

As far as topics for composition are concerned, important subjects can be found within the area of literary criticism or criticism of expository writing. An example of an exercise in composition is to give students a poem or editorial to study and to comment upon. Then, according to the type of subject, criteria for correction and guidance of content can be taken from the topics for analysis listed in Units 2 or 3 above.

In the case of literary criticism, it is unwise to insist upon a particular interpretation or valuation of a piece of literature, but after a few weeks of instruction on the characteristics of different kinds of literature, we can expect the student at least to *mention* something about such elements as the sense, form, imagery, and intention of a piece of writing.

Form. Considerable attention has been paid in recent years to the artificiality and inadequacy of classical grammar—"Incomprehensible abstractions, pretentious yet for the most part empty definitions, false rules,

indigestible lists of forms . . . sins against reason, truth, and education. . . ." [8]

Every English teacher knows the difficulty of teaching the elementary
parts of speech. "A verb shows action. Why isn't *explosion* a verb?" asks
the innocent pupil. Concepts with difficult Latin nomenclature like "ap-
position" are introduced merely to establish a name for a rule of the
comma. [9]

Another grievance against grammar teaching is that in the traditional
school the rules of grammar are often taught apart from actual composition
or use. Naming the parts of speech sometimes becomes an end in itself.
The exercises in grammar books are uniformly dull and disconnected. And
research has shown that the correlation between mastery of grammar rules
and the actual control of proper English is remarkably low. [10]

Enough verbal bloodshed has been spilled in both educational and
nonliterate circles (how to teach English is a popular subject with provincial newspaper editors) that we would like to dodge further discussion of
the subject except to point out that if grammar is defined as the study
of systematic peculiarities of language and its usage, it is impossible to discuss language structure without entering the realm of grammar. If this is
done, however, it seems clear that it should be done in what is called a
"functional" way, that is, in connection with actual writing done by the
students or considered by the class.

From the point of view of critical analysis of language, there are
certain important qualities of language structure which may be called
logical syntax, that is, the interrelationship of words considered from a
logical rather than a grammatical point of view. In Chapter 7 on inference,
we have already spoken of the kinds of propositions which assert something, of conditional sentences, and of alternation. *Conditional* is a common grammatical term which takes on special significance in logic. *Alternation* is a rare word in grammar but an important one in logic.

In Chapter 6 on facts, we have distinguished between *factual* and
nonfactual sentences. From a formal point of view, the two types might
be identical, but from a critical viewpoint they differ greatly.

In Chapter 10 on words, we have talked about the *neutral* and
emotive qualities of sentences, of symbols and referents. Also in this
chapter were words like *abstract, concrete, theoretical construct.* Such
terms could be the basis for a grammar of content rather than form. As

---

[8] Ferdinand Brunot, "L'Enseignement de la Langue Française," p. 3, translated
and quoted by I. A. Richards in *The Meaning of Meaning, op. cit.,* p. 251.

[9] See also Hans Reichenbach, *Elements of Symbolic Logic* (New York, Macmillan, 1947), Ch. 7.

[10] For a useful treatment of grammar see Robert C. Pooley, *Teaching English
Grammar* (New York, Appleton-Century-Crofts, 1957).

yet, such a vocabulary has not been developed, but the possibility deserves careful consideration. If such a movement ever takes place, care should be observed that it does not degenerate into a formalistic discipline, as grammar did.

The matter of "usage" should be handled in a sensible way and consistently with the semantic principles outlined in Chapter 10. The teacher should explain about levels of usage, about the changing norms of language and not insist that language is either "correct" or "incorrect" according to the dictate of the grammar books of fifty years ago, which in turn were based on the usage of the day. When usage is treated intelligently and is well explained, it becomes more interesting and fits in with the analytical study of language development.

EVALUATION

Evaluation of progress in critical reading is difficult to make, but there are several standardized tests on the market which will aid the teacher.

To test the achievement of pupils in the critical-thinking abilities of consistency of opinion, logical reasoning, sound inference, correct generalization, discrimination in argument, and evaluation of arguments, there is the Watson-Glaser Critical Thinking Appraisal. [11]

For testing interpretation of literature there is the Co-operative Literary Comprehension and Appreciation Test. [12] It will be described in Chapter 21. In terms of our language arts problem, this test is designed to test nine of the critical abilities which we have described in this chapter following suggestions by I. A. Richards.

There are other tests available, such as the Eight-Year Study Evaluation tests and the Co-operative Reading Comprehension test. See Chapter 21 on tests of critical thinking.

Naturally, if the teacher is interested in finding out whether the class has made progress during the term, he will want to give pretests and posttests and compare results.

A simple but less objective kind of test is to give the students at the beginning of the year a poem to react to, an editorial to analyze, or a story to read, and to compare their writing then with a similar exercise at the end of the year. Such a procedure has been carried out with encouraging results by one of the authors.

[11] Goodwin Watson and Edward M. Glaser, *Watson-Glaser Critical Thinking Appraisal* (Yonkers, N. Y., World Book, 1952).

[12] Hyman Eigerman, Mary Willias, and Frederick B. Davis, *Co-operative Literary Comprehension and Appreciation Test* (Princeton, Co-operative Test Service, 1941).

EXERCISES

1. List some common practices in English teaching which need revision.

2. Suggest alternative organization of course content from that on p. 349.

3. Select an editorial, and analyze it according to outline in chapter.

4. Suggest alternative specifications for term paper.

5. Answer questions in Cleanth Brooks and Robert Penn Warren, *Understanding Poetry* (New York, Holt, 1950), pp. 138, 203.

6. Devise intelligent questions for one of the poems in Brooks and Warren, Section viii.

7. Construct analytic questions to guide the study of *Hamlet*.

8. Compose specifications for a book review which would oblige students to do more in the critical line than merely summarize the plot and list the characters.

9. Analyze editor's point of view, and show shortcomings in the following editorial:

Fading Standards

Once there was a time when school teachers were particularly earnest that youngsters committed to their charge learn the difference between what was right and what might be passable but wrong.

That was before the advent of the theory of "usage" which holds there are no standards of good or bad English, only "levels" of usage appropriate to the occasion and atmosphere in which one finds himself at a given moment.

The depth to which this doctrine has penetrated education may be illustrated by a story in the *Detroit Free Press* in which the writer tells of a reader who sent him a letter she received from a firm of educational publishers.

The letter was written in response to the reader's objection to the use of "can" for "may" in the conversation used in her daughter's second-grade textbook.

"Our writers and editors," the firm replied, "think it advisable to observe, throughout the Basic Readers, the normal patterns of everyday speech. Particularly when a child is first mastering the reading process, they feel that the words he finds in print should be familiar and follow patterns of his daily conversation.

"It has been the observation of grammarians for a long time that in cultivated English "can" has been replacing "may". . . . If our primary-grade books use only "may," we feel the children would get an artificial usage of the word, and most of the pupils would eventually use "can" in spite of the textbook.

"Of course, these questions have different aspects at high school level. There one can teach students how our language has developed and can discuss with them what standards of usage they wish to adopt."

The implications of the explanation are, of course, ridiculous. In effect, it is suggested, children should be permitted to speak ungrammatically for a dozen years and then, when they reach high school, they will be told the difference between "can" and "may" and will be asked to vote on the way they care to speak English.

Reading (Pennsylvania) *Eagle,* July 5, 1959

10. Answer the questions and exercises at the end of the following "Letter to the Editor":

He Wants Facts, Not Opinions

Editor:

It would be interesting to hear some statement of fact instead of opinion as to the wisdom of our being in the U.N.

Opinions can be limitless in number, and controversial. Facts are few, and the undisputed basis for action.

Opinions can be contradicted—facts cannot.

Some facts are that the U.N. is costly to us; it allows representatives of Russia, our most dangerous potential enemy, to be in our country; it cannot prevent or stop wars; and it weakens us by our being a member of an organization whose members are opposed in principles and beliefs.

If we stay in the U.N. much longer we will be in the same predicament we are in now as regards to social security, income tax deduction (not reduction) strikes using pickets and other violations of American principles, i.e., we will not know how to act otherwise.

An individual is stronger than any group whose members must oppose any of their individual beliefs in order to abide by those of the group.

R. J.

    a. Which of the following propositions from the above letter are factual and which are statements of opinion?

        (1) ". . . the U.N. is costly to us. . . ." (line 6)

        (2) "[the U.N.] allows representatives of Russia . . . to be in our country. . . ." (lines 6, 7)

        (3) "[Russia is] our most dangerous potential enemy. . . ." (line 7)

        (4) ". . . it cannot prevent or stop wars. . . ." (line 8)

        (5) ". . . it weakens us by our being a member of an organization whose members are opposed in principles and beliefs." (lines 9, 10)

    b. Does the writer of this letter have a clear conception of the distinction between fact and opinion? What are the distinctions?

    c. In line 6, what is the meaning of the word *costly?*

    d. Which of the statements in Question *a* are value judgments and which predictions?

    e. What implicit assumptions are contained in this letter?

    f. Does the last paragraph make any sense at all?

    g. What does the writer consider to be "American principles" in line 14?

    h. Rewrite this letter taking the same viewpoint as the writer, but distinguish carefully between factual matters and matters of opinion.

    i. Reply to this letter, taking a different point of view.

11. The following paragraphs are taken from a letter which appeared in

the *Portland Oregonian* in March, 1959, written by Evelyn Marks Burke, and quoted by permission of the publishers.

> . . . we also had the opportunity to hear straight from the lips of the former national president of the NEA, why many of today's students lack a proper knowledge of their own English language— even after graduation from high school and in some cases even college.
>
> It was stated that at one time English was taught by the learning and application of specific rules, with failure resulting if passing grades were not attained. With the advent of "progressive" education, learning of rules was relegated to the background or abandoned entirely, and emphasis was placed on the passing of every student regardless of how little he or she knew. It was assumed that English could be learned incidentally.

The "former national president of the NEA," Miss Martha Shull, kindly supplied a typed copy of her remarks with permission to quote:

> Theories have changed from time to time. Once I was reproved for having too few failing grades. We used to drill like mad on subordinate clauses of cause, purpose, result, etc. More recently we have tried to have no failures and have taught grammar quite indirectly. Now we are somewhere between the two extremes. But through all the changes in emphasis we have had one major concern; how can we best help *everyone* to develop *all* his potentialities?

How might you account for Mrs. Burke's misinterpretation of Miss Shull's remarks? Develop several points in some detail.

12. A number of interesting experiments have been made in the field of aesthetic judgment. Advanced college classes were used in which students had had considerable experience with this type of judgment. Their likes and dislikes for a number of major poets were well known.

One experiment used a number of passages from the same writer but with many of the verses attributed to other writers. Many of the students made judgments which correlated more highly with their previously expressed likes and dislikes of the several authors than with their views on the real author.

Another experiment reversed this and used passages from several writers but attributed them all to one well-known poet. Students were asked to say in which cases this author had done his best and his poorest writing. Students who had an appreciation for this writer could not distinguish any great differences, evaluations being from "fair" and "pretty good" to "very good." Students who did not particularly appreciate this writer judged the selections in terms of their attitude and did not recognize or distinguish between verses written by others.

What is the explanation? This is a simple case, but the factor involved could be quite serious in political, economic, or social affairs. Illustrate.

13. A statement of the desirable aims for labor, originally prepared by an eminent and respected labor leader, was circulated among lesser leaders and the rank and file union members. The statement, however, was labeled as having been made by a nationally known capitalist and industrialist.

Several labor men agreed somewhat reluctantly that it was a sound and desirable statement of the aims of labor. Others condemned it in varying terms, a few doing so very harshly as a "smoke screen by some———owner or representative of management."

Again, what is the explanation? Possible methods of curing such blunders?

Illustrate from everyday affairs.

READINGS

All references used in this chapter are in the footnotes. These are not repeated here in order to save space.

CHAPTER 18

Teaching for Thinking: Social Studies

> I am aware of the difficulty of establishing in these fields (the social disciplines) rigorous criteria for competence and qualification. Nevertheless, at a time when the whole world realizes that many of its most vital problems depend upon an understanding of human behavior . . . and of the regularities which underlie the operations of our varied society, we should recognize the great benefits which may come from attracting men and women of prominence to the study of these questions.
>
> DR. J. R. OPPENHEIMER
>
> Politics is harder than physics.
> EINSTEIN

The remarks by Einstein and Oppenheimer are of profound significance for all education, particularly for education in critical thinking.

The layman tends to think of physics, mathematics, astronomy, and the like as extremely difficult areas. Students in secondary school and college tend to avoid them. The laymen and certain physical scientists also tend to look down on the social sciences as being "easy." Certain misconceptions may be at work here.

The physical scientists insist on precision, statistical reliability, controlled observations, predictability—and rightly so. Mathematics and physics deal with abstractions and with complex relationships among abstractions. Abstractness and complexity, together with possible poor teaching on lower levels may be responsible for the reputation of difficulty. No one denies the difficulty of these fields, but imposition of abstractions on little children in advance of maturity, and later upon college students similarly, is by no means uncommon. This contributes to the reputation for difficulty. Imposition of this type clearly interferes with insight and growth.

364

The materials of the physical sciences are far more stable than those of the social fields; facts and principles do stay put; their operations can be relied upon. This is true of closed systems, and particularly for everyday uses of these fields. Scientific thought on the frontiers of knowledge, on the creative level, is another story, but the average citizen does not reach that level. Physical scientists can and do, however, make a serious scientific error in ridiculing the partial findings and the new terminology of the emerging social disciplines. It is not easy to systematize the human equation. The materials in these fields are far, far less stable than in the physical sciences. Criteria are very difficult to establish. Facts and principles that will "stay put" do not come easily. The history of the physical sciences—for instance, chemistry and astronomy—show that the same groping and blundering appeared when they were on comparable levels of maturity with social sciences of today.

Human relations, the vastly intricate interplay of human thinking and motives, the interrelations between people from neighborhood to the world, cannot be reduced to formula. We need not here take space to note the considerable progress which has been made in getting increasing reliability, validity, and predictability when dealing with problems wholly within the social fields. Politics, economics, anthropology, sociology, group dynamics, comparative religion, psychiatry, and others are developing respectable bodies of information.

The study of human personality, of the conventions of civilized society, of the difficulties which men get into while trying to organize their lives together cannot be handled on a slide rule, or by perfectly controlled experiments, but suitable methods are arising. Critical thinking in these areas may have critical bearing on societal survival. Einstein and Oppenheimer among the physical scientists have been quoted. The late Ortega y Gassett of Madrid, Pitirim Sorokin of Harvard, and numerous other social scientists agree on this.

We need not engage in arguments as to the relative difficulty of physical and social sciences. We may be very emphatic, however, in saying that he who is unaware of or decries the difficulty of politics, human relations, and the social sciences generally is guilty of a serious and perhaps dangerous blunder.

The social studies a dynamic and emergent field. The emergent status of the field is revealed through the very large literature available on everything from ultimate aims to visual aids. Variation in the worth of this material is very great. Some is sharp and clear, some mediocre, and some plain muddled. Ample discussion, fortunately, is available in systematic presentations by competent writers.

New trends in content. The more traditional courses still show their origins in the social sciences, being largely adaptations from history, geography, civics, economics, and sociology. Today there are trends not only toward fused or integrated content but toward new areas. A few illustrative new areas are:

Community resources and use

Health and housing of the population

Regional studies of resources, problems, possible developments

Intercultural relations between nations and races

Foreign policy of the United States; United Nations; NATO; aid or trade

Consumer education

Newspapers and magazines, their objectivity in reporting, policy or slant, subservience to or freedom from special interests, and many other items

Advertising, facts or lack of them; special pleading, misleading or informative; relation to policies of publications carrying the advertising material

Propaganda, methods, clues for detection, methods of counteraction

World government and national interest

Pressure groups and lobbying

The effects of colonialism and exploitation; effect of breakup of modern empires

Many others could be listed.

Objectives of the social studies in elementary and secondary schools. Statements are available in great number in texts and in teaching guides. They vary from hopelessly vague, through mere adaptations of the aims of general education, to well-organized statements specifically related to the field. Lists below are illustrative only. General objectives include such things as:

To broaden and deepen informational background of student through introduction to cultural heritage and to current materials

To introduce principles and facts relating to the social studies through studying such areas as:

a. Man's relationship to the environment, physical and social

b. The development and status of the institutions of society, political, social, economic

To develop democratic values, processes, and attitudes

To develop the values, principles, attitudes, and skills of democratic citizenship, (includes everything from voting and civil liberties, to protective tariffs, to social welfare, to international relations)

To develop the ability to think critically in the social fields (This includes the types of problems and processes presented in Parts I and II of this volume)

More specific objectives include:

To develop alertness to problem of values, types, and alternative systems

To develop skill in determining what happened in historical problems and also in current controversies

To recognize that there will usually be more than one possible and plausible solution in problems involving groups.

To recognize problems which call chiefly for critical analysis

Critical thinking as aim. Critical thinking, the chief concern of our volume, is listed as a prime objective by writers in the social studies. Critical thinking, furthermore, undergirds practically all of the other aims, particularly citizenship, and the determination of one's beliefs and policies about social problems. Textbooks and teacher's guides which give any detail about critical thinking outline in general the processes we have presented in Part II of this volume.

Cogent observations are made on this point by Dressel and Mayhew: [1]

Little was being done to teach critical thinking . . . Attempts to teach critical thinking in social science by making minor changes in particular courses did not appear to result in greater growth than was found in courses not making overt attempts to teach this skill. Observations of classes and interviews with students suggest that students in typical humanities courses read assignments from textbooks, and then come to class either to listen passively to a teacher tell them *about* some work of art or to listen to or see a work about which they have studied . . . If the objectives of increased participation, analytical ability, or genuine appreciation are valid, then the way the humanities courses are conducted must be judged inadequate.

CURRICULAR IMPLICATIONS OF CRITICAL-THINKING THEORY

The inescapable ramifications and interrelationships of any problem or topic in the social sciences are such that curriculum and methods are inevitably affected. Questions, problems, and assignments cannot be confined to any one delimited area. The early correlated, fused, or unified curriculums were efforts to meet this situation. Today there is good effort to combine social studies and English (for instance), or to have a social studies core curriculum, or to insert social studies into a total core organized on other bases. Many interrelationships between fields will be apparent as we suggest topics and problems in the following pages.

SUGGESTED PROCEDURES FOR TEACHING CRITICAL THINKING IN THE SOCIAL STUDIES

The earlier that students can be brought into contact with the details of thinking in its various manifestation, the better. Units on problems or topics involving content which permits emphasis upon stating problems carefully, collecting data, noting semantic fallacies, and other similar factors should appear as early as possible. The following problem units on probing

[1] Paul L. Dressel and L. B. Mayhew, *General Education: Explorations in Evaluation* (Washington, D. C., American Council on Education, 1954), pp. 67, 170-171.

prejudice and on the detection of propaganda will, we hope, illustrate this procedure.

1. GIVE SPECIFIC UNITS ON CRITICAL THINKING, THAT IS, SEMANTICS, COLLECTION OF DATA, FALLACIES, AND OTHERS.

Propaganda. The literature on this is enormous and widely ramified. Several units can be organized with ease. Do not stop with identifying the typical devices of propaganda, an error made by many students of propaganda. Make wide application of the devices and principles derived from the literature. Material is available on every hand—books, including fiction, editorials, columns, news, letters to the editor, reviews, speeches, sermons, pamphlets, and many others. The analysis, for instance, of the book *McCarthy and the Communists* reveals that both McCarthy and the Communists were guilty of using the same devices: [2]

The multiple untruth	Attributing significance to the
The abuse of documents	irrelevant
Insinuation and innuendo	The bluff and diversionary gambit
The slander amalgam	The personal spy network
Intimidation	Contempt for the law
	The unfounded charge of treason

Another enlightening device is to examine the typical propaganda devices in the light of logical errors and fallacies. These were listed on page 357 of Chapter 17.

Use specific books, editorials, or other materials as a base for these comparisons.

Probing prejudice. Again the literature is voluminous and easily available. The volume *Probing our Prejudices,* by Hortense Powdermaker, an older discussion, is an excellent starting point. [3] It contains good questions, text adapted to secondary school students, and a list of sources for good pamphlets. Dealing with prejudice will lead into valuable related fields such as anthropology, racial myths, race and culture, race and biology, as well as the psychology of prejudice in immediate instances. The psychology of attitudes, learning and unlearning them, can be studied in some detail.

Scapegoating may be studied easily in connection with prejudice. There is a small literature, but much of it is valuable. The pamphlet, *The A B C's of Scapegoating,* published by the Central Y.M.C.A. College, 19 South La Salle Street, Chicago, Illinois, and undated, supplies an excellent start. A small selected bibliography is included. Another pamphlet, *They Got the Blame,* contains an excellent brief history of scapegoating with illustrations and a good bibliography. [4]

[2] James Rorty and Moske Decker, *McCarthy and the Communists* (Boston, Beacon Press, 1954).
[3] Hortense Powdermaker, *Probing Our Prejudices* (New York, Harper, 1944).
[4] Kenneth M. Gould, *They Got the Blame* (New York, Association Press, 1942).

Rumor, its nature and danger. This makes another excellent study in the general field of human relations, news reporting, and critical thinking. A first-class analysis with many experimental demonstrations which a group may utilize is found in *The Psychology of Rumor.* [5] The bibliography is good up to the date of publication.

An excellent illustration of rumor attached to a specific situation is found in *Far Corner,* by Stewart Holbrook, an Oregon historian. [6] The chapter "The Dead Were Stacked Like Cordwood" deals with the flood disaster at Vanport, Oregon, on May 30, 1948. City and county officials stated during the actual disaster at Vanport, "the buildings were clogged with bodies—many swept down river—total dead may never be known." One story widely circulated held that 457 bodies had been secretly shipped to Japan to be returned later as Army dead, thus covering up the size of the disaster. Oregon newspapers pursued this rumor with every facility at their command and found—nothing. The facts were that 15 were dead with no one missing or unaccounted for! The confusion, sorrow, and expense caused by senseless rumor were local in this instance but illustrate what can happen on a national scale.

Two students in a group studying such things with the writer decided to try out an idea. They stopped one student in front of the library and made a casual remark to him and spoke to no one else. The remark was that there would be "no more trains running out of town after nine P.M. *tonight.*" This was the truth; there were never trains after nine P.M. any night. Wartime Shortage of fuel had already curtailed rail service widely, thus sensitizing communities to the possibility of further curtailment. By seven o'clock that evening the college and the town were in an uproar with frantic long distance calls being made to state officials and transportation executives throughout the area. Frightened at the results, the two students confessed to the instructor, but it took several days to get things back to normal.

These illustrations, as stated, are but a drop in a bucket. Units are available in all fields in enormous number. The genius of the teacher will select those which have important cultural and informational benefits as well as opportunities for the continuous exercise of critical thinking.

2. Organizing a part of the course into problem units furnishes a helpful basis for teaching critical thinking.

Our analysis of thinking presents problem solving as a major phase of thinking, together with policy making and critical analysis. Courses in social studies organized at least in part around problems, real and vicarious, afford some of the best opportunities for training critical thinking. *Ordi-*

[5] Gordon W. Allport and Leo Postman, *The Psychology of Rumor* (New York, Holt, 1947).

[6] Stewart Holbrook, *Far Corner* (New York, Macmillan, 1952).

narily, problems should be real and pertinent to the lives of students. This is possible only in some areas—for instance, problems of childhood and youth. Needs growing out of the physical, intellectual, and emotional development of maturing children will furnish any number of real problems. [7]

The subject areas may also be used as sources of real problems, though not if taught under the traditional assign-study-recite procedure. The best guidance toward finding real problems in subject areas is in modern teacher's guides from kindergarten on. Many contain suggestions for getting inventories of problems in given subjects. The social studies area under discussion here is an excellent source of real problems. This will be analyzed further a few paragraphs below.

Artificial problems are not desirable if they remain artificial, unreal, and uninteresting to students. Some teachers, however, manifest considerable genius in developing artificial problems which "catch on" with the students who get good experience in critical thinking as well as information.

Long-term and short-term problems, projects, units. Many teachers favor carrying a few semester units in two or three major fields such as foreign policy of the United States, civil liberties problems, taxation policies (local, state, or national), transportation, and the like. Other teachers favor a larger number of smaller units.

A basic reason exists for utilizing long-term units, perhaps supplemented by several shorter ones. First, certain problems are so complex and materials so voluminous that they cannot be handled in a short unit. Second, some problems are developing day by day—for instance, as this is written, United States policy on Germany—so that new material for study emerges daily. The maturity and experiential background of the learner, the available resources, and the skill of the teacher, all affect choice of procedure.

Problems that cannot be answered. Objection is raised by many to certain areas and to certain specific problems in the social studies on the ground that the students cannot possibly solve them or act on the findings if they do get solutions. As for that, neither can their parents solve these problems, nor the state legislature, nor the courts, nor any other organization of adults. Constant study and effort over many years are necessary.

[7] See for illustration:

Ross L. Mooney, "Exploratory Research on Students' Problems," *Journal of Educational Research* (Nov., 1943), pp. 218-224.

Miles E. Cary, "Looking at Teen-age Problems," *Journal of Home Economics* (Dec., 1948), pp. 575-576.

W. H. Remmers and Benjamin Shimberg, *Examiner Manual for the SRA Youth Inventory* (Chicago, Science Research Associates, 1949), pp. 15-20.

Bruce Grant, "Problems of Freshmen in the Antelope Valley Joint Union High School." Unpublished but summarized in Grant's "Survey of Research Studies on Problems of Adolescents," *California Journal of Secondary Education* (May, 1953), pp. 293-297. Commentary on other recent studies also.

See also recent texts on childhood, youth, problems of learning.

The democratic nations were a long time in solving, and then only in part, the evils of unjust imprisonment and punishment by authoritarian rulers. Trial by jury and voting by the public on highly technical issues were solutions of early evils, but they now again need further study and new solutions. Civil liberties is an area in which solutions are still being sought. As this is written, the problem of school integration in the South is in process of being solved. Legal processes, social pressures, public discussion, police power, and mob violence have all been called in.

The important point is that individuals will never be able to solve this type of problem unless they get practice. People hardly ever solve difficult problems at the first approach. Solutions for some social problems which are current cannot be derived under present conditions and knowledge. Compromise and tentative working decisions are all that are possible by any group on any level. Another reason for using these problems in school is that students get practice in gathering pertinent information from different sources, in critical evaluation, and in making conclusions. Oddly enough, some critics of the schools which use these problems assert that students discuss them in an informational and conceptual vacuum. They seem to ignore the fact that informational and conceptual vacuums can be filled only through practice in gathering information and in developing concepts.

The real danger in discussion of these problems is that unskillful teachers may lead students to believe that such problems can be solved on the basis of superficial examination or, worse, that they can be solved at all without long, expert, analysis, and continuing reorientation.

A very few samples of such problems are given here:

Is lobbying a justifiable practice in local and national legislatures?

What are the facts about our foreign policy? About foreign aid?

Is a sales tax desirable, either in itself or as an offset to income taxes?

What problems and tensions persist in our society because of our transition from an agricultural to an industrial economy?

What advantages and what evils have attended the great growth of the cities?

To what extent are moral standards changing in our society? What are the reasons for this? Are the changes all, none, or partially good or bad?

What effect has the industrial system had on family life?

What is going on in China? Should we recognize Red China?

Should there be a pooling of world resources?

What is the relation between population, food supply, and birth control?

What might be the effects of peacetime use of atomic energy?

What is the relation between churches, Sunday school attendance, and delinquency in a given community?

What are the advantages of the free enterprise system? Evils that need correction?

Should we study socialism or communism in the schools?

Are the current criticisms of the school justified, wholly, partially, not at all? (Failure to teach the 3 r's; inability to maintain discipline; progressive education as cause of the evils; homework lacking).

Is membership in the United Nations and NATO in the national interest?

Big government, big business, and big labor often interfere with the free working of the law of supply and demand. Take several specific instances, and try to determine the advantages or evils.

What are the facts about U. S. foreign policy in regard to Red China? With regard to travel in Red China by U. S. newspapermen? With regard to recognition and trade? With reference to Formosa?

What are the facts about U. S. policy with reference to Berlin? In regard to internal disorders in Latin America? Foreign aid? Aid versus trade? Foreign alliances: farm subsidies and surplus products?

These problems are certainly not solvable by students at any level or, as has been said, by adults. But they must be given attention, must be under constant study, or certain evils will never be corrected, certain important social benefits never realized. Students working on these problems get the best possible training for continued attention to them in adult life. Every known study skill and every known process of critical thinking will enter. Group discussion with all its benefits will become thoroughly familiar.

Without discussion of these problems in school and college, students are bound to be ignorant of many critical issues of the day, but, what is worse, they will grow up holding many erroneous beliefs. As was shown in an earlier chapter, the questioning of many beliefs taken for granted is a real necessity today. Dr. H. J. Muller in his *Uses of the Past* points out that the uncritical acceptance of the concept of original sin is responsible in part for a callous and unrealistic acceptance of many social evils, the easy acceptance of slavery, and many hideous religious atrocities. Belief that "you can't change human nature" has caused irresponsible and unrealistic thinking in tragic amount.

Controversial problems in the classroom. The same general principles hold here as were summarized just above for problems for which no final answer is immediately available. A good deal of thinking must deal with controversial problems, varying from simple everyday affairs up to matters of political policy, social programs, and economic decisions. Adults—from average citizens to national leaders who do not always do too well in managing major controversial problems—should conceivably have done much better had they had school discussion of such problems. Everything that has been said in previous chapters about the nature of thinking and learning to think applies here. Children come into contact with controversial problems as soon as they can understand the conversation of older children and adults. They meet them as soon as they can look at pictures and read. Even the comic strips (so-called) often deal with current controversial problems, too often with a definite propaganda bias. Social, moral, economic, and political problems confront them at every turn. Children and youth will deal with controversial problems, and no one can prevent it; they will be conditioned by all manner of contacts and will form opinions in any event. They will do this, either on the basis of random and often biased contacts with street corner and neighborhood gossip or through honest and orderly discourse under the auspices of the school.

Schoolmen know that a school which does not boldly face up to controversial problems is not a school. Certain lay groups, on the contrary, are opposed to any and all discussion of controversial issues. Resolutions against it are often announced by various patriotic, religious, commercial, and fraternal organizations, clubs, and associations. Opposition sometimes goes as far as bullying teachers and administrators, book burning, and arbitrary dismissal of school personnel. The same groups are often equally violent in demanding that their own selfish interpretations of certain problems and doctrines be taught in the schools. Certain prominent newspaper publishers who create unlimited uproar over censorship or any threat to a "free press" have led fights for censorship of textbooks, demanding that statements of fact and historical record be changed to suit their views. Exponents of the "free press" have often openly led fights for the suppression of free discussion of facts in the schools. Some years ago the social studies field was under particular attack; textbooks were actually censored and in some instances destroyed. Legislatures have gone further and attempted by law not only to make sure that certain issues shall be included or excluded, but to prescribe the interpretation which should be presented. The enforced interpretation is often contradicted by several centuries of historical record, which seems to bother no one.

The reasons given for suppression of facts and free discussion of crucial problems are of great interest. It is said that (1) children are too young, (2) cannot get all the facts, (3) cannot solve problems which adults have not solved. These are superficial and trivial reasons which have been answered several times in preceding chapters. Another set of reasons includes (1) children are misled when given final answers to indeterminate problems, (2) children may be indoctrinated through biased presentations, and (3) such discussions "cause trouble." The answers are that the school has no intention of giving final answers to indeterminate problems but is interested in giving practice in the skills used in handling such problems. The same is true for indoctrination. Teachers found engaging in deliberate indoctrination should be dismissed. If fear of indoctrination were put forward in all honesty, the same critics would have to insist on suppression of many newspapers and magazines. The fear of "causing trouble" reveals far more than it shows on the surface! Let us not upset the *status quo* or disturb belief in accepted dogmas, slogans, and clichés!

The public is well within its rights in protecting children and youth from selfish propaganda, from bias and prejudice, from indoctrination, from perversions of thought of any type. The public can make, however, two tragic mistakes: first, in neglecting to attack the many, many easily available sources of indoctrination and prejudice in everyday publications, and, second, in attacking the school which can and should be so administered as to be free from these evils. It is a tragic and grievous mistake to exclude from the schools the free, honest, analytic, informative, judgment-training discussion of important problems which bear upon the course of our lives and of our society.

The real reasons which underlie opposition to free discussion in school are quite different from those often cited. The *first* one is simple and usually honest; it is plain ignorance of facts about the processes of learning. *Second* is the selfish fear that vested interests may be injured. *Third* is the desire of special interests to use the schools for their own ends. *Fourth* is the unfortunate and regrettable suspicion toward educated men, toward experts, toward creative thinkers, which characterizes large groups of the body politic. [8] Progress is being made, it seems, in conquering the widespread anti-intellectualism of the era.

The school is society's instrument for maintaining and bettering civilization. The merits and deficiencies of any phase of civilization must come up for discussion. The strength and weakness of capitalism and socialism, of "rugged individualism," of independent enterprise and of co-operative endeavor; the rights and wrongs of national policy, whether of internal economics or of foreign military alliances; and the methods of selecting and maintaining our government officers and mechanisms are all fit and necessary topics. Comparative standards of living, poverty in our own country, collective bargaining, the rights of free or "risk" capital, the practice of "Jim Crowism," anti-Semitic prejudices, and religious politics are all crucial problems. Schools blunder dangerously in omitting them.

The technique of democracy is free discussion, interchange of opinion, dissemination of fact, group judgment, common decisions, the reopening of discussion if experience warrants. Democracy among the masses is impossible without training in the techniques of democracy, including experience with free discussion of public issues. Suppression of discussion in the schools or anywhere else is the first move in the assassination of democracy.

Arguments over the inclusion or exclusion of controversial problems are silly if not dangerous. Controversial problems and materials must be included in the curriculum. The real and vitally important question is *how* to teach within controversial areas.

School systems in many places are developing policies and presenting

[8] In this connection, read and analyze recent surveys of teen-age opinions about intellectuals.

bulletins for the guidance of teachers. The following suggestions are made on the basis of our analysis of the problem.

1. *Take every opportunity to give practice in the processes of thought, particularly of critical discrimination and judgment.*

2. *Adhere to facts insofar as facts are available.* Control factual discussion through insistence upon sources and critical evaluation of sources. Insist that pupils back each statement with facts and the source of these facts.

3. *Label opinions as such, when opinion is all that is available.* Control discussions of opinion through the canons of logic and reference to the principles of probability, and through weighting of opinions in terms of sources, amount of data, and probability.

4. *Present both sides in equal detail.*

5. *Train in the use and evaluation of sources of opinion and fact.*

6. *Remember that ideas which entered the mind under emotional circumstances and with strong emotional accompaniment are not going to be easily modified or dislodged by fact and reason.*

7. *Know the local taboos, prejudices, and traditions, and plan to avoid shocking local groups through careless or deliberate defiance of local standards.* Subservience is not indicated here. Local taboos and prejudices are not to go unchallenged, but they are to be eliminated through reputable psychological and educational methods. Slow, tedious progress must be accepted as natural here. Useless disturbance and antagonism are to be avoided.

8. *Use the language of decent intercourse; avoid "fighting words."* The very same persons, organizations, and beliefs can be described in words which are insulting and an invitation to retaliation, or in words which are wholly acceptable to all.

9. *Avoid entanglement in public controversy.* Do not let pupils leave any discussion period without a summary or necessary explanation. Misunderstandings, with resultant misquotation, cause more serious trouble than open discussions of communism and birth control. Avoid wrangles with pupils. Keep the discussion among pupils as far as possible.

10. *Be as honest and impartial as is humanly possible; exemplify as well as teach suspended judgment and the open mind.* A teacher must express his own opinion on controversial matters in order to maintain his own self-respect, to retain the respect of his pupils, and to exercise leadership. The teacher's opinion should be treated as one of the several thrown into the discussion. The teacher as well as the class is studying the problem, seeking facts and guidance, and working toward a tentative conclusion. Teachers will freely accept facts contrary to their views. The teacher is under exactly the same obligation as the pupils to cite facts and sources.

11. *Aim at development of honest, careful thinkers, not converts.*

12. *Learn to compromise when basic principles are not at stake; learn to "roll with the punch."* Develop devices for allowing violent statements to die, for diverting discussion, for matching opposing statements.

13. *Drop any discussion or material if public opinion becomes belligerent and insistent.* Reinstate the discussion and material just as soon as the uproar blows over, profiting by the errors which precipitated the first difficulty.

Many projects or units are informational instead of problem solving in nature. Such topics as the following will result in excellent study and great amounts of information:

How is (our town) supplied with pure milk?
How can we predict tomorrow's weather accurately?
Do newspapers slant the news?
How can we keep from being misled by advertisements?

Critical skills enter at many points in the above projects, but the chief activity is study. Now, then, if we change the titles a little, we get another order of lesson.

Did the (local newspaper) suppress or slant the news regarding the recent action of the city council in dealing with local gambling spots?
Do *Time, Life,* and *U. S. News and World Report* give objective accounts on a given topic, or is there a constant slant?
Did pressure groups force the school board to change the graduation requirements?

With these there will be some genuine problem solving and critical thinking (if the authorities do not demand that the school stop dealing with such things!). The contrast can be shown further:

How can we detect propaganda in the news?
Does the (local or a selected national newspaper) mix propaganda in with the news?

The first can be answered reasonably well by typical study skills and through accessible sources. The second will necessitate the derivation of original data (if it can be gotten) the development of hypotheses, and the use of most careful inference.

A corporation or large business may be examined; the labor unions or a specific union, migrant workers—all are opportunities for case surveys. The health services of a community, a hospital or clinic, the organization for protection of person and property, or even such items as trash collection or off-street parking may be (and have been) the basis for useful case studies. Other possible topics include family, marriage, courts, or any of the several score listed and implied in earlier pages of this chapter.

The informational studies are commendable and useful. They usually constitute a large part of the curriculum in any field. They often lead to or suggest real problems in which critical thought predominates. The many excursions common to the elementary schools, and in some instances to the upper schools, are largely informational projects. Problems can, however, arise within them at any time. A visit to the post office supplies much information of interest and value to children, but with older students the question might arise as to the justice of certain subsidies given to certain classes of mail, and to certain public carriers. A visit to the police station and to the courts will supply much information and cannot fail to raise problems. One of the problems may be that the teacher is ordered to stop bringing students to such places! Students in several instances have raised embarrassing questions at home. Some of them came up for public discussion.

Illustrative subjects for large units or projects. Textbooks and teachers' guides contain literally scores of suggested units, together with considerable detail on organization and development with the learners of these units. To duplicate these would be a waste of space here. All we wish to do at this point is to illustrate the type of topics available with a very brief indication of possible procedure. Suggestions below are mere starters; far more can be done by the teacher and class group.

A study of news reporting. The basis can be a local newspaper, a national one if files are available, a chain, a weekly journal of opinion, or other type.

Care must be taken in studying newspapers not to confine study to materials prepared by critics of the newspapers, their ownership, bias, and methods of reporting. Excellent material is available written by editors, publishers, correspondents, and other members of the working press. Use of these is far more convincing than an outside criticism, though both must be used. The best material, for instance, on slanting the news, biased reporting, and the like is found in the writings of newspapermen and in the various columns by and about newspapermen. Major newspapers quite often print detailed exposés of news slanting by rival papers. Few things make newspaper publishers and editors more angry than the charge that news is sometimes slanted, suppressed, or fake news manufactured. The newspapers and newspapermen themselves are, however, the best sources of facts showing that these things do happen.

Another caution is that newspapers should not be commended or condemned in blanket fashion. Individual newspapers and the press generally have unquestionably fought courageously and successfully in the public interest at given times and on given issues. Individuals under vicious attack have often been saved by newspaper publicity and editorial support. Newspapers have also unquestionably served special interests with a vicious disregard for public interest. Individuals have suffered character assassination in newspaper columns. Individual newspapers have been, and still are, from time to time allied with the vice interests in a city, with a corrupt police force, with dishonest government. Careful study of the valid literature, plus analysis of newspapers will enable any sincere student to set up criteria for the objective evaluation of given newspapers. It is by no means difficult to set up criteria and earmarks which reveal very clearly the honesty or dishonesty of given papers.

The following is an extremely brief list of suggestions for getting started. Suggestions for the total study would fill several pages.

1. *Ownership.* Is the publisher or owner a local resident, or is he a manager sent in by the head office of a chain?

If the owner is a local citizen, has he other interests, industrial or political? Look him up in *Who's Who,* or any biographical reference, and in the tax records for local and federal returns; learn about his fraternal or religious connections.

Get any past history that can be found.

2. *Set up criteria,* after detailed study of appropriate literature, for determining if editorials are consistently reactionary, conservative, liberal, radical?

Note who is supported in local political campaigns and on local government issues. Note amount of space given to all parties in a campaign on local issues.

3. *Set up criteria, similarly, for the reporting* of national and local news. Which press association is favored?

Set up criteria particularly for detecting objectivity and full coverage, selectivity in the news, slanting, suppression, and the like. Note relationship between news coverage and editorial views.

4. *Make a study of space devoted to crime,* general national and international news, accidents, sensational items about obscure persons. Several studies are available as models.

Note particularly if there are differences in handling a murder or vice story involving an unknown or friendless citizen, a public figure, a prominent figure of the underworld. Some of the surest indications of honesty or dishonesty of the press are to be found here.

5. *Compare your own observations* of events which you observed or have direct knowledge about with coverage in the paper.

6. *Make a study of freedom of the press* both in general and, if possible, in specific cases.

Few topics should be of such vital interest to citizens of a democracy as this one. Everyone should be familiar with the literature on both sides. Newspaper publishers assert with vigor that there should be no control and fight censorship of any type. Charges of control by special interests are denied as sharply as the charge that news is slanted. Evidence exists in considerable volume, and the heated exchange of opinion should give way to the facts.

Summarize the ways the press of the United States is free as is no other press, except possibly the English.

Summarize the ways in which our press is not free. Get the facts on pressures from individuals, political, religious, patriotic, and economic groups, large advertisers. Ample materials are available.

Summarize cases of individual newspapers or magazines which have courageously resisted any of these pressures. Note particularly cases in which a publisher-owner has operated a censorship and slanting far more arrogant and arbitrary than any government control could be. Again ample material is available.

Should there be laws regarding the publication of fact, ignoring of fact, and particularly regarding defiance of known facts? Is there any similarity between controlling the publishing of statements which are flatly contradicted by facts and controlling publication of libelous statements as in the present laws?

Interview and pin down, when possible, speakers, writers, or citizens who write to the editor; who (a) extol our press as completely free and unbiased, as wholly objective, as "print the news as they see it," or those who (b) condemn in equally inclusive terms, "full of lies," "all propaganda," "don't dare print anything the bigwigs don't want printed."

The foregoing suggestions, it must be repeated, are but a brief and meager start. A good study of news reporting will involve extensive analysis of much literature, of many papers and magazines. Teachers' guides often have a good outline on this topic and upon others closely related.

The following are a few studies in which the writer has observed or participated:

> The History of the Development of Our Democratic Rights and Obligations
> Our Government in Action (any level, segment, or activity)
> The United Nations: A Study in International Co-operation
> What Our Community Does
>> How the Community Protects Persons and Property
>> How to Get There in My Community (Points of interest, cultural significance, suburban and slum areas, segregation of ethnic and national groups, housing, transportation, and many others.)
>> The Story Behind Greater Boston's Way of Living (Can be applied to any city.)
> Crime Presents a Problem
> Crime and Punishment (This turned into a study of punishment in human history covering many centuries.)
> Marriage and the Family in Our Industrial Civilization
> Fluoridization of City Water Supply (Despite the facts that large volumes of evidence are available, public discussion has developed some incredibly absurd remarks and arguments. Pamphlets have been published and widely circulated which not only amuse students, but raise the question of mental balance among those doing the writing.)

Grade placement of problems and informational projects. Learning situations should be adapted to the maturity and experiential background of the students. Nearness to typical life behavior is essential. Excellent references on grade placement are available in the periodical literature, and particularly in some of the older books on the teaching of history and geography.

Instructional resources and materials. The textbooks on teaching of the social studies, the teacher's guides for cities and states, as well as separate bulletins on materials, all contain huge, well-organized lists. Discussions are also given on the manufacture of one's own materials, and upon the use of all types of materials. The *chief error* to avoid in the social /

studies above all other fields is the use of *one textbook* for any course. A few study guides or courses of study advocate this, but the practice is condemned by every known authority. Many books, references, pamphlets, pictures, films, museum exhibits, are necessary.

3. ORGANIZE FACT-FINDING UNITS.

Units in which emphasis is on collection of data as well as upon the content are valuable. One example is given:

A study of freedom to do research and to teach as facts dictate. Closely related to free enterprise and freedom of the press is academic freedom. This, too, should be studied by citizens as part of the continuous analysis of the educational system. In certain colleges the faculty had better make frequent, stirring appeals for a return to the faith of the founding fathers, with frequent references to Plymouth Rock, and our standard of living. In still other colleges, the faculty may go so far as to make indignant remarks about sharecroppers, migrant workers, housing in South Boston, and our refusal to recognize Red China, but they must not do anything about these topics, particularly join organizations or give money to "causes." In still other colleges, faculty members may do research and make critical analysis on industrial democracy, civil rights, integration, and peaceful coexistence. They may write and speak freely on any topics where they have valid facts or reasoned conclusions. It is interesting to note that it is the third group of colleges which produce the vital new research facts which affect our lives, the books which change minds and move our civilization ahead.

Similar studies may be made of the operations of the Better Business Bureau, of various consumer research agencies; of the hearings under the Pure Food and Drug Act; of the activities of the Advertising Council, the National Industrial Conference Board, the League of Women Voters, and many others.

4. ORGANIZE NORMATIVE UNITS, USING GROUP PROCESSES.

5. ORGANIZE CRITICAL UNITS.

General principles and procedures were set forth in Chapter 15 on general methods. Illustrations are to be found in previous chapters and in many other sources.

6. THE CASE STUDY.

A case, as was defined in an earlier chapter, is a detailed account of events leading up to some type of difficult problem. The written or printed summary brings to the student realistic detail through which he can project himself into the situation and see the issues vividly. This brings him as close to actual participation as is possible. Students may also develop the case materials and tackle the problems revealed by the case as well.

The literature on teaching the social studies, in contrast to that on the physical sciences, has practically no mention of the case study. There are, however, some indirect discussions and some good illustrations, even though they are not labeled as case studies. See particularly:

Ruth Ellsworth and Ole Sand, eds., *Improving the Social Studies Curriculum,* 26th Yearbook of the National Council for the Social Studies (1955). Several abbreviated accounts of good case studies.

Howard H. Cummings, ed., *Science and the Social Studies,* 27th Yearbook of the National Council for the Social Studies (1956-1957). Deals with the physical sciences generally but is replete with leads to case studies in the social studies. The whole volume is useful but particularly Chs. 9 through 12.

Roy A. Price, ed., *New Viewpoints in the Social Sciences,* 28th Yearbook of the National Council for the Social Studies (1958). Whole volume.

Carter V. Good, *Introduction to Educational Research* (New York, Appleton-Century-Crofts, 1959). Pp. 177-181 contain brief illustrative paragraphs describing community surveys. Chs. 5 and 7 contain lists of procedures.

The best references are, as stated in an earlier chapter, introductory texts on research.

Case studies are time consuming, but an occasional good one teaches concepts clearly and provides excellent opportunity for developing good habits of critical thinking.

Example: The Westinghouse Strike. The following illustration of case materials can be used as the basis for thinking, defining terms, making critical analyses, and spotting assumptions and hidden bias. The case can be followed in library files of newspapers and magazines.

A BIG TWO-MONTH STRIKE—WHAT IT'S ALL ABOUT

On October 17, thirty plants of Westinghouse Electric Corporation, scattered through the country, were shut down by a strike of 44,000 workers. On October 25, ten other plants of the company were closed by a strike of 10,000 workers belonging to another union. In 58 other plants workers took no part in the strikes and stayed on their jobs.

Most of the 54,000 workers had received no company pay—but were drawing small strike benefits from their unions to help meet living conditions. A few thousand, in scattered cities, had accepted a company offer to go back to work.

More than 60,000 other employees were not out on strike, but many of them—especially office people—were working only half time.

Salaries of company executives had been cut 40 to 50 per cent.

Westinghouse, one of the largest manufacturers of electrical equipment, was opening the gates to strikers who were ready to go back to work, but was getting few takers. Meanwhile, company production and sales were sharply curtailed.

Shift by Unions. This was a strike that involved two unions that are bitter rivals, and it was one of the few nation-wide strikes of 1955. Three years ago union officials were praising Westinghouse for its "fairness" and "reasonableness" in wage negotiations.

Larger of the two unions is the International Union of Electrical, Radio, and Machine Workers—known as "IUE"—which struck 30 plants of Westinghouse. The other union is the United Electrical, Radio, and Machine Workers, or "UE".

Wages. The IEU demanded a pay raise of 15 cents an hour. The company countered with an offer of wage increases totaling at least 23.5 cents an hour, but spread over a five-year-period. For the first year, the company proposed a boost of 3 per cent, with everyone getting a raise of at least 4.5 cents an hour.

The company offer included a yearly increase of 3 per cent in 1956 and 1957, a raise of 3.48 per cent in 1958 and 3.46 per cent in 1959. The minimum raise would go to 5 cents an hour for 1958 and 1959. The average worker reportedly earned $2.10 an hour before the strike, or $16.80 for an eight-hour day.

Skilled workers, under the proposal, would get extra raises, ranging from a half cent to 12 cents an hour in raises, (extra).

Improvements were also offered in the pension and insurance programs, and in other "fringe" benefits. The company offered to make wage adjustments as living costs rise or fall.

A Five-year Contract, proposed by Westinghouse as part of its package, was criticized by IUE officials, however.

The union took the position that its contract with Westinghouse, signed last year, allowed discussion this year of wage increases and nothing else.

James B. Carey, president of IUE, argued that Westinghouse should grant a pay raise of 15 cents an hour at this time and leave other issues for discussion in 1956.

The company declared that Mr. Carey, in a letter to the management, had served notice prior to this year's negotiations that he intended to file demands on "other matters," involving rate of pay, wages, hours of employment, and other conditions of employment.

(The Westinghouse package was similar to a five-year deal made by General Electric with its employees, and accepted by IUE. Gwilym A. Price, president of Westinghouse, stated that the offer was costly, but that it would give Westinghouse five years of peace. Carey replied that the Westinghouse offer was not worth as much as the General Electric one.)

Work Standards—according to Mr. Carey have been the main issue in the dispute, aside from the general pay raise. The IUE has accused Westinghouse of wanting to cut wages and reduce the number of employees by setting new standards of production. The management denied that it seeks to cut wages. Westinghouse has stated that what it has wanted is to make "time studies" of certain jobs to determine if the jobs are being handled in the most efficient manner. The jobs involved are on a straight-wage basis, the worker getting a fixed wage per hour, regardless of the amount of output.

Violence also has increased. At Trenton, N. J., cars of workers were damaged when the workers tried to go through picket lines. Homes of the non-strikers were reported stoned. The automobile of an IUE official at Columbus, O., was damaged by a bomb when parked near a union hall. *

Other situations out of which case studies may be made can be illustrated thus:

> The dust bowl and its effect on our economy
> The farm policy and surpluses
> A (specified) impoverished community—or depressed area
>> company town
>> suburban area being deserted
>> ghetto
>> wealthy high tax community
> Specific cases of juvenile delinquency
> The divorce statistics and the law

SPECIAL REMARKS ON SPECIFIC SUBJECTS

The discussion of general principles and methods to this point is applicable alike to fused or core curriculums in the social studies, and to the special subjects when these are taught separately. Both types of curriculum in the social studies are widely distributed.

History. We are concerned with teaching critical thinking within this field and not with the totality of method in teaching history. History has been given different definitions and scope by various writers, but this is a problem for the historiographers. We will be concerned with critical thinking on historical problems and materials within any definition.

Thinking on historical problems has much in common with thinking in the physical sciences but has also significant differences. Similarities include definition of a problem, formulating hypotheses, gathering data, checking and testing hypotheses for the derivation of an acceptable conclusion. A basic difference is found in the nature and analysis of the data used. The historian cannot use direct observation or experimentation. He cannot recall the original actors or circumstances from the stage of history. The historian must rely on the recorded observations of others, upon the relics or remains from the past. The crucial problems in interpretation of data are to determine the authenticity of documents, relics, or other exhibits and to determine the qualifications and accuracy of the reporter whose statements are being studied. These problems give rise to the critical processes of the historian—external and internal criticism. Before listing

* Reprinted from *U. S. News and World Report,* an independent weekly news magazine published at Washington. Copyright 1955, United States News Publishing Corporation. Quotes were from issue of December 23, 1955.

the principles and procedures, let us examine a much-abbreviated list of typical source materials. [9] This list can be expanded to two or three pages by inserting detailed statements of types of materials.

1. Consciously transmitted information:
    a. Written sources: chronicles, annals, biographies, memoirs, diaries, genealogies, certain classes of inscriptions. The range is from papyri, bricks with cuneiform writing, vellum or parchments, to modern documents, printed books and papers.
    b. Oral tradition: ballads, tales, sagas, anecdotes.
    c. Artistic productions: historical paintings, portraits, scenic or portrait sculpture, figures on ancient coins.
    d. Motion picture films, microfilm, recordings.
2. Unconscious testimony or relics.
    a. Human remains, clothing, food, shelters, language, social institutions, products of the hand (such as utensils, arms, implements, furniture, pottery, machinery), industrial techniques, fine arts, manners, customs, ceremonials of all types, museum pieces.
    b. Physical remains, pyramids, aqueducts, fortifications, roads, historic sites, buildings (ruined or whole).

External criticism. The authenticity of historical materials must first be determined and is here illustrated with special reference to documents. Other classes of historical materials present their own problems and procedures.

1. Who was the author, not merely his name, but his personality, character, position, and so forth?
2. What were his general qualifications as a reporter—alertness, character, bias?
3. What were his special qualifications and disqualifications as a reporter of the matters here treated?
    a. How was he interested in the events related?
    b. How was he situated for observation of the events?
    c. Had he the necessary general and technical knowledge for learning and reporting the events?

[9] This list of materials has been compiled from three or four lists. Chief sources are:

Gilbert J. Garraghan, *A Guide to Historical Method,* Jean Delanglez, ed. (New York, Fordham University Press, 1946).

H. G. Good, "Historical Research in Education," *Educational Research Bulletin* (January 8, 1930).

L. L. Bernard, "The Sources and Methods of Cultural and Field Sociology," in *The Fields and Methods of Sociology* (New York, Long & Smith, 1934).

Allen Nevins, *The Gateway to History* (Boston, Heath, 1938).

Lists will be found in texts on the teaching of history and in texts on research methods. Excellent summaries are found in:

Carter V. Good and Douglas E. Scates, *Methods of Research* (New York, Appleton-Century-Crofts, 1954), Ch. 4.

Carter V. Good, *Introduction to Educational Research* (New York, Appleton-Century-Crofts, 1959). Ch. 4 contains abbreviated summary statements.

4. How soon after the events was the document written? For one purpose the century of the composition may be sufficient; for another the very hour may be essential.

5. How was the document written—from memory, after consultation with others, after checking the facts, or by combining earlier trial drafts?

6. How is this document related to other documents?
   a. Is it an original source, wholly or in part?
   b. If the latter, what parts are original; what borrowed; whence? How credible are the borrowed materials?
   c. How and how accurately is the borrowing done?
   d. How is the borrowed material changed; how used?

The document itself must also be examined to detect hoaxes, frauds, forgeries, borrowings, intentional or unintentional distortions. [10] Paper, ink, and paint may be subjected to ultraviolet rays or fluorescent photography. Dates of manufacture can thus be determined. Fraudulent documents purporting to be ancient can be exposed as modern forgeries or hoaxes. External criticism uses data and process from nearly every scientific field. Data from astronomy, chemistry, archaeology, and some twenty-five other fields have been utilized from time to time. Other sources of historical data are examined similarly.

Internal criticism. After the authenticity of a document has been established, internal criticism enters to determine value and accuracy of the contents. What does the document or other exhibit really say, and what does it mean? Meaning established, the reader must then determine the good faith and accuracy of the author. Honest and dishonest mistakes must be detected.

Certain general principles have been listed by Woody: [11]

1. Do not read into earlier documents the conceptions of later times.

2. Do not judge an author ignorant of certain events, necessarily, because he fails to mention them (the argument *ex silentio*); and, for the same reason, do not assume that certain events did not occur.

3. Underestimating a source is no less an error than overestimating it in the same degree, and there is no more value in placing an event too late than in dating it too early by the same number of years or centuries.

4. A single true source may establish the existence of an idea, but other direct, competent, independent witnesses are required to prove the reality of events or objective facts.

5. Identical errors prove the dependence of sources on each other, or a common source.

6. If witnesses contradict each other on a certain point, one or the other may be true; but both may be in error.

[10] The accounts of external criticism, particularly in the detection of forgeries and other fakes, are extremely interesting. Illustrations are found widely distributed in texts on history, history writing, teaching of history, historical research.

[11] Thomas Woody, "Of History and its Method," *Journal of Experimental Education* (Mar., 1947), pp. 175-201.

7. Direct, competent, independent witnesses who report the same central fact and also many peripheral matters in a casual way may be accepted for the points of their agreement.
8. Official testimony, oral or written, must be compared with unofficial testimony whenever possible, for neither one nor the other is alone sufficient.
9. A document may provide competent and dependable evidence on certain points, yet carry no weight in respect to others it mentions.

The specific problems of internal criticism obviously overlap with those of external analysis. [12]

1. What did the author mean by this particular statement? What is the real meaning as distinguished from its mere literal meaning?
2. Was the statement made in good faith?
   a. Had the author any interest in deceiving the reader?
   b. Was the author under pressure to tell an untruth?
   c. Was he influenced by sympathy or antipathy to tell an untruth?
   d. Did vanity influence him?
   e. Was he influenced by public opinion?
   f. Is there evidence of literary or drastic motives to distort the truth?
3. Was the statement accurate? Or, more particularly:
   a. Was the author a poor observer because of mental defect or abnormality?
   b. Was the author badly situated in time and place to observe?
   c. Was he negligent or indifferent?
   d. Was the fact of such nature that it could not be observed directly?
   e. Was the author a mere witness or a trained observer?
4. When it appears that the author was not the original observer, it is necessary to determine the truth and accuracy of his sources of information.

We have already referred in an earlier chapter to the difficulty that even trained observers have in reporting what happens in their immediate presence. Add to this the many conscious and unconscious influences which influence men when they observe and report, and we have a large and difficult problem. [13]

Geography. Old-time geography which once dominated the elementary schools might be called "sea captain" geography. It developed in the fifteenth and sixteenth centuries when captains were venturing out from Europe in search of a new way to the Orient and to circumnavigate the

---

[12] F. S. Chapin, *Field Work and Social Research* (New York, Century, 1920), pp. 37-38.

[13] As with external criticism, the accounts of analysis of utterances and documents are extremely interesting and revealing. The factors which have contributed to dishonest reports are enlightening, but it is the factors which influence reporters who are not clearly aware of these factors which are the most valuable. Many sources are available.

globe. Emphasis was on landfalls useful in navigation. The subject matter consisted in latitude and longitude, location, area, topography, capes, bays, islands, continents. Identification and memorizing were the learning processes. This type of encyclopedic geography is an effective block to thinking.

Modern geography deals with man living in his physical or geographic environment. How is life affected by climate, soil, topography, and vegetation either natural or cultivated? Man's cultural environment interacts with his physical, and consequently geography is sometimes called a physical-social science.

Instead of memorizing the facts, we have children try to derive them. Why do people live as they do in different climates, in areas with differing natural resources? This includes study of clothing and housing, agriculture, and other aspects of the total situation. Social grouping is often dependent on land ownership; hence, social structures are related to the geographic environment. The relation of population, birth control, and food supply to world peace, and these, in turn, to soil and climate, topography, and location on land masses are all geographic questions.

The general methods to be used are, in general, those already set forth—problem solving and the case study. As with history, much of the data must be observed at second hand. Excursions through the neighborhood and, with older students, into a region are increasingly used to approach subject matter directly. Books, pictures, models, and the like must still play a large part. Good research studies exist concerning the choice of content for geography courses. Cross reference can be made to literature as is done from history to literature.

Two good texts are available in which exercises, bibliography, and suggestions for problems may be found.

Roderick Peattie, *The Teaching of Geography* (New York, Appleton-Century-Crofts, 1950).

Zoe A. Thralls, *The Teaching of Geography* (New York, Appleton-Century-Crofts, 1959).

In addition, help may be secured from some of the texts in the teaching of social studies, from manuals accompanying textbooks, and from the periodical literature.

Preston E. James, ed., *New Viewpoints in Geography,* 1959 Yearbook of the Council for the Social Studies, Washington, D. C.

This volume points out that the space age has invalidated many of the familiar concepts of physical geography. The need is emphasized for human geography, economic geography, and regional geography. The space age and serial navigation have outmoded the familiar flat maps and globes, just as they replaced Mercator's projection long ago.

Other social studies. Summaries such as the above may be made for any other subject by a student or small class committee.

Evaluation of critical thinking in social studies. Tests for critical thinking are listed and described in Chapter 21. The chief points to re-emphasize here are, first, that memory tests and fact tests are largely useless for testing critical thinking. Problem-situation tests of various types and exercises involving use of actual materials are necessary. The improved essay-type examination which calls for judgment or critical discrimination of any sort is a valuable instrument. Details over and beyond our Chapter 21 are found in standard tests on evaluation, and on principles of teaching.

QUESTIONS, EXERCISES, AND REPORTS

Discussion following this chapter, as with Chapter 15 on general methods, should turn upon actual or proposed methods for teaching critical thinking in connection with social studies materials.

Teachers may report for class analysis any units or other type lessons which they have used. They may report on units now under development. These units may deal with major problem-solving sequences, with extensive critical analysis of materials, with analysis of local governmental policies. Other illustrations may deal with specified aspects of the total process—for instance, with gathering data in difficult situations; with the spotting of errors and fallacies; with special difficulties in handling informational surveys, indeterminate problems, controversial issues, case studies.

Reports may be made illustrating the development and use of principles of internal and external criticism in history. The special issues in geography, or of any other separate social field, should be illustrated.

READINGS

A number of good books are available on teaching the social studies, of which the following are samples:

BINING, Arthur C., and BINING, David H., *Teaching Social Studies in Secondary Schools* (New York, McGraw-Hill, 1952).

MICHAELIS, John V., *Social Studies for Children in a Democracy* (Englewood Cliffs, N. J., Prentice-Hall, 1950).

WESLEY, Edgar B., *Teaching Social Studies in High School*, 3rd ed. (Boston, Heath, 1950).

The yearbooks of the National Council for the Social Studies are an excellent source. The following are examples.

ANDERSON, Howard A., ed., *Teaching Critical Thinking in the Social Studies*, 13th Yearbook (1942). Despite its date it is the best reference on this particular topic.

CARPENTER, Helen McCracken, ed., *Skills in the Social Studies*, 24th Yearbook (1953). Ch. 3 is an excellent résumé of the thinking process. Covers much the same material as texts in teaching social studies and can be used as such.

CUMMINGS, Howard H., ed., *Science and the Social Studies,* 27th Yearbook (1956-1957). Deals with physical sciences generally but contains many leads to case studies in the social studies. Whole volume useful, particularly Chs. 9 through 12.

ELLSWORTH, Ruth, and SAND, Ole., eds., *Improving the Social Studies Curriculum,* 26th Yearbook (1955). Good abbreviated accounts of some case studies. Very useful specific materials.

FERSH, George L., *Problems Approach in Social Studies* (Washington, D.C., National Council for Social Studies, 1955). A very fine pamphlet that treats the issue of basic concern in this chapter—namely, how to teach social studies in a way that will develop certain general problem-solving skills.

PRICE, Roy A., ed., *New Viewpoints in the Social Sciences,* 28th Yearbook (1958). Very useful advanced and provocative summary. Ch. 10 contains extensive discussion of methods. Chs. 11 and 12 also specially useful.

CHAPTER **19**

Teaching for Thinking: Mathematics

Mathematics is as much a method of reasoning as it is a body of conclusions.

HOLLIS R. COOLEY *

Mathematicians are like lovers. . . . Grant a mathematician the least principle, and he will draw from it a consequence which you must also grant him, and from this consequence another.

FONTENELLE †

As a school subject, mathematics has had a long and honorable tradition. Therein lies both its promise and its peril.

On a recent visit to a high school, one of the authors had the opportunity to observe a young mathematics teacher at work in a geometry classroom. Although this visit occurred one year after the launching of the first Sputnik, the book in use was copyrighted in 1926 and was organized according to the classic "Books" of Euclid. Our young teacher friend saw no cause for concern, nor did his superintendent. During the postvisit conference with the superintendent, the question was explored in some detail.

"But geometry is geometry," protested the superintendent. "It hasn't changed much since Euclid, has it?"

Of course, the tragedy of this incident is at least twofold.

First, it emphasizes the failure to recognize the dynamic nature of mathematics as a content subject. Indeed geometry has changed since

---

* Hollis R. Cooley and others, *Introduction to Mathematics* (New York, Houghton Mifflin, 1937), p. 599.

† Quoted in Eric T. Bell, *Men of Mathematics* (New York, Simon & Schuster, 1937).

390

Euclid! In fact, all mathematics continues to change. This has been dramatically underlined by the manner in which "modern mathematics" suddenly has thrust itself onto the secondary school scene. [1]

Second, and most significant for our present concern, it indicates a hopeless confusion regarding the objectives of mathematics education. The products of mathematical thought have not been distinguished from the processes which created these products. Unwittingly, both the superintendent and his teacher have accepted subject matter mastery as the sole objective of mathematics instruction—and have even risked choosing the wrong subject matter for the twentieth century!

What point of view, then, must be adopted if such limitations are to be surmounted?

MATHEMATICS AS AN INTELLECTUAL ENTERPRISE

Our society tends to be basically a utilitarian one. The "practical" man is the man who usually receives both public acclaim and suitable material rewards. Hence, it is not surprising to find that mathematics sometimes is considered to be the "handmaiden." Viewed in this manner, its contribution is facilitative rather than fundamental, and its role specific rather than general. Educators have been led to coin the phrase, "tool subject," with all that such an expression implies.

When the emphasis is thus restricted, only one side of the coin is seen. Admittedly, application and the desire to maintain some sort of one-to-one relationship with physical reality have served both to motivate and to justify many mathematical endeavors. But other equally important, though somewhat obscure, benefits are within our grasp. To overlook them would be a costly indulgence.

The essential point is that mathematics is a way of thinking. Hence, it is reasonable to anticipate that mathematics has some contribution to make to the art of thinking, even as thinking has some contributions to make to mathematics. Several mathematicians and mathematical philosophers have developed this idea in considerable detail, but none in a more direct manner than C. J. Keyser: [2]

Mathematics may be viewed either as an enterprise or as a body of achievements. As an enterprise, mathematics is characterized by its aim, and its aim

---

[1] See, for example, *Insights Into Modern Mathematics,* 23rd Yearbook of the National Council of Teachers of Mathematics (Washington, D.C., National Council of Teachers of Mathematics, 1957).

Newspapers, as these pages were being written, carried accounts of the selfsame criticism of geometry teaching being made in the Russian schools. The Russian curriculum is often held up as an example for us to follow, but many weaknesses found in our schools are duplicated in the Russian schools and curriculums.

[2] C. J. Keyser, *The Human Worth of Rigorous Thinking* (New York, Columbia University Press, 1925), p. 3.

is to think rigorously whatever is rigorously thinkable or whatever may become rigorously thinkable. . . .

. . . to challenge the human worth of mathematics, to challenge the worth of rigorous thinking, is to challenge the worth of all thinking, for now we see that mathematics is but the ideal to which all thinking, by an inevitable process and law of the human spirit, constantly aspires.[3]

Virtually the same point has been presented with somewhat varying emphasis by others. [4]

These claims that mathematics will serve well as a vehicle for improving thinking usually rest on the grounds that mathematics is a superbly, even perfectly, developed deductive-postulational system. Keyser, for example, argues that it is an ideal system which can serve as the basis for handling the problems of life with order and rationality. Several analogies are suggested: constants and variables are compared to fixedness and change in life; equations are compared to certain natural and spiritual laws; limits are compared to the ideals of life (approached, but never truly attained. [5]

Without denying the value of thus viewing mathematics, three qualifying points need to be kept in mind. *First,* there is an element of equivocation in appearing to assert that mathematics is a perfected logical system, or that in some respects it is virtually so. While none of the writers cited do make such a categorical assertion, the appearance of one persists: there remains the clear possibility that teachers will present even elementary mathematics as the "ultimate truth," and the axiomatic-deductive procedure as the only road to that truth. Suffice it to say that both Black [6] and Stabler [7] have presented careful critical refutations of such a formalist or logicalist interpretation.

Second, and more crucial in respect to its educational implications, is the resulting tendency to overemphasize the deductive aspects of mathematics. Strictly interpreted, this point of view will lead the teacher to ignore or disparage the empirical features of mathematical thinking; it will suggest that mathematics has few, if any, potential contributions to the improvement of inductive thinking. Courant and Robbins [8] warn against this

[3] *Ibid.,* p. 14.

[4] Robert D. Carmichael, "The Larger Human Worth of Mathematics," in William L. Schaaf, ed., *Mathematics: Our Great Heritage* (New York, Harper, 1948), pp. 260-288.

    Cooley, *op. cit.,* pp. 9-10.

    E. R. Stabler, *An Introduction to Mathematical Thought* (Cambridge, Mass., Addison-Wesley, 1953), pp. 1-119.

[5] Keyser, *op. cit.,* pp. 60-79.

[6] Max Black, *The Nature of Mathematics: A Critical Survey* (New York, Harcourt, Brace, 1933).

[7] Edward R. Stabler, "The Educational Possibilities of Geometry," unpublished E.D. dissertation, Harvard Graduate School of Education, 1935, pp. 56-118.

[8] Richard Courant and Herbert Robbins, *What Is Mathematics?* (New York, Oxford, 1941), pp. xv-xix.

sort of inference, and Polya [9] has devoted two volumes to the argument that mathematics may with both justification and value be viewed as a model for the inductive method.

A *third* consideration also must be kept in mind. Many mathematicians either state explicitly or clearly imply that the transfer of logical thinking skills from mathematical learnings to life situations will be automatic. In view of our current understanding of the nature of learning and the phenomenon of transfer, such a conclusion is totally unwarranted.

What, then, can we deduce from the writings of the mathematicians? Obviously there is not complete agreement as to the extent that the methodology of mathematics has any substantial applicability outside the field of mathematics, and there are conflicting views as to the relative emphasis to be given to deductive and inductive methods. We do find, however, that there is shared a mutual conviction that the study of mathematics clearly can contribute to the improvement of thinking. But when we look for suggestions as to how we should order our instructional objectives, materials, and methodology to realize this brave hope we find little specific help.

Since this is apparently a task for the mathematics-educator, the psychologist, the curriculum worker, the classroom teacher, and only incidentally the task of the mathematician, let us turn to the issues involved.

A PATTERN OF MATHEMATICS EDUCATION

Clearly, mathematics is more than a body of knowledge. Not only does it have its unique content; it also has a characteristic methodology. If we accept as a fundamental objective of mathematics education the idea that students should gain an understanding of "the way of thinking that is mathematics," it must be recognized that this objective will best be achieved if we consciously organize instruction with that objective in mind. Educational research has clearly demonstrated that if teaching is to achieve any particular objectives, our efforts must be directed specifically toward those objectives. This is no longer a matter of opinion.

If we want our students to discover the facts and relationships of mathematics, then we must provide specific opportunities for their discovery; we must give the students a chance to formulate and test their generalizations. If we want the student to see mathematics as a way of thinking, we must stress those features which characterize *all* of mathematical thought; we must help him to see that mathematics is more than a loosely related sequence of subjects, each in its own tidy compartment. And if we want

[9] George Polya, *Mathematics and Plausible Reasoning,* Vol I: *Induction and Analogy in Mathematics,* and Vol. II: *Patterns of Plausible Inference* (Princeton, N. J., Princeton University Press, 1954).

the student to realize that this way of thinking may help one to solve many problems of human concern, then we must provide him with many illustrations of this fact; we must provide specific opportunity for transfer.

If we accept this point of view, several controlling principles emerge.

1. Mathematical relationships take on more meaning when they are discovered by the student.
2. Discovery and generalization are intellectual processes, not mechanical ones. Experimentation must be planned and guided; experimentation is more than manipulation.
3. Students will better understand the nature of proof if this concept is developed slowly, building on that which is already familiar to the pupil.
4. The student should recognize that algebra, geometry, and trigonometry, in particular, and mathematics, in general, are unified. They represent a complete and interrelated pattern of thought.
5. The student will become acquainted with several methods of discovery and proof. If these are to be transferred to nonmathematical situations, detailed attention must be given to teaching for transfer.
6. Mathematics should be taught so as to emphasize original and independent thinking. Particular care must be taken to avoid providing the sort of cues and organizing the original exercises in such a way that the subject is reduced to a "bag of tricks." Specific techniques of analysis should be identified, developed, used, and generalized.
7. The materials and methods of mathematics must stimulate the curiosity and interest of each student so that he will carry his study of the subject to a point compatible with his ability.

Unfortunately, not always have these principles received credence in mathematics education. Some have rejected the suggestion that mathematics can make a significant contribution to generalized critical-thinking skills. The reasons for this are varied; they may be rooted in the conviction that mathematics is to be taught as an exclusively content subject; they may have their basis in narrowly conceived theories of learning; they may develop from a discredited interpretation of "formal discipline" and the whole subject of transfer of training. Whatever the cause, the consequence is to promulgate a mechanistic, tightly structured, adult-oriented pattern of mathematics instruction.

However, the principles suggested gain significance in the light of recent thinking in both mathematics and learning theory. By encouraging the teaching of more basic and consequently more generalized concepts, it becomes possible to deal with concepts which apply well beyond what has been considered the normal domain of secondary school mathematics.

Fehr has suggested that philosophies of mathematics education which lie behind these two "schools" can be effectively contrasted by structuring them as in Figure 5.

Generalized Pattern		Specific Pattern
Child Society Universe	Order of Importance	Universe (physical) Society Child

Individual
  development
Social living
Vocational
Aesthetic
Tolerance
Self-direction
Creativeness
Reflective
  thinking
	Objectives	Ability to think
		  clearly
		Information, mathe-
		  matical concepts,
		  principles
		Fundamental skills
		Interests
		Appreciations

Formulation,
  solution
Data
Approximation
Function
Proof
Symbolism
Operation
	Subject
	Matter
		Number
		Geometric form, space
		  perception
		Graphic representation
		Elementary analysis
		Relational thinking
		Logic (deductive)
		Symbolism

Changing values
  and
Problem solving
	Primary
	Values
		Permanent values
		  and
		Organized subject
		  matter

Gestalt psychology Analysis Insight Closure Generalization	Implied Theory of Learning	Stimulus-response Specific-general Association

Configurational,
  integrated
  learning program
Difficult to
  evaluate
	Teaching
	Implications
		Well-organized,
		  firmly structured,
		  subject-matter-
		  centered program
		Easily evaluated

Fig. 5. A Comparison of Two Patterns of Mathematics Education. [10]

[10] Adapted from Howard F. Fehr, *Teaching High School Mathematics* (Washington, National Education Association, 1955), p. 9.

LANGUAGE IN MATHEMATICS

Efforts to communicate will be a part of most thinking. Sometimes thinking is motivated by efforts to communicate; very frequently it culminates in an effort to communicate. Language, in its broadest sense, is the means of relating ideas and communicating them. Although words are only one of many types of language symbols, they are perhaps of greater significance than all other types in the everyday thinking of most people:

Men use words to solve most of their perplexities, if not all of them. But it is not easy to use words properly in solving problems. . . . In helping students to think reflectively, therefore, the teacher should help them to understand the use of words. [11]

Mathematics is concerned with the careful use of words. Because its language is emotionally neutral, there are opportunities to emphasize particular attributes of language with conciseness. Even though mathematics is not and need not become involved in all the niceties of semantics, certain concepts can and should be developed. [12]

For those who find no urge to be precise, everyday living usually makes no extraordinary demands for careful use of language. Words such as "truth," "honesty," "conservative," "liberal," "democratic," are encountered regularly. Men use them in everyday discourse with only vague notions regarding their exact meaning. Although no obvious damage results, long-term complications plague the careless thinker. The stage is set for demagoguery, for the "hard sell," for social crises both large and small.

On the other hand, to know only that "mean," "median," and "average" indicate central tendency is to know very little. Without an exact definition, intelligent judgments as to which should be used would be difficult or impossible.

Or consider the question: Is it better to choose an income of $4000 per year with annual increases of $200 in preference to an income of $2000 semiannually with a semiannual raise of $50? The alert reader will analyze the two proposals clearly, in spite of the fact that language encourages the choice of the less desirable of the alternatives.

Thus, the need for clear definitions in mathematics is obvious. In fact,

[11] The Progressive Education Association Committee on the Function of Mathematics in General Education, *Mathematics in General Education* (New York, D. Appleton-Century, 1940), p. 214.

[12] Irvin H. Brune, "Language in Mathematics," *The Learning of Mathematics: Its Theory and Practice,* 21st Yearbook of the National Council of Teachers of Mathematics (Washington, D. C., National Council of Teachers of Mathematics, 1953), pp. 156-191.

Recall discussion of definition in Chapter 10.

this requirement is almost too obvious, and students often conclude that every word can and must be defined. Mathematics offers the ready opportunity to demonstrate the impossibility of doing this. Some terms are "primitive;" they must be accepted as undefined.

But even undefined terms are not just meaningless marks on paper. Consider the mathematical kind of *point,* a term usually accepted without definition. Suppose we draw a circle and divide it into three equal pie-shaped pieces. If the three pieces are shaded red, white, and blue, what color is the center of the circle? Examine a map of New England. There is a point where the boundaries of Vermont, New Hampshire, and Massachusetts meet. Who owns the "point"? Through experiences of this sort, students can be brought to see that undefined terms are perfectly reputable, even necessary. The student begins to comprehend that certain language symbols (or mathematical symbols) represent concepts which have significance in terms of his experiences with the real world and that they permit us to build definitions which can convey the same meanings to different people. In brief, here is a way to sensitize the student to the arbitrary and artificial nature of words, yet not give the impression that this necessarily implies chaos.

After a basic vocabulary has been agreed upon, students can be encouraged to build up a large assortment of definitions, generalizing from specific experiences. Students should experience an idea in a variety of problem situations before a name is given to it. This procedure helps focus the attention where it belongs, on the concept itself, rather than on the name we give to it. Confusion of words with the objects and concepts the words signify commonly cripples effective thinking. Instruction in mathematics should be planned to help students avoid this confusion in mathematics and to recognize it in nonmathematical situations.

Other opportunities exist. What of the student who has numerous experiences with exponents, who verbalizes readily that $a^2 = a \cdot a$ and that $x^4 = x \cdot x \cdot x \cdot x$, yet is at a loss to put into words the significance of y^N? What of the student who uses the expression *corresponding angles* to name certain related parts in congruent triangles and persists in using the same expression to identify a certain combination of angles formed by parallel lines and a transversal? In short, what of the problems of *vagueness and ambiguity?* Within reason, we must expect multiplicity of meaning. People do not possess identical backgrounds of experience. Yet we cannot dismiss the problem so casually.

After students have accepted the need for good definitions, they should attempt to formulate definitions of their own. Immediately they will meet face-to-face those twin demons—vagueness and ambiguity. As they struggle to minimize the limitations of language, they should be encouraged to develop a listing of at least five or six characteristics which are typical of a good definition. It is imperative that the mathematics student discover: [13]

1. A definition should name the term being defined.
2. The term being defined should be placed in the nearest and smallest known class.
3. A definition should give the crucial properties which distinguish the term from other members of that class.
4. A definition should give no unnecessary additional properties.
5. A definition should use only terms which have been previously defined (or accepted as undefined).
6. A definition should be reversible; the converse should be true.
7. A definition should be stated positively; it should avoid telling what the term "is not."
8. A definition should avoid circularity; the term being defined must not be used either directly or indirectly in an explanatory role.

Teachers must, of course, recognize that even mathematical language should be precise only to the degree that such preciseness is meaningful to the student. Students without background will gain no meaning from the elegant accuracy of Bertrand Russell's "The number of a class is the class of all classes that are similar to it." Only confusion and possibly contempt will result if the student is confronted with "Under suitable restriction, a continuous function of a continuous function is continuous." [14] Language is successful only when meanings are conveyed, and meaning is grounded in experience. The teacher of mathematics must recognize this principle if the study of mathematics is to give the student a genuine insight into the art of communication.

Even this brief discussion suggests that the language of mathematics is more precise, more cogent, more "correct" than the language of everyday usage. But the two are related; the language of mathematics, which tends to be concerned with quantities, amounts, and abstract relationships, complements ordinary language, which tends to be concerned with kinds or sorts. It serves as a model both to underscore limitations and to suggest procedures for an orderly treatment of the problem of language.

If this possibility is to be realized, teachers will have to consider at least three requirements:

1. Teachers themselves must use language effectively. Preciseness without pedantry, scholarliness without sophistry, caution without cynicism—these the teacher should exhibit consistently.
2. Teachers must provide experiences which help students develop their own individual mastery of language concepts. Memorization of meaningless symbols no longer suffices; mathematics no longer can abound with verbalisms.

[13] Recall summary on definition in Ch. 10.
[14] Lyman M. Kells, *Analytic Geometry and Calculus* (Englewood Cliffs, N. J.: Prentice-Hall, 1950), p. 68.

A significant understanding of the specific vocabulary of mathematics is necessary.

3. Teachers must help the student generalize his language skill. This consciousness of the ground rules of communication should be transferred outside the mathematics classroom.

POSTULATIONAL BASIS OF MATHEMATICS

Ask a group of mathematics teachers "What are the values of mathematics?" Almost certainly many will mention the logical beauty of the subject. The austere correctness of it all suggests to some that here is *one* occasion in the school life of the youth when he meets, face-to-face, *Truth*. After all, does not our mathematics square with everyday experience *and* with common sense? Is not two plus two always four?

Sadly, this is but a shimmering mirage for our Truth seekers. Not only do they fail to grasp a fundamental facet of mathematical thought, but also they let slip away a golden opportunity to teach a basic lesson in the laws of logical thinking.

The popular myth is that mathematical proof is absolute because it grows out of logical reasoning applied to self-evident truths. These supposedly self-evident truths are the axioms and postulates of mathematics. And the application of logical reasoning to these assumptions generates results that are supposedly "True."

The only trouble with this comfortable analysis is that recent developments in both science and mathematics have shown it to be invalid. It is now evident that some of the "self-evident" assumptions are not obviously true and that oftentimes hidden assumptions, not consciously recognized, are accepted.

Probably the most dramatic illustration of this phenomenon is the rise of non-Euclidean geometry over the past century. We now know there are several distinct geometries, each with its own set of assumptions and its own "truths." The details of these developments are not of immediate concern to us, but the reader may wish to learn more of the mathematical issues involved. [15]

The significant fact to be recognized is that in deductive branches of thought (and much of mathematics is taught as a deductive science) conclusions depend upon assumptions. A fundamental aim of the deductive method is the development of a body of propositions which are consistent. Obviously, just as no doctrine can define every one of the terms used in developing it, neither is it possible to prove all of its propositions. Undefined terms have to be introduced. Similarly, some sets of propositions must be taken for granted; not every one can be demonstrated. The essen-

---

[15] A good discussion, requiring no more than a reasonable background of high school algebra and geometry, may be found in Stabler, *An Introduction to Mathematical Thought, op. cit.,* pp. 11-24.

tial requirement is that the assumptions be consistent with one another.

Mathematics is not unique in this respect. Other areas of thought, in fact all thought, proceed out of certain initial assumptions. Unfortunately, it still is generally true that the students' prior work has not been presented so as to give any useful background in deductive thinking. There are opportunities, then, both to turn attention to the postulational basis of the arithmetic and algebra already known to the students, and also to help them to see some of the ways that assumptions influence thinking in nonmathematical situations.

The question of just which propositions are to be assumed is one not easily answered. Even as we recognize that "a doctrine can have maximum clarity and cogency when and only when it has a minimum of undefined terms and undemonstrated propositions," [16] we must also recognize that we are dealing generally with adolescents. As Reeve warns: [17]

> To select the "irreducible minimum" of assumptions, however, is to offer a set of statements quite unintelligible to students beginning geometry or any other branch of elementary mathematics. Such an effort is laudable when the results are intended for the advanced students in the university, but it is merely suggestive to teachers rather than usable by students when it touches upon the primary steps of any science.

The crucial matter *is not* whether a specific proposition such as "Vertical angles are equal" is proved or is assumed from the outset. Rather, it is (*a*) whether the students understand the need for a consistent set of assumptions, and (*b*) whether they realize that the nature of their conclusions is inevitably shaped by the assumptions which precede them. In short, it is fully as important for the student to perceive the role of assumptions and their function in the development of a body of propositions as it is for students merely to grasp the content of these propositions in order to accumulate additional content mastery.

The opportunities available to the teacher of mathematics are manifold. Consider the simple question of whether $1+1=2$. Even junior high school students can be introduced to the rudiments of the binary system and see that, under the new set of assumptions (and definitions) concerning the number system, it is perfectly logical to conclude that $1+1=10$. [18]

Another illustration might be taken from the field of geometry. Often, students are encouraged to "discover" that the sum of the angles of a triangle is 180° by measuring the angles in several triangles and noting that the sum of the angles is independent of the size and shape of the tri-

---

[16] C. J. Keyser, *Thinking About Thinking* (Washington, D. C., special edition by Scripta Mathematica for the National Council of Teachers of Mathematics, 1953), p. 15.

[17] William D. Reeve, *Mathematics for the Secondary School* (New York, Holt, 1954), p. 337.

[18] For a further treatment, see Courant and Robbins, *op. cit.,* pp. 4-9.

angle. But, what if the students draw their triangle on a globe, or a football? A little reflection concerning the conclusions when triangles are drawn on flat surfaces and on spheres will crisply show the significance of any assumption regarding the nature of the surface we have under consideration.

It is equally simple to illustrate the difficulties of inconsistent assumptions. Consider, for example, the proposition:

> Every sentence in this rectangle is false.

If we accept the proposition, then the sentence is "true"; yet the fact that it is "true" is not consistent with the sense of the statement, which requires that the sentence be "false." Conversely, if we deny the proposition, then the sentence is "false"; but now the fact that it is "false" in effect makes the statement "true." Another inconsistency. Thus, while we have the right to choose any assumptions we please, discretion is needed if any sensible results are to be achieved.

This whole matter of assumptions also is closely related to the psychological phenomenon called "set." [19] In effect, set is a blindness to certain possibilities. Apparently set is induced by the unconscious acceptance of unnecessary limiting conditions. Mathematics abounds with simple illustrations of this difficulty.

"Arrange six match sticks to form four equilateral triangles."

"Draw four connected straight lines so that they contain all points in this array."

> . . .
>
> . . .
>
> . . .

In the first problem, it is critical to avoid assuming this must be done on a flat surface, such as a desk top. In the second, it must not be assumed that the array of dots defines the boundary of the completed sketch.

However, presentations of this type will remain only interesting puzzles unless the student can generalize the lessons conveyed. The real value is gained when the student examines the assumptions, open and hidden, which lie behind slogans such as "Buy Brand-Name Products" or until he can bring them to bear on the analysis of questions such as "Why is it that relatively few women have achieved great distinction as artists?"

Thus, the relationship between mathematical thinking and the type of thinking encountered in the everyday world can be better understood. Even though mathematics, per se, has nothing to do with reality and is capable of proving nothing about the world, it constitutes a powerful scheme for discovering and testing relationships which may be observed in

[19] Recall discussion of assumptions in Ch. 7 and of "set" in Ch. 12.

the real world, and it suggests a standard for thinking processes against which many nonmathematical processes may be judged.

To conclude, then, the postulational plan of organization which characterizes mathematics is useful for the systematic development of ideas and principles in many fields of thought. Essentially, the postulational plan implies that three criteria are met:

1. The postulates which support any body of thought must be *consistent*. To the extent that contradictory and incompatible assumptions are accepted, we risk arriving at conflicting conclusions.

2. The set of postulates should be *complete*. In effect, this criterion demands that no hidden assumptions be included in our field of logical inquiry. It is important to recognize that the presence of hidden assumptions probably will lead us to what may be termed extraneous conclusions.

3. The postulates should be *independent*. Generally speaking, this requirement may be thought of more as an ideal than an imperative. Still, it is desirable to avoid overlapping assumptions. Redundancy rarely is an attribute, and tests for independence often may serve to clarify matters of consistency and completeness.

Even though only mathematics and science may demand precise conformity to these criteria, these disciplines hold no monopoly on the characteristic features of axiomatic-deductive organization. Many areas of human thought may be made more effective if attention is given to a list of "official assumptions," to the development of adequate definitions (founded on accepted undefined terms), and to the application of logical reasoning to formulate significant conclusions.

DEDUCTIVE REASONING IN MATHEMATICS

Thus, through mathematics we can make it clear that the deductive system consists of a collection of defined and undefined terms, certain initial assumptions, and conclusions which follow from logical explication. Although the methods of deductive logic have been reviewed in Chapters 7 and 11, it will be helpful to develop certain ideas within the context of mathematics education.

Mathematics is the very essence of what Keyser has termed "postulational thinking." [20] Its fundamental mode of operation rests on the principle that "if p is true, and if p implies q, then q is true."

There are three rather distinct ways to apply this syllogistic argument commonly encountered in mathematics. Usually these are labeled the methods of *analysis, synthesis,* and *indirect proof.* Each will be considered briefly.

Analysis. The method of analysis is the common manner of aiding students in the discovery of proof. It should be made clear, however, that

[20] Keyser, *op. cit.,* p. 14.

to suggest this manner of attack as an aid in discovering proofs is not to be interpreted as suggesting that it always yields a proof. An examination of the pattern of analysis given below will make this point self-evident. It is equally important to recognize that this procedure is of no help in discovering, a priori, what conclusions are plausible enough to warrant efforts to prove them.

Actually it is not necessary to rely on an intuitive judgment as to whether analysis, or any other technique, can equip a student with rules for discovering proof. There are no such rules, and none are possible. Not only is there no possibility of any "mechanical" means of discovering proofs in mathematics generally; it has been demonstrated by Gödel that in some areas of mathematics there can exist no general mechanical test of the correctness of proofs once they have been presented. [21]

Gödel's proof does not, of course, dictate that it is impossible to improve a student's ability to discover and judge proofs. It still remains that some approaches tend to be more fruitful than others as a matter of general procedure, and the method of analysis is one such method. It seems reasonable to anticipate that this procedure for attacking the problem of proof can be taught to others.

The method of analysis may be represented in the following way:

Suppose it is desired to establish that "if A is true, then D is true." (A implies D.)

If C is true, then D is true, because C implies D.
If B is true, then C is true, because B implies C.
If A is true, then B is true, because A implies B.
But, A is true (assumed).

Therefore, since A is true, D is true.

This method could be used by the student in solving the following simple example in geometry.

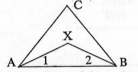

ASSUMED: AC=BC
AX bisects Angle A
BX bisects Angle B
PROVE: Triangle AXB is isosceles

The student might analyze the problem as follows:
1. If AX=BX, then triangle AXB would be isosceles.
2. If Angle 1=Angle 2, then AX=BX.
3. If Angle A=Angle B, then Angle 1=Angle 2.
4. If AC=BC, then Angle A=Angle B.
5. But AC=BC because this was assumed; therefore triangle AXB is isosceles.

[21] Willard Van Orman Quine, *Methods of Logic* (New York, Holt, 1950), pp. 242-248.

Synthesis. Synthesis is the utilization of the syllogistic pattern in order to present a completed proof in an orthodox logical sequence. In effect, it is the step which concludes the enterprise, for it merely affords a concise and formal means for expressing the results of the analytic stage.

The synthetic method can be represented in the following way:

Suppose it is desired to establish that "if A is true, then D is true." (A implies D.)

If A is true (assumed), and A implies B, then B is true.

If B is true, and B implies C, then C is true.

If C is true, and C implies D, then D is true.

Therefore, since A is true, D is true.

Thus, the proof we just considered might now be presented in synthetic form. One scheme for doing this is illustrated in Figure 6. This method of presenting a proof, incidentally, is very helpful in bringing

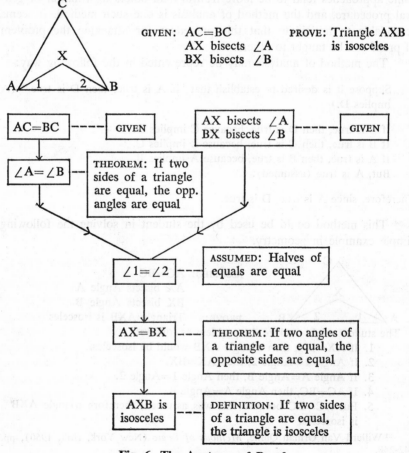

GIVEN: AC=BC
AX bisects ∠A
BX bisects ∠B

PROVE: Triangle AXB is isosceles

Fig. 6. The Anatomy of Proof

students to see the proof as "a logical whole." Variations of it can be used equally effectively to summarize arguments in nonmathematical settings.

It will be readily noted that the methods of analysis and synthesis are inversions of one another. The mathematics student often will use the former as the means of discovery, the latter as the means of checking and presenting a proof.

Indirect proof. Both analysis and synthesis actually represent direct applications of conventional syllogistic reasoning. By accepting the assumption that it is not possible for a proposition to be both true and not-true, it is possible to develop a method of proof which is indirect.

The method of indirect proof can be represented in the following way:

Suppose it is desired to establish that "if A is true, then B is true." (A implies B.)

Assume the statement is false so that "A and not-B are both true."

If it can then be shown that, as a consequence, we must conclude that "C and not-C are true" (or A and not-A are true), this is an impossibility which indicates that at some point a fallacy has been introduced. Since the only possible fallacy is the assumption that "A and not-B are both true," this must be rejected.

Hence, it is concluded that "if A is true, then B is true."

In mathematics we begin many proofs with a statement such as "Suppose that . . ." and then we proceed with the deliberate intent of showing the supposition to be false. By so doing, we demonstrate its contradiction to be true. Consider the proposition "If the square of a number is even, so is the number." To prove this we may start by saying "Suppose there is an odd number whose square is even." From this point on, our efforts are directed toward showing this to be a false statement. In this simple illustration, such a result is readily accomplished if we let N represent an odd number which supposedly has an even square. Because N has been assumed to be an odd number, there must be some non-negative integer (x) such that $N = 2x + 1$. It then follows that

$$N^2 = (2x+1)^2 = 4x^2 + 4x + 1 = 2(2x^2 + 2x) + 1 = 2(\text{some number}) + 1$$

Thus, N^2 must be an odd number, which is a contradiction. In turn, this means that our initial supposition is false and that the proposition is true.

As Kershner and Wilcox point out, the indirect method rests on the establishment of a contradiction. [22] Merely to arrive at a fact known to be true or valid permits no conclusion; the establishment of a contradiction, however, permits a conclusion to be drawn. Although the methods of indirect argument, *reductio ad absurdum* and proof by elimination, sometimes are considered separately, [23] there seems to be no good reason to at-

[22] R. B. Kershner and L. R. Wilcox, *The Anatomy of Mathematics* (New York, Ronald Press, 1950), p. 80.

[23] See, for example, Max Black, *Critical Thinking* (Englewood Cliffs, N. J., Prentice-Hall, 1952), pp. 82-93; and E. R. Stabler, *An Introduction to Mathematical Thought, op. cit.,* pp. 70-73.

tempt this in high school mathematics. Presumably students can develop a useful understanding of indirect reasoning in mathematical and non-mathematical situations without a detailed consideration of the logical subtleties involved. [24]

Much more could be written about other details of the deductive method which may be considered during the study of mathematics. [25] Just one additional example will be suggested.

Frequently we state mathematical propositions in forms like the following: "A necessary condition that p be true is that q be true," or "A sufficient condition that p be true is that q be true." Because the concepts of necessary and sufficient conditions have possibilities of wide application, they merit closer examination. Although individual teachers will vary in their judgment as to how much emphasis this particular concept merits, mathematics certainly should help the student understand that valid "if-then" conclusions follow from sufficient conditions, whereas valid "if not-then not" conclusions follow from necessary conditions.

Consider the following simple illustrations from elementary algebra.

> a. A *necessary condition* for a given integer N to have 6 as a factor (multiplier) is that it have 3 as a factor. Note that the presence of 3 as a factor is necessary, but guarantees nothing about the truth of the proposition that N has 6 as a factor. For example, N might be 15.
>
> b. A *sufficient condition* for N to have 6 as a factor is that it have 12 as a factor. Note now that the fact that 12 is a factor guarantees that 6 will be a factor also; but it is entirely possible that 6 could be a factor even if 12 is not. For example, N might be 42.
>
> c. A *necessary and sufficient condition* that N have 6 as a factor is that it have the integers 2 and 3 as factors. Note that this condition guarantees that any number which meets this requirement must have 6 as a factor *and* that any number which does not meet this requirement will not have 6 as a factor.

Through a carefully planned elaboration of selected mathematical propositions, the whole pattern of logical relationships which connect a proposition, its converse, its contrapositive, and its inverse may be developed out of these basic concepts which underlie necessary and sufficient conditions. [26]

---

[24] An older but still useful discussion may be found in an article by C. B. Upton, "The Use of Indirect Proof in Geometry and Life," *The Teaching of Geometry,* 5th Yearbook of the National Council of Teachers of Mathematics (New York, Bureau of Publications, Teachers College, Columbia University, 1930), p. 102-133.

[25] For a more thorough development see Carl B. Allendorfer, "Deductive Methods in Mathematics," in *Insights Into Modern Mathematics, op. cit.,* pp. 65-99.

[26] A helpful and explicit analysis of these logical relationships and their significance in demonstrative geometry has been presented by Lazar. See Nathan Lazar, "The Importance of Certain Concepts and Laws of Logic for the Study and Teaching

Again, it must be emphasized that the students' opportunities for deductive thinking are not to be restricted to mathematical situations. Because the deductive method is an essential part of mathematical thinking, it should be given emphasis at every opportunity. There is considerable evidence from the field of educational experimentation to indicate that illustrations alone will not teach students the essential structure of the deductive method. Much less will they equip a student to use such methods in his everyday thinking.

An organized, systematic discussion of deductive thinking as an intellectual activity unquestionably is needed. Equally important, reinforcement and elaboration of this topic through experiences with a wide variety of applications are essential. Even though the first steps will be informal, perhaps opportunistic, an adequate mathematics curriculum will provide for a planned sequence of experiences which will make the deductive method a part of each student's "mental furniture."

INDUCTIVE ASPECTS OF MATHEMATICS

For many years the instructional emphasis in mathematics was exclusively on its deductive aspects. Even today this is largely true. An examination of current textbooks and discussions with typical classroom teachers will readily substantiate this point.

At least three major difficulties tend to develop when the deductive approach is the only one considered. In the *first* place, modern educational psychology has increasingly emphasized the importance of discovery in the teaching of mathematics. And yet, discovery is not ordinarily a deductive process, although confirmation often is. The heuristic method is accepted as an effective means of promoting discovery; experimentation, measurement, manipulation, analogy, and comparison are the techniques. Ultimately, the purpose of this method is to guide the student to discover for himself the procedures and principles to be learned.

Not only is it psychologically questionable to treat high school mathematics in a purely deductive manner. For, *secondly,* this procedure results in overlooking a major educational opportunity to acquaint the student with some of the possibilities, limitations, and techniques of inductive reasoning—with what Polya has termed "plausible inference." [27] Polya, in fact, has expressed real concern that we may have become so enamored with the deductive features of mathematical thinking that we overlook its potential contributions to improved induction.

---

of Geometry," *Mathematics Teacher,* Vol. XXXI (1938), pp. 99-113, 156-174, 216-240.

Recall discussion of inference, Chapter 7; discussion of transfer, Chapter 15.

[27] George Polya, *op. cit.,* Vol. I, p. vi.

Everyone knows that mathematics offers an excellent opportunity to learn demonstrative reasoning, but I contend also that there is no subject in the usual curricula of the schools that affords a comparable opportunity to learn plausible reasoning. . . . Finished mathematics presented in finished form appears as purely demonstrative, consisting of proofs only. Yet mathematics in the making resembles any other human knowledge in the making. . . . The result of the mathematician's creative work is demonstrative reasoning, a proof; but the proof is discovered by plausible reasoning, by guessing. If the learning of mathematics reflects to any degree the inventiveness of mathematics, it must have a place for guessing, for plausible inference. [28]

Thirdly, exclusive attention to deductive reasoning may lead the teacher and the student to the belief that deduction is somehow a superior form of reasoning and induction is an inferior method. Sometimes this distortion is carried to the point where deductively established propositions are labeled as "true" while those based on inductive processes are considered "approximate" and therefore of questionable acceptability. The following excerpts from recent textbooks illustrate how this curious distinction sometimes is presented:

Thus inductive reasoning . . . is not a method of proof. It is a method of arriving at a tentative conclusion by experiment, by examining many cases. The tentative conclusion is made *certain* by *logical proof.* [29]

As has been stated before, a proof by induction, which is based upon observation and measurement, is subject to error. For this reason we shall, in the main, study geometry by the demonstration method, which is deductive. [30]

Black offered an explicit warning against just this sort of confusion when he wrote:

. . . the reader should now be on guard against the temptation to regard induction as a kind of inconclusive or otherwise inferior form of deduction. The point to emphasize is that induction and deduction are processes directed toward two different ends. In deduction we discover what is logically involved in given propositions: it supplies us with a valuable means of organizing and reorganizing our assumptions and our beliefs. By means of induction we try to discover those generalizations that are true of the world in which we actually live. [31]

Earlier it was suggested that one aspect of critical thinking is facility in suggesting hypotheses; a necessary skill is the capacity for formulating tentative solutions or conclusions in the light of available data or evidence.

[28] *Ibid.,* pp. v-vi.

[29] Virgil S. Mallory and Chauncey W. Oakley, *Plane Geometry* (Chicago, Sanborn, 1953), p. 74.

[30] A. M. Welchons and W. R. Krickenberger, *New Plane Geometry* (Boston, Ginn, 1952), p. 36.

[31] Max Black, *Critical Thinking, op. cit.,* pp. 306-307.

Yet in conventional mathematics instruction, students often are deliberately deprived of this experience. The present procedure may be summarized briefly in one or two sentences. Ordinarily the student is presented with some general proposition. This proposition is, or readily may be changed to, a statement of certain "given" conditions (curiously labeled as the "hypothesis") and a certain set of conclusions. The student's task is thus reduced to preparing some proof of the already-accepted conclusion.

The limitations of this procedure are clear. The student has no opportunity for experience in taking the crucial step, namely, the invention of one or more plausible conclusions which might reasonably follow from the given data.

Because the conclusions presented are always "true" (mathematics textbooks generally do not encourage consideration of problems presenting conclusions which cannot be proved), there is no reason for the student to adopt a questioning, open-minded point of view; there is no reason for him to suspend judgment. And because the given data always is precisely adequate for the solution, never too much and never too little, the student's experience tends to be a very sterile one where relevancy of data, selection of appropriate information, and discrimination between alternatives only inadvertently enter the picture. [32]

Concern for the restricted and artificial mode of thinking presented in the typical goemetry textbook led Fawcett to propose a completely different way of proceding. His suggestion is that we make the discovery and statement of the general proposition the *culmination* of the learning experience rather than to present it to the student as an inviolate truth which he obediently and perhaps blindly attempts to prove. The following four stages constitute the essential aspects of Fawcett's suggested procedure. [33]

1. A statement of the "assumed data."
2. A statement of one or more hypotheses suggested by the data (these statements formulated by the students).
3. A test of each hypothesis leading to proof or rejection (this testing may include experimentation, analogy, logical elaboration, and the like).
4. A statement by the student of the general proposition which follows from the conjunction of the assumed data and the proved conclusion.

[32] Luchins contends that there is evidence that conventional instruction in geometry not only fails to develop flexibility and originality in thinking, it actually fosters the sort of psychological rigidity which impairs ability to handle unusual problem situations. See A. S. Luchins and E. H. Luchins, "New Experimental Attempts at Preventing Mechanization in Problem Solving," *Journal of General Psychology,* Vol. XLII (1950), pp. 279-297.

Henri Poincaré made the same statement in one of his mathematical discussions.
[33] Harold P. Fawcett, *"Quod erat demonstrandum," The Mathematics Teacher,* Vol. XLIX (1956), pp. 1-6.

Only two textbooks are known to the writers which make a careful and consistent effort to present geometry in the manner suggested above. [34]

It should be kept in mind that the kind of induction under consideration is empirical in nature. It should be distinguished from the more formal method of mathematical induction. If student discovery is to be emphasized, then induction also will be emphasized. In mathematics, the process is largely confined to simple enumeration and analogy, but even in this limited setting a fruitful educational opportunity exists.

Thus, genuine learning may occur when the student is asked to discover and prove some relationship between the hypotenuse of a right triangle and the median drawn to the hypotenuse. If necessary, hints should be given to direct the student's problem-solving efforts. For instance, if the student is making no effective progress, it might be suggested that he prepare several careful drawings and make some measurements, or that he examine again the characteristics of the diagonals of a parallelogram, of a rectangle. How much more profitable than simply being instructed to prove that the median is one-half the length of the hypotenuse!

THE PROBLEM OF TRANSFER

An attempt has been made to point out some of the characteristics of mathematics which seem to indicate that this subject offers a means of improving the ability of the student to think reflectively. It is clear that any such contention, however it may be formulated, ultimately rests on the premise that some form of transfer is possible.

Enough experimental evidence has been accumulated during the past several decades to establish conclusively that transfer does occur, and that certain learning situations are favorable to transfer while others are not. Because transfer is of central importance, a brief discussion of the problems and issues was given in Chapter 15.

INTERPRETATION OF DATA

In the foregoing sections we have suggested a variety of ways whereby certain basic principles of mathematical thinking may be generalized and applied to nonmathematical situations. Very little consideration has been given to the techniques of manipulating numbers and quantities, even though this activity often is judged by many to be "mathematics." Teachers should not overlook this aspect of the mathematical enterprise; it, too, has a contribution to make as an aid to straight thinking. Urged on by the

[34] Myron F. Rosskopf, Harold D. Aten, and William D. Reeve, *Mathematics: A First Course* (New York, McGraw-Hill, 1952).

Leroy H. Schnell and Mildred G. Crawford, *Plane Geometry: A Clear Thinking Approach* (New York, McGraw-Hill, 1953).

popular maxim "Figures don't lie," many persons stand in awe of quantitative presentations. This is merely a manifestation of numerical illiteracy. Surely mathematics is concerned with this problem.

The function concept. When one quantity is related to another such that for every value of the former there is some corresponding value of the latter, the mathematician says one is a function of the other. Thus we have relationships between speed and time, radius and area, volume and pressure, and so on. We often note apparent relationships such as that between intelligence and scholastic achievement, although now the relationship seems less precise, less reliable. Many times the relationship is appropriate over certain limits, but not for the totality of values. For example, when the earth's atmosphere is explored, we find a rather well-defined temperature-pressure variation. This relationship holds until we reach a height of about 40,000 feet. Then, while the pressure continues to drop with altitude, the temperature remains nearly constant, at least to about 75,000 feet.

Thus, although the function concept is fundamental in many mathematical operations, and its usefulness as a tool of analysis has been well established, there are limitations which should be recognized. Students should understand that functional relationships do not necessarily imply or establish cause-effect associations; that accuracy of measurement, the nature of the phenomena, and the influence of miscellaneous variables all must be fully considered. In short, outward appearances of mathematical preciseness must not be confused with logical validity or scientific maturity.

Statistical inferences. The host of errors that may be perpetrated in the name of statistics almost defies cataloguing. Certainly no attempt to do so will be attempted here. Interested readers may turn to other references which consider the problem in detail. [35]

Even though each variety of statistics has its own logical pitfalls, Larrabee has suggested a number of questions which will help to reveal illegitimate procedures. Perhaps these questions always should be asked whenever a set of figures is offered as evidence to support or disprove a particular proposition. [36]

1. *What are their sources?* Is anyone trying to "prove something" by their use? Are all the figures on one side of the argument? Were they gathered especially, or merely in the course of daily routine? Just how much has bias, conscious or unconscious, affected their worth?

2. *Are the quantities used representative of the qualities under discussion?* Are additive and nonadditive qualities kept distinct? Are the units (of meas-

[35] See, for example, H. A. Larrabee, *Reliable Knowledge* (Boston, Houghton Mifflin, 1945), pp. 356-472; Darrel Huff, *How to Lie With Statistics* (New York, Norton, 1954).

[36] Larrabee, *op. cit.,* pp. 401-402.

urement) well chosen with respect to the material? Clearly defined? Stable enough to be comparable?

3. *Are the data sufficient in volume to support the conclusions drawn from them?* Enough instances? Covering enough time? From a sufficient number of sufficiently independent observers? If samples, are they representative?

4. *Has a definite effort been made to discover and present data which might overthrow the conclusions reached?*

5. *Have any of the common fallacies in making inferences from data been committed?* Recall here the extensive listing of errors in making inferences enumerated in Chapter 11, pages 218-222.

EXERCISES

1. Some years ago an American mathematician named Benjamin Pierce said "Mathematics is the science of necessary conclusions."

    a. If we accept Pierce's idea, is mathematics based on deductive or inductive reasoning, or both? Give your reasons.

    b. What is the significance of observation, measurement, and experimentation in the field of mathematics? In the teaching of mathematics?

2. When Albert Einstein was asked to explain how he came to formulate the Theory of Relativity, his answer was, "I never believed an axiom." What are the implications of this creed?

3. Find illustrative problems or examples from one or more textbooks of high school mathematics which resort to subconscious assumptions, introduce undefined terms, or violate the principles of sound postulational organization in some manner. Indicate how your illustrations might be developed into a meaningful experience for learners.

4. The following statement of the characteristics of a good teacher was adopted in 1948 by the National Conference on Education of Teachers. Analyze the list with regard for the principles of postulational organization:

A good teacher should

    1. Possess human qualities—love of children, sympathetic understanding for all, fairness, patience, humor, and a sense of justice.

    2. Have emotional stability and adjustment.

    3. Possess outstanding native ability together with adequate professional training and should like to teach.

    4. Be intellectually alert and curious.

    5. Have pleasing personality and appearance, enthusiasm, vigor, vitality, poise, and charm.

    6. Be able to develop love for the democratic way of life and be a full participating member of the democratic society.

    7. Have the ability to think critically and objectively.

    8. Have a healthy physical and mental outlook on life, with well-rounded interests.

    9. Keep up to date with modern educational trends and philosophies, participate in professional affairs.

10. Understand the importance of developing world citizenship and better human relationships.

(Adapted from E. R. Stabler, *An Introduction to Mathematical Thought* (Cambridge, Mass., Addison-Wesley, 1953), p. 172.

5. Prepare in a form suitable for use in a school mathematics class an account of the historical development of some significant mathematical concept, illustrating not only the concept itself, but also the thought processes which created it. (For example, consider the rise of non-Euclidean geometry.)

6. Prepare a sequence of learning activities to clarify and generalize the concept of necessary and sufficient conditions.

7. Report on the indirect proof that the square root of 2 is irrational. See, for example, Richard Courant and Herbert Robbins, *What Is Mathematics?* (New York, Oxford, 1941), p. 22. Prepare other illustrations of this type of reasoning (*a*) using the subject matter of mathematics, (*b*) using everyday experiences.

8. Prepare a sequence of learning activities which will help a student *discover for himself* a particular mathematical relationship or concept. Discuss the techniques of logical inquiry which you anticipate the student might use. Explain how you would help the student to recognize, master, and generalize these techniques.

BIBLIOGRAPHY

The references given *do not* include any which appeared in footnotes.

FEHR, H. F., *Secondary School Mathematics, A Functional Approach for Teachers* (Boston, Heath, 1951). Largely devoted to mathematical content material. Excellent as subject matter background resource for high school teachers.

FAWCETT, H. P., *The Nature of Proof*, 13th Yearbook of the National Council of Teachers of Mathematics (New York, Bureau of Publications, Teachers College, Columbia University, 1938). Rapidly becoming a classic account of how geometry may be taught for critical thinking without loss of content mastery.

HADAMARD, J., *The Psychology of Invention in the Mathematical Field* (Princeton, N. J., Princeton University Press, 1945). Stimulating and penetrating account of the experiences of outstanding mathematicians as they discovered major new contributions in the mathematical field. Considerable attention is given to the matter of "insight." Generally nontechnical.

HOGBEN, L. W., *Mathematics for the Millions* (New York, Norton, 1937). Semitechnical discussion of the development of mathematical thought and principles. Contains many ideas useful in classroom instruction.

KASNER, E., and NEWMAN, J., *Mathematics and the Imagination* (New York, Simon & Schuster, 1940). A clearly written, nontechnical account of mathematical thought. Excellent for teachers and better students.

KATONA, G., *Organizing and Memorizing* (New York, Columbia University Press, 1940). Provides detailed descriptions of a variety of experiments related to problem solving as interpreted by the Gestalt school. Not quite as directly useful as *Productive Thinking* by Max Wertheimer.

KLINE, M., *Mathematics in Western Culture* (New York, Oxford, 1953). An unusual and outstanding book. Demonstrates the influence of mathematical thought on the development of our culture. Contributions of both content and methodology receive consideration.

The Mathematics Teacher, the National Council of Teachers of Mathematics. All issues of this monthly journal of the National Council of Teachers of Mathematics are worth quick reading. Many articles dealing with teaching mathematics to cultivate critical thinking have appeared over the years; many more will be written.

The Place of Mathematics in Secondary Education, 15th Yearbook of the National Council of Teachers of Mathematics (New York, Bureau of Publications, Teachers College, Columbia University, 1940). Although some aspects of this report are now outdated, most of the proposals still are valuable. Worth reading to trace the development of certain emphases which still control the teaching of high school mathematics.

POLYA, G., *How To Solve It* (Princeton, N. J., Princeton University Press, 1945). A trained mathematician attempts to analyze the problem-solving process as it applies to mathematics. Crisp, readable discussion, based largely on experiences with college students.

SCHNELL, L., and CRAWFORD, M., *Clear Thinking: An Approach Through Plane Geometry* (New York, Harper, 1952). This high school geometry textbook makes a very unusual and determined effort to structure instruction so as to emphasize critical thinking skills. Well worth examining.

WERTHEIMER, M., *Productive Thinking* (New York, Harper, 1945). Brilliantly written report of several subjective investigations of the thought process by an outstanding Gestaltist. Illustrations using mathematical problems and elementary principles of science should give teachers helpful insights regarding problem solving.

CHAPTER **20**

Teaching for Thinking: Science

In the teaching of science, the art of thought should be taught; namely the art of forming clear conceptions applying to first-hand experience, the art of divining the general truths which apply, the art of testing divinations, and the art of utilizing general truths by reasoning to more particular cases of some peculiar importance.
The thought which science evokes is logical thought. Now logic is of two kinds: the logic of discovery and the logic of the discovered.

ALFRED NORTH WHITEHEAD *

INTRODUCTION

The twentieth century has seen science come of age. Dramatic conquests of dreaded diseases, production of unbelievable amounts of energy, the launching of earth-girdling satellites, probes into outer space—each is a manifestation of the power and versatility of modern science. And each causes man to inquire: What is this activity called science? Why has its progress been so spectacular? Can these techniques be applied to other intellectual concerns?

It now seems apparent that discovery of science as an intellectual discipline is perhaps the most significant development in the whole history of science. Clearly, however, this discipline is complex, subtle, elusive. Even as it is not easily attained, it is not easily taught. Indeed, in a conventional sense, it probably cannot be taught at all! If teachers are to communicate successfully to students what we sometimes call "the scientific method," far more than oversimplified rules and prescriptions are necessary. A reasonable comprehension of the methods (note the plural!) of

* Alfred North Whitehead, *The Aims of Education and Other Essays* (New York, Macmillan, 1929).

415

science is the first prerequisite; appropriate content and methodology make up the second; and effective designs for evaluation are a third.

Comprehension of the methods of science is but the *first* objective for science education. A *second* general objective is concerned with the citizenship aspects of science. For example, in 1955 some $5.4 billion were spent in the United States for scientific research and development. Of this amount, just about one-half was spent by the federal government. Stated another way, some $2.7 billion of public funds were spent, by public decision, to foster scientific research and applications. Many fields were embraced—public health, nuclear development, public power, air-traffic control, agriculture. Participation in this type of decision making, even though indirectly, is the obligation of each citizen. Economic, moral, even philosophical questions arise. A general science background for each citizen is necessary, and science education must be organized to provide this.

There is yet a *third* general objective of science education. It has its basis in the needs of citizens as consumers. Science already has thrust itself into our everyday affairs. Every consumer item from high fidelity radio and color television to toothpaste and household detergents derives from applied science. With some minimal background of scientific facts, and some acquaintance with science methods, intelligent consumer decisions may be possible. Without these, the consumer will be hard pressed to make reasonable selections. In other words, living in a world of science, the individual who knows some science will probably get along a little better than the person who knows no science.

The special objectives of science education relating to the matter of training talented students to be future scientists are obviously a further, and somewhat distinct, concern of the science educators. Important as these objectives may be, they have but limited relevance for our present discussion.

Summarizing briefly, we have pointed out that science education has both general and specific objectives:

A. General Objectives of Science Education
  1. Growth in understandings and skills relating to the methods of science and the ability to apply those skills to nonscience problems.
  2. Growth in science knowledge needed to accept citizenship responsibilities in a scientific era.
  3. Growth in science knowledge appropriate for making reasonable decisions as a consumer of the products of applied science.
B. Specific Objective of Science Education
  1. Development of the science skills and knowledge needed by those who will be practicing scientists and technicians.

Except for incidental attention to allied objectives, this chapter deals somewhat exclusively with the first of the objectives suggested above. Many excellent books already present effective discussions of the other.

THE METHODS OF SCIENCE

Step with us for a moment into a typical junior high school science classroom. Along one wall we see a variety of growing plants; in the corridor display case we note a neatly prepared set of posters depicting the constellations; a modern science demonstration table is at the front of the room, fully equipped with gas, electricity, water and waste disposal facilities. The atmosphere of science is evident. Surely science is being taught effectively here.

But on the blackboard something is carefully written. We read the following:

STEPS IN THE SCIENTIFIC METHOD
1. Define the problem.
2. Form some possible solutions to the problem.
3. Collect the data needed to solve the problem.
4. Test these solutions.
5. Select the correct solution to the problem.

What do these words really mean to children? We decide to make a few inquiries of our young friends in the science class. "Just *how* does one define a problem, Johnny?" "Tell us, Sue, what ways do you use to determine whether data have any bearing on a problem you want to solve?" "And you, Bill, what is the best way to think up some good ideas which may be the answer to the problem you have?"

Soon we see that the steps suggested on the blackboard really have little significance to these young learners.

What has gone wrong?

Perhaps it is an oversimplification to suggest that the teacher has been the victim of a most unscientific legend. This legend suggests that scientists have discovered a magic formula for solving problems. And, further, this formula can be dispensed to one and all as the scheme for success. Not so! Scientists make no such claim—and neither should those who teach science.

Yet the scientist does profess fidelity to certain intellectual principles. His general statements of these principles are interesting, but not particularly helpful in the classroom. Jacob Bronowski, British scientist and philosopher suggests, "Science is the creation of concepts and their exploration in the facts." He points out that the authority of "experimental fact as a face of truth" constitutes the driving force of the scientific movement. [1]

[1] J. Bronowski, *Science and Human Values* (New York, Julian Messner, 1956).

Harvard University's Nobel Prize winning physicist, Percy Bridgman, has another way of saying it: "The scientific method, as far as it is a method, is nothing more than doing one's damnedest with one's mind, no holds barred. [2]

Despite the modest claims which scientists themselves advance in support of "method," it is clear that the process of scientific thought is not exclusively individual. Certain attributes concerning relevance of data, controlled experimentation, matching logical consequences with observable facts, and a commitment to a recognizable pattern of intellectual integrity do characterize science and scientists. The ethic of modern science is not like some political code, to be put aside when irksome. At that crucial moment when the scientist addresses the unknown, the failure to observe the "morality" of scientific method is absolute; nature cannot be cheated into revealing her secrets. And it is just because of this that science can make significant contributions to that human skill we call rational thinking.

We have already noted that this contribution cannot be realized simply by telling students the rules of the game. How, then, can we accomplish this? The answer is both simple and complex: *experience,* vicarious or direct. The central thesis of our chapter is that growth in scientific-thinking abilities will occur through those experiences which permit a student to "be a scientist." Many of the problem-solving experiences provided in normal science instruction will help to achieve our goal. A second approach, the case study technique, is gaining acceptance as a means of providing a sort of vicarious experience, a reliving of great moments in science. In this connection, again it is important for us to emphasize that we will not achieve results automatically. Throughout the learning process we must help students identify, specify, verbalize the principles of rational thinking which emerge from their learning experiences. It may even be appropriate to write on the blackboard some five steps which characterize scientific methods.

But this will come at the end of the learning experience, not at its beginning! It will be a conclusion, not a recipe.

THE CASE STUDY APPROACH

It has been suggested by James B. Conant that for the great majority of our students a historical approach to science may lead to the best understanding. The subject matter of modern science is heavily burdened with technical and logical complexities. Only the talented science specialist can hope to penetrate the field deeply. "Philosophic and mathematical minds will prefer the logical approach, but it is my belief that for nine people

[2] P. W. Bridgman, *Reflections of a Physicist* (New York, Philosophical Library, 1950), p. 342.

out of ten the historical method will yield more understanding of a complex nature." [3]

It is important to bear in mind two qualifications: (1) The "historical method" is intended for the student who is a nonscientist, the student who has relatively limited aptitude and interest in science and whose science education is to be a part of his general educational experience; (2) By "historical method" we do not imply a chronological account of the development of science, but rather a series of case studies which permit a student to look in on selected critical developments in science when that subject was in its formative era. By such an approach, the student is afforded an opportunity to "look over the shoulder" of the scientist as he perceives and clarifies a major concept; yet the concept is within the intellectual and experiential framework available to the learner.

The learner thus experiences, albeit vicariously, what Conant has termed "the tactics and strategy of science." Through such experiences he may comprehend what science is and distill out those principles which represent the methods of science. There still remains the task of generalizing these principles of scientific thinking so that their wide application is realized.

Although detailed case studies have been worked out for use with college students, [4] relatively little has been done with this technique in public school instruction. This need not constitute an unsurmountable barrier. Case studies ranging from simple to fairly complex can readily be introduced in all science courses, in the social studies courses, and in the elementary school program. Initial steps can be limited in emphasis, detail, and objective without damage to the purpose they are intended to accomplish.

It may be helpful to consider, in much simplified form, one of the case studies presented in the Harvard volumes. We shall take as our illustration an account of the overthrow of the theory of transmutation of substances as it was accepted by the alchemists of the sixteenth and seventeenth centuries. In particular, we shall consider the investigations which established that water cannot be transmuted into earth. [5]

Our story starts with Johann Baptista van Helmont (1577–1644), a Belgian physician. He performed the famous willow tree experiment and offered the following account:

I took an earthen vessel, in which I put 200 pounds of earth that had been dried in a furnace, which I moistened with rainwater, and I implanted therein

[3] James B. Conant, *On Understanding Science: A Historical Approach* (New Haven, Yale University Press, 1947).

[4] James B. Conant, ed., *Harvard Case Histories in Experimental Science*, Vols. I and II (Cambridge, Mass., Harvard University Press, 1957).

[5] For a detailed account of the role of these experiments in regard to a larger scientific problem, see Conant, ed., *Harvard Case Histories in Experimental Science*, Vol. II, *op. cit.*, pp. 325-436.

the trunk or stem of a willow tree, weighing five pounds. And at length, five years being finished, the tree sprung from thence did weigh 169 pounds and about three ounces. When there was need, I always moistened the earthen vessel with rainwater or distilled water, and the vessel was large and implanted in the earth. Lest the dust that flew about should be co-mingled with the earth, I covered the lip or mouth of the vessel with an iron plate covered with tin and easily passable with many holes. I computed not the weight of the leaves that fell off in the four autumns. At length, I again dried the earth of the vessel, and there was found the same 200 pounds, wanting about two ounces. Therefore 164 pounds of wood, bark and roots arose out of water only.

Here we have an experiment of crude design, to be sure, but nonetheless an effort to "ask a question of nature." The facts of his experiment caused van Helmont to conclude that he had demonstrated an actual transmutation of water into wood (an earthy material). His hypothesis of transmutation, itself a natural historical outgrowth of the natural philosophy he knew, was compatible with the facts as he observed them.

The English scientist, Robert Boyle, carried out variations of this experiment with growing plants. He went an additional step:

. . . and if we consider that not only men, but even sucking children are, but too often, tormented with solid stones, and that diverse sorts of beasts themselves may be troubled with great and heavy stones in their kidneys and bladders, though they feed but upon grass and other vegetables that are perhaps but disguised water, it will not seem improbable that even some concretes of a mineral nature, may likewise be formed of water."

Boyle is thus engaged in the elaboration of the hypothesis. Through this generalization he suggests the new hypothesis—that transmutation of water into earthy substance may occur through other means than growing plants. Soon Boyle presents evidence with regard to this proposition:

I thought it then worthwhile to prosecute this matter a little farther; and having put a pretty quantity of distilled rainwater in a clean glass body, and fitted it with a head and a receiver, I suffered it to stand in a digestive furnace, till by the gentle heat thereof the water was totally abstracted, and the vessel left dry; which being taken out [of the furnace], I found the bottom of the glass covered over with a white (but not so very white) substance, which being scraped off with a knife, appeared to be a fine earth, in which I perceived no manifest taste, and which, in a word, by several qualities seemed to be earth.

Following this experiment, Boyle discussed the phenomenon with colleagues. He reported that they, too, had observed similar deposits, even following repeated distillations of the same initial quantity of water. And so another requirement of science, confirmation by independent observations, is illustrated.

Even so, Boyle suspended judgment. Other hypotheses also might explain these strange deposits, and he candidly presents these alternatives.

If I had leisure and indulgence enough, I could, I confess, add many things in favour of some thoughts [on the possible ways of turning liquids into solid bodies]: yet I would not have you wonder, that whilst I was mentioning the many particulars that seem to evince the change of water into earth, I should let fall some words that intimate a diffidence about it. For to disguise nothing unto you, I must confess, that having in spite of an unusual care unluckily lost a whole paper of the powder I had made myself, and having unexpectedly been obliged to remove from my furnaces before I had made half the trials I judged requisite in so nice a case. I have not yet laid aside all my scruples.

For 1. I would gladly know whether the untransmuted rainwater, by the deposition of so much terrestrial matter, were grown lighter in specie than before [that is, whether its density had decreased after the deposition of the solid matter], or sharp in taste. Next I would [want to] be thoroughly satisfied . . . whether and how far insipid liquors (as rainwater is) may or may not work as menstrums [solvents] upon stones or earthy bodies . . .

2. It were also fit to know whether the glass body, wherein all the distillations are made, do lose of its weight anything near so much as the obtained powder amounts to over and above the decrement of weight which may be imputed to the action of the heat upon the substance of the glass, in case it appear by another glass, kept empty in an equal heat, and for the same time, that the glass loses by such operations anything worth reckoning.

Despite Boyle's judicious reservations, the theory of transmutation prevailed until the French chemist Antoine Lavoisier (1743–1794) reported on experiments which substantially destroyed the hypothesis that water could be transmuted into earth, or other mineral matter. As we have seen, the hypothesis rested on two circumstances: first, the apparent transformation of water to earth by means of plant growth, and, second, the direct conversion of water into earth by heating, as in distillation. Unhappily, Lavoisier gives Boyle no credit for stimulating his own inquiries, which perhaps indicates that scientists, too, suffer from the common human frailties.

Nonetheless, Lavoisier's development of the ideas suggested by Boyle was splendidly conceived and beautifully executed. As a first step, he repeated the process of successive distillations and noted the deposits of a white, mineral-like substance. *But,* Lavoisier measured the density of the distillate at each stage, and found no real difference. Here was a significant clue! If the solid matter were truly a transmutation of the water, how was it that the density of the water did not decrease at each successive stage?

Let us examine Lavoisier's own account of the matter:

I thought that I might be able to deduce from this experiment one of two things. Either the earth that I separated by distillation was of such a character that it could be held in solution in the water without increasing the density, or at least without increasing it as other substances do. Or else that this earth was not yet in the water when I determined its density, that it was formed during the distillation, and, in short, that it was a product of the operation. To decide with certainty which of these views I should adopt, no means has seemed more suitable to me than a repetition of the same [distillation] experiment in hermetically sealed vessels, keeping an exact account of the weight of the water used in the experiment. For if it should be a case of the fire-matter passing through the glass and combining with the water, there must needs occur, after many distillations, an increase in the total weight—that is, in the combined weight of the water, the earth, and the vessel. Physicists know that the matter of fire augments the weights of the bodies in which it is combined.

The same thing should not occur if the earth is formed at the expense of the water or of the vessel. If so, there must be found a diminution in the weight of one or the other of these two entities, and this diminution must be exactly equal to the quantity of earth separated.

Note the penetrating insight of Lavoisier's experimental design. If the repeated distillations of water within the system produce a mineral residue, three significant possibilities may be encountered: First, the weight of the system may increase, indicating that some new material, presumably the substance of "fire particles" has entered the system and combined with some part of the water to form the mineral. Secondly, the weight of the total system may remain unchanged, and likewise the weight of the container may not change, thus indicating that the water constituted the source of the mineral deposit—support for the transmutation theory. Third, the weight of the total system may remain unchanged, but the weight of the containers may be less. This result would indicate that the mineral matter was formed from the container itself, presumably because the water dissolved a tiny portion of the glass container during the experiment.

Upon completion of his experiment, Lavoisier found no change in the weight of the total system, but the glass container had been reduced in weight by a significant amount. Actually, the weight of the residue was slightly larger than the loss noted for the glass, but this was readily explained by Lavoisier.

Therefore it was clearly shown that it was the substance of the glass itself which had furnished the earth separated from the water during the operation. What had happened was merely a dissolution of the glass. But in order completely to attain my objective it still remained for me to compare the weight of the earth which had separated from the water during the digestions with the loss of weight suffered by the pelican. These two quantities should, of course, be equal; and if a considerable excess in the weight of the earth had been found, it would have become necessary to conclude that the glass alone had not furnished all the earth.

There is an excess of three grains in the weight of the earth which cannot be attributed to the solution of the substance of the pelican. However, a little reflection on the conditions of the experiment reveals the origin of this excess; and, indeed, shows it to be inevitable under the circumstances. On its removal from the pelican the water was poured into another glass vessel, and it was afterwards transferred, for the evaporation, to a glass retort. But these different operations could not have been conducted without the solution of a small portion of the substance of these two vessels . . .

It follows from the experiments described in this Memoir that the major part, and possibly the whole, of the earth separated from rainwater by evaporation is due to the dissolution of the vessels in which it has been collected and evaporated . . . the earthy matter that MM. Boyle, Eller and Margraff have separated from water was nothing but glass dissolved during the operation. Thus the experiments that these investigators have used to support their conclusion, far from proving the possibility of changing water to earth, rather lead us to suppose that it is unalterable.

Thus the alchemy of transmutation was discredited and a foundation erected for more productive investigations concerning the fundamental relationships between vegetation and the atmosphere which characterize the economy of plant growth.

Let us review briefly the essential contributions which this case history makes toward an understanding of the methods of science. (It should be clear that this particular case history makes no real contribution to a student's knowledge of the facts of science, and its basic purpose is to offer teacher and learner an opportunity to discover certain generalizations which permit one to think more effectively.)

1. Preconceived notions, in this case first formulated by the Greek philosophers, seemed never to have been subjected to empirical demonstration. Van Helmont undertook to present factual evidence in support of the concept of transmutation. It is significant to note that van Helmont did not suggest other hypotheses to explain the "willow tree" results. Apparently his exclusive concern for the cherished principles of alchemy limited the scope of his thinking.
2. Boyle's work produces results which appear to confirm and generalize the hypothesis of transmutation. Yet he directs attention to certain inadequacies in the experiments conducted, emphasizing that other explanations might reasonably account for all results thus far reported. Just why he did not pursue his own doubts is not entirely clear.
3. Preliminary experiments by Lavoisier with successive distillations of water cast doubt on the transmutation hypothesis. The old explanations are not adequate to account for the new results.
4. The doubts suggested by this preliminary work prompt Lavoisier to attempt a "crucial experiment," designed to permit conclusive logical elaboration of the results in terms of support for a particular hypothesis. The skillful design of the experiment, not to prove a point, but to clarify an issue which is vague and ambiguous, is most significant.
5. A new working hypothesis is confirmed, and an incorrect hypothesis is set aside.
6. Our story is far from complete. The next chapter in this case study

really is the most significant, for Lavoisier's results make clear that the willow tree experiment, and in fact all plant growth, must be explained by some hypothesis other than transmutation. And so a whole new experimental effort was set in motion as scientists sought a valid explanation of the fundamental processes of plant growth.

THINKING IN SCIENCE

Although the sample of scientific activity which we just examined is most limited in scope and significance, the pattern of thinking which we have identified is not. Further study of additional case histories will suggest numerous refinements, elaborations, and special applications. Still, all will yield a common core of principles and procedures which we may reasonably label "the methods of science." A basic goal of all science instruction is to communicate to students the essence of these methods; to encourage the degree of understanding, mastery, and acceptance which makes it both possible and probable that students will apply these scientific methods to all appropriate problem situations which characterize everyday living.

Broadly speaking, the steps involved can be discerned. In practice, of course, these steps occur in no fixed sequence. A subtle interplay among the steps always occurs, generating an infinite number and variety of operations which derive their sequence and form from the nature of the problem and the talents and disposition of the thinker. Nonetheless, there is sound reason to examine briefly, apart from any specific problem setting, the activities we have been calling "the methods of science." It is only through an awareness of these methods that a teacher may hope to communicate them to the learner.

Problem recognition. Obviously, problems must be recognized before they will be solved. In any field, and particularly in science, this assumes familiarity with facts and concepts which pertain to the problem. Given adequate familiarity, problems will grow out of casual observation, curiosity, inconsistency, or need. For school students, a learning problem must not only be recognized, it must be sufficiently simple to permit pupils with limited background and experience to formulate significant hypotheses concerning the problem.

Hypothesis formulation. Once a problem has been recognized, made explicit, and reduced to workable dimensions, proposed solutions usually suggest themselves to the prepared mind. Certain relevant data ordinarily are available, the processes of deductive logic may be applied, mental concepts may be created, analogies and insights occur—a host of intermingling mental activities direct the scientist toward feasible hypothesis.

Hypothesis testing. Even before a scientist turns to experimentation, preliminary tests are used. Available data is examined, analyzed, classified.

Compatibility between these data and suggested solutions should be reasonably substantial.

But crucial experiments eventually must be designed and completed. These must meet certain common tests of preciseness, completeness, predictability, reproducibility, cogency, and workability.

Hypothesis becomes theory. When a hypothesis is found to be consistent with observed data, with related and accepted theory, and with logic, the scientist has achieved a solution to his problem. The solution itself usually is tentative, for subsequent developments in experimental design, laboratory devices, and scientific knowledge frequently lead to refinement or rejection of well-established theories. Rarely, if ever, will problem solutions be certain and enduring.

ABILITIES AND ATTITUDES

It is clear that in order to think there must be something to think about. In a sense, this truism is just another way of saying that a necessary condition for critical thinking is that the individual have experience in or knowledge of the subject of inquiry.

If the matter is pursued no further, the danger is that "knowing as a prerequisite to thinking is all too easily misinterpreted to mean that thinking follows naturally out of knowledge—or, at least, that it should. A logical extension of such reasoning is that critical thinking is a by-product of instruction rather than an immediate objective." [6] Just this point of view has been vigorously put forth in an article by Wood and Beers who contend that "the best if not the only way by which teachers can promote fruitful thinking is to promote knowledge. . ." [7] The task, however, is not quite as simple as Wood and Beers suggest. Something more than factual knowledge is needed if critical thinking is to occur.

Concern for this point has led several writers to develop carefully prepared lists of the particular behaviors which constitute critical thinking. [8] Each of these efforts presents critical thinking as a generalized pattern of behavior abstracted from any particular body of subject matter.

[6] Paul L. Dressel and Lewis B. Mayhew, *General Education Explorations in Evaluation* (Washington, D.C., American Council on Education, 1954), p. 176.

[7] B. D. Wood and F. S. Beers, "Knowledge vs. Thinking," *Teachers College Record,* Vol. XXXVII (1936), p. 496.

[8] Dressel and Mayhew, *op. cit.,* pp. 174-181.

Mary A. Burmester, "Behavior Involved in the Critical Aspects of Scientific Thinking," *Science Education,* Vol. XXXVI (1952), pp. 259-263.

Hilda Taba, "The Evaluation of Critical Thinking," in H. R. Anderson, ed., *Teaching Critical Thinking in the Social Studies,* Part Four, 13th Yearbook, National Council for the Social Studies (Washington, D. C., National Council for the Social Studies, 1942), pp. 123-175.

Harold P. Fawcett, *The Nature of Proof,* 13th Yearbook, National Council of Teachers of Mathematics (New York, Bureau of Publications, Teachers College, Columbia University, 1938), pp. 10-14.

In many respects, the following description of critical thinking has been influenced by the publications cited above.

Characteristics of critical thinking. A person may be said to think critically to the degree that he exhibits the following skills and attitudes:

1. Recognizes and defines problems.

   He is sensitive to problem situations; he recognizes and makes explicit the nature of any difficulty which blocks his attainment of a desired goal; he locates the crucial aspects of the problem; he defines key terms and issues; he breaks complex problems into workable parts.

2. Formulates adequate hypotheses.

   He approaches problems in a flexible manner; he formulates or recognizes feasible hypotheses; he is skillful in establishing an appropriate "solution model."

3. Makes pertinent selections.

   He is aware of the need for facts, for evidence; he is adept at devising methods for obtaining and judging evidence; he is able to keep a problem clearly in mind; he consistently discriminates between relevant and irrelevant assumptions, materials, techniques, and issues; he distinguishes between reliable and unreliable information; he exhibits good judgment.

4. Draws valid conclusions.

   He is rational; he makes reasonable generalizations from specific data (induction); he applies judiciously the canons of logic (deduction); he recognizes the influence of emotions and values; he suspends judgment; he is cautious in asserting the generality of a conclusion because he is aware of the limited data supporting the generalization; he extends the scope of his generalizations only as he discovers additional supporting data.

5. Applies conclusions.

   He grasps the general principles which relate to a problem; he is apt in applying these generalizations whenever they are appropriate; he is capable of decisions, of action consistent with his conclusions.

The above description of critical thinking has been couched in terms of certain skills and abilities, many of which constitute measurable educational outcomes. It is to be noted, however, that while this description deals primarily with the cognitive aspects of the matter, selected effective aspects have been implied. Quite possibly an individual may possess the requisite skills and knowledge; he may be aware of the correct forms of thought, yet fail to be an effective critical thinker. The explanation lies in the fact that critical thinking depends in part upon the possession of certain *critical attitudes*.

An attitude may be considered as an inferred state of readiness to react in a characteristic way toward particular types of situations or objects. Without a disposition to "act critically" there is little likelihood that a person will consistently respond to situations in a manner which can be properly described as "critical thinking."

A brief elaboration of this matter of "critical attitude" is appropriate and was given in detail in Chapter 3. Another outline of characteristics of critical thinking was given in the introduction to Part III.

HOW TO DO AN EXPERIMENT

The average person tends, almost automatically, to associate the word *science* with *experiment*. Actually this association does not always exist. Certain sciences are not experimental at all; consider astronomy, anthropology, archeology, geology, or cryptanalysis. And yet, the popular conception is not entirely unfounded. The experimental sciences are the more numerous, and they have had the greatest impact on the material world we live in. Planned experimentation has been the key which opened the door to our most spectacular technological advances. And certainly the bulk of our public school science instruction is concerned with the experimental sciences.

Carefully chosen case histories, as we have seen, can be used to help students identify reflective thinking skills. Teachers of nonscience subjects —for example, social studies teachers—may find it necessary to rely exclusively on the case study technique. Opportunities to teach scientific methods in nonscience courses naturally are limited.

For the science teacher, no such limitations exist. As we just noted, science traditionally has been a laboratory oriented school subject. Skillful teaching can make the laboratory experience most rewarding. Through it, students can meet on a one-to-one basis the "process of travail" which is the essence of scientific method.

We say, this *can* be accomplished. Too often it is not. School science laboratory problems have become sadly stereotyped. Unimaginative teaching, mechanistic workbooks and laboratory manuals, limitations of equipment and supplies, and an obsession for "demonstration" reap a sad harvest. The spirit of inquiry, the thrill of discovery, the challenge of creative and imaginative effort—all are overlooked in many traditional science laboratories. If our teaching patterns continue to embody the very antithesis of scientific method, what can the student learn about scientific method?

Our best defense against these difficulties depends upon a clear recognition of the nature of planned experimentation. Fundamentally, the school science experiment should yield answers to specific questions. It will do this because it has been designed to control all variables except for the one under scrutiny. This requirement does not necessarily imply complexity. Many outstanding science experiments have been amazingly simple; some have been extraordinarily complex. Regardless of this, certain basic characteristics underlie all scientific experimentation. If we look at a relatively simple experiment, most of the salient characteristics become clear.

Suppose we choose for our example, "Is water necessary for seeds to sprout?" As an experiment, we might plant a seed in a jar of dry soil, water it periodically, and discover that it actually did sprout. Does this permit us to conclude the seed needed the water?

Clearly this conclusion is questionable. We have no knowledge about the behavior of seeds when no water is added. That is, we have no experimental control. Many factors could have accounted for the phenomenon. For example, it is possible that this particular seed was going to sprout spontaneously, perhaps the warm temperature caused it; maybe the action of sunlight is the explanation.

So we add an experimental control. Two jars of similar dry soil are selected. A seed is placed in each; they are exposed to the same conditions of light and temperature; but only one jar is watered regularly. Again we observe that the moistened seed sprouts, but the dry one does not. [9] Is this experiment adequate?

A bit of reflection suggests it is not. Because only one seed was used in each jar, it is possible that the one we placed in the dry jar was dead and would not germinate under any conditions. More cases are needed.

So we do the experiment a third time. Now we select several bean seeds, several corn seeds, several tomato seeds and several pumpkin seeds. These are divided at random and planted in jars as before. Again we make all variables similar except for the amount of water. And again we note that all moistened seeds sprout, but none of the dry ones do. Now we are nearing a defensible conclusion. At least for the types of seeds we have tested, it appears that moisture is needed for them to sprout. We might wish to attempt further verification of our tentative conclusion. Seeds could be planted in dry and moist sawdust, samples could be placed between sheets of dry blotting paper and between sheets of moistened blotting paper, and so on. If each experiment associated sprouting with moisture and no sprouting with dryness, our conclusion is thereby strengthened.

Even the brief, oversimplified situation we have just considered suggests certain "ground rules" for adequate controlled experimentation:

1. The experiment should be planned in terms of a specific hypothesis or objective.

[9] One teacher, a strong prohibitionist, extended a similar experiment to include a jar in which alcohol was placed on the seeds to show its deadly effects. The alcohol destroyed soil pests and harmful insects also, leading the children to conclude that alcohol was very useful in cases of infection!!

2. The experiment should permit a comparison of phenomena observed under experimental and control conditions.
3. The only significant difference between the experimental and control conditions should be the variable which is under study. Extraneous influences should be held constant in both samples.
4. Enough cases should be examined to avoid chance errors due to small samples.
5. The design and conduct of the experiment should be such that other independent investigators can repeat it.
6. Conclusions must not be generalized beyond the specific limits of the experiment.

The foregoing is hardly a sophisticated analysis of the subtleties of scientific experimentation. Still, it represents a reasonable framework for much introductory work. As students come to understand these basic requirements (and limitations) of scientific work, this understanding can lead to more effective and more rational thinking in many problem situations.

A somewhat more mature approach to this same problem has been fostered by a collection of teaching aids recently produced under the auspices of the Manufacturing Chemists' Association, Inc. These teaching aids present a series of "open-ended experiments" intended as much to get the student to do what a scientist must do as to provide him with subject matter information. Each experiment is designed to direct the attention of the student to some scientific principle, to encourage and assist him to investigate the matter, to help him arrange and analyze data, and to set the stage so that he may reach a reasoned conclusion regarding that principle. Often the experiment has no "right answer" in the conventional sense.

The most elementary experiment in the series merely raises the question "What is the optimum height to place a beaker of water above a bunsen burner to obtain the most efficient heating?" A simple experimental design produces data relating time intervals and rate of temperature increase for various heights above the burner. Necessary experimental precautions are pointed out, and effective ways to treat the data are suggested. Because the results vary somewhat with each student's equipment, there is no right answer to this particular question.

Subsequent experiments in the series are concerned with more complicated chemical phenomena, but each is built around the "open-ended" concept. Through them, the student can learn what it is to do a scientific experiment. [10]

[10] These resource materials are published in loose-leaf notebook form under the general heading "Scientific Experiments in Chemistry." They may be obtained by writing to Director of Education, Manufacturing Chemists' Association, Inc., 1625 Eye St. N. W., Washington 6, D. C.

TEACHING SCIENCE TO DEVELOP PROBLEM-SOLVING SKILLS

Perhaps the most significant reason why science teaching frequently does not help students improve their understanding of scientific methods is because teachers believe that achievement of this outcome will happen in the natural course of events, or that an occasional lesson on the subject will be sufficient, or that observation of science demonstrations teaches scientific methods. [11] Even though the study which established these conclusions was made almost thirty years ago, our observation of much science teaching today does not indicate any substantial change of viewpoint. And the results of this viewpoint are just as threadbare and unproductive now as they were then.

One experiment after another, in science and in other instructional fields, has made it apparent that improvement of reflective thinking results from a planned effort. Incidental lessons, wishful thinking, and faith in the traditional notwithstanding, the evidence says we must clarify in our minds just what we wish to accomplish, then set about purposefully to do so.

We have already seen that the phases of problem solving are not discrete, sequential, or self-evident. Methods of science do not resolve into a neat package of rules which can be handed to the student to learn and apply.

How does the science teacher get at this difficulty? First of all, he identifies for his own understanding the abilities, skills, attitudes, and activities which are the methods of science. Next, he devises a sequence of learning situations which may be expected to develop them. As students experience these learning opportunities, he helps them to identify, specify, generalize those skills, abilities, and attitudes. Finally, he develops techniques and instruments which will evaluate the extent of their achievement.

Obourn has suggested a comprehensive checklist of problem-solving practices which a science teacher might use for continuous self-appraisal. Conscientious use of this list will provide a reliable basis for improving classroom practice. [12]

A. *Sensing and Defining Problems*
   To what extent do you:

[11] W. L. Beauchamp, *Instruction in Science,* U. S. Office of Education Bulletin No. 17, Monograph No. 22 (Washington, U. S. Government Printing Office, 1933), pp. 57-58.
   [12] E. S. Obourn, *An Analysis and Check List On the Problem-Solving Objective,* U. S. Office of Education, Circular No. 481 (June, 1956). Presumably Obourn intended this check list to present an inventory of desirable teaching practices rather than to serve as a description of thought-in-process. In actual problem solving, it is necessary to formulate some hypotheses prior to collecting data. Otherwise the thinker would have no guides in his search for meaningful data. Thus it might be better to consider Point E immediately following Point A: Sensing and Defining Problems.
   The subquestions under each heading are excellent.

1. Help pupils sense situations involving personal and social problems?
2. Help pupils recognize specific problems in these situations?
3. Help pupils in isolating the single major idea of a problem?
4. Help pupils state problems as definite and concise questions?
5. Help pupils pick out and define the key words as a means of getting a better understanding of the problem?
6. Help pupils evaluate problems in terms of personal and social needs?
7. Help pupils to be aware of the exact meaning of word-groups and shades of meaning of words in problems involving the expression of ideas?
8. Present overview lessons to raise significant problems?
9. Permit pupils to discuss possible problems for study?
10. Encourage personal interviews about problems of individual interest?

B. *Collecting Evidence on Problems*
   To what extent do you:
   1. Provide a wide variety of sources of information?
   2. Help pupils develop skill in using reference sources?
   3. Help pupils develop skill in note taking?
   4. Help pupils develop skill in using reading aids in books?
   5. Help pupils evaluate information pertinent to the problem?
   6. Provide laboratory demonstrations for collecting evidence on a problem?
   7. Provide controlled experiments for collecting evidence on a problem?
   8. Help pupils develop skill in interviewing to secure evidence on a problem?
   9. Provide for using the resources of the community in securing evidence on a problem?
   10. Provide for using visual aids in securing evidence on a problem?
   11. Evaluate the pupils' ability for collecting evidence on a problem as carefully as you evaluate their knowledge of facts?

C. *Organizing Evidence on Problems*
   To what extent do you:
   1. Help pupils develop skill in arranging data?
   2. Help pupils develop skill in making graphs of data?
   3. Help pupils make use of deductive reasoning in areas best suited?
   4. Provide opportunity for pupils to make summaries of data?
   5. Help pupils distinguish relevant from irrelevant data?
   6. Provide opportunity for pupils to make outlines of data?
   7. Evaluate the pupils' ability to organize evidence on a problem as carefully as you evaluate their knowledge of facts?

D. *Interpreting Evidence on Problems*
   To what extent do you:
   1. Help pupils select the important ideas related to the problem?

2. Help pupils identify the different relationships which may exist between the important ideas?
3. Help pupils see the consistencies and weaknesses in data?
4. Help pupils state relationships as generalizations which may serve as hypotheses?
5. Evaluate the pupils' ability for interpreting evidence as carefully as you evaluate their knowledge of facts?

E. *Selecting and Testing Hypotheses*
   To what extent do you:
   1. Help pupils judge the significance or pertinency of data?
   2. Help pupils check hypotheses with recognized authorities?
   3. Help pupils make inferences from facts and observations?
   4. Help pupils devise controlled experiments suitable for testing hypotheses?
   5. Help pupils recognize and formulate assumptions basic to a given hypothesis?
   6. Help pupils recheck data for possible errors in interpretation?
   7. Evaluate the pupils' ability for selecting and testing hypotheses as carefully as you evaluate their knowledge of facts?

F. *Formulating Conclusions*
   To what extent do you:
   1. Help pupils formulate conclusions on the basis of tested evidence?
   2. Help pupils evaluate their conclusions in the light of the assumptions they set up for the problem?
   3. Help pupils apply their conclusions to new situations?
   4. Evaluate the pupils' ability to formulate conclusions as carefully as you evaluate their knowledge of facts?

EXERCISES

1. Prepare a case study tracing the development of some significant scientific concept, principle, or discovery. The case study should include the proper detail and be of suitable scientific content to make it a basis for either an elementary or secondary school science-learning experience.

2. Many frauds, hoaxes, fictions, superstitions, and just plain honest blunders have been perpetrated in the name of science. These range from flying saucer stories and Martian "invasions" to elaborate proofs concerning the origin and nature of the universe. There are even instances where political or religious dogma has distorted the scientific enterprise to support its own promulgations. Analyze one example of this type of pseudoscientific procedure. Suggest some of the learning activities which might grow out of a consideration of this type of problem.

3. Throughout this chapter we have implied that the formulation of relevant hypotheses is the crucial step in scientific inquiry. The function of any scientific hypothesis is to give direction to problem-solving efforts. Suggest as many criteria as you can identify which must be met by any hypothesis if it is to fulfill productively its function.

The reader may wish to consult various references such as Morris R. Cohen and Ernest Nagel, *An Introduction to Logic and Scientific Method* (New York, Harcourt, Brace, 1934), Ch. 11; and H. A. Larrabee, *Reliable Knowledge* (Boston, Houghton Mifflin, 1945), Ch. 6. There are others.

4. Enumerate the significant differences between scientific method and formal logic.

5. Generally speaking, teachers of mathematics mean one thing when they use the word *hypothesis,* teachers of science mean another. Clarify this difference.

6. Science is sometimes taught as a descriptive, demonstration-oriented subject; sometimes it is taught as a laboratory-oriented subject. Discuss the possibilities and limitations of each of these approaches as a way of improving students' thinking.

BIBLIOGRAPHY

BRANDWEIN, P. F., and others, *Teaching High School Science: A Book of Methods* (New York, Harcourt, Brace, 1958). Discusses the ways of scientists and suggests teaching techniques and resources which will help students understand the methods of science.

BROWNELL, W. A., "Problem Solving," in *The Psychology of Learning,* 41st Yearbook of the National Society for the Study of Education, Part II (Chicago, University of Chicago Press, 1942). Defines problem solving and discusses research in problem solving. Issues in teaching for problem solving are discussed, and eleven practical suggestions are offered.

CAMPBELL, N. R., *What Is Science?* (New York, Dover Publications, 1952). A brief account of the essential characteristics of science as an intellectual discipline. Nontechnical, but scholarly.

COHEN, I. B., *Science, Servant of Man* (Boston, Little, Brown, 1948). A good source of case histories.

COHEN, M. R., and NAGEL, E., *An Introduction to Logic and Scientific Method* (New York, Harcourt, Brace, 1934). Book I is concerned with formal logic. Book II relates logic to the method of science. Excellent chapters on "Hypotheses and Scientific Method" and "The Methods of Experimental Inquiry."

CONANT, J. B., ed., *Harvard Case Histories in Experimental Science,* Volumes 1 and 2 (Cambridge, Mass., Harvard University Press, 1957). Written for college use, but still a superb source of case histories which the teacher can adapt for elementary and high school classes.

CONANT, J. B., *On Understanding Science* (New Haven, Yale University Press, 1947). The initial development of Conant's proposal for a historical approach to science as the means of developing an understanding of science and the ability to use its methods.

CUMMINGS, H. H., ed., *Science and the Social Studies,* 27th Yearbook of the National Council for the Social Studies (Washington, D. C., National Council for the Social Studies, 1957). Develops a point of view that science is of fundamental significance to the social studies teacher because of the nonscience applications of scientific thinking and because of the impact of science itself on the world in which we live.

EASLEY, J. A., *A Study of Scientific Method as an Educational Objective.* Unpublished Ph.D. thesis, Harvard Graduate School of Education. A careful analysis of the nature of scientific method with particular attention to the possibilities of developing skill in scientific method as an educational outcome.

GARDNER, M., *In the Name of Science* (New York, Putnam, 1952). Discusses and exposes a wide variety of fictions which have been perpetrated by the "pseudoscientist." A good source of study materials to illustrate the misuse of scientific method in the twentieth century.

GOLDSTEIN, P., *How To Do An Experiment* (New York, Harcourt, Brace, 1957). A book written for teachers and students. Contains many helpful suggestions for planning, conducting, and reporting on scientific investigations appropriate at the secondary school level.

HEMPEL, C. G., *Fundamentals of Concept Formation in Empirical Science,* International Encyclopedia of Unified Science, Volume II, No. 7 (Chicago, University of Chicago Press, 1952). A very careful, and sometimes difficult, treatment of the process of concept formation in experimental science. Does not require extensive technical background in science, however.

LARRABEE, H. A., *Reliable Knowledge* (Boston, Houghton Mifflin, 1945). An extensive account of the ways by which man achieves reliable knowledge. Many excellent examples and illustrations. Contains a very fine, detailed discussion of the role of the hypothesis in reflective thinking.

Progressive Education Association, Commission on Secondary School Curriculum, *Science in General Education* (New York: D. Appleton-Century, 1938). Offers a broad look at the role of science as one aspect of general education. Contains a helpful chapter on reflective thinking.

REICHENBACH, H., *From Copernicus To Einstein* (New York, Philosophical Library, 1942). A concise history of the ideas that have led to the formulation of the theory of relativity. Gives an insight into the grand strategy of science as mankind groped toward a discovery of a major unifying principle.

CHAPTER 21

Evaluating Critical-Thinking Skills

Evaluation, as contrasted with measurement, embraces a wider range of technique and evidence.

PAUL L. DRESSEL and LEWIS B. MAYHEW*

PURPOSES OF EVALUATION

Testing of students now is as much abused as any single activity in the teaching process. Many circumstances account for this, but two seem particularly important. First of all, testing has frequently done more than measure outcomes; *it has shaped them.* The student concludes that examination-passing is the major purpose of education. Subject matter triumphs over all, and students and teachers find themselves committed to a battle of wits in which the superficial intricacies of content dictate the strategy. Significant outcomes regarding improved critical and creative skills are ignored—even penalized.

A second reason for our difficulty is sheer ignorance of sound methods of measurement and evaluation. Even when teachers identify their basic educational objectives, oftentimes they lack the technical skill to devise ways to measure just how well a student has achieved these objectives. Teachers, like students, can become enmeshed in meaningless verbalisms. At no time is this more clearly demonstrated than when a teacher attempts to report on a student's educational progress. Just join a group of parents during the monthly PTA visiting hour. Each, you will observe, asks the same question. "How is Billy coming along?"

And the replies: "He is doing fine." "Well, Billy just needs to be a

---

* Paul L. Dressel and Lewis B. Mayhew, *General Education: Explorations in Evaluation* (Washington, D. C., American Council on Education, 1954), p. 21.

little more careful." "Arithmetic seems to bother Billy. I guess he needs to work a little harder at it." "Billy doesn't seem to be interested in the work. He always has his mind on something else." "That little Billy of yours is a fine student. Did he tell you that he made 100 in the last spelling test? He never gives any trouble in class, and it is just good to see how much he likes school."

Are these evaluations? For some people they may seem to be. Probably on the next morning Billy would claim in no uncertain language that he had been evaluated. Yet, only a moment's consideration suffices to convince us that no truly useful judgment of Billy has been offered. The significant questions have not been answered. And worthwhile evaluations must answer significant questions. The fact that Billy's mother did not ask a significant question is beside the point. A good teacher could help to educate her, too.

Over 40 years ago Thorndike postulated that "whatever exists at all exists in some amount," with the obvious implication that it therefore can be measured. [1] Perhaps this is an overstatement. Certainly many human attributes cannot *now* be measured, even though they exist, for example, attitudes of appreciation, love for one's wife, and the like. Whether we can ever hope to measure all dimensions of the human mind and personality is a moot question. Regardless of this, if Thorndike's assertion has any merit at all, it surely suggests that we can make a more productive effort at evaluating than our teacher friend did for Billy. After all, Billy exists!

Even though evaluation of critical-thinking skills is the real concern of this chapter, it will be helpful to spend a few moments examining the larger problem of evaluation. Without attempting to offer an abridged text in educational measurement, a few of the more important issues may be reviewed. Even this general review, however, will be undertaken from the somewhat special viewpoint suggested by our interest in evaluating critical-thinking activities.

At the outset it should be recognized that evaluation has certain purposes. Both the nature of the evaluative activity and the method of summarizing and interpreting the results should be controlled by the purpose of the evaluation. Four general purposes may be considered:

1. *Clarification of Instructional Objectives*

Conventionally, the first step in evaluation is to state the objectives of the particular course or unit. This may lead one to assume that careful identification of objectives must come *before* we evaluate, that never can objectives be a consequence of the evaluation. Yet we shall find that some of the activities and behaviors which we label "critical

[1] Edward L. Thorndike *The Nature, Purposes, and General Methods of Measurement of Educational Products,* 17th Yearbook of the National Society of Education, Part II (1918), pp. 16-24.

thinking" are nonspecific; our efforts to evaluate these activities will help us continuously to improve our understanding of the very objectives we seek to evaluate. This point will become clear as we discuss the methods and materials now used to measure critical-thinking skills.

2. *Assessment of Knowledge and Skills*

When we specify our objectives, we will find it both appropriate and possible to state the kind of subject matter and knowledge, the intellectual skills, the attitudes and dispositions which these objectives signify. Evaluation of these attributes will permit teachers to estimate the likelihood of success in more advanced work (prognosis); it will permit an analysis of the student's strengths and weaknesses (diagnosis); and it will provide a means for estimating the extent to which a given student has attained the course objectives (reporting outcomes).

3. *Motivation*

Because tests so often have been used in a threatening manner, we usually see them as an extrinsic, authoritarian type of motivation. This need not be the case. Intrinsic motivation, healthy and constructive, can grow from effective evaluations. When students understand the real objectives of education, and when they are helped to see a reasonably precise estimate of their own progress in achieving these objectives, evaluation becomes a part of the teaching process. It is a disturbing fact that this rather obvious possibility is generally neglected.

4. *Improvement of Instruction*

The results of evaluation can give teachers new insights into what they are doing. Every evaluation of a student is also an evaluation of the instructional program. Unfortunately, teachers (who so casually rate their students) live in such dread of being rated themselves that often they fail to see the great potential which their own evaluations offer for their own improvement.

EVALUATING CRITICAL-THINKING BEHAVIOR

The general purposes of evaluation need to be sharpened considerably before any specific act of evaluating is likely to be productive. No evaluative efforts should be attempted before this is done. Under most circumstances this will mean the teacher must clarify the particular behavior he wishes to assess. It follows, then, that to evaluate critical-thinking skills, we must first stipulate the kind of things people do when they think critically. Much attention has been given to this matter in earlier chapters (see Chapters 4-12; 19).

This aspect of evaluation is tremendously demanding. Only if it is carefully and adequately done is it probable that really useful results can be attained. Although competence in critical thinking can in one sense be viewed as a generalized skill, the skill itself will be apparent only when applied in specific situations. Once we establish the nature of the behavior we wish to examine, the crucial step is to devise questions, situations, and experiences which, when successfully undertaken, provide evidence with respect to this behavior.

All of this may be stated a bit differently. Each teacher must analyze the tasks of critical thinking within the frame of reference established by particular school subjects. Science teachers will have to stipulate the kinds of knowledge, behavior, and attitude that characterize critical thinking *in science,* perhaps even in a particular field of science. Social studies teachers will need to do this for the various social studies, English teachers for the language arts, and so on.

Fortunately, some help is available. Other writers have given thought to this problem. A list of the more helpful references includes:

Science
> Mary A. Burmester, "Behavior Involved in the Critical Aspects of Scientific Thinking," *Science Education* (Dec., 1952), pp. 259-263.

Social Studies
> Hilda Taba, "The Evaluation of Critical Thinking," in H. R. Anderson, ed., *Teaching Critical Thinking in the Social Studies,* 13th Yearbook of the National Council for the Social Studies (Washington, National Council for the Social Studies, 1942), pp. 123-175.
>
> Paul L. Dressel and Lewis B. Mayhew, *General Education: Explorations in Evaluation* (Washington, D. C., American Council on Education, 1954), pp. 35-41.

Mathematics
> Harold P. Fawcett, *The Nature of Proof,* 13th Yearbook of the National Council of Teachers of Mathematics (New York, Bureau of Publications, Teachers College, Columbia University, 1938), pp. 10-14.

English
> Edward M. Glaser, *An Experiment in the Development of Critical Thinking* (New York, Bureau of Publications, Teachers College, Columbia University, 1941).

To summarize, the teacher who would evaluate critical-thinking skills must achieve three things. *First,* there must be a comprehension of the general nature of critical thinking, of the behaviors it implies. If the reader has been attentive and the authors successful, this volume has already achieved this end. *Second,* there must be an understanding of the unique function of critical thinking within the setting of a particular body of knowledge, a particular subject, a particular problem situation. The present volume, supplemented by the many references which have been suggested will meet this need. *Third,* the teacher must reflect on the significance of these ideas; he must interpret, modify, elaborate, and implement them according to the practical realities of his own teaching situation.

PRINTED TESTING MATERIALS FOR EVALUATING CRITICAL THINKING

From time to time, tests have been published which are directly concerned with evaluation of certain aspects of critical-thinking ability. Although relatively few tests of this sort are available (in comparison with the plethora of subject matter tests), some are very good. Any teacher with concern for the problem of evaluating critical thinking should be acquainted with these materials.

It is not possible for us to analyze in detail each published test in critical thinking. This section will present a limited discussion of the more significant ones. However, only a careful examination of the test, the manuals, and other related materials will be adequate to permit the reader to judge whether a particular test is appropriate for his purposes.

GENERAL TESTS OF CRITICAL-THINKING SKILLS

Several tests have been devised that are intended to measure some aspects of critical thinking, apart from a particular subject matter area. The more important of these include the following.

Watson-Glaser Critical-Thinking Appraisal, World Book Company, Yonkers, N.Y., 1952. [2] This test is designed for use with high school and college students. The test items, which are of a multiple-choice type, present problems, statements, arguments, and data similar to that which a citizen might encounter in daily life. Five subscores can be obtained for (1) Inference, (2) Recognition of assumptions, (3) Deduction, (4) Interpretation, and (5) Evaluation of arguments. The test is easily administered and readily scored. Excellent normative data is presented. Of the tests currently available, probably this one is the most widely used.

Test of Critical Thinking, M. T. Macey and H. B. Wood, School of Education, University of Oregon, Eugene, Oregon, 1951. Available in mimeographed form, this test is designed for use in the junior high school grades. Part scores are obtainable on (1) Inquiry, (2) Interest, (3) Relationships, (4) Open-mindedness, (5) Generalizations, and (6) Accuracy. The test is easily administered and can be scored quickly, although no printed answer sheets are available. All items are objective. Only very limited normative data is presented by the authors, and it is unlikely that the norms are of any useful significance.

A Test of Critical Thinking, American Council on Education, Cooperative Test Division, Educational Testing Service, Princeton, N. J.,

[2] For a review of an earlier edition, see O. K. Buros, ed., *Third Mental Measurements Yearbook* (New Brunswick, N. J., Rutgers University Press, 1949), p. 544.

1952. Although this test was developed for use with college freshmen, it has been used successfully with high school sophomores. Objective type test items and answer sheets make the test simple to administer and score. Part scores are available for (1) Defining problems, (2) Selection of information, (3) Recognition of assumptions, (4) Inventing and evaluating hypotheses, and (5) Making and judging inferences. Normative data is available for college students, but none is published for high school students.

Interpretation of Data Test: General Education Series, Co-operative Test Division, Educational Test Service, Princeton, N. J., 1950. [3] This test is an adaptation of the excellent evaluative instruments developed in conjunction with the Progressive Education Association's Eight-Year Study. Despite the fact that scoring is complicated, and norms are not published, this test is of considerable interest because it attacks the problem of evaluation with real ingenuity. Forms are available for use at college level as well as for junior-senior high school students. Part scores can be obtained for (1) General accuracy, (2) Recognition of true-false statements, (3) Accuracy with insufficient data, (4) Overcaution, (5) Overgeneralizing, and (6) Crude errors.

Inductive Reasoning Test, G. B. Baldwin, Education Test Bureau, Educational Test Publishers, Inc., Philadelphia, Pa., 1946. [4] Because it provides only items dealing with completion-of-number sequences, this test will be of limited interest. The test is for high school and young adult use. Easily administered and easily scored, it may produce significant results concerning ability to reason inductively with quantitative concepts. There is no evidence that more general skills are measured. Norms are provided but are of limited value because they are not fully reported.

Test of Practical Judgment, A. J. Cardell, Science Research Associates, Chicago, Illinois, 1950. [5] This test is designed to measure capacity for practical judgment in everyday situations. It is intended for high school and college use. Although the evidence to support the validity of this test is somewhat inconclusive, some indications of face validity can be noted.

Ohio Thinking Checkup for Intermediate Grades, Ohio State Department of Education, 1946. [6] A subtest of the Ohio Guidance Tests for Elementary Grades, this instrument is for grades 4-6. Common aspects of critical thinking such as interpretation of data, overgeneralization, and overcaution are evaluated. Normative data are not published.

Logical Reasoning Test, Co-operative Test Division, Educational Testing Service, Princeton, N. J., 1950. [7] Essentially, this test measures

[3] For reviews, see O. K. Buros, ed., *The Fourth Mental Measurements Yearbook* (Highland Park, N. J., Gryphon Press, 1953), p. 581.

[4] For review, see Buros, *Third Mental Measurements Yearbook, op. cit.,* p. 232.

[5] For reviews, see *Ibid.,* p. 694.

[6] For review, see *Ibid.,* p. 63.

[7] For review, see Buros, *Fourth Mental Measurements Yearbook, op. cit.,* p. 582.

ability to handle formal logic of an elementary sort. Ten scores are obtainable, but the very nature of the scores makes some dependent upon others; for example, "right conclusions" and "wrong conclusions" appear as two distinct scores although they are merely opposite sides of the same coin. As the manual suggests, this test seems to be appropriate primarily for senior high school students with some training in formal logic. A limited amount of normative data is presented.

Logical Reasoning, Sheridan Supply Company, Beverly Hills, Calif., 1955.[8] This is a brief test (20–25 minutes) consisting of 40 logical syllogisms. The items test ability to handle 15 different syllogistic forms. Easily administered, the test items are of the multiple-choice type, and thus the test is also easy to score. It is intended for use in grades 9–16. Because the items deal only with syllogistic logic, and because relatively limited normative data are available, it is unlikely that this test will be of general value. In special situations it would make an interesting teaching device. Quite possibly it would be a valuable research instrument.

SPECIALIZED TESTS OF CRITICAL THINKING SKILLS

Often it is possible to evaluate certain critical-thinking skills best in terms of a specific subject or problem. More than a dozen tests have been published which make a specific effort to measure some aspect of critical thinking as it pertains to a particular sphere of school instruction. The following section briefly describes the leading tests of this type.

A. Critical Thinking in the Language Arts

Interpretation of Literature Test, Co-operative Test Division, Educational Testing Service, Princeton, N. J., 1950. [9] Adapted from the Eight-Year Study, this test is based on a detailed analysis of a summary of an O. Henry story. Seven scores dealing with understanding, recognizing point of view, grasp of motivation, weighing evidence, and literary analysis can be obtained. Although some sections of this test relate more closely to technical skills in literary competence, many aspects of it are significant to the more general problem of critical thinking. Norms are not available.

Test of Critical Analysis in Reading and Writing, Co-operative Test Division, Educational Testing Service, Princeton, N.J., 1953. This test is designed for use at the college level, although it might be effective with better students in senior high school. It assesses the student's ability to read rather difficult materials with comprehension and, by requiring judgments of writing effectiveness, attempts to measure ability to write clearly. Norms are not available. No part scores can be obtained. In its present form this test probably is of more value as a teaching device than as an evaluative one.

Interpretation of Literary Materials, Test #7 of the Iowa Tests of Educational Development, Science Research Associates, Chicago, Ill.,

[8] For review, see Oscar K. Buros, *Fifth Mental Measurements Yearbook* (Highland Park, N. J., Gryphon Press, 1959), pp. 694-695.

[9] For reviews, see Buros, *Fourth Mental Measurements Yearbook, op. cit.,* p. 187.

1951. [10] This test is one of a nine-test battery designed to sample ability to think critically and to apply factual information in specific subject matter areas. It is intended for high school use. Rather than depending upon an analysis of specific course content as a basis for these tests, the test writers have attempted to judge what an educated person should know or understand about significant areas of knowledge, and the tests are constructed in terms of these judgments. Substantial normative data are available to help in interpreting the test results.

Co-operative Literary Comprehension and Appreciation Test, Co-operative Test Division, Educational Testing Service, Princeton, N. J., 1941. This test was constructed by Frederick B. Davis and others on the basis of applying nine critical principles suggested in part by I. A. Richards' writings to the purposes of evaluation. It attempts to measure knowledge of word meaning; ability to reason abstractly; ability to understand explicit statements; ability to determine the writer's purpose, intent, and point of view; ability to draw inferences from the passage about the content of the passage; ability to grasp detailed statements; ability to follow the organization of a passage and to identify antecedents and find references in the passage; ability to recognize the literary devices used in a passage and apprehend its tone and mood; and ability to synthesize the main ideas of a passage.

B. Critical Thinking in the Social Studies

A Test of Critical Thinking in Social Science, American Council on Education, published by Co-operative Test Division, Educational Testing Service, Princeton, N. J., 1951. Like the *Test of Critical Thinking* reviewed above, this is another of the instruments developed for the American Council on Education's Co-operative Study of Evaluation in General Education. It is intended for early college use but seems to have applicability for high school students. Although certain items are less appropriate now than when the test was written because the material is somewhat "dated," the test still merits attention. Specialized knowledge of social studies is not required. No part scores are obtainable, but the test manual gives a description of the particular critical-thinking skill tested by each item. Some normative data from colleges are published.

Interpretation of Reading Materials in the Social Studies, Test #5 of the Iowa Tests of Educational Development. See the general comments given above with respect to another test from the same battery, *Interpretation of Literary Materials.*

C. Critical Thinking in Arithmetic and Mathematics

Many publishers provide one or more tests of arithmetic. Generally these tests purport to give part scores on computational skills ("arithmetic fundamentals") and problem-solving skills ("arithmetic reasoning"). The latter type of score does measure some very specific skills which constitute

[10] For a general review of entire battery of Iowa Tests of Educational Development, see *Ibid.,* p. 17.

a small part of general critical-thinking ability. Because the problem situations tend to be highly artificial, and because the problem setting is unusually limited, it is questionable whether these tests contribute much to the evaluation of the larger objectives of critical thinking as these have been suggested in this book.

By and large, it appears that no tests presently available really get at the problem, either at the elementary or at the high school level. Most of the published tests in this general area contain only a few items which appear to be truly appropriate. Perhaps discriminating use of pupil's performances on these items will serve as a basis for making judgments about their critical-thinking abilities in quantitative and mathematical situations, but much experimental work could be done in this area.

D. Critical Thinking in Science

A Test of Reasoning and Understanding Natural Sciences, American Council on Education, Co-operative Test Division, Educational Testing Service, Princeton, N. J., 1952. Another test from the Co-operative Study of Evaluation in General Education, this one also is designed for use with entering college students. For the most part it consists of excerpts from science articles written for the general public with questions to evaluate a student's ability to analyze the problems in terms of the broad principles of science. Part scores can be obtained for (1) Problem recognition, (2) Selection and use of information, (3) Hypothesis formation, (4) Development of conclusions, and (5) Attitudes. Although the vocabulary of the test is a bit difficult, it seems reasonable to consider using this test with better high school students. Some limited normative data for college freshmen are published.

Test of Application of Principles in General Science, Co-operative Test Division, Educational Testing Service, Princeton, N. J., 1950. [11] This test, like the following two, is part of the General Education Series of tests which developed out of the Eight-Year Study. Students are presented with science problem situations similar to those occurring in everyday living. Statements of causes, predictions, or possible courses of action are presented, and a variety of supporting reasons also are presented. The student selects the best statement and the reasons which justify that selection. Although this seemingly provides an excellent way to get at process as well as product, it does lead to involved administration and scoring procedures. Norms and part scores are not available. The test may be more useful as a teaching tool than an evaluative one.

Test of Application of Principles in Biology, Co-operative Test Division, Educational Testing Service, Princeton, N. J., 1950. [12]

Test of Application of Principles in Physical Science, Co-operative Test Division, Educational Testing Service, Princeton, N. J., 1950. [13]

[11] For review, see *Ibid.,* p. 629.
[12] *Ibid.*
[13] *Ibid.*

Each of these tests is similar in construction to the general science test. Of necessity, the tests do not give consideration to all principles of science which might be considered worthy. Further, they in no way should be considered as tests of subject matter mastery (this latter point is not to be interpreted as an indictment, however). In view of the lip service which science educators pay to the objective of scientific attitude, it is perhaps significant to remark that very few tests have been published which evaluate this skill. These tests make a significant contribution.

Interpretation of Reading Materials in the Natural Sciences, Test #6 Iowa Tests of Educational Development. See the general comments given above with respect to other tests from this same battery.

E. Miscellaneous Tests

The alert teacher will find that a variety of other tests also can be helpful in diagnosing and evaluating critical-thinking activities. Tests dealing with study skills, use of library materials, use of sources of information and similar techniques will give an objective appraisal of the student's capabilities in this important phase of careful thinking. Likewise, tests and inventories of attitudes, beliefs, and interests will provide the teacher with helpful insights. Finally, certain subtests on reasoning or problem solving appear in many intelligence and aptitude tests. These, too, can give significant information regarding the learner. There are many dozens of tests in these general categories, and it is quite out of the question to summarize each. Suffice it to observe that if the teacher will take the time to examine carefully the individual items and the major subsections of many published tests, she will note that much can be learned about students' critical-thinking skills from their responses to these items.

TEACHER-TECHNIQUES FOR EVALUATING CRITICAL THINKING

PENCIL-AND-PAPER TESTS

For many years teachers have used their own written tests of one type and another as one of the major techniques for evaluation. Even though these have often been shown to be unreliable, incomplete, and even unvalid, this fact hardly signifies that teacher-made tests should be abandoned. When used properly, they may be as valuable as any other evaluative technique. In fact, under some circumstances, they are absolutely essential. Consider, for example, the fact that no other person knows the student *as a learner* as well as the teacher, and no other person knows the objectives of a particular course as intimately as the person teaching that course. Only the classroom teacher is in a position to develop the tailor-made evaluation procedures fully sensitive to these points.

How is the classroom teacher to meet this challenge? Many excellent books and articles have been prepared which discuss the use of standardized tests, which suggest ways to summarize test scores, which stress in a general way the function of evaluation in a well-balanced program of instruction. The bibliography at the end of the chapter lists many sources, and only a brief discussion of these matters will be presented.

But there is relatively little well-organized and readily accessible material which gives specific help to the teacher in developing teacher-made testing materials. Some down-to-earth instruction in how to plan and prepare for classroom evaluation is needed. It is the intent of this section to provide such help, although detailed suggestions and illustrations cannot be given. If they encourage further thought and reading, they will have served their end.

The test items. Several factors should be considered in determining the types of test items to be used. Perhaps these factors can be emphasized best by suggesting certain questions which should be answered by the person preparing the test:

1. Specifically what is the purpose of the particular question? What objective does it relate to? What does this objective mean in terms of definite, concrete behavior?
2. Does the test item require this behavior in order to be completed successfully? Are other types of behavior also required? If so, can the behavior under consideration be distinguished by a response to this item?
3. Can the behavior under consideration be measured by a more realistic problem situation?
4. Are the directions clear? Are there any word patterns, grammatical clues, or other hints which tend to make the problem either too easy or unnecessarily confusing?
5. If test items have been used previously, have they been revised and refined on the basis of earlier results? Have teaching colleagues examined them for clarity, suitability, agreement on significance of response, and the like?

As the above questions imply, preparing test items is a continuous process. If a teacher will remember this, many effective testing items will be suggested through class discussions, through leisure-time reading, in conferences, and while reviewing or supplementing subject matter. When ideas for testing occur, by all means record them immediately, and file them for subsequent use.

It is recommended that each test item, or problem, be recorded on a 4 x 6 index card. As the various items are used from one class to the next, appropriate notes should be made regarding the suitability of the item, its apparent difficulty level, and possible revisions. After a brief period of time the teacher will have an excellent inventory of test items, all carefully refined. Some, of course, will deal with material which is "perishable," but even these often make useful models for similar items using different content.

Many different types of test items have been devised. Not all are useful in testing for critical-thinking outcomes; some are much better than others.

1. *Simple recall items.* Items of this type require the student to give an answer in the form of a single word or number, or a brief phrase. An illustration: "If a proposition is true, its contrapositive is . . . ."

   Clearly, although this type of item is easy to prepare and score, and usually eliminates the "bluffing" which we sometimes get with true-false or multiple-choice items, it is limited to material of a simple descriptive nature. Any widespread use of such items to test critical thinking is unwise.

2. *True-false items.* Items requiring a simple indication of truth or falsity permit the examiner to sample a wide range of material. Thus, if we were interested in learning of students' proneness to accept superstitious beliefs, they might be given a true-false test using items such as: "One should be especially careful on Friday the 13th," and "Eating carrots will help a person see better at night."

   Of course, there is always the problem of guessing. This problem is aggravated if the items are carelessly prepared. An adaptation of this type of response ("always true," "always false," and "sometimes true and sometimes false") avoids certain difficulties, but, generally speaking, different items will serve better to measure critical thinking.

3. *Sequential or rearrangement items.* Items of this type, including matching items, are best adapted to evaluating a grasp of chronological sequences of events or the procedural sequence of a set of operations. For example, the steps in the development of a particular theorem in geometry might be presented in scrambled order and the student directed to arrange the steps in logical sequence. This may be a useful means to present a very intricate problem, one which a student might not be able to solve without this limited assistance.

   A major weakness with this type of test item is that it requires a complicated scoring procedure. If many steps are involved in the sequence, scoring will be very complicated. Thus the usefulness of this type of item is limited.

4. *Multiple-choice items.* The multiple-choice test item presently enjoys wide popularity because it offers most of the advantages of the other objective items and at the same time reduces the significance of many of the disadvantages. A little ingenuity, amplified by a study of the ideas illustrated in various commercially printed tests, will permit a teacher to construct a versatile assortment of test items based on the multiple-response structure.

   Effective evaluations of critical-thinking skills often can be made by basing a series of questions on a carefully developed selection which the student reads before attempting to answer the questions. Many of the standardized tests reviewed in this chapter use this technique.

   Some teachers have expanded the testing possibilities of these items by providing the opportunity for the student to write out a defense of his choice. This gives the teacher considerable insight into troublesome situations where simple knowledge of "right" and "wrong" responses does not give enough information about the student's method of attack.

5. *Essay items.* The essential characteristic of the essay item is that it requires the student to create his own answer rather than merely to choose an answer from a few specific alternatives. It permits testing powers of decision, discrimination, interpretation, organization, and development. It permits the teacher to appraise perception of significant and subtle distinctions. These characteristics make the essay item an unusually effective way of testing critical-thinking skills.

Unfortunately the scoring of essay-type items has many well-known shortcomings. Scores are influenced by penmanship, grammar, spelling, fluency, general neatness, and other possibly extraneous circumstances. Careless scoring of essay questions has given them a notorious reputation of unreliability.

Nevertheless, with care and common sense, this type of item can be very useful. Teachers should construct *in detail* the correct answer before correcting papers. A specific listing of all appropriate points, with recognition of the needed sequence, must be available. Papers should be rated in five or more general categories, thus separating the problem of obtaining raw scores from the problem of grading or ranking. Once a good distribution of raw scores has been obtained, the assignment of grades can be handled as for any other type of test.

Excellent treatments of the essay examination and its use are to to be found in many modern texts on principles of teaching and on evaluation.

Administering tests. A well-constructed test can be made worse than useless through improper administration. Special pains must be taken to be certain that directions are clear; students should understand what is expected. Distracting interruptions should be avoided. These may occur in the guise of group activities, health examinations, counseling interviews, casual visitors, and the like. A check with the principal often will help avoid unnecessary confusion during formal evaluations and testing.

Many arguments have turned on the most suitable length of a test. As a rule, longer tests give more reliable results. Obviously, practical considerations cannot be ignored, and usually the length of a single class period controls the time of testing.

A related question is the one of time-limit tests versus work-limit tests. No hard and fast rules can be defended. Probably most teacher-made tests should be of the work-limit type. Although there are certain skills where speed is a crucial factor, in the area of critical thinking teachers should not have primary interest in how fast students can read and respond to test items.

Usually tests are administered on a carefully supervised basis. This is as it should be. But the results have been sterile. The almost complete absence of "open book" testing is unfortunate. Certainly in school there should be much more testing designed to permit and even to require the student to use whatever references, texts, notes, or other materials he considers necessary to solve the problem facing him. This is a real-life situation, and testing should not lose sight of this fact. Perhaps the testing of critical-thinking skills, more than of other school outcomes, should be arranged with this in mind.

Analyzing test results. There is no sense in carefully preparing and administering a test if the results are not then put to use. Actually, a test will be more effective if the planning as to how the results will be analyzed and applied is done *before* the test is prepared. A basic analysis should be made for every test, including at least the following points:

1. A distribution of the raw scores should be prepared.
2. Some sort of average should be computed. Generally, the median will be preferable to the arithmetic mean, although each has its uses.
3. The raw score distribution should be used to derive other scores with greater intrinsic significance. For many years percentile scores have been one of the most popular kinds of derived scores. Recently, the use of stanine scores has been gaining wider acceptance, and they may be the best of all for classroom teachers. Elementary books in educational measurement should be consulted for additional suggestions concerning derived scores.
4. Some form of item analysis should be made to provide a basis for both group and individual diagnosis.

Obviously, corrected tests should be returned and discussed with the class just as soon as possible. Careful attention should be given to helping students understand the purpose of the test questions, how each relates to a clearly established objective, and the type of intellectual behavior which the teacher had in mind to appraise. There should be ample opportunity to go over tests with individual students to help them experience a satisfactory learning situation.

OTHER EVALUATIVE PROCEDURES

It would be inaccurate to leave the impression that evaluation is restricted to answers given on pencil-and-paper tests. Many less formal methods are available and should be used. Project work, committee activities, research papers, reports on individual reading, and related activities present excellent evidence on critical-thinking skills. Anecdotal records, questionnaires, and rating scales will serve to give a balanced picture of the student. That is, they will do this if they are developed and evaluated with the same thoroughness which has been indicated for written tests. A random and haphazard collection of teachers' impressions, based on a few special occurrences, is not what we mean.

Sociometric techniques. Various quasi-mechanical devices can be used to measure both the quality and quantity of class discussion. A chart similar to the one illustrated below will reveal patterns of participation in group thinking by the individuals in the group. Probably it is not feasible to use this type of evaluation frequently, and certainly the spots for using it should be carefully chosen in terms of the nature and purposes of the discussion. The results can be useful to the class as a group and to individuals as they have a good look at the role they play as members of a group attempting to solve a problem.

Name	Factual Statement	Valid Inference	Invalid Inference	Irrelevant Point	Statement of Opinion	Incorrect Information
John	x x	x			x x	
Mary			x	x		x
Ray	x		x x		x	
Jean	x x	x x x				

(Each cross indicates one contribution in the category where it appears.)

The variations possible in this technique are probably infinite in number. Even though it is not as easy to interpret these results in terms of numbers which may be handled as we do test scores, this detracts not at all from the usefulness of sociometric methods. Critical-thinking objectives are admirably suited for this type of behavioristic evaluation.

Evaluations based on audio-visual presentations. With radio, motion pictures, television, and tape recordings commonly used to strengthen instruction, we must not overlook the role of these devices in evaluation. Once again, the opportunities are manifold. Only one specific illustration will be discussed, a technique which has sometimes been called the "interrupted showing method."

This technique requires only a thought-provoking film dealing with a subject within the experiential range of the class, and some very careful planning by the teacher. For instance, we might select a film which deals with the teaching of controversial issues. One such film presents a case study of how a history teacher taught about the United Nations, the consequent criticism she received, intervention by the school board, the sometimes acrimonious testimony at a public hearing, and ultimately the school board's disposition of the case. By interrupting the film at key points and asking the class to evaluate the quality of the thought processes exhibited, by inviting the class to suggest desirable courses of action on the basis of evidence then available, it is possible to involve them directly in the events portrayed on the film. As new evidence unfolds, as varying points of view are brought to light, as judgments are made and actions taken, the students

A CRITICAL-THINKING SCALE

Name of student: ....

DIRECTIONS:

The following items describe certain kinds of behavior associated with the skill we often call "critical thinking." A careful rating of a student on each item will give an index of his or her critical-thinking skill.

The ratings should represent your best estimate of the student's typical, day-in-and-day-out behavior. Do not rate a person according to his or her performance in one unique or spectacular situation. To help obtain ratings which represent typical behavior, it is requested that no ratings be prepared until at least one week after you receive this rating blank.

For each of the items you are to place a check (√) at the point on the scale which seems best to describe the person being rated.

1. Ability to recognize a problem.

/	/	/	/
Rarely notices any sort of problem	Identifies only superficial problems	Notices obvious problems; overlooks subtle ones	Maintains questioning attitude; is intelligently curious	Has penetrating mind; consistently identifies problems

2. Tendency to stick to a problem.

/	/	/	/
No capacity for a sustained attack on most problems	Many problems not held clearly in mind; wanders, introduces irrelevant ideas	Solves average problem efficiently	Is persevering; is reluctant to leave a problem without completing it	Is unusually persistent in all problem-solving efforts

3. Tendency to be rational.

/	/	/	/
Is gullible; easily swayed by own beliefs, values, prejudices	Makes clear effort to be rational; is hampered by limited intellectual ability	Attacks most problems in rational, objective manner; troubled by highly controversial issues	Regularly attacks all problems in a logical manner	Is unusually adept at logical analysis; attacks all types of problems in a logical manner

4. Ability to clarify a problem.

/	/	/	/	/
Does not attempt to make a problem specific, precise, definite	Usually unable to select and clarify key ideas	Usually grasps central idea in ordinary problems	Detects and clarifies central ideas even in complicated problems	Consistently locates and clarifies very obscure points

5. Ability to attack a problem in a flexible and original manner.

/	/	/	/	/
Abandons problem after one attempt to solve	Relies on steady plodding, shows little ingenuity	Shows average resourcefulness	Has only occasional trouble suggesting new, effective ways to attack problems	Is highly imaginative; displays unusual ingenuity

6. Awareness of need for evidence, for facts.

/	/	/	/	/
Feels "one opinion is as good as another"	Rarely presents or demands any sort of supporting evidence	Generally seeks the facts of the situation	Regularly seeks evidence; is a good judge of reliable and pertinent data	Consistently bases conclusions on all facts, properly evaluated

7. Ability to draw accurate conclusions.

/	/	/	/	/
Often reaches conclusions contrary to the known facts	Does not interpret data carefully; draws unjustified conclusions	Usually forms acceptable conclusions	Regularly forms acceptable conclusions after sound analysis of all facts	Competently organizes and interprets even complicated data, notices obscure inferences

8. Willingness to suspend judgment.

/	/	/	/	/
Jumps to conclusions	Considers alternate solutions only very superficially	Usually makes reasonable choice among obvious alternatives	Critically examines most possibilities	Reaches decisions only after a careful analysis of all available data

will have several opportunities to express their own thoughts. When thoroughly and skillfully planned, the teacher can evaluate many aspects of critical-thinking behavior. Of course, as is the case with all good evaluations, the students will also enjoy an effective learning experience which will help to improve the very skills being evaluated.

Rating scales. Rating scales of one form and another have been used for many types of evaluation. Fundamentally, such scales are intended to provide a way for an observer to report his impressions about a person and to do so according to certain guidelines which assure a degree of objectivity in the rating.

Although no rating scales which relate directly to critical-thinking skills are generally available, one of the authors developed a scale which was used effectively in a separate research study. [14] This scale is presented on pages 450-451. It was developed in terms of the significant characteristics of critical thinking as defined in this volume [15] and presents possible categories of critical-thinking behavior expressed in language commonly used by teachers.

EXERCISES

1. Select a test of critical thinking that is designed for use at the grade level and in the subject area of greatest interest to you. Prepare a careful, item-by-item, analysis of the test:
   a. Which critical thinking behaviors are sampled?
   b. Which behaviors are not tested adequately?
   c. Does each item test only one or more critcal-thinking abilities, or do other skills and knowledge play a predominant role in solving the item?
   d. What items could be improved? How?
   e. What items might be added? Omitted? Why?
2. Choose a critical-thinking skill which seems to permit pencil-and-paper testing. Describe a problem situation suitable for testing for mastery of this skill. Write test items of various types (true-false, multiple-choice, completion, essay, etc.) based on this problem situation.
3. Suggest additional techniques for evaluating critical-thinking behavior other than those given in this chapter.
4. What evidence is there that satisfactory performance on pencil-and-paper tests of critical-thinking skills is a reliable indication that the person will think and act critically in real-life situations?
5. Comment on the following, with particular reference to evaluating critical-thinking skills:

[14] R. B. Kimball, "An Investigation of the Relationship Between Certain Aspects of Critical Thinking and Instruction in Geometry." Unpublished Ed. D. thesis, Harvard Graduate School of Education, Harvard University, 1958.

[15] See, for example, the list in Ch. 20, p. 426.

"The school must devise means for continuously evaluating pupil growth. The primary consideration is to devise instruments and techniques which as nearly as possible approach lifelike situations. Lifelike here means like the life of immature but growing children, not the life of mature, organized society. Unable to secure final and conclusive evaluations, the school will endeavor to gather as much presumptive and symptomatic evidence of learning as possible. The problem of evaluation and the devising of instruments is clearly one of the most prominent and dynamic educational problems of the moment." From W. H. Burton, *The Guidance of Learning Activities,* 2nd ed. (New York, Appleton-Century-Crofts, 1952), p. 575.

6. Describe how the promotional and evaluative practices in your school give recognition to the critical-thinking objective of education. Suggest modifications if you consider the present practices inadequate.

BIBLIOGRAPHY

AMERICAN COUNCIL ON EDUCATION, *A Guide for the Teaching and Evaluation of Critical-Thinking Abilities in Social Science* (Washington, American Council on Education, 1952). A mimeographed bulletin describing the work of Co-operative Study of Evaluation in General Education in the area of the social sciences. Contains many suggestions and illustrations concerning both objective and nonobjective evaluative techniques. Although written from the viewpoint of college teaching, most ideas are readily adaptable to public school situations.

AMERICAN EDUCATIONAL RESEARCH ASSOCIATION, *Technical Recommendations for Achievement Tests* (Washington, National Education Association, 1955). Despite the title, most of the recommendations are not so highly technical. Teachers with rather limited background in educational measurements will find these suggestions very helpful in judging the worth of published tests.

ANDERSON, H. R., ed., *Teaching Critical Thinking in the Social Studies,* 13th Yearbook of the National Council for the Social Studies (Washington, 1942). Part Four, written by Hilda Taba, discusses the evaluation of critical thinking. Specific suggestions and helpful illustrations are included.

BARON, D., and BERNARD, H. W., *Evaluation Techniques for Classroom Teachers* (New York, McGraw-Hill, 1958). A practical treatment of the problem of evaluation in the classroom.

BUROS, O. K., *The Fifth Mental Measurements Yearbook* (Highland Park, N. J., Gryphon Press, 1959). A very useful reference. A great number of published tests and books or articles dealing with evaluation are carefully reviewed by experts. Earlier editions of this volume often contain information not repeated in later issues, so all editions should be consulted.

CRONBACH, L., *The Essentials of Psychological Testing* (New York, Harper, 1949). A clear and authoritative discussion of many types of tests, including intelligence, interest, aptitude, achievement, and personality.

DRESSEL, P. L., and MAYHEW, L. B., *General Education: Explorations in Evaluation* (Washington, American Council on Education, 1954). A full account of the evaluative studies made during the Co-operative Study of Evaluation in General Education. This volume contains several sections which give detailed and thoughtful analyses of the nature of critical thinking and the problems associated with attempts to evaluate this complex skill. An excellent treatment.

FURST, E. J., *Constructing Evaluation Instruments* (New York, Longmans, Green, 1958).

LEFEVER, D. W., and others, *Measuring Pupil Achievement* (Chicago, Science Research Associates, 1957). A nontechnical little pamphlet prepared for teachers and administrators at the secondary school level. Contains many practical suggestions.

LINDQUIST, E. F., ed., *Educational Measurement* (Washington, D. C., American Council on Education, 1951). This handbook has become a standard reference in the field. Leading authorities have contributed chapters.

MAYHEW, L. B., *Developments in Testing for Critical Thinking and Attitudes*, Program and Proceedings of Conference on Higher Education, 1954, pp. 37-47. An especially appropriate reference.

MORSE, H. T., and McCUNE, G. H., *Selected Items for Testing of Study Skills and Critical Thinking* (Washington, D. C., National Council for the Social Studies, 1957). A source of samples and suggestions for social science teachers.

NOLL, V. H., *Introduction to Educational Measurement* (Boston, Houghton Mifflin, 1957).

SMITH, E. R., TYLER, R. W., and others, *Appraising and Recording Student Progress* (New York, Harper, 1942). This volume reports steps taken by schools in the Eight-Year Study to measure the progress of students toward accepted goals. Even though an older reference, contains many refreshing suggestions.

WALKER, H. M., *Mathematics Essential for Elementary Statistics* (New York, Holt, 1951). A good refresher on selected topics from simple arithmetic and mathematics needed to understand and use the elementary statistical concepts which underlie educational measurement.

WEITZMAN, E., and McNAMARA, W. J., *Constructing Classroom Examinations* (Chicago, Science Research Associates, 1949). Simple and straightforward discussion of the techniques of constructing objective test items. Written for teachers.

WRIGHTSTONE, J. W., *Evaluation in Modern Education* (New York, American Book, 1956).

WRIGHTSTONE, J. W., *What Tests Can Tell Us About Children* (Chicago, Science Research Associates, 1954). A brief and readable review of some major purposes and techniques in evaluation.

Appendixes

APPENDIX A

Questions for Preliminary Discussion

Several days may be spent profitably on these questions. Beware of answering any of them quickly and glibly. All will repay time spent in analysis and exchange of views.

Three continuing questions to be used throughout the course.

1. What is the author trying to accomplish in this chapter (or any assigned materials)? Put it as briefly as possible in your own words.
2. Summarize as briefly as possible the major points, or concepts, or principles, or conclusions developed in this chapter (or assigned materials).
3. Do you think the author achieved his purpose reasonably well? Tell why— or suggest additions and/or rearrangements.

Preliminary Discussion, A

1. You, as experienced teachers, will all assert that you try to teach your students to think. Outline specifically how you go about this. (Time will be given for the preparation of this outline before class discussion starts.)
2. Scholars agree that reason and the intellect are not the chief factors in reaching decisions, in controlling our behavior. Why, then, study the processes of reasoning or, more broadly, thinking?

Preliminary Discussion, B

1. This course will deal in part with the process of thinking and with teaching for the improvement of thought. Students often say enthusiastically: "Just the course I am looking for! I wish to improve my thinking." Or, "I wish to learn how to think."

   This course which deals with thinking and its improvement will not and cannot teach you to think. Can you explain this seeming paradox? If you can, you are on the way to understanding thinking and how to improve your own processes. If the question baffles you so that no start can be made, it might be well to take a preliminary course in Principles of Teaching.

2. After you know and understand what may be said about the processes of thinking, there is still one item outside thinking itself, which is necessary before you may think well, or at all. This factor is, indeed, a *sine qua non*. What factor is indicated?
3. It has been said that the greatest obstacle to thinking is to have no obstacles at all. What are the implications of this statement?

Preliminary Discussion, C

1. According to one popular conception, Heaven is a place where everything is calm and peaceful, all desires are satisfied, no problems will annoy. A prominent thinker states, therefore, that thinkers will probably not be ad-

457

mitted and if admitted would be quite unhappy. What is the basis for his humorous statement?

2. A well-known political leader once said: "Do not ever appoint ministers or priests to public boards if it can be avoided." Can you develop some of his reasons for saying this?

3. An engineer is called upon to determine the nature of a bridge necessary to span a deep canyon. A sociologist is trying to determine the influence of the Negroes of Birmingham on Southern culture. Summarize in organized manner the likenesses and the differences in the processes likely followed by the two men.

4. Do fish sleep? The answer to this question is not important. The essential thing is an account of how you went about finding the answer you finally accepted. Bring in a detailed account of everything you did in attempting to develop an answer. (The discussion will not be allowed to digress to the question itself, but will be held to the process of answering).

After developing an answer and your method for deriving an answer for Question 4—"Do fish sleep?"—select any one of the following and proceed as in Question 4. Remember that the essential thing is the account of your method of proceeding to find an answer.

    a. Can children below the age of five reason?

    b. At what age does syllogistic reasoning appear among children? (That is, processes which could be thrown into syllogistic form by adults.)

    c. Can critical thinking be taught?

    d. Can critical (or scientific) thinking be tested?

    e. Which students are likely to be the more effective thinkers—those who read slowly or those who read rapidly?

    f. What percentage of the school population is probably capable of critical thought? Creative thought?

    g. Do the comic strips and books affect the thinking of children who read them? Moving pictures? Television?

    h. A proportion of children is often asked to repeat a grade. What is the effect of this on their learning and thinking?

    i. When a child makes a mistake or gets the wrong answer, the failure is pointed out. Show how this aids thinking.

    j. What is the effect, if any, on thinking of tension or emotional stress? Of given attitudes? Of prejudices for or against anything?

    k. What part does one's experiential background play in thinking?

5. What have you learned about thinking from the foregoing question? Apply what you have learned to any one of the current criticisms of our schools and educational system. What would happen if the critics applied what you have learned?

6. The great majority of men:

    a. Are able to maintain in their minds, with no embarrassment whatever, two flatly contradictory sets of opinions, convictions, values. (This is known as compartmentalization of the mind.)

    b. Are able to state consistently and persistently a set of convictions and values and, at the same time and without embarrassment, are able to act in flat contradiction of the announced convictions and values.

c. Are able to substitute words (verbalisms) for action in situations which actually can be solved only by appropriate action.

d. Flatly refuse to accept moral responsibility for either speech or action, in fact are usually unaware of what is known as moral responsibility.

e. Are unable to distinguish between:

(1) Fact and opinion.

(2) Evidence and hearsay.

(3) What they observed and their opinions of what they observed.

(4) The canons, controls, and processes of logic—and the complete absence of these things in their personalized thinking.

Explain each of these items as best you can at this preliminary stage of the course. Outline as far as you can some of the results and implications for life. Outline the educational implications.

NOTE: The following questions may and should be answered without any mention of your church affiliations, political party, or social conventions. We are not at all concerned with your affiliations and memberships. We are concerned with the general texture and attitudes of your mind. The areas used supply excellent opportunities for testing this. Any student who wishes may be excused from answering the question on religious beliefs.

7. State any principle, doctrine, or conviction upheld by your political party, but with which you *disagree*. Tell very briefly why you differ.

8. State any principle, doctrine, dogma, firm conviction upheld by the church of your affiliation, but with which you *disagree*. Tell briefly why.

9. State any belief, conviction, convention, or social usage which is firmly believed in by the general social class to which you belong, but with which you *disagree*. Tell briefly why.

10. What is meant when a man is labeled a "free thinker"?

11. What comment do you care to offer on Francis Bacon's statement: "If we begin with certainties, we shall end in doubts; but if we begin with doubts, and are patient in them, we shall end in certainties."

12. Write out in a few numbered statements what you have learned about thinking so far.

Preliminary Discussion, D

The next set of questions may strike you as simple, even somewhat absurd. The questions are to introduce a number of phases of thinking as ordinarily carried on, with implications for improvement. Do not be led away from the processes involved because of the trivial content in some of the anecdotes.

1. Consider these two simple anecdotes:

a. A New Yorker staying at one of the early dude ranches years ago casually stated that he had paid $5 for dinner in New York on a number of occasions. Several cowpunchers stalked off in disgust and thereafter regarded the visitor as an unprincipled liar. Said they, "No man could eat $5 worth of ham and eggs and canned peaches."

b. An early auto tourist, dressed in plus fours, stopped in a remote village, whereupon a local resident said in disgust, "That's the first time I ever seed a growed man in knee pants."

The judgments' expressed exemplify a number of errors in thinking which unhappily are quite common in more exalted places. One blunder in particular is very widely found in the thinking of the everyday citizen. Analyze the incidents to show several errors in the thinking, and try to spot the one major blunder.

2. Many individuals, in trying to explain a given situation, say, "Why it's a natural."
   a. Tell first explicitly what is meant. (If you do not know, skip this question.)
   b. Analyze as in No. 1 to show the various errors. This story brings out some new ones.
3. An ancient poem widely known as "Mother Shipton's Prophecies" was written long, long ago in England. Mother Shipton referred among other things to—"carts without horses shall go"—"ships without sails will run"—"men flying in machines through the air."

This is taken almost universally as a remarkable prophecy—seeing into the future. Generations before they appeared, Mother Shipton was credited with foreseeing automobiles, steamships, airplanes, and many others. A far more sensible explanation can be made.

   a. Can you think out a better explanation than prophecy?
   b. If so, outline your own thinking—and particularly what probably happened in the thinking of the so-called prophet.
   c. Any guidance here for interpreting other prophecies? Other factors in prophecy?
4. The dock loafers in Palos laughed at Columbus when he asserted that the world was round. "Everyone can see that it is flat," said they.
   a. Outline the facts which led Columbus to believe it round.
   b. Why, do you suppose, others of his time did not react as he did?
   c. Any guidance in this for us?
   d. Can you cite other "ridiculous hypotheses" in history which turned out to be right? Any which did not? Is there any possibility of distinguishing between the two types before experiment or life processes have gone so far as to be wasteful in the case of the erroneous items?
   e. Cite some widely held educational beliefs which are similar in their error to the dock loafers' belief in a flat world.
5. A school principal says he never heard of such nonsense as pupil participation in management, in planning class procedures, in evaluating. He has never seen creative education which was anything but chaos. He knows that all "progressive" classrooms are disorderly and unproductive.
   a. To what extent is he a brother under the skin to the cowpunchers and the villager in the first stories above?
   b. To what extent is he notably different?
6. Individuals often say of something they meet, "I never heard of it." Can

you see what this may do to thinking? Give several reasons why persons make this reaction.

7. How does the savage ward off disease, calamity, war? Bring needed rain, safety on the warpath?

How do you do it? What are the differences and likenesses in the two cases?

Preliminary Discussion, E

SUMMARY. The foregoing discussions were to introduce you through common-sense, everyday experiences to the principles and processes involved in reflective thought. Let us attempt a preliminary summary before entering the systematic discussion.

1. Argument arises, it is commonly believed, when two or more persons disagree. The fact is that disagreement prevents argument. Argument can arise only when two or more persons agree on something. (The last sentence deliberately omits something but is correct for our purpose here.)

Explain the statements in the last two sentences. Guidance for our everyday affairs? For aiding students to improve their thinking?

2. Define in a sentence each:

truth	proof
fact	explanation
knowledge	illustration

3. Why do you believe so many things which are not so and concerning which simple evidence is easily and immediately available?

4. Make a brief listing of any principles of thinking, aids to thinking, and errors to avoid which you may have derived from these preliminary discussions.

5. Make a similar listing of educational implications. Individuals or committees should make an organized list of inferences drawn from the preliminary discussions which would be of direct assistance to teachers in aiding pupils in thinking. The list here will be incomplete, and we will repeat this at the end of the course.

6. Report briefly to the class any accounts of thought-in-process which you may have run across anywhere. These will usually be found incidentally in one's general reading. Poets, prose writers, scientists, inventors, and other creative thinkers occasionally leave detailed accounts of their own thinking in arriving at problem solutions, beliefs, or other conclusions.

END OF PRELIMINARY DISCUSSIONS

Special Additional Exercises on Details of Process

The ordinary class of good background will grasp the general nature of the process from the three or four simple problems at the beginning of this list. Instructors and students who need or wish to go further will find the following problems both interesting and enlightening. Answers may be oral or written. Class discussion is essential. Individuals or committees, preferably the latter, may report.

GENERAL DIRECTIONS TO THE STUDENT. Select any one of the

following, and work out an answer. Think it out, ask others, get group discussion if you can. The *answer* to the question is not so important as the *process* of securing it. Keep a record, and analyze the process in terms of the foregoing discussion of problem solving. Do not quibble over words if the general meaning and setting of the problems are clear.

After writing this analysis, make a brief but adequate summary of inferences regarding teaching. In other words, specifically what guidance for teaching can you derive from this exercise?

1. *Situation.* The twenty-one-year-old son of a millionaire, a college graduate, is wrecked on a remote island, peopled by a primitive race. This man has always lived in a large city; his money has procured him anything he needed or wanted. He has never done a day's work, though not lazy, and has always been much interested in the type of life he led.

   There is no chance for rescue for years, if at all. He must either work, play, and live as the natives do or die. He takes up their existence, comes to like the active outdoor life, and marries a native.

   Ten years pass. A ship loses its way and finds the remote island. The man can be taken back to civilization to take up his old life.

   Question. Will he return or stay?

2. *Situation.* A book is published anonymously and becomes famous. A disappointed man, a failure in life, tells his wife in order to regain her respect and love that he is the unknown author of the book. The true author hears of this statement, makes the acquaintance of the faker, and in due time reveals who he is. The false author commits suicide. Meanwhile, the real author has fallen in love with the wife, now widow. She believes passionately in the integrity and ability of her dead husband and will not remarry.

   Question. Will the author tell her the truth, or will he allow her to go on believing her husband the author of the book, arranging that part of the royalties go to her to keep up the deception?

3. *Situation.* A housewife is faced with the choice of giving her family a sketchy, inadequate dinner in order to get away to a very important business engagement or giving them a good meal and being late to the engagement.

   Question. Which will she do?

4. *Situation.* (This one is not original but appeared in a story some time ago.) A renowned scholar has spent a lifetime compiling notes for an authoritative book in his field of research. The notes are complete. A drunken butler accidentally sets fire to the house. By the time the scholar discovers the fire it is clear that he can save his notes or the drunken butler who is lying in a stupor. No one else is there; so there would be no witnesses.

   Question. Which will he save? (This one affords a good opportunity to trace the scholar's thinking, no matter what decision he chooses.)

   NOTE. These exercises may be tried on groups of individuals who are not studying this text. Note differences between their procedures and those of the students.

   Instructors or students may make up many similar situations.

APPENDIX B

The Baconian Idols

These are to be used in connection with the exercises for Chapter 11, "Errors and Fallacies in Thinking."

The roman numerals in parentheses refer to the original paragraphs in Bacon's statement. The statements have been reworded for the sake of brevity and clarity.

Idols of the Tribe

Foundation in human nature itself, tribe or race of men.

The sense of man is *not* the measure of the universe or of things—on the contrary all perceptions are according to the measure of the individual—the human understanding is a false mirror which distorts by mingling its own nature with the perceptions.

1. (XLI) Tendency to rely on sense—to rely on limited personal data—to judge by appearances. ("Seeing is believing"—"common sense tells us"—"my experience shows"—all of this the opposite of critical analysis and evaluation which must be learned.)

2. (XLV) Tendency to suppose more order and regularity in the world than we find.

3. (XLVI) Tendency to support a belief once accepted; notes supporting illustrations, ignores or decries opposing data.

(XLIX) Tendency to believe what he wants to be true; to believe as one wishes. (Affections color understanding.) Becomes rationalization. Rejects difficult or careful processes and beliefs; accepts popular beliefs; superstitions. Tendency to be more moved by affirmatives than negatives.

4. (XLVII) Tendency to be influenced by the striking, the bizarre, the forceful; to be unduly influenced by first contacts. Imagines all to be thus—overgeneralizes. (Need for gathering of sufficient, varied cases must be learned.)

5. (XLVIII) Tendency to seek first or final causes. (Is not satisfied to state laws and principles as derived from experience, or discovered, but must seek beyond this. This confuses thought on the remote levels, just as failure to seek causes in the limited and closed systems of everyday experience does.)

6. (L) Tendency to stop speculating when sensory observation ceases. Sense is incompetent and limited but (see No. 1 above) outweighs influence of things not immediately apparent. (The practical man makes his best blunders here.)

7. (LI) Tendency to set up abstractions and then to reify or personify them; accepts forms which are really figments of the mind and ignores actuality.

Idols of the Cave or Den

Foundation in the particular mental or bodily constitution of each individual; also in his education, his conversation with others, reading; in authority of those he admires; in differences in impressions made on his mind when pre-occupied and predisposed, or when indifferent and settled. Heraclitus: "Men look for sciences in their own lesser worlds and not in the greater or common world."

1. (LIV) Tendency to be attached to certain sciences or speculations because they think they invented them; or because they worked hard upon them. (For example, "I am a student of the Bible," or "of the war," or "of health foods," or "of Mexico.")

2. (LV) Tendency to note resemblances—or to note differences. The one catches at shadows; the other at gradations.

3. (LVI) Tendency to admire antiquity—or to strive for novelty.

Tendency to conservatism, unwillingness to change, to distrust new ideas, to be satisfied with what is (particularly when dealing with familiars long in use and ministering to comfort, security, profit, or prestige). Tendency to hasty acceptance of new (where no trusted old idea is attacked)—to take a chance. (May sometimes be ignorance of facts and implications.)

4. (LVII) Tendency to study structure and neglect the part—or study the part and neglect the structure. Tendency to deal only in broad generalizations —or to be submerged in specifics. Tendency (again) to overgeneralize—or to fail to rise to general notions or statements.

5. (XLII) Tendency to evaluate optimistically and to overstate—to evaluate pessimistically and to understate.

6. (XLII) Tendency to revere authority—to differ with authority.

7. (XLII) Tendency to be narrow-minded—closed-minded.

8. (XLII) Tendency to avoid effort, inertia (laziness, mental or physical, so-called)—or to long, overarduous work—or to the "too-busy" complex. (Others may be added.)

9. Tendency to "jump to conclusions." (May be a part of Nos. 2, 4, 5, and possibly 1.)

Idols of the Market Place

These spring largely from one cause: languages through intercourse. Confusion arises from lack of definition of words, improper definition, or the substitution of words for facts.

"Here is the first distemper of learning, when men study words and not matter." Francis Bacon.

"The great disease of knowledge is that in which, starting from words, we end up with them." I. A. Richards.

". . . men believe that their reason governs words; but it is also true that words react on the understanding. . . . " Francis Bacon.

". . . definitions cannot cure this evil in dealing with natural and material things; . . . the definitions themselves consist of words and series and order. . . ." Francis Bacon. (Comenius stated this positively, "things—ideas—words.")

Words are inherited from use by the crowd and do not conform to nature. The word stands in the way of improvement by minds which are acute enough to see better organizations. (Paraphrase.)

1. Tendency to name things which do not exist: For example, Fortune,

Luck, Fate, Democracy, The Reds, Uncle Sam, London. (May be Tribal Idol, see No. 7.)

Tendency to reify or personify abstractions. (Tribal?)

2. Tendency to use words with ill-defined meaning, or several meanings, or confused meanings.

3. Tendency to base thinking on limited, personal, or bizarre interpretation of words, passages in the Bible or other basic volumes, codes, laws, contracts, and the like.

4. Tendency to judge the depth of thought by difficulty or size of words, versatility or glibness of speech. (Tendency to mistrust same with some people.)

5. Tendency to think in terms of slogans, proverbs, verbalisms. Complicated by failure to distinguish between subjective and objective thinking; ideas in the head and facts in the world. This probably stems from Tribal Idols.

6. Tendency to use a word and to think or to imply that the thing or action implied by the word is actually present, i.e., meeting a situation through use of emphasis upon such words as "logical," "careful," "clear-cut," "sound," "critical," "experimental," "democratic," "moral." Similarly to meet a situation through demand that "we pass a law," "make a protest."

Idols of the Theater (or of Systems)

Basis in learned or taught philosophical systems or inadequate or inaccurate demonstrations.

Acceptance of the teachings is based in part on other causes: primitive credulity; reliance on sense; reliance on limited data; confusion of subjective with objective; jumping to conclusions; rejecting careful, tedious processes of checking, measurement, experimentation; unawareness of emotional biases; reliance on authority; and others.

1. (LXIII) Three species of false philosophy:
   a. (v) The sophistical school—overworks a few cases—leaves much to speculation. Sets up systems, classifications, or categories based on too-few instances and then tends to force facts into these classifications. The inductive derivation of principles and categories from reality and sufficient experience tends to be ignored.
   b. (LXIV) The empirical school—overworks a few experiments. Sets up systems, classifications, and categories based on the careful analysis of insufficient number of instances.
   c. (LXV) The superstitious school—involves theology, traditions, spirits, genii. Sets up systems, classifications, and categories based on theological dogmas, accepted beliefs, and on popular superstitions.
2. Excesses of two schools:
   a. Dogmatic, or
   b. Hyperskeptical.
3. (LXIX) False demonstrations:
   a. Impressions of senses are erroneous.
   b. Notions are improperly abstracted from the senses and confused.
   c. Principles arrived at by the method of simple enumeration.
   d. General propositions established first and axioms added later.

APPENDIX C

Term Paper Topics

Students are urged to suggest and select other similar topics which appeal and which are within the field of the course.

Term papers of this type are far more brief than is the typical term report. The essence here is critical analysis of the meager literature available.

1. How children develop concepts. (Material is available, both experimental and descriptive, on concepts in social areas, in mathematics, in magnitude, of time, of cause and effect, and others.)

Students may select any one area if sufficient material can be found. Otherwise take two or more areas.

2. Methods of teaching designed to aid children in developing concepts. (This may be combined with No. 1, if desired, or treated as a separate paper. Sufficient material is probably available.)

3. Critical analysis of studies of children's reasoning. This may deal with problem solving as a process, or with any phase such as inference, judgment, definition of problem, proving conclusions.

4. Critical analysis of studies or descriptions of the appearance of new ideas, of insights, of creative contributions, with children or adults.

5. Methods of teaching designed to aid children or adults in improving problem solving, or any phase thereof. (Student may decide how much to include after examining available literature.)

6. Methods of teaching designed to encourage creative thinking, invention, discovery.

7. Methods of teaching designed to train in habits of critical evaluation. The development of habits of critical reading may be included or treated separately.

8. Critical summary of studies of superstitions among children or adults, of unfounded beliefs. Analysis of methods designed to aid students in criticizing these beliefs. Analysis of methods designed to aid students in criticizing these beliefs and developing rational substitutes.

9. A separate paper as in No. 8 may, if desired, be confined to the popular delusions, widespread myths, and the like among adult populations.

10. An analysis of studies or discussions dealing with what is commonly labeled "stupidity."

11. A summary of the chief factors in the historical method with special reference to critical analysis and derivation of tenable conclusions; together with analysis of methods designed to aid students with this method.

12. A paper may be written putting into simple everyday language the statement and implications of the logical fallacies; the rhetorical fallacies; the psychological fallacies.

13. Critical analysis of studies and discussion of methods designed to bring about changes in values, social or intellectual stereotypes.

14. Summarize studies showing how emotional maladjustment (as anxiety, frustration, outside tensions) influence thinking.

15. What is the effect of emotionally toned materials on critical thinking? (Some good materials are available in studies of judgment of poetry, of judgment of political statements when sources have been concealed or falsified.)

16. Summarize the material which can be found dealing with the ways people respond to problems which surpass their intellectual capacity and/or experiential background.

17. Make a critical summary of recent discussions of cause-and-effect relationships.

18. Summarize materials which might suggest methods for improving the act of judgment.

19. Summarize the literature on luck as a factor in human affairs and in thinking. If possible, make, at the same time, a brief popular summary of the mathematics of probability.

20. Summarize and interpret any current case studies of scientific discovery, of insight, of hunch or intuition. Discussion here is not on general principles or interpretation but no specific cases as described in the literature.

21. Make a similar summary of cases of difficult problem solving, or of critical thinking. These will usually be found in current scientific literature but may appear anywhere.

22. Describe and analyze any illustration or illustrations of good thinking in everyday affairs. Cases should be, preferably, those which you have observed.

23. The letter columns to newspapers and magazines are rich mines of material.

   a. Make a study of letters to a given paper over a period of time, and analyze in the light of this course.
   b. Follow a series of letters dealing with some controversy.
   c. Note especially the flat contradictions between letters. (The *Saturday Evening Post,* for instance, pointedly prints contradictory letters next each other.) Attempt to expain the grounds on which such letters are written. Pay particular attention to matters of fact and interpretation.

24. Make an extensive study of honesty or factualness in advertising. Include accounts of hearings before the Food and Drug Administration, or any accounts you can secure from Better Business Bureaus. There are two or more associations of advertisers whose views should be included.

25. Make studies, similar to those suggested above in No. 23, dealing with editorials over a period of time; with commentators' columns.

26. Propaganda—both techniques and specific illustrations—is a wide field. Choose any angle, and make a summary.

27. A paper on thinking as related to decision making.

   Students are encouraged to take any topic or problem of interest to them, dealing with current affairs or historical illustrations.

APPENDIX D

Sample Unit Outlines

A very few sample units are supplied in the hope that they will (*a*) be of use when properly elaborated, and (*b*) suggest many others. Many other units are listed by title in several chapters in Part III of the book. Textbooks in the teaching of various subject areas contain still other valuable suggestions.

The first six units are extremely abbreviated; in fact, the barest outline is given. They are designed to serve as guides and suggestions. Teachers will need to supply much more detail.

The last two units are resource units and contain more detail. These units on mathematics are from a series prepared by Kimball for use in New Hampshire secondary schools. The first six were used by Wing in high school teaching.

Units I and II are primarily in language arts, though No. 1 has suggestions for the science and mathematics fields as well.

Unit III is useful in history, the social studies, and English.

Units IV, V, and VI may be used in any field.

The two resource units (VII and VIII) are obviously for mathematics.

Unit I. Definition

A. *Introduction.* Many pointless arguments and misunderstandings occur when one person has one idea of what a word means and another person thinks it means something else. Definition is the process of explaining the meanings of words so that confusion does not result. It is always necessary when new words are introduced, but it is also important with familiar words which have different senses and shades of meaning.

B. *Objectives.* The following understandings, attitudes, and abilities are fundamental to the proper use of definition.

  1. Understandings

    a. Key terms should be defined or their meanings made clear in order to avoid:

      (1) Ambiguity (uncertainty of choice between two clear meanings for one word).

      (2) Vagueness—fuzziness.

    b. There are several kinds of definition:

      (1) Class and detail (*genus* and *differentia*).

      (2) Example.

      (3) Comparison.

      (4) Negative.

      (5) Description.

    c. Temporary (nominal) definitions are useful.

    d. Dictionary definitions:

      (1) Attempt to show how good writers happen to use words.

      (2) Are not always complete; for example, they sometimes fail to give the emotive connotations of words.

       e. Word meanings shift:
          (1) From time to time.
          (2) From place to place.
          (3) Within a piece of writing or a speech.
  2. Attitudes
     a. The student should be disposed to define terms and look for the other person's meaning when necessary.
  3. Abilities
     a. The student should acquire the ability to define terms of average difficulty.
     b. The student should learn to apply understandings listed above.

C. *Procedures.*
  1. Introducing unit
     a. Give obvious instances of controversies in which confusion resulted from failure to define key terms. Max Black in *Critical Thinking* (Englewood Cliffs, N. J., Prentice-Hall, 1946) gives an illustration on page 185.
     b. Read a passage containing a word which needs definition, and ask the class what the word means. From the discussion draw out the need for definition.
  2. Basic information
     a. If it is not possible to obtain books and other printed materials for the students to read, the teacher may wish to give basic information about definition in the form of a lecture. References for the teacher are given at the end of this unit.
  3. Activities. The following activities for the class are suggested:
     a. Have the class look in newspapers for articles in which key terms need definition.
     b. Have the class keep a list of common terms whose meanings shift in different contexts.
     c. Examine history and literature texts for terms needing further definition.
     d. Give words to class, and have them practice defining.
     e. Mimeograph passages; give them to the class, and have them look for definitional problems.
     f. In all subsequent analyses of selections, check for definitional needs.
  4. Special activities for exceptional students
     a. Have superior students read at the library some of the references at the end of this unit.
     b. While other students are busy, discuss certain more-difficult aspects of definition, such as real and nominal definition, nominal definition within theoretical systems, and others.

D. *References.*
  1. Black, Max, *Critical Thinking* (Englewood Cliffs, N. J., Prentice-Hall, 1946), pp. 185-208.
  2. Cohen, Morris R., and Nagel, Ernest, *An Introduction to Logic and the Scientific Method* (New York, Harcourt, Brace, 1934), pp. 136, 224-241.

3. Larrabee, H. A., *Reliable Knowledge* (Boston, Houghton Mifflin, 1945), pp. 248-261.

4. Ogden, C. K., and Richards, I. A., *The Meaning of Meaning* (New York, Harcourt, Brace, 1946), pp. 109-138.

5. Walpole, Hugh R., *Semantics* (New York, Norton, 1941), pp. 121-140.

6. Burtt, E. A., *Right Thinking,* 2nd ed. (New York, Harper, 1946), pp. 148, 541-559.

7. Hemple, Carl G., "Fundamentals of Concept Formation in Empirical Science," *International Encyclopedia of Unified Science,* Vol. II, No. 7 (Chicago, University of Chicago Press, 1952), pp. 1-20.

Unit II. Emotive Language

A. *Introduction.*

The solution of many problems involving communication between persons is hampered by the use of language with an emotional or "affective" tinge which colors the basic meaning and leads people to conclusions they might not make if the language were not so emotively colored.

B. *Objectives.*

1. Understandings
   a. Many words have shades of meaning not quite the same as the pure sense of the word but which affect the reader or hearer in an emotional way.
   b. Sometimes the presence of an emotive quality in language interferes with the exchange of clear ideas.
   c. It is important to understand the emotive qualities of certain key words.

2. Attitudes
   a. The student should be disposed to look for emotive connotations and be wary of them.
   b. The student should be disposed to be aware of the affective senses of the words he uses.

3. Abilities
   a. The student should be able to apply the understandings above to his everyday reading.
   b. The student should be able to recognize the emotive content of certain commonly used terms, such as "socialistic," "democratic," "capitalistic," "left wing," "reactionary," "American."

C. *Procedures.*

1. Introduction to unit
   a. Ask the class what the difference is between the following pairs:
      house—home
      teen-ager—juvenile
      misbehavior—delinquency
      red as a rose—red as a tomato

2. Lecture materials: see this heading under Unit I.

3. Activities
   a. Explain the emotive effects of these terms: "communist," "liberal," and others.

      b. Compare the emotive effect and plain sense of the following pairs:
            bureaucrat—government official
            fib—lie
            pig-headed—determined
            executioner—murderer
      c. Try out the procedure in Max Black, *Critical Thinking* (Englewood Cliffs, N. J., Prentice-Hall, 1946), pp. 160, 161.
      d. Have the class look in newspapers for examples of emotive usage.
      e. Have the class keep a list of common terms which arouse emotive reactions.
      f. Examine materials in history and literature for emotive terms.
      g. In subsequent analyses, look for emotive uses.
    4. Special activities for exceptional students: further reading in references
D. *References.*
    1. Black, Max, *Critical Thinking* (Englewood Cliffs, N. J., Prentice-Hall, 1946), pp. 154-160.
    2. Hayakawa, S. I., *Language in Thought and Action,* rev. ed. (New York, Harcourt, Brace, 1949), pp. 82 ff. (Hayakawa uses the term "affective" language.)
    3. Ogden, C. K., and Richard, I. A., *The Meaning of Meaning* (New York, Harcourt, Brace, 1946), *passim.*
    4. Walpole, Hugh R., *Semantics* (New York, Norton, 1941), pp. 38-62.
E. References for superior teachers and exceptional students:
    1. Morris, C. W., *Foundations of the Theory of Signs* (Chicago, University of Chicago Press, 1938), pp. 29-42.
    2. Morris, C. W., *Signs, Language, and Behavior* (Englewood Cliffs, N. J., Prentice-Hall, 1946).

Unit III. Inductive Method

A. *Introduction.* The procedure by which general conclusions are arrived at by examining individual data and pieces of evidence is called induction.
B. *Objectives.* The students should become familiar with the following understandings:
    1. Kinds of data used to authenticate historical generalizations include reports of eyewitnesses, public records, documents.
    2. The reliability of the kinds of data mentioned above depends on several things, including nearness to event, known bias or lack of it, genuineness, and the like.
    3. Newspapers are historical writings in the sense that they collect data on events and generalize from them to produce a description of what is happening at a period in time.
    4. One cannot take for granted that what is printed in newspapers is completely reliable.
    5. There are certain standards concerning the degree to which one can trust the testimony of witnesses:
      a. Correspondence of testimony to known fact.
      b. Reputation of witness.
      c. Absence of inconsistency in witness's report.

       d. Objectivity of witness's attitude.

       e. Known bias of witness.

   6. Sometimes we depend upon an authority for our information. The reliability of authorities depends on recognition by other authorities, agreement with other authorities, and special competence.

   7. The standards by which we judge evidence vary from one field to another, that is, according to whether the problem is in the field of science, law, history, language, or the like.

C. *Procedure.*

   1. Introduction of units

       a. Ask class how historians 100 years from now will know what the events of this year were, that is, what will be the sources of their information.

   2. Activities

       a. Study documents of history, such as letters, contemporary statements, drawings, public records.

       b. Discuss the standards of news reporting.

       c. Examine the evidential content of editorials.

       d. Study the testimony in legal cases.

       e. Take a newspaper headline, and attempt to trace the evidence upon which the news summary was based.

       f. Discuss the problems of reporting for the school paper.

D. *References.*

   1. Black, Max, *Critical Thinking* (Englewood Cliffs, N. J., Prentice-Hall, 1946), Pt. III.

   2. Burtt, E. A., *Right Thinking,* 2nd ed. (New York, Harper, 1946), Pt. III.

   3. Cohen, Morris R., and Nagel, Ernest, *An Introduction to Logic and Scientific Method* (New York, Harcourt, Brace, 1934), Bk. II.

   4. Larrabee, H. A., *Reliable Knowledge* (Boston, Houghton Mifflin, 1945), Chs. 4, 10-16.

Unit IV. Fact-Opinion Analysis

A. *Introduction.* This subject logically belongs under the unit on inductive methods. But it corresponds to a popular distinction and is useful as a separate process in analyzing materials.

B. *Objectives:* Understandings.

   1. A definition of fact: A fact is a statement about an event in the physical world for whose truth there is considerable evidence and small disagreement.

   2. The following factors make evidence about facts strong:

       a. Independent observers agree on it.

       b. The evidence can be reproduced without significant change (science field).

       c. Many observations have been made on the evidence.

       d. Observers agree on the definition of the nature of the evidence.

       e. The observations are made objectively, that is, with a minimum of personal bias.

3. An opinion is a conclusion drawn from evidence which may or may not be factual.
4. The opinion itself may be sound or unsound.
5. Sometimes it is hard to draw the line between a factual statement and an opinion.
6. Statements may be considered factual now, but, at a later time in the light of new evidence, what was once considered fact may be thought to be nonfactual.
7. A statement may be unproved but be capable of being tested. This kind of statement may be called "of a factual type."
8. Facts in different fields of knowledge may be established by different kinds of evidence.

C. *Procedure.*
   1. Introduction of topic:
      a. Read passage written by someone who misuses the word *fact.*
      b. Ask class what a fact is to a policeman (for example, Jack Webb).
   2. *a.* Mimeograph newspaper editorials and other materials, and have class classify each statement as to whether it is factual or not.
      b. Analyze news reports, and see if the reporting is objective.
      c. Have a class member describe in completely factual terms a person known to all.
      d. Discuss kinds of evidence, e.g., in court.
      e. Discuss the difference between data in science and data of history and social, economic, and legal matters.

D. *References.*
   1. Cohen, Morris R., and Nagel, Ernest, *An Introduction to Logic and Scientific Method* (New York, Harcourt, Brace, 1934), pp. 199, 201, 391-392, 215-221.
   2. Larrabee, H. A., *Reliable Knowledge* (Boston, Houghton Mifflin, 1945), Chs. 4, 5.

Unit V. Assumptions

A. *Introduction.* This unit is scarcely more than a single lesson as far as the time required to present the ideas is concerned. Checking for assumptions is a practice which should be carried on whenever an analysis is made during other lessons.

B. *Objectives.* Understandings.
   1. It is desirable in analyzing an argument to bring out unstated ideas which are taken for granted.
   2. Stated assumptions should be examined to see whether they are acceptable or not.
   3. If the assumptions behind an argument are not acceptable, the whole argument may be worthless.
   4. Certain entire value systems are assumed in the discussion of certain literary and social problems.

C. *Procedure.*
   1. Introduction. Give example of argument in which something crucial is assumed.

2. Activities. Examine assumptions whenever close analysis is undertaken.
D. *References.*
   1. Black, Max, *Critical Thinking* (Englewood Cliffs, N. J., Prentice-Hall, 1946), *passim.*
   2. Fawcett, H. P., *The Nature of Proof* (New York, Columbia University Press, 1938), *passim.*

Unit VI. Errors and Fallacies

A. *Introduction.* Errors occur in all the processes of critical thinking. This unit summarizes these errors and fallacies using as a model the basic table of critical abilities. It should be stressed that the individual fallacies should be discussed with the units to which they apply. Here we have a kind of summary—of a negative sort—of the different units.
B. *Objectives.* The student should understand the following kinds of errors and fallacies:
   1. Failure to examine problem, define it, and locate crucial points.
   2. Failure to formulate or recognize suitable hypotheses.
   3. *a.* Failure to select or recall relevant data accurately.
     b. Failure to differentiate between reliable and less-reliable sources of information.
     c. Failure to tell the difference between statements that give observations, draw conclusions, make definitions, and make no sense.
   4. Failure to make or recognize careful experimental plans.
   5. Inductive fallacies
     a. Insufficient cases
     b. Cases not typical
     c. Contradicting cases ignored
     d. Post hoc, ergo propter hoc
     e. False analogies
   6. Deductive fallacies
     a. Taking for granted:
       (1) Exceptions ignored
       (2) Exceptions overvalued
       (3) Begging the question
       (4) Complex question
     b. Off-the-point:
       (1) Red herring
       (2) You're another
       (3) Name calling (*ad hominem*)
       (4) Appeal to prejudice
       (5) Employment of threat
       (6) Appeal to reverence
       (7) Appeal to pity
       (8) Mercenary appeal
     c. Various negative types
       (1) Objections (trivial)
       (2) Appeal to ignorance
       (3) *Non sequitur*

7. *a.* Failure to recognize assumptions
   b. Failure to recognize pertinent value systems, as in criticism of literature
8. Failure to come to a conclusion
9. Failure to test conclusion
10. Failure to apply conclusion to new situation
11. Interpretation
    a. Failure to define
    b. Quoting out of context
    c. Failure to penetrate emotive coloration
    d. Failure to note complexity of term
    e. False classification
    f. Failure to amplify abstract terms
    g. Failure to make terms of quantity specific
    h. Taking figures of speech literally
    i. Ambiguity
    j. Quibbling
    k. Jargon
    l. Mistranslation
    m. Failure to understand tone
12. Attitudinal errors
    a. Lack of curiosity
    b. Narrow-mindedness
    c. Intellectual dishonesty
    d. Gullibility
    e. Lack of objectivity
    f. Failure to demand explanations in terms of universal laws of cause and effect
    g. Lack of persistence
    h. Inflexibility

C. *Procedures.*
1. Introducing unit. Present cases of error and fallacies. The references supply many illustrations.
2. Basic information. It might be worthwhile to mimeograph the list of errors and fallacies above, possibly with illustrations of each.
3. Activities.
   a. Go over list of fallacies and errors. Explain. Have students provide examples.
   b. Examine newspapers, especially editorial sections and letters to the editor for fallacious arguments.
   c. Discuss advertisements that make misleading statements.
   d. Mimeograph materials for group discussion.
   e. Have students listen for fallacious arguments they hear in everyday conversation.
   f. Check political speeches.
   g. Look for errors in other unit materials.
4. For exceptional students. Take up the syllogism and its uses and misuses.

D. *References.*

1. Beardsley, M. C., *Practical Logic* (Englewood Cliffs, N. J., Prentice-Hall, 1950), *passim.*
2. Black, Max., *Critical Thinking* (Englewood Cliffs, N. J., Prentice-Hall, 1946), pp. 209-224.
3. Burtt, E. A., *Right Thinking,* 2nd ed. (New York, Harper, 1946), pp. 141, 247, 269 ff., 481 ff., 733 ff., 731, 503 ff.
4. Cohen, Morris R., and Nagel, Ernest, *An Introduction to Logic and Scientific Thinking* (New York, Harcourt, Brace, 1934), pp. 316-322, 376-382, 382-390.
5. Larrabee, H. A., *Bentham's Handbook of Political Fallacies.* Revised and edited by H. A. Larrabee (Baltimore, Johns Hopkins University Press, 1952). Entire.
6. Thouless, Robert H., *How to Think Straight* (New York, Simon & Schuster, 1940), *passim.*

Unit VII. Similarity, Proportion, and Analogy

Overview for the Teacher

The sequence suggested in these resource units introduces the topic of similarity earlier than in the conventional course. This has been done to encourage even more regular use of algebra to develop at an earlier stage the relationship between congruence and similarity, to acquaint the student with simple trigonometry which can be used in later work in the course, and to provide an earlier insight into a frequently used and frequently misused type of thinking.

Objectives

A. General understandings and appreciations
   1. Reasoning by analogy is one of the most common methods used to reach conclusions.
   2. The basic pattern for reasoning by analogy is to identify situations which are similar with respect to certain relationships and then apply this similarity to reach conclusions regarding other relationships.
   3. Analogy often may help us to discover relationships without explaining (proving) them.
   4. Situations sometimes are similar in some respects but *not* similar in other respects. This condition may lead to invalid conclusions because of false analogy.
B. Specific knowledge and skills
   1. An understanding of the proof and application of theorems of proportion.
   2. An understanding of similarity in geometry, particularly with respect to the conditions which yield similar triangles.
   3. Ability to solve practical problems involving ratio and proportion, and similar figures (including simple trigonometric examples).
   4. Minimum list of specific theorems to be studied

    a. If three angles of one triangle equal three angles of another, the triangles are similar.

    b. If an angle of one triangle is equal to an angle of another triangle and the sides including the angles are in proportion, the triangles are similar.

    c. The altitude upon the hypotenuse of a right triangle:

        (1) Forms two triangles, each similar to the original triangle and similar to each other.

        (2) Divides the hypotenuse so that each leg of the given triangle is the mean proportional between the hypotenuse and the projection of that leg on the hypotenuse.

        (3) Is the mean proportional between the segments of the hypotenuse.

    d. The square of the hypotenuse of a right triangle is equal to the sum of the squares of the legs.

    e. The perimeters of two similar polygons have the same ratio as any two corresponding sides.

    f. Theorems relating to the 30-60-90 and the 45-45-90 right triangles.

Suggested Problem Areas and Learning Activities

1. The idea of comparing familiar situations with unfamiliar ones is an old one. When properly used, this is an excellent way to discover conclusions. One of the most common uses of comparison, or analogy, in mathematics is through the use of ratio and proportion. You are already acquainted with problems of this general type:

    a. If apples sell at 6 pounds for 35 cents, what is the price of 10 pounds?

    b. Mr. Jones's house was valued at $4500, and his property tax was $210. If Mr. Smith's house is valued at $5300, what will his tax be?

    c. If an airplane has a glide ratio of 13:2, what distance can it glide from an altitude of 2800 feet?

2. In algebra we learned that the ratio of two numbers is their quotient. When two ratios are set equal, we have a proportion. Consider the proportion:

$$a/b = c/d$$

Derive as many properties of proportions as you can.

Note to teacher: Most books give some attention to ratio and proportion. If the material in a particular text seems too limited, supplement it freely with material drawn from first and second year algebra books. This is a splendid opportunity to review linear equations, fractions, radicals, and related ideas from elementary algebra. Obviously, many practical examples can be devised to give meaning to the ideas being considered.

3. The basic ideas of ratio and proportions which you encountered in algebra are equally important in geometry. This was recognized even 2400 years ago. For instance, about that time a Greek mathematician

named Thales was traveling in Egypt. When he saw the great pyramids, he was amazed at their size, and at the physical labor and the engineering skill which they represented. He wondered how high the tallest one was. (Can you find the name and the height of the tallest?). He stuck his walking stick erect in the sand and then measured its height and the length of its shadow. Next he measured the length of the shadow of the pyramid, and added to it one-half the length of the base of the pyramid (Why?). With these measures, and a knowledge of ratio and proportion in geometry, he computed the height of the pyramid.

a. Even though you cannot really prove the method is correct, can you explain the analogy which Thales used?

b. Make up some similar examples which apply this idea.

c. Measure the height of a building, a flagpole, or some similar object using this method.

Note to teacher: Even though the development of similar triangles cannot be logically rigorous at this point, it seems wise to build on the intuitive experiences with indirect measurement which the students have had in earlier grades. It helps emphasize the nature of "reasoning by analogy," and it provides a concrete picture to give meaning to the more abstract development soon to follow. It is recommended that several "practical applications" be worked out on this intuitive basis.

4. You have seen how we can arrive at what appears to be sensible answers by using certain characteristics which make two triangles very similar, even though they are not identical (that is, they are not congruent).

a. Work out your own definition for these "similar triangles." Remember the characteristics of a good definition.

b. Now make your definition more general, so that it describes any "similar polygons."

c. Explain how congruent triangles may be viewed as a special case of similar triangles.

Note to teacher: Assist the students in formulating the conventional definition. Then help them see that if the corresponding sides are in proportion we have

$$\frac{AB}{A'B'} = \frac{BC}{B'C'} = \frac{AC}{A'C'} = k$$

and congruence becomes the special case where $k=1$.

5. Note to teacher. The preceding exercises lead to an intuitive acceptance of the concept of similarity. It is desirable, however, that the student also see a more rigorous development of the theorems pertaining to similar triangles. From time to time, our instruction in geometry should stress the logical structure exhibited by a chain of propositions. There are many ways that this can be accomplished. A recognition of the definitions and assumptions on which the sequence is based, the logical order of the theorems which make up the sequence, and the

possible interchange of certain theorems in a sequence without destroying the validity of the reasoning are some of the points to be stressed in presenting this feature of geometry. The topic of similarity provides an excellent opportunity to stress the concept of sequence. The sequence might be presented as follows:

Definition: Similar polygons are polygons having corresponding angles equal and corresponding sides in proportion.

Assumption: A line parallel to one side of a triangle and intersecting the other two sides divides these sides in proportion. (Some texts prove a portion of this as a theorem, but the incommensurable case arises and has to be accepted as an assumption. It is recommended that the entire proposition be treated as an assumption.)

Derived Theorems:

1. If two angles of one triangle are equal to two angles of another, the triangles are similar. (Of course, this could have been accepted as the basic assumption, and then the assumption given above could have been proved as a theorem. This procedure may even be best, since it reduces the need for proofs by superposition or coincidence of lines.)
2. If in a right triangle the altitude is drawn upon the hypotenuse
   a. The two triangles thus formed are similar to each other and similar to the original triangle.
   b. Each leg of the original triangle is the mean proportional between the hypotenuse and the projection of that leg on the hypotenuse.
3. In a right triangle, the square of the hypotenuse equals the sum of the squares of the legs.
4. a. The hypotenuse of a 45-45-90 triangle equals $\sqrt{2}$ times the leg.
   b. In a 30-60-90 triangle, the side opposite the 30° angle is one-half the hypotenuse, and the side opposite the 60° is one-half the hypotenuse times $\sqrt{3}$.

6. All of your work in similarity has been a sort of "thinking by analogy." There was nothing very risky about it, because the properties of similar figures were carefully stated, and only those properties were used in reaching conclusions. Sometimes, however, the resemblance between two situations cannot be stated quite as clearly as in geometry, but still we feel justified in reaching conclusions based on the resemblance. The following examples will illustrate the method of reasoning by analogy, and some of its strengths and weaknesses.
   a. Ice is a solid. When heated it becomes a liquid and, at a still higher temperature, becomes a gas. Iron is also a solid, and therefore we

should expect that it will become a liquid and then a vapor if it is heated sufficiently. Notice that the basic pattern of reasoning can be diagrammed like this (adapted from Max Black, *Critical Thinking;* Englewood Cliffs, N. J., Prentice-Hall, 1946; pp. 320-321):

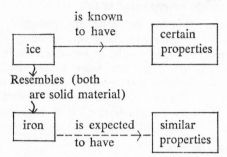

It is obvious, then, that the nature of the resemblance between the things compared is crucial. Only when the basis of the resemblance bears a direct connection to the properties being considered are we on safe ground.

Thus we might rearrange our diagram like this.

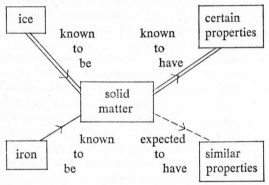

The key question now is evident: Is it the characteristic of being a solid which accounts for the property of changing to a liquid and then a vapor when heated? Or is it some other characteristic, *not common to iron,* which accounts for this property?

Give several examples of reasoning by analogy. Try to select ones where the reasoning is valid, and diagram them.

  b. Do teachers have the right to inflict corporal punishment on students? In one case, which was taken to court in New Hampshire, the court ruled as follows: "The law clothes the teacher, as it does the parent in whose place he stands, with power to enforce discipline by the imposition of reasonable corporal punishment."

    (1) Do you think the analogy between a teacher and a parent is a proper one to support the conclusion? Discuss.

    (2) What key words used in the court's ruling need careful definition? How would you define them?

c. It is quite clear that reasoning by analogy can lead to many difficulties when a person becomes the least bit careless. Reasoning using "false analogy" is quite common. It may take several forms, as the following examples illustrate.

(1) If Mr. Doe was a good mayor, then he will be a good governor.

(2) John was arguing with his parents about what time he should be in bed. "Look at Edison," he said, "and Napoleon. They usually slept only three or four hours a night. Why should I have to go to bed so early?"

(3) A man claimed he had scientific proof that a "crash" in the stock market would come. Asked for his proof, he tossed a ball up in the air, pointed, and said, "What goes up must come down."

Find three or four arguments which are based on reasoning by analogy. Try to find some examples where you consider the argument valid and some where you consider it invalid.

d. Most news cartoons are analogies. In them current events are simplified into pictures of easily understandable "parallel cases." Often the picture also suggests some conclusion; it will be more than a simple report of the event. Find several cartoons which illustrate reasoning by analogy. Be prepared to analyze the analogy and judge the validity of the conclusion implied by the cartoon.

e. For discussion

(1) "Analogy is an extremely fertile source of new ideas; but it is also extremely prolific in error, having yielded a large part of the myths, allegories, parables, and superstitions which comprise the endless history of human stupidity." H. A. Larrabee

(2) "Men, taken historically, reason by analogy long before they have learned to reason by abstract characters." William James

(3) "Lunacy grows worse at full and new moon because the brain is the microcosmic moon. Paracelsus

(4) "Imagination is more important than knowledge." Albert Einstein

(5) ". . . though analogy is misleading, it is the least misleading thing we have." Samuel Butler

(6) "Science is nothing but analogy. . . ." Ralph Waldo Emerson

7. What is the main value of analogy?

Note to teacher: Students should see that perhaps the main value of analogy is that it helps us formulate a new *hypothesis*. When we attack a strange problem, analogy or comparison with a familiar situation reveals the clue needed to develop the solution; rarely does it provide the solution directly.

Additional Points of Strategy

1. One high school geometry textbook approaches geometry through five basic assumptions. The "theorem" that "two triangles are similar when an angle of one equals an angle of the other and the sides including these angles are in proportion" is one of the five assumptions. From

this point, all of the conventional theorems are proved, though often in an unconventional manner. Teachers and better students would be amply rewarded for several hours' study of this highly original treatment of the subject. The book is George D. Birkhoff and Ralph Beatley, *Basic Geometry* (Chicago, Scott, Foresman, 1940).

2. Space does not permit a detailed development of all points, but the class should be encouraged to discover and develop many theorems and applications based on similarity. Certainly this may include an introduction to both numerical trigonometry and a few basic identities such as sin A^2+cos A^2=1. Considerable work which utilizes the skills of algebra should be introduced.

3. Never overlook opportunities to stress originality, flexibility and creativeness. The Pythagorean Theorem probably has been explored in more ways than any other given topic. Share with the students some of these unique proofs, and encourage them to create new ones. In addition, some may find the proof of the converse of this theorem a real challenge. Others will find that, even with the limited trigonometry which has been introduced, they can generalize the Pythagorean Theorem by developing the law of cosines.

4. Students can develop rules for testing arguments based on analogy. The following ones are adapted from Max Black, *Critical Thinking* (Englewood Cliffs, N. J., Prentice-Hall, 1946), pp. 322-323.
   a. Distinguish between the use of analogy to justify a conclusion and the use to present an assertion in a more vivid manner.
   b. State explicitly the properties which represent the "basis of resemblance."
   c. State explicitly some ways in which the things being compared *do not* resemble each other.
   d. State the "linking generalization" which gives the argument whatever force it may have.
   e. Check carefully all possible "dissimilar factors" which might upset the argument.

Unit VIII. A Pattern For Effective Thinking

Overview for the Teacher

The characteristics of sound, clear thinking have been emphasized throughout this course. Geometry has been the vehicle for acquainting the student with an effective pattern of logical reasoning. This final unit is intended to help the student see that pattern in a very general manner. It presents the *process* of thinking as something which is quite distinct from the *product* of thinking. This distinction is crucial because it is what permits us to anticipate that "transfer of training" through geometry actually is possible.

Objectives

A. General understandings and appreciations
   1. The process of reflective thinking usually follows this general pattern:

       a. Recognizing and clarifying the problem (identification).
       b. Analyzing the problem—defining terms, identifying assumptions, breaking a big problem into several little ones, and the like (Analysis).
       c. Collecting the facts and thoughts which have some bearing on the problem (Directed search).
       d. Interpreting the facts and thoughts in order to suggest an answer or conclusion to the problem (Formulating hypotheses).
       e. Testing the proposed answer to be sure it is a valid one (Testing or proving hypothesis).
   2. Effective thinking is hard, slow work; only when a person wants to think effectively is he likely to do so (necessary, but not sufficient).
   3. Not all problems will have solutions that are clearly "correct".
  B. Specific knowledge and skills
   1. There are many factors which may cause us to reach faulty conclusions.
   2. We may assess our own thinking, and the thinking of others, by seeking answers to these questions:
       a. What is the problem?
       b. What are the possible solutions?
       c. What is the evidence for accepting (rejecting) each possible solution?
       d. Is the evidence sufficient to justify acceptance of one particular proposed solution?
         (1) Is the evidence pertinent?
         (2) Is the evidence reliable?
         (3) Has all relevant evidence been considered?
         (4) Is the evidence properly interpreted?

Suggested Problem Areas and Learning Activities

   1. We have spent considerable time this year studying geometry, attempting to discover some facts about mathematics. These conclusions about mathematics are important. But even more important are the different steps we went through as we discovered these conclusions and tried to build effective arguments which would prove that these conclusions were reasonable.
       a. In view of our work this year, write a brief report, or outline, with the title, "A Guide to Effective Thinking." Try to emphasize five or six steps which people should follow when they attempt to figure out *any* problem (not just problems in geometry).
       b. Try to apply your steps to solve a problem in geometry. For example,

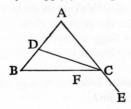

Given: AB=AC
       BD=CE
Prove: Something about
       point F

Note to teacher: Once the student has clarified the steps in reflective thinking (see the "objectives" on first page of the unit), it is a good experience for him to try them out on relatively strange problems, such as the one given here. As has been emphasized in earlier units, the problems should require the student to *discover* the conclusion, *then* prove it.

c. Examine some account of the process of reflective thinking taken from the field of science. See if you can point out the "typical" pattern of reflective thinking. Possible sources are:

(1) Cohen, Morris R., and Nagel, Ernest, *An Introduction to Logic and Scientific Method* (New York, Harcourt, Brace, 1934). A fine analysis of how Herodotus tried to explain the flooding of the Nile River is given on pp. 197-204. A briefer description of Galileo's work with falling bodies is discussed on pp. 204-206.

(2) Larrabee, H. A., *Reliable Knowledge* (Boston, Houghton Mifflin, 1945). Discusses Fridtjof Nansen's research into ocean currents in the polar regions which was stimulated by curiosity about a piece of driftwood on an ice floe near Greenland (see pp. 10-12 or the writings of Nansen).

(3) DeKruif, Paul, *Microbe Hunters* (New York, Harcourt, Brace, 1932).

(4) Any good biography of a scientist or history of scientific thought.

d. Examine a problem in the field of the social sciences (human behavior). Even though the process of problem solving is no longer as clear-cut, the same underlying pattern can usually be detected. There are a wide variety of problems which might be considered, for example:

(1) Why was Lincoln murdered? (See Otto Eisenschiml, *Why Was Lincoln Murdered?* New York, Grosett, 1957.)

(2) What can be done to overcome our shortage of trained scientists? (Analyze the proposal of James Killian in *Life,* May 7, 1956, pp. 147-150.)

(3) What can be done about juvenile delinquency?

Note to teacher: This business of analyzing the way in which people go about solving problems can be both time-consuming and fruitful. Probably the classwork on this point will have to be limited to helping students see that the pattern of reflective thinking which has been suggested is applicable to a wide range of problems from many areas of human concern.

2. One way to describe the steps in reflective thinking might be as follows: (1) Identify the problem; (2) Make the problem clear—"sharpen it up"; (3) Examine the evidence; (4) Suggest some possible solutions; (5) Determine the correct solution by logical reasoning or some other type of test.

a. In your judgment, do people usually follow this sequence as they try to solve different kinds of problems?

    b. Can you suggest certain kinds of problems which probably could not be solved by this method of attack?

    c. Will this procedure guarantee correct solutions to all problems? Explain your answer.

    d. Discuss some of the kinds of errors in reasoning which people may make even when they try to follow the pattern we have suggested. How can we reduce the frequency of the errors you have noticed?

Note to teacher: This question opens the way to reviewing the common errors made in geometry. Students enjoy examining proofs containing varying types of errors to see if they can detect them—and surely the average class will hand in an adequate supply of incorrect proofs. Some of the "standard" fallacies, such as the "proof" that "all triangles are isosceles" and that "two equals one" are excellent devices for directing attention to sources of error.

3. One of the things which makes thinking such a challenge is that the opportunities for making errors are unlimited. Whole books have been written on the subject of straight and crooked thinking. In our course, in geometry, only a few of the pitfalls have been examined in detail. Here are some interesting books for those who wish to know more:

Beardsley, M. C., *Thinking Straight* (Englewood Cliffs, N. J., Prentice-Hall, 1950).

Black, Max, *Critical Thinking* (Englewood Cliffs, N. J., Prentice-Hall, 1946). See particularly Ch. 12.

Chase, Stuart, *The Power of Words* (New York, Harcourt, Brace, 1954).

Doub, Leonard W., *Public Opinion and Propaganda* (New York, Holt, 1948).

Flesch, Rudolf, *The Art of Clear Thinking* (New York, Harper, 1951).

Huff, Darrell, *How to Lie with Statistics* (New York, Norton, 1954). A book as witty as the title suggests, dealing with the many ways that figures can lie—when someone wants them to.

Mander, Alfred, *Logic for the Millions* (New York, Philosophical Library, 1947).

Miller, Clyde, *What Everybody Should Know About Propaganda,* rev. ed. (New York, Methodist Federation for Social Action: Committee for Propaganda, 1949.) An entertaining description of the seven common tricks of propaganda.

Reilly, William, *Twelve Rules for Straight Thinking* (New York, Harper, 1947).

Robinson, James, *Mind in the Making* (New York, Harper, 1921).

Schopenhauer, Arthur, *The Art of Controversy.* Various editions available. A brief, splendid catalogue of common tricks used to twist our thinking.

Shanner, William, *A Guide to Logical Thinking* (Chicago, Science Research Associates, 1954). One of the Science Research Associates' Life Adjustment Booklets, written especially for high school students.

Thouless, Robert, *How to Think Straight* (New York, Simon & Schuster, 1947). An effective, popular treatment; contains some good test items.

a. Read and report on all, or part, of one of these publications.

b. Many of the errors in reasoning have popular labels. Some of them are listed below. Find out what each is, and give an illustration.

   (1) *Non sequitur*

   (2) *Post hoc ergo propter hoc* ("after, therefore caused by")

   (3) Fallacy of accident

   (4) Begging the question

   (5) Circular reasoning

   (6) Name-calling

   (7) Fallacies of circumstance

4. Experience seems to show that the most difficult phase of reflective thinking is the one we have placed fourth on our list. Once we have pinpointed our problem and examined the evidence, how do we think up possible solutions to the problem? Several suggestions can be made. After studying them, see if they help you with examples 5 and 6.

   a. Use your previous experience. How have similar problems been handled successfully in the past?

   b. Use your imagination. Be bold, and even reckless, in proposing possible solutions. Often we develop a "mind set" which closes off the the best solution.

   c. Prepare yourself well. Be sure your mind is well stocked with facts pertaining to the problem.

   d. Allow time. On some occasions it may be helpful to cease thinking about the problem for a while. Let your thoughts go through a period of "incubation".

5. Try to prove these examples in the shortest number of steps:

a. Given: AC=BD

   AC and BD perp. AB

   M is midpt. AB

   Prove: MC=MD

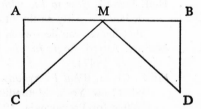

b. Given: AB bisects ∠B   (use diagram below)

   BC=BD

   Prove: ∠1=∠2

c. Given: ∠C=∠D

   ∠1=∠2

   Prove: ∠3=∠4

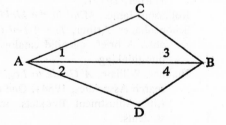

    d. Did you use congruent triangles to prove each of these examples? If so, you did not use your imagination. The last one can be done in just two steps, without congruent triangles. The first two examples tend to produce a "mind set" which cuts our ability to think imaginatively.

6. *a.* Examine the nine crosses marked below. Can you place your pencil point on one of the crosses and then, without lifting your pencil from the paper, draw four successive straight lines so that a line passes through each cross? (Diagram on right illustrates the idea but does not give the correct solution.)

This is another test of your ability to devise many alternate solutions. (Hint: If your imagination fails to tell you to try drawing lines long enough to extend outside of the "nine-cross rectangle", you will never solve the problem.)

    b. In "The Episode of Dr. Watson's Watch," Sherlock Holmes is complimenting a certain French detective of whom he says, "He has considerable gifts. He possesses two out of the three qualities necessary for the ideal detective. He has the power of observation and that of deduction. He is only wanting in knowledge, and that may come in time. He is deficient in the wide range of exact knowledge that is essential to the higher developments of his art." After a little discussion, Dr. Watson challenges Holmes to put his theories to a severe test. He states that he has just come into possession of a watch which he hands to Holmes with the request that the latter give him an opinion upon the characteristics or habits of the late owner of that watch.

Holmes begins: "I would judge that the watch belonged to your elder brother, who inherited it from your father."

"That, you gather, no doubt, from the *H. W.* upon the back."

"Quite so; the *W* suggests your own name. The *date* of the watch is nearly fifty years back, and the initials are as old as the watch, so it was made for the last generation. Jewelry usually descends to the eldest son, and he is most likely to have the same name as the father. Your father has, if I remember right, been *dead* many years. It has therefore been in the hands of your elder brother."

"Right so far," said Watson. "Anything else?"

"He was a man of untidy habits—very untidy and careless. He was left some good prospects, but he threw away his chances; lived for some time in poverty with occasional short intervals of prosperity and finally, taking to drink, he died. That is all I can gather."

At this point, Watson charges Holmes with having looked up the brother and thus really having information from another source. Holmes replied that he did not even know the brother lived until the watch was handed on to him. He goes on to say that he never guesses and that all he had said was derived from an examination of the watch.

"What seems strange to you is only so because you do not follow my train of thought or observe the small facts upon which large inferences may depend. For example, I began by stating that your brother was careless. When you observe the lower part of that watchcase, you notice that it is not only *dented* in two places but is *cut and marked* all over from the habit of keeping other hard objects such as coins or keys in the same pocket. Surely it is no great feat to assume that a man who treats a *fifty-guinea watch* so cavalierly must be a careless man. Neither is it a very far-fetched inference that a man who inherits one article of such value is pretty well provided for in other respects."

Watson nodded to show that he followed Holmes's reasoning.

"It is very customary for pawnbrokers in England, when they take a watch, to *scratch the number* of the ticket with a pinpoint upon the inside of the case. It is more handy than the label, as there is no risk of the number being lost or transposed. There are no less than *four such numbers* visible to my lens on the inside of this case. Inference—that your brother was often at low water. Secondary inference—that he had occasional bursts of prosperity, or he could not have redeemed the pledge. Finally, I ask you to look at the inner plate which contains the keyhole. Look at *the thousands of scratches all around* the hole—marks where the key has slipped. What sober man's key could have scored these grooves? But you will never see a drunkard's watch without them. He winds at night, and he leaves those traces of his unsteady hand—clears the mystery in all this."

EXERCISE. Disregard the discussion of the initials which would be the same in any case. Take all the other facts which Holmes found by looking at the watch, and see if you can construct another explanation which is equally or nearly as plausible.

c. Look up the story of the *Marie Celeste,* a mysterious ship whose crew and passengers vanished for no apparent reason. Try to suggest some explanations of this strange occurrence. (Recall references and questions at the end of Chapter 5.)

d. Many farmers have observed that the flow of water from a spring increases prior to a storm. Suggest some possible explanations.

e. How much does Ted Williams mean to the Red Sox? Early in May,

1956, Joe Reichler, Associated Press Sports writer, said, "The inescapable truth is that the Red Sox, without Ted Williams are a second division club. With him, they are a pennant contender." To support this conclusion, Reichler cited the following facts:

> "From the start of the 1952 season to date, the Red Sox have won 316 games while losing 305 for a .509 percentage. With Williams in the lineup, they won 144 and lost 111. That's a .565 gait. Without him, they won 172 and lost 194 for a .470 percentage."

Has Mr. Reichler proved his point? Explain your answer.

7. A college president once wrote, "Most of the problems facing the human race could be solved if men would only think."

a. Do you agree with this statement?

b. Why do so many people seem to find it difficult or impossible to think effectively? Make a list of the different factors which seem to reduce our ability to think clearly. (Notice that some, like lack of adequate intelligence, cannot be completely remedied; others, like lack of accurate information, can be.)

c. Very often we are exposed to efforts to influence our thinking, to convince us of a certain point of view. This is the main task of many politicians, salesmen, writers, lawyers, and next-door-neighbors. Ordinarily we should examine their arguments carefully before we accept or reject them. Write a paper on the topic "How to Judge the Thinking of Other People."

d. Prepare a list of "The Ten Demandments of Effective Thinking." These should be the ten principles which, in your judgment, are most important for straight thinking.

Additional Points of Strategy

1. Although geometry has emphasized mathematics as a mode of thought, the task of teaching students to think logically is shared with the other areas of the school curriculum. Geometry teachers should be aware of the ways that this problem is being met by teachers in other subjects. For example, in English, the *Living Language* textbook series presents work, a four-chapter sequence, on straight thinking intended to help the student detect and avoid vagueness and hasty generalizations and to distinguish fact from opinion. Many social studies books also give explicit attention to the problem-solving approach. For example, see Chester D. Babcock and James I. Quillen, *American Values and Problems Today* (Chicago, Scott, Foresman, 1956), pp. 7-28, or Lavone A. Hanna, *Facing Life's Problems* (Chicago, Rand McNally, 1955), pp. 1-5. The tie-in with science courses is too obvious to warrant further discusison.

2. Often school and local libraries are limited in the variety of books which bear on the issue of effective thinking. But there is a fascinating variety of paper-bound books which will serve the purpose. Probably the Mentor Books are most helpful. Since they are very inexpensive,

quite a few could be added to the school's mathematics library with very little trouble. For a copy of the complete catalogue write to The New American Library of World Literature, Inc., 501 Madison Avenue, New York.

3. Do not overlook mystery stories as a good source of examples of reflective thinking. A good collection for school use will be found in Mary Y. Sandrus, ed., *Famous Mysteries* (Chicago, Scott, Foresman).

4. Present the students with arguments which have a similar logical structure, but which have varying degrees of "emotional toning." It is surprising to them to see how this emotional toning distorts their ability to reason logically.

   Illustration: Each of the following examples presents an argument. Judge whether each conclusion arrived at is warranted by the statements given in support of it.

   a. Only if a government completely ignores the best interests of its people can it enter into any kind of friendly relations with the communists. Since India has signed certain agreements of friendship with Russia, it is not acting in the best interests of the Indian people.

   b. If a vessel is made of material lighter than water it will float. The steamship Queen Elizabeth floats. Therefore we can be sure that the Queen Elizabeth is made of material which is lighter than water.

   (Notice each argument is of the same form and is invalid, but the first one tends to get wider acceptance because its conclusion is "emotionally appealing.")

5. Superior students may enjoy testing their powers of critical thinking on a system of finite geometry. The following ideas are adapted from E. R. Stabler, *An Introduction to Mathematical Thought* (Cambridge, Mass., Addison-Wesley, 1953), Ch. 7.

   A restricted (finite) geometry can be developed, using the deductive methods we have studied, by starting with this list of carefully chosen postulates (let "S" represent our "system," and our "lines" are not necessarily the "straight" lines of ordinary geometry):

   > Postulate 1: Each pair of lines in S has one and only one point in common.
   > Postulate 2: Each point in S is on two and only two lines.
   > Postulate 3: The total number of lines in S is four.

   We know we can reason out answers to these questions:

   a. How many points are there in S? (six)

   b. How many points are there on each line in S? (three)

6. Some publishers make available display material which is related to the topic of critical thinking. For instance, Scott, Foresman and Company of Chicago publishes a large wall chart on "Propaganda Devices That Can Mislead you" (#516). Of course, bulletin board displays prepared by the students can be extremely effective.

APPENDIX E

Principles of Really Sound Thinking

(A humorous statement written by Professor Max Black and first appearing in the *Scientific Monthly* for March, 1948, pages 232-234. Reprinted here through the kind permission of Professor Black.)

There is thinking and thinking; we shall be concerned with the second kind. Textbooks are still full of impracticable principles of logic for which men of affairs have unqualified contempt. It is time to be more realistic. But for the dead hand of Aristotle and the lingering influence of medieval scholasticism, logicians would not have the impudence to refer to practical thinking as "invalid" or "poor." Such emotive language should be avoided. The principle of identity should have taught academic logicians that Really Sound Thinking can be nothing if not Really Sound.

We are interested in the way the man in the street should think. Formal logic should be left to mathematicians and scientists who get paid for trafficking in abstractions. Symbolic logic should be left to those lonely thinkers who understand the symbols.

There are two major principles of really sound thinking:

A. Think only as a last resource.

B. Trust your feelings.

Think Only as a Last Resource

The really sound thinker knows thinking to be an uncomfortable, disturbing, and antisocial occupation. Consider the attitude of Rodin's statue "The Thinker." This is not the favorite posture of a successful executive or a regular guy.

Modern life fortunately provides a number of defenses against the early onslaught of thinking. The radio is always close at hand—use it. The company of others, preferably of the opposite sex, is to be strongly recommended. If the irritation is too severe, one may retreat to bed until restored to a healthier frame of mind.

It has to be confessed, however, that complete protection against thinking still remains to be achieved:

> But men at whiles are sober
> And think by fits and starts
> And if they think, they fasten
> Their hands upon their hearts.
> —A. E. Housman

Conscientious adherence to the next principle will go far to palliate the discomforts of unavoidable and involuntary thinking.

Trust Your Feelings

The logic texts have created the fiction of Logical Man, coldly calculating the probabilities of alternative hypotheses, willfully blind to human sentiment and passion. Do you want to be this kind of philosophical monster, interminably vacillating between conflicting conclusions? Of course not. In any matter of serious concern, you will *feel* strongly that a certain conclusion *must* be right. This is the clue to success in really sound thinking. Let yourself go—think in technicolor.

Suppose you are worried about the possibility of war with Russia. You will notice in yourself a tendency to think of Stalin as a bloodthirsty ruffian, dripping with the gore of murdered innocents. Dwell upon the notion—let your blood pressure rise. In a short time you will *feel* strongly enough to be able to stop *thinking* altogether. In really sound thinking, it is the conclusion that counts, not the premises. Trusting your feeling will quickly provide you with satisfying, heart-warming conclusions.

The two principles of really sound thinking can be illustrated by the following maxims, widely accepted by successful practitioners.

1. *If you must stick to the point, be sure it's blunt.* The natural human reaction to contact with a sharp point is violent motion in reverse. Such animal wisdom is deeply significant. It's the dead butterfly that stays on the point. Cultivate judicious irrelevance.

Example: Does John Smith deserve a raise in salary?

Blunted point: Doesn't everybody deserve a raise?

Really sound reasoning: Of course they do! Who is John Smith to be favored at the expense of everybody else?

2. *What's in it for me?* Remember that a really sound thinker is practical. And what can be more practical than concern for one's own interests? The chief advantage of this maxim is the strong light it throws upon the truth of many a debatable proposition.

Example: Should educational facilities be improved in the South?

Really sound reasoning: What's in it for me? Nothing—I don't live in the South.

Conclusion: NO. (Notice the directness and incisiveness of the method.)

3. *It all depends on who says it.* Men are easier to classify than arguments—attend to the man, not the argument. (For classifying the speaker, see principle B above.)

Example: Should Congress be reorganized?

Really sound reasoning: Who says so? X? Oh—he ran for Congress three times unsuccessfully.

Conclusion: You can't trust *him.*

4. *A million people can't be wrong.* It would clearly be undemocratic, not to say snobbish, to think otherwise. We can't all be Gallups, but we have a ready fund of popular wisdom to hand in the form of proverbs. Make frequent use of such axioms as "Human nature never changes," and "An ounce of experience is worth a peck of talk," and, especially, "It will all be the same in a thousand years." The last is particularly consoling.

Example: Can we prevent another war?

R.s.r.: I've *seen* men fighting. You'll never change human nature. After all, it will all be the same in a thousand years.

This method can be usefully supplemented by the use of identical propositions, such as "East is East, West is West," "Business is Business," "A man's a man for a' that." These are best introduced by the words "after all." Even a logician can hardly dispute the truth of such tautologies.

5. *The exception proves the rule.* Corollary: The more exceptions, the better the rule. This popular maxim hardly needs recommendation. It has the great advantage of allowing us to make simple generalizations in an intolerably complex world. (See also Maxim 8 below.)

Example: You say women are no good at physics. What about Madame Curie?

R.s.r.: The exception proves the rule! (Absolutely conclusive, as r.s.r. should be.)

6. *It's all right in theory, but it won't work in practice.* We might almost say: *Because* it's right in theory, it won't work in practice. This maxim is very useful in puncturing the pretensions of experts.

Example: Would we support the United Nations?

R.s.r.: (You know what!)

7. *Consistency is the hobgoblin of little minds.* None of the great thinkers from Socrates to Korzybski have been consistent. Who are you to improve upon their practice? The sciences are notoriously full of unresolved contradictions. If scientists don't care, why should you?

Example: You say that we ought to work for universal free trade, but insist on raising American tariffs.

R.s.r.: I contradict myself? Very well, I contradict myself.

8. *Truth is always pure and simple.* Notice the purity and simplicity of this maxim. Oscar Wilde denied its truth, and see what happened to him (compare Maxim 3). Anything too complicated for translation into Basic English is unworthy of the attention of a really sound thinker. The truth must be incapable of shocking the Johnston (formerly Hays) Office. In any case, truth is too precious to be lightly squandered. It is better to hold it a closely guarded hostage far back in reserve. *

Example: Is there anything in psychonanalysis?

R.s.r.: Of course not. Why, I can't even understand it. And it isn't fit to print.

* With acknowledgments to Peter Fleming.

9. *Take care of the sound, and the sense will take care of itself.* This is perhaps the most important of all the maxims of really sound thinking. "There is a great advantage in names" (Mark van Doren). Be sure you get the greatest benefit out of the names you use.

If you trust your feelings as you should (principle B above), you should have little trouble in finding the right name. Thus, the *Management Review* lately recommended the use of "Income Account" instead of "Profit and Loss Account," "Earnings" instead of "Profits," "Reinvested in the Business" instead of "Added to Surplus." You get the idea?

Example: On being questioned about the implications of a legislative program no really sound thinker would say, "I don't know." This is better: "It is totally unreasonable to expect a blueprint which answers every question which can arise day after tomorrow in this distraught earth, when no man knows for twenty minutes at a time what is going to happen" (Senator Vandenberg, quoted in the *New York Times*, April 18, 1947).

10. *Never argue with a man who is wrong.* Corollary for married ladies; never argue with a husband. For the purposes of this maxim, a man who is wrong is easily identified as one who (a) is an unsound thinker, (b) refuses to see that you are right, or (c) has an unwholesome look (see Maxim 3 above).

The careful reader will have noticed that the reasoning used in the above exposition of the principles of really sound thinking provides numerous further illustrations of the principles discussed.

(*Scientific Monthly,* March, 1948, pp. 232-234)

APPENDIX F

General Bibliography

Space simply prohibits inclusion of a total bibliography. The listing for Chapter 12 alone runs over 250 titles. The general references would total over 300. The following is therefore a sampling only of the total available. No research studies are included.

Some readers will wish to disagree with the classification of certain references, and in fact a few have been included in two groupings.

Instructors and students should note current references as they appear and add them to the proper listing.

A. Classic References

BACON, Francis, *Novum Organum.* Kitchins' translation (Oxford, University Press, 1885), pp. 19-45, is a good one. A popular edition based on Spedding, Ellis, and Heath, Vol. I, Pt. 2, pp. 72-102, is also good. Any number of translations of editions are available. Use the index to find the discussion of "Idols."

BAIN, Alexander, *Logic, Deductive and Inductive.* Various editions and revisions.

DESCARTES, René, *Discourse on Method.* Various editions by several publishers are available.

GALTON, Francis, *Inquiry into Human Faculty and Its Development* (New York, Macmillan, 1883).

HUME, David, *Inquiries Concerning the Human Understanding, and Concerning the Principles of Morals* (Oxford, Clarendon Press, 1902).

LOCKE, John, *The Conduct of the Understanding* (an abstract of *Essay on Human Understanding*). Available separately and in collections.

——, *Thoughts Concerning Education.* Available separately and in collections.

MILL, John Stuart, *A System of Logic* (London, Longmans, Green, 1925). Other editions are available.

SCHOPENHAUER, Arthur, *On Thinking for Oneself.* In various collections of essays or translations of his works.

B. Older References

BOSANQUET, Bernard, *The Essentials of Logic, Judgment and Inference* (New York, Macmillan, 1914).

CARNAP, Rudolph, *The Logical Syntax of Language* (New York, Harcourt, Brace, 1937).

CREIGHTON, James E., *An Introductory Logic,* 4th ed. (New York, Macmillan, 1920).

FIELD, G. E., *Prejudice and Impartiality* (New York, McBride, 1932).

FOWLER, Thomas, *Logic, Deductive and Inductive* (Oxford, Clarendon Press, 1904).

HARTMAN, Sylvester J., *A Textbook of Logic* (New York, American Book, 1936).

HOBHOUSE, Leonard T., *Mind in Evolution,* 2nd ed. (New York, Macmillan, 1915).

JAMES, William, *Psychology.* The chapter on reasoning. There are several editions available.

JEVONS, W. S., *Elementary Lessons in Logic* (New York, Macmillan, 1877).

———, *The Principles of Science* (New York, Macmillan, 1924).

JOSEPH, H. W., *An Introductory Logic,* 2nd ed. (Oxford, Clarendon Press, 1931).

KELLEY, T. L., *Scientific Method* (New York, Macmillan, 1932).

LORIMER, Frank, *The Growth of Reason* (New York, Harcourt, Brace, 1929).

PEARSON, Karl, *The Grammar of Science* (London, Adam and Charles Black, 1900).

POINCARÉ, Henri, *Science and Method* (New York, Scribner, 1914).

RICHARDS, I. A., *Basic Rules of Reason* (London, Kegan Paul, Trench, Trubner, 1933).

THOMSON, J. A., *Introduction to Science* (New York, Holt, 1911).

WESTAWAY, F. W., *Scientific Method: Philosophy and Practice,* 3rd ed. (Blackie and Sons, 1924).

WHEWELL, William, *The History of the Inductive Sciences* (London, John W. Parker, 1857; New York, D. Appleton, 1874, 1901).

C. *More Recent References*
Moving Toward Discussion of Thought-in-Process
(Sometimes Called Dynamic or Functional Logic
in Contrast to Formal Logic)

BALDWIN, James M., *Thought and Things,* three vols. (New York, Macmillan, 1906-1911).

BELL, E. T., *The Search for Truth* (Williams Company, 1934).

BLACK, Max, *Critical Thinking: An Introduction to Logic and Scientific Method* (Englewood Cliffs, N. J., Prentice-Hall, 1946).

———, "The Principles of Really Sound Reasoning," *American Scientist* (Winter, 1948).

BOAS, George, *Our New Ways of Thinking* (New York, Harper, 1930).

BOGOLSLOVSKY, Boris B., *The Technique of Controversy: Principles of Dynamic Logic* (London, Kegan Paul, Trench, Trubner, 1928).

BURTT, E. A., *Right Thinking,* 2nd ed. (New York, Harper, 1946).

CARMICHAEL, R. D., *The Logic of Discovery* (Chicago, Open Court, 1930).

COHEN, Morris R., *A Preface to Logic* (New York, Holt, 1944).

COHEN, Morris R., and NAGEL, Ernest, *An Introduction to Logic and Scientific Method* (New York, Harcourt, Brace, 1936).

COLUMBIA ASSOCIATES in Philosophy, *An Introduction to Reflective Thinking* (Boston, Houghton Mifflin, 1923).

DEWEY, John, *Logic: The Theory of Inquiry* (New York, Holt, 1938).

——, *Studies in Logical Theory: And Essays in Experimental Logic* (Chicago, University of Chicago Press, 1903). Briefly summarized with special reference to education in *How We Think*.

FAWCETT, H. P., *The Nature of Proof* (New York, Columbia University Press, 1938).

FRYE, A. M., and LEVI, A. W., *Rational Belief* (New York, Harcourt, Brace, 1941).

HAZLITT, Henry, *Thinking as a Science* (New York, Dutton, 1915).

HOLMES, R. W., *The Rhyme of Reason* (New York, Appleton-Century-Crofts, 1939).

JUDD, C. H., *Education as the Cultivation of the Higher Mental Processes* (New York, Macmillan, 1936).

KANTOR, J. R., *Psychology and Logic* (Principia Press, 1945).

MURPHY, A. E., *The Uses of Reason* (New York, Macmillan, 1943).

RAUP, Bruce, and others, *The Improvement of Practical Intelligence* (New York, Harper, 1950).

REISER, Oliver S., *Humanistic Logic for the Mind in Action* (New York, Crowell, 1930).

RITCHIE, A. D., *The Natural History of the Mind* (New York, Longmans, Green, 1936).

ROBINSON, Daniel S., *The Principles of Reasoning*, 3rd ed. (New York, Appleton-Century-Crofts, 1947).

STEBBING, S. L., *Thinking to Some Purpose* (London, Penguin Books, 1939).

WERKMEISTER, William H., *The Basis and Structure of Knowledge* (New York, Harper, 1948).

WERTHEIMER, Max, *Productive Thinking* (New York, Harper, 1945).

WILLIAMS, D., *The Grounds of Induction* (Cambridge, Mass., Harvard University Press, 1947).

D. Popular Discussions of Thinking or of Some Given Aspect of Thinking

ANGELL, Norman, *The Public Mind* (New York, Dutton, 1928).

——, *The Unseen Assassins* (New York, Harper, 1932).

BARNARD, Chester I., *Mind in Everyday Affairs* (Princeton, N. J., Guild of the Brackett Lecturers, 1936).

BEARDSLEY, M. C., *Thinking Straight* (Englewood Cliffs, N. J., Prentice-Hall, 1950). An abbreviation in part of the next reference.

——, *Practical Logic* (Englewood Cliffs, N. J., Prentice-Hall, 1950).

CLARKE, Edwin L., *The Art of Great Thinking* (New York, Appleton-Century-Crofts, 1932).

CRAWSHAY, William R., *The Comforts of Unreason* (London, Kegan Paul, Trench, Trubner, 1947).

EVANS, Bergen, *The Natural History of Nonsense* (New York, Knopf, 1946).

HOGBEN, L. T., *Retreat from Reason* (New York, Random House, 1937).

——, *Dangerous Thought* (New York, Norton, 1940).

HUSE, H. R., *The Illiteracy of the Literate* (New York, Appleton-Century-Crofts, 1933).

JASTROW, J., *The Betrayal of Intelligence* (New York, Greenburg Company, 1938).

——, *Effective Thinking* (New York, Simon & Schuster, 1931).

————, *The Story of Human Error* (New York, Appleton-Century-Crofts, 1936).

JORDAN, David S., *The Higher Foolishness* (Indianapolis, Ind., Bobbs-Merrill, 1927).

KEYES, Kenneth S., *How to Develop Your Thinking Ability* (New York, McGraw-Hill, 1950).

KEYSER, C. J., *Thinking About Thinking* (New York, Dutton, 1926).

KNOWLSON, Thomas S., *Originality: A Popular Study of the Creative Mind* (Philadelphia, Lippincott, 1918).

————, *The Origins of Popular Superstitions and Customs* (London, Laurie, 1910 and 1930).

LERNER, Max, *Ideas Are Weapons* (New York, Viking Press, 1939).

LIEBER, Lillian, *Mits, Wits and Logic* (New York, Norton, 1947).

MACKAY, Charles, *Extraordinary Popular Delusions and the Madness of Crowds* (Boston, Page, 1932).

MANDER, Alfred E., *Logic for the Millions* (New York, Philosophical Library, 1947).

McCLURE, M. T., *An Introduction to the Logic of Reflection* (New York, Holt, 1925).

————, *How to Think in Business* (New York, McGraw-Hill, 1923).

MULFORD, Prentice, *Thoughts Are Things* (London, G. Bell, 1911).

PITKIN, Walter, *A Short Introduction to the Study of Human Stupidity* (New York, Simon & Schuster, 1932).

REILLY, William J., *Twelve Rules for Straight Thinking* (New York, Harper, 1947).

RICHET, Charles, *Idiot Man, or the Follies of Mankind,* translation (New York, Brentano's, 1925).

ROBINSON, James H., *Mind in the Making* (New York, Harper, 1921).

————, *The Humanizing of Knowledge,* 2nd rev. (New York, Doran, 1926).

SMITH, Henry Bradford, *How the Mind Falls into Error* (New York, Harper, 1923).

STEFANSSON, Vilhjalmur, *Adventures in Error* (New York, McBride, 1936).

————, *Standardization of Error* (New York, Macmillan, 1929).

SWIFT, Edgar J., *The Jungle of the Mind* (New York, Scribner, 1931).

THOULESS, Robert H., *How to Think Straight* (New York, Simon & Schuster, 1947). A revision of his older and well-known book called *Straight and Crooked Thinking.*

WEIL, Richard, *The Art of Practical Thinking* (New York, Simon & Schuster, 1940).

NOTE. Recall here the several books, old and modern, listed within the body of Chapter 13, "Skill in Thinking as an Aim of Education." These have not been included in the list above.

E. Educational Methods and the Improvement of Thinking

BEARDSLEY, Monroe C., *Thinking Straight* (Englewood Cliffs, N. J., Prentice-Hall, 1950).

BORAAS, Julius, *Teaching to Think* (New York, Macmillan, 1924). This is one of the first books to undertake this problem. It is now out of date and probably out of print. It is very simple but contains a wealth of good material for the everyday classroom teacher.

DEWEY, John, *How We Think,* rev. ed. (Boston, Heath, 1933). This is the great classic in the field but actually covers only one of the three major types of thinking. Treatment will be extended through the references by Raup and others, and by the Smith, Stanley, and Shores chapter listed below.

JUDD, Charles H., *Education as Cultivation of the Higher Mental Processes* (New York, Macmillan, 1936).

MILLER, Irving E., *The Psychology of Thinking* (New York, Macmillan, 1912). This is one of the oldest books in the field and of interest now chiefly for historical reasons. The treatment of logic is a little formal, but the book still contains a large number of excellent discussions and illustrations.

RAUP, R. B., and others, *The Improvement of Practical Intelligence: The Central Task of Education,* rev. ed. (New York, Harper, 1950). Somewhat difficult to read in spots but one of the best treatments available.

SCHAEFFER, Nathan C., *Thinking and Learning to Think* (Philadelphia, Lippincott, 1901).

SMITH, B. O., STANLEY, William O., and SHORES, J. H., *The Fundamentals of Curriculum Development* (Yonkers, N. Y., World Book, 1950). Ch. 23 is an exceptionally able compact treatment of three types of thinking and the educational implications thereof. Very valuable to all students.

SYMONDS, Percival M., *Education and the Psychology of Thinking* (New York, McGraw-Hill, 1936). This is the account of the experiences of a class dealing with this topic. It is a little bit rambling and discursive but contains a very important and useful body of material.

TROW, William C., *Scientific Method in Education* (Boston, Houghton Mifflin, 1925). Another of the older books, very brief, but contains much excellent material.

F. Books from Which May Be Gained Considerable Insight Into the Nature of Thinking and Particularly into Certain Obstacles and Pitfalls to Thinking

BAGEHOT, Walter, *Physics and Politics.* Various editions available from 1873 to 1948.

BAILEY, Alice A., *From Intellect to Intuition* (New York, Lucis Press, 1950).

BARROWS, Dunham, *Man Against Myth* (Boston, Little, Brown, 1948).

BELL, E. T., *The Search for Truth* (Baltimore, William & Wilkins, 1934).

BRIDGMAN, Percy, *The Intelligent Individual and Society* (New York, Macmillan, 1938).

CARPENTER, C. E., *Dollars and Sense* (New York, Doubleday, Doran, 1928).

CASSIRER, Ernst, *Language and Myth* (New York, Harper, 1946).

CHASE, Stuart, *Democracy Under Pressure* (New York, Twentieth Century Fund, 1945).

CHASE, Stuart, and SCHLINK, F. J., *Your Money's Worth* (New York, Macmillan, 1927).

CHASE, Stuart, *The Nemesis of American Business* (New York, Macmillan, 1931).

COMMAGER, Henry Steele, *The American Mind* (New Haven, Conn., Yale University Press, 1950).

CURTI, Merle, *The Growth of American Thought* (New York, Harper, 1943).

DARROW, Floyd L., *Thinkers and Doers* (New York, Silver Burdett, 1925).

DEKRUIF, Paul, *Microbe Hunters,* text ed. (New York, Harcourt, Brace, 1932). See other accounts by scientists and inventors; also biographies and autobiographies.

DORSEY, George A., *Man's Own Show: Civilization* (New York, Harper, 1931).

EISENBERG, Philip, *Why We Act as We Do* (Kingswood Press, 1950).

GASSETT, Ortego y, *The Revolt of the Masses* (New York, Norton, 1932). Various editions are available in Mentor Book.

GIBSON, Alexander B., *Thinkers at Work* (New York, Longmans, Green, 1946).

HANKIN, E. H., *Common Sense and Its Cultivation* (New York, Dutton, 1926).

HIRSCH, N. D. M., *Genius and Creative Intellect* (Sci-Art Publishers, 1931).

HUMPHREY, George, *Directed Thinking* (New York, Dodd, Mead, 1938).

———, *The Story of Man's Mind* (New York, Dodd, Mead, 1932).

JUDD, C. H., *The Psychology of Social Institutions* (New York, Macmillan, 1926).

KELLER, A. G., *Man's Rough Road* (New York, F. A. Stokes, 1933).

LEBON, Gustave, *The Psychology of the Crowd* (New York, Macmillan, 1896).

LIPPMAN, Walter, *The Phantom Public* (New York, Macmillan, 1927).

———, *Public Opinion* (New York, Macmillan, 1922; also Penguin Books, 1946).

MARTIN, E. D., *The Behavior of Crowds* (New York, Harper, 1920).

MOSZKOWSKI, Alexander, *Einstein the Searcher* (London, Methuen, 1921).

NOTCH, Frank, *King Mob* (New York, Harcourt, Brace, 1930).

PATRICK, Katharine, *Creative Thought and Poetry* (New York, Columbia University Publication, 1935).

RANDALL, John Herman, *The Making of the Modern Mind* (Boston, Houghton Mifflin, 1940).

RIBOT, Th. A., *The Evolution of General Ideas* (Chicago, Open Court, 1899).

———, *Essay on the Creative Imagination,* translation (Chicago, Open Court, 1906).

RIES, E. H., *Mother Wit* (New York, Century, 1930).

SPEARMAN, C., *Creative Mind* (New York, Appleton-Century-Crofts, 1931).

STEBBING, L. S., *A Modern Introduction to Logic,* 2nd ed. (Humanities Press, 1933).

STODDARD, Lothrop, *Luck, Your Silent Partner* (New York, Liveright, 1929).

THORNDIKE, Lynn, *A Short History of Civilization* (New York, Crofts, 1926), or any other good history of civilization.

VANLOON, Hendrick, *Tolerance.* Various editions and publishers, 1925 to 1939.

TRATTNER, Ernest R., *Architects of Ideas* (Carrick and Evans, 1938).

VEBLIN, Thorsten, *The Higher Learning in America* (B. W. Huebsch, 1918).

———, *The Place of Science in Modern Civilization* (B. W. Huebsch, 1919).

———, *The Theory of the Leisure Class.* Various editions and publishers, 1899 to 1945.

WHEWELL, William, *The History of the Inductive Sciences* (London, John W. Parker, 1857; New York, D. Appleton, 1874, 1901).

WHITEHEAD, Alfred N., *Science and the Western World* (New York, Macmillan, 1925).

———, *Adventures of Ideas* (New York, Macmillan, 1933).

WILLISON, George, *Saints and Strangers* (New York, Reynal Hitchcock, 1945).

WOODWARD, W. E., *Bread and Circuses* (New York, Harper, 1925).

———, *Bunk* (New York, Harper, 1923).

WYLIE, Philip, *Generation of Vipers* (New York, Farrar and Rinehart, 1942, 1944).

Name Index

Subject Index

TEXTBOOKS IN EDUCATION
William H. Burton, *Consulting Editor*

An Approach to Guidance, by Edna Dorothy Baxter.

Growth and Development of the Preadolescent, by Arthur Witt Blair and William H. Burton.

The Diagnosis and Treatment of Learning Difficulties, by Leo J. Brueckner and Guy L. Bond.

Student Teaching in the Elementary School, 2nd ed., by James R. Burr, Lowry W. Harding, and Leland B. Jacobs.

Guidebook for Elementary Student Teachers, by Isabel Miller, George E. Dickson, and Loren R. Tomlinson.

The Guidance of Learning Activities, 2nd ed., by William H. Burton.

Supervision, 3rd ed., by William H. Burton and Leo J. Brueckner.

Education for Effective Thinking, by William H. Burton, Roland B. Kimball, and Richard L. Wing.

Education and Morals, by John L. Childs.

Public Education in America, by George R. Cressman and Harold W. Benda.

The Third Curriculum, by Robert W. Frederick.

Educational Psychology, by Karl C. Garrison and J. Stanley Gray. Also accompanying *Workbook,* by Karl C. Garrison, Ira E. Aaron, and Joseph C. Bledsoe.

Introduction to Educational Research, by Carter V. Good.

Methods of Research, by Carter V. Good and Douglas E. Scates.

Human Relations in School Administration, by Daniel E. Griffiths.

Guidance in Democratic Living, by Arthur Hollingshead.

The Guidance Function in Education, by Percival W. Hutson.

Early Elementary Education, by Myrtle M. Imhoff.

The Child and His Curriculum, 3rd ed., by J. Murray Lee and Dorris May Lee.

The Child and His Development, by J. Murray Lee and Dorris May Lee.

The Preadolescent, by Mary Jane Loomis.

Changing the Curriculum, by Alice Miel.

Teaching Adolescents in Secondary Schools, by Harry N. Rivlin.

The American Secondary School, by L. O. Taylor, Don R. McMahill, and Bob L. Taylor.

Education and the Democratic Faith, by Ephram Vern Sayers and Ward Madden.

Statistical Methods in Educational and Psychological Research, by James E. Wert, Charles O. Neidt, and J. Stanley Ahmann.

TEXTBOOKS IN EDUCATION
William H. Burton, Consulting Editor